Dedicated to Captain James T. Kirk, Spock, and Scotty

CONTENTS

Social Work Research and Evaluation

SECOND EDITION

Social Work Research and Evaluation

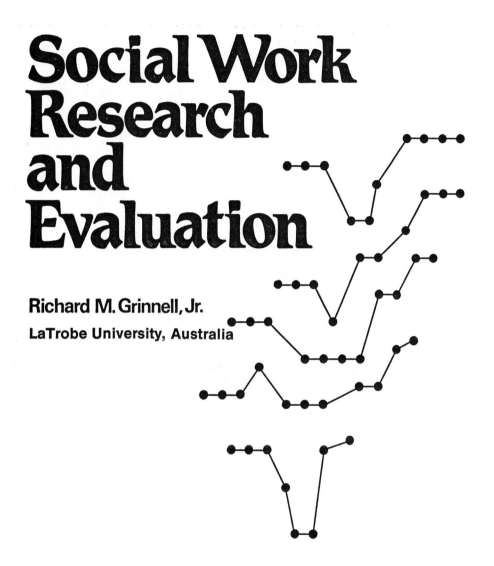

Richard M. Grinnell, Jr.

LaTrobe University, Australia

F.E. PEACOCK PUBLISHERS, ITASCA, ILLINOIS 60143

Pp. 3, 4, 6
"Curriculum Policy for the Master's Degree and Baccalaureate Degree
Programs in Social Work Education," 1982, Council on Social Work Educa-
tion, 1744 R. Street, N.W., Washington, DC 20009.

Pp. 34, 381–382
Martin Bloom, Joel Fischer, *Evaluating Practice: Guidelines for Accountable
Professional,* © 1982, pp. 14–15, 118, 119, 121, 126, 190, 228, 477.
Reprinted by permission of Prentice–Hall, Inc., Englewood Cliffs, N.J.

Pp. 276, 277–278, 309, 320–322, 323–324
Reprinted with permission of the Free Press, a Division of Macmillan, Inc.
from Methods of Social Research by K.D. Bailey. Copyright © 1978 by The
Free Press.

ACKNOWLEDGMENTS

Many individuals have contributed to the development and preparation of this text. For individual chapters, a number of people in addition to the contributors, aided in the production of this text by critiquing and reacting to chapter drafts, suggesting text and/or chapter content, and encouraging others to contribute. These include: David M. Austin; Donald W. Beless; Martin Bloom; Floyd Bolitho; Edgar F. Borgatta; Edwin G. Brown; Harry Butler; Harris Chaiklin; Kayla Conrad; Kevin J. Corcoran; Richard F. Dangel; Inger P. Davis; Liane Davis; Paul H. Ephross; Roland Etcheverry; Michale Fabricant; Phillip A. Fellin; John Flanagan; Charles D. Garvin; Neil Gilbert; Thomas Givler; Dianne H. Glisson; Richard L. Gorsuch; Donald K. Granvold; Ernest Greenwood; Lynda Hacker; Joseph Heffernan; Srinka Jayaratne; Alfred A. Kadushin; Rosalie Kane; Shanti Khinduka; Stuart A. Kirk; Michael S. Kolevzon; Michael L. Lauderdale; E. E. LeMasters; Charles S. Levy; Rona L. Levy; Harold Lewis; Duncan Lindsey; Anthony N. Maluccio; Rachel Marks; Robert R. Mayer; John L. McAdoo; Clyde O. McDaniel; Thomas P. McDonald; Robert Morris; Edward J. Mullen; Donald M. Pilcher; Norman A. Polansky; Joan Robertson; Sheldon D. Rose; Aaron Rosenblatt; Martha L. Royer; Adrea Savage-Abramovitz; Beatrice N. Saunders; John R. Schuerman; Judith Sears; Fredrick W. Seidl; Larry Shulman; Max Siporin; Harry Specht; Paul Stuart; Richard B. Stuart; John E. Tropman; Barbara Turman; Margaret Whelan; Stanley L. Witkin; Sidney E. Zimbalist; and Louis A. Zurcher.

Within the limits of time frames and resources, we have tried to follow the suggestions offered by these colleagues. However, they should not be held responsible for our sins of omission or commission.

Finally, and most importantly, special thanks go to the contributors for their obvious hard work and scientific contribution. This text is a product of their experiences and their desire to introduce others to social work research, which they have found so challenging and stimulating.

Scott Briar

FOREWORD

Research is becoming accepted as an integral part of the social work profession. As we know, research was, of course, a part of our profession from its earliest beginnings, but more often than not we regarded research as a less than welcome intruder whose presence we ignored, avoided, and even openly rejected.

Such attitudes toward research stemmed, in part, from two beliefs. One idea was that research was somehow incompatible with the human elements central to our profession (especially social work practice)—the feelings, emotions, and intense relationships that are an inherent part of the social worker's daily practice. The other source was the belief that what social workers do, what their practice objectives are, and even the nature of problems that social workers deal with are too complex and elusive to be studied and measured by "scientific research techniques." These beliefs were widespread among social workers until quite recently.

We have discovered that research *can* generate findings (knowledge) that have a direct and immediate use for us. The skepticism about research among social workers was not unfounded. Little of the social work research that had been conducted, produced data that we could find useful in practice. In recent years an increasing number of research findings have appeared that have direct, useful, and constructive application to social work practice. As this trend continues, social workers can be expected to look to research findings (and actually engaging in research studies) for solutions to practice problems. Also, the emergence of research methods and techniques (presented in this text) make it more feasible for social workers to conduct research on their own practice *and* in their own agencies. This development, which makes possible the incorporation of research techniques into the normal routine of practice, provides the necessary foundation not only for the generation of a body of knowledge based on practice research but also for the use of research techniques by social workers to solve their practice problems. Until quite recently, most social work students graduated with the belief that they lacked the resources and skills to conduct a research study and, in any event, research would not be of much help to them.

The contributors of this text have studied social work research from two vantage points: one, through the eyes of social work researchers actively engaging in research projects; the other, from the view of social work practitioners and educators striving to build a coherent practice knowledge base. This text is an outgrowth of both experiences in that it endeavors to bridge the gap between social work practice and research by providing a basic set of principles and concepts from which can be developed a foundation of general social work research knowledge. It includes original chapters with illustrative and rich material from the literature in the field with the notion that social work practice and research are both a problem-solving process.

More than any other research text in the field, the second edition of *Social Work Research and Evaluation* emphasizes the four important elements of the social work research process that are most relevant to practice: problem formulation; conceptualization; operationalization; and measurement. This text is written *by* social workers *for* social workers with an emphasis on readability and usefulness in actual practice and research situations. As a result of the text's efforts to bridge the practice-research gap, we hope to see more social work students and graduates who regard research as a useful and essential component of effective social work practice.

CONTRIBUTORS

AUSTIN, MICHAEL J., School of Social Work, University of Washington, Seattle, Washington 98105.

BISNO, HERBERT, Department of Social Work, La Trobe University, Bundoora, Victoria 3083, Australia.

BOROWSKI, ALLAN, Department of Social Work, La Trobe University, Bundoora, Victoria 3083, Australia.

BOSTWICK, GERALD J., JR., School of Social Work, Michigan State University, East Lansing, Michigan 48824.

BRIAR, SCOTT, School of Social Work, University of Washington, Seattle, Washington 98105.

CROWELL, JILL, Mental Health Division, Department of Social and Health Services, Olympia, Washington 98105.

DUEHN, WAYNE D., Graduate School of Social Work, University of Texas at Arlington, Arlington, Texas 76019.

EPSTEIN, IRWIN, School of Social Work, The City University of New York, Hunter College, New York, New York 10021.

FISCHER, JOEL, School of Social Work, University of Hawaii at Manoa, Honolulu, Hawaii 96822.

GOCHROS, HARVEY L. School of Social Work, University of Hawaii at Manoa, Honolulu, Hawaii 96822.

GRINNELL, RICHARD M., JR., Department of Social Work, La Trobe University, Bundoora, Victoria 3083, Australia.

HOSHINO, GEORGE, School of Social Work, University of Minnesota at Minneapolis, Minneapolis, Minnesota 55455.

HUDSON, WALTER W., School of Social Work, Florida State University, Tallahassee, Florida 32306.

KYTE, NANCY S., East Lansing, Michigan 48824.

LYNCH, MARY ANN, Dallas County Mental Health and Mental Retardation Center, Dallas, Texas 75221.

LYNCH, MARY MARTIN, Ramsey County Community Human Services, Saint Paul, Minnesota 55101.

MINDEL, CHARLES H., Graduate School of Social Work, University of Texas at Arlington, Arlington, Texas 76019.

MOSS, KATHRYN E., School of Social Work, University of Texas at Austin, Austin, Texas 78712.

POLSTER, RICHARD A., Graduate School of Social Work, University of Texas at Arlington, Arlington, Texas 76019.

RAMOS, REYES, Department of Chicano Studies, University of Colorado at Boulder, Boulder, Colorado 80309.

RAYMOND, FRANK B., College of Social Work, University of South Carolina, Columbia, South Carolina 29208.

REID, WILLIAM J., School of Social Welfare, State University of New York at Albany, Albany, New York 12222.

SCHINKE, STEVEN PAUL, School of Social Work, University of Washington, Seattle, Washington 98105.

SEABERG, JAMES R., School of Social Work, Virginia Commonwealth University, Richmond, Virginia 23284.

SMITH, NORMAN J., Department of Social Work, La Trobe University, Bundoora, Victoria 3083, Australia.

THOMAS, EDWIN J., School of Social Work, University of Michigan at Ann Arbor, Ann Arbor, Michigan 48109.

TOSELAND, RONALD W., School of Social Welfare, State University of New York at Albany, Albany, New York 12222.

TRIPODI, TONY, School of Social Work, University of Michigan at Ann Arbor, Ann Arbor, Michigan 48109.

WATTS, THOMAS D., Graduate School of Social Work, University of Texas at Arlington, Arlington, Texas 76019.

WEINBACH, ROBERT W., College of Social Work, University of South Carolina, Columbia, South Carolina 29208.

PREFACE FOR INSTRUCTORS

The favorable reception given to the first edition of *Social Work Research and Evaluation* has provided the courage for us to attempt another. Based on new developments in the field of social work, on numerous comments from colleagues and students, but mostly on the basis of the data generated from in-depth interviews with many of the instructors who adopted the first text, numerous changes have been made in this edition. Hopefully the current changes will make this text even more useful than the first one. As in our first edition, every conceivable effort has been utilized to tie together concepts not only within chapters, but across chapters as well. In order to accommodate new ideas and to eliminate older, less-useful, and less-relevant content, a tremendous amount of new material and editing has occurred; this edition has been so substantially updated and revised that it would be impractical to discuss the differences between the first and second edition of this text.

Once again, we feel very fortunate to have secured the collaboration of a diverse group of practitioner/researchers in assembling more knowledge than any one of us pretends to have alone. All contributors worked seriously, promptly, and well, and have subjected themselves to a discipline uncommon in compendia—that is, writing in terms of what is most needed for an integrated research and evaluation text, rather than in line with one's own predilections. There have been changes in the list of contributors based on a variety of reasons which would be too tedious to recount. None was dropped lightly from the original list, and it is a source of satisfaction to know that their contributions are readily accessible in the many copies of the first edition which still survive.

PREFACE FOR STUDENTS

Most students who are obtaining a degree in social work study research reluctantly and regard it as a necessary evil encountered in the course of becoming prepared as professional social workers. In fact, few courses arouse more apprehension than the one that has required you to purchase this text. There are undoubtedly two simple reasons for these feelings. First, you may have heard through the student grapevine that the required research courses are abstract, dry, and hard. Second, and probably most importantly, you may have heard that these courses are irrelevant for social work students. The research course you are now taking is intended to put these two rumors (yes, rumors) to rest once and for all. Even though the material presented in this course is vitally important to your future success as a social worker, you will probably have little chance to apply what you learn until later in your career. Only actual social work experience will give you enough exposure to the various problem areas in our profession to make you fully appreciate the knowledge and skills you have gained through the material presented in this course and provide you with opportunities to utilize it.

This text is not a set of rules or a do-it-yourself manual. Rather, it considers many different methods of social work research and presents the different ways in which you can use them in your efforts to become an effective social worker. It also provides opportunities to develop the appropriate language, knowledge, and skills for the application of these methods in actual social work practice.

It is likely that you want a degree in social work because you want to help people help themselves; this is what social work is all about. But at this time you probably do not see the value of having to have a sound knowledge base in research. Nevertheless, acquaintance with this specialty will widen your knowledge of our profession and open up new vistas for helping people help themselves.

In this spirit, we offer this text to you—the future social worker. We hope you will keep it on your bookshelf and refer to it from time to time when you need to review particular concepts. If this text helps you to expand your knowledge and assists you in becoming more effective with your clients, our efforts will have been more than justified. If it also encourages you to do research in order to continue the pursuit of a stronger, better-knit theoretical base for social work practice, our task will be fully rewarded.

Richard M. Grinnell, Jr.

1. BECOMING A PRACTITIONER/RESEARCHER

This text is designed for social work students and practitioners who have never before studied or done research; no previous research knowledge or experience is necessary. This text does not comprise a reference manual or an aggregate of readings on general research methodology. Instead, it forms a beginning textbook that provides an integrated, general overview of the social work research process. Compared to the first edition, this edition is more straightforward, uses less jargon, and is easier to read. Those who have had some training or experience in research will also gain from the basic level of discussion. Going back to the fundamentals of social work research will widen their practice and research perspectives.

ACCOUNTABILITY

Since its beginning, the social work profession has attempted to develop its own knowledge base for practice (Rein & Peattie, 1981; Rein & White, 1981). This goal has remained an enduring ideal even though progress toward it has been, at the most, very modest (Grinnell, 1983). Despite the growing output of research findings during the past half century from the social sciences and the other helping professions, a solid quantitative knowledge base for social work practice has yet to be formed (Bloom & Fischer, 1982). More importantly, the majority of relevant research findings produced *by* and *for* social workers are not being effectively utilized (Reid & Smith, 1981).

Accountability—demonstration of our effectiveness—has most frequently been given as the rationale for the movement in social work education toward the training of empirically based social work practitioners (Grinnell, 1981a; Kim, 1977; Thomlison, 1984; Tripodi, 1983). Less frequently mentioned is another rationale at least as important as that of accountability: the need to develop an empirically oriented knowledge base for social work practice theory (Reid, 1983; Wood, 1980). The social work literature is almost embarrassingly rich in qualitative detail on what social workers need to *know,* to *do,* and to *feel* (Reid & Hanrahan, 1982, 1983). However, the borderline between a social worker's intuitive *hunch* and a *fact* which is derived from quantitative means is often tenuous. In our profession, a seemingly truthful and self-evident hunch often seems to achieve the status of a fact by sheer repetition (Hudson, 1982c; Laird, 1984; Middleman, 1984).

THEME OF THE TEXT

The major theme of this text is that knowledge of the research process enhances the effectiveness of professional social work practice (Schinke, 1981a). The issue is not whether social workers should do research. Rather, it is whether or not social workers can engage the full spectrum of knowledge and skills available to them to continually improve their practice (Duehn, 1981). Thus, this text is based on the assumption that the best way to become an effective social worker is to be knowledgeable of the research process (Weissman, Epstein, & Savage, 1983).

Professional versus Semiprofessional Practice

The social work research process simply applies a set of rational procedures to social work practice (Compton & Galaway, 1984). The research process as presented in this text employs the four components of the research process which are most relevant to practice—problem formulation, conceptualization, operationalization, and measurement (including validity and reliability). Thus, the knowledge of the research process makes it possible for professional social workers to conceptualize, put into practice, and measure problem formulations, practice methods, and outcome goals (Welch, 1983). The extent to which they are guided by the research process marks the essential distinction between professional and semiprofessional social work practice. In other words, professional social workers utilize research procedures in their practices—semiprofessional social workers do not. The purpose of this text, therefore, is to enable social work students and practitioners to become professionals who will utilize research procedures (and hopefully, research findings as well) in their practice (Eldridge, 1983; Mandell, 1983).

Professional social workers maximize their own potential for becoming effective social workers (Bloom & Fischer, 1982). Unlike semiprofessional social workers, they owe no allegiance to any one particular theory or dogma. Professional social workers cannot, and will not, exclude practice methods of demonstrated efficacy from their practice merely on grounds of newness or because they are "uncomfortable with them" (Fischer, 1978, 1984). In short, professional social workers are effective only to the degree that they are open to new ideas (Siegel, 1983). And to be truly open to new ideas requires them to have a solid knowledge base of social work research and evaluation, as it is this base that is needed to assess the validity of new practice methods and their corresponding treatment techniques (Council on Social Work Education, 1982; Imre, 1984).

To some of us, research procedures may seem like a bag of tricks. Indeed, they can be quite technical. This text will make it easier to understand research articles that use those procedures. However, its overarching purpose is to introduce a set of relevant, rational research concepts and procedures and to demonstrate how they can be utilized in social work practice and research. Thus, this text describes how social workers who have knowledge of the basic principles of the research process utilize this knowledge to enhance practice methods and their corresponding treatment techniques, to generate new knowledge, and to become part of a professional community that is working to advance the effectiveness of all its members (Weinbach & Gandy, 1980).

PROFESSIONAL SOCIAL WORK RESEARCH ROLES

The contents of this text have been formulated to conform to the "Research Component" of the "Curriculum Policy for the Master's and Baccalaureate Degree Programs in Social Work Education," that became effective on July 1, 1983 (Council on Social Work Education, 1982):

7.15 Informed criticism and a spirit of inquiry are the basis of scientific thinking and of systematic approaches to the acquisition of knowledge and the application of it to practice. Every part of the professional foundation curriculum should therefore help to bring students to an understanding and appreciation of the necessity of a scientific, analytic approach to knowledge building and practice. The ethical use of scientific inquiry should be emphasized throughout.

7.16 The content on research should impart scientific methods of building knowledge for practice and of evaluating service delivery in all areas of practice. It should include quantitative and qualitative research methodologies; designs for the systematic evaluation of the student's own practice; and the critical appreciation and use of research and of program evaluation. The plan for teaching research should be explicit in showing how content on research relates to the knowledge base and practice skills that are included in the curriculum content of social work practice.

7.17 The professional foundation content in research should thus provide skills that will take students beyond the role of consumers of research and prepare them systematically to evaluate their own practice and contribute to the generation of knowledge for practice.

This text prepares schools of social work in meeting the research content that is required to be taught in all graduate schools of social work by presenting three research roles (Garvin, 1981) within the text's general theme and within the spirit of the Curriculum Policy statement mentioned above by the Council on Social Work Education (1982). The three research roles are: (1) the role of the consumer of research; (2) the role of the disseminator of knowledge; and (3) the role of the contributing partner.

The Consumer of Research

The first professional role is that of the consumer of research. This role stems from the conviction that social workers have an obligation—to self, to society, and to the recipients of services—to base their efforts on knowledge in the field (Teigiser, 1983). The obligation to self is to strive to be a person whose work is as effective as current knowledge allows. The obligation to society, which sanctions our profession and supplies the resources we require, is to justify such societal support. We must always remember that our greatest obligation, however, is to the persons, families, groups, and larger social systems that are seeking solutions to the problems that confront them. They have invested time and energies in their struggles, which may be related to their very survival (Gordon, 1983, 1984). Thus, the consumers of research must know how to search for appropriate studies and publications, how to determine whether they are valid and reliable and how to translate them into treatment techniques to use in their practice which, in turn, will enhance their own effectiveness. We agree with the Council on Social Work Education (1982) when they state:

7.26 The advanced student should be proficient in applying the foundation content to the area of concentration. In addition, graduate students should develop the ability to assess critically the practice theories associated with their concentrations, to evaluate their own practice, and to identify those areas of knowledge and skill that should be the focus of continuing personal and collective professional development beyond graduation.

The central issue is to reduce the randomness that has typified the proliferation of untested practice methods in social work (Fischer, 1973b). The social work profession needs to be more efficient in generating the kinds of effective practice methods clients and society really require (Fischer, 1973a). As Gochros (1978b) observed:

> As a practice teacher in social work, I have long been concerned with the dangers of indiscriminate teaching of treatment fads simply because they're new or exciting. Each year the list of practice "theories"—or, more accurately, tested or untested postulates from the social and behavioral sciences, or from the experiences of some articulate, innovative, exciting practitioner—grows longer and longer. Many social work practice faculties seem to feel responsible for presenting all these modalities to their classes for fear of leaving something out. One is led to the image of practice teachers waiting by their mailboxes for the latest announcements from the Behavioral Science Book Club to see what they may be able to add to their syllabus for the following semester.

One of the major problems such an explosion of practice methods creates is that the additions far outnumber the subtractions. As in our wardrobes, we are eager to add but reluctant to throw away (Gambrill, 1983). The result is that social workers run the risk of learning progressively less about progressively more. Until they learn the principles of research and evaluation, they will lack the knowledge required to separate practice fads from proven methods and will be left without any sense of professional competence or direction (Council on Social Work Education, 1982; Gochros, 1978b).

The Disseminator of Knowledge

The second professional role is that of a disseminator of knowledge. Social workers have a responsibility to initiate and participate in systematic efforts to determine effective practice methods for social work problems. The results of such efforts are then communicated to other social workers in ways that will be useful to them (Stern, 1979). *Systematic* means that the techniques used to identify effective practice methods are planned in advance and are both communicable and replicable. As the social worker gains experience, knowledge dissemination may range from a simple, carefully written report of what was done, to a report based on a single-subject design, to a report of a large multiple-group study (Kane, 1978, 1980). Whether a report is sent to a few colleagues or submitted to a professional journal for possible publication, social workers have the responsibility to disseminate their experiences so that the pool of information available to all social workers becomes more comprehensive (Schinke, 1981b).

The social worker's obligation to communicate experiences and add to the shared knowledge of the profession may be satisfied in many ways: through staff conferences, workshop presentations, and professional publications, to name a few. Many kinds of professional writings are also useful: carefully prepared practice descriptions; statements of problems facing social work; expositions of practice methods or models; and reports of research efforts. We agree with the Council on Social Work Education (1982) when they state:

> 8.4 The effectiveness of any profession's services depends on its carrying out systematic and high-quality research to assess its practice and develop new knowledge. Such knowledge-building and service-development enterprises are also natural and essential complements to the primary function of educational programs—the training of new practitioners.

The Contributing Partner

The third professional role is that of a contributing partner. This role helps to broaden the knowledge base of our profession. This means joining with others who have similar tasks and problems to rank the importance of gaps in knowledge and to determine appropriate ways of filling them. Social workers who fulfill this colleaguial role help to create a firmer knowledge foundation for all social workers. It also provides a source of support for their own work.

The most effective advances in practice are achieved when many persons are involved at one stage or another in the research process (Beckerman, 1978). This is why the third role is described as contributing partner in the process of knowledge development. There are many subroles social workers fill. Some workers are skillful at identifying and giving priority to important practice problem areas. Others are creative in seeking possibilities for new social work practice methods from obvious as well as unlikely sources. Still others are excellent as promoters of new, yet *tested,* practice methods.

The attention to the development of practice methods in social work is enhanced by knowledge of social work research and evaluation (Downs & Robertson, 1983). The need for an understanding of how knowledge is disseminated, of how theories are developed, and of how practice and research interface is strongly recognized (Mullen, 1978, 1981, 1983). Thus, our profession must continue to generate institutions and mechanisms for systematically developing, integrating, and disseminating knowledge (Council on Social Work Education, 1982; Mullen, Bostwick, & Ryg, 1980).

Relationship between the Three Roles

The three research roles above are not independent of one another. They are and must be related if the knowledge base of our profession is to be extended (Geismar, 1982). Professional social workers share their experiences and their findings with others who, in turn, are able to evaluate such presentations in terms of their own problems and needs (Reid, 1981). They work together to advance the state of theory for practice, the quality of technical operations employed in practice, and the appropriateness of the criteria that guide the selection of technologies in practice situations (Reid, 1978a). The contribution that simple research procedures can make to all of these tasks is enormous (Aronson & Sherwood, 1967; D. Austin, 1978; Baker, 1975; Basom, Iacono-Harris, & Kraybill, 1982; J. Brown, 1975; L. Brown & Levitt, 1978; Carr, 1980; Chambers, 1976; Crane, 1966; Weinbach, 1981).

THE KNOWLEDGE BASE FOR PROFESSIONAL RESEARCH ROLES

This text provides the beginning knowledge base that is needed for social workers to perform the three research roles mentioned above. The text therefore presents six generic avenues for increasing this knowledge base. The text helps to: (1) increase the research skills of social workers; (2) make research courses more relevant; (3) teach students to become professionals; (4) present quantitative and qualitative methods; (5) present research *and* evaluation strategies; and (6) present research and evaluation to social work students who have different practice interests.

Increasing the Research Skills of Social Workers

Research training of social work students has been less than successful (Grinnell, 1982b). Research courses are often viewed by students as the least helpful courses in the entire curriculum (Grinnell, 1982a). After graduation, few practitioners either conduct or read research studies, consult, utilize, or share research findings, especially when faced with difficult practice situations (Briar, Weissman, & Rubin, 1981). And even when they do read research, their judgments of the quality of the research findings and their implications for practice are strongly influenced by whether or not the findings support their own biases (Rosenblatt, 1968; Rosenblatt & Kirk, 1981). In short, social workers are neither skilled producers nor consumers of research after they leave school (Grinnell & Kyte, 1977).

The extent to which social workers use the procedures and findings of research and evaluation in shaping their practices will have a profound impact on our profession's future growth and development. Any profession (and especially ours) that bases its credibility on faith or ideology alone will have a hard time surviving, even though believers and followers can sustain their efforts for a very short time. Although an empirically oriented knowledge base of our profession will not guarantee us achievement of public acceptance, the absence of such a base and the lack of vigorous quantitative efforts to expand it will—in the long run—undoubtedly erode our credibility (Wood, 1980).

Making Research Courses More Relevant

In response to the negative reaction to the place of research in social work practice, social work education as an institution seems to have shrugged its shoulders and given up (F. C. Johnson, 1981). The proportion of the graduate curriculum devoted to research courses is continually decreasing (Zimbalist, 1974; Zimbalist & Rubin, 1981). Thus, there is a decrease in the number of *professional* social workers entering our profession as time goes by. Unfortunately, however, the number of *semiprofessional* social workers entering the same market is increasing. To make matters worse, many schools of social work have dropped any requirement for students to complete a research project in order to graduate. This regrettable trend persists despite the fact that the Council on Social Work Education (1982) in its 1983 accreditation standards recognizes the importance of research as a critical component of the social work curriculum.

Research studies have focused on how research is taught in a few schools of social work (Barth, 1981; Bogal & Singer, 1981; Seidl, 1973). The main objective of most master's level research courses is to help students understand and utilize research, not necessarily to produce it or apply it in practice (Rubin & Zimbalist, 1981). When research is taught in schools of social work there are basically three approaches (Rubin & Rosenblatt, 1979) in teaching the subject: (1) consumer approach; (2) producer approach; and (3) practitioner/researcher approach.

Consumer Approach. According to this viewpoint, professional social workers need to know how to utilize social work research and therefore, they should be prepared to assess, understand, and apply its results. The main concern in this approach is to prepare professional social workers as *consumers* of research (Tripodi, Fellin, & Meyer, 1983).

Producer Approach. The second major approach to teaching social work research provides instruction in basic social science research with examples from the field of social work. This approach demonstrates an interest in training *producers* of social work research. It is generally derived from statistics or methodology courses in academic departments such as education, mathematics, psychology, or sociology

(Babbie 1979; Bailey, 1978; Kerlinger, 1973; Selltiz, Wrightsman, & Cook, 1976; Walizer & Wienir, 1978).

Adopting teaching strategies and textbooks from other departments for social work research, however, is not satisfactory because the various components of the research process (especially problem formulation, conceptualization, operationalization, and measurement) differ from one discipline to another. Each academic discipline, therefore, must develop research courses which stress the content its students need most. Thus, a rationale has been established for social work research courses and texts that will respond to the distinctive needs of our profession—the practitioner/researcher (Arkava & Lane, 1983; Atherton & Klemmack, 1982; Grinnell, 1981b; Reid & Smith, 1981; Schuerman, 1983; Tripodi & I. Epstein, 1980; Wechsler, Reinherz, & Dobbin, 1981)

Practitioner/Researcher Approach. The above two traditional orientations in teaching research (consumer and producer approaches) to social work students fail to recognize the distinctive characteristics of the contemporary social work profession and the practice needs of its practitioners. Thus, in integrating the consumer *and* producer approaches in teaching social work research, we have adopted the concept of the *professional* social worker as a *practitioner/researcher.* The strength of the consumer approach is that it has emerged out of basic social work problems. The strength of the producer approach is its focus on methods and analyses of research and evaluation that are theoretically based, objective, and replicable. In the concept of the practitioner/researcher, emphasis on the practice character of the research and evaluation effort places the components of the research process within a framework specifically designed for social workers (Bloom, 1975; Bloom & Block, 1977; Bloom & Fischer, 1982; Dea, 1981; L. Epstein, 1981; Fischer & Hudson, 1983; H. K. Goldstein & Horder, 1974; Gottlieb & Richey, 1980).

The idea that research and evaluation are too important to leave to specialists runs throughout this text. Even more important, however, is the idea that knowledge development in the field is too critical to be left to those who are not themselves professional social workers. It is the practicing professional who encounters and struggles with current issues and who is most sensitive to the critical knowledge gaps in our profession. Thus, professional social workers are in the best position to formulate and conduct the needed research and evaluation. They are committed to acquiring the research knowledge and skills necessary to guide the helping effort. To rely on research specialists from other fields technically trained to "do research" is therefore unacceptable.

The centrality of research to social work practice has been stressed for many years (Gripton, 1978; Grossman, 1980; Hollis & Woods,

1981; Kirk & Kolevzon, 1978; Kirk, Osmalov, & Fischer, 1976). This orientation views social work practice as linked closely with study, diagnosis, and treatment. The concept of the practitioner/researcher emerges naturally from this continuing perspective on the interrelations of research and social work practice (Kolevzon, 1975; Kolevzon & Maykranz, 1982; Levitt & Reid, 1981; J. C. Nelsen, 1978, 1981).

Both social work practice *and* research are based on factually verifiable information (Duehn, 1981; Northwood, 1966). Social workers use research methods to try to acquire knowledge of how to obtain and process information and how to apply this knowledge in interpreting findings, making decisions, and reporting the results obtained (Perlman, 1957, 1970, 1972, 1976). Thus, the process of social work practice is identical to the process of social work research. It includes formulating the problem for study, collecting and analyzing data, evaluating the outcome, and drawing conclusions supported by these data.

In the practitioner/researcher model, therefore, good social work practice and good research are united (Schinke, 1983). This text presents the beginning knowledge and skills needed to become a professional social worker via the practitioner/researcher model. As defined by Briar (1980), competent practitioner/researchers:

1. Use with their clients the practice methods and techniques that are known to be most effective.
2. Continuously and rigorously evaluate their own practices.
3. Participate in the discovery, testing, and reporting of more effective ways of helping clients.
4. Use untested, unvalidated practice methods and techniques cautiously and only with adequate control, evaluation, and attention to client rights.
5. Communicate the results of their evaluations.

By participating in the professional dialogue that accompanies the practice of the practitioner/researcher model, professional social workers can keep alive an active interest in knowledge development in our field through research. By seeing how other professionals have attempted to examine and resolve related issues, social workers will refine their own practices. Thus, the concept of the practitioner/researcher provides a framework for the continuing education of all social workers (Rosen & Proctor, 1978).

Social workers who base their practice in careful evaluations of outcome with each and every client, and who carefully select practice methods and their corresponding treatment techniques according to the results of quantitative and qualitative research findings are more than just social workers. They are social workers who let themselves be guided, as much as possible, by quantitative and qualitative data. Professional social workers understand that research is a useful tool to be utilized to guide and enhance—but not to rule—practice. These social workers are *practitioner/researchers,* or more appropriately, *professional* social workers, as they recognize that the efficacy of their services cannot be left to chance. Too much is at stake.

This text meets the research needs of our profession by providing content which is entirely relevant to social work. The integration of research content and relevant social work examples helps social work students and practitioners find their identities as professional social workers. Thus, this text contains highly integrated chapters written by social workers who have strong, diverse social work backgrounds and interests. They have one major thing in common, however—all agree that the best way to become a professional social worker is to have a basic understanding of the social work research process, and, more importantly, to utilize the research process in practice.

Teaching Students to Become Professionals

The text's guiding principle is to enable social work students and practitioners to appreciate, and hence utilize, the tools of research in professional social work practice. We see this as another, possibly more important purpose than the traditional goals of preparing social work students and practitioners as *consumers* or *producers* of research. Indeed, our purpose encompasses the other two: social workers need to be trained to consume *and* produce research because their professional roles require them to gain the latest knowledge from social work research, to conduct evaluations to improve their practice, and to answer critical questions which are not being researched in other professions.

Throughout the text there is a continuing emphasis on the idea that professional decisions are derived from the best knowledge base possible, and one's intuition alone may be misleading (Posavac & Carey, 1980). Professional social workers are concerned with their impact on people or situations and with obtaining objective feedback on that impact. Indeed, this is the major distinguishing characteristic between a professional *career* in social work practice and an approach which treats it just as another *job.* To put it less tactfully, *professional* social workers have careers—*semi*professional social workers have jobs.

The purpose of social work education is to teach professional practice methods which are more effective than those based on the layman's intuitive approach or the ideas of social workers some 30 years ago (McCord, 1978; Reid & Hanrahan, 1982, 1983). Students who are being trained as professionals must be able to separate knowledge that is firmly founded in appropriate research designs and analyses from untested concepts or fads based primarily on people's enthusiasm for their own ideas. The only way to differentiate effective from noneffective practice methods is to have a sound understanding of the research process (Fischer, 1984; Grinnell, 1981b).

The perspective of this text is compatible with most social work curricula. It can be used at both the undergraduate and graduate levels, and it can maintain continuity from one level to another. It is also suitable for research courses of various lengths, styles, and emphases (Downs & Robertson, 1983). While it is designed to be used over two semesters, instructors are encouraged to select various chapters and to tailor their own research courses to fit the needs of the students in their social work curricula (Grinnell & Kyte, 1977).

Quantitative and Qualitative Methods

Some research courses favor quantitative research methods (based on quantifiable observations). Others favor qualitative research methods (based on nonquantifiable observations). We neither support nor deny the merits of either of these two approaches to social work research. Rather, we maintain that both methodologies are needed to strengthen our profession's knowledge base and the effectiveness of all social workers. Neither type of methodology is inherently more efficient than the other, and both have a place in the research arsenal of the skilled social worker (Lindsey, 1978b). Thus, we have included chapters on quantitative and qualitative methods (Weissman, 1981). Professional social workers master a variety of research methods, selecting the method according to the problem area rather than trying to fit the problem area to the method (Rosenblatt, 1981).

Dual Emphasis: Research and Evaluation

The title of this text, *Social Work Research and Evaluation,* indicates its orientation to evaluation as well as research. We are concerned with principles of relevance to all professional social work information, or data, gathering and processing, not just the classical group research situation. Therefore, we have included chapters on research methods which are generally referred to as evaluation. This broader definition of research implies application of the basic principles of research and evaluation throughout the social work profession.

Research Education for Two Types of Social Work Students

The distinctive needs of social work students can be related to the dual focus of our profession: community organization, administration, and planning (CO) and direct practice with individuals, families, and small groups (DP). The research needs of these two types of students have been generally ignored in planning research and evaluation courses and texts. For CO students, classical group research methods are needed most. But for DP students, who are primarily concerned with individuals or at most very small groups, single-subject design techniques are also needed.

Our continuing experiences and thinking, interactions with other faculties, and feedback from students have led us to base the rationale for the utilization of this text for both types of social work students on five tentative conclusions.

First, most principles of data collection and processing transcend the classical group—single-subject distinction. There is a set of basic research principles that is relevant for both types of students. For example, chance can produce seemingly important results in either setting; this has been obvious in the classical group approaches, but it is also apparent in single-subject analyses (Kazdin, 1982). And the principles of good measurement, including both validity and reliability, are equally important whether the concern is with observations on one client or a group. This text provides a diversity of examples so that both CO and DP students can see the generalizability of such principles (Mandell, 1983).

Second, the single-subject approaches are potentially just as important for CO students as for DP students. An agency administrator constantly needs to track the agency's progress over time and evaluate how well its goals are being accomplished. To increase the impact of the agency, the administrator may initiate a major intervention that could produce agencywide results. If these results are realized, a plot of the degree to which the goals are achieved over time should show a major jump after the intervention. In this way single-subject analyses are useful in agency and community settings.

Third, the ability to utilize group research approaches is also important for DP students. New practice methods and techniques are often developed and tested with group designs, and up-to-date social work professionals in direct practice need to learn about and apply such findings. In addition, many DP social workers are supported by agencies requiring group evaluations as a basis for grants. Professional practice is sure to be undercut if methodologically poor evaluations are conducted on it. Professional social workers, therefore, must be able to raise critical questions to ensure appropriate evaluations.

Fourth, there is a lack of consensus among social work research instructors about the essential content to be taught at either the undergraduate or graduate level (Nelson, 1983). Consequently, many graduate research courses needlessly duplicate undergraduate preparation, while others assume too great a degree of research knowledge. This lack of fit between undergraduate and graduate training ought to be reduced. The research exit requirements of undergraduate schools should be the research entrance requirements of graduate programs. In short, graduate research courses should start where undergraduate research courses end (Duehn & Mayadas, 1977a). This text can help bridge the gap between undergraduate and graduate social work research courses by providing a basic frame of reference if it is utilized at both levels (Grinnell & Kyte, 1977).

Fifth, and most importantly, to teach research effectively, the entire faculty must be committed to the concept that social work practice is indeed professional only when it is knowledge based and it utilizes data (broadly defined) as feedback for improvement. This text can only introduce the topic and help social work students and practitioners learn the research language. Courses in all content areas and, especially, field work placements must build on its main points to show how these concepts are utilized in practice. It is much like learning to write a good case narrative. The essential knowledge of grammatical principles such as spelling and punctuation is best provided in a general course. But the utilization of these skills must be developed throughout the educational experience, particularly in advanced courses and field settings where research and evaluation reports are required.

PLAN OF THE TEXT

While trying to develop a working definition of a practitioner/researcher via the chapters in this text, and at the same time emphasizing the need to integrate practice and research, our major objective has been to produce a text that is comprehensive and detailed enough to be useful in social work research situations and plainly written enough to be readable. Students are often faced either with a text that is too simple to prepare them for the complexities of the real world of social work research or too complex and abstract to be understood.

Thus, this text is divided into four main parts. Part One, "Formulation of Research Problems," presents the process of formulating and measuring social work research problems with an emphasis that is most closely related to practice: problem formulation, conceptualization, operationalization, and measurement (including validity and reliability). Part Two, "Measurement of Research Problems," presents how to measure the research problems as formulated in Part One. Part Three, "Methods of Data Gathering," presents the various types of social work research methods that can be utilized to gather data for the various research questions, formulated in Part One and measured in Part Two. Part Four, "Proposals, Reports, and Knowledge Utilization," presents how to write and evaluate empirical research studies and how to incorporate the knowledge gained from research studies into social work practice.

SUMMARY

Teaching students and practitioners to become practitioner/researchers through the use and application of research techniques in their practices is not an easy task (Hudson, 1977, 1978a, 1978b). The approach utilized in this text, however, has been extensively class tested, and we have had more than encouraging reports from colleagues and students. Research courses are a valuable part of the educational package for social workers if the courses are oriented to social work practice, and if other instructors are concerned with producing professionals who have an established knowledge base and can learn from their experiences through appropriate evaluative techniques.

We hope this text will help relieve students' anxiety about a research course and counteract their skepticism about the use of research in practice (Grinnell & Kyte, 1979). We also hope that as professional social workers they will use the knowledge they gain from it to provide clients with the most effective services. Incorporating the content of the following chapters into their own frame of reference, according to their professional interests or aspirations, will guide them in becoming practitioner/researchers. As discussed in the next chapter, social work practice and research are based on factually verifiable data, and the process of social work practice and research are one process; namely, systematic problem solving.

PART ONE

Formulation of Research Problems

Contents of PART ONE

Chapter

Wayne D. Duehn

2. PRACTICE AND RESEARCH

Social workers help people who seek their services, even though there is precious little evidence that what social workers do is effective. Because empirical studies to provide such evidence are few in number, inconclusive, and usually have methodological limitations, there is little choice but to view the knowledge on which social work skills are based as impressionistic, probabilistic, and tentative (Butler, Davis, & Kukonnen, 1979). But as members of a responsible, knowledge-based profession, social workers are ethically committed to rigorous investigation and objective evaluation of their practice activities (Bloom & Fischer, 1982). It is questionable for social workers to offer clients ineffective treatment interventions or to base their practice on unsupported evidence if other interventions whose efficacy has been established are available. All social work interventions are accountable both to the clients served and to the accepted conventions and standards of systematic, rigorous evaluation (Jayaratne & R. L. Levy, 1979).

THE PRACTICE-RESEARCH PARADIGM

In the past, social work research and evaluation was conceptualized as consisting of research tasks to be carried out by highly specialized personnel, apart from ongoing practice. Recently, however, a new perspective or paradigm which calls for social workers to rigorously analyze and study their own practice activities with research methods is receiving attention. The basic proposition is that it is well within the realm of possibility for a social worker to be both a practitioner *and* a researcher, or a practitioner/researcher. The focus is on the social worker's problem-solving process in formulating problems, selecting strategies, implementation, and evaluation to resolve social work issues (Eaton, 1962).

A paradigm is an exemplar of the concrete puzzle-solving directions which define what should and should not be studied. The paradigm directs where to look, prescribes the methods of how to look, and describes the entities when they are found (Kühn, 1970, 1977). Those whose research is based on shared paradigms are committed to the same rules and standards for scientific practice. As presented in the preceding chapter, professional social workers are adopting systematic research procedures to shape, direct, monitor, and assess their problem-solving activities. The paradigm, which can be applied to virtually all practice methods allows for the use of theory to guide practice and permits rigorous verification of change results.

If this paradigm becomes fully understood and generally accepted, it will have a far-reaching influence on our profession and ultimately on the clients served. It will affect the kinds of activities social workers engage in, the agencies and settings in which their work is done, the type of social work education offered and the institutions in which it is delivered, and the directions professional organizations take and the functions they perform. Conducting practice within this paradigm will not only contribute to the advancement of professional knowledge but will enable social workers to gain a more objective, less biased evaluation of their own practice effectiveness (Gambrill, 1983).

The Practice and Research Perspectives

There is no real dichotomy of social work practice and research. Social work *practitioners* employ the same methods and modes of thought in approaching problems as *researchers* do when they undertake a study. The practitioner/researcher's problem-solving process consists of four phases, as illustrated in Figure 2.1: (1) problem identification, definition, and specification; (2) generation of alternatives and selection of strategies for problem solution; (3) implementation; and (4) evaluation and dissemination of findings. In the ongoing process, the four phases are not separate entities but interconnected parts of a cycle which gradually blend together. There is no agreement as to the number of identifiable phases in the process, but this should not obscure its underlying commonalities. The number of phases and the identifying terminology used here are for analytical purposes and descriptive convenience (Perlman, 1957).

Practice and Research as an Orderly Thought Process

Our thought process begins with uncertainty or dissatisfaction with what is—doubt, perplexity, or confusion. A value decision about

FIGURE 2.1

Phases of the Problem-Solving Process Used by
Social Work Practitioner/Researchers

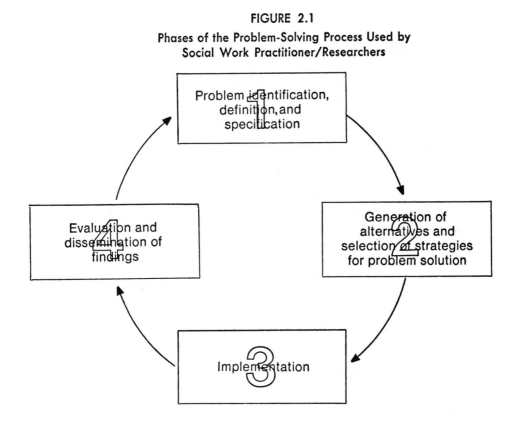

the importance of the uncertainty may impel us to lessen our dissatisfaction, and to do this a rational procedure must be followed. If we act
impulsively, uncritically, or unsystematically, we invite inappropriate
conclusions and inaccurate problem definitions. When errors and biases
are allowed to multiply and become compounded, we can be misled
into searching for solutions to the wrong problems, and this ultimately
compromises our ability to improve the situation.

Well-defined, orderly thought procedures reduce observational
biases, resist premature conclusions, and leave open the possibility of
alternative solutions. Many years ago Dewey (1933) formulated the
concept of reflective thinking as having five phases: (1) recognition of
a difficulty; (2) definition or specification of the difficulty; (3) generation
of suggestions for possible solutions and rational exploration of the
ideas; (4) selection of an optimal solution from among many proposals;
and (5) implementation of the solution. This list does not include

evaluation of effort and continuous feedback processing, and it fails to specify how modifications or adjustments are to be made when incoming data indicate that the intended objectives are not being met or the problem is not being resolved.

Nevertheless, the sequence does indicate the contingent relationship between phases in the process. The satisfactory completion of one phase is intrinsically tied to success in the preceding phases (B. S. Phillips, 1976, 1979, 1984). The explicit phases also force the problem solver to direct attention to the problem-solving process rather than becoming immersed in the situation (Perlman, 1957). Thus, it serves as a guide to help locate deficiencies or gaps in procedure. All social work problem-solving activities, both practice and research, are organized around this central assumption: There is a preferred order of thinking and action which, when rigorously and consciously pursued, will increase the likelihood of achieving objectives.

This way of looking at practice is far from new. Social work practitioners *and* researchers base their conclusions on careful observation, experimental trial, and intelligent analysis. Both observe, reflect, conclude, try, monitor results, and continuously reapply the same process until the problem in hand is solved or abandoned (H. Miller & Tripodi, 1967; Tripodi & H. Miller, 1966).

The Social Work Approach to Problem Solving

In social work, the approach to professional problem solving began many years ago. This approach makes not only every social worker but every successfully treated client a researcher in spirit. Figure 2.2 compares an excerpt from the writings of Richmond (1922) which illustrates this genetic problem-solving stance and the phases of the problem-solving process identified in Figure 2.1.

Professional problem solving has in effect been accepted by the Commission on Social Work Practice of the National Association of Social Workers, which makes no distinction between practice and research. As Bartlett (1958) notes:

> Social work methods include systematic observation and assessment of the individual or group in a situation and the formulation of an appropriate plan of action. Implicit in this is a continuing evaluation.... This evaluation provides the basis for the professional judgment which the worker must constantly make and which determines the direction of his activities. The method is used predominantly in interviews, group sessions, and conferences.

Unfortunately, the commission used *implicit* in its definition and did not spell out the operations of these evaluative procedures. This omis-

FIGURE 2.2

Comparison of Generic Problem Solving and the Phases in the Practitioner/Researcher's Problem-Solving Process

Illustration of Generic Problem Solving*	*Phases in the Practitioner/Researcher's Problem-Solving Process†*
Maria Bielowski's probation officer had to know which facts in her probationer's past were most likely to reveal the innate make-up of the girl, and which would show the effects of environment upon her personality. She also had to know how, setting appearances aside, to get evidence bearing upon these points from relatives, teachers, and employers; and how, after discarding irrelevant testimony, to draw the correct inferences from the relevant. It was important, moreover, to find the right home for Maria to live in, since her own seemed to be the wrong one, and to induce those in charge of that home to receive her. Further, the probation officer had to report all these facts and procedures to the judge, doing this so concisely, clearly, and without bias that he would be able to arrive promptly at a just decision. Omitting all mention of the training given to Maria at the school during the next eight months, consider also what her guardian had to know about the use of medical and mental specialists, about the careful selection of working homes for a difficult girl, about cooperation with her teachers, and the discovery of suitable recreational opportunities. None of this specialized experience was any more important, however, than were the skill, insight, and patience required in dealing with the girl herself. It was necessary to know what Maria was doing without discouraging her own initiative.	1. Problem identification guided by theory. 1. Investigator neutrality and objectivity to prevent sample biasing. 1. Data collection and classification; multiple baseline measures in the natural environment. 1. Problem specification and hypothesis formulation. 2,3. Generation of alternatives, selection of strategy, and implementation. 4. Evaluation of strategy and dissemination of findings. 1,2,3. Problem identification and specification, selection of strategies, and implementation of intervention. 3. Implementation, worker skill. 4. Evaluation, lessening reactivity effects.

Source: Richmond (1922).
Source: Courtesy of Russell Sage Foundation.

sion in itself may suggest that research procedures have little validity or relevance for current practice, when the opposite would be more accurate.

Observations based on experience or "felt knowledge" remain a primary function in present-day practice. Without the systematic, rigorous testing demanded by research, observational biases and errors go unchecked. The workers' practice skills may serve them well in various settings and with a variety of clients, but they often are far removed from and irrelevant to the ever-expanding body of knowledge identified as research findings (Tripodi & I. Epstein, 1978).

Many social workers remain largely unaware of the basic principles and processes of research and view the activities of practitioners and researchers as incompatible. With this stance, they seldom apply any of the knowledge available from research in social work and other social and behavioral sciences to practice situations (Rosenblatt, 1968). Knowledge related to interpersonal influence, assessment, decision making, and outcome is seldom taken into account (Mayadas & Duehn, 1975). There is evidence that social workers value personal experience, consultation, and supervision more than research findings as a source of practice knowledge. Until recently, outcome studies have had little visible effect on practice behaviors.

As social workers have continued to rely on practice wisdom instead of research findings, the procedures used by most social workers have been not self-correcting but, in many cases, self-perpetuating (Kirk & Fischer, 1976; Kirk & Rosenblatt, 1981; Rosenblatt, 1968; Thomas, 1981). Rare are the social workers who know of even two research studies in their area, and rarer still are those whose practices have changed as a result. In light of this evidence, it is not surprising that the adequacy of the social work knowledge base to accomplish our profession's stated ends is increasingly being questioned.

CASE A: THE PRACTICE PERSPECTIVE

Bette and Donald had had 12 years of marital strife at the time they sought assistance from a local family service agency; there had been a nine-month separation early in their marriage. They were the parents of three children: Amy, 10; Jennifer, 8; and Richard, 6. Donald worked on the assembly line at an automobile manufacturing plant, while Bette occasionally earned money as a seamstress.

Phase 1: Problem Identification, Definition, and Specification

Donald called the agency because a friend at work had suggested it could "straighten Bette out." Over the telephone, he complained that she was irritable, bitchy, not affectionate, and too tied to her parents. He was finding it increasingly hard to tolerate her conversation, which, he said, consisted mainly of complaints and tears. As a result, he worked a lot of overtime "to get away from her bad mouth."

The following dialogue illustrates how a rather vague and abstract description of a problematic situation began to be defined and spelled out in detail by the worker in the first interview.

> *Worker:* Before I can begin to help the two of you in your marriage, I need to learn as much as possible about each of you, your lives together, and what you hope to gain by being here today. That's why I will ask you a number of questions, and I'll also ask you to help collect additional information related to your problems and concerns.
>
> *Donald:* Like I told you on the phone, I'm tired of fighting. And that's all this lady seems to want to do. It starts the minute I get home. After standing on my feet all day long, working in all that noise, I've had it. I'm tired! I want to be left alone. I'm not up to any "meaningful interactions." And, what she calls "meaningful" is really her gripes and bitches. She doesn't seem to get it through her thick head that I need some time just for me—time to relax!
>
> *Worker:* Sometimes two people see things differently and have different ideas or notions about what's going on. Bette, I'm interested in why you feel *you* and Donald are here today.
>
> *Bette:* He makes everything sound so simple. If I'd only shut up when he gets home, then there would be no problem. We don't have a communication problem because we don't talk. I think Donald expects me to be some kind of maid who is supposed to follow him around the house picking up after him. I'm expected to fix *his* meals, wash *his* clothes, clean *his* house, and raise *his* children, without so much as even a thank you.
>
> *Worker* (talking to both Bette and Donald): How long have you both had these feelings?
>
> *Donald:* For years. I'm just a paycheck to Bette, or somebody she can kick around.
>
> *Bette:* That's not so. But to answer your question, for a long, long time. I can't even remember when they began. Donald refuses to admit that there are any problems. I'm surprised he even called.
>
> *Worker* (to Bette and Donald): You both indicate that talking with each other has been and is a big problem. Does this lead to other conflicts?
>
> *Donald:* You bet. Name anything and it's a problem for Bette.
>
> *Bette* (to Donald): That's because over the years you've become less involved in us. Everything is left up to me. I, too, get tired, irritable, and depressed. We never talk. There's no affection. Our sex life is next to nil. We're in debt. I try to budget, but I always come out short. You disapprove of the kids' behavior and somehow this is my fault too. Yet, you're never there to help out. You resent anything I do outside the house. We never go anywhere, except to visit my family, which you hate. We never have any fun together.

As this excerpt illustrates, from the first moment clients and workers begin to interact, a process of problem identification, definition, and specification is underway. This process is described in a variety of ways in the social work literature. The central aim of interview data is to specify details of the problem situation and to formulate a tentative problem area by identifying major goals and conflicts in the situation. Specifically, it consists of ordering events which provide data about where the couple has been, where they are now, where they want to be, and how the parents feel about these issues. This phase also includes a description of some of the factors that stand in the way of realizing the clients' objectives.

Relying heavily on the data in this first interview, the worker formed tentative impressions and then shared them with Bette and Donald. The worker's impressions were that they were experiencing considerable marital distress, and it could be attributed to four factors.

First, their expectations had not been met. Donald, who worked 10 hours a day, saw no need to discuss or help out with budget, household, or child management problems. He came from a family where such activities were labeled "women's work." Bette, who was home all day, expected Donald to be interested in her activities, however routine, and to participate actively in manners pertaining to the children, household, money, recreation, and the giving of affection.

Second, their exchanges within the interview as well as their individual descriptions of their problems were characterized by minimal support and lack of positive feedback from one another.

Third, they displayed a number of communication deficits. Their speech was marked by interruptions, countercomplaints, and failure to listen to one another.

Fourth, they had few negotiation and problem-solving strategies.

As a result, the worker surmised that Bette's and Donald's dissatisfaction centered in the areas of work, parenting, social and recreational activities, financial matters, sex, relationships with the extended family, and individual independence. On the positive side, Bette valued her husband's loyalty (fidelity), ambition, and devotion to his children. Donald said that he was only pleased with Bette's ability to socialize. She made friends easily, had a sense of humor, and was independent. In collecting interview data, the worker prodded the couple to give specific examples of their problems which could be observed and measured. If the problems could not be observed and measured, the worker believed they could not be treated (Hudson, 1978a, 1981, 1982a, 1982c).

The worker confirmed these tentative observations with the couple by reviewing the problems and goals each had identified. Donald's stated goals were: more private time, pleasant conversation with Bette, less time with Bette's parents (operationally defined as only one visit per month), and agreement on how the children should be disciplined. Bette's stated goals were: more "meaningful interaction" with Donald (operationally defined as mutual participation in problem solving, expressions of opinions and feelings, acknowledgment of her own contributions, and less criticism), increased affection and sexual expression, and the development of a mutually shared, active social and recreational life.

Bette and Donald (with the help of the worker) chose to concentrate first on improving their communication skills. They reasoned that improvement in communication would make the most positive difference in their relationship. In the worker's judgment, also, improvement in communication was a prerequisite to subsequent problem solving and resolution. The worker speculated that Bette's and Donald's conflicts in general problem solving, sexual relations, child rearing, money, personal independence, and recreation were affected by their communication patterns. Good communication skills could facilitate problem-solving activities, lessen or eliminate conflict areas, and ultimately contribute to increased marital satisfaction (Mayadas & Duehn, 1977). This rationale was shared with the couple.

The couple made the standard contractual commitment to cooperate and then was asked to supplement the interview data by collecting additional personal information with several measuring procedures and standardized measuring instruments. The worker requested Bette and Donald to complete, independently, two subjective self-report data collection devices: Hudson's (1982a) Index of Marital Satisfaction scale (IMS), and Richard Stuart's (1973) Marital Precounseling Inventory (MPI). The two data collection devices were chosen on the basis that a broadly based and varied approach to data collection was required in order to evaluate the aspects of marital functioning which went beyond those specifically defined by the couple as problematic. Data from the IMS and MPI provided the worker with an understanding of the overall scope of the problem which facilitated plans for sequencing the treatment strategies. The alternative would have been to operate blindly by attacking the problem of greatest immediacy as perceived by the clients.

A major advantage of the standardized measuring instruments was that they provided a simple, low-cost, and low-effort data collection method. They also served as a stimulus for discussions by the worker and the couple in definite substantive issues. In addition, the instruments required the couple's active participation in data collection activities and so served as a basis for introducing the concept of the client as data collector, problem assessor, and solver. The MPI was chosen for this couple because of its focus on positive relationship

TABLE 2.1
Index of Marital Satisfaction (IMS)

Name: _____ Today's Date: _____

This questionnaire is designed to measure the degree of satisfaction you have with your present marriage. It is not a test, so there are no right or wrong answers. Answer each item as carefully and as accurately as you can by placing a number beside each one as follows:

1. Rarely or none of the time
2. A little of the time
3. Some of the time
4. Good part of the time
5. Most or all of the time

Please begin:

1. I feel that my partner is affectionate enough. _____
2. I feel that my partner treats me badly. _____
3. I feel that my partner really cares for me. _____
4.
5.
6.
7.
8.
9.
10.
11.
12. $\Big($ Permission was granted to reproduce only the $\Big)$
13. first 3 items of the 25-item scale.
14.
15.
16.
17.
18.
19.
20.
21.
22.
23.
24.
25.

Source: From Walter W. Hudson, *The Clinical Measurement Package: A Field Manual,* (Homewood, IL: The Dorsey Press, 1982). Copyright © 1982.

aspects (social workers have long extolled the principle of starting with the client's strengths), its emphasis on self-change and self-determination, and its direct relationship to treatment outcomes and objectives. The IMS, which is presented in Table 2.1, was chosen because it was short and easily administered and scored, provided almost instant feedback, was valid and reliable, and was standardized so that evaluative comparisons could be made (Tripodi, Fellin, & Meyer, 1983).

The worker selected the above two data collecting instruments (IMS and MPI) after asking and then answering five questions:

1. Does the instrument provide me with information that will help me in my assessment or intervention planning?
2. Is the instrument relatively easy to use?
3. Will the data obtained indicate whether or not I have to make changes in my intervention program?
4. Is the instrument suitable for the resources available? Is it financially affordable? Are there people available who can and will accept and use it?
5. Do the data derived from the instrument provide the clearest and most accurate picture possible of the problem the client wants changed and the factors that may be affecting or maintaining the problem?

There are several reasons why it is particularly advantageous to use measuring instruments such as the IMS and MPI.

1. They enhance assessment and intervention planning, particularly by providing a focus on specific targets and outcomes.
2. They allow the social worker to determine case progress and to record plateaus or regression.
3. They can alert the social worker to the need for changes in the intervention program.
4. They can serve as a motivating factor for client and social worker as they see the results of their work.
5. They can keep track of small but steady changes that might be overlooked.
6. Recording of several cases by one social worker or several in one agency can provide data that can be analyzed to determine the dimensions of a range of effective interventions.
7. They provide clear evidence about the effectiveness of our practice.
8. They allow us to demonstrate our accountability.

The assessment data provided by the couple, consistent with the interview content, indicated high distress, with IMS scores of 47 for Bette and 40 for Donald. Data from the MPI showed high discrepancy scores on decision making (i.e., Bette's and Donald's perceptions differed greatly on how decisions were made and how they wanted them to be made). The MPI also revealed low general satisfaction ratings for Bette (25 percent) and Donald (35 percent).

In the next interview, Bette and Donald were asked to exchange their completed inventories and discuss their responses. The worker audiotaped this discussion to provide further evidence of their communication styles. Using a verbal communication-style checklist, the worker was able to obtain a detailed interactional profile of this discussion which pinpointed their conversational deficits (Mayadas & Duehn, 1977). Then they were given a daily homework assignment to audiotape 15 minutes of their conversation and rate it independently with an interactional log which is presented in Figure 2.3. They were to provide a brief analysis of the conversation such as time, place, who was present, what was said, other following events, and reactions.

Phase 2: Generation of Alternatives and Selection of Strategies for Problem Solution

After Bette and Donald left the agency, the worker began the arduous task of examining available intervention strategies to use with them. From these options, those that best fit the specific characteristics of the couple and its set of problems would be selected. Consideration would be given to the resources and constraints of the agency and the community, as well as the worker's personal skills and abilities. This process involved a series of compromises and trade-offs between the ideal and the possible. For example, the worker traded off data collection procedures that were more methodologically desirable for those that were more efficient to administer and less intrusive to treatment. Procedures with increased objectivity could necessitate a number of trained observers and elaborate recording equipment which would be far too time-consuming and expensive.

To choose the intervention strategies as intelligently as possible, the worker generated a list of all possible interpretations of the problematic situation and known practice methods for bringing about planned change. The first entries came from the worker's educational background and practice experience of "what works." This information was necessarily biased, dated, and limited, however, so a literature search was conducted at a university library. Using the card catalog and various social and psychological journal indexes, the worker reviewed material pertaining to such topics as marital counseling, marital interaction, problem solving, communication, communication skills, and communication skill training (Truax & Mitchell, 1971). The literature search yielded a wide variety of descriptive case studies, theoretical essays, and a few quantitative research studies. Practice models and techniques derived from psychodynamic, communication, structural, and cognitive-behavioral theories were among those reviewed.

The worker then applied the framework presented in Chapter 24 to analyze the interventions suggested in these studies which empha-

FIGURE 2.3
Example of an Interactional Log

Client Name: _____ Day and Date _____

Time	Place	Who Was There?	What I Said	What They Said	What I Said	Other Events That Followed	Your Reaction

Source: Martin Bloom, Joel Fischer, *Evaluating Practice: Guidelines for Accountable Professional*, *1982. Reprinted by permission of Prentice-Hall, Inc., Englewood Cliffs, N.J.

sized relevancy, objectivity, observability, manipulability, replicability, accessibility, and effectiveness. Relevancy pertains to the ability of an intervention to have an immediate, direct bearing on the problem. Objectivity refers to the extent that the intervention has been evaluated without bias or prejudice. Observability determines whether problems, intervention activities, and results can be seen, observed, recorded, and measured. Manipulability and accessibility pertain to the degree of worker control and the ways or means by which the problem can be approached. Replicability refers to the extent to which an intervention has repeatedly resulted in similar outcomes. Effectiveness is determined by the extent to which the intervention could bring about the desired outcome.

Next an inventory of the worker's own current skill level was made, time and cost factors of implementation were estimated, existing agency resources and constraints were appraised, and most important, the potential suitability of the procedures for the couple was considered. For example, an assessment of the couple's literacy was required before pencil-and-paper data collection methods could be used. The worker also observed that Bette and Donald were not particularly introspective about their relationship and surmised that they would probably experience some discomfort and would be less likely to follow through with interventions requiring extensive cognitive skills (Duehn & Mayadas, 1976, 1977b).

Based on this assessment, the worker decided that the first step in helping the couple would be an educationally oriented systems approach directed at improving Bette's and Donald's verbal communication skills. The three components in this approach were: (1) videotape-focused feedback; (2) modeling and instruction; and (3) behavioral rehearsals and home practice.

Videotape-focused Feedback. In videotape-focused feedback clients are presented with a video replay of themselves interacting with others discussing a relevant substantive area. They not only receive verbal critiques from others and the worker but can verify these perceptions with the taped reproductions of their behaviors. The instant replay capability of videotape makes it possible to compare these perceptions with data undistorted or filtered by perceiver bias. As clients become aware of the effects of their responsive behaviors, the worker guides them through focused feedback to alter problem-causing interactional patterns. The impact of watching and reexperiencing such exchanges, followed immediately by nondiscrepant feedback, makes the technique a potent reinforcer for learning skills.

This procedure was demonstrated in Bette's and Donald's first treatment session. During the video playback of the couple's discussion of Bette's extra sewing work, the worker repeatedly stopped the tape at points where one partner failed to acknowledge or respond to the other's comments and asked them to observe the effects of this failure. For example, Donald noted that when he didn't comment on Bette's efforts, she stayed on the subject until she got a reaction from him. Bette observed that it wasn't necessarily *what* she had said but rather *how* she said it that prompted a defensive reaction in her husband.

Modeling and Instruction. Modeling and instructional procedures are based on the notion that much social learning occurs vicariously through observing the behaviors of others. A modeled performance provides substantially more relevant and clearer cues to learning a task or skill than can be conveyed by verbal description alone. Making the modeled behavior vivid and explicit and minimizing competition stimuli accelerate skill acquisition. Video modeling adds another dimension because it not only standardizes and structures a depicted skill, but it can be presented repeatedly to clients. Model presentation in itself usually is not sufficient, however. Clients often need to be guided by instructions from the worker specifying which part of the performance is to be imitated.

Bette and Donald were shown videotapes of a couple modeling active listening skills. As the tape was viewed the worker pointed out the components of active listening displayed by the modeling couple (body posture, eye contact, verbal acknowledgment, reflected content, etc.) and the positive effects such listening had for the participants.

Behavioral Rehearsals and Home Practice. Behavioral rehearsals and home assignments are based on the rationale that one learns best what one practices most. Through guided, systematic, structured situations, clients are asked to practice a specific communication skill, first during a treatment session and subsequently in the real-life interactional situation at home. These procedures serve several purposes: They provide direct feedback to the worker on the level of skill mastery or deficit; they provide clients with structured opportunities to enact skills; and they promote the transfer and generalization of a skill to the real world.

A major criterion in selecting these treatment strategies for Bette and Donald was their proven efficacy with similar clients confronted with similar problematic situations. In social work, the problem configurations are far too varied and complex to be solved by a single intervention approach. Priority must always be given to interventions that have successfully demonstrated their effectiveness in a specific client-problem configuration. Thus, the most effective intervention cannot be chosen until the problem has been thoroughly explored and defined.

Phase 3: Implementation

Before implementing the treatment, the worker discussed with the couple the treatment process and was very careful to protect the rights of the couple, as described by Bloom and Fischer (1982):

1. Clients have the right to know what the *problem* is (from the perspective of the practitioner) in clear language that they can understand.
2. Clients have the right to participate in selecting *goals* and *objectives* of their treatment.
3. Clients have the right to know specifically what is going to happen during the *intervention process*—who is supposed to do what to whom and under what conditions?
4. Clients have the right to know how long the intervention is likely to last (*time* dimensions).
5. Clients have the right to know *alternative methods* of dealing with their problems, and what the probability is that the one(s) selected will lead to successful resolution of the difficulties.
6. Clients have a right to know how much the intervention will *cost* them. If they do not directly pay fees, it is equally a right to know the value of the services being provided.
7. Clients have the right to know what *records* will be kept and who will have access to them.
8. Clients have the right to know in advance about *termination* of services.
9. Clients have a right to take increasing *control* over their own lives, so far as they are able, or to know (or have a guardian know) why this is not so.
10. Clients have a right to be a part of and informed about the *evaluation* of their own situations, in order that they may profit from and make decisions based on these data.

The worker described what would take place in the treatment sessions; what would be required of the couple, both at home and during sessions; what tasks the worker would perform; and how the intervention procedures would relate directly to their initial request for help. The couple was informed of the need for ongoing data collection, and procedures were instituted for systematic retrieval of the data. The worker also requested Bette *and* Donald to complete a postsession evaluation form (see Figure 2.4) at the end of each treatment session. These evaluation forms helped the worker to see how Bette *and* Donald felt about each treatment session. Bette and Donald agreed to complete the IMS on a weekly basis and to prepare short individual daily activities records to provide data on time spent talking, recreational and social activities, free time, sexual activity, and so on. The communication program was focused on the three skills they wanted to improve: (1) listening and verbal acknowledgment, (2) opinion expression, and (3) positive expression. The worker emphasized that the first two skills are necessary for any problem-solving activity.

FIGURE 2.4
Postsession Evaluation Form

Client's Name   Practitioner's Name   Date

Please circle the number that comes closest to describing your feelings about the session you just completed.

    1   2   3   4   5   6   7   8   9

Not Productive   Moderately   Extremely
   At All   Productive   Productive

Please try to describe at least one positive and one negative incident or a part of the discussion that occurred during the session that might help explain your rating.

Positive Incident

Negative Incident

Source: Martin Bloom, Joel Fischer, *Evaluating Practice: Guidelines for Accountable Professional,* ●1982. Reprinted by permission of Prentice-Hall, Inc., Englewood Cliffs, N.J.

Following the assessment phase, the couple met for eight 90-minute weekly sessions, the first three of which are summarized in Figure 2.5. The program emphasized the three components in the intervention strategy identified above: videotape-focused feedback, video modeling and instruction, and behavioral rehearsal and home practice.

With the subject focused on the couple's immediate concerns, there could be considerable flexibility in each session. The interactional logs were used by the worker and the couple to critique the taped interactions, which provided immediate data on the extent to which a skill was being performed. Throughout this period, the worker con-

FIGURE 2.5
Contents of Three Treatment Sessions for Case A

	In Session	*At Home*
SESSION 1:	A. Introduction to skills of verbal acknowledgment (active listening)	A. Complete daily activities record
	B. Videotaping of couple discussing Bette's extra job using skill of verbal acknowledgment	B. Complete IMS
	C. Video replay and critique	C. Practice skill of verbal acknowledgment
	D. Video model presentation and discussion	D. Rate skill on checklist
	E. Taped practice	
	F. Replay and critique	
	G. Repeat procedures 1B–1F; subject matter—Donald's opinions related to kids' behavior	
SESSION 2:	A. Review and feedback of Week 1	A. Complete daily activities record
	B. Review of daily activities record, IMS, and checklist	B. Complete IMS
	C. Review skill of verbal acknowledgment	C. Practice skill of verbal acknowledgment
	D. Repeat procedures 1B–1F; subject matter—the in-laws, from Bette's and Donald's perspectives	D. Rate skill on checklist
SESSION 3:	A. Review and feedback of Week 2	A. Complete daily activities record
	B. Review of daily activities record, IMS, and checklist	B. Complete IMS
	C. Introduction of skills of positive expression	C. Practice skill of verbal acknowledgment
	D. Repeat procedures 1B–1F; subject matter—child management	D. Rate skill on checklist
		E. Practice skill of positive expression

Source: Duehn (1981).

sciously attempted to keep the focus on improving communication skills rather than actual problem resolution and monitored this focus by periodically reviewing audio recordings of the treatment sessions. When, in the fifth session, Donald asked for the worker's opinion on how much free time was reasonable, for example, he was reminded of their decision to work first on communication skills and was asked to evaluate the extent to which his taped responses reflected the skill of verbal acknowledgment.

Phase 4: Evaluation and Dissemination of Findings

Client self-reports not only served to guide and adjust the ongoing intervention but provided a means for evaluating the final outcome. During the eighth session, the worker noted how many of the couple's statements reflected change. Bette and Donald commented positively on how their marriage had changed and indicated that their children were better behaved; they spent more time together (and surprisingly, liked it); they went out more frequently; and they were more affectionate toward each other ("Sex couldn't be better").

Data from the IMS and MPI instruments and the daily activities records supported this encouraging pattern, as shown in Table 2.2, which summarizes pretreatment (Phase 1) and posttreatment (Phase 4) data for Bette and Donald. The IMS data revealed substantial decreases in their global perceptions of marital dissatisfaction, as reflected in scores of 21 (originally 47) for Bette and 24 (originally 40) for Donald. Although the intervention had not been directed toward problem solving, greater congruence was achieved on the MPI decision-making scale. Bette and Donald were in agreement on their perceptions of the decision-making process and were satisfied with the results. From this data, the worker surmised that the hypothesis that listening or verbal acknowledgment and expression of opinions were necessary components of problem solving for this couple was correct. As expected, MPI satisfaction ratings were markedly improved (up from 25 to 75 percent for Bette and from 35 to 85 percent for Donald). Data from the daily activities record indicated that both Bette and Donald had increased the amount of time spent talking together to an average of 96 minutes on weekdays (from the 10-minute average before treatment), were having sexual intercourse more frequently, and were engaging in more social and recreational activities apart from the children.

Observational ratings obtained from the videotapes indicated steady improvement in all three communication skills areas: verbal acknowledgment, opinion statements, and positive expression. There was a substantial increase in Donald's verbal acknowledgments (from 6 to 32)

TABLE 2.2
Pre- and Posttreatment Measures for Case A

Measure	Pretreatment	Posttreatment	Change
MPI:			
Bette	25%	75%	50%
Donald	35%	85%	50%
IMS:			
Bette	47	21	−26
Donald	40	24	−15
Verbal acknowledgment:			
Bette	12	38	26
Donald	6	32	26
Opinion statements:			
Bette	20	35	15
Donald	4	18	14
Positive expression:			
Bette	2	35	33
Donald	0	39	39
Daily time spent together:			
Talking	10 minutes	96 minutes	86 minutes
Sex	Next to nil	3 times/week	
Social activities	Very few	Increased	

Source: Duehn (1981).

and opinion statements (from 4 to 18), and they both raised their rates of positive expression.

Although the initial treatment plan called for continued intervention, with a focus on the development of problem-solving skills, treatment was terminated with the completion of the communication skills program at Bette's and Donald's request. In a six-month follow-up session which was videotaped and rated utilizing the observational checklist, they agreed to repeat all the self-report measures. All levels on these measures had been maintained, with one exception; the IMS measure indicated that Bette's dissatisfaction had increased. Observational data on the three communication skills indicated little change after termination.

CASE B: THE RESEARCH PERSPECTIVE

One afternoon two social workers began discussing a concern

related to the one in Case A. They noted that although increased atten- tion was being directed to developing more effective intervention ap- proaches to marital problems, specific treatment goals and measurement procedures were largely lacking. They reasoned that the need for these services would grow, due to increasing divorce rates, more openly acknowledged marital dissatisfactions, and the problems being encoun- tered by adults and children experiencing these disruptions. While they reached no conclusions, they agreed to explore this situation.

Phase 1: Problem Identification, Definition, and Specification

After numerous visits to the local library and talking to col- leagues, the workers concluded that the literature and practice wisdom were rich in global theories of marital dysfunction and general practice methods, often supplemented with anecdotal case histories. However, little quantitative evidence was available to explain or suggest tested methods of intervention for ameliorating these problems. Within the profusion of theoretical explanations, however, one common thread emerged—marital discord was seen primarily as a function of inade- quate or problematic communication. Here the literature ended. Be- cause measurable indicators of specific communication skills were by and large absent, interventional practice methods, as well as their intended objectives, were often cast in such global and vague terms that they defied measurement and evaluation. One exception was the work of a research group which had derived a provisional list of 27 problematic marital verbal behaviors (Thomas, Walter, & O'Flaherty, 1974).

As the workers continued to review the relevant literature, they were confronted with accumulating evidence of the efficacy of modeling procedures in learning new and complex social skills. And there was evidence that when these modeling procedures were combined with video feedback and guided practice, the learning rate was accelerated. On the assumption that specific verbal skills could be identified and reliably measured, combined with accumulating evidence of the effec- tiveness of modeling procedures, video feedback, and guided practice, they spent six months developing and testing a valid and reliable video- tape that could be used in practice with couples requiring training in communication skills. The final videotape showed a couple modeling 19 pairs of commonly occurring functional and dysfunctional verbal behaviors. For example, one segment depicted a husband and wife discussing money management using the dysfunctional verbal behav- iors of countercomplaining, and the scene was repeated without the countercomplaints.

Their exploration led the investigators to pose additional research questions. Whereas the literature reported the use of videotape feedback in marital counseling and the efficacy of modeling, the two techniques had rarely been combined, and their separate effects had not been measured. Few (if any) modeling procedures had utilized videotape technology. They narrowed their concern to the following research question: Could video modeling procedures and video-focused feedback alter certain problematic marital communication patterns? Specifically, if marital communication patterns could be altered, were these procedures more effective than traditional counseling approaches?

Phase 2: Generation of Alternatives and Selection of Strategies for Problem Solution

The two social workers then stated the research problem in a testable form. This required putting the research question in the form of a hypothesis—a statement which predicts a relationship between an independent and a dependent variable (see Chapter 3). The hypothesis in this study was that videotape modeling procedures and video-focused feedback (independent variable) are more effective in altering the problematic communication patterns of marital-distressed couples than traditional verbal counseling procedures (dependent variable).

In order to test this hypothesis, the investigators faced the task of generating a number of alternative research strategies and then selecting those that offered the greatest degree of experimental control (see Chapter 7). Included in this task were questions related to study design, use of a control group, methods of sample selection and sample size, data sources, data classification, and analysis procedures. In the same way the worker in Case A generated a list of possible interventions appropriate for Bette and Donald, these workers explored feasible research methodologies. Throughout these deliberations they were confronted with the rigorous demands of research on the one hand and the realities of what was available and feasible on the other. Thus, like the worker in Case A, they also arrived at all their decisions through a process of negotiation which resulted in a series of compromises (Toseland, 1981).

They decided to carry out the study in a marital counseling agency rather than a laboratory setting. Although this allowed for far less control over the experimental conditions and left room for the influence of extraneous variables, the research question called for an applied practice setting. Thus, the study's generalizability to other practice situations could be measured (Fischer, 1976b).

A research design was chosen on the basis of agency, practice, and data processing constraints. No maximum limit was set on the number of clients treated; this was subsequently determined by the availability of clients requesting such agency services. Clinical and methodological considerations made it impossible to examine the separate effects of video-focused feedback and video modeling (Thomas, 1983). As a result, the basic research question had to be modified so that comparisons could be made between the effects of videotape modeling and videotape modeling combined with focused feedback. The worker in Case A was similarly required to make several modifications in treatment programming which directly influenced how that problem was eventually formulated (Gambrill, 1983).

A number of decisions were made to minimize extraneous variables and to rule out factors that could explain away changes attributed to their intervention. Couples were randomly assigned to one of three conditions to control for possible pretreatment client differences: (1) videotape modeling; (2) videotape modeling combined with video-focused feedback; and (3) verbal counseling (attention placebo). Individual social worker effects were minimized by having each worker deliver all three treatment interventions. The specific details of the study and research hypothesis were not shared with the workers, to control for investigator bias effects.

Phase 3: Implementation

Like the worker in Case A, they next translated the decisions made in the two preceding phases into action. Through peer contacts, they gained access to a practice setting which was interested in testing the treatment interventions. Close collaboration among the agency, the workers, and other colleagues was required in all phases of the process, from problem identification, definition, and specification to evaluation and dissemination of findings.

Decisions had to be made in relation to staff allocation, service disruptions, secretarial time, technical hardware, and supportive funding. To ensure that the social workers were delivering separate treatment interventions so that adequate comparisons could be made, considerable time was spent teaching and monitoring the video modeling and video-focused feedback procedures. Decisions regarding case assignment and equalization of workers' skills were based on research requirements to minimize the influence of extraneous variables. The social workers made frequent checks throughout the study to determine if the interventions were being systematically varied and if established data collection procedures were being maintained. Workers were required to submit a pre- and postintervention videotape on each couple for data analysis.

The two social workers employed a combination of research knowledge and interpersonal skills to accomplish these collaborative tasks (Tripodi & I. Epstein, 1980). Similar interpersonal skills were required of the worker in Case A to ensure the continued cooperation of Bette and Donald.

Pre- and posttreatment percentage changes of the clients' most frequently occurring problematic verbal behaviors were chosen as the measures for testing intervention effects. These percentages were computed from ratings made by three independent observers (raters) who had no knowledge of the study's purpose, hypothesis, or tape sequence (pre or post). Tapes were rated only after the observers had reliably mastered the measuring procedures.

Phase 4: Evaluation and Dissemination of Findings

In order to compare the effects of the three treatment interventions (videotape modeling alone and combined with feedback, as compared with verbal counseling) the social workers organized the data in such a way that objective comparisons and analysis could be made (see Table 2.3).They were adopting an explicit, standardized method for making a planful and rigorous comparison which would allow for evaluation of the stated relationships between the various interventions (independent variable) and the couple's communication patterns (dependent variable). These activities were similar to the worker's comparison of Bette's and Donald's pre- and postcommunication patterns on a number of dimensions in Case A (see Table 2.2). The results of these comparisons indicated video modeling in combination with video-focused feedback was the most effective method for improving communication skills. Skill acquisition occurred in all five areas measured: (1) countercomplaining, (2) being abstract, (3) dogmatic assertion, (4) failure to express acknowledgment, and (5) ancient history-distant future. Couples exposed only to the video modeling procedures improved in the first, fourth, and fifth areas, whereas those receiving traditional verbal counseling improved in only the fourth one. As part of the evaluation in their subsequent written report the two social workers pointed to the study's limitations, discussed the applicability and generalizability of their findings to other social work practice situations, and raised a number of additional research questions which had emerged from their study. Thus, the research process was again set in motion (Toseland, 1981).

TABLE 2.3

Pre- and Posttreatment Averages for Three Treatment Methods for Case B

	Type of Treatment								
Verbal Behavior	*Stimulus/Modeling Videotape and Feedback*			*Stimulus/Modeling Videotape Only*			*Verbal Counseling*		
	Pre —	Post =	Change	Pre —	Post =	Change	Pre —	Post =	Change
Counter-complaining	28	6	22	30	5	25	26	28	−2
Being abstract ..	11	4	7	13	11	2	11	10	1
Dogmatic assertion ..	13	2	11	11	9	2	14	9	5
Failure to express acknowl-edgment ..	32	6	26	30	4	26	33	10	23
Ancient History—distant future	21	3	18	22	5	17	23	24	−1

Source: Duehn (1981).

THE SOCIAL WORK PRACTICE PROCESS IN RESEARCH

The word *research* is composed of two syllables, *re* and *search*. The dictionary defines the former as a prefix meaning again, anew, or over again and the latter as a verb meaning to examine closely and carefully, to test and try, or to probe. Together they form a noun describing a "careful, systematic, patient study and investigation in some field of knowledge, undertaken to establish facts or principles." In social work, this field of knowledge broadly consists of people, their actions and reactions to external situations, the external world, and methods that bring about change. To avoid becoming too philosophical, we will simply note that knowledge of these four areas does exist. Further, we can assume that social workers must apply this knowledge to attain certain ends. It follows, then, that the attainment of these ends is predicated on a thorough understanding of this existing knowledge, or reality.

Paradoxically, this reality can never be fully known: it can at best only be approached or inferred (Kühn, 1970). In the process of defining "the real," we are unable to make a distinction between the thing and the thought. Attributes that characterize even the simplest of things contain internal processing elements in addition to the externalities or "givens" that are supplied by sensory perception. This has crucial implications for social work. If social workers are to base their actions primarily on the facts and principles of what exists, "the real," rather than on inferences and thoughts, it is imperative to adopt the most rigorous procedures for obtaining the closest approximations of "the real."

As presented in detail in the next three chapters, social workers have available a number of ways of arriving at knowledge about what is. But all practice methods have built-in biases and limitations which create errors and keep us from being absolutely certain. And although research emphasizes objective data, objectivity, public observability, empirical verifiability, and testing through measurement, it too is subject to error. Thus, error can occur both in the kinds of observations we make and in how we think about what is real (Garfield & Bergin, 1978).

Research, therefore, can be operationally defined as the repeated use of objective, rigorous, and systematic procedures by which what we think about reality is tested against what we observe, and conversely, what we observe is examined in the light of what is known. To qualify, the procedures must conform to the conventions and standards of sciences that stress controlled observations, verifiability, representativeness, and measurement. This process of repeated testing of what is known and what is observed seeks to eliminate errors and biases. All of the elaborate testing procedures which have been developed are designed to protect us from making errors or obtaining wrong answers. The aim of the social work practice *and* research process is to produce data about reality as it is, unbiased by error.

THE SOCIAL WORK RESEARCH PROCESS IN PRACTICE

As the two case studies above indicated, social work practice and research have many similarities. Both seek to add knowledge through systematic problem solving, and both require identifying problems, posing questions, making observations, selecting data sources, selecting clients (samples), classifying observations, analyzing data, making inferences, and validating theories. In the practitioner/researcher model, the methods of research are explicitly incorporated into practice activities. Thus, the processes cease to be similar and become one, as practice activities are directed, monitored, and evaluated by the standards and methods of scientific inquiry (Fellin, 1984; Fischer, 1983; Karger, 1983; A. Rosen & Proctor, 1978).

The practice perspective of Case A consistently embodied the four elements of the problem-solving process, from problem identification, definition, and specification to evaluation and dissemination of findings. The worker's observations served as a major source of data throughout the problem-solving process. By listening and interacting, the worker obtained reports on the couple's perceptions of themselves, each other, the problems, and the helping process. The worker could perceive subtle discrepancies among the reports as well as changes in them as treatment progressed and could use the data to formulate provisional notions or hypotheses related to the couple and their problem. This problem definition, arrived at through abstraction and generalization of the events, pointed out connections with similar situations and helped direct the change efforts.

Sources of Error

Observations and theories are riddled with errors and biases, however. First, the worker's behavior, indeed the very presence of the worker, creates sampling biases in the interview, and this opens up possibilities for observational errors. Considerable evidence has been accumulated to suggest that even in the most nondirective, passive kind of interviewing, the social worker acts on implicit assumptions and hypotheses (W. Gingerich, Kleczewski, & Kirk, 1982). In fact, every interview question supports some implicit or explicit hypothesis. It has also been shown that client responses are affected by the social worker's eye contact, body posture, vocal phrasing, verbal inflections, and facial expressions. To lessen these sources of error, the worker formulates questions which are as measurable as possible and utilizes interviewing skills which are most likely to produce undistorted data. For example, in Case A the worker simply asked Bette and Donald, "Give me some examples of how you each discipline the children."

A second source of bias and errors is the worker's knowledge base, practice orientation, and belief system. The worker's ideas about marriage, communication, behavior, change, and so on provide much of the stimuli for the questions asked (Duehn & Mayadas, 1976). Virtually all practice frameworks attempt to control for these effects through the use of structured interviews or well-spelled-out strategies for data collection which emphasize breadth, objectivity, representativeness, and comprehensiveness. Nevertheless, there is ample evidence that social workers are more responsive to client data that are consistent with their

own beliefs (Duehn and Mayadas, 1979). Since the worker is predisposed to select questions that confirm existing hypotheses, care must
be taken to ensure that problem formulation is a process of discovery
rather than justification (Fischer & Gochros, 1975).

The format for seeking help is a third source of error in client data.
Much of the interview data is determined by the social structure in
which help is given. The "hello-goodbye" effect, whereby clients begin
treatment emphasizing problems and leave treatment convinced of its
efficacy may be in part an artifact of social convention. Clients want to
believe that they have benefited from treatment. They also want to
please their workers. Bette and Donald, for example, may have had
difficulty in objectively separating actual treatment effects from the
inherent social expectations that dictate to them that they have been
helped.

A fourth bias and sampling error source is the worker's perceptual
and cognitive limitations for processing data. The literature provides
abundant evidence of the effects of channel capacity, primary-recency,
anchoring, cognitive style, perceptual set on information processing,
decision making, and clinical judgment (Duehn & Proctor, 1974). The
worker's assessments of the "realities" of Bette's and Donald's problem
were influenced by situational complexities, amount of information,
order of timing of information, and perceptions of other clients in other
situations.

Minimizing Errors

To counteract the possible sources of data error inherent in personal observations and inferences and in the subjective self-report instruments, the worker in Case A augmented the interview data with
data collected from other sources, such as self-report schedules, checklists, records, home observations and the electromechanical devices of
videotapes and audiotapes.

In generating the list of possible solutions to the problem in Case
A, the worker conducted a literature search which culminated in a list
of suitable treatment strategies. Such a search is based on the assumption that professional social workers are ethically bound to be as fully
informed as possible. It is supported by evidence that indicates the
greater the number of possible solutions to a problem, the greater is the
likelihood of effective plans for problem resolution. Interventions are
selected on the basis of such criteria as proven efficacy, client values
and objectives, situational constraints, time-cost considerations, self-
assessed knowledge, and skill competencies, rather than the worker's
personal preference or comfort.

In addition to the worker's observations and the client's self-reports, the intervention in Case A was monitored and assessed with several other data collection procedures chosen on the basis of their relevance to the defining situation, the couple's abilities, and the worker's assessment of measurement reactivity (changes that result from applying the measuring instruments). The monitoring procedures used should be beneficial to clients and unlikely to create situations which could cause them additional pain or intensify their problems. If treatment activities are to be meaningful, the worker and the clients must have verifiable, observable data of what is going on in the process and what changes are taking place.

Throughout implementation, these observations, verbal statements, and data points serve as minitests of the adequacy of the original problem formulation. In Case A, by careful, systematic, and rigorous (and as well as biased, unsystematic, and impressionistic) observations, the worker and the couple were testing their assumptions of how to effect change in marital communication patterns and how these patterns were related to the couple's marital satisfaction and problem-solving activities.

The evaluation of social work practice rests on the identification of precise measurable objectives. When outcomes are clearly specified, the process is less likely to drift, and workers are less able to impose, inadvertently or otherwise, their own values. Research studies have shown that social workers are notoriously susceptible to their own "hello-goodbye" effects and can be grandiose in estimating their positive impact on clients.

The built-in objective measures and research procedures used in Case A had two advantages: They enhanced the rigor of social work practice, and they were consistent with the ethical principle that clients have a right to the most unbiased assessment possible. Thus, evaluation efforts are not viewed as a set of research procedures imposed on practice but as an integral aspect of professional social work accountability.

SUMMARY

The processes of social work practice and research are one process, namely, systematic problem solving. The extent to which the activities have explicitly incorporated rigorous, systematic conventions and standards of science has characterized them as practice or research, rather than any underlying differences. Social workers must become aware of the "oneness" of this generic problem-solving process if our profession is to demonstrate its effectiveness and thus survive (Fischer, 1981b).

There are available procedures social workers can use to vigorously analyze and study their practice activities. These procedures cannot only advance social work knowledge and practice but also provide for objective and unbiased evaluation of individual practice effectiveness. The chapters in Part One of this text show how the initial phases of the practitioner/researcher's problem-solving process can lead to the construction and use of empirically based instruments in social work practice and research.

Conceptualizing the social work practice and research processes into separate and sometimes divergent activities has had unfortunate consequences. Adoption of the practitioner/researcher problem-solving model will have far-reaching effects on the knowledge-building efforts of the profession, the practice of social workers, and the clients social workers serve.

Norman J. Smith

3. RESEARCH GOALS AND PROBLEMS

The social work profession has always been concerned with various social problems and how to solve them. As presented in the previous chapter, the different methods social workers adopt to solve these problems predominantly focus on a problem-solving approach. However, the term *problem* is much used in our everyday vocabulary. According to the *way* it is used, it can have different meanings to different people (Thomlison, 1984). For example, "researchers" talking about a child abuse problem are more often using the term (*child abuse*) differently than, say, "practitioners" facing difficulties surrounding their work with their child abuse clients. The social work researcher may be talking about the problems associated with ways of explaining or examining child abuse in order to add to our profession's knowledge base in reference to child abuse as a social problem. On the other hand, the practitioner may have a problem deciding what can or should be done to help in child abuse cases in order to change their situations and to stop the abuses from reoccuring.

At a basic level, a problem is an expressed difficulty. The problem must be expressed either in thoughts to one's self or in communication with others. A problem cannot exist until it is recognized as one, therefore, recognition precedes expression. A dilemma may arise since there is usually more than one way a specific problem can be solved. Thus, we must make a decision on how to solve a specific problem (see Phase 1 in Figure 2.1 in Chapter 2) based on a choice of alternatives and selection of strategies for the problem's solution (see Phase 2 in Figure 2.1 in Chapter 2). The very process of choosing from the different alternatives to solve a problem, each with its own advantages and disadvantages, is what makes it a problem. Obviously, no problem exists if there are no alternative decisions or choices available to solve a specific problem situation.

For example, a person who has only enough money to pay for a bus fare may have a problem in deciding whether to walk and save the money or to take the bus. On the other hand, if the person had enough money for a bus or a cab fare and decided to ride, a dilemma may arise in choosing between the bus or the cab. Each of the two available options has its own advantages and disadvantages. This overly simple example demonstrates that the differential use of the word problem surrounds the different kinds of questions formulated in particular problem situations.

The type of question (i.e., how or what) constructed in addressing a specific problem determines the kind of knowledge and data needed to answer the question. *How* a person travels from *A* to *B* (e.g., riding or walking), or *how* a social work practitioner helps a specific client (e.g., behavior modification or person-centered therapy) are different types of problems than *what* means of transportation a person utilizes to travel, or *what* treatment methods can be utilized to help a specific client.

What topic a social worker chooses to study is much different from how the same topic is studied. As presented in Chapter 13, each question (what and how) requires a different kind of knowledge base. Knowledge can be defined as the cumulated information or understanding of a subject. The what question surrounds a decision to be made over various areas to be studied. The how question presupposes that the subject area has been chosen (Stinchcombe, 1968).

RESEARCH GOALS

The many problem areas studied within our profession never occur in isolation (Blalock, 1969). They are usually influenced by a particular goal the worker may wish to achieve. Additionally, the worker's own goal may be influenced by our profession's goals. Thus, research problems must always be seen as being influenced by the social worker's goals which in turn are influenced by the goals of our profession (Welch, 1983). It is always the purpose of the required answer to a specific problem that determines the type of problem formulated (what or how) and the means for its solution. Thus, one must be aware of the nature of problems (e.g., mental illness) and the different kinds of data (e.g., why do some people become mentally ill) required to answer different questions. If the main goal of social workers in a particular probation department is to help juveniles with their delinquency, then the strategies adopted to answer the problem of, say, *what* to do and *how* to do it, will be the criteria utilized to evaluate whether the social workers achieved their goal.

In order to reduce the complexity of life, we may order the goals we set into specific areas. For example, we talk about health problems, housing problems, relationship difficulties, and so on. At certain times, we change the order of the importance of these areas as their value to us changes (Clark, 1983). At one time we may lay a greater value on our future career as compared to the geographical area we live in. Another time it may be that the value of our health is of greater importance than a sport or leisure interest (C. S. Levy, 1976). In reality, however, many areas impinge on each other. The impinging of problem areas on each other is particularly so for social workers intending to do a research study in the many possible problem areas covered in our profession (Lowenberg & Dolgoff, 1983).

Evaluative and Truth Goals

The first task facing social workers is determining what their goals are. There are two ultimate but alternative goals, each with its own advantages and disadvantages: (1) evaluative goals; and (2) truth goals. Evaluative goals are directed at enhancing social work practice for the *direct* benefit of a specific client system because we believe in the value of helping others. Truth goals, on the other hand, increase the general knowledge base of our profession for the *indirect* benefit of all clients systems. It is extremely important to realize that the two goals are not incompatible; they are two opposite poles of applied (evaluative) and pure (truth) research inquiries. Each goal has implications for, and effects on, the nature and conduct of all research studies that are subsequently executed. Each goal generates different needs requiring different decisions, although the type of question (i.e., *what* or *how*) is the same. When evaluative goals are established, professional accountability claims are addressed. Evaluative goals relate to specific practice methods and their effectiveness in terms of how or whether they have helped clients. Social workers who evaluate their own practices in terms of specific outcomes are essentially establishing evaluative goals (see Chapters 20 and 21). The establishment of truth goals center around conditions relating to knowledge generation and add to our profession's knowledge base through generalizations (Tripodi, 1981).

From the very outset, these respective goals influence *what* problem is studied and the *way* it is studied. The remainder of this chapter focuses on the formulation of problems into researchable terms for truth goals with the theme of meeting the standards required by the knowledge-generating paradigm presented in Chapter 2. This does not imply that the structure and process of "practice" and "research" are distinctly different. In both cases, the phases are the same (see Figure

2.1 in Chapter 2); it is the goals of the two kinds of research that are different.

RESEARCH PROBLEMS

Central to the entire process of any research endeavor is the specific problem that is the subject of the study. The formulation of a problem is usually more essential than its solution (Kaplan, 1964). What problem is chosen to study and how the problem is studied becomes the two main criteria on which to judge its usefulness in advancing our profession's knowledge base (Polansky, 1975c). In considering the way a problem is conceptualized and operationalized into researchable terms we have to distinguish between the problem's authorized version and its reality version (Blalock, 1982). The authorized version is the way the study should be done; the reality version is that way that the study actually takes place (Merton, 1957).

The authorized version envisages the research process as a number of discrete and sequentially linked phases beginning with problem formulation, identification, and specification in which the overriding stance of detachment and objectivity shapes its composition (see Figure 2.1 in Chapter 2). In reality, social work research is in itself a social activity (Beckerman, 1978). The phases of the practice and research process are not clear cut in formulation and they are heavily influenced by the social worker's and our profession's value systems. For example, it may be that several social workers notice an increase in their case loads and decide to analyze why this was occurring. As a result, they became interested in explaining this increase and began to search the literature to see if other social workers were experiencing the same increase. Following the literature review and after analyzing their data, the project was written for possible publication. The manuscript was written in the accepted format for professional papers (see Chapter 23). The specific format of the manuscript may give the impression that their inquiry was conceptualized, operationalized, and executed after they reviewed the literature. However, this was not the case.

Selection of Subject Area

The selection of a subject area to study and the subsequent formulation of a specific problem to be studied from the subject area must precede the selection of the method to gather data needed to answer the specific problem (Greer, 1969). As presented in Chapter 7, the selection of a specific problem and the method utilized to gather data to answer the problem heavily interact (Billups, 1984; Chatterjee, 1984; Blalock & Blalock, 1968).

It is the current state of knowledge of a subject area that ultimately determines the specific problem to be studied (Tripodi, 1981). It is the way a problem is expressed for examination that determines the method chosen to gather data to answer the problem. As presented in Chapter 13, if little is known about a subject or problem area, it is usually not feasible or desirable to utilize a cause-effect experimental design until hypothetical-developmental studies have been done first (see Table 13.1 in Chapter 13).

Issues surrounding the feasibility of a specific study interacts with the way it can be done (E. G. Brown, 1981). This, in itself, causes the problem to be reinterpreted and adapted. For example, if we wanted to find out how clients evaluated social work services, it would not be feasible to interview every social work client in the United States. First, we would not be able to identify or contact every existing client. Second, it would raise ethical issues surrounding the questions of "outside" contact and interference with their present receipt of social work services (Schinke, 1981b). Therefore, we would be required to either look for ways that we could draw a sample of clients, which in itself would possibly require some modification to our problem statement, or we could restate the problem in such a way as to avoid the requirement of sampling by examining ex-clients who were seen by one organization and/or in one geographical area (see Chapter 8).

Throughout the entire research process it is important to constantly address the paramount position of the problem as the initiator of the study and not as the subject matter for a particular method (e.g., quantitative or qualitative).

There is no single rational process to select a specific problem area for any study (Reynolds, 1971). Many factors influence a particular choice since ideas emerge from many sources such as reading, discussion with colleagues, and inspiration. Research problems are dealt with through the rules of a knowledge building paradigm in such a way as to reduce or minimize the biases that arise from subjective factors (Charlesworth, 1982). For example, we must always state the aims of our study in a clear manner. We must also ensure that the operational definitions we use are unambiguous (to be discussed later in this chapter). In reality, there is no one major source of problems offering themselves up ready for study. As presented in depth in the next two chapters, there are many extrinsic (e.g., role in an organization's policies) and intrinsic (e.g., personal preference, professional interest) factors that influence the way problem areas are translated into specific researchable terms.

FORMULATING RESEARCH PROBLEMS

The process of problem formulation is akin to the cognitive and emotive aspects of the research process in miniscule (Stinchcombe, 1968). This is because social workers find themselves moving out from ideas in a problem area into the process of how to study them through a series of mind experiments. This constant feedback process both refines the problem area as well as the subsequent research design utilized to study the problem. A danger arises in that a particular type of research design may be chosen first and the problem area is refined and tailored for the chosen design.

There are three ways one can become interested in a research problem: (1) some statement, observation, or finding from a written or verbal source; (2) observation of something leading to a feeling of interest, puzzlement, or curiosity; or (3) a seemingly sudden idea that holds one's attention. Whatever the source of ideas, there are seven phases needed in order to refine what may be a fairly general and vague idea into a more specific researchable topic for study. The seven phases are: (1) identifying the general topic areas; (2) identifying the personal interest areas; (3) reviewing the literature; (4) refining the problem area; (5) examining relationships between concepts; (6) relating the research problem to existing theory; and (7) constructing the hypothesis.

Phase 1: Identifying the General Topic Areas

The first phase in formulating a research problem is to identify the subject area, on a very general level, in which the idea is located. For example, if our interest was in the professional career patterns of social workers, then our specific area would be social workers as opposed to psychologists or sociologists. Our interest would also be concerned with their professional work milieu as opposed to a social or educational one. Therefore, we might define professionalism as our general topic area. It is advisable to keep a research logbook during all phases of the research process (S. J. Wilson, 1980). A logbook is similar to a diary in which one's ideas, comments, thoughts, and more importantly, decisions about any proposed study can be chronologically recorded. Not only is a logbook an aid in the task of preparing and designing a study, it is necessary in order to develop important ideas and concepts concerning the general problem area itself (Kagle, 1984a, 1984b). Additionally, the logbook constitutes a piece of historical research in its own right in terms of how the research problem was conceptualized (P. Stuart, 1981). By undertaking this process, it is possible to delineate the specific area of a study by the exclusion of other areas. It also helps in the identification of the potential independent and dependent variables or, more importantly, concepts.

Concepts. Words or ideas that we utilize to communicate the reality we experience and explain events are called concepts. Concepts connect a particular experience or observation to a theoretical explanation for it. For example, people seeking services from a social work agency may be conceptualized as clients, teenagers, or members of minority groups. As well as these, they may be conceptualized as depressed, insecure, or aggressive. The actual meanings depend on the characteristics the people share with other individuals and the purposes for which the concepts are formulated. Concepts relate anticipated research questions to an existing knowledge base (E. G. Brown, 1981). They also help to define an area for subsequent study. Concepts are measured in one of two forms: (1) abstract definitions, or (2) operational definitions.

Abstract and Operational Definitions. Abstract definitions are concepts relying on other concepts for meaning. Take for example the statement:

> Social workers (concept) are professionals (concept) who work (concept) in the area of human relationships (concept).

Thus, there are four concepts in the preceding statement. Operational definitions specify explicitly how the major concepts of a study are observed and subsequently measured. They are considered adequate if, and only if, the instrument or procedures based on them yield data that are deemed to be satisfactory representatives of the concepts they stand for. Operational definitions eliminate any ambiguity in the meaning of key variables (B. Phillips, 1976). Not only do some words have several meanings but the contexts in which they are used can affect comprehension (Mindel, 1981). One way to alleviate this difficulty is to be extremely clear about what is being considered. For example, the social workers mentioned above could be operationally defined as:

> All people who hold an M.S.W. degree from an accredited graduate school of social work who have been employed on a full-time basis for the last 24 months within Agency A.

The above statement is fairly straight forward and eliminates much, but not all, of the ambiguity that was present in the first statement. However, we must be aware that the operational definitions that we utilized must be selected for use on a rational basis (Reid & L. Epstein, 1972; Reid & Shyne, 1969). Why were social workers operationally defined as those people who hold an M.S.W. degree? Why not include B.A., B.S.W., D.S.W., or Ph.D., for example? Why did they have to work on a full-time basis? What is the specific rational for this—why not part-time social workers? Why only Agency A and not Agencies B, C, D, or E? Why did the social workers have to graduate from an accredited graduate school of social work? How about those who graduated with a counseling psychology degree from an accredited graduate school of psychology?

All of the above operational definitions must be able to generate valid and reliable data. They must also have been selected on a rational basis—that is, they must have been selected for a logical reason—not for convenience only. If at all possible, the operational definitions should have been selected from the theoretical framework of the study (Clark, 1983).

Phase 2: Identifying the Personal Interest Areas

The second phase in formulating a research problem is to brain-storm and to ask questions to establish what particular aspects of the area chosen creates personal interest and why; this technique allows new ideas and associations to be examined. The emphasis in this phase is establishing an answer to "why the interest area?" An answer to this question may uncover ideas associated with the area which could have been assumed; that is, taken for granted. In our example, the interest may stem from results of previous work in an allied area surrounding attitudes workers develop toward their clients after they have been in practice a number of years. *Why* is it that some of the workers seem to maintain positive attitudes toward their careers or our profession while others develop negative attitudes?

Coupled with this is extensive reading from recent studies in other professions. One may have found in the literature that during the professional socialization process, two time periods were important: (1) the educational period itself; and (2) immediately after the educational period during the first job. The latter period (reality shock) might have been said to be the most significant of the two periods because begin-ning social workers have been exposed to new value sources and bu-reaucratic pressures. Could it be that the interplay between the professional educational process of social workers (Independent Varia-ble 1) and their initial work experiences (Independent Variable 2) affect some social workers in such a way that they develop negative attitudes toward their careers or our profession (Dependent Variable), thus caus-ing some social workers to leave the profession? If it were possible to establish if this process did occur, and how it did occur, these findings could have the ability, in terms of social work education, to refine our educational and student selection processes.

By expressing the ideas to one's self, it is possible, in a general way, to observe the *kinds* of questions we are asking since the questions provide clues as to what *knowledge* will be required to answer them.

In our example, we may try to determine what independent variables are related to our dependent variables (positive and negative attitudes of workers toward their careers). We may ask *why* the negative attitudes develop, if we are sure we know they do occur. This type of questioning leads back to identifying additional concepts such as attitudes, professional socialization, and values. It is also the beginning stages in which we are starting to think about various operational definitions of these concepts (Parsons, 1949, 1964).

Phase 3: Reviewing the Literature

The third phase in formulating a research problem requires that one's searching and questioning becomes both wider and yet narrower. One must also be critically accepting yet questioning what one reads. Having established a general but as yet imprecise area for study, it is advisable to read around the problem area utilizing the general concepts identified in the previous phase as guides. We must also critically evaluate the studies that utilized the concepts we identified in the previous phase. The evaluation applies both to the topics covered and to the *ways* the studies were conducted (see Chapter 24). The literature search may include psychological and sociological literature. This process is, paradoxically, both liberating and confining. However, it helps us see how other studies operationalized their concepts we identified in the previous phase (Heffernan & Turman, 1981). It awakens us to new insights but focuses us more specifically. In our example we may find that the two-year period immediately after graduation seems a crucial time for the development of social worker's attitudes toward their work although we are only specifically focusing on one small part of the professional socialization period.

Phase 4: Refining the Problem Area

The fourth phase in formulating a research problem is refining the problem area. As a result of the literature search process (Phase 3), it is now possible, on the basis of the presence or absence of similar studies, to refine the problem area more sharply (Reid, 1975b). A number of studies may have investigated the anticipatory stage of socialization (i.e., *during* the professional educational process). Also, a number of studies may have examined the reality shock phase (i.e., *after* the professional educational process). From these studies, it may be hypothesized that there are differences in attitudes toward the social work profession between social workers who value a social institutional change model and social workers who value an individual client change model.

Also, that the development of negative attitudes in other professions seemed closely allied to that of social work and that a time period of about two years after graduation seemed to be a crucial time period in the development of these attitudes. Thus, the problem area is becoming more specific in that we are now concerned with the professional socialization of social workers and the relationship between the professional model they value (i.e., social institutional change model or individual client change model) and the subsequent emergence of specific attitudes (i.e., positive or negative) toward our profession.

Closely allied to the literature search is the discussion with all people willing to critically listen to our ideas. These people can also be fellow colleagues and professionals from other disciplines and professions. This process is necessary because through the act of having to express one's ideas and the critical questions that this procedure generates, we are forced into a more specific and rigorous appraisal of the study's ideas, concepts, variables, and operational definitions. It also helps to test the possible theoretical utility of the study (Mannheim, 1936). In our example, besides the relationship between the variables of the professional models valued by social workers, their socialization, and their attitudes, it may have also been found that there were possible links with other variables such as the type of their professional social work education, and their career choices. The firmer the ideas take shape in terms of the ability to relate the concepts into a theoretical framework based on previous work and satisfactory explanations, the nearer the problem is to its final form (Labovitz & Hagedorn, 1976).

Phase 5: Examining Relationships between Concepts

The fifth phase in formulating a research problem is examining the possible relationships between the various concepts we have obtained from the process of the first four phases. This procedure can be done diagrammatically or by assigning each concept to a plain card and shuffling the cards around. The principal aim is to identify all possible relationships that may arise among the concepts we have defined thus far. We are, in effect, creating a number of possible models to explain what we *think* may be a reasonable explanation for the phenomena we are studying (Kerlinger, 1973).

Could it be that the social worker's professional education and values *precede* their work satisfaction and career choice? Also, is there some dynamic relationship between these variables to *cause* specific attitudes toward the profession to develop? Maybe values can be identified according to where the social workers feel they should be working (social institutional change model or individual client change model). If so, what is the relationship between the variables of, say, age, sex, and job chosen? Again, depending on the existence or absence of previous knowledge derived from quantitative and qualitative research studies, we may be able to decide that we think we know *what* the relationship is but we may want to know *why* the relationship exists for some social workers and not for others. For instance, we may have found that female social workers go into line-level clinical agency settings and male social workers go into administrative positions within the same agencies. Why is this? Is it related only to gender, or are there other variables present? *What* questions precede *why* questions in the hierarchy of knowledge building; this, it is important to be satisfied that the *what* type of question has been adequately dealt with. If in doubt, the goal of a study should be to answer the *what* type of question first.

As before, the type (what and why) of question formulated determines the level of knowledge that will be needed to answer the question. Also, having established the type of question, it then takes us into the formal process of problem formulation adhered to in the present paradigm of knowledge building. In attempting to explain the relationships among the concepts in our example we are in the process of creating the theoretical framework from which our research question will eventually emerge.

Phase 6: Relating the Research Problem to Existing Theory

The sixth phase in formulating a research problem is relating the research problem to existing theory (Philliber, Schwab, & Sloss, 1980). A theory is nothing more than the linking of observations to generalizations, or more formally, a set of concepts, definitions, and propositions which are interrelated (Rossi, 1979). For example, one "role theory" might explain the aging process as individuals adapting to situations by conformity to the roles that are expected of them. They lose some roles such as parenting, work, and friendship, when children grow up, full-time work ceases, and friends die. Thus, an individual gradually disengages from the mainstream of life and adopts an aging role. From this role theory it is also possible to make similar logical statements or propositions about other phases of life such as adolescence, all within the same theory.

By theorizing, we can limit the scope of events to be considered or described such as roles. We can also clarify phenomenon as well as being able to explain or specify sequences of events covered within the phenomena (e.g., aging or adolescence). Theorizing also enables us, by interconnecting the logical propositions, to develop greater leverage to produce further possible explanations of the phenomenon, and, just as important, to produce new ideas (Fay, 1975; Sidman, 1960; Wallace, 1973).

From the above example, the theory is concerned with role relationships specifically related to aging and the sequence of events leading up to it (Siegel, 1983). We can deduce that the same could apply to other periods of life. From a social work point of view, we might use this theory to help us develop new ideas about helping the aged deal with "disengagement" by introducing educational and/or counseling services.

Returning to our example of the social workers' attitudes toward their profession, we might well relate it to a simple theory which *explains* the phenomenon. This theory may maintain that a person's choice of a profession carries with it an initial set of values, or expectations of that career which are subsequently modified over time. This modification occurs through professional education and experience on the job. Modification of attitudes occurs because individuals are able to refine and change their values in the light of new information, or meanings, via cognitive skill and experiential learning. Social workers in practice who have been unable to modify the dissonance of mismatch between their values and reality may utilize some forms of adaptive strategies to deal with this mismatch. Adaptive strategies could range from changing jobs or avoiding some clients, or working closely to the rules of the organization at the expense of the clients.

Deductive and Inductive Logic. From this sketchy theoretical outline relating to our example and the information we have already gleaned in the literature from other studies and discussion, we are now in a position, by the use of deductive and inductive logic to state what we *think* should happen if the theory is a good explanation of what *actually* happens in reality.

Deductive logic begins with two statements or premises derived from a theory and by reasoning arrives at a third statement or conclusion which is logically valid. The conclusion can then be tested quantitatively to determine whether the theory is an adequate systematic view of what pertains in reality.

For example, using deductive logic, we could construct two premises from our theory about the development of social workers' attitudes toward our profession:

Major Premise: The individual client change model is still paramount as an ideology in social work education.

Minor Premise: Social workers whose value system is different from the paramount ideology will have negative attitudes toward the social work profession.

From the above two premises it is possible to deduce a third statement, or conclusion:

Conclusion: Social workers whose values do not identify with an individual client change model will have negative attitudes toward the social work profession.

or,

Conclusion: Social workers whose values identify with an individual client change model will have positive attitudes toward the social work profession.

Obviously, this simple example is not the end of the logical process. Certain other premises may emerge by making one deduction the major premise of another argument. From the major premise we can add another minor premise such as: negative attitudes toward the social work profession are one form of exhibiting dissonance. Therefore, we can conclude a third statement or conclusion such as: those social workers who do not adhere to an individual client change model will exhibit negative attitudes toward the social work profession rather than those who adhere to an individual client change model.

This process makes it possible to narrow the logical ideas down, by approximating or getting nearer and nearer by gradual steps to the most logically strong explanation that can be envisaged. Thus, we are now in a position of stating in a fairly categorical form what we believe happens in reality.

We may reason that social workers who hold similar values toward our profession assimilate new information during their professional social work education similarly. In some instances, assimilation is minimal to the point that values and the realities of practice become dissonant. This may be evidenced by those who do not hold similar values to the dominant educational ideology. In order to adjust to the dissonance, the group in which it is minimal must adopt strategies in practice to deal with these which are evidenced as negative attitudes.

It follows, if this is true, that we should be able to identify the two groups in terms of specific values and attitudes. Social institutional change-oriented values should give rise to adaptive strategies, which are evidenced as negative professional attitudes toward the profession. By contrast, inductive logic starts with specific *observations* about singular events or things from which inferences or more general statements are made. Thus, if one noticed on a number of occasions that colleagues who valued the social institutional change model were apathetic about their work, the worker may infer, rightly or wrongly, that all social workers who valued this model were apathetic. On the other hand, if the social worker found one colleague who was not apathetic but valued this model, then the worker's inference could not be accepted as a general conclusion.

As a general rule, we use deductive reasoning with theory in order to arrive at specific statements for empirical testing. Inductive reasoning is usually applied to our results in order to try to make general statements from our results to see if they fit the theory (see Chapter 19). At this point it is back to reading, thinking, and discussion. We then take it a step further and state more categorically that social workers whose values are more social institutional change oriented rather than individual client change oriented, will have more difficulty modifying their values in practice and thus, will develop adaptive strategies associated with negativism. We may infer that they will be identified by the way they react to their professional social work education. Naturally, all this presupposes that our concepts are clear and that we have meaningful operational definitions of our independent and dependent variables (Babbie, 1982; Bailey, 1982; Kerlinger, 1973).

Assumptions.   Certain assumptions are taken for granted within any study. They are usually formed as a result of reading the literature, talking to others, and as a result of the social worker's values along with our profession's values. In our example it may be assumed that the current social work education value system is not in itself that much different than the values that we actually uphold in professional practice. It also makes no assertions or claims at this stage about the changes in values in the work place, although this can be deduced:

Major Premise: Values can be modified through socialization.
Minor Premise: Professional employment itself is a process of socialization.

From the above two premises, it is possible to deduce a third statement, or conclusion:

Conclusion: Values can be modified through professional employment.

Naturally, important considerations are the assumptions and assertions which constitute the context of a particular research problem formulation. If, for example, we were planning to study how social workers make decisions and we assumed that the workers were influenced by their personal judgments in their decisions, we may be led to focus our study on "personal judgement" variables. On the other hand, if we assumed that the variables surrounding the nature of the social work role were more important in their decision making, we would concentrate on "social work role" variables. It depends upon the assumptions which underlie a particular proposed research study what variables we decide to focus on. We can easily acknowledge the fact that "social work role" variables may influence decision making. However, we must assert that attention was only being paid to "social work role" variables, and not to "personal" variables. Assumptions must be made clear in any study. This helps set limits to the study and enables further deductive analysis of the theory itself.

Phase 7: Constructing the Hypothesis

The seventh phase in formulating a research problem is constructing a hypothesis. A hypothesis is tested for its truth content. Hypotheses are tentative propositions in testable forms that need to be answered. Whether a general question or a specific hypothesis is to be tested is determined by the existing knowledge base and previous research activity on the topic. Some studies are designed to answer general questions (Knowledge Level 1, as presented in Chapter 13). These general questions help us acquire an understanding and the data needed to formulate more specific hypotheses for use in subsequent, and more refined and focused studies (Knowledge Level 4, as presented in Chapter 13). Research hypotheses are stated in the form of a proposal. In our example, a hypothesis might be:

Major Hypothesis: Social workers who value a social institutional change model of social work practice will evidence more negative attitudes toward the social work profession than those social workers who value an individual client change model of social work practice.

It is contended that the two types of social workers (social institutional change oriented and individual client change oriented) will differ in respect to attitudes (negative and positive) they hold toward our profession. A hypothesis must contain an independent and a dependent variable. Hypotheses can be stated in various forms. In our example, we are proposing a specific associative relationship. Other hypotheses might propose causal relationships; A causes B. Or, A is always present with B.

Independent, Dependent, and Intervening Variables. All types of hypotheses consider some form of dependence of Variable B (dependent variable) on Variable A (independent variable). Hypotheses must contain an independent and a dependent variable. Therefore, we may assume that the values held by the social workers (social institutional change model or individual client change model) are the independent variable which influences the attitudes (positive or negative) they hold toward our profession which is the dependent variable. We must assume that their values occur *before* their attitudes toward the profession (Campbell & Stanley, 1963; Champion, 1970; Durkheim, 1966; Reynolds, 1971).

Obviously, in our study there are other variables called intervening variables which may intervene in the relationship between the independent and dependent variable. Such intervening variables could give rise to spurious or misleading results. Thus, the independent variable may be dependent upon other intervening variables such as the professional social work training (e.g., B.A., B.S.W., or M.S.W.) of the social worker, or the socioeconomic background of the worker (e.g., lower, middle, upper).

Therefore, each of these intervening variables can themselves be made into separate subhypotheses with each serving as an independent variable while the dependent variable remains the same (Schuerman, 1981). Thus, we could state:

Subhypothesis 1: The type of professional social work training of social workers is not related to their attitudes toward the profession.

and,

Subhypothesis 2: The socioeconomic status of social workers is not related to their attitudes toward the profession.

This procedure eliminates the possibility of these two intervening variables affecting the major hypothesis stated earlier (Hays & Winkler, 1971). By testing the subhypotheses first, we could then account for the influence on the major hypothesis. We could substitute other variables such as sex or age of the social workers, personality types, length of time in practice, type of job; in fact, any intervening variable which could be justified for inclusion on a theoretical basis.

Null Hypotheses. Subhypotheses are stated in "null" form (Isaac & Michael, 1971). Stating subhypotheses in null form is based on the logic that no difference exists between an independent and dependent variable. The present state of knowledge of a problem area always stands until it is capable of being proved otherwise. Also, since social work researchers usually believe that differences exist, it may be possible that somehow the researcher consciously or unconsciously biased the studies to prove what they believe rather than to find out what really exists. By specifying the opposite to beliefs and ideas and attempting to prove the opposite, they can, if *unsuccessful,* argue that since differences exist, their explanation of the differences may justifiably be considered (Schuerman, 1981).

Thus, if the null hypotheses were upheld, that there were no differences associated with the intervening variables chosen and the dependent variable, we would be in a stronger position to make a pronouncement about our major hypothesis since we would have eliminated possible intervening variables by showing they did not contribute the differences. The major hypothesis itself would then be tested in its null form.

If, however, after testing the major hypothesis seemed to hold true, we can look on the theory as probably offering a good explanation of reality. However, although theories are logically constrained by fact, they are not determined by them. A theory may still be in existence, even though quantitative findings have cast doubts on the theory's ability to explain phenomena. It is the confidence in the theory that has changed. Other future studies with different methodologies, concepts, and operational definitions may cause the theory to be further studied (Mayer & Greenwood, 1980).

SUMMARY

The formulation of a problem into acceptable and useful research terms is the hardest but most important part of any research study. The formulation of a problem to study constitutes the only truly original part of the research process. As such, it requires a range of skills: imagination, tenacity, interest, and an ability to reason. One must be prepared to abandon favorite ideas, but only after rigorous scrutiny. Creative and imaginative ideas coupled with critical appraisal of these ideas is a good combination. Social workers must share and discuss their ideas with others and by using logbooks they can see what specific ideas are changing and why. In the problem formulation stage, we are constantly finding ourselves drawn to theories in psychology and sociology in order to test possible explanations of social work. However, all the necessary work associated with research into and on social work practice, the first and necessary step of problem formulation, is not such an insurmountable feat judging by the growing amount of research now starting to be undertaken.

Robert W. Weinbach

4. THE AGENCY AND PROFESSIONAL CONTEXTS OF RESEARCH

In order to execute a research study in a social work agency, one needs to understand more than the practice and research process as presented in Chapter 2 and how to formulate meaningful research problems as presented in the previous chapter. More importantly, it is impossible to execute a research study in a social work setting without an understanding of the environment in which the study will take place. To be sure, social work research is unique because social work practice and practice settings are unique. There are unique opportunities to execute research studies in social work settings (Glisson, 1982). However, there are also constraints inherent within the same settings. The social worker who desires to do a research study in a social work agency and who ignores the unique characteristics of executing such a study within the agency is destined for failure.

SOCIAL WORK RESEARCH

As discussed in the previous three chapters, social work research is neither psychological nor sociological research, nor research of some other academic discipline "tailored" to a social work setting. Social work research is applied research undertaken by social workers in order to advance practice theory and methods for our profession. As presented in Chapter 1, social work research is not executed by "research specialists" from other fields who are usually unfamiliar with the uniqueness of our profession. Many people who have taken research courses in fields other than social work are familiar with only the traditional psychological and sociological research methods. However, these people usually lack the capacity to carry out research projects success-fully within social work agencies because they are not familiar with the central aim of all social work research: to build a social work knowledge base to improve practice theory (E. G. Brown, 1981; Reid & Smith, 1981; Wood, 1980).

What Is Social Work Research?

Sociological research is descriptive and, to some degree, predic-tive. Research in psychology and in the medical sciences is also aimed at improving treatment (it is in addition prescriptive, but concerns itself with relatively limited areas of human functioning). Social work research, if it is truly to assist the social work practitioner and, ultimate-ly, the wide range of clientele served, provides knowledge that reflects a balance of descriptive, predictive, and prescriptive methods (Tripodi & I. Epstein, 1980). Ideally, social work research must guide social workers to intervene in client problem situations more effectively. It should also reflect a balance between the practice skills needs of the "direct practitioner" and the "community organizer" as well as the majority of the social workers who fall between these two extremes (Rein & Peattie, 1981; Rein & White, 1981).

Given the wide diversity of the knowledge and hence, practice needs of social workers, research studies cannot afford the luxury of obtaining financial resources for pursuits that represent "knowledge for its own sake" (Polansky, 1975a, 1975c). While some social workers understandably may desire to pursue special interest areas, they must constantly ask whether such pursuits are commensurate with the needed practice skills of our profession's practitioners (E. G. Brown, 1981). Since we are a service profession, all of our activities (including re-search) should be those which have the highest potential for resolution of social problems and for improvement of the social conditions of individuals and groups (Mullen & Dumpson, 1972).

The phases in the social work research process directly reflect practice priorities (see Figure 2.1 in Chapter 2). As in this text, psycho-logical and sociological research texts also cite problem identification, definition, and specification as Phase 1 in the research process. Howev-er, in psychological and sociological research, this is often an *ideal* rather than a *reality*. It is no secret that psychological and sociological research methodologies have often been selected first, and the search for appropriate problems to use the predetermined methods selected second. Also, favorite data collection instruments may have been chosen before a problem has been adequately conceptualized and operationalized (Hudson, 1982a). Social work research cannot afford this reversal of sequence. Only meaningful problems in service delivery should legitimately compete for limited financial resources. No research design or instrument in search of a problem need apply. In social work research the identification, definition, and problem specification phase *must* precede any other phase in the research process as identified in the previous chapter and elaborated upon substantially in the following chapter.

The ultimate phase in the research process—utilization of the study's findings for the improvement of services—also underlies the overall priorities which dominates all research in social work. While knowledge building in some fields may emphasize publication of a good report as being the final activity of the research process, social work research requires two additional steps—it must be *read* and *evaluated,* and if appropriate, *utilized* by social work practitioners (Thomas, 1981). Research findings that are not read have little potential for improving practice (see Chapters 23 through 25). But, its having been read and even understood is not a sufficient guarantee that clients will benefit from research efforts. The social worker disseminates research findings in a form conducive to being read (see Chapter 23) and evaluated by the consumer (see Chapter 24) and, if deemed worthy, applied to the practice of the individual social worker practitioner (see Chapter 25).

Recent efforts by such professional organizations such as the National Association of Social Workers and the Council on Social Work Education have been trying to identify and understand obstacles to research utilization by social workers (Briar, Weissman, & Rubin, 1981; Fanshel, 1980). The dichotomy between social work "practice" and social work "research," whether real or imagined, has provided a launching platform for "practitioners" and "researchers" to attempt to identify areas of common concern. They are also seeking to work toward acceptance of methodologies which may bridge whatever gap may exist between the generation of knowledge and its ultimate application in practice—thus, the concept of the practitioner/researcher.

Research utilization is not only desirable for our profession it is absolutely imperative (Rothman, 1978, 1980a, 1980b). The improvement of social work services to clients is the only legitimate reason for social workers to engage in any research study. A research study is worthless, but actually represents a loss (given other needs for social work personnel and resources), unless it is disseminated in a way which allows it to be read and utilized to help resolve human problems (Rothman, 1980b).

FACTORS AFFECTING SOCIAL WORK RESEARCH

There are three factors that shape social work research, and it is not always possible to view the three factors as either single or even partial influences on potential research studies. They interact (as do components in any system) to create a research environment whose potential for support of research endeavors ranges all the way from complete enthusiasm and support to virtual sabotage. This interaction is compounded by the individual personalities, values, and needs of persons involved in social work agencies, both as members of our profession and the practitioners. The three factors which serve as major shaping forces for social work research are: (1) the social work agency; (2) the social work profession; and (3) the social work practitioners themselves.

The Social Work Agencies

The first factor that affects social work research is the social work agencies where the research studies take place. The majority of social workers are employed by social work agencies. The rare self-employed private practitioner remains the exception in our profession (Grinnell, 1982b). Some social work agencies, particularly in the private sector, have demonstrated a strong commitment to research over the years. As voluntary financial support has decreased in a time of recent economic problems for many citizens, traditional research roles and responsibilities are being examined. It cannot yet be ascertained whether research in private agencies will move in the direction of the "luxury" status that it currently enjoys in many public agencies. The future of agency-generated (and -supported) research remains at best tenuous for the foreseeable future.

But what of the social worker who may merely be seeking to conduct a research study without requesting extensive agency and/or financial support? What climate exists within agencies that can affect the potential for at least minimal support of research? Generalizations regarding agencies (which range from public social service settings employing thousands to two- or three-person counseling offices) are always dangerous and rarely apply perfectly to any one setting. However, there are six general characteristics that are appropriate to the majority of agencies. These six characteristics are: (1) agencies have accountability concerns; (2) all research has evaluative potential; (3) accountability pressures create a market for research; (4) agencies have hostile environments; (5) agencies have scarce financial resources; and (6) agencies have client files.

Accountability Concerns. Accountability, the need to demonstrate both effectiveness and efficiency to those who pay the bills, has resulted in a mixed blessing for social work research. Evaluative research, or program evaluation, has been a logical response to demands that an agency demonstrates that it is doing what it claims to be doing and that it is doing it relatively inexpensively (Weiss, 1972a, 1972b). At the same time, agency administrators are acutely aware of the threat of unfavorable program evaluations and are fearful that such evaluations may provide justification for funding cutbacks or termination of inefficient, but needed, social programs (M. Austin, Cox, Gottlieb, Hawkins, Kruzich, & Rauch, 1982; Raymond, 1981; Tripodi, 1983). Social work practice is often inefficient, and a real fear may be that evaluation may emphasize inefficiency without adequate attention to the necessity for services upon which clients depend upon (Grinnell & Hill, 1979a, 1979b).

Evaluative Potential. Social workers are suspicious of research studies that are clearly evaluative in nature. They fear that it will have negative consequences for the workers and their clients, for many of the same reasons that agency administrators fear it (Tripodi, 1983). These fears within agencies are not limited to program evaluations, however. Despite widespread agreement regarding the need for research, particularly in the evaluation of social programs, the social worker's attitude toward research remains typically one of anxiety, distrust, apathy, or misgiving (Brenner, 1976). In fact, a generalized fear of research is not totally unfounded. Even simple research designs which seek only to describe (Knowledge Level 1 as presented in Chapter 13) or to identify a relationship between an independent and dependent variable (Knowledge Level 3 as presented in Chapter 13) have the potential to embarrass individuals and agencies alike. If data are incorrectly (or correctly, but tactlessly) interpreted or made available to an audience hostile to the agency or one or more of its personnel, research of *any type* can be a legitimate threat (Tripodi, 1974). An agency's administrator "once burned" can be expected to be extremely wary of a proposed research study, no matter what assurances are made and what controls are included in the study's design. Only after past negative experiences are explored and the appropriate assurances are made, can any reasonable level of approval and support be anticipated from an agency (Attkisson, Hargreaves, Horowitz, & Sorensen, 1978).

It must be emphasized that social work researchers may have far different perspectives and needs from those of agency administrators. The questions that obsess researchers and comprise the most important issues for them may not be mirrored in a similar burning interest of the administrators of the agencies where they wish to execute their research studies. Agency administrators may prefer (and need) to see requests for research studies in terms of cost/benefit ratios (Thompson, 1980).

Agency administrators are especially concerned with what and how agency resources will be diverted from normal client service to support the study. They may have difficulty in justifying such a reallocation of funds and/or personnel, especially if previous research studies within their agencies resulted in a promised research report that was never delivered. Or worse, they may have received a report that was written in such an esoteric form that it had little potential for utilization by anyone but the researchers themselves (Marks, 1975; Reid, 1981; Tallent, 1983). Many agency administrators have had at least one negative experience with research studies which have either embarrassed the agency, its programs, or the very administrators who risked their reputations to support them. Sometimes, unfortunately, all these experiences have occurred to the point that the next, well-meaning intended potential social work researcher has an especially difficult sales task.

Sometimes, it is not past experience, but a genuine fear that threatens support for a research study within an agency. While accountability pressures have successfully eliminated some agencies which were ineffective and/or inefficient (and some that were not), few agencies still remain because they have been able to cover up their shortcomings. Having suspected the existence of such an agency, a social worker seeking to do a research study might as well recognize that support for the study is potentially nil, and thus, better look elsewhere for an applied research setting. It will and must remain true that good evaluation will pose a serious threat to poorly administered programs and its administrators (J. Gilbert, Mosteller, & Tukey, 1976). Since all research is potentially evaluative in nature, resistance to any and all suggestions for knowledge building will be opposed in the agency that is simply unable to demonstrate accountability.

Market for Research. On the positive side, pressures for accountability and resultant fears regarding it in social work agencies have created an environment of interest in research, particularly in program evaluation (Suchman, 1967a; Weber & Polansky, 1975). Agency administrators, faced with the need to demonstrate accountability, have searched for evaluative methods which would be fair to their agencies while providing useful feedback for improvement of its services to clients.

At first, there was a tendency to try to apply systems-oriented evaluation methods developed for use in business (i.e., profit-making) to social work agencies. This seemed logical, given a renewed emphasis on efficiency, and was supported and even imposed by persons in funding organizations. Their advocates had little understanding of the unique nature of social work agencies committed to a *public service* rather than to a *private profit*. Use of such evaluative techniques such as planning, programming, budget systems (PPBS), program evaluation review techniques (PERT), and other systems analysis-oriented methods provided proof to agency administrators and their practitioners that evaluation was legitimately to be feared. The specter of cost efficiency being used as a criterion for evaluation of human services was threatening, and was resisted unless mandated (I. Epstein & Tripodi, 1977). Agencies which knowingly offered services (e.g., counseling of alcoholics) which were "inefficient" on a unit basis and with a relatively low "success" rate (effectiveness) were especially fearful.

Obviously, only profit-oriented measurements of success within social work agencies is totally inappropriate (Thompson, 1980). A renewed interest in different types of program evaluation methods that take into account such factors as the need for services (*despite* efficiency) is becoming apparent. There now are many books and other literature written by social workers proposing program evaluation methods which agency administrators feel are infinitely more fair and reasonable than those utilized in business. A changing attitude within social work agencies is now being observed. Agency administrators, faced with the need for evaluation, have correctly turned to persons in our own profession to provide it. Social workers, who are more familiar with both the strengths and limitations of practice provide evaluations which are not excessively rigid or critical. They also generate more meaningful recommendations which have greater utility for improving services to clients than do researchers outside our field who may be utilizing criteria inappropriate to a social work agency. Unlike researchers in other fields, social work practitioner/researchers understand the limits of knowledge which exist within our profession. They will not mistakenly assume that cause-effect knowledge exists (Knowledge Level 4 as presented in Chapter 13) and that this knowledge can be applied in a given situation where professional judgment is really the only measurement tool currently available.

The development of social work agency evaluation methods and the increased interest among social workers in doing program evaluation (there may be more funding available for evaluation than for many other areas of research), have contributed to agency administrators seeming less fearful of evaluation now than in the late 1970s. Some even welcome it as an important skill to upgrade service delivery. The widespread resistance to accountability, especially evaluation of our effectiveness, is passing. It has been replaced by an increasing acceptance of the importance of evaluation and research activities for the future development of our profession (Briar, 1973).

While support for the evaluation of social work programs has been affected more than other areas by the emphasis on accountability within agencies, more positive attitudes toward the potential benefits of research for improving services have spilled over into other areas of research as well. Professional social workers have begun to look more critically at the effectiveness and efficiency of their individual practices. With encouragement from the professional literature, they have shown an increased interest in both group- and single-subject research as vehicles to evaluate their daily work and to generate suggestions for improving it (Bloom, 1975; Bloom & Block, 1977; Howe, 1974; Jayaratne & R. Levy, 1979; R. Levy, 1983; Reid, 1983; Schinke, 1979a, 1979b, 1981a, 1983).

Accountability has sensitized social work agencies to what research can do. Individual agency attitudes continue to range from complete enthusiasm and support for research activities all the way to virtual paranoia. The politics of the organizational climate within any given agency will very much affect receptivity to and support for any research endeavor.

Hostile Environments. While some social work agencies are accepted and valued within their communities, many are not. Public, tax-supported agencies such as public assistance and criminal justice facilities are nearly always misunderstood and, frequently resented. They may be perceived by the general public as giving away the public's tax dollars to undeserving and undesirable clients (D. Austin, 1981). Letters to the editor columns in local newspapers illustrate the low regard and even outright hostility reserved for these agencies and the clients they serve. A common theme is one of wasteful, self-serving bureaucracies, seeking to perpetuate themselves and, perhaps, to grow even larger and more wasteful.

Research which has potential to dispel commonly believed mythology about social work agencies may be especially useful, particularly in the agency's ongoing public relations struggle. Any data which can improve the credibility and the overall image of an agency are useful. Program evaluation and descriptive research (e.g., client characteristics and needs and utilization of services) have this potential.

Scarce Financial Resources. Some social work agencies which suffer from a public image problem could benefit from research which would result in a more accurate portrayal of themselves to the general public. However, financial resources that are needed for such projects are often simply not available. Research related to advancing practice theory must often compete with other activities which appear more politically desirable (e.g., policing of clients, fraud investigation) within the critical spotlight of the community. Resources which are available for a research study may be committed almost entirely to the tasks of data compilation, storage, and retrieval, an especially large undertaking in a large public agency. Overall experience seems to demonstrate that social work agencies are barely able to provide the continuity of financing and size of staff that are minimal for research studies to advance practice theory (Posavac & Carey, 1980).

Social work agencies usually cannot afford the type of research that is designed to directly build knowledge for improving its services. However, social workers may find an unexpected receptivity to research suggestions (or topics), providing they are willing to conduct the studies with minimal resource support. Agency administrators would often like to improve the agency's image by showing a commitment to greater accountability, but cannot because they lack the personnel to conduct the studies. The social worker who is interested in working in an area that may potentially improve the agency's image may be permitted access to data otherwise inaccessible for purely research purposes. Research activities which can suggest interest in improving quality of services and a commitment to more efficient use of funds are a valuable tool for an administrator seeking to improve community relations, dealing with suspicious board members, or negotiating next year's budget.

Client Files. The bureaucratic nature of social work agencies (particularly the larger public ones) provides a desirable resource for social work research. As presented in Chapter 19, there is often a tendency on the part of social work researchers to think in terms of collecting *original* data. However, a wealth of *existing* data in the form of case records (client files) and regularly gathered statistics often go untapped (Hoshino & Lynch, 1981; Reid, 1978b). Data may be gathered within agencies because of federal or state mandate or because administrators may feel they need to have sufficient records in case of legal actions. Social workers themselves are accustomed to recording voluminous notes, whether out of custom or because they may actually serve some need such as "jogging the memory" about a client seen only occasionally.

For legal and other reasons, client files are not and should not be readily available. However, since research has many advantages for agencies in the present environment, client files can usually be obtained (Reid, 1974, 1978b). An agency administrator is charged with both safeguarding confidentiality of client information and with creating a good public image for the agency. Research which threatens either of these will result in denial of access to the data residing in the client files. Thus, it is essential that tact be used and all necessary assurances be given when proposing a research study to an agency administrator (M. Austin & Crowell, 1981).

Agency administrators are aware that research involving agency data will usually require time of agency personnel (Hoshino & Lynch, 1981). To safeguard confidentiality, a staff person will probably be needed to be present when client files and other data bases are utilized in a study. If data are computerized, agency personnel may be required simply to obtain the desired information in a form usable to the researcher. Agency data are a relatively economical data source, but various limitations in the use of such data bases need to be noted (P. Stuart, 1981).

First, generalizations of the study's findings to other agency clientele may not be possible. Every social work agency and its clientele is unique. While some phenomena (e.g., certain human problems and behavioral characteristics) transcend the boundaries of a given agency, factors such as catchment areas (i.e., geographical areas served) and eligibility criteria (e.g., unemployed youths) of individual agencies may result in a research sample unlike any other. As presented in Chapter 8, social workers must be attuned to any biasing effects that arise from all samples used.

Second, client files often lack standardization. As presented in Chapter 19, data in some agencies are abundant, but not in a sufficiently standardized format to be readily accessible or analyzed (S. J. Wilson, 1980). Data within client files tend to change as federal and state requirements are modified (Kagle, 1984a; 1984b). Sometimes it is more economical to collect original data in the usual standardized format than it is to use already existing data from somewhere in the agency.

Third, client files may be biased. The sources for most agency records and client files are the individual social workers. Social workers' effectiveness is evaluated in part on what is reflected in their clients' case files. As with most human beings, few social workers are sufficiently honest (or masochistic) to record their failures and errors of judgment in agency records. Client files may be biased so as to present the social work practitioner in the best possible light. Certain data which result in the evaluation of the effectiveness of social workers are especially suspect. Even if every effort has been made to record data in client files as accurately as possible, it must be remembered that the social work researcher who uses client files still has no firsthand knowledge of the client. The data ultimately used for a research study may easily become distorted in the necessary chain of translations from the actual behavior of the client to the practitioner's perceptions of these behaviors (case files) to the researcher's measurement instruments (categorizations) to the data analyses.

Fourth, client files may contain deliberate omissions. Sensitive client data which may be subject to court subpoena may never appear in clients' files. Sometimes, data (variables) which would be most valuable (e.g., assignment of clients to diagnostic categories) are deleted as a matter of agency policy or worker discretion. In short, client files, for reasons of political and client interest, must be assumed to be inconsistently incomplete data sources.

Increase in computerization of client files and legal concerns regarding the safeguarding of client data may not portend well for social work researchers using agency records (Smith, 1983). Every time an agency must defend itself in court, either for refusing to release data (client and/or agency) or for releasing data with questionable authorization, the climate for the storage of accessible client information worsens. Issues of confidentiality have led to questions of whether written client files are not a dangerous anachronism now that these necessary data can be stored in coded form capable of limiting access to all but a few selected employees (S. J. Wilson, 1978). While this is not yet a common practice, if it were to become widespread, it would have negative implications for what is currently a favorable attribute of the context of social work research.

The Social Work Profession

The second factor that affects social work research is the social work profession. What is possible and desirable in social work research is shaped by professional values, standards, and definitions which differ from those in any other discipline (Schram & Mandell, 1983). There are five characteristics inherent in our profession which shape social work research. These five characteristics are: (1) the profession's values and ethics; (2) the profession's beliefs and practices; (3) the treatment relationship; (4) beliefs about practice; and (5) the rewards for doing research. Membership in our profession carries certain responsibilities. Combined with professional objectives, they constitute supports and obstacles which exist for those who seek to advance social work practice-relevant knowledge through research.

Values and Ethics. Physical scientists need not concern themselves with the rights of their research subjects. Nonorganic matter may be manipulated in a way that will minimize the researcher's three enemies which are: investigator bias; intervening variables; and chance. Chapter 6 presents many of the ethical issues which must be addressed in the use of human subjects for research purposes. Our profession reflects special concerns relating to the protection of clients whom we are committed to help—not to harm. Some of these concerns are quite legitimate; others are somewhat less so. Nevertheless, our profession and its protectiveness toward its clients tend to set limits on research studies that exceed a generalized concern for protecting the rights of human research subjects. Specifically, there are research situations that our profession generally will not (and should not) tolerate, despite the apparent potential for building knowledge for practice theory. For example, research studies involving the random assignment of clients to different practice methods to compare their relative effectiveness is usually opposed. Professional judgment regarding the most desirable practice method for the client cannot be set aside. What if this judgment suggests that a given client group would be more likely to benefit from a particular practice method (e.g., psychotherapy or behavior modification) than the one to which they are due to be assigned (e.g., primal scream or trust fall) on the basis of randomization?

Probably the most dramatic example of a conflict between professional values and responsibilities and research requirements relates to the issue of the denial of services (Rosen & Mutschler, 1982). In evaluating the effectiveness of a social work practice method it would be highly desirable, from a research perspective, to randomly form a group of persons seeking help but who are denied it (control group) so that a comparison can later be made to those who received help (experimental group). Such a decision would be a violation of professional social work ethics. As presented in Chapters 5 and 6, services to those in need cannot ethically be denied, or individual problems ignored or deliberately mistreated in the interest of knowledge building (Reinherz, Regan, & Anastas, 1983).

Beliefs and Practices. Some characteristics of our profession are not written down or so easily identified as its value and ethics. Certain beliefs, traditions, and professional definitions, while elusive, nevertheless have their effect on the shaping of research investigations in our profession (Geismar & Wood, 1982). Whether they are based on a verifiable *fact* or have their basis in *mythology* is really unimportant (McLoed & Meyer, 1967). As is so often true, what is perceived to be true, is true in its consequences, especially as it influences the research process (Grinnell, 1983).

Treatment Relationships. Social work practice, particularly at the direct practice level, is believed to be highly dependent on the social worker-client relationship (Kadushin, 1983). Not surprisingly, any practice (even in the interest of knowledge building) that might be perceived as threatening or in any way changing this relationship will be opposed. While it is easy to build a logical case for evaluation of practice methods or for describing the nature of social work practice through direct observation of social worker-client interaction, requests for permission to do this are usually not well received. Students in field work courses may observe a similar resistance when making what appears to be a perfectly reasonable request to learn treatment techniques (e.g., active listening) of a particular method (e.g., nondirective therapy) by observing their field instructors in action.

The rationale most frequently given for not permitting onsite observation of direct treatment, even in the interest of research, is that it would jeopardize the treatment relationship. While the cynic might see this as an effort to avoid exposure to the errors that even a very experienced social worker inevitably makes, it is more likely a sincere belief, based in part on professional tradition and folklore. Despite the fact that skilled observers are rarely an impediment to any treatment relationship (they are soon ignored), the belief persists. The belief presents an obstacle to research studies where firsthand observation of treatment techniques that are utilized with a particular practice method would be the best means to collect data for the study.

Beliefs about Practice.   While accountability pressures have recently tended to prod our profession to examine and evaluate our practice methods, the nature of our practice is such that effective practice remains difficult to conceptualize and operationalize (Compton & Galaway, 1984; H. Goldstein, 1973; Pincus & Minahan, 1973). Such vague outcome measures such as progress and growth when applied to client problem areas equally as vague such as communication, self-esteem, and social functioning become especially elusive (Eldridge, 1983). A tremendous amount of progress has been made in the measurement of these and many other concepts (see Table 11.3 in Chapter 11). However, our profession has a certain folklore that remains somewhat distrustful of measurement packages which do not take into consideration the professional judgment of the social worker. Some social workers may prefer to perceive improvement in client functioning subjectively rather than objectively. Research methods which rely heavily on objective measures are likely to be suspect; thus, quantitative research findings may be readily dismissed as to their utilization potential solely because they are based on such quantitative data sources.

Research Rewards.   Research has not always been synonymous with status in our profession as it has in many other fields (Grinnell & Kyte, 1976). Rewards in the form of promotions and recognition have more often gone to skilled practitioners, especially to those who have evolved a new practice method (e.g., primal scream, trust fall) or pioneered practice methods with a newly discovered client group (e.g., "Boat People").

Professional social work journals publish fewer reports of quantitatively based research studies than qualitatively based studies (sarcastically referred to as "show and tell" or "I once had a case"). Whether this phenomenon occurred because of editorial preference or the unavailability of quality quantitative research reports for publication is not really the issue (Else, 1978, 1979; Grinnell, 1983; Lindsey, 1976, 1977a, 1977b, 1978a, 1979). What is important is that there has been a message within our profession which tends to say that published reports of research findings may be of secondary importance to other forms of communication (Geismar, 1982; Geismar & Wood, 1982).

A constant pressure for more and better research endeavors in social work has come from ongoing efforts to further professionalize the field (Reinherz, Grob, & Berkman, 1983). No matter which of several available lists of attributes of a profession are applied, social work appears especially vulnerable to accusations of nonprofessional status because of its heavy reliance on knowledge derived from fields such as psychology and sociology. The lack of a clear-cut body of knowledge unique to social work practice, and hence the concern about this shortcoming, will continue to foster practice-relevant research. Current emphasis on single-subject research methodologies for use by the social worker is but one example of this trend (R. Levy, 1983). The popularity of program evaluation is another example (Tripodi, 1983). As more social work professionals become involved in doing research, they will see its value to professionalization, and thus, to practice. Our profession can be expected to become even more supportive of research efforts as professionalization and professionals need research. Individuals seeking to conduct research studies would be well-advised to use this point in gaining acceptance and support for their research aspirations (Gottlieb & Richey, 1980).

The Social Work Practitioners

The third factor that affects social work research is the social workers themselves. As in the case of the agencies and the profession, generalizations about the characteristics of social work practitioners are dangerous. Of course, there are always exceptions, but social workers, as a group, seem to have three characteristics that are useful in understanding their role in affecting social work research. These three characteristics are: (1) social workers are people oriented; (2) social workers have a vested interest in practice; and (3) social workers need research.

People Orientation. A certain selection process takes place when any career is chosen. People committing themselves to our profession have done more than choose an academic field or a knowledge area in which to work. Statements about themselves have been made in regard to the personal needs and values they possess.

In general, people choose our profession because they feel a need and a responsibility to help other people help themselves. They believe themselves as capable of interacting meaningfully with others, either on a one-to-one basis (direct practice) or on a more indirect level of helping (community organization). Furthermore, they desire this type of interaction and probably believe that the helping process and the interaction will provide gratification for them. The selection of our profession is, in part, an acknowledgment of a person's desire to work with the real and the human, rather than with the abstract or the inanimate.

Social work research usually involves working with social workers, either as research subjects, as research collaborators, or as researchers themselves (K. Nelson, 1983). The people orientation of social workers is an important point to remember for social workers wishing to gain entry into an agency to conduct a research study. Because of this orientation, relatively few students in social work programs would elect to concentrate in a study of social work research (Perlman, 1972). In fact, we can only speculate as to how many social work students would choose to take even a single research course were it not part of their degree requirements (see "Preface for Students").

Social workers have a certain amount of disinterest (or even terror) of research (Grinnell & Kyte, 1979). They have not generally exhibited either the reliance on or the interest in research that would be reasonable to expect among those seeking to professionalize our profession by attempting to move toward a more knowledge-based practice. Rather than using research-based practice knowledge, social workers usually prefer to rely on what they describe as a combination of humanitarian impulse, occupational folklore, and common sense (Geismar & Wood, 1982; Heineman, 1981; Watts, 1981). As presented in Chapter 1, social workers prefer not to be involved in research, do not like to read research reports and do not understand reports of statistical analyses when they do read them (Fischer, 1976a).

These phenomena should not be viewed as "anti-research" so much as "pro-people." To many social workers, research is abstract, dry, theoretical, and totally unrelated to practice. This impression is not without basis in reality. Unfortunately, some social work research has lacked relevance to practice and has had little potential for utilization (see "Foreword"). The combination of researchers not always in tune with social work practitioners' practice needs, and practitioners disinterested in and uninformed about research, has resulted in attitudes of apathy and even antagonism toward research. However, this attitude has begun to change in recent years as social work graduates have a better understanding of research and have a knowledge of more practice-relevant methodologies; the people orientation of social workers can be expected to continue.

Social workers have a tendency to be advocates for clients, and co-workers alike; they reflect optimism and hope that their clients' situations are improving and will continue to improve. While this characteristic is necessary and desirable for social work practitioners, it can drive social work researchers to frustration if they are unaware of the potential biasing effects that this tendency can have. As presented in Chapter 2, social workers are notoriously poor resources for the measurement of their clients' success. Social workers tend to subjectively view clients in a positive light which interferes with their ability to objectively evaluate their clients' success. In evaluating the functioning level of clients, objectivity seems to be compromised even further

by a need to somehow reward past client growth or even client effort by unrealistically favorable current measurements. Research measurements involving social workers' perceptions of clients' functioning must be viewed as suspect, and in need of corroboration. The characteristics of emphasizing strengths and the good in people, absolutely essential to good social work *practice,* may be almost diametrically opposed to what is necessary for valid and reliable success measures in social work *research.*

Vested Interest in Practice. Social workers not only believe in people, they believe in practice methods. This results in a confidence which is as desirable for practice as are optimistic evaluations of clients. Unfortunately, this confidence gives rise to a resistance to certain types of research and the acceptance of research findings which are not supportive of commonly employed practice methods. It can result in an unwillingness or even an inability on the part of social workers to question, and hence, to revise practice methods and their treatment techniques based on emerging quantitative data.

Social workers have employed various practice methods for many years. They have become skilled at them through repetition and experience. Some social workers have gone even further, writing papers and books about practice methods and their corresponding treatment techniques. They have also been acknowledged by peers as experts in their specializations. Some social workers have sought to become more proficient at what they do and have made personal and financial sacrifices to receive advanced training in specialized practice methods. The social worker who wishes to evaluate whether a practice method is truly effective will likely meet a wall of resistance, based upon one or a combination of these investments.

Research that evaluates a practice method and/or its corresponding treatment techniques must be totally objective. Its findings can challenge accepted practice and, in some cases, threaten the reputation and status of those most associated with its theory (if a theory exists). While this type of research may be what is most needed in our profession, researchers must anticipate that some social workers will refuse to participate in the study and will demonstrate a reluctance to utilize those findings that are not a resounding endorsement of their favorite practice methods (Fischer, 1978).

Research Needs. It would be erroneous to suggest that the characteristics of social workers present the only barrier to research. There is another side, based in part on the same attributes, which can provide support for those wishing to build a social work knowledge base for practice theory. Generally, social workers will welcome research that is clearly aimed toward the objective of improving client services. Having been convinced that a proposed research study has this goal,

social workers will more than likely support the study, and participate in it.

Until quite recently, there were few research studies that represented methodologically sound evaluations of practice methods (Reid & Hanrahan, 1982; Schinke, 1981a). The paucity of these evaluations and the need for them represents an excellent opportunity for research activity. Positions by professional organizations such as the National Association of Social Workers on the need to evaluate social work practice methods may be having an effect on the attitudes of the practitioners. Our profession needs to incorporate into agency operations, and the daily routine of practice, the developing means for continuously monitoring and assessing the results of our efforts (Briar, 1968). Research will help social workers in their difficult task of explaining to others what they are doing, with what success, and its importance.

As a group, social workers are more humble than arrogant, more open to learning from others than smug about their own knowledge. They are generally realistic about the effectiveness of their helping skills, particularly in working with client groups and problems where experience in the field is limited. The nature of our profession is such that a large percentage of those who practice in it are forced to make decisions and to intervene without the assistance of a vast body of knowledge. They will welcome research which promises to assist them in functioning less on instinct and good intention, and more on the basis of knowledge.

SUMMARY

Research in social work is unlike that in any other discipline. What can be done—and what should be done—is shaped by factors which are unique to our profession, both individually and in concert. The social work research environment has been presented as resulting from the characteristics of social work agencies, the profession, and the social work practitioners themselves. Now that the issues and concerns related to each of the three factors which provide both constraints and supports for knowledge building through research have been presented, it is now necessary to have an understanding of how social and psychological variables affect social work research endeavors. Thus, the next chapter is a continuation of this chapter as it places the social work research process into a much broader context which allows for recognition of the fact that both social and psychological variables are embedded in the essence of the social work research endeavor itself.

Herbert Bisno and Allan Borowski

5. THE SOCIAL AND PSYCHOLOGICAL CONTEXTS OF RESEARCH

The mid-1970s witnessed an intensification of our profession's long-standing flirtation with research studies on social work practice. The impetus for such research activity arose in response to growing and appropriate demands for accountability and as a result of increasing concern over the utility of numerous social work practice methods that were beginning to appear. In addition, the limited research that had been done in regard to direct social work practice raised serious questions about the efficacy of the practice methods and techniques being employed (Mullen & Dumpson, 1972).

Other sources of influence included competitive claims from other professions and client self-help groups, as well as the emergence of a socioeconomic milieu characterized by constraints on funding and political and ideological support for those segments of the community that were hostile to social programs and services. Some social workers even questioned the legitimacy of social work as a professional activity (Fischer, 1981c).

In response to the above, the emphasis on the practitioner/ researcher model has developed rather rapidly and has found considerable support within our profession. A broad characterization of this overall trend is the emergence of social workers who directly introduce an empirical base to their practices. Empirically based social work practice refers to a reliance on a foundation of findings, derived from scientific inquiry, as the basis for effective and efficient practice. The spirit of this thrust is captured in some of its terminology, such as objectivity, precision, specification of goals and outcomes, feedback, and measurement (Bloom & Fischer, 1982; Grinnell, 1981b).

The practitioner/researcher model as presented in this text seeks to ensure the integration of practice and research so that there will be a constant interplay between both aspects until, in fact, they become indivisible. Although the model is appealing and, as a goal seems unobjectionable, some social workers question the compatibility of these two roles (the practitioner and researcher) believing, that in practice, one or the other role will dominate. Regardless of differences as to the feasibility of the model, the important fact is that there is a widespread belief within our profession as to the importance of practice-research linkages. Thus, a broad and realistic understanding of the research process is of particular importance at this time.

This chapter seeks to foster a better understanding of social work research by considering the meaning and nature of science and then proceeding to an examination of both the social and psychological factors that are embedded in the social work research enterprise.

WHAT IS SCIENCE?

Science is a way of acquiring and/or confirming knowledge; it is neither static nor fixed. Knowledge in this sense refers to a body of principles, facts, and truths. Yet science is not the only way of knowing, of acquiring, and of confirming knowledge.

Other Methods of Knowing

Besides science, there are three other methods of knowing: (1) tenacity; (2) authority; and (3) the a priori method. Science *and* each of these three methods of knowing rests on a foundation of a particular set of assumptions about the way the validity of knowledge is established. As presented in Chapter 2, the set of assumptions, both stated and unstated, on which ideas rest are called paradigms (Kerlinger, 1973; B. Phillips, 1979).

Tenacity. The first of these other methods of knowing is referred to as the method of tenacity—holding firmly to the truth, the truth that people know to be true because they hold firmly to it, because they have always known it to be true. This position emphasizes the subjective certainty of beliefs as a criterion of truth, and/or the importance of tradition in the acceptance of the validity of knowledge. Many past claims as to the efficacy of certain types of social work practice (e.g., psychotherapy) seem to have been based on this mode of knowing. However, the willingness, within our profession, to continue to put reliance on this manner of determining the effectiveness of the activities of social workers appears to be rapidly eroding under the impact of the practitioner/researcher model of social work practice.

Authority. A second of these other methods of knowing is reliance on authority and public sanction. This is a variant of the tenacity approach and involves the relatively uncritical trusting of those in positions of authority, whether this be an authority of expertise, charisma, or social position. A characteristic of this way of knowing is that it is "other" directed insofar as there is acceptance of the validity of the knowledge of others, without requiring further proof.

A Priori. The third method of knowing is the a priori approach. This method of knowing relies on conclusions arrived at by rational reasoning processes. The difficulties of dubious premises, or competing rational arguments, none of which are required to be subjected to external testing, confront those trusting this method of knowing. A variant of this approach is found among groups of people who rely on supposedly self-evident truths or intuitional certainty. The statement in the U.S. Declaration of Independence, "We hold these truths to be self-evident," is an example of the rationalistic version of this method of knowing.

Definition

The precise definition of science has been a long-standing focus of concern among historians and philosophers of science. However, no neat definition on which there is a high degree of consensus has been arrived at. But this lack of a universally accepted definition of science need not discourage us. Not only is the search for one definition of the scientific method probably futile but also there are other ways of making meanings clear than by defining them. The danger in a conventional definition is that, on the one hand, it may be too tight and, on the other hand, it may not be broad enough to accommodate all of the procedures that may potentially be employed by scientists (Kaplan, 1964). This very open view of the scientific enterprise does not mean, however, that anything goes in its name. Indeed, the avoidance of a constraining definition does not imply that science is without identifiable characteristics (Bronowski, 1973).

Characteristics

Science has a diversity of characteristics including: (1) it contains an empirical component; (2) the knowledge generated by science is always provisional; and (3) it is a public way of knowing.

Empirical Component. A prevailing view of science, critical to the conception of research in social work, is that it contains an empirical component. Empiricism rests on a particular constellation of assumptions which, in turn, serve as a basis for meaningful scientific inquiry. According to Goode and Hatt (1952), some of these assumptions are:

1. The world exists and is external to the observer.
2. We can know the world [an assumption that is the subject of profound discourse among philosophers].
3. We can know the world through our senses [sight, sound, touch, taste, smell].
4. Phenomena are causally related [poverty has a diversity of causes, delinquency has a diversity of causes, poverty may be an important cause of delinquency].

Perhaps the essence of empiricism is that reality can be known only as experience is processed through human intelligence; that is, human experience and observation rather than belief, authority, or reasoning per se are the source of our knowledge of the world. Knowledge founded on observation and experience provides it with independence—of our subjective thinking processes and fantasies. Thus, knowledge founded on observation and experience is objective and, hence, valid or true. Consider the following example. Many people subjectively believe that the poor do not want to work. In attempting to confirm whether this is valid or not, researchers would seek to come to know the world of the poor, to observe and experience it through using their senses. On the basis of listening to and talking with the able-bodied nonworking poor, monitoring their job search behavior, and examining job vacancy figures provided by local employment offices, they might find that the poor, like the population at large, do want to work but that there are too few jobs to go around. This finding would represent scientifically valid knowledge.

Provisional Knowledge. A second characteristic of the scientific method of knowing is that valid knowledge (principles, facts, and truths) is always provisional. This is a fundamental characteristic of the scientific stance. The evidence in support of a particular piece of knowledge must be both of sufficiently high quality and have a sufficiently high probability of being accurate to warrant acceptance of that piece of knowledge (Kerlinger, 1973). If the finding above, that the poor want to work, was based on two or three interviews in one locality, the quality of the data and the probability of its general accuracy would be rendered suspect. In practice, the quality/quantity of evidence in a given case appears to reduce that uncertainty. However, absolute and final truth cannot be offered in the name of science.

Public Way of Knowing. A further characteristic of science is that it is a public way of knowing. Scientific knowledge is public and shared as contrasted with strictly private knowing that contains within itself its own authority and validity. An example of strictly private knowing is divine revelation. In such instances, there is no means available for the researcher to experience and observe this very private, individualized manifestation with a view to objectively concluding on its validity.

Procedural Aspects of Science

The conduct of a research study demands that the social worker employ appropriate research methods and techniques. Acquiring or confirming valid knowledge according to the scientific method of knowing requires objective observations or evidence. Many of the methods and techniques utilized in the course of a research study are designed to control for errors of observation attributable to the observer. These methods and techniques presuppose that the process of observation can be purged of biases, attitudes, prejudices, and the like—those human influences that may lead to the distortion of reality.

Methods and Techniques. Research methods are broad procedures of sufficient generality to be shared by all (see Part Three). Research methods include such activities as theory building (see Chapter 3), the operationalization of concepts, the formulation of hypotheses, observation, measurement, experimentation, explanation, and prediction (Toseland, 1981). Methods may also refer to principles of inquiry specific to the science and distinguish it from other activities and ways of knowing. In contrast, research techniques are more specific procedures. Examples include the construction of a questionnaire and its pretesting (see Chapter 12), the various means of drawing a sample from a population (see Chapter 8), and tests of validity and reliability (see Chapter 10).

All research studies require a command of the research methods and techniques presented in this text. However, while competence in such technical operations is an essential requirement, there is a danger that rather than being seen as instrumental, the procedures may become dominant over, or confused with, the ends. As presented in Chapter 3, many research studies are undertaken because of the availability of a research technique rather than the significance of the research problem. A study of psychological functioning that employed an existing pretested, valid, and reliable instrument, rather than one devised de novo and more suited to the specific focus of the study in question, is an example of this potential danger (Polansky, 1975b).

Theory. Theory is very much implicated in the use of scientific procedures; it is pervasive. It serves to give coherency and meaning to an otherwise unclustered group of observations (Becker, 1958; Clark, 1983; Parsons, 1949). However, social workers must never view theory as the last refuge of the impractical. The choice for the worker is not "to be or not to be a theoretician" but rather the choice is which theories are going to be utilized and why were they selected for the research study (see Chapter 3).

Measurement. A critical element in the procedures of science is measurement. Indeed, many of the techniques employed by the social work researcher are directly related to measurement. The importance of measurement flows from the assumptions of quantification. As presented in Chapter 9, measurement links physical observation to the real world. It involves the assignment of numerals and symbols, according to some rule, to properties of objects and serves to increase the objectivity of observations, the potential replicability of studies and the effective communication of findings (Bostwick & Kyte, 1981). Measurement is also a device for standardization but it is no contradiction to point out that it also makes possible more subtle discrimination and, hence, more precise description. For example, a group of policy analysts may, in principle, support equity (or fairness) in social arrangements as reflected in their response to an interviewer's question. However, a more carefully cast question may identify that subgroup which also acknowledges that equity may still be seen to apply in a situation where the most disadvantaged are advantaged by a social policy initiative. Of course, the difficulty of measuring certain types of phenomena should not be denied. Thus, measuring romantic love among those recently afflicted by gathering data on blood pressure, pulse rate, and sex drive may completely fail to capture the essence of this construct—romantic love.

In considering measurement as a procedural aspect of science, it is important to point out that measurement has been described as being bedeviled by two mystiques—the mystique of quantity and the mystique of quality (Kaplan, 1964). The mystique of quantity refers to the tendency in the sciences to place quantitative data on a pedestal above qualitative data, as if the former had an intrinsic scientific value in some way superior to that of the latter. The mystique of quality is based on the notion that the qualitative and quantitative are essentially antithetical and that in the human sciences measurement is inappropriate or pointless—or even worse, a distortion of what is really important. As presented in Chapter 14, both quantity and quality are misconceived when treated as opposites.

A primary concern associated with the mystique of quality appears to be that something of the qualitative essence will be left out in the quantitative description. Of central importance is that the quantitative account includes everything contained in the corresponding qualitative one. There are, of course, formidable obstacles, in some instances, of accomplishing this as the example above on those recently afflicted with romantic love illustrates.

Another source of the qualitative mystique involves the value sphere, that numbers debase the unique humanity of individuals by standardization. Thus, a number depicting the size of the juvenile offender population in a given region fails to capture the variation within this population in terms of life circumstances, age, sex, seriousness and frequency of offending, and so on. But assigning a number to a behavior does not in any inherent sense rob the behavior of its worth or value or meaning. In fact, measurement may enhance it. Thus, a number that simply depicts the size of the juvenile offender population serves to indicate the magnitude of this problem.

Division of Labor.   The extent to which an individual social work researcher employs particular methods and techniques, draws on theory, and engages in quantitative or qualitative measurement during the course of a research study is dependent on the division of labor among social workers. Knowledge-development requires a wide range of abilities, competencies, and styles (Garvin, 1981). A division of labor among social work researchers is not only necessitated by the scope of the requisite knowledge and skills but also by varied interests, differences in intellectual work habits, temperamental preferences and styles of problem solving. Some workers in the process of knowledge development may spend most of their time on theoretical problems (the meaning of equity or fairness, for example). Others may concentrate on experimental designs, or on research in the natural milieu (Moos, 1974; Webb, Campbell, Schwartz, & Sechrest, 1966). Yet another group may devote its energies to sharpening treatment techniques of practice methods, or developing computer software packages for management information systems (MISs). There is an ample amount of work to go around (Hudson, 1982d). When one considers what is still to be known, particularly in our profession, one is struck by the magnitude of the task of getting ahead with the development of requisite knowledge and skills and the importance of diverse contributions to this task.

Style and Orientation.   Differences in style and orientation are another procedural aspect of social work research. For example, some researchers prefer to work boldly on a large canvas (undertaking large-scale, cross-national, social policy studies, for example), while others are more concerned with meticulous attention to finely wrought miniatures. An example of the latter stylistic orientation is the sole social worker employing a single-subject design in a casework agency. Nevertheless, we all applaud these differences.

The emphasis on stylistic differences and a necessary division of labor should not, of course, obscure similarities in at least a basic knowledge of research methodology, and an understanding of key theoretical issues shared by most social work researchers. Nor is the recognition of a division of labor intended to imply that only large-scale, organized research employing many social workers and heavily funded, is worthwhile. Fortunately, there remains an important place for the solitary or small-scale social work researcher, sometimes working along on a minimal financial support (e.g., Sigmund Freud), and for the creative and sometimes quite deviant thinker who, in splendid isolation, may make quite seminal contributions to scientific thought (e.g., psychoanalytical theory), including inspirational ideas later developed by large-scale research undertakings.

RESEARCH AS A SOCIAL AND PSYCHOLOGICAL ENTERPRISE

Social work research has a number of features which, considered separately or jointly, point to the social/psychological nature of the research enterprise itself. These features include: (1) the link between knowledge development and the social environment of which it is a part; (2) researchers proceed with their work according to a system of orientation; (3) objectivity is the product of intersubjectivity; (4) values impinge on all research studies; (5) researchers are members of a scientific community and this membership influences their activity; (6) research activities are socially organized; (7) research is subject to fads or fashion; and (8) personal psychological considerations can directly enter into the conduct of research.

The Social Context of Ideas

The ideas of knowledge in and about social work and its research activities are linked to the social milieus of which they are a part and from which they emerged. This is true of all professions, as well as of other types of idea systems.

The relationship between ideas and the social milieu is complex and the process of trying to sort out the tantalizing interplay between them is frequently elusive. One of the *particularly* complicating factors is that it is much easier to overlook social linkages of ideas which are very much a part of our profession. Thus, it is frequently easier to spot the relationships between ideas and the social milieu when analyzing events and belief that are sociologically, psychologically, or historically removed from the observer. To put it simply, we more readily perceive implicit assumptions in, and see the social roots of, another person's ideas than our own.

This tendency to take for granted so many of our own assumptions and to attribute an almost totally self-generating quality to our accustomed ways of thinking becomes more understandable if we imagine people who have been thoroughly immersed in water all their lives, and compare them with a group of people who go in and out of water. Which group is more likely to be consciously aware of water as we usually think of it? In a very important sense the group who shifts from one environment to another would be in a better position to become *self-conscious* about the water. This is at least partly due to the fact that the water becomes distinguishable, as such, when differentiated from nonwater. The very separation of water from nonwater becomes a defining attribute that is itself part of our conception of water. In a somewhat similar manner children acquire a personal identity, a sense of self: through the process of interaction with others, they are able to separate themselves from them and to discover they have "boundaries." A further example is provided by social workers engaged in the settlement of new immigrants or refugees. They are often struck by the perceptiveness of the new arrivals in making subtle distinctions between the new host country and their native country in terms of the degree of nationalism, social fragmentation, and the like. Since reflective thinking involves a consideration of alternatives, it suggests a new way for social workers to think about their own country, a process whereby a nondifferentiated "field" (country) is broken down into separate elements.

All this implies that we may be most "unaware" of that with which we are most familiar. This would apply to group (including disciplinary/professional) assumptions and modes of thinking as well as to other phenomena. There is even a subbranch of sociology, the sociology of knowledge, which has as its primary focus the study of the connections between mental productions (systems of theories, values and other ideas, and beliefs) and the characteristics and social position of groups/categories/classes in society which hold and share such ideas. A premise basic to the sociology of knowlege is that knowledge (including what constitutes adequate evidence of knowledge—the method of knowing) is related to or determined by the social position of the group of which the person is a member. Individuals differentially located within a social structure (blue-collar worker, politician, physicist, social worker, theologian) tend to view society, and even what constitutes valid knowledge, differently (Mannheim, 1936).

The sociology of knowledge approach is useful as a sensitizing mechanism which may result in social workers looking at their own work and that of others with "new eyes." Yet, even this provides no certainty of an objectivity "freed" from its social and historical roots and even less does it assure us of having found the royal road to truth (Polansky, 1975a). Science must rely primarily on other means to reach its objectives. Although the insights offered by the sociology of knowledge can be a useful supplement to the more usual methods of scientific knowing there are certain cautions that need to be kept in mind. For example, the demonstration of a relationship between a scientific idea and its social roots, even if these are firmly embedded in group or class interest, does not, in itself, determine whether or not the scientific notion is valid (Popper, 1945, 1961). Truth and falsity have to be judged by customary scientific standards. A related point is that the sociology of knowledge approach, if misused, may have an irrational impact on research disputations insofar as arguments may be summarily dismissed as being tied to the interests of a particular social group rather than being debated in terms of substantive merits and judged by accepted scientific standards. Thus, conservatives tend to attribute poverty to individual deficiencies while liberals/radicals tend to point to prevailing inequitable social arrangements as the prime cause of poverty. Of course, accepted scientific standards are themselves "social."

When all is said, though, an understanding of the social psychological context and roots of our ideas and methodology has the potential of making a significant, if not decisive, contribution to social work research and an understanding of our profession, its past, present, and future.

The Social Sources and Functions of Systems of Ideas

Social workers, like other people, operate within "systems of orientation." In other words, a constellation of diverse knowledge, values, norms, and attitudes facilitates their assessment of a given situation and guides their choice of appropriate action (Gould & Kolb, 1964). Thus, one system of orientation would impel all social work practitioner/researchers to honestly report all of their practice and research findings and avoid "fudging" of their data (Agnew & Pyke, 1969).

As a part of their system of orientation, social work researchers carry around in their heads a conception of what social work research is all about (Bucher & Strauss, 1961). This conception may also be referred to as a paradigm and is analogous to a model which, according to Kühn (1970), effectively dictates what is considered to be science at any particular time. Kühn also argues that there are points in time in which there are sharp breaks in these basic scientific models and describes the process in terms akin to the stages of a social "revolution" with a new reorganized scientific view eventuating (Friedrichs, 1970). Thus, even these fundamental frames of reference are socially linked.

Regardless of the extent of one's agreement with Kühn's view of the ways in which scientific paradigms have changed, three things are clear: (1) there is an indisputable relationship between these scientific frames of reference and their social/cultural milieus; (2) these paradigms are crucial in determining the scientific concerns, the research ideas and techniques, the principles of verification and even the very conception of what constitutes the scientific enterprise during a given point in time; and (3) scientific models themselves are always changing.

Hence, it is appropriate to think of the conception of social work research that exists at a particular point in time as the result of tacit negotiation between researchers (Charlesworth, 1982).

Objectivity through Intersubjectivity

The view has often been expressed that since social work researchers are human they must necessarily be subjective. This apparent inevitability of subjectivity has raised questions as to the possibility of objectivity in observation (and other aspects of research activity). It would appear obvious that if objectivity, which we have already indicated is a critical attribute of research procedures, requires purging of all human influences (e.g., attitudes, values, prejudices, cultural perceptions) then objectivity is likely to be as elusive a goal as the fountain of youth. Even carefully controlled observation can be no guarantor of success in such a quest. Fortunately, the situation is not that bleak. The key is that of scientific objectivity through *intersubjectivity*. This requires that social workers define and describe their research techniques with sufficient clarity and specificity to permit replication by others. If replication is possible, then objectivity is a result—an objective investigation has been carried out (Hudson, 1982c). Thus, different social work practitioner/researchers can and do achieve similar results when they employ accepted standardized research techniques in practice and research (Grinnell, 1981a; Howe, 1974).

It is of interest to note that intersubjectivity implies that more than an independent isolated researcher is required and points to the collective or communal nature of the scientific enterprise, a point to which we shall return later.

The similarities between the findings of replicated studies may provide strong evidence that objectivity has been achieved. This becomes even more evident, however, when such results eventuate from the work of social workers whose values and attitudes may be quite different—or even antagonistic (C. Levy, 1976).

Values

As presented in Chapter 3, tradition suggests that social work researchers deal with facts (quantifiable observations), that is, they deal with what is, while others (e.g., philosophers, political ideologues, the average citizen in the street) deal with values; that is, with what ought to be. This traditional view amounts to an assertion that research is, or should be, devoid of values. However, this value-free position is not advanced as frequently or extensively as was once the case. Indeed, values *are* involved in social work research studies in a number of different ways. For example, the values of social work students may be the subject matter of a study and values are certainly associated with the ethics of scientific inquiry (e.g., integrity in complete reporting of results).

We will focus our discussion on how values impinge on the research process at three different phases: (1) the selection of the research topic; (2) the use of research techniques (e.g., in the course of measurement); and (3) the conclusions drawn from the data. Values will also be discussed in program evaluations.

Selection of a Research Topic. As presented in Chapter 3, the selection of a topic for investigation by the social work researcher is a fundamental part of any research endeavour. The importance of this phase of the research process is underscored by the fact that the nature of the research problem, the way it is posed, has ramifications for the kinds of solutions that are possible. The selection of the topic is a product of the complex interaction of many elements. Thus, the personal preferences, value judgements and theoretical presupposition of the social worker are important factors bearing on the choice of the topic for study and the way in which it is posed. Drawing on a previous example, one social worker deeply concerned with the plight of the poor and disadvantaged may conceive of poverty as a product of individual deficiency and undertake a research study on the most effective practice methods to overcome these deficiencies. Another similarly concerned worker may conceive of poverty as a product of extant institutional arrangements and undertake a study on the determinants of the prevailing pattern of income distribution with a view to identifying the institutional arrangements which both merit and are amenable to change.

Values beyond those held by the individual worker also enter into the selection of the research topic. While the researcher's agenda in the physical and biological sciences is more likely to be shaped by theoretical developments and empirical findings, the selection of the research topic in all scientific disciplines is shaped by the values of both the relevant scientific community and society at large (H. K. Goldstein, 1969).

The influence of the values held by fellow social workers is likely to be considerable. In large part, this is attributable to the fact that the reports and papers that are the products of research studies are generally consumed by other social workers within our profession.

The choice of a research topic is also influenced by broader social values (e.g., a concern for the disadvantaged, the pursuit of an egalitarian society, serving the physically and developmentally disabled in the least restrictive environment). In the realm of social work, the types of problems which social workers deal with are social constructions which, in turn, are rooted in social values. Mental illness and delinquency are human inventions designed to capture specific types of socially unacceptable behaviors. Thus, values play a major role in creating the social problems social workers may potentially study. However, whether these social problems or the issues surrounding them actually become the subject of research further depends, in part, on broader social values. Certain social values tend to dominate during particular epochs and certain groups in society are more influential than others in getting their definitions of phenomena as social problems accepted. For example, individualism, libertarianism, and populism are constellations of values that assumed ascendancy in the early 1980s in Thatcher's Britain, Reagan's America, and Fraser's Australia at the expense of social concerns. Consequently, research studies oriented toward facilitating optimal efficiency in the delivery of ever-shrinking human services are more likely to be fostered than, say, research into optimal environmental designs for public housing estates. Thus, current social reality can be important in determining what our profession will focus upon.

Measurement.   An example of how values impinge on measurement techniques is provided in a study of the adequacy of social security retirement benefits (Borowski, 1980). The study accommodated both absolute and relative measures of adequacy, the former being premised on notions of minimal requirements while the latter assumed the maintenance in retirement of accustomed preretirement living standards. These two measures clearly reflect differing social valuations of the aged and views on the quality of life that institutional arrangements should provide for this segment of the populace.

Conclusions.   The endings, or conclusions, of social work research are also value laden, and influenced by considerations of likely outcomes. For example, the specification of the desirable means for dealing with the poverty reported by a poverty survey will be hedged in by considerations of the legitimate means of social change. Thus, while poverty may be attributed to the particular society's institutional arrangements that generate a given income distribution pattern, the conclusions of the study will not, in all probability, be cast in terms of solutions that require means deemed illegitimate or impractical by the political system (Rein & Peattie, 1981).

Evaluative Research.   The role of values in social work is perhaps nowhere more clearly evident than in the area of evaluative research (see Chapter 21). The measurement of a program's impact on its clients is inextricably bound up with the values of the social program, its clients and the evaluative researchers themselves. Zimbalist (1977) illustrates this point in citing an evaluative research finding that the marital counseling provided by a family agency increased the incidence of divorce among a sample of clients. Zimbalist asked the question, "Is this good or bad?" and goes on to point out that if one of the agency's goals is to reduce divorce, then the finding is clearly unsatisfactory. However, if an agency goal is to strengthen healthy family relationships then, in some cases, dissolving destructive relationships may not be inappropriate.

Even seemingly objective measures in evaluative research are value laden (H. Goldstein, 1969). Consider, for example, the measure of efficiency; that is, the ratio of the amount of work performed to the total energy expended. The ratio can only have meaning when another standard is provided in terms of which work and energy are identifiable and measurable. Most importantly, this can only be done in terms of some agreed upon value. Thus, a measure of efficiency only has meaning if one is able to answer the question, "Efficient in terms of what?"— financial cost? suffering? human labor? therapists' time? clients' rights? or what? Whatever the answer, it necessarily entails an extra-scientific judgement (Fay, 1975).

The foregoing examples suggest that a consensus regarding the goals of the program subject to an evaluation and the values underpinning those goals is a prerequisite if the findings of an evaluative research study are to be acceptable to the parties concerned (Tripodi, 1983).

It is apparent from the preceding discussion that values are an inherent part of scientific activity and cannot be from such investigations. Rather, we need to recognize them, make them explicit, understand them (including their social/personal roots) and attempt to prevent them from intruding in a manner that corrupts scientific inquiry and to subject our work to the public scrutiny of our professional (and larger) community (Bell, 1983).

The Scientific Community

It is evident from everything that has been argued thus far that social work research is very much a social enterprise. As a community and "subculture," social work researchers reach consensus by sharing the same general norms for both research activity and acceptance of scientific findings and explanation. Kühn (1970, 1977) originally defined scientific communities by subject matter (e.g., the social work professional community) but later concluded that common social patterns of education and communication, not subject matter, are critical. Thus, a social work researcher becomes a member of such a community by acquiring an arsenal of "exemplars" of how to proceed (Kühn, 1977).

Communication within a scientific community is in the form of refereed professional journal articles, lectures, and various peer review mechanisms (Lindsey, 1978b). Professional associations such as the National Association of Social Workers and the Council on Social Work Education frequently play important roles in scientific socialization and social control, as well as in transmitting the content of their respective subcultures. The social control function is supported by a range of social and social-psychological rewards and deprivations. Through all these means the norms are perpetuated, including those governing the research activities, accepted explanations, and the prestige hierarchy within the community. In turn, those who deviate from such norms may be subject to intense pressures, formal and informal.

The exercise of the social control function is illustrated by Galileo's difficulties with the Roman Catholic Church during the first half of the 17th century. In Galileo's time, the theologians were the guardians of the route to certain knowledge, albeit knowledge *not* based on the scientific method of knowing. Galileo is credited with proving that the earth revolves around the sun. This conclusion was reached on the basis of observational evidence gathered with the use of a telescope. Galileo's findings conflicted with traditional church doctrine which viewed the earth as the center of the universe. Galileo was eventually called before an inquisitional tribunal and was forced to recant. Clearly, it was the theologians who determined what was to pass for valid knowledge during the first half of the 17th century; they had the power to enforce their own paradigm.

Despite the strength of the forces encouraging or demanding normative adherence, however, conflicts often quite intense, do break out from time to time in our profession. In certain periods the changes emerging from these differences may be quite abrupt and dramatic. Among the community of social work researchers recent debates have centered around the utility of empirically based practice in social work, the value of single-subject designs (see Chapter 20) and the role of qualitative research (see Chapters 14, 17, and 18).

The Social Organization of Research

The social organization of research refers, in part, to the sponsors of research and their constituents. The sponsors and their constituents in interaction can play an important part in encouraging the pursuit of research on one topic or another.

In the United States, the federal government and a few large foundations are the major sponsors of research in areas spanning the entire spectrum of social welfare. As a result, these organizations are highly influential in determining the problems on which research is done. The U.S. Department of Health and Human Services, for example, allocates hundreds of millions of dollars annually for research on *selected* topics. This department may either solicit research proposals (RFPs) or fund regional research institutes which are mandated to carry out particular types of research. The constituents are the beneficiaries of the grants—the researchers. Indeed, a situation of mutual dependency may develop between the bureaucrats charged with disbursing research funds and the beneficiary—researchers who require these funds so that they may continue to ply their trade.

The role played by the social organization of research in shaping research topics may be seen in what is called hegemonic structure of problem definition (Rein & Peattie, 1981). This implies a tacit agreement between sponsor and grantee as to the research topics deemed worthy of pursuit. Thus, federally funded institutes of poverty research have undertaken research on the administration of the welfare system, negative income taxes, and the integration of the tax and transfer systems, rather than, for example, the structural causes of poverty, to the mutual satisfaction of sponsor and grantee. It should come as no surprise to discover that social work researchers have a proclivity to formulate research topics in a way which is likely to attract funding and which requires those very techniques in which they are most skilled.

Research Fadism

Just as what passes for science is likely to change with the passage of time, so do the topics chosen to study. Fad and fashion pervade our culture (Gordon, 1984). Witness the changes in clothing styles, hairstyles, music, dance, film, even preferred vacation resorts, over the last decade alone. The pressures of fad and fashion are just as evident in our profession. Zimbalist's (1977) study of research fashions in American social work between the 1870s and mid-1960s found six reasonably self-contained and coherent research themes. The themes were:

1. Research on the causes of poverty.
2. Measurement of the prevalence of poverty.
3. The social survey movement.
4. Quantification and indexes in social work.
5. Evaluative research on social service effectiveness.
6. Study of the multiproblem family.

Why is social work research subject to the vagaries of fad and fashion? In part, the answer lies in the fact that social work is a social profession ultimately dependent on public sanction for its legitimacy and viability. Consequently, social work researchers tend to follow the lead provided by public perceptions of problems and needs. These, in turn, also reflect the dominance of different interests. Because the perceptions of problems and needs and their salience change over time, different societies accordingly place different premiums on research on different topics (Selltiz, Wrightsman, & Cook, 1976). For example, research on manpower issues in general and youth unemployment in particular, is a relatively recent phenomenon in Australia. The fact that Australia experienced an average unemployment rate of only 1.5 percent (a full-employment economy) between the end of World War II and 1974, obviated the need for such research. Today, unemployment and what to do about it are major social issues and, hence, a growing area of research activity.

Since this text seeks to foster professional social work practice in accord with the thrust of the practitioner/researcher model, it is important to note that this model, be it desirable or undesirable, is yet another expression of fashion in our profession. As society at large has increasingly demanded accountability from the social work profession, the community of social work researchers has, in consequence, acknowledged the need for effective and efficient practice (Haselkorn, 1978). A practice model deemed capable of realizing these values has been developed.

A cautionary note must be sounded in relation to fadism. Researchers in all of the sciences are, in varying degrees, preoccupied with enhancing their prestige, securing research funds, publishing their findings, being promoted, and improving their personal income. The confluence of all these preoccupations may lead to a kind of compromised intellectual integrity in the bending of research pursuits to such exigencies of the moment as the availability of federal or foundation grants or to subject areas that will yield the largest payoffs in dollars and professional prestige (Rothman, 1979). In general, however, changes in the political and social spheres are likely to have the greatest influence in shaping future research fashions in social work (Hershey & Miller, 1976).

Social Psychological Considerations

Social work researchers are not made in a different mold from other persons (Fischer, 1984). As noted above, they frequently compete with each other for position, prestige, and money. Some of these competitive struggles have become classics in the scientific community, told and retold. When such intense activities lead to important discoveries or the acceptance of progressive policies, or the development of promising new professional practices, then the costs appear to be compensated for by the benefits. But there is a less pleasant side to these intense strivings. As presented in the next chapter, a number of serious frauds in scientific research (not social work) have been uncovered in the past decade. More subtle costs have been the distortion of research activities (e.g., avoiding long-term research with slow results, or difficult subjects) in order to further one's career in congruence with the university reward systems. Even the neglect of the teaching function by university-based researchers is not unknown, or is the spewing out of trivial publications in order to build up an impressive curriculum vitae. Fierce ideological clashes which lose sight of scientific norms are also frequently encountered. And, as we have already suggested, the thrust of the researchers' interest may be diverted into less significant directions by the siren call of the prospect of funding (Kelman, 1968).

The above cataloguing of dangers is not intended to suggest that personal considerations more often fall on the cost side of the account book than in the benefit column. Much positive motivation, with important contributions for society and self, has emerged from these same considerations. But since discussion of the costs is frequently overlooked in the formal transmission of the cultural expectations and norms (even in research texts) it appears to be important to make this informal "in-group" knowledge more generally available.

SUMMARY

This chapter has sought to broaden the reader's understanding of the social work research enterprise through identifying both its foundation in the scientific method and the social and psychological factors that are embedded in it. The intent has been to show that these factors are not illegitimate or extraneous. On the contrary, they are part of the essence of social work research. If in the course of reading this chapter there is a loss of innocence about what is involved in social work research, then the better for it—the chapter will have achieved its goal.

6. ETHICS

Social workers abide by clearly defined ethics in all practice and research activities (C. Levy, 1974). Since practice and research focus on actual client populations, problems, and real-life settings, social workers are in a vulnerable position to transgress ethics (Diener & Crandall, 1978). Ethical principles and guidelines help prevent abuses to clients, delineate the social worker's professional responsibilities, direct data gathering, and point change efforts toward worthwhile goals (Reamer, 1979, 1982, 1983; A. Schwartz, 1976).

As presented in the previous five chapters, the notion that social work practice and research are discrete activities, so that some social workers conduct research and others do not, has long been a disservice to our profession. This delineation of roles falsely divides social work practice and research, alienates social workers who would profit from working together, and results in poor research production, use, and publication. Every social worker is a researcher, and any dichotomy between research and practice is absurd (Briar, 1981).

ETHICS IN THE PROBLEM-SOLVING PROCESS

When practice is viewed as compatible with research rather than as a distinct undertaking, the concept of the practitioner/researcher naturally emerges (Reinherz, Regan, & Anastas, 1983). Social work research and evaluation are best approached as integral components of practice. Social workers engage in research activities during every phase of the practice and research problem-solving process (Schinke, 1983). Research ethics apply to all problem-solving activities identified in Figure 2.1 in Chapter 2: Phase 1, Problem identification, definition, and specification; Phase 2, Generation of alternatives and selection of strategies for problem solution; Phase 3, Implementation; and Phase 4, Evaluation and dissemination of findings.

Phase 1: Problem Identification, Definition, and Specification

As presented in the previous three chapters, the identification, definition, and specification of a research problem is often more essential than its solution. Responsible ethics in social work research also rely on soundly formulated research problem areas (E. G. Brown, 1981). For problem areas to be testable and socially relevant is not sufficient. Research questions and issues such as racial superiority, homosexuality, and drug abuse warrant attention in developing ethically grounded research questions and hypotheses (Lowenberg & Dolgoff, 1983). Less controversial issues may also require careful consideration, depending on research goals, underlying theories, and practice methods.

Evaluating a research question's ethical values is difficult. In most instances, social workers have to put time and effort into reviewing available literature, lay and professional (Heffernan & Turman, 1981). In addition, it is critical to consult with professional colleagues, clients, and any persons who may be affected by attempts to answer the research question and by the answers these attempts might yield (Blalock, 1982, 1984).

One possible dilemma is suggested in the case example below.

Example. A social worker employed by the Children's Service Division to help evaluate family therapy and other agency programs has been asked to study the direction of future planning for client services. These services are based on the belief that placement in foster care of referred children from lower socioeconomic homes would break the cycle of poverty and would allow social workers more time for intensive services to children without parent interference. The social worker is asked to test relevant hypotheses in practice situations.

After careful consideration, the social worker decides that such a study is not ethical. This conclusion is based on values and codes questioning the removal of children from their parents without substantial evidence of abuse or neglect solely for research purposes. To investigate whether separating children and parents from lower socioeconomic homes will break the poverty cycle and permit better social work services to children is unethical.

The social worker suggests conducting a longitudinal study to examine differences between the socioeconomic status of abused or neglected children placed in foster care and those remaining in their own homes. The two groups would then be compared for the children's functioning and the quality of social work services. Such a design allows the research question to be answered without violating ethical standards.

Phase 2: Generation of Alternatives and Selection of Strategies for Problem Solution

Most of the concern with research ethics surrounds how social workers arrive at alternatives and strategies for hypothesis testing. Within this area, ethicians, government, and the public concentrate on the participants in research studies. Certainly, the human element deserves greatest attention when social workers conduct a research study.

Past misjudgments in the treatment of human participants in research caused the U.S. Congress to create the National Commission for the Protection of Human Subjects of Biomedical and Behavioral Research (American Psychological Association, 1973, 1977). Since its inception, this body has examined documentation on the treatment of research participants, held hearings and conferences on related issues, and developed detailed safeguards for research with individuals. Other professional organizations and interested lay groups have also focused on ensuring the physical safety and emotional well-being of individuals taking part in biomedical, behavioral, and social research (Beecher, 1966).

The emphasis on protecting research participants is quite appropriate, given earlier instances of maltreatment. Nazi experiments of the 1930s and 1940s epitomize the worst biomedical research conducted in this century. Infamous medical experiments in the United States include a 1960s study where live cancer cells were injected into elderly patients in a New York hospital, a series of drug studies conducted with uninformed and nonconsenting patients in a Georgia psychiatric institution, and an Alabama-based experiment denying treatment for persons given syphilis spirochetes (Edsall, 1969).

Behavioral and social research is not without violations of human rights and welfare. Tight control exercised in psychological laboratory experiments makes such studies prey to negative examples. Illustrative was a research project that coerced research participants into ostensibly delivering near-lethal shocks to another person (Baumrind, 1964; Milgram, 1963). Psychological laboratory research has induced high levels of fear, anxiety, and anger in individuals who were led to believe that emotion-eliciting situations were real (Hess, 1965; Lazarus, 1964; Lindzey, 1950). The ethics of such manipulations are evermore suspect when participants are inadequately debriefed after the study (Ring, Walston, & Corey, 1970).

Social research in the field, as well, displays dubious ethics. For example, U.S. Army stress research convinced soldiers aboard an airplane that they were going to crash-land; other recruits were exposed to alleged live artillery shelling (Berkum, Bialek, Kern, & Yagi, 1962). Large-scale programs evaluating effects of family planning and income maintenance, federally controlled housing, and police brutality have been criticized for ethical transgressions (Reiss, 1971). To avoid repeating these mistakes, social workers must be vigilant to protecting participants' welfare, rights, and confidentiality throughout the research process.

Informed Consent. Social workers must acquaint study participants with every aspect of the project. Full permission for involvement should be obtained via informal-consent procedures prior to initiation of the study. Informed consent ensures protection for social workers and participants alike in any setting (Afidi, 1971; Sammons, 1978).

The U.S. Department of Health and Human Services codes provide lengthy and detailed operational definitions of consent. Essentially, informed consent requires that study participants know what research participation entails, and that they freely agree to participate. Consent is obtained prior to the initiation of any research procedure, and it is documented by signed statements from participants indicating they have read or heard a complete description of the research project (American Association on Mental Deficiency, 1977). Participants' signatures follow a written summary of intended research procedures, including the social worker's name and telephone number for further information. Since review boards develop standards appropriate to their individual needs, the organization and wording of informed-consent statements varies among institutions and agencies.

Nonetheless, the National Commission for the Protection of Human Subjects requires all informed-consent statements to meet three criteria: (1) participants are competent to consent; (2) social workers provide sufficient information to allow for a balanced decision; and (3) participant consent is entirely voluntary.

First, competency encompasses the legal and mental capabilities of research participants to give permission for activities affecting their rights and welfare. Minors or prospective participants with legal guardians, for instance, are not legally capable of signing or entering into agreements of any type. Assessing mental competency is much less obvious, and it is a complex problem if participants are mentally handicapped or institutionalized because of mental disorders. Changing laws concerning these groups' legal rights increase the difficulty of competency assessment. Responsible and conservative social work researchers gain informed, written consent from at least one significant person in such participants' lives—a parent, guardian, court-appointed social worker, or spouse, for example.

The second informed-consent criterion, that participants receive adequate information about the proposed study before consenting, also entails specific standards (Afidi, 1971). Differences among formats required by individual review boards are determined by whether the sponsoring institution is a university, medical school, hospital, public school system, or social agency. Operationally, adequate information means detailing what the study will demand regarding time, activities, and disclosure of private facts and attributes, and its risks and benefits. Participants get opportunities before signing and during the research study to ask questions about any facet of the study (Grinnell & Lieberman, 1981). They are assured they can decline involvement and told that personally identifiable information will be destroyed on request. Should individuals decline to participate or withdraw from the study, they are guaranteed access to benefits, services, and funds available to the usual clientele of the sponsoring organization (Reamer, 1979).

The third informed-consent criterion of voluntary participation guards researchers from coercing, deceiving, or fraudulently recruiting participants. This requirement is the most difficult one to meet, since study involvement often brings explicit or implicit rewards. Research participants may receive cash payments for their time, or they may be promised less immediate but equally tangible benefits such as a guaranteed income, special social work services, differential treatment in a health-care facility, or enriched educational curricula. Despite the worker's good intentions, extra payoffs for participation can represent powerful reasons for volunteering. When target groups are from lower socioeconomic levels or other deprived populations, even small inducements may be too great to refuse.

The line between voluntary and involuntary participation is less well defined if potential participants are institutionalized or have their freedom restricted. Captive populations of school children, mental hospital patients, treatment center residents, and prisoners may volunteer for unpleasant research tasks to escape institutional tedium. The timing of a request to participate in a research project can also result in extra pressure to volunteer. A couple just ready to enter a hearing on termination of parental rights because of child abuse may have difficulty turning down a social worker's invitation to examine their case file for research purposes. Or, women awaiting abortion may agree to provide private nonmedical information about themselves, their families, or their partners.

The neutrality of the context and setting in which informed-consent requests are obtained are also considered. The presence of such influential people in the client's life as parents, spouse, social worker, teacher, or physician is likely to make the voluntary participation decision less objective. Admittedly, social work researchers cannot control all the factors that could possibly influence voluntary consent. Agency settings especially limit the social worker's ability to orchestrate environmental influences. But these complexities do not deter workers from removing as many coercive influences as feasible and giving potential research participants maximum freedom to accept or refuse offers of participation.

The case material from a proposed social work study presented below depicts major precautions to be considered when working with research participants.

Example.   Two graduate students were satisfying their field placement requirements at a Community Action Commission. The agency primarily served single-parent families in a federal housing project. Part of the students' responsibilities was facilitating monthly tenant meetings. The students received an assignment to design and conduct a field research study. The Community Action Commission meetings appeared to be a logical site for the study, and the students planned procedures to collect observational data on various interactional patterns: who attended the meetings, who spoke, who assumed leadership roles, and so forth. One student asserted that telling meeting members about the study in advance would alter interactional patterns and so suggested that the study should not be revealed until after data collection. The other student opposed such deception and advocated disclosure regarding the study's intent, and proposed obtaining informed consent from all members who went to the monthly meetings before beginning. Unable to agree, the two students deferred to their instructor.

The instructor listened to both sides and agreed that awareness of the study would change interaction patterns of the participants. Nevertheless, the instructor said that informed consent was absolutely necessary and noted that interaction patterns of the participants would be ethically examined by collecting data in two different formats: in front of the consenting participants, and out of their sight. Comparing data collected under both conditions would show how the level of awareness affected interactions, at no cost to research ethics (Van Maanen, 1983).

Phase 3: Implementation

Sound ethical choices go beyond participant recruitment and informed consent. The actual implementation of social work research is risky in terms of ethics. During implementation, social workers have to scrutinize their research designs, procedures for data collection, analyses, presentations, and practice methods.

Research designs are vulnerable to problems in several respects. As presented in Chapter 13, research designs refer to the plan, structure, and strategy of attempts to answer questions of interest. Accurate and reliable conduct of research requires control. To generalize conclusions beyond the individuals who participate, sampling procedures (see Chapter 8) must be considered. Exercising control and selecting samples in line with scientific methods and ethical considerations requires much deliberation.

Control groups allow greater confidence in study findings. An experimental group of individuals exposed to treatment is contrasted with a control group of individuals not receiving treatment. If the two groups are equivalent in every way except variation of treatment, the study may conclude that differences between the two groups are due to treatment. Omission or variation of treatment may violate the rights of participants. For example, control group participants may be denied essential social work services, funds, or such adjunctive resources as food stamps. The research design, therefore, must be studied for potential participant abuses.

Data collection demands attention to ethical issues in selecting and using collection instruments and in analyzing and presenting data. Data collection instruments such as those presented in Table 11.3 in Chapter 11 must accurately measure the relevant concepts under study. In addition, the instruments must be unbiased (see Chapters 9, 10, and 11). Literature on similar research and pilot work is invaluable in choosing precise measures. Investigations with psychological and social data collection instruments have stimulated critical assessment of measures for bias against racial, cultural, and handicapped groups (French, 1979; Hobbs, 1975). Such concerns suggest care at this stage of the research process. All data collection instruments selected for a study should closely follow administrative protocol. Research integrity and respect for participants' rights and privacy rest on cautious data collection procedures.

The analysis and presentation of data demand extra attention, since these processes are most impervious to external monitoring (Marks, 1975; Reid, 1983; Souther & White, 1977). Recent transgressions provide evidence of how easily data are faked (Evans, 1976; Gibbons, 1975; Haywood, 1977; Jensen, 1977; Steiner, 1972; Warwick, 1975). Pains must be taken when constructing tables, drawing graphs, and presenting findings through other data displays (American Psychological Association, 1983; Katzenberg, 1975; Reid, 1981).

Unlike finite research designs and data collection procedures, the practice methods adopted by social workers have been limited only by the imaginations of practitioners and policymakers. Over the years, social workers have tried to solve human problems via macrolevel income maintenance, separation of public assistance and social services, increased police patrols, street lighting, day care, food stamps, preschool education, and community mental health services. Microlevel practice methods have included therapeutic strategies of psychoanalysis, behavior modification, guided-group interaction, psychosurgery, transactional analysis, electric shock, token economies, rational-emotive therapy, biofeedback, family and group counseling, primal scream, trust fall, and psychotropic drugs, to name only a few.

Unfortunately, many practice methods have been delivered without being evaluated. Worse yet, some practice methods social workers dream up are so questionable—ethically and therapeutically—that they contraindicate any human service application, even on an experimental basis.

The responsibilities of social workers at this juncture are twofold: untried practice methods must undergo rigorous evaluation; and potentially harmful or irreversible practice methods should be supported by previous research literature, grounded theory, or multiple case studies (Fischer & Hudson, 1976). The responsibility for assessing potential practice methods risks places workers in roles heretofore not considered within the research bailiwick (Martin, 1975). For social workers, conducting ethical research studies means questioning value and underlying theories and assessing possible harm resulting from the research process and any experimental intervention (Vigilante, 1974).

The case below highlights key issues in implementation.

Example. A school social worker has earned a reputation as being knowledgeable and effective in helping teachers use various behavior management techniques. One of the kindergarten teachers seeks the social worker's assistance in controlling an unruly afternoon class and asks advice on maintaining an orderly classroom.

The social worker agrees to help the teacher develop and implement an improved learning environment but explains that careful assessment is necessary first. The intervention would reflect this assessment data and conventional procedures. But the teacher wants a quick response and opposes assessment because it will delay classroom intervention. Knowing the harm a poorly planned intervention might cause, the social worker agrees to become involved only if they devise a plan to assess the problem, develop an appropriate intervention program, and evaluate its efficacy. Unless they systematically follow each step, they may base their decisions on insufficient data. They also will not be able to pinpoint exactly what worked and what did not, and other teachers with similar problems will not be able to benefit from their experience.

Phase 4: Evaluation and Dissemination of Findings

Not surprisingly, social workers often believe ethical responsibilities end with data collection. This is simply not true. Social workers who exemplify high standards continue their moral and professional commitments long after the research study per se is over. Three issues that warrant a careful eye to ethics are: (1) follow-up; (2) publication; (3) and collaboration.

Follow-Up. Follow-up necessitates fulfilling agreements made with all those involved in the research project: study participants; co-workers; those assisting, consulting, and advising at various stages; and representatives of sponsoring agencies and external funding sources. When final outcome data have been collected, participants are interviewed regarding their views of beneficial and adverse effects of the study. A specific welfare program may have changed their interactions with family and friends; completing a survey on attitudes toward sex education may have stimulated discussions between parents and children. Through written, telephone, or face-to-face contact, participants are told how the study findings may shape programmatic and policy changes. Specific data given individuals on their own or others' results are carefully couched to obviate negative interpretations. Revealing assessment instrument scores could raise more questions than answers, and confidentiality agreements might be violated by divulging personally identifiable information.

Agency co-workers and auxiliary personnel are queried about a research project's positive and negative ramifications. Feedback to these people is best kept to aggregated data and interpretations. Revealing the substance of specific results or detailed feedback risks damaging participant and worker confidentiality and could launch unfortunate comparisons among individuals and collaborating sites.

Follow-up with sponsoring and funding agencies demands formal presentation of major findings, cost accounting, and suggestions for future projects the organization could underwrite. Since the bulk of social work research is applied, social work researchers translate study results into possible implications for social programs and policy (Tripodi, 1983). Many agencies require final written reports, and most would benefit from them if available.

Publication. Regardless of individual agency requirements, the social worker's responsibilities to our profession remain unmet until the study findings have been written and reproduced in retrievable form. Briar and Miller (1971) noted:

> Commitment to the method of science requires that one's professional work be made open to examination within a professional arena. New theory and new techniques are of no value if such developments perish with their creators. The accumulation of knowledge is not a private effort, and a professional ethic demands that such accretions become part of the public domain.

Government policy has given added weight to the need for dissemination of research findings. The Federal Council of Science and Technology, for example, states that the publication of research results is an essential part of the research process. This has been recognized with authorization to pay publication costs from federal research grants and contract funds (Arkava & Lane, 1983).

Collaboration. Multiple collaborative relationships are numerous in social work research. Workers soon learn, planfully or by trial or error, how and when to delegate responsibilities and tasks to peers, research assistants, and adjunctive support personnel. Judging how much to rely on others, assessing in advance individual expertise, and tactfully but quickly terminating unworkable relationships can mean the difference between successful and less than successful projects.

Ethical concerns encountered in collaborative relationships in research are not unlike those in any professional contact. Still, social workers are often faced with rather special considerations. Colleaguial consultations about ethical issues can be of help in selecting an appropriate research problem, study population, and research method. Advice and counsel from colleagues having different racial, sexual, and cultural perspectives are especially helpful. If pitfalls cannot be obviated, social workers can at least anticipate them and prepare contingency plans. Positive collaborative arrangements with agencies are fundamental during planning, data collection, and follow-up operations. Ethical workers ensure that all agency personnel receive frequent, candid project status reports. Withholding key information, such as whether the study's review application has been denied or that some data have been lost and must be recollected, will cause much damage when it eventually leaks out.

Directing and supervising research assistants demands consummate skill and might seem to require more time than doing the tasks alone. Because social workers cannot personally attend to every detail of conducting a research project, they teach others to perform specified tasks and to exercise ethical principles in everything they do. Pressures on research assistants to meet tight deadlines may lead them to temporarily set aside ethics in order to achieve the overall objectives. "Forgetting" to ask to see a signed informed consent statement before administering a questionnaire is one example.

Sharing authorship with collaborators may become an issue, since research activities frequently yield grant applications and publication possibilities. Ambiguous guidelines for determining authorship complicate this delicate matter (Reid, 1981). Potential coauthors meet together, review their relative contributions, and jointly decide on how authorship is to be stated. All contributors are contacted before being listed on a document to authorize proper use and placement of names—in footnotes, title or text—and to demonstrate how their contributions will be acknowledged. Correct spellings, credentials, and institutional affiliations are verified at this time. Evaluation and dissemination activities that operationalize ethics are evident in the following case example.

Example. A social work supervisor at a Department of Social

Services (DSS) staff development center was responsible for training caseworkers in three regional offices. To evaluate a specific training program, the supervisor and DSS administrators designated that social workers in each office were to be trained in sequence, with one month between phases. This interval allowed training to be measured. Measurement included knowledge questionnaires, attitudinal scales, and skill performance tests.

Results showed that staff in each office improved only after they had been trained. In short, training was deemed successful. Findings also revealed differences among the three offices, with social workers at two offices improving more than those at the third. Further, workers in the same office increased their skills at varying rates: some improved a great deal, others very little.

The supervisor wanted to share evaluation findings with each office on the basis that the workers, supervisors, and agency administrators involved would appreciate seeing how research and evaluation methods were applied in their agencies. But showing and explaining findings can easily have negative effects by highlighting differences among the participating workers and agencies. Thus, the supervisor compromised by collating all data into composite results across staff and agencies. This procedure reduced the likelihood of generating between-worker or between-staff competition, yet gave everyone an objective glimpse at the training program.

IMPLICATIONS FOR THE FUTURE

Doubtless, future social work research enterprises will be greater occupied with ethical questions, issues, and procedures. Proposed legislation, federal regulations, and modified professional codes suggest that research with human participants will require more careful ethical safeguards for all activities. Some fear social work research will become so encumbered by externally imposed constraints that only unimaginative and irrelevant studies will be launched. Indeed, evidence indicates that people are highly suggestible and that information alone changes attitudes, moods, feelings, and perceptions. Thus, efforts to obtain informed consent may have negative effects if participants adversely react to information. If protection of the individual is the reason for obtaining informed consent, the possibility of harm as a direct result of the consent process must be considered. Criticisms from the professional community will surely intensify as government agencies and professional associations require additional ethical safeguards. The federal government continues to release regulations on social research. For example, recent guidelines direct all institutions receiving U.S. Department of Health and Human Services (formerly Department of Health, Education, and Welfare) funds to inform research participants not only of study risks but of medical treatment and financial compensation available should any harm take place (Department of Health, Education, and Welfare, 1978).

Since institutionalized, mentally handicapped persons are highly vulnerable to abuse of their welfare, rights, and privacy, significant changes in federal regulations protect these populations when they participate in research efforts. One measure aimed to safeguard institutionalized, mentally handicapped persons requires advocates—to audit the protection given participants during any research procedure. To ensure objective assessment of risk, regulations set explicit criteria for selecting advocates: no one may serve as an advocate who has an interest in or association with the institution conducting or sponsoring the research study. And where the individual is a ward of a state or of another agency, institution, or entity, the advocate may not have any interest in that entity. Advocates must also be familiar with the physical, psychological, social needs, and legal status of the individuals under study.

Other federal regulations increase lay representation on institutional review boards from a minimum of one member to at least two thirds of total membership, with institutionally affiliated persons and outside consultants comprising the remaining third. Institutional review boards have to make all meetings open to the public and keep five-year records of their deliberations. Not unexpectedly, debate over many of these revised regulations is sharp. Putting some of the more unwieldy laws into practice may alienate those who wish to remain their own ethical watchdogs.

Professional association efforts match government moves toward awareness, attention, and positive action to prevent ethical transgressions. For a few associations with members serving in multiple human services capacities—service, administration, research, teaching, consultation—one procedure has been the establishment of separate ethical codes for various professional roles. The American Psychological Association has three sets of ethical guidelines to help direct the work of its members. These cover areas in which all psychologists share responsibilities; responsibilities of clinicians, supervisors, and administrators in community and institutional service programs; and issues relevant to laboratory and field investigations (American Psychological Association, 1973, 1977).

The National Association of Social Workers' ethical code demarks various professional roles. Code revisions include categories for social workers' general responsibilities and their obligations to clients, colleagues, employers, the profession, and society (National Association of Social Workers, 1980). In the first category, scholarship and research are covered in six ethical guidelines. The code deals with client rights and prerogatives, confidentiality, and privacy, as germane to both practice and research. Recognition of the special ethical problems encountered in the research process is an important advancement for the code:

E. Scholarship and Research—The social worker engaged in study and research should be guided by the conventions of scholarly inquiry.

1. The social worker engaged in research should consider carefully its possible consequences for human beings.

2. The social worker engaged in research should ascertain that the consent of participants in the research is voluntary and informed, without any implied deprivation or penalty for refusal to participate, and with due regard for participants' privacy and dignity.

3. The social worker engaged in research should protect participants from unwarranted physical or mental discomfort, distress, harm, danger, or deprivation.

4. The social worker who engages in the evaluation of services or cases should discuss them only for professional purposes and only with persons directly and professionally concerned with them.

5. Information obtained about participants in research should be treated as confidential.

6. The social worker should take credit only for work actually done in connection with scholarly and research endeavors and credit contributions made by others.

Despite added vigor in government and professional association standards for ethical social work research inquiries, the ultimate burden to infuse ethics throughout the practice and research process rests on the individual social worker. Government regulation is certainly necessary; without it, workers would have less sensitivity to ethical issues. Professional associations must refine and disseminate ethical codes and standards appropriate for their members. Codes might be even stronger, with sanctions for violations. But neither government nor professional associations can continuously monitor how ethical guidelines are translated into the conduct of the research process, especially research done by social workers in the field. The social worker's responsibilities to question, assess, plan, implement, monitor, and evaluate all activities involved in the research process must be underscored.

SUMMARY

Social work research ethics address concerns and questions raised throughout the research process. On a par with high-quality research, ethical principles permeate each aspect of social work inquiry. Ethical social workers are mindful that they alone can apply and monitor ethical standards. Social workers who practice research within this conceptual framework limit the risk of harming clients, themselves, or the lay, professional, and scientific communities to which they are accountable.

Ethics are not merely derived from a pretentious etiquette—they express our beliefs and guide us in achieving them. As an integral part of our profession, they foster practice and research endeavors which are compatible with our profession's goals and values. Thus, they are applicable in all four phases of the practitioner/researcher's problem-solving process, from problem identification, definition, and specification to evaluation and dissemination of findings. Social workers committed to ethical practice and research search for the most valid and reliable data as possible without deceiving others, causing harm, or being dishonest in any way.

Ronald W. Toseland

7. RESEARCH METHODS

The systematic process for choosing an appropriate social work research method serves as a guide to various aspects of the several kinds of methods that can be used for collecting data. The research method chosen provides a way to deal with a research problem derived from situations encountered in practice. The choice represents the second phase in the social worker's problem-solving process as outlined in Figure 2.1 in Chapter 2: generation of alternatives and selection of strategies for problem solution.

Knowledge about the selection, application, and implementation of social work research methods is a powerful tool which can be applied throughout the research process. Research methods provide the initial data on a social problem and guide selection of the most effective treatment intervention. They help the social worker evaluate an intervention's effectiveness in the delivery of services to a target population and provide data about who is being served by a social program. The method used may determine the extent to which results can be disseminated and the study can be replicated by other social work researchers. Thus, the practical utility of research methods for social workers is enormous (Thomas, 1975).

DEFINITION OF SOCIAL WORK RESEARCH METHODS

In its broadest sense, a research method is a plan or design for the process of finding a solution to the research problem posed by the social worker (Suchman, 1967b). The research problem or question may be as simple as wanting to know the demographic characteristics of the client population of an emergency shelter program, or as complex as defining and testing the effectiveness of a specific treatment technique such as "effective use of self" in social work practice.

There are many definitions and classifications of research methodology in the literature. Some of these definitions limit research methodology to a consideration of classical experimental methods (Fairweather, 1967). Classical experimental methods are characterized by active manipulation and measurement of independent variables through the comparison of experimental and control groups to assess the effects of an independent variable on a dependent variable. In recent years it has become quite clear that experimental research methods are insufficient for the variety of questions and problems faced by practicing social workers.

Broader definitions of research methodology often consider different levels of research methods. These levels imply that some research methods, such as participant observation (Chapter 17) or ethnomethodology (Chapter 18), are at a lower level of sophistication than rigorous experimental research methods (Finestone & Kahn, 1975). While it is true that some research methods provide for greater control of variables, for many research problems greater control is neither desirable nor possible. A second basis for classifying levels of research methods comes from the link between a research method and the causal inferences which can be drawn from that method. Although extensive control over a closed system may provide greater confidence about causal inferences than research methods which are designed for open systems where less control is possible, a variety of research methods permit causal inferences (Tripodi, Fellin, & Meyer, 1983). Participant observation, single-subject research (Chapter 20), survey research (Chapter 15) ethnomethodology, and classical experimental research (Chapter 13) may all yield data about cause-effect relationships.

Choosing an appropriate social work research method must never be a process of trying to fit a particular question to a particular level of research methodology. The choice must be based on the nature of the problem confronting the social worker. The research method should provide the most complete and appropriate data about the research question. A careful exploration and analysis of the research question prior to the choice of an appropriate research methodology is essential. Just as a social work practitioner chooses an intervention strategy based on the nature of the problem confronting the worker, rather than forcing the problem to conform to a particular social work intervention strategy, the process of deciding on an appropriate social work research methodology should not force a research question to fit a particular research method.

It is important that the methodology or plan for answering the research question be made prior to, rather than after, data on the research question are collected. A well-chosen, clear research method will provide a much better answer to the social worker's question than an unplanned, unsystematic method (Finestone & Kahn, 1975). Haphazard, unsystematic attempts to answer social welfare questions or resolve social welfare problems can lead to erroneous data or result in the collection of data that do not address the original question. A clear, systematic research procedure helps to ensure that the social worker will be provided with relevant answers to the practice issues in question. There is no substitute for taking time to evaluate alternative methods carefully and choose the method that will provide the most complete data about the research question being investigated.

THE PROCESS OF SELECTING A RESEARCH METHOD

As an aspect of the practitioner/researcher's problem-solving process, the choice of an appropriate research method can itself be viewed as a problem-solving process in which the problem is to choose a plan or a design for a research study (Suchman, 1967b). The end product of this process is the selection of a method which is effective for collecting the necessary data about the research question. Systematic use of problem-solving processes has been shown to improve decision making in a variety of situations and contexts (Spivack, Platt, & Shure, 1976). What is more important, problem-solving processes are used implicitly by all workers when they are confronted with a research problem. Making the process clear, systematic, and explicit can help to ensure that all factors are considered in decision making.

The problem-solving process used to decide on a research methodology can be divided into nine phases, as illustrated in Table 7.1. After this problem-solving process has been completed, the researcher is ready to implement the plan and then to analyze the results.

The problem-solving process is not a linear one. Feedback is possible at each phase, as the arrows indicate, and various phases may occur simultaneously. For example, in considering the practical issues involved in choosing an appropriate research methodology for a problem of how to reach out to a client group not currently being served, the worker may decide that time and money are severely limited and would not be available for a continuing outreach program. This feedback may help the social worker redefine the research question to consider ways to ensure full access to services once a client makes contact with the agency. Simultaneous changes might also occur in the social worker's assumptions about how potential clients can be served by the agency. Similarly, the context of the study often affects assumptions and theories about how the question may be pursued. Therefore, although the phases in the problem-solving process are presented successively, interaction between them is essential for choosing the most appropriate research plan for a specific research question.

TABLE 7.1

Phases in Choosing a Research Method
(from Figure 2.1 in Chapter 2)

---

1. Problem identification, definition, and specification

    1a. Defining the research question

2. Generation of alternatives and selection of strategies for problem solution

    2a. Gathering a knowledge base
    2b. Choosing a methodological approach
    2c. Gathering data on the research context
    2d. Listing alternative methods
    2e. Considering practical issues
    2f. Deciding on a research method

3. Implementation

    3a. Ensuring proper implementation

4. Evaluation and dissemination of findings

    4a. Specifying the strengths and limitations of the method

---

Phase 1a: Defining the Research Question

The selection and formulation of problem areas for social work research, as presented in Chapter 3, provides for the operational definition of concepts and variables. How research questions are defined affects the research method chosen and the results of the entire project. There are two important questions social workers must consider while attempting to define a research question:

What am I really trying to find out?

For what purposes will the findings be used?

The first question requires a very specific answer so a definite research question can be devised. Vague questions do not tell us what we need to know (Simon, 1969). For example, in trying to define and evaluate the skills which comprise "effective use of self" a social worker might really want to know what direct-service workers perceive these skills to be and their assessment of the value and importance of each skill. Research questions might also be stated as workers' desire to find out whether or not a particular skill which might be considered a part of the effective use of self affects their practice with particular clients.

Collecting data on these two different definitions of the research question requires the use of different social work research methods.

While defining the research question clearly and specifying all the variables (independent and dependent) relevant to the question are essential, it is also important to be clear about the purposes of the study, which are determined by its intended uses (Simon, 1969). The central question to be answered is whether the specific research problem, as defined, will provide useful data about the problem being investigated. Social workers must consider not only how they might use the data but also how the results will be used by professionals, administrators, policymakers, and clients. If the results are intended exclusively for the use of the worker who conducts the study, the choice of a research method may reflect only the needs of the worker and the clients who may be affected by the study. In most instances, however, research results are useful to and used by others. In these cases, the choice of a research method should attempt to reflect the needs of those who are most likely to use the study's results.

An example of the problems that can arise when a detailed specification of the intended purposes and uses of a research project is omitted from the design of the study is the New Jersey-Pennsylvania negative income tax experiment (Rossi, 1982). This social welfare experiment was carried out to evaluate the effects of various levels of guaranteed income on the work incentives of low-income, two-parent families. The study took three years to conduct, and final results were not available until some time after its completion. During the development and implementation of the project, policymakers in the federal government became increasingly interested in the consolidation of welfare programs and less interested in the question of work disincentives as a result of a guaranteed income. While the extent to which the researchers attempted to analyze how the results of the study would be used by policymakers prior to data collection is unclear, obviously the study did not answer the questions in which the policymakers were most interested (Kershaw & Fair, 1976; Mahoney & Mahoney, 1975).

Phase 2a: Gathering a Knowledge Base

The choice of a research method is also affected by the worker's knowledge of the subject being investigated, the theory or theories the worker believes affect the research question, and the assumptions made. The knowledge base a social worker is familiar with affects the choice of a research method in a variety of ways. For example, previous research knowledge may suggest that two variables appear to be related. This knowledge could be used to design a research project to test the extent to which one of the variables (dependent) is a cause of the other variable (independent). For this purpose, an experimental design method might be most appropriate. However, if little is known about the variables affecting the research question, such a method would be inappropriate. Instead, the social worker is much more likely to choose a method, such as survey research or participant observation, which will describe the relevant variables in the situation. Familiarity with the knowledge base allows the social worker to examine ways in which others have answered similar research questions. This examination may suggest similar or innovative ways of investigating the question at hand.

Although it is sometimes assumed that social work research is value free, assumptions and theories are a part of any worker's conception of a research question, and they affect the choice of the method that will be used in the study (see Chapter 5). Assumptions or hypotheses which remain untested form a base from which the project begins. For example, assumptions about the boundaries of the problem being investigated, about relationships between the concepts and variables involved in the research question, and about how the issues, problems, and questions developed and progressed will all affect the choice of a research method.

Theories that the social worker knowingly or unknowingly applies in practice can also influence how a problem is investigated. For example, social workers who use existential models of social work practice may be more likely to choose participant observation or ethnomethodology, whereas those who employ a social learning theory model may tend to use experimental or single-subject designs. Given the fact that there is no one correct way to design a research project, or any one answer to a complex research question, it should be clear that differing assumptions and theories bring a variety of perspectives to the investigation of any social work phenomenon (Suchman, 1967b). Assumptions and theories should not, and cannot, be prevented from influencing a social worker's choice of a method. In fact, specifying a theory which is addressed by the research problem helps accumulate knowledge by adding to the empirical validation of the theory. Assumptions and theories should be made explicit, however, so that anyone utilizing the research results can see how the worker's assumptions and theories influence the way in which the research question was studied.

Phase 2b: Choosing a Methodological Approach

The method chosen to investigate the research problem is also affected by how the methodological issues which affect the research process are resolved. Social workers who are attempting to choose among a variety of research methods should be familiar with three important issues which can affect their decision. The first issue is whether a descriptive or an experimental method of scientific investigation provides the best answer for the problem being studied. Descriptive methods attempt to specify and delineate the relevant variables affecting a research question, while experimental methods attempt to specify relationships between variables in a causal fashion. Any research method may include both descriptive and experimental characteristics, but some methods, such as survey research, are more often associated with descriptive approaches, while others, such as classical experimental methods, are more often associated with causal approaches.

Another issue that is often confronted when choosing a research method is that of quantitative versus qualitative methods. This has been described as the rigor versus vigor debate and the scientific versus humanistic approach to the study of people (see Chapter 14). The quantitative approach stresses rigorous control of the research situation and a focus on the elements or parts of a complex research question. It is most often associated with the scientific study of human behavior and is clearly evidenced in classical experimental methods. The qualitative approach emphasizes attention to clinical intuition and a holistic, humanistic approach to investigation. Attention is focused on the unique aspects of the research situation. As presented in Chapter 14, proponents of each approach assume that these are two different methods for investigating the same research question, but in fact the two approaches are complementary and lead to different ways of conceptualizing the problem.

The methods presented in Part Three contain elements of both quantitative and qualitative approaches to the study of human behavior, and all of them can be considered both scientific and humanistic. Some research methods are more closely associated with one or the other approach, and it is the social worker's responsibility to determine which method is most appropriate for the research problem under investigation. For example, a worker who is investigating the relationship between two variables which affect recidivism (relapse into criminal behavior) may use an experimental method to investigate the magnitude of this relationship. The worker who is investigating the effects of nursing home placement on the lives of older persons may choose ethnomethodology or participant observation for describing the changes which occur.

Another methodological issue which often affects the choice of a method is the social worker's decision about the most appropriate data collection method, such as through direct observation or self-reports. Surveys, for example, rely heavily on self-report data, while participant observation methods rely to a much greater extent on direct observation. Other research methods fall between these extremes. The choice of a research method must be guided by the type of data to be collected. The critical issue is whether the data collected will be appropriate to the aims, purposes, and definition of the research question and whether the choice of research methodology will permit meaningful conclusions about the research problem under investigation.

Phase 2c: Gathering Data on the Research Context

The next phase in choosing a method is to examine the context in which the research problem is being investigated. Just as social workers must be aware of the problem-person-situation context in social work practice, they must also be aware of the context in which the research study will be conducted. The research context consists of the social welfare problem being investigated, the clients who may be affected by the study, and the setting in which the study is taking place. All of these may affect the selection of the research method.

Particular social work problems can have a significant impact on the method. Domestic violence, for example, is an extremely sensitive issue. Research methods to study aspects of domestic violence must consider how valid and reliable data can be obtained, what the ethical issues involved are, how the research methodology can preserve the anonymity or confidentiality of the participants, how research on domestic violence will be viewed by the community and society in which it takes place, and how the data will be used. The type of social work problem investigated may also narrow the choice of a method. For example, to find out how the historical development of settlement houses is related to modern multiservice community centers, the social worker may be limited to the historical methods (P. Stuart, 1981).

Clients, who may be affected either directly by participating in the research study or indirectly by experiencing the results of the project, should also be considered carefully when selecting a research method. As presented in the preceding chapter, any methodology for investigating a research problem should carefully consider how ethical issues will be resolved. The needs of the social worker for precise data to improve social work practice must be balanced by the needs of clients for privacy, self-determination, and the highest quality service possible. In choosing a research method, the extent to which different methods will affect services to the clients must be evaluated.

The agency in which the social worker is employed and the setting where the study will be conducted are also important determinants in the selection of an appropriate method. A great deal has been written about the politics of social research (Beals, 1969). The social work setting can support or hinder the research process in a number of ways. Financial support; the cooperation of staff, clients, and administration; facilities for the study; and dissemination of the research results—these are just a few of the areas which can be affected by the worker's relationship to the agency where the study will be conducted. Modifications in ideal research methods, based on the social worker's assessment of the research setting, must often be made, but the research methodology should not be compromised to the point where it will not be able to provide valid and reliable data on the research question. As presented in length in the two preceding chapters, the process of deciding on a research method is one of give and take, where the ideals of sound research methodology and the needs for precise data are balanced by the context in which the study is to be conducted.

Phase 2d: Listing Alternative Methods

Before making a decision to use a particular method and after considering how practical issues such as time and money could affect the choice of a method, it is helpful to list the methods which could possibly be used to investigate the research question. The strengths and weaknesses of each alternative for collecting data on the research problem being investigated should be analyzed. This process is useful because it helps provide a clear grasp of the advantages and disadvantages of each method and prevents the development of unrealistic expectations.

The social worker may want to share the list with others who are knowledgeable about research methods in order to gain additional perspectives on the choice. Sharing options and allowing input and feedback from administrators and professionals who will be asked to help with the implementation of the study is also useful. Others can often identify problems which have been overlooked, and they may be able to suggest additional sources of support to overcome barriers which might have been considered insurmountable. Active participation in decisions, such as participating in the choice of a research method, will enhance the commitment to the option finally selected (Heap, 1975).

Phase 2e: Considering Practical Issues

After the advantages and disadvantages of all the potential research methods have been examined, the social worker is ready to analyze the practical barriers which may affect the final choice and can proceed by modifying or overcoming them before they can interfere with implementation. If it does not seem possible to change practical barriers which stand in the way of implementing a specific method, alternative methods which reduce or eliminate the impact of the barriers should be considered.

Five practical barriers which are particularly relevant to the problem-solving process for selecting a method are: (1) the size and scope of the proposed study; (2) the cooperation needed to implement the method; (3) the extent to which the study will intrude on the participants in the project; (4) the financial and physical resources required; and (5) the time needed to implement and conclude the project.

Size and Scope. The size and scope of the study are important practical issues for several reasons. The more systems affected, either directly or indirectly, by the proposed study, the more likely it is that the worker will encounter practical barriers in implementing it. The social worker is likely to find it difficult to designate responsibilities and gain cooperation from various participants in a large research project. Political barriers are also more difficult to surmount when a large project involves several competing interest groups who might be affected by the results. One must attempt to select research questions that are meaningful and manageable, as well as methods to investigate questions that are clearly possible with the resources available. Novice social workers often attempt to study questions which are so broad that there is little chance of obtaining meaningful data. When complex research questions are unavoidable, several different research methods performed simultaneously or consecutively may be needed to answer them. It is often useful to view complex issues as a set of two or more separate research questions and to select a method which is appropriate for each one.

Cooperation. The degree to which cooperation from sources other than the worker is needed and the extent to which cooperation can be obtained have a direct bearing on the choice of a research method. A classical experimental design, for example, requires significantly more cooperation from staff and clients than a survey of workers in the agency where the social worker is employed. Gaining the cooperation of those who are responsible for the resources needed for implementing the project and the support of those who will be involved in carrying it out is not easy. If the research study must obtain data which are representative of the entire population being studied, the social worker will be particularly interested in choosing a method which ensures a high response rate from those who are selected for the study. For example, the choice of a research plan calling for the use of a mailed questionnaire, which normally yields low return rates (from 10 to 60 percent), would not be appropriate if the worker wants to obtain data from every potential respondent.

Intrusion. The amount of intrusion into the setting where the research study is being conducted is also a factor in choosing a method. Some research methods necessitate a great deal of cooperation and participation by agency staff and clients, while other methods may go virtually unnoticed. The extent to which unobtrusive methods of research should be used depends on the type of problem being investigated, ethical issues, the cooperation of those who will implement the study, the funding available for extra staffing, and the degree to which intrusion in the setting affects the services rendered. Whenever possible, a research method which minimizes unwanted intrusions into the normal operations of the agency should be selected. In some cases, an unobtrusive method also can reduce biases that can arise from implementation of the study. This is particularly true when knowledge about the study may distort or bias the results obtained (see Chapters 17 and 18).

Financial and Physical Resources. Financial and physical resources are always a central concern in planning for an appropriate method. Without adequate financial and physical resources, a method cannot be implemented properly. A social worker must estimate the costs of personnel, equipment, subject costs or participant fees, space rental, data analysis, and report writing, as well as any additional costs projected for a particular research plan. Funding from outside the agency may have to be sought. Often local planning agencies, a United Way agency, or a community development group can be helpful in locating sources of funding. It should be emphasized, however, that a great deal of research can be done with agency cooperation and a small amount of funding for supplies, typing services, and data analysis. Many excellent research projects have been conducted on extremely limited budgets, and social work practice problems often can be addressed by the researcher within an agency without any outside sources of funding (Grinnell & Jung, 1981).

Time. The time needed to undertake a project is another important practical consideration when choosing a method. Research methods vary considerably in terms of how long they take to implement and conclude. For most practicing social workers, case loads are large, and there is always too much to do in too little time. In these circumstances, research may be seen as a luxury or an added burden. Without solid practice research, however, new practice methods cannot be developed and tested.

Responsibility for freeing time to pursue both small and large research efforts rests both with the workers and the administrators in social programs. Professional social work standards clearly stipulate that service to clients is the primary goal of the social service agency. But when that service has not been evaluated, or when a possibly more effective or efficient method is proposed, these standards indicate the need for research. Social workers in an agency can plan to cooperate in a specific research endeavor, and the choice of a research method can in part be based on the time and resources available to conduct the study. Thus, although client service is paramount, the researcher, recognizing professional social work standards and concern for the development of more effective practice methods, will balance service to present clients with a commitment to developing and testing methods to serve future generations more effectively. Along with client service, therefore, the worker should attempt to carry out some developmental research (Chapter 25) for practice innovation.

Phase 2f: Deciding on a Research Method

The problem-solving process for selection of the research method that is best suited for investigation of a research problem climaxes with this phase. It is helpful to refer back to the listing of possible alternative methods developed in Phase 2d and examine their strengths and weaknesses. The social worker should also consider how practical issues might affect the implementation of each alternative.

A procedure has been developed for choosing among alternative solutions to a problem which can be used by the researcher (Carkhuff, 1973). Alternative solutions, in this case different research methods, are listed and assigned numerical scores, based on the method's strengths and weaknesses, for each factor being considered. Each factor can be differentially weighted; for example, practical issues could be considered four times as important as the choice of a quantitative approach to the problem in deciding on the method to be used in the study. In addition to helping the workers decide on a method, this process is useful in presentations to administrators and funding bodies and at board meetings and staff meetings in order to show that all the alternative methods were analyzed and fully considered.

Table 7.2 illustrates a decision table used in choosing among four research methods for investigating the effectiveness of a peer counseling program for runaway adolescents. The social worker was attempting to choose among: (1) a survey of the adolescents who had been in the program for the last four months; (2) an experiment comparing the innovative peer counseling program to a more traditional program for adolescents sponsored by a neighborhood center in another section of town; (3) a single-subject method which would be applied to the next five adolescents who became involved in the program; and (4) a program evaluation method using a prepost measure to evaluate the progress of 40 adolescents during the next four months of program operation.

TABLE 7.2

Decision Table for Choosing a Research Method to
Investigate the Effectiveness of a Peer Counseling Program

Factors Possibly Affecting Choice of Method	Effect of Factor on Method*			
	Survey	Experiment	Single Subject	Program Evaluation
	(Chapter 15)	(Chapter 13)	(Chapter 20)	(Chapter 21)
1. The research problem ...	+1	+1	+1	+1
2. Existing data	−1	+1	0	+1
3. Relevant theory	0	0	0	0
4. Researcher's assumptions	−1	+1	+1	+1
5. Preference for an experimental approach	−1	+1	+1	+1
6. Preference for a quantitative approach	+1	+1	+1	+1
7. The preferred method of data collection	−1	+1	+1	+1
8. Nature of the problem ...	+1	−1	−1	−1
9. The client	+1	−1	−1	0
10. The setting	0	−1	0	0
11. Size and complexity of the research problem	0	−1	+1	−1
12. The extent of cooperation.	+1	0	+1	+1
13. The intrusiveness of the method	+1	−1	0	0
14. The resources available..	0	−1	+1	0
15. The time necessary to implement the study ...	−1	−1	+1	−1
Totals	1	−1	7	4

*Key: Positive = +1
      Neutral =   0
      Negative = −1

The worker carefully analyzed 15 factors which affected the choice of method and assigned values of +1, 0, or -1 on each factor for the four alternative methods. For example, on Factor 15, concerning the time necessary to implement the study, the worker decided that all the methods except the single-subject approach would take a long time to implement and results would not be available in time to present with an annual report to the Division of Youth and Children Services.

Since the program director had requested that some evidence (data) be submitted with the annual report, the survey, experimental, and program evaluation methods were scored -1 and the single-subject method, which appeared to be feasible within the time constraints, was scored +1. The 15 factors were weighed equally and the total score for each method was calculated. The results in Table 7.2 indicate that for this particular research question, a single-subject method would be the best alternative method for determining the effectiveness of the peer counseling program.

For some social work research problems, particularly in cases where the research effort is quite limited, the entire process of choosing a research design can be accomplished quickly. As the social worker gains experience, the process becomes less tedious. Even for the experienced researcher, however, it is essential that careful attention be given to the choice of a research method, because the method affects the entire research process and the quality of the data obtained. Novice and experienced social work researchers alike have a tendency to rely on one or two research methods for all research problems. While personal style and preference have a place within both social work practice and research, reliance on one or two methods, such as surveys or experimental designs, without considering alternatives limits the capacity of social workers to resolve research questions effectively.

Phase 3a: Ensuring Proper Implementation

The research method problem-solving process does not end when a method is chosen. Who will carry out the procedures? If the social worker is going to implement the study, a variety of unanticipated problems and issues may arise; the research problem may require the development and implementation of new intervention strategies, new practice procedures, or entirely new programs. Even when these do not have to be developed, the arduous task of administering data collection instruments may prove difficult for the researcher.

When other staff are involved in carrying out the method selected, additional problems can arise. The staff may not know what is expected of them or may, by choice or by error, fail to adhere to all the procedural details. There is a common tendency for staff members to slip back into previous ways of performing services. In research studies which compare different practice methods, some may feel more comfortable with one or the other, and preconceptions about the effectiveness of new intervention strategies can lead to improper implementation. All of these problems can lead to biased or erroneous data.

Well before the final decision is made about choosing a particular method, the social worker must attempt to recognize and deal with any potential problems in implementation. Inviting feedback and sharing plans with those involved in the project is essential. Although workers at the lower levels of human service bureaucracies can make few essential changes in human service organizations, they can greatly influence the proper implementation of innovations in direct services which are suggested by management (Brager & Holloway, 1978). Therefore, it is important to gain the understanding, trust, and cooperation of staff members who have direct responsibility for implementing the method chosen. Without such cooperation the project runs the risk of being sabotaged from within. Once the method has been chosen, the researcher should develop procedures for sharing information about the progress of the study, channels for dealing with issues and problems which may arise, and mechanisms for monitoring the proper implementation of the research procedure.

Phase 4a: Specifying the Strengths and Limitations of the Method

The final responsibility of the social worker in choosing a research method is to be aware of how its strengths and limitations will affect the study and the generalizations that can be made from the findings. There are no perfect research methods. Every one has its limitations, and it is the worker's responsibility to state the limitations of the method as well as to highlight its strengths. For example, a single-subject research method may provide some excellent data with regard to the effectiveness of a practice intervention, but it should not be assumed the same intervention would be effective for all clients with similar problems. It is better to be concerned about the unverified efficacy of a procedure than to attempt to use an intervention based on an overly broad interpretation and generalization of findings from a single research project. Social workers must always stay within the limitations of the method they choose when analyzing results and drawing conclusions from a study.

SUMMARY

Social work researchers can view the different methods of approaching a research question as alternative frames of reference about research. These frames of reference allow a variety of perspectives on a given research question. The guidelines presented in this chapter can help social workers decide which research method is best able to answer the specific question being considered. The essence of the multidimensional nature of the problems which confront social workers can ultimately be captured by the cumulative effect of asking a variety of questions about particular social welfare problems and using a variety of research methods to respond to these questions.

PART TWO

Measurement of Research Problems

Contents of PART TWO

James R. Seaberg

8. SAMPLING

Once a research problem has been stated in researchable form, the next step in the research process is the generation of data that are relevant to the research problem. A necessary part of this process is the determination of what or whom to observe, or who will answer the questions posed in the investigation of the problem. This component is commonly referred to as sampling (Bailey, 1978).

A sample is a small portion of the total set of objects, events, or persons which together comprise the subjects of the study. The total set from which the individuals or units of the study are chosen is referred to as a population. Although only a portion of a population comprises a study's sample, the portion is assumed to be representative of the total set. The notion of a sample, therefore, suggests that all appropriate subjects or individuals of the total set will not participate in the study. The reasons for this are fairly obvious, mainly having to do with efficiency, time limitations, and restricted financial resources. In most instances, it is unnecessary to include all appropriate individuals if a sample can be identified which is representative of the population (Yeakel & Ganter, 1975).

DEFINING A POPULATION

A fundamental prerequisite for good sampling is a precise specification of the population from which the sample will be drawn. The population is the totality of persons, events, organizational units, case records, or other sampling units with which the research problem is concerned. Thus, a sampling unit is an object, event, or person which is the subject of the study, and the population is composed of sampling units (Selltiz, Wrightsman, & Cook, 1976).

A clearly defined population increases the probability of selecting a representative sample. When a sample adequately drawn from a population is studied, the findings can be generalized to the population. That is, if the sample is representative of the population from which it was drawn, the experiences, beliefs, changes, or whatever factors are observed for the sample can be assumed to be very similar for the entire population (Slonim, 1960).

Ecological Fallacy

One of the potential major pitfalls in moving from population to sample and then generalizing from sample to population is what has been labeled the *ecological fallacy*. The ecological fallacy occurs when reports of results about one unit of analysis (or sampling unit) are based on the examination of another unit of analysis (Babbie, 1979). While this is a conceptual problem which is observed most often in the interpretation of research results, it also can be found in other aspects of the research process, including sampling. If a population is not clearly defined, the probability increases that confusion may arise, for example, between studying families as units and persons in specific roles in the family; between a specific deviant behavior as a phenomenon and the individuals who engage in that deviant behavior; between child abuse perpetrators and reported child abuse perpetrators; and in innumerable other instances.

A related but slightly different problem is the practice of studying a sample that is available and easily accessible, and then attempting to define the larger population of which that sample is a subset. Approaching population definition in this way can result in very circumscribed population definitions which do not truly represent the populations to which social work researchers wish to generalize study results (Seaberg, 1981).

In a study to test the comparative effectiveness of two forms of marital counseling, for example, the sample included all applicants requesting marital counseling from a family service agency in an urban setting (Wells, Figurel, & McNamee, 1977). The sample was selected by eligibility requirements: At least one spouse was from 18 to 50 years of age, both spouses were willing to enter counseling, and the couple was available for evening interviews. In discussing the generalizations of the findings, the authors describe the population as "middle-class married couples applying for marriage counseling." The accuracy of the definition of the population could be questioned in several respects, especially whether middle-class married couples seeking marriage counseling who chose this specific agency or this type of agency are somehow systematically different from other middle-class married couples seeking marriage counseling through other resources.

Obviously, it is much better to begin with a clear description of the population rather than to have to create a population to fit an easily accessible sample. The process of selecting and formulating a research problem must always include at least an implicit definition of the population (Simon, 1969). The degree to which generalizations about the population can be made from the study of a sample is the same as the degree to which the sample is representative of the population from which it was drawn (Slonim, 1960).

REPRESENTATIVENESS

A sample is representative of the population from which it is drawn to the extent that it contains the same distribution of variables of substantive concern to the study as does the population. It is rare to draw a sample that perfectly represents the population from which it is drawn. However, there are sampling procedures, especially those within the broad class of probability sampling procedures, that greatly increase the chance that the sample will approximate perfect representation (Kish, 1965).

In the problem formulation stage of the research process, the variables with which the study will be concerned are identified. Age, sex, delinquency severity, marital adjustment, and organizational structure are a few examples. They are referred to as variables because each is composed of two or more different values or different categories which are presumably exhaustive of all possible values or categories and which are mutually exclusive (H. K. Goldstein, 1969). For example, age is a variable which is usually measured by one-year intervals; sex is a variable which is measured by two categories, male and female; delinquency is a variable which can be measured in several ways, one of which is a score representing the total severity of delinquent acts in a specified time interval; and so on.

For a specific population, there will be unique frequency distributions (frequency counts for each category of the variable) for all variables of concern in the study. A study of adjudicated delinquents, for example, may include the variable of delinquency severity. For a specific population, say all adjudicated delinquents in Chicago, there will be a specific distribution of delinquency severity scores. A representative sample of this population would have to closely approximate the distribution of delinquency severity scores found in the population, as well as similar distributions of variability for other variables pertinent to the study.

The importance of understanding the nature of variability and distributions for variables, as they pertain to the degree of representativeness a sample has of a population, cannot be overemphasized. Lack of appreciation of this factor has contributed to the severe limitations which must be imposed on the quality and generalizability of the results of much social work and social welfare research to date.

PROBABILITY SAMPLING

The first major classification of sampling procedures is probability sampling. In the most general sense, a probability sample is one in which each person (or other sampling unit) in the population has the same known probability of being selected, and the selection of persons from the population is based on some form of random procedure.

Simple Random Sampling

Simple random sampling is the least complex of the several forms of probability sampling. It is the selection, at random, of a specific number of persons (or other units) from the complete list of persons in the population. Before simple random sampling and other forms of probability sampling can be used, a list of the persons from which the sample will be drawn must be available. This list of the population is often referred to as a sampling frame. Obtaining or creating a sampling frame might seem to be a straightforward and relatively easy task, but, unfortunately, this is rarely the case. There are no lists of all persons living in the state of Illinois, or all residents in the city of Chicago, or all minority persons in Cook County, for example. In fact, the need to obtain or create a sampling frame which will remain constant until the sampling is completed presents one of the most serious problems in the research process for conscientious social work researchers.

Random Numbers Table. Once a sampling frame is available, each person in the population is assigned a number. For example, if the population consists of 575 persons, the first person would be numbered 001, the second person 002, and so on through 575. Then a table of random numbers is consulted to begin the random sampling process. It is the usual practice to select a page of the table and a starting point on that page by some unbiased process, such as flipping to a page at random and arbitrarily selecting a point at which to start selecting numbers. Table 8.1 is an example of the first half page from a random numbers table (Grinnell, 1981b). The numbers, of course, represent the persons in the population.

In the following illustration, we would need to use three columns of numbers to satisfy the three-digit identification number usage. We would move down (or up) the same three columns of numbers looking

TABLE 8.1

First one-half page of a Random Numbers Table

02584	75844	56012	44269	76402	33228	96152	76777	50479
66791	44653	90947	61934	79627	81621	74744	98758	65294
44306	88222	30967	57776	90533	01276	30525	66914	08136
02471	15131	38577	03362	54825	27705	60680	97083	12376
65995	81864	19184	61585	19779	08641	47652	27267	17622
45567	79547	89026	70767	25307	33151	00375	17652	94391
12542	90218	20878	13335	15646	16325	80926	49893	16936
33171	52348	72412	95958	84085	81763	70482	48630	39339
32255	22611	83967	56626	00918	97100	35798	21074	60368
11580	73961	27661	34664	23436	22431	32474	70200	92580
61413	05518	07369	15387	75399	02097	74620	54875	07117
38996	48862	53772	12594	43274	40348	52622	90538	11132
57118	46467	11099	55037	13554	15088	52094	25561	73353
38586	84378	78470	82178	36353	05104	03588	01877	43386
55647	61604	25976	99305	25318	06965	55363	26115	14395
60552	07946	13082	89325	94217	61802	60534	89222	23331
92101	78676	77017	93990	02335	39620	34007	45002	98112
60192	37922	96107	68664	19802	98434	06223	47837	09356
46879	94921	68237	81643	47359	54273	86671	83285	31115
85506	88963	26970	54724	92651	60790	87046	62976	28651
23961	55703	26555	17861	31905	65508	64454	38930	90583
60863	78397	44209	00315	24410	37793	86356	34633	36326
99656	59752	70987	27574	85938	02405	43000	70420	11325

Source: Grinnell (1981a).

for three-digit numbers between 001 and 575, inclusive. Every time we came to such a number, the person with that number would be included in the sample. This process would continue until we had achieved the desired sample size. As we exhausted one set of three columns, we would move one column right (or left) to the next set of three columns. If we were sampling without replacement, we would omit repetitions of the same number.

For a more specific illustration, assume the three circled digits (087) in Table 8.1 are selected at random by looking away from the table and placing a pencil on a single digit (0 in this instance), and then including the two digits to the right of it (8 and 7). Since 087 is within the range of identification numbers (001–575) representing persons in the population, the person with the identification number 087 is included in the sample. We then proceed down these three columns checking each three-digit number directly below the first one for possible inclusion in the sample. In the next 15 rows down, persons with identification numbers 241, 396, 377, 109, 308, and 420 are included in the sample because they fall in the range of 001 to 575. To complete the sample, this procedure would continue until a predetermined sample size (say 115 persons) is selected.

This seemingly easy way to obtain a simple random sample is not utilized often in social work research because there are numerous substantial difficulties in obtaining a sampling frame. Nonetheless, an understanding of this sampling procedure provides essential background for understanding other probability sampling procedures.

Systematic Sampling

In systematic or interval sampling we would proceed down the sampling frame (or population list) selecting for the sample every kth person, starting with a person randomly selected from among the first k persons. The symbol k represents the size of the sampling interval. It is the ratio of the population size (N) to the desired sample size (n):

$$k = \frac{N}{n}$$

Where:

$$k = \text{Size of the sampling interval}$$
$$N = \text{Population size}$$
$$n = \text{Sample size}$$

Thus, if we had a population of 575 persons and we desired a sample of 115 persons, k would equal 5.

Substituting values of letters:

$$k = \frac{575}{115}$$
$$= 5 \text{ (size of sampling interval)}$$

Among the first five persons in the sampling frame we would select one at random, say the fourth person listed. Then we would select every 5th person from that point on down the list—the 9th, 14th, 19th, 24th, and so on—through the 574th person. If the systematic sample did not utilize random selection of the first person, the result could not be considered a probability sample, since most of the persons would have a zero probability of being included in the sample. Unlike the simple random sampling procedure, systematic sampling does not give all possible combinations of persons in the population the same chance of being included, only those combinations k units apart on the sampling frame.

There is a potential bias in systematic sampling which calls for caution. The source of this bias is any systematic ordering of sampling units in the sampling frame which might correspond to the sampling interval. For example, if a study of the need for emergency public assistance funds is based on the number and dollar amounts of such requests for particular days (sampling unit) of the year, and the sampling interval happens to systematically select days which fall in the last week of each month, the need might appear much greater than it is on the average (and vice versa). The potential for bias is also apparent if a mental health needs assessment survey is being conducted in which households in a neighborhood with a specific apartment-single household mix are systematically sampled, but the sampling interval and construction patterns happen to coincide so that apartment complexes are rarely or never included. The possibility that these types of biases might exist in the sampling frame should be ruled out before the systematic sampling procedure is used.

If the ordering used in creating the sampling frame can be considered to be essentially random with regard to the key variables in the study, then a systematic sample will be roughly equivalent to a simple random sample. Systematic sampling is obviously easier to use when the sampling frame is lengthy or the sample size is large. It is often used as one phase of a sampling design which includes combinations of two or more sampling procedures.

Stratified Sampling

Stratified sampling involves application of the simple random sampling procedure to two or more strata (or categories) of the sampling frame. The stratification is based on mutually exclusive categories of the pertinent variables (Lazerwitz, 1968). For example, if a community mental health center is interested in studying the effects of different treatment methods on its clientele, it would be desirable to learn what these effects are not only for the clientele as a whole, but also for different categories of the clientele (such as various problem diagnostic categories). Sampling from different strata of problem diagnoses can assure that a sufficient number of cases with each diagnosis will be included in the sample to permit the desired analyses.

The implementation of the stratified random sample requires definition of the stratification categories such that a specific person will appear in one and only one stratum. When this has been accomplished, the simple random sampling procedure is employed to select an independent sample for each stratum. The strata samples are then combined to form the total sample.

To the extent that the persons within a stratum will tend to be more homogeneous with respect to the variables under study (which is often the case), the amount of sampling error can be decreased and the efficiency of the sampling can be increased. In the example above, we can assume that there will be less variation (greater homogeneity) within specific problem diagnostic categories and greater variation between such categories. This allows the utilization of a smaller number of persons from each stratum for a more efficient sampling procedure.

Stratified sampling can be either proportional or disproportional (Kerlinger, 1973). The proportion of persons for each stratum can be the same for the sample as for the population (proportional), or intentionally different for the sample as compared to the population (disproportional).

Assume that the problems of 1,000 clients in a mental health center can be classified into eight major diagnostic categories, and we have knowledge that the entire client population is distributed in each of these categories in the pattern shown in column *a* of Table 8.2. If we choose to select a proportionate sample of one-tenth (1/10) of the client population from these eight strata, we would randomly select 25 clients from Diagnostic Category 1, 20 clients from Category 2, and so on,

TABLE 8.2

Stratified Random Sampling Situation

Diagnostic Category	(a) Number	(b) 1/10 Proportionate Sample	(c) Number and (Disproportionate Sampling Fractions) for a sample of 25 per category
1	250	25	25 (1/10)
2	200	20	25 (1/8)
3	150	15	25 (1/6)
4	150	15	25 (1/6)
5	100	10	25 (1/4)
6	50	5	25 (1/2)
7	50	5	25 (1/2)
8	50	5	25 (1/2)
Totals . .	1000	100	200

Source: Seaberg (1981).

down to 5 clients from Category 8 (column *b*). These numbers represent one-tenth of all clients in each diagnostic category.

In some cases the concern may be less with the entire population than with a comparison between the subpopulations represented by the strata (Lazerwitz, 1968). This is probably true in this example. In such an instance it is desirable to sample disproportionately. We might decide, for example, to select equal numbers from each diagnostic category in order to facilitate a more accurate comparison of treatment effects. If we randomly select 25 clients from each category the procedure is straightforward, but we must be aware that the sampling fraction will not be the same for each category. For Diagnostic Category 1 the sampling fraction will be one tenth; for Category 2, one eighth; for Categories 3 and 4, one sixth; for Category 5, one fourth; and for Categories 6 through 8, one half (column *c*). A major actor in disproportional stratified sampling is that in generalizing findings to the entire population, estimates of population characteristics must be weighted to counteract the effects caused by variation in the sampling fraction for each stratum.

The decision to utilize stratified random sampling is determined by several factors. The first is whether the data necessary for stratification (diagnostic classifications, in this example) are available for the population prior to the study. If they are not, stratification is impossible unless the necessary data are gathered, and this would add to the cost and time requirements for the study. A second factor is the relative homogeneity of the strata. If the stratification process does not result in reasonably homogeneous strata, little can be gained through the stratification process. Third, stratification should result in gains of sampling efficiency through reduced sample size and a related reduction in data collection costs. Caution must be exercised that these savings are not offset by the costs of developing the stratification data base for the sampling frame. Finally, stratification which involves more than one variable tends to be extremely difficult with regard to the homogeneity criterion (Isaac & Michael, 1971).

Cluster Sampling

The difficulty of locating or creating a sampling frame for the population relevant to a study is probably most obvious in relation to surveys of national opinion but it is equally problematic for regional, state, or local surveys. Cluster sampling, often in combination with other sampling procedures, provides a means of dealing with this situation. Clusters of the population, such as census tracts, can be listed to create a sampling frame. In its simplest form, cluster sampling involves randomly selecting a cluster from among the clusters listed and implementing the research procedure (e.g., questionnaires), with all persons in that cluster who meet present criteria such as age, sex, or family role.

Cluster sampling not only provides a means of dealing with the problem of not being able to obtain or create a sampling frame of specific persons, but it usually reduces costs in the data collection phase of the research process. There is a trade-off, however; the potential for sampling error is considerably increased. In stratified sampling, for example, to reduce sampling error, persons within each stratum are sampled, and a stratification process is sought which will yield homogeneous strata that are as markedly different as possible. In simple cluster sampling, there is no sampling error within each cluster because every appropriate sampling unit is included in the cluster, but there is a source of sampling error in variability between clusters. To decrease this source, the ideal situation would be to include both clusters in which the sampling units within each cluster are heterogeneous, and clusters which are homogeneous with regard to critical variables. With natural clusters, however, this is usually not the case. It is more common to find homogeneity among the sampling units within a cluster and great heterogeneity between clusters. For example, it can be reasonably assumed that residents of a specific city block are more alike than residents of all city blocks are, or that users of public day-care centers are more alike than users of all forms of day-care services, including private, for-profit facilities, licensed family day care, unlicensed family day care, and so on. The conventional resolution of such dilemmas is to maximize the number of clusters sampled while limiting the number of sampling units sampled from each cluster (Lazerwitz, 1968).

Simple cluster sampling is infrequently utilized. In usual applications, cluster sampling is combined with one or more other sampling procedures, a combination referred to as multistage cluster sampling. The liability of increased potential for sampling error with simple cluster sampling can generally be contained through combination with other sampling procedures. An oversimplified example of multistage cluster sampling would be a community needs assessment with the following steps:

1. A disproportionate random sample of census tracts stratified on a ratio of average income per person is drawn.
2. A simple random sample of blocks within the census tracts is selected.
3. The households on each selected block are listed, and a simple random sample is taken of households per block.
4. Within each selected household every person of a specified age or older is interviewed as to their perceptions of their own and the community's needs.

In a multistage cluster design the particular combination and sequence of the various sampling procedures used depends on a carefully reasoned approach to obtaining the data necessary to address the research question, sensitized by the need to reduce sampling error. In seeking a balance between cost and efficiency, the procedure that yields the smallest sampling error for a given cost should be used.

NONPROBABILITY SAMPLING

The second major classification of sampling procedures is nonprobability sampling. When these procedures are used the probability of inclusion in the sample is unknown and is usually different for each person or unit in the sample. The procedure is usually utilized where the expense of probability sampling would be too great or where less than precise representation of the population is temporarily justifiable. Nonprobability samples are suited to exploratory studies where investigators are merely interested in obtaining as much unique data on a research question as possible (Knowledge Level 1, as presented in Chapter 13). They are also useful in studies in which the sampling units represent the extremes of a particular phenomenon or are in key positions to observe or experience the phenomenon being investigated.

Availability Sampling

The simplest nonprobability sampling procedure is called availability or accidental sampling. The label is very descriptive and almost self-explanatory: The worker uses the first available appropriate sampling units. A large proportion of social work research and evaluation relies on this type of sampling procedure; studies have been based on the caseload of an individual social worker or the clientele of a particular agency, for example. In such instances, self-selection in utilizing the services of the agency, caseload assignment procedures, and other factors enter into the sampling process. Applied to a survey of community needs, accidental sampling might be implemented by interviewers stationed in a location of high public usage such as a shopping center or auditorium to interview as many persons as can be induced to cooperate.

Quota Sampling

Quota sampling is another form of nonprobability sampling which is described by its label; quotas are set for the inclusion of a certain number of persons who possess preset characteristics. This type of sampling is useful where the research problem suggests that variation on specific characteristics of persons appropriate to the study should be associated with patterns of variation on the variables of concern. For this reason, quotas are set for the number of persons to be included in the study who possess the desired characteristics or combination of characteristics. Often the quotas set reflect the proportions of the desired characteristics known to exist in the population. Once they are set, the researcher is only obligated to locate as quickly and easily as possible the specified number of persons with the preset characteristics.

For example, in a study of public attitudes toward the disposition of child abuse cases, there might be reason to believe these attitudes will vary according to income level and whether the respondent is a parent. A matrix can be formed with three levels of income and the two categories of parenthood, as in Figure 8.1. After quotas are set for each cell, the job of the worker is simply to locate n_1 persons with income below $7,000 who are also parents, n_2 persons with income between $7,001 and $17,000 who are also parents, and so on through n_6 persons with income in excess of $17,001 who are not parents. Which persons are selected for each cell is left to the discretion of the interviewer, as long as they meet the two criteria. The interviewer must, of course, satisfy the quota for each cell. The potential for interviewer bias in selecting persons within each cell should be apparent. The interviewer might avoid persons above the first floor of apartment buildings, persons not at home during the day, neighborhoods considered undesirable or dangerous, and so on.

FIGURE 8.1
Quota Sampling Matrix of Three Income
Levels by Parenthood

	Parenthood	
Income Level	Yes	No
Below $7,000	n_1	n_4
$7,001–17,000	n_2	n_5
$17,001–over	n_3	n_6

Source: Seaberg (1981).

Purposive Sampling

Another type of nonprobability sampling is known as purposive (or judgmental) sampling. Purposive sampling is predicated on the assumption that the social worker has sufficient knowledge related to the research problem to allow selection of "typical" persons for inclusion in the sample. For example, a social worker studying a phenomenon such as child abuse may decide, on the basis of previous empirical data, that child abuse is more of an urban phenomenon than a rural one and arbitrarily include all cases from the 10 largest cities in the country as part of a national sample.

In other applications of purposive sampling, the worker may want to seek out persons who represent extremes of a phenomenon as a means of gaining insights into why they differ from the norm, such as social workers who experience burnout quickly in working with a particular clientele in contrast to those who stick with it five years or more. Purposive sampling might also be used if it is desirable to check the clarity and comprehensibility of a questionnaire which will later be used with another sample. In this instance, the widest variety of respondents might be sought with regard to reading skill level. A primary assumption in purposive sampling is that by selecting persons who are "typical" with regard to the study's variables, any errors of judgment in selection will tend to counterbalance one another. Investigations of this assumption have not confirmed its validity.

Snowball Sampling

Snowball sampling, another nonprobability sampling procedure, is particularly useful if a social worker is interested in a very special population of limited size and only knows of a handful of appropriate persons from that population. The procedure is simply to gather data from the known persons and to request information from them as to other appropriate persons. This cycle is repeated until the social worker has exhausted the potential respondents or has a sample of the desired size. The sample increases in size, or snowballs, with each repetition of the cycle. An example might be a follow-up study of persons who were participants in a loosely structured social action program 10 years ago in a particular community (LeMasters, 1976).

SAMPLE SIZE

The determination of sample size has received relatively little attention by social work researchers, in part because of the frequent use of nonprobability sampling procedures. When a probability sampling procedure is used, the question of sample size may ultimately be dealt with in a precise manner.

The correct sample size is dependent on the characteristics of the population and the nature of the research question. If the research problem deals with an extremely limited population, it would be desirable and possibly feasible to include the entire population in the study, as in studying the reaction of patients and families to a highly specialized medical social work service for victims of a rare disease. Usually, however, the population is large enough to require sampling, and the general rule of thumb is, the larger the sample the better.

Some professionals have made the case that in order to use basic statistical procedures the sample size must be at least 30, but more conventional wisdom suggests a minimal sample size of 100. These guidelines must be qualified, however, because sample size is affected by knowledge about the population and the extent of categorization of the sample necessary in the analysis of data. Generally speaking, the greater the variance in the population on the main variables under study, the larger the sample size must be; and, of course, the converse is equally true. In other words, the greater the likelihood of sampling error, the larger the sample size should be. In the extreme case that there is no population variance on critical variables, a sample of only one person would suffice. This, of course, is never a reality.

A fairly common problem related to sample size is failure to consider the number of categorizations of the sample which may be required to analyze the data appropriately. The result of such a situation often is a category with only one or two persons. By anticipating the categorization features of the analysis, the sample size can be adjusted to supply the minimal number of persons per category. This situation can be handled with the disproportionate stratified random sampling procedure.

There are formulas available for the calculation of sample size, based on such statistical concepts as confidence intervals and levels, z scores, and normal distributions, in addition to the standard error. A thorough understanding of these background concepts is necessary to apply these formulas, and they are difficult to use in their own right because they depend on knowledge of the standard deviation for the population on the variable under study. Since these data are usually unknown and usually estimated from the sample data, they cannot be determined until the samples have been drawn and the data have been collected and analyzed. For this reason, a convention on sample size has been adopted; in most instances, a sample of one tenth (1/10) the size of the population will give reasonable control over sampling error. This proportion also applies in various categories of the population; one tenth of each category can be sampled (Lazerwitz, 1968).

Nonsampling Errors

It is important to be aware of and to attempt to control nonsampling as well as sampling errors. Even the most carefully planned sampling design can be weakened by nonsampling errors. And, while it is possible to estimate the sampling errors for a probability sample, there is no basis for estimating the nonsampling errors.

Nonsampling errors are errors produced in collecting and processing data from the persons or units included in the sample. Some sources of such error are intended and unintended response errors (lies or mispreceptions), interviewer bias, poorly worded questions, refusals to participate in the study, partial or illegible responses to questions, inability to contact selected respondents, and clerical errors in processing or coding interviews. The social worker must strive for control of such sources of error, because there is no point in selecting a large sample as a means of reducing sampling error only to have it offset by a large nonsampling error. Since the total error is a function of both sampling and nonsampling errors, it cannot be reduced unless they are controlled simultaneously. The control of nonsampling errors is discussed in the following chapters of this text.

RANDOM ASSIGNMENT

Random assignment or randomization is a concept which is often confused with random sampling. This procedure is used in assigning individuals to experimental and control groups where an experimental design or some variate is used (see Chapter 13). In the simplest case, a pool of appropriate individuals is derived, identification numbers are assigned to each person and then, using a table of random numbers, individuals are randomly assigned to either the experimental or the control group. The random feature of the assignment to experimental and control groups, given a sufficiently large number of individuals, makes it possible to rule out investigator bias in the assignment process. It also assures that the two groups are roughly comparable on the dependent variable and associated variables prior to the introduction of the experimental variable (e.g., a social work intervention of some type). If there are minor differences in the two groups on the dependent variable, the use of random assignment permits the assumption that these differences are random or due to chance.

Often the pool of individuals will be stratified on some dimension of the dependent variable (say, severity of delinquency), with persons from each stratum randomly assigned to the experimental or control group. This added step further assures the comparability of the two groups prior to the beginning of the study.

SUMMARY

The major forms of probability sampling that have been described and illustrated in this chapter are simple random sampling, systematic sampling, stratified sampling, and cluster and multistage cluster sampling. They are all predicated on the use of a nonbiased random procedure in selecting sampling units, the known probability of the inclusion of each sampling unit in the sample, and the possibility that the degree to which the sample is representative of the population can be estimated in the form of the standard error (Seaberg, 1981).

It is seldom possible to execute perfect sampling procedures in the practice of social work research. Lack of an adequate sampling frame, refusals and other forms of attrition, prohibitive costs, and other factors are constant problems for the conscientious worker in the application of probability sampling procedures.

The nonprobability sampling procedures described and illustrated are availability sampling, quota sampling, purposive sampling, and snowball sampling. Nonprobability sampling procedures are the least desirable means of producing samples which are demonstrably representative of the population. A primary problem is the absence of a basis for estimating the sampling error (Seaberg, 1981).

Gerald J. Bostwick, Jr. and Nancy S. Kyte

9. MEASUREMENT

Measurement is a pervasive and important part of our daily lives. Each day we make informal and implicit use of various standardized or individualized measures: Our morning routine, for example, may include weighing ourselves, adjusting the water for a shower, and making breakfast. Although we may not give much thought to these activities, we are in fact measuring our weight, the temperature of the water, and the amounts and proportions of the foods we prepare. The scale, our heat-sensitive finger, and the measuring cup or spoon are all instruments which help make such measurements possible.

What distinguishes this type of measurement from that engaged in by social workers? Put simply, it is the nature of the measuring procedures used. For social workers, measurement is a systematic (formal) and scientific (explicit) process involving the assignment of symbols to properties of objects, according to specified rules (Stevens, 1951). As presented in Part One of this text, such rules are designed to increase the probability that goings-on in the world of concepts will correspond accurately to goings-on in the world of reality. The closer the rules bring these two worlds together, the more helpful the resultant measures will be in explaining what has been observed in the empirical world or in predicting what has not yet been observed (Kogan, 1975).

Thus, formal measurement is one of the most crucial components of social work practice and research. It is intimately related to the four phases of the social worker's problem-solving process, as presented in Figure 2.1 in Chapter 2. The development of good measurement procedures is an intricate process in the physical sciences, but it is even more complex in the social sciences. In physics, for example, measurement is largely concerned with such fundamental variables as weight, length, time, density, volume, and velocity. In social work, however, we are primarily interested in psychosocial variables, such as ego strength, achievement, motivation, dependency, racial conflict, alienation, interpersonal communication, organizational structure, social status, aggression, and group cohesion. Social workers focus, therefore, on the many, multifaceted properties of individuals, families, groups, organizations, neighborhoods, communities, and institutions. Not surprisingly, the accurate measurement of such properties is often extremely problematic.

MEASUREMENT IN SOCIAL WORK

Definition of Measurement

As might be expected, definitions of measurement vary widely. Some define measurement as the assignment of numerals to objects or events according to rules (Stevens, 1951). Others contend that numerals should be assigned not to objects or events but to their properties or attributes (Nunnally, 1978). Most would agree, however, that the numerals assigned take on a quantitative meaning. This position has led many professionals to use the terms measurement and quantification as if they were interchangeable. Recent efforts to get away from what many social scientists believe to be a very restrictive view of measurement have culminated in definitions of measurement which are broader in nature and reflect a decreased emphasis on quantification. Examples include the systematic assignment of symbols to observations, the assignment of quantitative or qualitative values to attributes, and the assignment of numerals to either quantitative or qualitative response categories (Wallace, 1973).

Common Components

Whether or not a qualitative component is included, these definitions reflect three common, interrelated themes. First there is the assignment of numerals (e.g., 1, 2, 3) or symbols (e.g., A, B, C). The two are basically synonymous because a numeral has no intrinsic quantitative meaning and therefore is nothing more than a label when used to identify something. Thus, the numeral 1 is simply a symbol of a special kind, as are + or $ when used to refer to addition or money. The letters A, B, and C could be used just as easily as the numerals 1, 2, and 3. Measurement, however, has traditionally used numerals which, after being assigned quantitative meaning, become numbers.

Second, these numerals or symbols are assigned to properties of objects rather than to the objects themselves. Put another way, we do not measure objects per se but rather their properties or characteristics. To be even more precise, we actually measure indicants of these properties. This point is important when we are concerned with the measurement of a complex property where direct observation is impossible. For example, hostility, depression, and intelligence are variables which cannot be directly observed. We must always infer these properties from observations of their presumed indicants, such as fighting, excessive crying, or responses on an achievement test (Polster & Lynch, 1981).

Third, numerals or symbols are assigned to (indicants of) properties of objects according to specified rules. The importance of these rules, often referred to as rules of correspondence or assignment, cannot be overemphasized (Kaplan, 1964). Measurement is a game we play with objects and numerals. Games have rules—rules which can be good or bad. Other things equal, good rules lead to good measurement, and bad rules lead to bad measurement. At its most basic level, then, a rule is a guide, method, or command that tells us what to do (Kerlinger, 1973).

Suppose that a client is asked to identify five possible solutions to a problem and then rank order them according to some criterion, such as probable effectiveness. We might formulate a rule which states that the range of numerals (1-5) should be assigned in such a manner that the highest (5) represents the solution judged to be the most effective, and the lowest (1) represents the solution judged to be the least effective. This rule clearly tells us how to assign the range of numerals to the domain of problem-solving options the client has identified.

It is important to realize that while a definition of measurement stipulates the formulation of and adherence to rules, it does not restrict the kind of rules that can be used. Rules can be developed deductively, can be based on previous experience, can stem from common sense, or can be pure hunches (Kogan, 1975). Whatever the origin, the utility of any measure is contingent on its ability to explain adequately the phenomenon being studied. Therefore, no measurement procedure is any better than its rules.

In summary, any endeavor attempting to assign numerals or symbols to (indicants of) properties of objects according to specified rules qualifies as measurement. Measurement of anything is theoretically possible if rules can be set up on some rational or empirical basis. Whether that measurement is good or bad will depend on the formulation of clear, unambiguous rules of correspondence that can themselves be empirically tested (Hudson, 1982a).

FUNCTIONS OF MEASUREMENT

Measurement is not an end in itself. Its scientific worth can only be appreciated if we consider what it is intended to do, and to know what role and function it has in social work. Just what is it that measurement allows us to achieve?

Correspondence

First, and perhaps foremost, measurement theory mandates the delineation of rules and procedures whose application will increase the correspondence between the real world and the world of concepts. The real world provides social workers with their empirical evidence; the world of concepts provides them with a theoretical model for making sense out of that segment of the real world that they are trying to explain or predict. And it is measurement's rules of correspondence which connect this theoretical model with the world of reality. Thus, it is largely with regard to these rules that measurement plays one of its most significant roles.

Objectivity and Standardization

By facilitating correspondence between the world of theory and the world of reality, measurement (and in particular, standardized measurement) also helps take some of the guesswork out of scientific observation. This in turn makes the observations themselves considerably more objective than, for example, personal judgments. A key principle of science is that any statement of fact made by one social worker should be independently verifiable by other social workers. This principle is violated if there is room for disagreement about observations of empirical events.

In the absence of a standardized measurement of narcissism, for instance, two social workers may disagree strongly about how narcissistic a particular client is. Obviously, then, it would be impossible to make any empirical test of theories of narcissism. This, unfortunately, is frequently the case in social work. Social workers have a myriad of theories at their disposal, but the theories often involve concepts which, at present, cannot be adequately measured. Consequently, the theories go untested. However, since research results are inevitably reported in terms of functional relationships among measured variables, our profession will progress neither faster nor slower than it becomes possible to measure important variables and theoretical constructs accurately (Perlman, 1972).

Quantification

Measurement increases not only the objectivity of observations but also the ability to describe observations precisely. Different types of measurement result in different types of data. One type of measurement is classification, which makes it possible to categorize variables (such as sex and religion) into subclasses (such as male-female and Protestant-Catholic-Jewish). A second, higher level measurement operation makes it possible not only to define differences between variable subclasses but also to determine more than—less than relationships. Thus, we might be able to classify a particular behavior as not just occurring or not occurring but also as never, rarely, sometimes, often, or always occurring. Another type on an even higher level makes it possible to rank order certain variable characteritics and specify the exact distances between the variable subclasses. We could, therefore, say that a family with an income of $13,000 has $5,000 more than a family with an income of $8,000—or that a social agency employing 20 social workers has twice as large a professional staff as one employing 10 social workers.

Each type of measurement provides important data which enable social workers to describe physical, psychological, or social phenomena empirically. The precision of the measurement increases as it moves from the lower (less sophisticated and refined) to the higher levels.

A related advantage of measurement is that it permits the use of powerful methods of statistical analysis (Blalock, 1972). Numbers render information amenable to statistical manipulation.

Suppose that we are conducting a study to determine what characteristics differentiate clients who continue in family therapy from those who drop out. To do this, we collect data from a variety of sources (clients, therapists, independent judges), using questionnaires, in-person interviews, case records, and tape recordings of family therapy sessions. We must then be able to make some sense out of all this information, in order to explain what is going on and why. Before the data can be analyzed with statistical techniques, however, they must be reduced to numerical form, so we need to quantify the variables we are studying. Once the data are in numerical form, we are in a position to test the hypothesis we have formulated.

When a hypothesis is supported in social work practice or research, the theory or theories from which it was derived are also supported, at least tentatively. Supporting a theory, moreover, is tantamount to endorsing the explanations provided for why certain events occur as they do. Thus, measurement greatly facilitates the ability to discover and establish relationships among phenomena. Numbers, when properly applied, permit use of the full range of mathematics in constructing and testing theories aimed at explaining or predicting the phenomena of the real world.

Replication and Communication

The research process is concerned not only with conducting tests of theories but also with replicating and disseminating the results of those tests. Obviously, the more objective and precise the measurement procedures used in a particular study are, the easier it will be for others to replicate the study and thereby to confirm or refute the results obtained. And the more rigorous the specification of the measurement procedures is, the greater will be the potential for increasing the effective communication of the study's findings.

LEVELS AND SCALES OF MEASUREMENT

Measurement is the assignment of numerals or symbols to properties of objects according to specified rules. These rules in turn define the kind of scale and the level of measurement to be used. There are four major levels and accompanying scales of measurement: nominal, ordinal, interval, and ratio (Stevens, 1951).

Because these levels vary in the extent to which they quantify a variable, they are often ranked from lowest (nominal) to highest (ratio). The higher levels of measurement (interval and ratio) permit a greater variety of mathematical operations to be performed with the data. Moreover, the statistical procedures that accompany the higher measurement levels are generally more sophisticated than those that accompany the lower levels (nominal and ordinal). Generally, therefore, more powerful kinds of statistical analyses can be used when interval- or ratio-level measurements underlie the data.

Statistical techniques have been developed for use with each of these four levels and scales of measurement. It is essential for social workers to understand them and to be able to determine which is most appropriate for the variable to be measured.

Nominal Measurement

The simplest level of measurement is nominal measurement. The word *nominal* refers to the assignment of names; it is through this process that properties of objects can be categorized. Thus, nominal measurement is essentially a classification system which involves the categorization of variables into subclasses. Characteristics such as sex, race, ethnic origin, and political party affiliation are usually treated as nominal variables. Other examples include marital status, referral source, diagnosis, occupation, family composition, source of income, and type of treatment.

The requirements of nominal-level measurement are simple. A nominally measured variable must have at least two categories, and the categories must be distinct, mutually exclusive, and exhaustive (Black & Champion, 1976). Exhaustive means that there must be an appropriate category for each case. Mutually exclusive means that each case must appropriately fit into only one of the categories. For example, empirically there are only two classes of the nominal variable sex— male and female. These categories are clearly exhaustive and mutually exclusive, as every person distinctly fits into one of the categories (exhaustiveness), but only one (exclusiveness).

In nominal measurement, numerals (or other symbols, such as letters) may be assigned to distinguish one category from another. Suppose we have divided a variable, type of treatment, into three categories: individual therapy, group therapy, and family therapy. We could then assign the numeral 1 to individual therapy, the numeral 2 to group therapy, and the numeral 3 to family therapy. We cannot imply, however, that Category 2 is greater than Category 1 or less than Category 3—just that they are different. The numerals we have used are merely labels and serve only to classify. They have no inherent quantitative meaning and cannot be manipulated mathematically (i.e., added, subtracted, multiplied, divided). It would be meaningless in this case to say that $1+2=3$. This would be the equivalent of contending that individual therapy plus group therapy equals family therapy. All we can really do is make counts of the numbers of cases falling into each category.

Technically speaking, nominal measurement is not accompanied by a scale in the same way as the other levels of measurement are. The scales designated for ordinal, interval, and ratio measurement use numbers to represent differing degrees or amounts of a particular property. In nominal classification, the categories have no such magnitude or amount referents. About all the nominal measurement can make use of is the simple "none-some" scale, wherein one category characterizes an object by the absence of a particular property and the other characterizes it by the presence of that property. In its most literal form, the first category should represent 0 percent of the property and the second category, 100 percent. However, since few objects of interest show such all-or-none characteristics, objects are usually assigned to the first category if they possess none or a negligible amount of the given property and to the second category if they show a discriminable or minimal amount of the property (Jones, 1971). Thus, a group of clients might be classified as group therapy continuers or group therapy noncontinuers, or a group of cases might be categorized as having terminated on either a planned or an unplanned basis.

Quality versus Quantity.   Since nominal-level measurement only involves classification, and since the assigned numbers have no intrinsic quantitative meaning, it is not considered by some to be a legitimate form of measurement. Those taking this stand emphasize quantification and contend that the more precise a measure is, the better it is. An underlying assumption is that the social work profession will advance only when higher levels of measurement are used. Others have taken issue with this, noting that qualitative and quantitative measurement have always worked hand in hand and are not synonymous with the terms *vague* and *precise,* respectively. They contend that classification is fundamental to any science and that all other levels of measurement basically involve classification as a minimal operation. Moreover, every measurement involves some degree of abstraction and, therefore, both quantitative and qualitative descriptions fail to tell everything about a phenomenon.

Since the definition of measurement is satisfied, however, and since the numbers of labeled sets can be counted and compared, our position is that nominal procedures constitute a legitimate form of measurement.

Ordinal Measurement

Ordinal-level measurement not only classifies observations but also rank orders them from high to low or from most to least. That is, it places them in categories that have a greater than—less than relationship to one another. Variables frequently measured on an ordinal scale are social class, social distance, attitudes, and occupational prestige. Other examples might include educational degrees received (bachelor's, master's, doctoral); ratings of change (considerable, some, little, none); agreement on problem definition (high, moderate, low); ratings of service effectiveness (very effective, somewhat effective, somewhat ineffective, very ineffective); ratings of client satisfaction with therapy (very satisfied, somewhat satisfied, somewhat unsatisfied, not at all satisfied); and rankings of problem severity (very severe, severe, mild, very mild).

Numbers used at the ordinal level of measurement make it possible to define not only differences between variable subclasses but also their relative positions. In nominal measurement we can say that a 2 is different from a 1. In ordinal measurement we can say that a 2 is not only different from a 1 but is in a higher or lower position relative to that 1. Thus, whereas the numerals on a nominal scale represent names, the numerals on an ordinal scale represent rank values. A rank value indicates whether an object has more of a particular property or characteristic than another object has. However, it does not indicate how much more. And it is not possible to determine how far apart the objects are with respect to that property or characteristic. Put another way, rank values do not indicate absolute quantities and do not assume equal intervals between the ranks. Thus, we do not know the exact distances between ranks, and we cannot assume that these distances are uniformly equal.

Consider, for example, the widely used Index of Social Position, developed by Hollingshead and Redlich (1958). This index purports to rank social class according to a set of categories ranging from Class I (upper) to Class V (lower). Since the intervals that separate classes need not be equal, we cannot say that Class I is two class intervals higher than Class III or that this interval is exactly the same distance that separates Class IV from Class II. While Class V may be nearly equivalent to Class IV, there may be a wide gap between Classes I and II. Suppose that we wanted to order a group of children from shortest to tallest. The resultant ordinal scale would give no indication of average height (as a group, the children might be relatively tall or relatively short) and would tell us nothing about how much the children vary in terms of height.

In summary, ordinal measurement goes a step beyond nominal measurement by making it possible to rank order observations. The resultant rank values provide a convenient shorthand for designating relative positions of those observations, but the values do not indicate their absolute quantities or exact distances from one another. Ordinal numbers, thus, indicate rank order and nothing more.

Interval Measurement

Interval measurement not only classifies and rank orders properties of variables but places them on an equally spaced continuum. Unlike ordinal scales, interval-level scales have a common unit of measurement (e.g., year, degree of temperature, dollar). Therefore they indicate exactly how far apart one rank is from another. We can say that an object has not only "more" or "less" of a given property than another object, but how many units more or less. With equal distances between the units, a 1 will be the same distance from a 2 as a 2 is from a 3, and so on. On an interval scale designed to measure intelligence, the difference between IQs of 100 and 105 would be equal to the difference between IQs of 115 and 120, and two individuals with achievement test scores of 50 and 60 would be the same distance apart as two individuals with scores of 80 and 90. In addition to intelligence and achievement, other variables often measured on an interval-level scale include calendar time, anomie, group morale, and social attitudes.

One disadvantage of interval-level scales is that they do not have an absolute zero. That is, we do not know where the zero is located on the scale. This means that we cannot say that a 2 is twice as much as a 1—only that it is one unit more. Since 0 degrees on a Fahrenheit (F.) thermometer does not represent the absence of temperature, a temperature of 60 degrees is not twice as high as a temperature of 30 degrees. Similarly, since a zero on a statistics test does not necessarily signify a complete absence of statistical knowledge, we cannot say that a student with a score of 90 knows twice as much about statistics as a student with a score of 45.

Interval measurement, then, rank orders properties of objects and determines how far apart they are from one another. However, it does not indicate anything about the absolute magnitude of a property for any particular object or person. Without the absolute (nonarbitrary) zero, moreover, the interval-level scale does not allow ratio statements about variables. This is permissible only with the most sophisticated type of scale, the ratio scale.

Ratio Measurement

The existence of a fixed, absolute, and nonarbitrary zero point constitutes the only difference between interval-level and ratio-level measurement. Indeed, if an interval scale has a natural origin at 0— representing zero amount of the property being measured—it is called a ratio scale. Therefore, numbers on a ratio scale indicate the actual amounts of the property being measured. With such a scale we can say not only that one object has so many units more of a property than a second object but that the first object is so many times greater or smaller. Typical examples of ratio scales are age; weight; height; income; birth, death, or divorce rates; number of children in a family; and number of behaviors emitted during a particular time period.

Since the absolute-zero point has empirical meaning, all arithmetic operations are possible—addition, subtraction, multiplication, and division. This permits the valid use and meaningful interpretation of ratios formed by two scores. For example, a country with a birthrate of 2.4 children per couple has twice as large a birthrate as a country with a rate of 1.2 children per couple. Similarly, a person 30 years old is half as old as a person 60 years old, and a family with an income of $15,000 has twice as much income as a family with $7,500.

Most of the scales used in social work research are not ratio scales because their zero points are arbitrarily chosen. One way to conceptualize the ratio scale is to think about the possibility of negative values. In other words, if negative values can be assigned (e.g., a temperature of -25 degrees F.), then a ratio scale does not exist for that particular variable. The same holds true for age and weight. Since no one can have a negative age or weight, these properties can legitimately be measured on a ratio scale. The best test, then, of whether a measurement is at the ratio level is whether or not a zero can be thought of as measuring "none" of a particular variable's property.

SUMMARY

Measurement is a fundamental requisite for social work. It facilitates correspondence between the world of concepts and the world of observations. It also plays a meaningful role in the operationalization of concepts, the testing of hypotheses, and the selection of appropriate methods of data collection and statistical analysis. Through its rules of correspondence, measurement serves to increase the objectivity of observations, the potential replicability of studies, and the effective communication of findings. Thus, measurement is intimately related to virtually all aspects of the research process. And, since the quality of social work practice and research is no better than its weakest phase (see Figure 2.1 in Chapter 2), careful consideration of measurement theory and the proper application of its rules and operations are essential.

The four major levels and accompanying scales of measurement—nominal, ordinal, interval, and ratio—together form a cumulative continuum, each building on its predecessor(s). Thus, ordinal scales possess all the characteristics of nominal scales, interval scales possess all the characteristics of nominal and ordinal scales, and ratio scales possess all the characteristics of the first three. Since no one level or scale dominates the research process—and since certain statistical analyses are permissible with some scales and not others—we must be familiar with the underlying assumptions of all four.

Qualitative variables are always measured (i.e., classified) on a nominal scale. Ordinal, interval, and ratio scales are appropriate for quantitative variables but vary in the degree to which they express the magnitude of a variable's property. Ordinal scales are the least informative of the quantitative scales because they simply designate ordered ranks or positions. Interval-level scales preserve distance between two measurements, but they lack an absolute origin. The most informative quantitative scale is the ratio scale, which possesses an absolute-zero point and which allows for truly meaningful use and interpretation of ratio statements. The four scales differ, therefore, in their ability to quantify a variable. The nominal scale represents the least quantification and the ratio scale the most.

Ratio scales are considered to be ideal because the numbers assigned correspond exactly with the property values; that is, the numbers represent the actual amounts of the property being measured. Thus, operationalization of the conceptual world is identical (isomorphic) to that of the empirical, or real, world.

Significantly, most of the scales used in social work are nominal or ordinal. The reason is derived in part from the fact that, with the exception of certain physical objects, the assumptions of interval (equal-distance) and ratio (absolute-zero) measurement are difficult to achieve. Indeed, some social workers view ratio-level measurement as basically unrealistic, since many of the psychosocial variables they are concerned with are not amenable to "complete" measurement. Others take a more flexible and pragmatic approach; they suggest that since many of the ordinal scales developed to measure social and psychological variables probably approximate interval measurement, they could be used as though they were interval-level scales. Doing this, of course, might not always meet the assumption of interval equality, and thus there is a risk of introducing distortions and errors into statistical analyses of the resultant data. In such a situation, however, it is often possible to use certain scaling methods to technically transform ordinal scales into interval scales. Therefore, ordinal-level measurements can be treated as though they were of the interval-level type, but provided constant attention is given to the possibility of gross inequality of intervals.

Gerald J. Bostwick, Jr. and Nancy S. Kyte

10. VALIDITY AND RELIABILITY

The degree to which a measuring instrument is doing what it is supposed to do and the degree to which it is free from error is called *measurement validity* and *reliability*. If social workers do not know how valid and reliable their measures are, they can put little faith in the results they obtain and the conclusions they draw from those results. They may not be sure of what they have measured; furthermore, they may not have measured the concepts consistently. It is essential, therefore, to not only choose measurement procedures carefully but to assess the validity and reliability of the instruments used to make the measurements (Kogan, 1975).

VALIDITY

A valid measuring instrument has been described as doing what it is intended to do, as measuring what it is supposed to measure, and as yielding scores whose differences reflect the true differences of the variable being measured rather than random or constant errors (Anastasi, 1976). An instrument such as a questionnaire, achievement test, personality inventory, or problem checklist is valid to the extent that it actually measures what we want it to measure. If we say that a test measures a certain variable such as dominance, the instrument is valid to the degree that it truly measures this trait. If, however, the test actually measures some other variable, such as sociability, then it is not a valid measure of dominance (although it may be a valid measure of sociability).

Thus, the definition of validity has two parts: the instrument actually measures the concept in question, and the concept is measured accurately. Obviously, it is possible to have the first without the second, but not vice versa. That is, a concept cannot be measured accurately if some other concept is being measured instead.

How, then, can a social worker go about establishing the validity of an instrument? To begin with, it is necessary to become accustomed to thinking not of an instrument's validity but rather of its *validities*. This is because validity refers broadly to the degree to which an instrument is doing what it is intended to do—and an instrument may have several purposes which vary in number, kind, and scope (Mindel, 1981). Various classification schemes have been developed in an attempt to categorize the validities underlying measurement. One of the most common and useful specifies three types of validity: content, criterion, and construct. The different types of validity relate to the different purposes of measurement because the purpose dictates the type of evidence (logical or statistical) needed to demonstrate that the measuring procedures are valid.

Content Validity

Content validity is concerned with the representativeness or sampling adequacy of the content (e.g., topics, items) of an instrument. To determine content validity we ask two questions: Is the instrument really measuring the concept we assume it is? Does the instrument provide an adequate sample of items that represent that concept? Thus, the concept being measured must be capable of definition, and the data being gathered must be relevant to that concept. If the properties of the concept being measured are not equally represented in the instrument, a biased sample of responses will result.

Suppose, for example, that we are interested in constructing an instrument that will measure a student's general social work knowledge. We operationally define general social work knowledge as including knowledge about social welfare policy, social work research, casework, group work, and community organization. Before administering the instrument we ask several colleagues who are experts in policy, research, casework, group work, and community organization to evaluate the content of the instrument. The community organization expert points out that no mention is made of several important functions of community organization, and the group work expert advises us that we have failed to include questions dealing with group cohesion and the normal phases of group development. Is this instrument content valid? No, because its intended purpose—to measure general social work knowledge—will not be achieved. Assuming that the other areas of the instrument were judged to be adequate, could we use the data obtained for a different purpose? In particular, could we validly determine a student's knowledge about social casework, social work research, and social welfare policy? Here the answer is yes. Although we would not be justified in using the instrument to determine general social work knowledge, we could use it to assess knowledge about these three areas. Thus, the instrument is content valid for one purpose but not for another.

Content validation is, by and large, a judgmental process. When we asked colleagues to assess our instrument we were relying on their judgments to establish its content validity. Content validation can be determined by the social worker alone or with the help of others; the decision as to which approach to follow is often pragmatic. In this case, however, if we had not asked for the judgments of colleagues or consulted with experts in each of the major areas of social work, the items on our instrument would not have been representative of general social work knowledge, and our resultant interpretations would have been open to question.

Establishing content validity is not as simple as it may appear. First, since content validity is determined largely by subjective judgments, in the same instrument it may be assessed as high by one person but low by another. Second, content validity requires—at least in principle—a complete specification of the universe of items from which the instrument's items will be drawn. That is, the instrument must contain a logical sampling of items from the entire universe of items that presumably reflect the concept, trait, or behavior to be measured. And that sampling of items must correspond with the universe of items in some consistent fashion.

Unfortunately, this is no easy task. Consensus about the definition of the concept to be measured may be lacking, and it may be difficult to identify the universe of items that theoretically make up that concept. Moreover, the potential number of representative items to be included in the measuring instrument can conceivably approach infinity. This is particularly apropos when we attempt to measure constructs which are complex and multidimensional in nature, such as ego strength, prejudice, alienation, and anxiety.

Personal judgments of the social worker (alone or with others) determine how a concept is to be defined, how the universe of items is to be identified, and how the sample of representative items from that universe is to be drawn. Thus, the general content validity of any instrument rests to a large extent on the skill and judgment of the person who constructs it. If poor judgment has been used—and this is always a possibility—then the instrument is likely to have little, or no, content validity.

Face Validity. The terms *face validity* and *content validity* are often used interchangeably in the research literature, although some methodologists argue that they should not be thought of as synonymous. They claim that face validity is not technically a form of validation since it refers not to what an instrument "actually" measures but rather to what it "appears" to measure (i.e., it appears relevant to those who will complete or administer it). Nevertheless, face validity is a desirable characteristic for a measuring instrument. Without it, we may encounter resistance on the part of respondents, which may in turn adversely affect the results obtained. Consequently, it is important to structure an instrument so that it not only accurately measures the attributes under consideration but also *appears* to be a relevant measure of those attributes.

Suppose, for example, that we want to assess the effects of a communication skills training course being offered at a school of social work. We decide to do this by administering a communication skills assessment form to each social work student at the beginning and end of the course. After carefully searching the literature we locate an instrument that has been validated and that measures the types of skills our course is designed to teach. The instrument, however, was originally developed for use with upper- and middle-management business personnel. If we were to ask social work students to answer questions that reflect situations occurring in the business world, they would undoubtedly ask us, "How do you expect these questions to tell you anything about how we work with clients?" To avoid such skepticism, we would need to rephrase the questions to reflect clinical situations typically encountered by social workers. In this way we would increase the face validity of the assessment form by making it appear more relevant to the respondents.

Thus, it is important to consider face validity in developing or adapting a measuring instrument. It should be remembered, however, that face validity alone does not ensure content validity—and vice versa.

Criterion Validity

Criterion (or criterion-related) validity, which involves multiple measurement, is established by comparing scores on an instrument with an external criterion known to or believed to measure the concept, trait, or behavior being studied. It is essential in this approach to validation that there be one or more external, or independent, criteria with which to compare the scores on an instrument. Suppose that we want to validate a test purporting to predict a social work student's success in a B.S.W. program. To do this, we administer the test to students entering their first semester and then compare the test scores with subsequent grade point averages. Here, the external criterion (or dependent variable) is grade point averages. Other potential criteria might be individual or combined ratings of academic and field work performance and graduation from the program.

It should be apparent that the criterion used should itself be reasonably valid and reliable. If we had chosen a criterion that was inaccurate or undependable, we would have been unable to validate our instrument adequately. Unfortunately, valid and reliable criteria may not exist or may not be thoroughly tested. In this case the one which seems most adequate (keeping in mind its limitations) should be chosen and, if possible, supplemented with other relevant criteria. The nature of the predictions the worker wants to make and the techniques available for checking them out will generally determine which criteria are relevant and which are not.

Criterion validity is frequently subdivided into two categories: concurrent validity and predictive validity.

Concurrent Validity. Concurrent validity refers to the ability of a measure to accurately predict an individual's current status. An example of an instrument with concurrent validity would be a psychopathology scale which is capable of distinguishing between adolescents who are in need of psychiatric treatment and those who are not.

Suppose that we want to predict how well students are using interviewing skills in their field work placements. To assess their use of these skills we develop an instrument comprised of excerpts of four simulated worker-client interviews, each of which consists of a series of statements made by the client and a corresponding set of responses by the worker. The student is required to select, from among those responses, the ones that are most appropriate.

Since we cannot assume that the instrument is measuring what we think it is (i.e., interviewing skills), we must evaluate its validity. First we ask the students' field work supervisors to make a separate assessment of each student's interviewing skills. We compare this assessment with the results obtained from our instrument and then ask an independent judge, such as a social work instructor, to listen to a tape recording of an interview held by each student and, on that basis, to rate the adequacy of the student's interviewing skills. If the supervisor's ratings and the independent judge's ratings agree with the student's performance on the simulated-interview instrument, we can say that the instrument has concurrent validity. If, however, the ratings do not concur, we cannot assume that it does. It may not be measuring the students' use of interviewing skills but rather their knowledge of how such skills should be used.

Predictive Validity. Predictive validity denotes an instrument's ability to predict future performance or status from present performance or status. An instrument has predictive validity if it makes it possible to distinguish individuals who will differ at some point in the future. An example of an instrument with predictive validity would be a psychopathology scale which is capable of differentiating adolescents who will need psychiatric treatment one year from now from those who will not.

To illustrate the establishment of predictive validity, let us take as an example a social work study carried out by Ewalt, Cohen, and Harmatz (1972), at a child guidance clinic. This study evolved from the staff's concern that over 50 percent of the clients were dropping out before the fourth interview. The staff wanted to identify those clients who would probably drop out early so they could initiate a structured form of short-term treatment from the beginning, thus maximizing the time they would have with these clients. Essentially, what they wanted was an instrument which would help them predict continuance in treatment.

Before initiating the study the social workers conducted an extensive review of the literature and identified a variety of factors alleged to predict continuance in treatment. They then developed an instrument containing 58 items which were representative of those factors and administered this instrument to 146 families during the intake interview. Of the 58 items, 14 proved to be related to continuance. When a new instrument comprised of these 14 items was developed and administered to another 127 families, only 5 of the 14 items accurately distinguished families who dropped out before the fourth interview from families who continued. Through this process of elimination, they ended up with five items which were good predictors of continuance. The resultant five-item instrument can be said to have predictive validity, since its scores compared favorably with the external criterion the workers used, namely, the family's status as continuer or discontinuer at the end of the fourth interview.

In summary, both concurrent and predictive validity, the two forms of criterion validity, are concerned with prediction, and both make use of some external criterion which is purportedly a valid and reliable measure of the concept, trait, or behavior being studied. What differentiates the two is time: Concurrent validity predicts current performance or status, while predictive validity predicts future performance or status. Moreover, concurrent validity involves administering an instrument and comparing its scores, at approximately the same time (i.e., concurrently), with an external criterion. In contrast, predictive validity entails comparative measurement at two different (present and future) points in time. It is important to remember, however, that the major concern of criterion validity is not whether an instrument is valid for current or future discriminations. Rather, it is primarily concerned with the use of a second measure as an independent criterion to check the validity of the first measure.

Construct Validity

Of the three major approaches to validation, construct validity is perhaps the most difficult because it involves determining the degree to which an instrument successfully measures a theoretical construct (hence the term *construct validity*). The difficulty derives in part from the highly abstract nature of constructs. A construct can be thought of as referring to a characteristic or trait which does not exist as an isolated, observable dimension of behavior. It cannot be seen, felt, or heard, and it cannot be measured directly—its existence must be inferred from the evidence at hand. Thus, the construct hostility must be inferred from observations of presumably hostile or aggressive acts, and the construct anxiety must be inferred from test scores, galvanic skin responses, observations of allegedly anxious behaviors, and so on. Other examples of typical constructs of concern to social workers are intelligence, alienation, political conservatism, cohesion, conformity, achievement, motivation, social class, delinquency, prejudice, and organizational conflict.

Construct validity is evaluated by determining the degree to which certain explanatory constructs account for variance, or individual differences, in the scores of an instrument. Put another way, it is concerned with the meaning of the instrument—that is, what it is measuring and how and why it operates the way it does. Suppose, for example, that we want to assess the construct validity of the Rorschach inkblot test. To do this, we would ask what factors, or constructs, account for differences in responses on the test. We might further ask if the test measures emotional stability, sociability, or self-control, and whether it also measures aggressiveness. In short, we are asking what proportion of the total test variance is accounted for by the constructs emotional stability, sociability, self-control, and aggressiveness. With construct validity, we are usually more interested in the property, or construct, being measured than in the instrument itself.

Thus, construct validity involves validation not only of the instrument itself but also of the theory underlying it. To establish construct validity, the meaning of the construct must be understood, and the propositions the theory makes about the relationships between this and other constructs must be identified. We want to know what predictions can be made on the basis of these propositions and whether the measurements obtained from using the instrument will be consistent with those predictions. Obviously, if the predictions are not supported, there is no clear-cut guide as to whether the shortcoming is in the instrument or in the theory.

Suppose we conduct a study to test the hypothesis that self-referred clients are more likely to have favorable attitudes toward treatment than those who are not self-referred. And suppose our findings do not show the predicted relationship between self-referral and attitude toward treatment. Should we conclude that our measure is not valid, or that the hypothesis is incorrect? In such a situation we would probably reexamine the construct of attitude toward treatment and the network of propositions that led to this prediction. The results might well be a refinement of the construct (with more detailed hypotheses about its relationship to other constructs) and changes in the measuring instrument.

Construct validation is a lengthy, involved procedure which makes use of data from a variety of sources. It is a painstaking building process much like theory construction—an attempt to ferret out the underlying dimensions that an instrument is tapping and thereby to validate the theory behind the instrument. This can be accomplished through a three-step process developed by Cronbach (1970): (1) suggesting what constructs might account for performance on an instrument, (2) deriving hypotheses from the theory surrounding the constructs, and (3) testing these hypotheses empirically. The testing of the hypotheses can in turn involve several procedures, including convergent-discriminant validation and factor analysis (Fiske, 1971).

Convergent-Discriminant Validation.   Convergent validity means that different measures of a construct yield similar results (i.e., they converge). Put another way, evidence gathered from different sources and in different ways leads to the same (or a similar) measure of the construct. Thus, if two different instruments, each alleging to measure the same construct, are administered to a group of people, similar responses or scores should occur. And if one instrument is administered to two groups of people in different states, it should yield similar results. If it does not, the theory underlying the construct being measured should be able to explain why.

Discriminant validity means that a construct can be empirically differentiated (i.e., discriminated) from other constructs. Here, the test is to see if an instrument is or is not related to other constructs which, according to theory, should differ. Thus, if it can be shown that an instrument measures a construct in the same way other instruments measure it and that it is not related to any other constructs from which it should theoretically differ, it has convergent and discriminant validity.

Factor Analysis.   Another powerful method for determining construct validity is factor analysis. Basically, factor analysis is a statistical procedure which reduces a large number of items or instruments to a smaller number (called *factors*) by discovering which ones go together (i.e., measure the same or similar things) and by determining what relationships exist between the clusters of items or instruments that go together (Kerlinger, 1973).

Suppose that we administer 10 different instruments, ours included, to a group of clients. Factor analysis would allow us to identify the different constructs that are being measured by these 10 instruments. It would also allow us to determine which of these instruments, if any, are essentially measuring the same constructs. We can then look at the relationships between our instrument and the other nine to determine which construct or constructs our instrument actually measures. And, the more we know the degree to which other constructs are or are not related to the one we are interested in, the greater our understanding of that construct.

To illustrate construct validation, let us take as an example the development of an index of client motivation for treatment. Krause (1966a, 1966b, 1966c, 1967) began by articulating a theoretical link between two variables, motivation for treatment and client role performance, and then identified four universal areas of client role performance: (1) attending all therapy sessions, (2) providing detailed problem descriptions, (3) listening and responding to the therapist, and (4) working on problems outside therapy sessions. This led to the construction of the Client Behavior Inventory (CBI), an instrument designed to measure the construct motivation for treatment, which required the therapist to assess a client's role performance in each area.

After assessing the inventory's content validity, Krause went on to establish its construct validity with several interrelated procedures. First, using a validation technique known as internal (or interitem) consistency, the CBI was examined to determine if each item differentiated a client in the same direction as did the entire inventory. Second, factor analysis was used to validate the underlying dimensions of the CBI (i.e., the four-client role performance areas). Third, the researcher explored the relationship between responses obtained from the CBI and therapist global ratings of client motivation for treatment, client satisfaction with treatment, and current success of treatment. With theory as a guide, a positive relationship between all three ratings and the CBI was anticipated. Finally, the social worker divided 216 family counseling agency clients into two groups, experimental and control. The experimental group was exposed to an intake procedure designed to enhance motivation for treatment; the control group was not. Both groups were given the CBI at intake. Again according to theory, it was expected that clients in the experimental group would score higher on the CBI than clients in the control group.

The results of these studies revealed a high degree of CBI internal (or interitem) consistency; a positive relationship between responses on the CBI and therapist ratings of client motivation, client satisfaction, and therapy success; and generally higher scores on the CBI for clients exposed to the experimental intake procedure. While further validation is probably warranted, this evidence strongly suggests that the CBI is, in fact, measuring the construct motivation for treatment.

In summary, construct validity is concerned with the degree to which an instrument successfully measures a theoretical construct. What sets construct validity apart from content and criterion validity is its preoccupation with theory, explanatory constructs, and the testing of hypothesized relationships. Thus, while one social worker may be interested in validating a test to determine whether or not it effectively distinguishes between individuals as high and low on a particular variable, another social worker interested in construct validity would want to know why the test succeeds in differentiating these individuals in the first place.

Overview of Validity

Content, criterion, and construct validity are three interrelated approaches to instrument validation. They are only conceptually independent—rarely is just one relevant to a particular kind of measure. Because each type of validation functions in a different capacity, it is difficult to make any blanket generalizations as to which is the best to use. However, as Thorndike and Hagen (1969) have noted, when we ask how valid an instrument is, we are really proposing three questions:

1. How well does this instrument measure what we want it to measure?
2. How well does this instrument compare with one or more external criteria purporting to measure the same thing?
3. What does this instrument mean—what is it in fact measuring, and how and why does it operate the way it does?

The questions chosen to be answered dictate which types of validation are of primary concern. That is, the worker's objectives and planned use of the instrument will determine what kinds of validity evidence are most needed. When an instrument is employed for different purposes, it should be validated in different ways. If an instrument is used for any purpose other than that for which it was intended—or if it is used with a different client population or in a different setting—it is the user's responsibility to revalidate it accordingly.

RELIABILITY

Reliability has been defined as the accuracy or precision of an instrument, as the degree of consistency or agreement between two independently derived sets of scores, and as the extent to which independent administrations of the same instrument (or highly similar instruments) yield the same (or similar) results under comparable conditions (Kerlinger, 1973). Synonyms for reliability are dependability, stability, consistency, predictability, accuracy, reproducibility, repeatability, and generalizability. Thus, an instrument is reliable to the extent that independent administrations of it or a comparable instrument consistently yield similar results.

In its broadest sense, instrument reliability indicates the degree to which individual differences in scores are attributable to "true" differences in the property or characteristic being measured and to errors of measurement. As will be discussed later in this chapter, errors of measurement involving reliability are random (as opposed to constant) and are the product of a number of causes and conditions which are essentially irrelevant to the purpose of the instrument, such as fatigue and fluctuations of memory or mood. Thus, scores will tend to lean now this way, now that way. It is important to remember that since these random errors are present in all measurement, no instrument is ever perfectly reliable. The data yielded by an instrument will be dependable only to the extent that the instrument is relatively free from errors of measurement. Consequently, every instrument should be tested for its reliability before, rather than after, it is formally administered.

Several procedures exist for establishing the reliability of an instrument. These include the test-retest and alternate-form methods and the split-half technique. Of related importance are the procedures used to determine observer reliability, which is of particular relevance to the social worker.

Test-Retest Method

As the term *test-retest* suggests, one way to estimate reliability is through repeated measurement. The same instrument is administered to the same group of individuals on two or more separate occasions, and the results are then compared by calculating what is known as a reliability coefficient (correlation). The reliability coefficient indicates the extent of the relationship between two sets of scores. If the reliability coefficient is high, it can be concluded that the instrument has good test-retest reliability.

Test-retest reliability thus estimates the stability of an instrument by showing the extent to which its scores are consistent over time. The higher the reliability, the less susceptible the scores are to random daily changes in the condition of the individual (e.g., fatigue, emotional strain, worry) or the testing environment (e.g., noise, room temperature). And the less susceptible the instrument is to such extraneous influences, the more reliable it is.

How is it possible to determine if a difference between first and second measurements is due to extraneous factors or to a genuine change in the variable being measured? To answer this question we must first consider the possibility that the first testing has influenced the second; the very process of remeasuring may have increased the influence of extraneous factors. For example, individuals may be less interested, less motivated, and less anxious during the second testing simply because they are already familiar with the instrument. Moreover, if the time interval between retests is fairly short, they may remember their answers and simply repeat many of the responses given the first time. There is also the possibility that the first testing has actually changed the variable being measured. For instance, a questionnaire assessing attitudes toward the elderly may raise questions people have never thought about before, thereby heightening their interest in the issue and stimulating the development of definite opinions. Consequently, a "don't know" response on the first testing may be replaced by a "definitely agree" or "definitely disagree" response on the second. And it is always possible that genuine change due to influences unrelated to the testing has occurred.

To minimize these potential influences on the temporal stability of an instrument, it is necessary to determine whether or not the measures obtained will be appreciably affected by a repeat testing. If they will, the conclusion must be that the instrument does not lend itself to the test-retest method. If they will not, careful consideration must be given to the time interval between retests. The shorter this interval, the more likely it is that the first testing will have an effect on the second one, and the longer the interval, the more likely it is that real change will have occurred. Thus, in the first case (short-time interval), we are likely to err in the direction of overestimating reliability; in the second case (long-time interval), we are likely to underestimate reliability.

There are no hard and fast rules for judging the optimal time interval. A two- or four-week interval is generally considered suitable for most psychological tests, and the waiting period should rarely exceed six months. A basic rule of thumb is: Wait long enough for the effects of the first testing to wear off, but not long enough for a significant amount of real change to occur. A good example can be seen in intelligence testing. If we administered an IQ test to a group of children on two separate occasions, approximately one month apart, we would not anticipate a significant amount of change. But what would happen if we waited two years?

To illustrate the use of the test-retest method in social work practice, let us briefly consider a series of instruments recently developed to help social workers assess the presence and extent of a client's problems and to obtain ongoing evaluative feedback on therapeutic progress.

The Clinical Measurement Package: A Field Manual written by Hudson (1982a) consists of nine 25-item scales to assess marital and sexual satisfaction, self-esteem, depression, and family problems. They are designed to be used as repeat measures; clients complete them every week or two weeks, and after they are scored by the social worker they can be used to monitor and guide the course of treatment on a continuing basis.

The test-retest reliability of these scales was established by asking clients to complete them at one sitting, wait a minimum of 2 hours and a maximum of 24 hours, and complete them again. The resultant reliability coefficients were high. In clinical applications, neither clients nor social workers have reported being bored with or frustrated by repeated use of these scales. And most importantly, their reliability does not appear to change markedly as a result of repeated administrations (Fischer, 1978). Hudson and others are continuing to evaluate the validity and reliability of these scales, but the evidence to date seems to support their use as measures for assessing client problems and monitoring the course of treatment.

In summary, the test-retest method is one of the most common approaches to establishing reliability. It permits an instrument to be compared directly with itself, and it reveals the continuity, or stability, of the instrument over time. Although test-retest reliability is relatively simple and straightforward, it is subject to a number of biases accruing from the potential effects of recall, practice, and repetition. Thus, tests which are appreciably affected by memory or repetition would not lend themselves to the test-retest method.

The Alternate-Form Method

One way to avoid some of the problems encountered with test-retest reliability is to use alternate (or parallel) forms. This method involves administering, in either immediate or delayed succession, supposedly equivalent forms of the same instrument to the same group of individuals. The obtained reliability coefficients indicate the relationships between the scores on these forms.

Alternate forms can be thought of as content-equivalent instruments which are constructed according to the same specifications. The forms contain items which are different (thus eliminating exact recall) but are intended to measure the same phenomenon equally. Thus, Form A and Form B of a reading comprehension test should contain passages of equal difficulty and should ask similar types of questions. If Form A uses a passage from a novel and Form B uses an excerpt from a philosophy text, we would expect the levels of difficulty to be quite different. Any observed differences, then, could be explained as a result of the test's content and not as a result of differing levels of reading comprehension.

For reliability purposes, alternate forms of an instrument are usually administered during a single session, with a brief intervening rest period. Under such circumstances, the strength of the relationship between the obtained scores provides an indicator of the instrument's item reliability. If the interval between testings were increased from several minutes to several days or weeks, the scores would provide a measure of both the consistency of response to different items and the temporal stability of the instrument, that is, reliability across forms and across occasions (or administrations). Thus, the use made of alternate forms will dictate the choice of a time interval between test sessions.

Consider, for example, the following two situations. In the first, our objective is to assess the research knowledge of 40 master's-level social work students enrolled in two separate sections of a first-year research course. Although each section is taught by a different instructor, we can develop a general test of research knowledge because the course's format and content are identical for both sections. But, since these two sections meet at different times, we really do not want to use just one instrument, because we will be unable to administer the instrument at the same time to all 40 students. To minimize the possible influence of discussions between students who have completed the test and those who have not, we develop two equivalent forms. To make sure that these forms can be legitimately compared (i.e., that the items on the two forms are essentially equivalent), we ask students who have recently finished the course to complete both forms at one sitting, with a one-hour rest period in between. Such a procedure is justified because we are assessing research knowledge at only one point in time; that is, we do not want to know whether we will obtain the same results over several different administrations of the test. The purpose of the one-hour rest period is to minimize transient differences (such as boredom or fatigue) and not to provide data on the temporal stability of the research test.

The situation and our objective in the second example are somewhat different. Here we want to design an instrument that will help a family service agency measure the effects of a community educational program designed to increase service utilization. Since this evaluation requires knowledge of the community's attitudes toward mental health services before and after intervention by program teams, we decide to administer the instrument on two separate occasions. We assume that any observed pre-post differences will indicate whether or not the community's attitudes have changed as a result of the teams' efforts. However, because the program lasts only three weeks, if the same instrument is administered both times the respondents may remember how they answered the questions initially, and this may bias their subsequent responses. The responses we would obtain might be influenced more by recall than by actual attitudinal change, so we decide to develop alternate forms of the instrument. And, since there will usually be a three-week hiatus between administrations, we decide to use a similar time interval to establish our reliability estimates.

In both of the above examples, the purpose of the instrument served as a guide for determining the appropriate time interval between test administrations. Since our research test was to be given at only one point in time, a one-hour interval was deemed sufficient for determining the test's item reliability. But because our agency instrument had to be administered at two different times, its reliability had to be established using a similar (three-week) interval. In the first case, then, we used the alternate-form method to assess item reliability, that is, consistency of response to different but supposedly equivalent items. Since the alternate forms were to be administered in almost immediate succession, the resultant reliability coefficient would show reliability across forms only, not across occasions. Thus, any observed differences would only represent fluctuations in performance from one set of items to another. In the second case, the alternate-form method allowed us to establish not only item reliability but also temporal stability, that is, consistency of response over time. Since the alternate forms were to be administered in delayed succession (i.e., at a three-week interval), the resultant reliability coefficients would show reliability not only across forms but also across occasions. Any observed differences would represent fluctuations not only in performance but also over time.

Use of the alternate-form method requires both appropriate time intervals and equivalent sets of items. Each alternate form must contain a sampling of items that is truly representative. Items must be randomly drawn from the universal pool of potential items in such a way that if the same procedure were followed a second or even third time three essentially equivalent sets of items would result. Each set would then qualify as an alternate form of the instrument. In addition to content-equivalent items, it has been suggested that alternate forms should contain the same number of items, items expressed in a similar form, items of equal difficulty, and comparable instructions, format, illustrative examples, and time limits.

Developing and administering truly equivalent forms requires considerable time and effort. All the problems of measuring social and psychological phenomena are compounded by the need to construct two instruments. We must be concerned not only with intratest reliability but also with the comparability of the different reliabilities of both measures. In addition, presenting measures as separate tests (whether or not the respondents are told they are alternate forms of the same instrument) may affect responses more than presentation of all the items as if they constituted a single test. Finally, we must carefully consider the degree to which the nature of the measuring instrument will change with repetition. In certain types of tests, for example, any items involving the same principle can be readily solved by most respondents once they have worked out the solution to the first one. Just changing the content of the items in the other form would probably not eliminate this carry-over. For these reasons, other techniques for estimating reliability are often required.

The Split-Half Technique

Another way to establish instrument reliability is with the split-half technique, which involves administering an instrument to a group of people. The items on the instrument are divided into comparable halves, and the scores on the two parts are compared to determine the extent to which they are equivalent. This is in many ways analogous to alternate-form reliability because each half is treated as if it were a parallel form of the same instrument. If the halves are not equivalent, the instrument may not have a representative sampling of items, and an individual's score may be influenced more by the items than by the variable being measured. If the scores obtained from the halves are similar, it can be assumed that the individual's performance is not appreciably affected by the sampling of items in either half of the instrument. Split-half reliability thus provides a measure of the instrument's internal (interitem) consistency. Temporal stability is not assessed, since only one administration of only one form of the instrument is required.

One of the main problems encountered with split-half reliability is how to divide the instrument into equivalent halves. The first thought might be to divide the instrument in half by counting the total number of items and dividing by two; a 30-item instrument would be split so that Items 1 through 15 would make up the first half and Items 16 through 30 the second half. While such a procedure seems fairly easy and straightforward, what happens if the nature or level of difficulty of the items is different at the beginning and end of the instrument? And how can such extraneous factors as fatigue and boredom, which may exert varying degrees of influence on responses at the beginning and end, be controlled for?

Potential problems such as these have led to the adoption of the odd-even procedure. All the even-numbered items are assigned to one group and all the odd-numbered items to the second group. Then the scores from the odd-numbered half are compared with the scores from the even-numbered half. This procedure has been used to provide an additional estimate of the reliability of the nine scales in *The Clinical Measurement Package: A Field Manual* (Hudson, 1982a). The social workers obtained an odd-half test score and an even-half test score for each client who completed the scales, compared these scores, and found that the two halves of the scales were very similar.

Observer Reliability

Observer reliability is analogous to the test-retest and alternate-form methods of establishing reliability in that it is concerned with the stability of observations made by one individual (intraobserver reliability) at several points in time or the equivalence of observations made by two or more individuals (interobserver reliability) at one point in time. While an extensive discussion of the many facets of observation (e.g., structured versus nonstructured; participant versus nonparticipant) is beyond the scope of this chapter, it should be noted that this process of data collection is frequently used when the phenomenon under consideration is not readily amenable to more traditional measurement techniques such as questionnaires, interviews, and tests, or when an outside, presumably more objective, assessment seems necessary. For example, if we are interested in the aggressive behavior of small children we might ask an observer to watch a group of them through a one-way mirror and record acts of aggression according to a prescribed set of instructions. Or the director of a social service agency might identify the intervention techniques commonly employed by the staff by having trained observers watch videotapes (or listen to audiotapes) of interviews and code the type and frequency of the various techniques used. In both instances, the observer would use an instrument and an accompanying set of instructions to make the ratings. In a sense, therefore, the reliability of the instrument can be estimated by determining the reliability of the observations made by the observers using that instrument.

Interobserver reliability (also referred to as interjudge, interrater, and intercoder reliability) is a specific type of observer reliability which has been widely used in social work research. In this approach, two or more judges use the same instrument to rate the same individual at a certain point in time. The reliability of their observations is assessed by calculating percentages of agreement or correlation coefficients.

An excellent example of interobserver reliability can be found in a study by Reid (1978c). The project was designed to evaluate the effectiveness of task-centered casework, a short-term, problem-oriented approach to practice. In this study, children and adults were provided with social work services in a variety of settings, including schools, mental hospitals, clinics, and family service agencies. A problem typology was developed, and this was used by independent judges to assign these clients' problems to such categories as interpersonal conflict, difficulty in role performance, and inadequate resources. The reliability of this typology was estimated by determining the percentage of agreement of two judges who had read and categorized the same problem statements. In another phase of the study Reid followed the same reliability procedures, but instead of reading case material the judges listened to audiotapes of a problem assessment interview and rated problem change. These ratings were made on 5- and 10-point ordinal scales which ranged from considerable improvement to considerable deterioration and from great improvement to great deterioration, respectively. A subsequent calculation of correlation coefficients to determine the strength of the relationship between these ratings (i.e., the extent to which the judges tended to agree) revealed quite satisfactory reliability for these scales.

Overview of Reliability

Reliability refers in general to the extent to which independent administrations of the same instrument (or highly similar instruments) consistently yield the same (or similar) results under comparable conditions. Put another way, reliability involves determining the degree to which variation in scores is due to transistory influences; that is, random errors. The less the scores are influenced by such extraneous factors, the more reliable the instrument is.

The term *reliability* is frequently used to refer to three different, but interrelated, concepts: stability, equivalence, and homogeneity. Underlying each of these is the notion of consistency. Stability refers to an individual's position from one administration of an instrument to another. It is determined by the test-retest method, which compares the results of repeated measurements. Equivalence concerns an individual's position on different instruments intended to measure the same thing. It can be established using alternate, or parallel, forms. Homogeneity focuses on the internal consistency of an instrument and can be determined with the split-half technique. All three concepts and procedures essentially involve establishing the degree of consistency or agreement between two or more independently derived sets of scores.

Reliability is primarily concerned not with what is being measured but with how well it is being measured. Obviously, the more reliable our instruments and observations, the more consistent and dependable our results. High reliability does not guarantee valid results, but there can be no valid results without reliability.

THE VALIDITY-RELIABILITY RELATIONSHIP

Although validity and reliability have been treated as separate properties of a measuring instrument, they are clearly related. One cannot have validity without reliability, but one can have reliability without validity. Put simply, high reliability does not guarantee validity. Reliability can only show that something is being measured consistently, but that "something" may or may not be the variable we are trying to measure. Thus, an instrument that is reliable may not measure what we want it to. On the other hand, it is *not* possible to have an instrument that is valid but not reliable. If an instrument measures what we say it measures, then by definition it must be reliable.

The interrelationship between validity and reliability can be summarized in the following manner: An instrument that is valid is always reliable; an instrument that is not valid may or may not be reliable; an instrument that is reliable may or may not be valid; an instrument that is not reliable is never valid. Since high validity cannot result from unreliable instruments, we can safely say that high validity is indicative of satisfactory reliability. Reliability, then, is a necessary, but not sufficient, condition for good measurement. Although a valid measure with low reliability is more useful than a reliable measure with low validity, it is important to make every effort to maximize both properties of any instrument used.

SOURCES OF MEASUREMENT ERROR

Measurement error can be thought of as any variation in responses, such as answers on a questionnaire or ratings made by an independent observer, which cannot be attributed to the variable being measured. Thus, measurement error is inversely related to the validity and reliability of an instrument. As the amount of variation due to extraneous (error) factors increases, the validity and reliability of the measurements decrease. Consequently, the ultimate goal is to develop instruments which are free from these outside, unwanted influences. However, most measurement occurs in relatively complex situations, where numerous factors operate to affect both the variable being measured and the process of measurement itself, and thus it is virtually impossible to construct a perfectly valid and reliable instrument. Because measurements will never be totally free of error, we must try to identify potential sources of error and control or lessen their impact (contamination). Put simply, we want to minimize error and maximize accuracy.

A myriad of extraneous influences could be operating in any measurement situation, and only some of the more common sources of error will be reviewed here. Basically, all of the factors that obscure the "true" differences in the attributes we are interested in measuring can be categorized as either constant (systematic) error or random (variable) error.

Constant (Systematic) Error

Constant error refers to those factors that consistently or systematically affect the variable being measured. These factors, by their very nature, are concerned with the relatively stable qualities of respondents. Demographic characteristics and personal style are the two most common sources of constant error.

Intelligence, education, socioeconomic status, race, culture, and religion are examples of demographic variables that may influence an individual's responses. Consider, for example, the effect reading level might have on an evaluation of the effectiveness of a job training program. Suppose we want to assess the job performance of a group of young men and women who have dropped out of high school and enrolled in this program. The instrument we decide to use requires an ability to read at the eighth-grade level. If we administer this instrument to the trainees without determining their reading levels in advance, we will probably end up with a set of confounded scores. That is, the scores will not reflect job performance but rather the trainees' ability to read and understand the instrument's questions. We must not assume, therefore, that respondents represent a homogeneous group with respect to demographic characteristics or that these characteristics exert little influence on our measurements. Put another way, we would not be justified in assuming that since all of the trainees dropped out during their sophomore and junior years of high school, they can all read at the eighth-grade level.

Personal style (also referred to a *response style* or *response set*) as a source of error has received most of the attention of test constructors and research methodologists. This is partly because response sets have been found to bias test results systematically and partly because different response sets have come to be viewed as indicants of different personality traits.

Some of the more common personal styles that can consistently affect responses include social desirability (a tendency to give a favorable impression of oneself), acquiescence (a tendency to agree with statements regardless of their content), and deviation (a tendency to give unusual or uncommon responses). Others are concerned with the reactions of observers: contrast error (a tendency to rate others as opposite to oneself in regard to a particular trait or characteristic), halo effect (a tendency to be unduly influenced by a single favorable trait or to let one's general impression affect one's ratings of a single trait or characteristic), error of leniency (a tendency to rate too high or to always give favorable reports), error of severity (a tendency to rate too low or to always give unfavorable reports), and error of central tendency (a tendency to rate in the middle, thus avoiding any extreme positions).

Some controversy continues to revolve around the actual biasing (error) effects of response sets, especially since there is support for the position that they only explain a small portion of the variance in measurement and are not general across different types of instruments. Ideally, every measurement situation should be examined for such sources of error, and appropriate steps should be taken to minimize their impact. Because constant errors are generally detectable, numerous methods have been developed to reduce their confounding effects. These control procedures include development of subtle or socially neutral questions and items, incorporation of various response set or "faking" indicators, and concealment of the instrument's true purpose. Other control efforts are the rank ordering of ratings, the careful training of observers, and the use of multiple observers.

Random (Variable) Error

Random error refers to those unknown or uncontrolled factors that affect the attribute being measured and the process of measurement in an inconsistent (variable) fashion. Unlike constant error, random error effects have no uniform trend or direction. This variation affects measurements in such a way that both overestimates and underestimates of the "true" differences in the characteristic being measured may result. Thus, these errors are self-compensating; that is, they tend to cancel each other out, especially with a relatively large sample of respondents. This phenomenon has led some methodologists to regard random measurement error as tolerable. Others suggest that since we do not know for sure that these factors are operating to cancel one another out, we must try to minimize their potential effects.

Most of the random errors identified in the literature can be classified as involving transient qualities of the individual, situational factors, or administrative factors.

Transient Qualities. Transient qualities of the individual include physical or mental health, mood, motivation, attention span, and degree of alertness, boredom, or fatigue. These can vary from day to day—indeed, from moment to moment. This is not to say that all of these factors operate simultaneously or have equal effects on a respondent's performance. Rather, each must be considered separately and a judgment must be made as to how germane or influential this type of error is to any particular measurement situation.

Situational Factors.   The respondent and measurement process can be influenced not only by internal conditions but also by external, or situational, factors. The physical setting (e.g., seating arrangement, work space, noise level, lighting, ventilation, presence of a tape recorder) and the social setting (e.g., degree of anonymity, presence of peers) can introduce unwanted sources of variation into the measures. For example, it would not be surprising to find that adolescents give different responses to questions about gang behavior when interviewed on the street or at a police station, as a group or individually, or in the presence or absence of family members.

Administrative Factors.   The third major source of random error involves the actual administration of the instrument. This source of error often stems from a lack of standardization. In part, standardization is concerned with the establishment of uniformity in the instrument's application. For instance, an absence of detailed instructions and training may lead some interviewers to add, omit, or change the wording of certain questions (see Chapter 16). Administrators of tests or questionnaires might improvise their own instructions, and observers might use different criteria or types of information to classify relevant behaviors. The issue revolves around the amount of subjectivity influencing the measurement process. Obviously, the goal is to minimize the subjective element and maximize the comparability and objectivity of measurements to the greatest extent possible.

The influence of administrative factors also concerns the administrators themselves. It has been found, for example, that an administrator's demeanor and physical appearance (as well as such other characteristics as sex, age, and socioeconomic status) can affect how an individual will respond. Administrators of instruments, therefore, should be aware of the image they present and should take into account any major demographic dissimilarities between themselves and the respondents.

Although random errors may cancel each other out, it is still advisable to take steps to minimize their potential effects. Basically, we want to create a situation where an individual's physical or emotional state, the testing environment, and the procedures used to administer the instrument exert little or no influence on the measurement process. One way to reduce random errors is to foster rapport with the respondents by arousing interest in the instrument, eliciting cooperation, spending time getting acquainted, increasing motivation, reducing anxiety, and making sure the respondent is capable of completing the tasks required by the instrument. Another is the selection of a setting which is conducive to the types of responses desired, such as interviewing husbands and wives separately to determine differences in attitudes toward marriage. Other effective procedures are the use of clear, standardized instructions and the advance preparation of interviewers, observers, and administrators of instruments with rehearsals, trial runs, or memorization of instructions.

Overview of Measurement Error

Measurement error refers to variations in responses that cannot be attributed to the variable being measured. These variations can either systematically (as with constant errors) or inconsistently (as with random errors) have unwanted influences on measurements. Thus, measurement error is inversely related to validity and reliability; as the amount of error increases, the reliability and validity of the instrument decrease. Since it is virtually impossible to eliminate these undesired influences completely, measurements will never be totally free of error. Nevertheless, the social worker must try to identify any potential sources of error that may be operating and take all possible steps to minimize their impact on the measurement process.

SUMMARY

Measurement is fundamental to social work practice and research. It facilitates correspondence between the world of theory and the world of reality and helps increase the objectivity of observations, the precision of interpretations, and the effective replication and communication of findings. Thus, measurement is intimately related to virtually all aspects of the social work research process. It plays a crucial role in the formulation of research questions, the operationalization of variables and concepts, the testing of hypotheses, and the selection of appropriate methods and techniques for data collection and statistical analysis.

Since measurement involves the assignment of numerals or symbols to properties of objects according to specified rules, it is essential that the rules be carefully formulated and appropriately applied to the variables to be measured. This in turn requires familiarity with the underlying assumptions and procedures of nominal, ordinal, interval, and ratio measurement. Unfortunately, however, proper application of these procedures will not lead automatically to good measurement. If an instrument is measuring something other than what it is supposed to measure, or it is measuring a variable inconsistently, we can have little confidence in the results we obtain and the conclusions we draw from those results. Thus, good measurement involves not only choosing measurement procedures that minimize error, but also assessing and maximizing the validity and reliability of the instruments used to make those measurements.

This chapter has provided an introduction to the use of measurement in social work. The principles of measurement are applicable in all four phases of the social worker's problem-solving process. They must be understood before they can be used in actual practice, and they are especially needed for an understanding of the next chapter, which discusses the development and application of indexes and scales.

11. INDEXES AND SCALES

Indexes and scales are composite measures of variables in which the principles of measurement introduced in Chapter 10 are applied to develop measurement instruments the social work practitioner/researcher can use in formulating problems, selecting strategies, and implementing and evaluating practice efforts. The instruments considered are to be used in social work practice *and* in social work research, not the other way around. This deliberate distinction reflects the purpose of this text: to make research directly relevant to the conduct of social work practice (Hudson, 1978a). Since the study of measurement is necessary to achieve this purpose, the focus is on the use of measuring instruments in direct social work practice.

EIGHT FUNDAMENTAL MEASUREMENT AXIOMS

An axiom is an assumption or principle that is accepted as self-evidently true (Siporin, 1975). Statements such as the eight fundamental axioms presented in this section can help social workers structure their thinking about the use and role of measurement in their professional practice. These axioms take the worker out of the realm of theory and into the world of practical utility, where problems are assessed, measured, and treated.

Validity and Reliability

Axiom 1. If instruments are to have any practice utility they must have two fundamental characteristics: they must be valid, and they must be reliable.

The concepts of validity and reliability should be familiar from the preceding chapter. If they are not, Chapter 10 should be reread, as this chapter assumes a sound understanding of these concepts.

Practical Utility

> Axiom 2. In order for instruments to have maximum utility for social workers, they must be short, easy to administer, easy to understand, easy to score, and easy to interpret.

Many instruments used in the social sciences are unnecessarily long and complicated. Some are designed in such a way that they are very difficult to interpret, score, or administer, and some are so technical that they can be successfully used by only a relatively small number of persons who have acquired the necessary specialized advanced training. Sometimes it is necessary to employ such instruments, but their general utility for social work practitioner/researchers is extremely limited. Some instruments also require clients to spend too much time on them. Many single-subject designs (see Chapter 20) call for periodic use of instruments to determine or assess the severity of clients' problems, and it would be ludicrous to require responses every week or so to an instrument that takes 45 minutes to complete, for example.

Problem Assessment

> Axiom 3. There are only two ways to determine whether clients have problems: watch them, or ask them.

Although this is not technically an axiom of measurement it is intimately connected with the validation of instruments. Social workers must continually be concerned with the definition and measurement of client problems because social work is a practice-based, problem-solving profession. There are only two ways a social worker can measure some feature of a client's problem in order to treat or study it: by making direct observations about the problem (watching), or by requesting the client to report on one or more features of the problem (asking). That is, the worker can decide, on the basis of direct observation, whether a client has a problem in some area of personal or social functioning or can ask the client to decide and report whether such a problem exists (W. Gingerich, 1978).

Self-report instruments have a number of distinct weaknesses (Hersen & Barlow, 1976). However, when they are skillfully devised and used in social work practice they are extremely useful and powerful devices for measuring client problems. Although their risks and shortcomings must be clearly understood and appreciated, their use and importance must not be underemphasized.

Client Problem Measurement

> Axiom 4. There are only four ways of measuring a client prob-
> lem: in terms of its switch, frequency, magnitude, or
> duration.

The simplest way to measure a client's problem is in terms of its
presence or absence. This can be referred to as a *switch* problem. The
switch is in the on position if the client has a problem, and it is off if
the client has no problem. Although this is a very crude level of
measurement (the client's situation is given a value of 1 if a problem
exists and a value of 0 if no problem exists), there are many cases in
which this is the highest possible level of measurement. More important, virtually all client problems can be measured at least at this crude
level. Thus, measurement is always available to help us deal with client
problems and improve the likelihood of positive outcomes (Hudson,
1978a).

A frequency measure of a client problem is obtained by simply
counting the number of times the problem occurs within some specified
time interval (Gottman & Leiblum, 1974). An example of a frequency
measure might be: "How many times did you and your spouse quarrel
during the past week?"

A magnitude or intensity measure of a client problem characterizes it in terms of some underlying dimension representing degree of
presence or absence. For example, "On a scale from 0 to 10, how
serious is the marital problem you claim to have? Let 0 = No problem
and 10 = A problem so serious that the marriage could terminate in
divorce."

A client problem also can be measured in terms of duration,
which is simply the length of time the problem is continually present.
A duration measure might be represented, for example, by the following instructions to a client: "During the next week, write down the
number of minutes from the outset to the end of each migraine head-
ache you have. Be as accurate as you can in recording these time
intervals."

Treatment

Four treatment axioms based on measurement are included here
to dramatize the powerful relationship which exists between measurement and social work practice. All are useful in thinking about the
structure and conduct of social work treatment (W. Gingerich, 1978).

> Axiom 5. If you cannot measure a client's problem it does not
> exist.

Axiom 6. If you cannot measure a client's problem you cannot treat it.

Axiom 7. If you cannot measure an intervention it does not exist.

Axiom 8. If you cannot measure an intervention you cannot administer it.

These axioms do not help workers to develop or select instruments; they merely point to the need to use measurement concepts to structure and carry out social work treatment. They identify a direct linkage between measurement theory and application, on the one hand, and the assessment of client problems and social work intervention, on the other.

INDEXES AND SCALES

In certain areas of the literature on research, distinctions are made between an index and a scale. As an instrument, a scale is always regarded as superior to an index. Indexes and scales are both composite measures which are constructed from two or more single indicators or data items. An index produces only an ordinal level of measurement, whereas a scale provides an interval or ratio level of measurement.

Consider, as Example A, the following simple measure of a child behavior problem, which is based on five data items.

A. Rate your child by assigning a score of:

    0. Less than most children
    1. About the same as most children
    2. More than most children

to each of the following five statements (place a number on the line to the right of each statement):

    1. MY CHILD WETS THE BED.   _____
    2. MY CHILD STEALS FROM OTHERS.   _____
    3. MY CHILD SCREAMS AT ME.   _____
    4. MY CHILD BREAKS THINGS.   _____
    5. MY CHILD WON'T OBEY ME.   _____

If we add the five item scores for a particular client, we will have (at best) only an ordinal-level measure of a behavioral problem for the client's child, and that total score is called an index. If one client obtained a total score of, say, 3 and another obtained a total score of 8, it would seem clear that the second client's child has a greater behavior problem (with respect to the five behaviors represented by the five items) than the first client's child. However, we should not attempt to draw any conclusions about the size of the difference between the two scores; ordinal distances have no meaning.

Now consider Example B, which is based on the same five data items as Example A:

B. During the last two weeks, how many times did your child (place number of times on the line to the right of each statement):

1. WET THE BED   _____
2. STEAL FROM OTHERS   _____
3. SCREAM AT YOU   _____
4. BREAK THINGS   _____
5. DISOBEY YOU   _____

If we add up the frequencies reported by a client for each of these five times, the total score is called a scale because it is an interval-level measurement; the score interval from, say 0 to 1 is the same as the interval from 8 to 9. Moreover, if we restrict our statements exclusively to the five behaviors represented by the five items, the total score can be properly seen as a ratio scale; a score of zero means that the child has no behavioral problem over the two-week period with respect to these five items. That means we can perform all the operations of arithmetic with such scores (Nunnally, 1978). Thus, a client who obtains a score of 30 is properly seen as having a child whose behavior problem is six times greater than that of the child of a client who has a score of 5 (assuming, of course, that both report completely accurate frequencies).

Client Scaling and Stimulus Scaling

Confusion may arise from a failure to distinguish between two entirely different tasks: the scaling of people and the scaling of stimuli. In the former, we are asking how much of the characteristic (say, physical abuse) is possessed by a client. In the latter, we are asking how much of a characteristic is represented by an item (stimulus). Consider the following three items in Example C:

C. During the last two weeks, how many times did your spouse exhibit the following three behaviors? (Place the number of times on the line to the right of each statement.)

1. PUSH OR SHOVE YOU AROUND   _____
2. SLAP YOU WITH AN OPEN HAND   _____
3. HIT YOU WITH A CLOSED FIST   _____

Most would agree that being pushed or shoved around represents less physical abuse than either being slapped or struck with a fist (depending, of course, "how hard" one is shoved, slapped, or hit with a fist). Thus, the items are already listed in terms of an ordinal level of abuse. These items could be scaled in a simple way by having a large number of persons complete the following task:

D. Rate each of the following three behaviors on a scale from 0 to 20 in terms of the degree of physical abuse represented by the behavior, where 0 = No physical abuse and 20 = Extreme physical abuse. (Place your rating on the line to the right of each statement.)

1. BEING PUSHED OR SHOVED AROUND   _____
2. BEING SLAPPED WITH AN OPEN HAND   _____
3. BEING STRUCK WITH A CLOSED FIST   _____

The average rating given to each behavior by, say, a few hundred clients could be regarded as the "scale" value for each item, but it is extremely important to recognize that in this task stimulus items are being scaled, not clients.

If we know the items' means, we can use them in a refined method of scaling clients. Suppose, for example, that the means obtained from a large sample which carried out Task D were:

$$M_1 = 9.2$$
$$M_2 = 12.1$$
$$M_3 = 17.4$$

Where: M_1 = Mean of item's score for "being pushed or shoved around"

M_2 = Mean of item's score for "being slapped with an open hand"

M_3 = Mean of item's score for "being struck with a closed fist"

If the actual frequencies a client gives for Task C are regarded as F_1, F_2, and F_3, then a refined physical-abuse score can be computed as:

$$RS = M_1F_1 + M_2F_2 + M_3F_3$$

Where: RS = Refined score

F_1 = Frequency of "being pushed or shoved around"

F_2 = Frequency of "being slapped with an open hand"

F_3 = Frequency of "being struck with a closed fist"

Suppose that two clients' responses to Task C were as shown in Table 11.1. In terms of a simple frequency scale, both clients have had about the same amount of physical abuse; they each have a total frequency score of 13.

However, because the stimulus items have been scaled, we have more data which can be used to scale the responses of these two clients (see Table 11.2). By multiplying a client's frequency response for each item by the item's mean rating value (number in parentheses) and then adding the three products together, we get a very different picture. Now it can be observed that the second client has experienced more physical abuse over the past two weeks than the first client has.

TABLE 11.1
Ratings for Task C

Item	*Client 1*	*Client 2*
1	9	4
2	3	2
3	1	7
Totals	13	13

Source: Hudson (1981).

TABLE 11.2
Client Responses to Task C Weighted by Mean Responses to Task D
(from Table 11.1)

Item	*Client 1*	*Client 2*
1	(9.2) 9 = 82.8	(9.2) 4 = 36.8
2	(12.1) 3 = 36.3	(12.1) 2 = 24.2
3	(17.4) 1 = 17.4	(17.4) 7 = 121.8
Totals	136.5	182.8

Source: Hudson (1981).

Some theoreticians would claim that the total scores (13) in Table 11.1 do not represent scales but are indexes, while the total scores (136.5 and 182.8) in Table 11.2 are true scales. Actually, both are scales, although the second is a better one because it provides more precise data about the quantity we are trying to measure—the amount of physical abuse suffered by a client. The essential difference between these two measures is that Table 11.1 scales clients only in terms of the frequency of abusive behaviors and Table 11.2 scales clients in terms of both the frequency and seriousness of those behaviors.

Some types of stimulus items differ from one another quite radically in terms of some dimension like seriousness, attractiveness, or hardness. In such cases the scaling of stimuli can be used to markedly improve the ability to scale clients. In most instances, however, it is rather difficult to make a strong case for using differential stimulus weights, and attempts to do so usually produce no apparent gains in the ability to scale clients.

Some researchers have become so concerned, enamored, or puzzled by the use of scaled stimuli that they urge its routine use. Some even claim that if stimulus items cannot be scaled in certain ways, it is doubtful that they can be used to scale clients. One of several methods which can be used to scale stimulus items is the Guttman scalogram technique. It is attractive to many investigators because its theory and logic are very elegant but it is based on some very stringent assumptions which may not be apparent, and it has been advocated much more frequently than it has been used. As a matter of fact, it is very difficult to employ, it has rarely been found helpful in social work practice, and many people have been misled or misdirected by those who advocate its use. Nevertheless, students should learn how to use the Guttman scalogram technique and should know about the problems associated with it. Though this information is not presented here, it can be obtained from the references.

Thus, the use of stimulus scales in the task of scaling people is a potential advantage in some cases, but the decision to use them most often reduces to the problem of developing appropriate weights for the items comprising the scale. Most often the effort is not needed or helpful.

To conclude this section, the following simple rules are suggested. If a value for a client variable is computed on the basis of two or more data items and that variable represents an ordinal-level measure, it is called a client index. If the variable is an interval- or ratio-level measure, it is called a client scale. If stimulus items can only be ordered in terms of the amount of a specific characteristic they represent, that order is called a stimulus index. If the items can be separated by meaningful intervals in terms of a specific characteristic, those interval values are called a stimulus scale (Torgerson, 1958).

The essential point to remember is the distinction between the scaling or indexing of clients and the scaling or indexing of stimulus items. Sometimes the two can be combined to produce more effective client scales, and sometimes they cannot.

THE USES OF MEASUREMENT

Measurements of client characteristics can be taken with respect to a potentially infinite number of variables. Fortunately, most of these variables (or at least a very large number) can be grouped into a fairly small number of categories. The major categories social workers are familiar with or need to be concerned about include:

- Physical characteristics.
- Biological characteristics.

- Social characteristics.
- Knowledge.
- Ability.
- Achievement.
- Attitudes.
- Beliefs.
- Values.
- Feelings.
- Perceptions.
- Behaviors.
- Problems in personal functioning.
- Problems in social functioning.

The last two categories (problems in personal and social functioning) are somewhat unique; at least they are rarely mentioned in standard texts in measurement or social work as categories of variables requiring measurement. They are listed here because social work is a practice-based, problem-solving profession whose major work literally springs from and is justified by these categories. Much work must be devoted to the measurement and quantification of such problems, both in practice and in research settings and applications. A large portion of the following sections of this chapter is related to the measurement of problems in the personal and social functioning of clients.

Types of Instruments

The variety of currently available instruments is so great that a complete listing would be unrealistic. Table 11.3 presents a very limited number of sources where one can find scales that are relevant for social work practice and research. In spite of the enormous variety of styles, formats, methods, purposes, and forms in use, most instruments break down into a relatively small number of types or classes. For purposes of this chapter the fundamental tool of all measurement will be referred to as a measurement item or simply an item. An item is any single indicator that enables a worker to assign a number to a client in a systematic way to order to represent some property of the client with respect to that specified variable. Thus, a measurement item can be, for example:

1. A question that elicits information about the size of a client's family.
2. A device used to measure the severity of a hearing loss.
3. A problem a client must solve on an arithmetic test.
4. A question that asks clients to report their age.

5. A statement responded to by clients designed to detect their value stance with respect to the necessity for teaching ethics in primary schools.
6. A question that seeks to determine whether a client has a problem in relating to a specific set of peers.
7. A report or judgment concerning one's own performance on an assigned or elected task.

Once it is understood that an item is a single indicator, and the most elementary one, which measures only one variable in only one way, it is possible to define several broad classes of instruments. Obviously, the simplest type of instrument is one that contains only one item. There are few of these around; nearly all instruments social workers use have more than one item. Another type of instrument uses one item to measure each variable; such an instrument might measure ten different variables and have only ten items. A third type of instrument is designed to measure only one variable but uses two or more items to do so. Finally, there are instruments which are designed to measure two or more variables and which use one or more items to measure each variable.

Unidimensional and Multidimensional Scales

Any instrument that is designed to measure only one variable is technically referred to as a unidimensional measure, regardless of the number of items to measure that variable. And any instrument that is used to measure two or more variables is technically referred to as a multidimensional measure, regardless of the number of items used to measure any of the variables.

Generally speaking, nearly all survey questionnaires (see Chapter 15) are multidimensional in nature, although they are practically never referred to as multidimensional scales. (Not that such a reference would be incorrect: it simply isn't done.) Most survey questionnaires also use only one item to measure each variable, but there are exceptions to this rule. Most other measurement scales used in the social sciences tend to be multi-item measures of one (unidimensional) or more (multidimensional) variables. There are good reasons for this which will be discussed later.

In the literature there are many discussions and examples of the use of multidimensional scales, which are sometimes referred to as multifactorial scales because they are constructed, scored, and interpreted with a data analytic method or tool called factor analysis. There continues to be a great deal of confusion about the need for such multifactorial scales and their construction, use, and interpretation. It

TABLE 11.3
A Few Sources of Existing Scales

Anastasi, A. (1976).
Arkava, M. L., & Snow, M. (1978).
Beck, A. T. (1967).
Beere, C. A. (1979).
Bloom, M., & Fischer, J. (1982).
Buros, O. K. (Ed.). (1968, 1978).
Chun, Ki-Taek, Cobb, S., & French, J. R., Jr. (1975).
Comrey, A., Barker, T., & Glaser, E. (1975).
Fischer, J. (1978).
Fiske, D. W. (1971).
Gambrill, E. D., & Richey, C. A. (1975).
Giuli, C. A., & Hudson, W. W. (1977).
Goldman, B. A., & Saunders, J. L. (1974).
Grinnell, R. M., Jr. (Ed.). (1981 b).
Haynes, C., & Wilson, C. (1979).
Hudson, W. W. (1982a, 1982b).
Hudson, W. W., & Glisson, D. H. (1976).
Hudson, W. W., & Proctor, E. K. (1977).
Hudson, W. W., Wung, B., & Borges, M. (1980).
Hunter, M., & Grinnell, R. M., Jr. (1978, 1983).
Hunter, M., Grinnell, R. M., Jr., & Blanchard, R. (1978).
Johnson, O. G., & Rommarito, J. (1971).
Lake, D. G., Miles, M. B., & Earle, R., Jr. (Eds.). (1973).
Levitt, J. L., & Reid, W. J. (1981).
Locke, H. J., & Wallace, K. M. (1959).
McReynolds, P., (Ed.). (1978).
Miller, D. C. (1977).
Rathus, S. A. (1973).
Robinson, J. P., Athanasion, R., & Head, K. (1973).
Robinson, J. P., & Shaver, P. R. (1973).
Shaw, M. E., & Wright, J. M. (1967).
Spanier, G. B. (1976).
Spielberger, C. D., Gorsuch, R. L., & Lushene, R. E. (1970).
Strauss, M. A. (1969).
Stuart, R. B. (1973).
Stuart, R. B., & Stuart, F. (1975).
Thorndike, R. L. (Ed.). (1971).
Thorndike, R. L., & Hagen, E. (1969).
Waskow, I. E., & Parloff, M. B. (Eds.). (1975).

---

is wise to beware of any instrument that claims to be multidimensional, since a multidimensional scale is nothing more than a collection of unidimensional scales, each designed to measure only one variable.

If it is really necessary to measure two different variables, then two different unidimensional scales or a multidimensional scale that has two factors which measure the two variables should be used (Giuli & Hudson, 1977). Such an instrument is readily constructed by simply putting together in one measurement package the items that comprise the two unidimensional scales. Failure to understand this fundamental fact concerning the nature and structure of multidimensional scales has contributed greatly to their abuse and misapplication. Much time has been wasted searching for multiple factors or dimensions or trying to develop multifactor scales, when it is often more efficient and effective to develop scales one dimension at a time. The point is that if only one variable is to be measured, the use of a multidimensional scale is a waste of time, money, and data.

PLANNING THE USE OR DEVELOPMENT OF A MEASURE

With the background information presented thus far, we can begin to address the problem of how to plan the use or development of a measurement instrument. Many questions come naturally to mind, but the first must be: What do we want to measure? Are we going to measure an attitude, belief, value, personal problem, ability—or what? In short, what types of variables are we going to measure? The answer comes directly from the practice issue, research question, or hypothesis being considered.

Once we decide what specific variables we are going to measure, the next question is whether there are valid and reliable instruments currently available in that area. Other questions concern the type of measure wanted or needed—whether the variables should be measured at the ordinal or interval level, and what the minimum validity or reliability of the measure should be. It may not be possible or even desirable to use a currently available instrument, and we may face the task of constructing our own. This section provides help in developing simple scales that can be both effective and efficient and in selecting currently available measures for use in practice.

As presented in chapter 10, the two most important characteristics of instruments are their validity and reliability. Thus, the primary emphasis in this section is on the use or development of valid and reliable instruments.

Identifying and Developing Content Validity

Seldom is enough attention given to development of the content of an item, yet it is the single most important step in developing a scale or selecting one for use. This is true for both single-item and multi-item instruments. If the item does not directly represent, in one way or another, the specific variable one wishes to measure, it cannot be a valid measure of that variable. An item which directly represents some aspect or feature of the variable to be measured is said to have high content validity. If the item or items comprising a scale do not have high content validity, the resulting measurement scale cannot be a measure of the variable or construct in question.

It is unfortunate that there are no formal rules to establish clearly the fact that an instrument has high content validity. Alas, this is solely dependent on human judgment, which is well known to be laden with frailty. Yet it's the best and only thing we have for assessing the content validity of a measurement tool.

There are a few general rules, however, that are quite useful. The first rule is to devise a clear and unambiguous definition of the variable or construct to be measured. The second rule is to examine each item and determine (with the best possible wisdom, training, experience, insight, and even intuition) whether it represents some aspect of the variable or construct being measured. If it does, it should be kept; otherwise it should be completely discarded.

Suppose we want to measure the severity of marital discord as seen, felt, or perceived by a client. Consider the five following items:

1. I am unhappy with my marriage.
2. My children cause me a great deal of distress.
3. I think my spouse is terrific.
4. Our income is not adequate to meet our needs.
5. My boss thinks I am a terrific worker.

Most married people would immediately discard some of these items because they do not appear to have any relationship to their own intuitive or implicit definitions of marital discord. There's the problem. We have not actually defined what we mean by marital discord, and until we do it is not possible to make good judgments about the content validity of these items. We might define it as follows:

> Marital discord consists of those affects, perceptions, and interactions among partners that relate to and potentially influence the quality of their dyadic relationship.

With this definition of the construct of marital discord (or satisfaction, depending on how we score the items), it would be immediately apparent that Items 2, 4, and 5 do not have content validity; none involves partner interaction. Now consider the item:

     6. My spouse washes my car.

This also is not a good item, in terms of the definition. First, it represents a service provided to one spouse by another, not an affective interaction between them. It has nothing to do with the expression or exchange of affect, and it does not deal with a perception about the quality of the dyadic relationship. Thus, the definition of marital discord helps to develop content-valid items for the measurement of marital discord or to select an available scale that claims to measure such a construct or variable.

     In developing a measurement scale to characterize the level or degree of marital discord on a magnitude continuum, we might decide to have clients merely rate themselves on a well-defined number scale to reflect the degree or intensity of their marital problems. In using a single item as an instrument it is extremely important to determine that the item has a very direct and completely unambiguous content validity. An example of such a single-item measure might be:

> On a scale from 1 to 5 (with 1 being low and 5 being high), rate the severity of the marital problem you say you have with your spouse on the line below:
>
> _____

Another example might be as follows:

> My spouse and I have problems in our relationship: (Circle one number below.)
>
> 1. NONE OF THE TIME
> 2. RARELY
> 3. A LITTLE OF THE TIME
> 4. OCCASIONALLY
> 5. A GOOD PART OF THE TIME
> 6. MOST OF THE TIME
> 7. ALL OF THE TIME

     It is important at this point to focus on the content of the item and not the rule or method used for assigning a value to the client's response. The first step is to determine whether the content of the item relates directly to the variable to be measured. This is the single most important step in assessing or developing the content validity of a scale.

Assigning Item Values

     If we want to develop a new scale and we've actually created a set of items, the next task is to develop some rule for assigning values to them. Sometimes this can be the most difficult task of all; if it is not handled well, an otherwise good scale can be made useless.

The most frequent purpose for assigning values to items is to obtain at least some crude notion of the level or magnitude of the variable for a specific person. These values should correspond to the degree of the response, so that a small value indicates the person has a low level or magnitude of the variable and larger values indicate the presence of a higher level or magnitude. Thus, the values are usually thought of as a degree, intensity, or magnitude continuum.

In the social sciences, it is extremely difficult to assign values for a single item in such a way that the resulting item scale is a truly continuous variable. A common procedure, therefore, is to partition the score continuum into a small number of categories, like:

1. NEVER
2. RARELY
3. OCCASIONALLY
4. FREQUENTLY
5. VERY FREQUENTLY

Items scored in such a manner are often referred to as Likert scales or Likert-type scales (Likert, 1967). They are more properly referred to as category partition scales, because this conveys direct information about the way the values are assigned to the scale items (Stevens, 1951).

The distinguishing feature of a category partition scale is that it is necessary to decide how many categories are to be used in dividing the continuum, and some means of defending the categories must be provided. One strategy is to devise a definition of each category, as in the above example. Another strategy is to define only the ends of the continuum, as in:

On a scale from 1 to 5 (with 1 being bad and 5 being good), how good is your marriage? (Place number on line below.)

_____

Or, as in an Osgood semantic differential scale:

My spouse is: (Circle one number on each line below.)

ATRACTIVE	5	4	3	2	1	UGLY
GENTLE	5	4	3	2	1	MEAN
BRIGHT	5	4	3	2	1	DULL

Of course, we are not bound to the use of category partition scales in assigning values to items. A number of ways have been developed which do not require the partitioning of a continuum into categories and which therefore circumvent entirely the need to define end points or categories. One technique, called magnitude estimation scaling, is represented by the following example:

Assign a low number to the following three items if you feel you do not have a problem, and assign a larger number if you feel you have a problem. The numbers you assign can be as large or as small as you like in order to indicate the seriousness or magnitude of the problem. (Place a number on the line to the right of each statement.)

1. MY SPOUSE NAGS ME TOO MUCH   _____
2. MY SPOUSE IS STINGY   _____
3. MY SPOUSE BEATS ME   _____

Magnitude estimation scaling has been most successful when all respondents are assessing the same stimulus object or entity and less successful in other measurement applications. Nonetheless, it illustrates an effort to avoid total reliance on the use of category partition scaling. Other schemes are available, but they will not be presented here (Shaw & Wright, 1967).

Overall, it is very difficult to find a better method of assigning values to scale items than the category partition method. It does have its problems, but most often they seem smaller than those associated with other methods. Some might dispute this assertion, especially in regard to the use of categories to partition a frequency continuum. Many feel it is much more scientifically valid to ask people to report (or to observe directly) the actual frequencies of specific events. Maybe so; it depends on what we want to measure. Consider the item:

A. My spouse nags me: (Circle one number below.)

    1. NEVER
    2. RARELY
    3. OCCASIONALLY
    4. FREQUENTLY
    5. VERY FREQUENTLY

Now compare Item A with Item B:

B. How many times each week does your spouse nag you? (Place number on line below.)

_____

Bette, who is nagged five times a week, might score the category item as 3, while Donald, who is also nagged five times a week, might score the category item as 5.

It must not be forgotten that the actual frequency of one or more events may be the same for one or more individuals, but the same frequencies may have very different psychological meanings. Consider, for example, people who have sexual intercourse once every two months and who report their sex lives to be satisfying, as compared to people who have intercourse twice a week and find that frequency deficient.

If there is a sound reason for measuring actual frequencies of events, then every effort should be made to obtain such frequency data. If, however, the real interest is in the psychological perceptions of the respondents, and the use of a frequency-oriented category partition scale will fill the bill, then it should be used. Failure to make these distinctions will produce misleading data (Nunnally, 1975).

Number of Response Categories

At a very minimum, every scale item must be scored with two response categories. If an item has only one response category it is defined as a constant and not as a variable; constants cannot explain variables. Thus, people are described as male or female, or they might make a right or a wrong response to a test item. Two categories—that's the bottom line. What about the top line?

There is no theoretical upper limit to the number of response categories we can have for any measurement item that is scaled as a magnitude continuum. Even so, most would agree that it is ludicrous to attempt to define, say, 200 response categories for a single item. How about 50, or 20? Some will say maybe, and others clearly say the magic number is seven, plus or minus two; that is, somewhere between five and nine. The literature is full of examples in which as many as 20 response categories per item have been successfully used, and the instances of success with only two categories are seemingly without limit. With this wide range to choose from, how is the number of response categories to be determined?

The first axiom cited in this chapter, that a measure must be both valid and reliable, is relevant here. The reliability of any multi-item, unidimensional scale is largely dependent on the number of items and the number of scoring categories used for each item. Increasing either number often improves the reliability of a scale. However, there appears to be a law of diminishing returns which operates in relation to increases in the number of response categories as a means of increasing the reliability of an instrument. It usually turns out, for example, that the gain in reliability is greater when we move from 2 to 9 categories (7 more) than when we move from 9 to 16 categories (also 7 more). Nonetheless, a general rule can be developed: It is better to have too many than too few categories. But, because of the law of diminishing returns, a really large number of categories may be of little benefit.

So there is no magic number of response categories, and perhaps the best advice is to be reasonable. The nine scales in *The Clinical Measurement Package: A Field Manual* uses five response categories. Seven or nine categories might have been better, but five are more convenient to complete and score (G. Miller, 1956). Since all nine scales have high reliabilities, the use of five response categories is adequate, and the use of seven or nine categories would probably not have much impact on their reliabilities.

Odd versus Even Number of Categories

One concern researchers seem to have is the choice between an odd or an even number of categories. This concern stems from their idea that clients will choose middle-of-the-road categories instead of committing themselves one way or another. They may question, for example, whether they should use four (even) categories, as in:

1. STRONGLY DISAGREE
2. DISAGREE
3. AGREE
4. STRONGLY AGREE

or they should use five (odd) categories and make the middle one neutral, as in:

1. STRONGLY DISAGREE
2. DISAGREE
3. NEITHER DISAGREE NOR AGREE
4. AGREE
5. STRONGLY AGREE

Some researchers try to resolve this issue by thinking along the lines of: "If I use five categories, too many people will respond in the middle, and the scale won't measure very well. So I'll use four categories and force the fence straddlers to declare themselves one way or the other." Clients who really are fence straddlers would blithely go down a list of items with four response categories and score them alternately as 2, 3, 2, 3, 3, 3, 2, 2, and so on. The fact that there are those who do not wish to state which side they are on should be clearly acknowledged, and they should be allowed the dignity of giving a forthright answer. If the scale really measures anything worthwhile, it will not be destroyed by using an even number of categories.

Defining the Continuum

Before we can define the response categories for a category partition scale, we must first define or decide what type of response continuum is desirable. Should we rate a number of items according to an agree-disagree continuum, for example, or should we use a frequency, severity, preference, desirability, or some other type of continuum? There is no fixed answer to this question, and the final decision is up to the investigator. This decision is best made after carefully considering and deciding what is to be measured, an effort that usually pays off with high dividends.

Suppose that we want to measure the severity of a parent-child relationship problem as seen by children with respect to their mother. Three items might read:

1. My mother yells at me.
2. My mother thinks I am terrific.
3. My mother beats me.

Should we consider scoring such items on an agree-disagree continuum? Maybe, but each of these items could be scored as a yes-no or true-false dichotomy. The use of an agree-disagree continuum for the measurement of human social or personal problems is a bit like trying to stretch a true-false or yes-no dichotomy to find out how much "yesness" or "noness" is present. It doesn't make sense. Moreover, the use of a neutral or "neither agree nor disagree" category makes even less sense. How could such a response to an item like "My father yells at me" be treated as a midscale value?

In the assessment of human personal and social problems, an especially fruitful approach seems to be, first, to write items so that a yes-no or true-false answer would indicate that a problem is either present or absent. Then the task is to score them to get some idea of their magnitude. The ordinary or common notion of degree or magnitude of such problems appears to rest largely in their frequency of occurrence. That is, if a problem occurs at all but does so very rarely (or it does not occur), we can say that the problem exists at a low level or magnitude; if it tends to occur with great frequency, we can say that it is present at a higher level or magnitude. Thus, a frequency rating appears to do a pretty good job of capturing data about the level or magnitude of problems with personal and social functioning.

None of this says anything about the "seriousness" of the behavior or event referenced by a particular item. An item that reads, "My spouse beats me so severely that I must seek medical assistance," would be regarded as very serious even if the event occurred quite rarely.

The use of such continua as agree-disagree, like-dislike, and sick-healthy raises the issue of bipolar versus unipolar items and scales. This can be very confusing, and it often leads to the fallacy of bifurcation. It may be quite correct, for example, to conceive and measure certain attitudes, values, and preferences as existing on true bipolar continua. However, for some types of human preferences and behaviors, the idea that they can be measured as existing at one extreme or another is absurd. Consider the issue of sexual orientation. It may be popularly acceptable to think of heterosexual and homosexual preferences as extreme end points on a bipolar continuum; bisexuals are then located (conceptually) near the center of such a scale. But such a conception of human sexual preferences is inaccurate. Men and women are two different sexual entities, and some people may love them both with equal or different degrees of fervor.

Whether a scale is a true unipolar or bipolar scale is a conceptual matter and not a "number" problem. We can always make the numbers look like a bipolar scale by simply subtracting their mean, but to do so thoughtlessly may dramatically reveal our ineptness. Consider the silliness of asking someone to report the frequency of any behavior on a bipolar scale. A general rule is to avoid bipolar scales and to use them only when absolutely nothing else will work—when the conceptual basis for the construct literally demands it.

Determining Scale Length

Perhaps the most frequent question that arises with respect to scale construction is how long the scale should be. Of course, it must have at least one item, but how many constitute the maximum number?

As noted above, the reliability of a scale is intimately related to the number of items it has. Generally speaking, the reliability of a scale increases with length—scales with many items are usually more reliable than those with only a few. As with response categories, the law of diminishing returns also appears to work in determining scale length. But unidimensional scales with 40 or more items, for example, are difficult to administer and score, and they obviously take more time, so there are also clear disadvantages to lengthy scales.

Some guidelines for choosing the number of items to be used are as follows: If a reliability of .60 or greater cannot be obtained by using 25 to 30 items for a single unidimensional scale, then the scale should be discarded, and the entire measurement task should be reconsidered (Kolevzon, 1981). To develop a multi-item scale, a minimum of five items is needed, and ten is even better. For a scale to be used by others, a large number of items may be necessary.

Single-item scales can be fantastic—or they can be worthless. Scale items with 5 to 20 categories can have reliabilities of .40 to .75, and in some instances the reliability can be much higher. The major problem with single-item scales is that their reliabilities tend to be low, and their validity and reliability are seldom questioned—most of us accept them uncritically.

Validating a Scale

Once we have developed a scale or selected one for use, how do we know that it measures what it is intended to measure? The answer concerns the validation of a scale or measure. Without a doubt it is the single most important issue in measurement and the one that probably receives the least attention. There are thousands of published scales currently available, but many do not provide evidence as to whether they in fact measure what they claim to measure.

In some cases, establishing the validity of an instrument is so patently obvious and simple that no one bothers to raise the issue. In others, the task is very difficult. Few would question the validity of an item such as "What is your age to the nearest birthday?" But the validity of a scale which attempts to measure the variables of depression, homophobia, degree of homosexual orientation, or anxiety would be open to question.

Generally speaking, variables that can be observed directly and those that relate to well-established empirical referents are comparatively easier to validate, and measures that represent higher order and more abstract concepts are more difficult to validate. Also, the extent to which we extrapolate from an observed phenomenon and interpret it as representing some other phenomenon is directly related to the difficulty of validating the latter construct. For example, respiration and pulse rate are excellent indicators of the level of physiological activity, but they cannot be considered good indicators of anxiety, or fear, or stress.

SUMMARY

Although this chapter has focused on the use of formal measuring instruments, virtually all the principles of measurement discussed are also directly applicable to the conduct of interviews with clients. Whenever we ask a question of a client and receive an answer, or we make an observation about a client and allow it to influence us, the first axiom cited in this chapter must be invoked: Both the client's answer and our observation must be valid and reliable.

12. INSTRUMENT DESIGN

In describing how to design and construct measurement instruments, this chapter applies two guiding principles based on the material on sampling procedures, measurement validity and reliability, introduced in Chapters 8, 9, and 10. First, the design and construction of the instrument should attempt to maximize the response rate of individuals in the sample or population. Second, the instrument should minimize the amount of measurement error in the responses of individuals. An instrument that embodies these principles can be said to be well constructed (Bailey, 1978, 1982).

In the research process data are gathered in order to test a hypothesis with the use of a research instrument, a generic term which covers a variety of data collection tools. In survey research, the instrument utilized to collect data is often called a *questionnaire*. When data are collected by means of face-to-face interviews, the instrument may be referred to as an *interview schedule*. Every research design, whether a survey, an experiment, or some form of observational study, involves the use of a research instrument to gather data. In this chapter, therefore, a research instrument is considered to be any type of data collection device or procedure designed to gather data on a social work research problem.

The type of research instrument used as an example in this chapter is primarily used in surveys. While the principles of design and construction are most appropriate to survey instruments, many of them can be applied to most other types of instruments as well (Babbie, 1979, 1982).

In the social work problem-solving process (see Chapter 2), the social worker does not consider constructing a research instrument until the problem area to be investigated has been formulated and converted into a clearly stated hypothesis (or general question) ready for testing. We must always remember that *only* after the problem area under investigation has been conceptualized and developed at an abstract and theoretical level can the development of a measurement instrument to test the hypothesis be considered.

In the development of the problem area and its associated hypothesis, the social worker is primarily working at a conceptual level. The concepts formulated are never directly tested as the study is carried out. Rather, they are converted into measurable independent and dependent variables by means of a process known as operationalization. The research process is really a test of the operational definitions of these theoretical concepts. To the degree that the operationalizations accurately and reliably measure the abstract concepts, the likelihood that the conceptual hypothesis itself is actually being tested is increased. If the measures are inadequate (i.e., invalid or unreliable), a true test of the hypothesis cannot be made.

INSTRUMENT FUNCTIONS

In social work research, the survey is the most common used form of data collection, because it provides a useful and convenient way to acquire large amounts of data about individuals or organizations (Atherton & Klemmack, 1982). A research instrument can make it possible to determine what people know, believe, or expect about a problem area. It also can provide data on how they feel, what they want, what they intend to do, what they have done, and why.

An effective instrument will serve numerous functions in the research process, all designed to give the social worker the necessary data on which to base empirical results of a study. These functions range from providing facts, determining beliefs and values and examining behavior, to ascertaining reasons.

Providing Facts

One of the most important functions of social work research is the determination of certain kinds of important facts about individuals or other units. For example, every 10 years the U.S. Census gathers demographic data on various variables in the population, such as sex, living arrangements, nationality, educational level, and family size. Social service agencies execute studies that are oriented to the collection of facts about individuals, gathering such data as the number and characteristics of individuals who have applied for social work services or the number who are child abusers or have applied for food stamps.

Determining Beliefs

In addition to determining the facts, the social worker is often interested in finding out what people believe the facts to be. In social service agencies, this is often an important distinction. For example, an agency may be having difficulty recruiting or serving an intended population, and a study might show that the beliefs of individuals in the community about that agency (whether or not they are based on fact) are quite negative. In terms of program planning, the existence of certain kinds of social problems may or may not coincide with the attitudes in the community about whether or not these problems exist. If an agency or worker is attempting to organize a social program to meet a certain social problem and important individuals in the community do not believe this problem exists, there will be difficulties in organizing the program. It is important, then, that as part of a needs assessment to determine whether a need for a program exists, the beliefs of important individuals and constituencies should be understood, as well as the current facts.

Exploring Feelings

In addition to understanding what the facts are and what people believe the facts to be, research instruments often explore their feelings and desires. Social workers, for example, might be interested in testing clients on a variety of feelings or states (e.g., depression). There are many well-established, tested instruments which explore different feelings such as those presented in Table 11.3 in Chapter 11.

Discovering Ethical Standards

Instruments also can probe individuals' feelings about what should be done or what is feasible to be done with respect to social policies. For example, many research instruments have examined attitudes toward abortion, women's rights, or education. A variation of these types of questions is represented by items which explore what individuals would do in certain situations. It is important to remember that items that explore what people should do or would do in certain situations do not necessarily indicate what they actually do. Although there might be a correspondence between what people say they do or would do and their actual behavior, this is by no means always so. Attitudes are *not* the same as behavior (LaPiere, 1934).

Examining Present or Past Behavior

In spite of the variance between expressed attitudes and observed behaviors in individuals, research instruments are useful for gathering reports about people's behavior, both from the past and in the present. These kinds of data are often needed in the field of social welfare, particularly in service utilization studies. For example, clients might be asked how many times they had visited a physician in the past year or the past month.

These types of data are very important, but there are potential problems with their accuracy. The instrument must not require individuals to reconstruct events from so far in the past that they cannot remember them accurately. It is much better to ask very specific questions within a reasonable time frame than to ask global, general questions ranging over a long period.

Ascertaining Reasons

A very important function of social work research is to ascertain why people behave, believe, or feel the way they do. Instruments often contain items exploring this "why" factor. For example, in a research study on elderly parents who live with their children, an important item asked why and under what circumstances they had formed this family arrangement. The history of the event, the types of reactions individuals felt at the time this event occurred, and what the process was were all relevant.

VALIDITY FACTORS IN INSTRUMENT DESIGN

Because a research instrument contains the operational definitions of the study's key concepts, as noted above, it is important to be cognizant of the external and internal validity factors in its design (Blalock, 1982). Internal validity refers to the degree to which the items contained in the instrument can accurately and reliably measure the underlying concept being studied; it is in this sense that the various validities of an instrument were presented in Chapter 10.

External validity goes a step further to consider the degree to which the answers to the items given by sampled individuals can be generalized to a larger population. The problems of external validity will not be dealt with very broadly in this chapter (the related issue of gaining an adequate response rate to the instrument will be considered in Chapter 15).

However, the way an instrument is designed (the subject of this chapter) can either increase or decrease the response rate, especially by the way the items are worded, designed, presented, and delivered to the individuals responding to the instrument.

External Validity

There are several reasons why an instrument will fail to achieve an adequate response rate, thus affecting the external validity of the research instrument, or the degree to which responses to the items can be generalized to a larger population. The external validity of an instrument can be improved by following the design procedures suggested in the following paragraphs.

Clearly State the Purpose of the Study. Individuals may not respond or may respond inaccurately to the instrument if they feel that it is being used for purposes other than those stated, or if they have suspicions about the researcher. This problem can be alleviated if a cover letter describing the study, written under the official letterhead of the sponsoring organization, is sent to those who are asked to complete the instrument (see Figure B in Chapter 15 and Figure 16.3 in Chapter 16). Public knowledge that the study is to take place also helps.

Minority group members are expressing a growing conviction that they are being exploited by social service studies. One solution to this complex problem is to demonstrate some exchange value for the study, or to show that there is something of value to the minority group or its members which justifies their participation. This might involve meetings with community members to discuss the purposes of the study and its value to them, hiring minority group members as staff, or other means of illustrating to the community that it is not being taken advantage of.

Keep Sensitive Items to a Minimum. Some individuals may feel that research studies are invading their privacy. The instrument may include personal items in sensitive areas, and respondents (those responding to the instrument) often perceive that they can be identified. Efforts must be made to alleviate these fears by omitting or reducing personal or sensitive questions and by assuring anonymity or confidentiality in a cover letter. On many mailed questionnaires, however, some form of identification is needed in order to do an adequate follow-up.

Avoid Encouragement of Socially Desirable Answers. Some individuals who respond to direct-service questionnaires in social work problem areas are relatively unsophisticated and are not familiar with the types of items or the format of questions in a research instrument. University students or graduates are used to taking tests and filling out answer sheets, but those who are unacquainted with this art are often at a loss as to how to fill out the forms. As a result they may respond in a way they think will not make them appear ignorant or undesirable. This increases the measurement error in the study. The purpose in asking the questions is not to elicit socially desirable answers but to get accurate responses. The instrument designer must word the items sensitively, so that socially desirable answers are not elicited. Assuring the respondent that there are no right or wrong answers is helpful.

Ask Only Relevant Questions. In social work policy studies, the population being studied often is not the general population but a subpopulation of professionals. These individuals have time constraints and may feel that they cannot justify responding to numerous or lengthy items. A solution to this problem is to emphasize the importance of the research question under study and the importance of their responses. In these instances, particularly, the instrument must not be too long or vague. Items should be to the point and should never attempt to gather irrelevant data. Under no circumstances should an item be included if it is not relevant to the study's research problem. Sending professionals an overly general questionnaire would demonstrate that the researcher is unsophisticated in the research process. The intended respondents would be apt to throw the instrument away, considering their time too valuable to be wasted.

Following these suggestions in designing the instrument will eliminate many of the reasons why people do not answer questionnaires. If too many in the sample chosen for a study fail to respond, it will be unavoidably limited. And if the response rate is low, it makes no difference whether the sample was selected in a probabilistic manner (see Chapter 8). Serious problems in generalizing the study's findings can be anticipated.

Careful design and construction of the research instrument, including the wording of the items and their format and layout, can do much to alleviate the problems of generalizability and to achieve external validity.

Internal Validity

The problems of internal validity are basically concerned with reducing and eliminating measurement error within the instrument itself. Ultimately, of course, a poorly constructed research instrument with problems which can produce measurement error will affect the response rate. It is possible, however, to distinguish between the problems of instrument design that affect response rate and those that produce measurement error.

The design procedures suggested in the following paragraphs will help ensure the internal validity of an instrument.

Make Items Clear. Aside from the fact that all items on an instrument must be relevant to a research problem, the most important factor in wording items to avoid measurement error is clarity of meaning. Words must not mean different things to different individuals; this applies to ambiguous or vague words and, particularly, to slang terms or colloquial expressions which may be known to certain groups but not to others. These can be a problem, for example, across different age levels, ethnic groups, and social classes.

Social work researchers may become so close to a study that they cannot perceive a lack of clarity in the items. Items that are perfectly clear to them are not clear at all to others. Consider the following example:

What is your marital status? (Circle one number below.)

1. MARRIED
2. DIVORCED
3. SEPARATED
4. WIDOWED
5. NEVER MARRIED

It is not clear whether the question is asking respondents if they were *ever* married, divorced, separated, or widowed or are *presently* married, divorced, separated, or widowed. The way the original item is stated, a person might in fact fit into the first four of the five categories. This question is more accurately stated: "What is your *present* marital status?"

Attention to simple detail such as this determine the degree to which the results will be subject to measurement error. Other problems of lack of clarity and ambiguity are apt to occur when social workers are studying a population with which they are not very familiar, such as elderly people, a minority group, or professionals. The worker's lack of knowledge about the population can result in the construction of items which will have little or no meaning to respondents.

Use Simple Language. Investigators also may word items using language that is much too complicated for individuals in the study population. The wording must be simple enough for the least educated respondent, while at the same time it does not insult the intelligence of any individual who will be presented with the instrument. For example, an investigator interested in the types of health-care services utilized by individuals might provide a checklist of types of health care with such medical specialties as ophthalmology, otolaryngology, dermatology, terms which may not be familiar to those who seek out the services. A more appropriate list would name specialists such as eye doctor; ear, nose, and throat doctor; and doctor for skin diseases.

Avoid Double-Barreled Questions. Double-barreled questions contain two questions in one. An example is: "Do you feel that the federal government should make abortion or birth control available to women whose households receive welfare?" The problem with this item is that some respondents might agree to tax support for birth control but not for abortion, or for abortion but not birth control. The way the question is worded, the social worker would never know which position the respondents hold. The solution, of course, is to present the two questions separately. A clue to double-barreled questions is the presence of an *or* or *and*. Such items should be reexamined to see whether they have two questions implicit in them.

Know the Knowledge Level of Respondents. Some measuring instruments ask individuals to respond to questions to which they have not given much thought or may not be competent to answer. Public opinion polls are good examples. For example, an unknowledgeable sample of the population might be asked to give opinions about psychotherapeutic techniques or issues in social welfare. In such cases the social worker runs the risk of being misled by the responses.

Keep Questions Short. A way of avoiding many of the problems in item construction is to make the questions short. This may appear to be an overly simple solution to a complex issue, but items that are kept short can quickly get to the point, and respondents will be more apt to read them thoroughly. A major problem with long questions is that they may not be read all the way through. Keeping questions short and to the point helps maintain the relevance, clarity, and precision of items.

Avoid Negative Items. Another way to minimize error by careful instrument construction is to avoid negative items, such as asking whether respondents agree or disagree with the statement, "The federal government should not pay for abortions for welfare mothers." It has been found that the word *not* is often overlooked in these kinds of questions. Obviously, when some people do not read the *not,* the error that is introduced can be considerable. This question should read, "The federal government should pay for abortions for welfare mothers," or "Abortions for welfare mothers should only be paid for by nongovernmental sources."

Pretest the Instrument. The traditional way in which the clarity of questions (and consequent internal validity) are examined is by pretesting the instrument on a sample of individuals who will not be included in the final study. The pretest is not concerned with the answers to the questions per se but rather with the difficulties respondents may have in answering the items. Are the items clear and unambiguous, and do respondents understand what the researcher is trying to say? The pretest should be followed by a debriefing to uncover any difficulties. In many research projects pretesting is performed in a perfunctory manner, when it should be seen as a crucial stage in the development of the research instrument. Pretesting the instrument can give a true indication of how well respondents in the actual study will understand the items.

OPEN- AND CLOSED-ENDED QUESTIONS

Questions or items in an instrument differ not only in form of wording but in the kinds of responses individuals are able to make. Two general categories are open-ended questions, where the response categories are not specified in detail and are left unstructured, and closed-ended or fixed-alternative questions, in which individuals are asked to select one of several response categories provided in the instrument. Each of these methods for responding has particular purposes, as well as certain strengths and disadvantages.

Open-Ended Questions

Open-ended questions are designed to permit free responses to questions and do not suggest any particular structure for replies. They serve various purposes and have some advantages over closed-ended questions. An example is:

> We would like to know some of your feelings about your job as an employee of the Department of Social Services.
>
> 1. What types of duties are most satisfying to you?
> 2. What types of duties are most dissatisfying to you?

The two open-ended questions ask for much information and considerable thought, since they deal with a complex issue which may reflect several dimensions of feeling.

Open-ended questions are often used when all of the possible issues (and responses) involved in a question are not known to the investigator, or when the worker is interested in exploring some of the basic issues and processes in a situation. Such questions are often used in a preliminary phase of a study (Knowledge Level 1, as presented in Chapter 13). If the investigator in the example is unaware of the various sources of satisfaction and dissatisfaction in the department, answers to the two open-ended questions should produce some clues. In addition, fixed-alternative or closed-ended questions often can be constructed out of such responses for use in a later phase of the study. An important function of open-ended questions, in fact, is the development of closed-ended questions.

An additional advantage of open-ended questions is that they put few constraints on individuals' statements of their feelings. A closed-ended question might list various sources of satisfaction and ask individuals to check how they feel about them. Open-ended questions allow respondents to go into detail and to express greater depth in their answers. They are not forced to choose among alternatives developed by the worker but can express their feelings on a matter more precisely. When an interviewer is present to administer the instrument, it is possible to probe responses and to elicit them by using appropriate attending behaviors. These techniques encourage respondents to give fuller and perhaps more thoughtful answers.

There are also some distinct disadvantages in this method which may lead to a lower response rate and decreased external validity. For example, research instruments with many open-ended questions take considerable time to complete, and a long questionnaire often discourages people who would be willing to answer a short one. In addition, some people may be discouraged from replying to an instrument because they are not naturally articulate. Because open-ended questions often require the ability to express oneself in writing, only those with higher levels of education may respond. In a study with an equally well educated population this is not a problem, and it is perhaps even advisable to take advantage of the respondents' expertise by using open-ended questions.

Internal validity, that is, the problem of measurement error, can also be a serious consideration with respect to open-ended questions. Unlike the numbered choices in closed-ended questions, the responses to open-ended questions introduce an element of subjectivity to the data. Suppose that 100 social workers at a department of social services complete a research instrument which asks for one-paragraph responses as to the sources of their satisfaction in the agency. The social worker is left with the problem of taking these individual replies and coding them into meaningful categories. There are several ways this can be done which have to do with the level of measurement. The worker could abstract from answers to the question, "Are you satisfied working in the department?" a list of different sources of satisfaction. The problem is that different individuals may state the same kind of satisfaction in diffrent ways. For example, one respondent may say, "I like the personal autonomy that is provided by this agency," and another might say, "They leave me alone here and the supervisor doesn't bother me very much." It is the responsibility of the investigator to decide whether or not answers such as these fall in the same category. The potential for error in this case is miscoding of responses or lack of rater reliability.

Interrater reliability (see Chapter 10) provides a way of minimizing this kind of error in the coding of open-ended questions by having more than one person (usually called a rater) code the responses. When several persons code the same responses and develop their own sets of categories, it is possible to calculate a measure of interrater relibility. This measure can simply be the percentage of times that the raters agree on the appropriate code.

Whenever open-ended questions are being coded, interrater reliability should be calculated in order to establish the degree of reliability in the coding. If low interrater reliability is found for a particular item, the investigator should try to ascertain the reasons why and, if it is impossible to solve the problem, should seriously consider eliminating the item. It makes no sense to try to use an item that different individuals will interpret in different ways.

Closed-Ended Questions

In closed-ended questions, in which the responses are limited to a number of specified choices, the responses can consist of a number of actions: expressing a simple yes or no, selecting degrees of agreement, or choosing one or more of a list of response categories. Some examples of closed-ended questions are:

1. If the abused child is out of the home, which situation best describes your current plan of action? (Circle one number below.)

   1. RETURN CHILD TO INTACT FAMILY
   2. RETURN CHILD IF ABUSER REMAINS OUT OF HOME
   3. CONTINUE FOSTER CARE
   4. SEEK ADOPTIVE PLACEMENT
   5. NONE OF THE ABOVE
   8. NOT APPLICABLE
   9. DON'T KNOW

2. Did the mother deny having knowledge of sexual abuse? (Circle one number below.)

   1. YES
   2. NO
   8. NOT APPLICABLE
   9. DON'T KNOW

The advantages of fixed-alternative questions are fairly obvious. These kinds of questions can often be presented in such a way as to attract and maintain reliable responses from individuals. The individuals' answers are easily compared from person to person, and there is no need for elaborate and time-consuming coding procedures such as those involved with open-ended questions. Because choices are provided, individuals are less apt to leave certain items blank or to express "don't knows." The problem of missing data can be very serious when analyzing the data of a study, particularly if the response rate is low.

An important advantage of closed-ended questions is that they can elicit data on topics that would be difficult to obtain by other methods. For example, it is often difficult in an open-ended question to get individuals to discuss various aspects of their sexual behavior. It is much easier to answer a series of short, closed-ended questions inquiring whether they agree or disagree with a statement or whether they participate in a certain behavior to a greater or lesser extent. A variable like income level is often difficult to obtain when asked as an open-ended question, such as "What is your present income?" or "How much money did you make last year?" It is much more effective to ask individuals to place themselves in a set of categories containing a range of income levels.

Survey respondents may also be reluctant to answer questions about their age, although whether this is a sensitive topic should be considered in relation to the study's population. As a rule, however, variables like age which are primarily measured at the interval or ratio level, such as years of education, income level, number of children in the home, or number of years married, should be gathered by open-ended questions. An open-ended question of the form:

What was your age at your last birthday? (Place number of years on line below.)

_____

will provide more usable data than a closed-ended question providing a range of responses, such as:

What is your age? (Circle one number below.)

1. 1 TO 5 YEARS
2. 6 TO 10 YEARS
3. 11 TO 15 YEARS
4. 16 TO 20 YEARS
5. MORE THAN 20 YEARS

Only when the items themselves are sensitive and there is reason to believe there will be a low or mistaken response to them should grouping of these kinds of variables into categories be considered.

Closed-ended questions are less suitable for sophisticated computer program packages which make it possible to group data by means of the computer. For statistical analyses which assume interval-level data, the open-ended responses are more accurate and usually produce more valid data. By grouping categories, one is throwing away important data; putting a person who is 10 years old into the same category as somebody who is 6 years old (Category 2 in the above example) is needlessly inexact, for instance.

There are other problems with closed-ended questions which must be considered. Individuals may not feel that the alternatives provided are appropriate to their answers. They also may be tempted to give an opinion on something they have never thought about before. This is a problem with open-ended questions as well, but the temptation to simply circle a fixed alternative is much greater than to answer an open-ended question where it is necessary to write something down. When closed-ended questions are used in interview situations, individuals who do not want to appear ignorant or socially undesirable may say they do not have answers to such questions.

Open- and Closed-Ended Questions Compared

Both open- and closed-ended questions have advantages and disadvantages, and one type of question is not overwhelmingly better than the other. Each type serves purposes which make it most appropriate for certain usages. Open-ended questions are appropriate in exploratory studies when questions are complicated and complex, and especially when all the alternative choices are not known to the social worker. Closed-ended questions are more efficient, especially when the choices are all known or limited in number, and when respondents have clear opinions on specific issues and feelings.

An important consideration in the choice of open- or closed-ended questions is, unfortunately, often more pragmatic. The factors are time and cost. Open-ended questions are time-consuming to code. They introduce error and require more personnel for data processing. Closed-ended questions can be designed so that they do not require extensive coding and can be moved to the data processing stage more quickly, since open-ended questions require an extra step in data processing.

The choice is not necessarily an either/or one. A typical research instrument might include both open- and closed-ended questions and need not consist entirely of one or the other. It is entirely possible to have the responses to a series of closed-ended questions processed and analyzed by a computer and to analyze the responses to open-ended questions on an individual basis.

INSTRUMENT DESIGN

There is a distinctive difference between a list of questions and a research instrument. How an instrument is constructed and what it looks like in an aesthetic sense is very important in determining whether or not those to whom it is administered or sent will respond. Individuals who receive a questionnaire in the mail or in person who answer the door to face an interviewer often consider whether completing the questionnaire or being interviewed is worthwhile or any of their concern. This is particularly so with a mailed instrument, which recipients can easily throw away without a second thought.

An instrument should be designed to provide immediate positive impressions about its importance, difficulty, and length. Each of these factors can be manipulated by careful attention to some important details. To some extent it is possible to indicate the importance of the instrument by how professional its appearance is, and the difficulty can be indicated by how the items are ordered. The length, of course, can be determined by the investigator, either by structuring the questions to save space or by including only those items that are absolutely necessary for studying the research problem.

Appearance

An important factor in maximizing the response rate is how the instrument appears to potential respondents. Unfortunately, dictates of cost often prevail. If the constraints of cost are set aside for the moment, however, a set of guidelines can be established concerning the best way to present the instrument.

The brief description of the design of a research instrument in this section is based on the work of Dillman (1978). While it is one of the more expensive designs to execute, it illustrates the preferred method of constructing instruments.

The instrument is printed as a booklet. It consists of $8\frac{1}{4}'' \times 12\frac{1}{4}''$ sheets of paper folded in the middle and stapled (when more than one sheet is used) to form a booklet, the dimensions of which are $8\frac{1}{4}'' \times 6\frac{1}{8}''$.

No items are used on the front or back pages. These pages are most likely to be seen first by individuals who receive the instrument and are reserved for material that has the specific purpose of stimulating their interest. As a result, the number of pages available for items is always two less than the number of pages available for printing.

The pages are printed in photographically reduced form. Each page is typed on an electric typewriter with a carbon ribbon, using 12 point (Elite) type in $7'' \times 9\frac{1}{2}''$ space on regular $8\frac{1}{2}'' \times 11''$ paper. To fit the booklet format each page is photographically reduced to 70 percent of the original size.

The instrument is reproduced on white or off-white paper by a printing method which appears very close to the original typed copy. A wide variety of printing machines produce quality work, and the preferred method depends on what is available.

This method has several important features which are useful even if one does not choose to follow it to the letter. For example, by photographically reducing the size of the page, the questionnaire appears to be shorter and uses less paper. The booklet format gives the appearance of a professionally produced document, and the use of a cover page maximizes this image. The professional appearance and quality printing tell the recipient that a great deal of thought has gone into the production of the document. The reduction in size and the consequent reduction in number of pages also has the advantage of lower postage costs if a mailed questionnaire is being used.

This method, or minor modifications of it, is the most preferred one. Unfortunately, many instruments are mimeographed and held together with a single staple in the upper-left corner. A particularly poor form consists of 8½″ × 14″ legal-size paper, folded several times to fit into a business envelope. Though it probably saves paper, its larger size also discourages respondents. Mimeographing gives a poor impression, particularly for mailed questionnaires, and it should be used only as a last resort. Under no circumstances should the instrument be typed on a manual typewriter, which will produce uneven type. A mimeographed questionnaire that has been typed on a manual typewriter results in a messy, unprofessional appearance which begs for a low response rate.

In interview studies some of these requirements for the instrument's appearance (see Figure 16.2 in Chapter 16) can be relaxed, but even then it is important for the interviewer to present a professional appearance. A good-looking document contributes greatly to an adequate response rate.

Question Order

How items in an instrument are ordered has generated much thought among social workers. There appears to be some general consensus on certain aspects of question ordering. Somewhat different procedures are recommended for interviewing individuals face to face (see Chapter 16), as opposed to a self-administered questionnaire (see Chapter 15).

It is generally agreed that a self-administered instrument should begin with items that are interesting to the respondent and relevant to the purpose of the study, as stated in either the cover letter accompanying the mailed instrument or the introductory statement delivered by the interviewer. It is not wise to begin by asking for demographic data such as sex, age, or educational level. Often this irritates respondents who are apt to feel that the instrument is an application form of some kind. The appearance of a routine form may well lessen the motivation of individuals to respond. Demographic data should appear at the very end of the instrument (but not on the back page).

Questions should be ordered along a descending gradient of social usefulness (or importance). That is, those items that appear to be the most important to the study's research problem are stated first, and the less important ones are stated last.

Another principle of ordering is that questions should be ordered by content area and by type of question. Respondents should not be forced to switch their train of thought or be faced by one question on one topic and another on a totally different one. Some investigators have believed that forcing individuals to switch from one topic to another would reduce the probability that they would consciously try to structure their answers so that they are all consistent. In fact, however, respondents are probably apt to give more thought to their answers if the instrument has consecutive items on a similar topic. If the items are organized by topic or content area, much less mental effort is required in responding to the instrument than if there is constant switching from one topic to another.

The questions should also be grouped by type of question (closed versus open ended) within the content areas. This means grouping together items that require a simple yes or no answer or those in which responses are asked on a range of agreement to disagreement. This eases the amount of mental effort required in responding to the questions and will signify that there is a logical order to the instrument.

Potentially sensitive or objectionable questions should not appear at the beginning of the instrument but should be positioned later. It would not be wise, for example, to begin an instrument by asking respondents to specify how many times they engaged in sexual intercourse last week.

Considering these constraints on question ordering, it should be apparent that at times certain compromises must be made; that is, it is not always possible to follow all of these principles all of the time. For example, it may not be possible to sort the questions by content area and then sort them again by type of question in such a way as to give the appearance of a well-thought-out instrument. The researcher must always try to strike a satisfactory balance.

Typographical Format

Typographical format is concerned with how the questions are laid out on the pages. This can be an important effort in producing a professional instrument which will encourage a high response rate.

The instrument must be constructed so that respondents do not skip over items or sections. Various levels of spacing can help keep sections of an item separate but related to one another.

Questions that start on one page and overlap onto another should be avoided if possible. Items in a series, particularly, should not be broken up. Confusion and mistakes often result when the parts of questions or questions and responses are not kept together. Nevertheless, large blank spaces on the bottom of pages should be avoided where possible for the sake of appearance.

Typographical considerations in the design of the instrument also can facilitate data processing procedures by making answers easier to locate and to score. Frequently little thought is given to how an instrument is to be processed once the items have been answered. Careful design of the instrument and planning with respect to data processing can save much time, energy, and money.

Question and Response Presentation

This section will discuss some of the problems in question and response format and suggest ways of solving them. Figure 12.1 shows both unacceptable and acceptable ways of asking five typical items in a survey instrument.

One of the most common problems in constructing items in a questionnaire reflects the mistaken assumption that people will know how to complete the instrument. Often detailed directions on how to answer the items are needed. Procedures that a social worker takes for granted may be mysteries to respondents (see Items 1-5 in Section A in Figure 12.1). This is not a serious problem in face-to-face interviews (Chapter 16), where explanations can be given verbally. But in a mailed questionnaire, if the respondents do not understand how to answer the items, serious error can be introduced. For example, in a question where the appropriate answer (and only one answer) is to be circled, unless this is explicitly stated in the instructions, respondents may circle more than one. Thus, for each item directions such as "Circle one number below" must be given (see Items 1-5 in Section B in Figure 12.1).

We suggest that answer categories should not appear on the same line as the question but rather should be placed on the line below. All too many research instruments squeeze questions onto a page with very little room between them and between the items and answers categories. In addition to a cluttered appearance, this increases the likelihood that respondents will skip over items and make mistakes in answering.

There are several ways answers can be selected. Some methods

FIGURE 12.1

Examples of Unacceptable and Acceptable Survey Instrument Items

A. UNACCEPTABLE ITEM FORMS

1. Sex: M_____ F_____

2. Number of children at home
   0–1 _____ 2–3 _____ 4–5 _____ 6 or more _____

3. Do you own your own home? Y _____ N _____

4. Religious preference:
   Protestant _____
   Catholic _____
   Jewish _____

5. Health: Good _____ Fair _____ Poor _____

B. ACCEPTABLE ITEM FORMS

1. What is your sex? (Circle one number below.)
   0. MALE
   1. FEMALE

2. How many of your children live at home with you? (Place number on line below.)
   _____

3. Do you own your own home? (Circle one number below.)
   0. NO
   1. YES
   8. NOT APPLICABLE
   9. DON'T KNOW

4. What is your religious preference? (Circle one number below.)
   1. PROTESTANT
   2. CATHOLIC
   3. JEWISH
   4. NONE
   5. OTHER (SPECIFY) _____

5. How would you describe your physical health? (Circle one number below.)
   1. POOR
   2. FAIR
   3. GOOD

call for blank lines, boxes, or brackets to be checked, but a better technique is to number the categories on the left and have the respondent circle the appropriate number. This technique, known as precoding, aids in the processing of the data. A number is preassigned to an alternative or response, and this number represents the response when it is coded for statistical analysis. Having respondents circle the number when they answer the question eliminates an additional step in data processing and another potential source of error. Instructions to circle the appropriate number should be included in the item (see Section B in Figure 12.1).

The number for each response should be placed at the left of the answer rather than the right or anywhere else because different responses may have different lengths (compare Item 4 in Section A with Item 4 in Section B in Figure 12.1). Having numbers at different places far away from the beginning of the response category can increase the chance of error. We prefer that response categories be typed in uppercase (all capital letters) with questions in lowercase letters. Because this sets off the items from the answers and clarifies the response categories, it aids respondents in answering the items correctly and completely.

As an aid to both respondents and coders, it is helpful if certain numbers are always used for certain responses. For example, if there are numerous questions asking for yes or no responses, the same value should be used for all the yes answers and another value for all the no answers. Thus, we might assign the value of 0 for no and 1 for yes and maintain this consistently throughout the instrument. We might also decide on a single value to be used for the "missing data" category, so that all "don't know," "no opinion," or "not applicable" answers would have the same value. This is an important aid in the later analysis of the data.

If at all possible, items should be arranged in vertical order with response categories in a vertical line, starting with Choice 1, rather than side by side. The questions also should be placed one under the other, for psychological reasons and to reduce measurement error. If there are several choices of response categories on the same line, respondents may circle the wrong number and skip certain choices inadvertently. Arranging questions vertically rather than side by side also makes the appearance less cluttered and helps respondents feel they are making progress on the questionnaire.

Edge Coding

Some survey instruments use a technique called edge coding for responses. A series of blanks is added on the right side of the instrument, directly to the right of the final response category (see Figure 12.2). The purpose of these lines is to aid in the processing of the data recorded on the instrument. Respondents are instructed not to write on these lines; rather, the social worker transfers the response number that has been circled for each question over to the line allocated for that question.

This usually simple procedure serves the function of eliminating the preparation of coding sheets, onto which the responses are transferred after being converted into numbers. The coding sheets are then keypunched onto computer cards. When the edge coding procedure is used, the instrument itself is the coding sheet. The keypunch operator simply punches in the values that are coded along the right side of the page.

While the inclusion of edge coding lines can give a somewhat sloppy appearance to the instrument, these lines do not have to be very obtrusive. Considering the savings of time and effort they provide, the possible disadvantage is minimal.

As a guide to the keypuncher, the column numbers on the computer data card in which the values will be keypunched should be added on some of the edge coding lines (as with 60 and 70 in Figure 12.2 and 1 and 10 in Figure 12.3). These column numbers need not be written in under every line but should appear at regular intervals, for example, every tenth column number. Keypunch operators often need to check every now and then to be sure they are on the proper column. If the operator misses just one column, every one thereafter will contain the wrong data.

Items in a Series

Many questionnaires use scales which ask individuals to respond to a series of questions. Respondents may be asked, for example, to choose whether they strongly agree, disagree, or strongly disagree on several items. If the guidelines given above for question and response presentation were all followed, this type of scale would be apt to take up a large amount of space, as well as being needlessly repetitive. There are, however, special ways to treat this type of question. Figure 12.2 illustrates how a series of items can be handled in a smaller amount of space and still appear uncluttered and be easy to follow.

In this example of a needs assessment within a specific community, it was decided that rather than asking 12 individual items regarding the severity of a problem in a community, the items would be set up in a single multi-item format. First there is an opening statement briefly describing the purpose of the questionnaire and providing directions

FIGURE 12.2
Survey Questionnaire with Edge Coding

This part of the survey is to learn more about your perceptions of the problems in the community. Listed below are a number of problems some residents of Northside have reported having. Please circle the number which represents how much of a problem they have been to you within the last year:

1. NO PROBLEM (or not applicable to you)

2. MODERATE PROBLEM

3. SEVERE PROBLEM

How Much of a Problem?

Questions	NO PROBLEM	MODERATE PROBLEM	SEVERE PROBLEM	
1. Finding the product I need ..	1	2	3	
2. Impolite salespeople	1	2	3	60
3. Finding clean stores	1	2	3	____
4. Prices are too high	1	2	3	____
5. Not enough Spanish-speaking salespeople	1	2	3	____
6. Public transportation	1	2	3	____
7. Getting credit	1	2	3	____
8. Lack of certain types of stores in Northside	1	2	3	____
9. Lack of an employment assistance program	1	2	3	____
10. Finding a city park which is secure	1	2	3	____
11. Finding a good school	1	2	3	____
12. Finding a good house	1	2	3	70

Source: Mindel (1981).

for answering the series of questions. Note that respondents are requested to circle the number which represents how they feel, and the three choices are given with their appropriate code numbers (1, 2, or 3). The questions are then listed consecutively on the left side of the page. The code numbers appear in columns, on the right of the 12 statements, and at the far right are the edge coding lines previously described.

FIGURE 12.3
Use of Single Format for Dual Responses

Into which occupational category do your father and mother presently fall? (Circle one number in each column.)

| | *Relationship* | | |
Occupational Category	Father	Mother	
PROFESSIONAL	1	1	——1——
MANAGER	2	2	——
SALES WORKER	3	3	——
CLERICAL WORKER	4	4	——
CRAFTSPERSON	5	5	——
OPERATIVE	6	6	——
LABORER	7	7	——
FARMER	8	8	——
SERVICE	9	9	——
UNEMPLOYED	10	10	——10——
DON'T KNOW	88	88	——
DECEASED (NOT APPLICABLE)	99	99	——
OTHER (SPECIFY)————————	13	13	——

Source: Mindel (1981).

Other techniques can be used when the same data are needed about a number of different people. It is possible to collapse these questions into a single matrix, as in Figure 12.3. The occupational categories of respondents' fathers and mothers are requested. Rather than repeating the list of occupational categories, it is given once and in separate columns there are series of numbers for father and for mother. It is important that the code numbers appear in the columns and that clear instructions be given to circle one number in each column.

Rank Ordering

An alternative way of gathering data concerning issues like those described in Figure 12.2 is the use of rank ordering. For example, respondents might be asked to consider the 12 problems listed and rank order them in terms of the severity the problem has for them.

We strongly suggest that you do *not* use this form of question, for several reasons. It is very difficult to juggle more than three or four different concepts in one's head at once for rank-ordering purposes. When the list consists of 12 or more of these problems (as in Figure 12.2), it is virtually impossible to consider the severity of so many problems adequately. In addition, rank ordering probably takes much more time than if each item is considered on an individual basis. And, for data analyses purposes, rank ordering restricts the type of analyses that can be carried out with the question. When a series of questions is used, the social worker can rank order the responses as well as carry out other analyses. By calculating the mean score for each of the 12 items listed in Figure 12.2 and then rank ordering these means, for example, the same result can be achieved as if individuals were asked to rank order the questions themselves. In addition, using a series of questions, it is possible to create an index or scale and to calculate its reliability, which could not be done if rank orders were used.

Transition Statements

Transition statements are used for several purposes, such as to lend an air of informality to the instrument and to reduce possible monotony. This type of statement attempts to converse and to engage respondents in the task. An example is:

> In this section of our survey we would like to develop a sort of thumbnail sketch of your everyday life, the things you do, the things that worry or concern you, and the things that make you happy.

Transition statements are also used when the instrument changes direction or introduces a new line of questioning. These statements in a sense tell people that they will be changing directions and forewarn them not to be surprised when they get to the next section. An example is:

> Now I would like to ask you a few questions concerning recreational activities.

A third type of transition statement should occur toward the very end of the questionnaire just before asking for the demographic data. This section should be introduced with a statement something like:

> Finally, we would like to ask you a few questions about yourself for statistical purposes.

This kind of statement should indicate that the end of the instrument is near.

While transition statements are important, they can be overdone. It is best to combine all three purposes into a single statement, if possible. Overly long statements and those that may inadvertently bias the response by pressuring the respondent toward a certain kind of answer should be avoided, however. Other problems with transition statements can be their tone, which should not be so didactic it alienates people and/or makes them appear foolish.

PRETESTING THE INSTRUMENT

Before a research instrument is submitted to the sample or population, it should be pretested to be sure that other individuals who are asked to answer the items understand them and have a favorable impression of the appearance and utility of the instrument. As noted earlier in this chapter, pretesting is a procedure which, unfortunately, most investigators do not follow very thoroughly. It often is done as an afterthought, as something which must be done because of the "research tradition." Often it does not fulfill the real purposes of a pretest, which, according to Dillman (1978), should provide answers to eight specific questions. These are:

1. Is each item measuring what it is intended to measure?
2. Are all the words understood?
3. Are questions interpreted similarly by all individuals?
4. Does each closed-ended question have a response category that applies to each person?
5. Does the questionnaire create a positive impression, one that motivates people to answer it?
6. Can the questions be answered correctly?
7. Are some items missed? Do some items elicit uninterpretable answers?
8. Does any aspect of the instrument suggest bias on the part of the investigator?

Some of these questions can be answered by mailing out the questionnaire to a sample of individuals who are similar to the study's sample or population. However, what the social worker is really concerned with is feedback from these individuals, and this kind of feedback can best be gathered by direct interaction with them.

There are essentially three types of groups that are best used in the pretest of a research instrument: (1) fellow colleagues; (2) the potential users of the data; and (3) individuals drawn from the population to be surveyed. Each of these groups can provide important feedback to the designer of the instrument which the others cannot.

Colleagues, whether they be fellow students, instructors, or colleagues at work, have specialized experience and understand the study's purpose and the type of hypothesis being tested. Potential users of the data include agency personnel, policymakers, clients, and professionals, among others. They can indicate whether any of the items are irrelevant to their purposes or reveal lack of knowledge on the investigator's part.

Feedback is also needed from those who might be the focus of the study to determine whether such individuals understand the questions and are positively impressed with the instrument. These people will provide information as to the difficulty of the items and whether they provide the right answer categories, and so on. There are several ways in which this feedback might be gathered, but it is probably best to administer the instrument individually or in groups and to follow with a debriefing session. This gives those who take the pretest an opportunity to discuss with the worker what they did and did not like about the instrument, what kinds of problems they had, and how they generally felt about the experience.

SUMMARY

The design and construction of measuring instruments is not something that should be or could be done carelessly or on the spur of the moment. These instruments require extensive planning, writing, and rewriting. The instrument construction process cannot be rushed, and the investigator must be continually amenable to the possibility of further revision. The development of an adequate measuring instrument is crucial to the ultimate goal of the study, which is to measure and thus to understand human behavior or attitudes. Designing an instrument that maximizes the response rate and minimizes measurement error can only be done by careful attention to the details considered in this chapter, which may seem to be minor but which in the long run are very important considerations.

Tony Tripodi

13. RESEARCH DESIGNS

Research designs are the plans, structures, and strategies of investigations which seek to obtain answers to various research questions (Kerlinger, 1973). They refer to the overall scheme of the research process, from problem identification, definition, and specification to evaluation and dissemination of findings. The purpose of research designs is to provide a set of systematic procedures for producing data pertaining to the development, modification, or expansion of knowledge (Finestone & Kahn 1975).

There are four levels of social work knowledge objectives, along with criteria for determining whether the level of knowledge sought by a specific research question is being obtained. Each of the specific knowledge objectives requires distinct research procedures. The 10 research designs presented do not exhaust the possibilities, but they do illustrate the major research approaches to the building of knowledge: case study designs for refining general concepts and formulating more specific hypotheses; descriptive survey designs for the provision of quantitative descriptions; comparative designs for defining empirical associations between variables; and experimental and quasi-experimental designs for generating cause-effect knowledge (Campbell & Stanley, 1963).

KNOWLEDGE OBJECTIVES

Social work research objectives can be specified on a continuum of knowledge objectives that has four distinct levels (Tripodi, 1974). These levels are:

Level	Knowledge Objective
1	Hypothetical-developmental
2	Quantitative-descriptive
3	Associational
4	Cause-effect

Although social workers may pursue one or more of these knowledge objectives in a particular study, generally not more than two are sought simultaneously.

Level 1: Hypothetical-Developmental Knowledge

The lowest level of knowledge is hypothetical-developmental. On this level, a worker may seek to describe social phenomena in a qualitative manner for the purpose of developing general concepts into more specific measurable variables or generating more specific research questions or hypotheses. As presented in Chapters 2, 3, 4, and 5, concepts are verbal labels for organizing and succinctly summarizing experiences. For example, social workers who work with individuals, families, and small groups use concepts such as social interaction, resistance, denial, reinforcement, and supportive treatment. Social workers who work with communities use concepts such as power structure, alienation, conflict resolution, and bureaucracy.

Concepts are the basic building blocks of communication. Their specification is necessary for the development of hypotheses and higher levels of knowledge. Concepts are definable in two ways: nominally or operationally. A nominal definition of a concept entails a verbal description, such as those available in a dictionary. An operational definition of a concept delineates all the specific procedures that are required for describing a particular concept so that it can be measured. For example, the variable called anxiety can be defined nominally as "an abnormal and overwhelming sense of apprehension and fear often marked by physiological signs (as sweating, tension, and increased pulse), by doubt concerning the reality and nature of the threat, and by self-doubt about one's capacity to cope with it." One operational definition of this variable may be the extent to which individuals agree with a predetermined series of statements reflecting their symptoms of anxiety (Spielberger, Gorsuch, & Lushene, 1970). Although operational definitions are usually arbitrary, they serve the function of translating global concepts into more specific measurable variables.

In addition to developing concepts and variables, this level of knowledge also seeks to formulate meaningful questions and generate testable hypotheses. Without meaningful questions and adequate hypotheses, the quest for higher levels of knowledge (Levels 2, 3, and 4) cannot be satisfied. The purpose of research questions is to seek simple facts. Research questions such as the following may be posed in a Level 1 study:

> What is the proportion of welfare recipients who are able to work?
>
> How many residents in a specific neighborhood are interested in participating in community organizations?
>
> Do female social work administrators earn less money than male social work administrators?

The function of hypotheses is to predict relationships between two variables. For example, we could hypothesize that there is a high positive relationship between the two variables of educational level and participation in community organizations. In other words, persons who have more years of formal education are more likely to participate in community organizations than those who have fewer years of formal education.

In the preceding hypothesis, there is a predicted relationship between the two variables of educational level (independent variable) and participation in community organizations (dependent variable). If there is simply a prediction about the existence of a relationship, the hypothesis may be regarded as associational. However, if we predict that changes in an independent variable cause changes in a dependent variable, the hypothesis is a prediction of a cause-effect relationship.

For example, we may hypothesize that an overweight client will lose a significant amount of weight as a result of a specific social work treatment method such as behavior modification. Hence, it is predicted that the use of behavior modification techniques (independent variable) will result in the client's weight reduction (dependent variable). Hypotheses are neither correct nor incorrect. Rather, hypotheses are hypothetical queries that await verification. Depending on the empirical evidence obtained in the research process, they may be refuted or verified.

Level 2: Quantitative-Descriptive Knowledge

Quantitative-descriptive knowledge is quantitative data that answer simple, descriptive questions. The answers to quantitative-descriptive questions are facts that state the existence of empirical relationships between two variables. They provide data about frequency counts and proportions within one variable, as identified by another variable.

For example, in a particular social work agency, it may be observed that 20 percent of the male social workers and 50 percent of the female social workers are active members in the National Association of Social Workers. The social workers' gender is the variable within which the frequency counts are tabulated. Membership activity (active or not active) is the variable utilized for identifying whether males and females should be counted.

Quantitative-descriptive knowledge may be specific to a particular community, neighborhood, organization, group, family, or client, or it may be generalizable. "There are more female social workers than male social workers in a specific social agency" is a simple fact. It is not generalizable, as there may or may not be more female social workers in other social agencies. A fact that contains a greater degree of generalizability would be: "There are more female social workers than male social workers in family service agencies." When these quantified observations can be generalized to other situations (such as agencies or communities), they are regarded as low-order empirical generalizations. Some examples of low-order empirical generalizations are:

> The largest proportion of patients in mental hospitals are schizophrenic.
>
> There are more male juvenile offenders than female juvenile offenders.
>
> Of the clients seen by social workers, 80 percent receive fewer than five treatment interviews.

Generalizable facts are thus low-order empirical generalizations. These hypotheses simply indicate or verify the presence of variables. Higher order empirical generalizations are indicative of higher levels of knowledge: verified associational and cause-effect hypotheses that are generalizable. These hypotheses seek to answer the "whys" of lower order empirical generalizations.

Level 3: Associational Knowledge

Associational knowledge involves empirical data which indicate a relationship between two variables. The empirical data are summarized by statistical techniques which show the degree of the relationship. Associational knowledge may also be expressed in terms of the direction of the relationship. There is a positive relationship when increases in the independent variable are associated with increases in the dependent variable. Furthermore, decreases in the dependent variable would also correspond to decreases in the independent variable. Conversely, a negative relationship is obtained when increases in the independent variable are associated with decreases in the dependent variable, and decreases in the independent variable are associated with increases in the dependent variable (Kolevzon, 1981; Royer, 1981).

For example, a negative relationship between the two variables of anxiety and learning ability signifies that increased anxiety is associated with decreased learning ability. Correspondingly, increased learning is associated with decreased anxiety. In contrast, a positive relationship signifies that increased anxiety is associated with increased learning (Leedy, 1980, 1981).

Like quantitative-descriptive and cause-effect knowledge, associational knowledge may be specific to a particular situation, or it may be generalizable to other circumstances. Associations that are generalizable are empirical generalizations of higher order (i.e., they include more information) than empirical generalizations of quantitative descriptions. They are at a lower knowledge level than generalizable cause-effect knowledge. While associations are necessary for cause-effect knowledge, they are not sufficient. Two variables that are associated are not necessarily causally related. In other words, changes in one variable do not necessarily lead to, produce, or cause changes in another variable. Some examples of associational statements are:

> Therapeutic progress varies as a function of therapist characteristics such as warmth, empathy, adequacy of adjustment, and experience.

> The larger, the more complex, and the more heterogeneous the society, the greater the number of organizations and associations that exist within it.

> The degree of congruence between the worker and the client in their definitions of the client's situation has been found to be strongly associated with continuance in all studies that have examined this factor.

Level 4: Cause-Effect Knowledge

Cause-effect knowledge is the highest level of knowledge that can be directly produced by means of social work research. This knowledge contributes to the development, refutation, and expansion of theories about social work phenomena. It can be specific or generalizable.

Cause-effect knowledge specifies that changes in the independent (or causal) variable are directly responsible for producing changes in the dependent variable. For example, it may be demonstrated within a psychiatric hospital that reduced anxiety in patients is traceable to the administration of certain drugs. If the drugs are shown to have similar effects on patients in other representative psychiatric hospitals, then the knowledge obtained from the study would have a greater degree of generalizability.

Cause-effect knowledge also contains associational, quantitative-descriptive, and hypothetical-developmental knowledge. Such knowledge is based on a verification of an initial hypothesis (hypothetical-developmental). Empirical regularities (quantitative-descriptive) within variables need to be described prior to the production of empirical relationships (associational), which, in turn, are required for cause-effect knowledge.

A special kind of cause-effect knowledge can be inferred when there is no relationship between two variables. For example, it may be reported that for community organizers there is virtually no relationship between the two variables of years of experience in developing neighborhood centers and clarity in the presentation of community issues to a public forum (Kolevzon, 1981). From this statement, it could also be inferred that there is no causal relationship between the two variables of years of experience and clarity in the presentation of community issues to a public forum. Some examples of cause-effect statements are:

> Psychotherapy may cause people to become better or worse adjusted than comparable people who do not receive such treatment.

> When a response is followed by punishment, the frequency or probability of recurrence decreases—where punishment is any event that runs counter to the existing set of motives, e.g., pain. Again, when punishment is withdrawn, the rate tends to recover.

> When caught in cross-pressures between the norms of different groups of which an individual simultaneously is a member, the individual will suffer some emotional strain and will move to reduce or eliminate it by resolving the conflict in the direction of the strongest felt group ties.

CRITERIA FOR PRODUCING RESEARCH KNOWLEDGE

For each of the above four research knowledge objectives, there are specific criteria that must be met to produce evidence that the desired knowledge objective is attained. These criteria include:

Level	Criteria
1	Conceptual translatability, hypothesis researchability
2	Measurement accuracy, representative sampling
3	Empirical relationships, replications
4	Time order, internal and external validity

A continuum of criteria exists in relation to each knowledge objective. That is, the more criteria that are satisfied, the higher the level of knowledge obtained.

Level 1: Conceptual Translatability and Hypothesis Researchability

Useful concepts, hypotheses, and questions are attained when the criteria of conceptual translatability and hypothesis researchability are satisfied. Conceptual translatability refers to the clarity, potential generalizability, and operationalization of concepts. Concepts must be clearly communicated and understood in terms of concise and specific nominal definitions. They must also have the potential of being generalized to a variety of social work practice situations. Concepts such as neighborhood, community, and client relationship can be defined precisely, and they can be used in a variety of social work practice settings in different states, countries, and nations. Operationalization is a delineation of the procedures involved in defining concepts so that they can be transformed into specific measurable variables. If different social workers independently use the same operational definitions, they should produce the same results. Hence, operationalization increases communication and sets the foundation for obtaining quantitative measurement.

Hypothesis researchability is the extent to which questions and hypotheses can be adequately investigated. Researchability entails the potential for research investigations that can be conducted for providing answers to research questions and producing evidence for the affirmation or refutation of hypotheses. Hypotheses are researchable when five conditions are met (Tripodi, 1974). They are:

1. The statement of relationship between two or more concepts is clearly articulated.
2. The concepts are operationally definable, and there are available procedures and techniques that can be used to measure them.

3. The concepts are clearly distinct and nonoverlapping.
4. The statement of relationship is specific in reference to population, time, and place.
5. The hypothesized phenomenon can be studied.

For example, the following hypothesis is researchable: "For low-income, second-generation, Italian females between the ages of 14 and 16 who live in urban areas of the United States of America in August 1985, there is a negative relationship between the two variables of knowledge of social service agencies and academic performance in public schools." The hypothesis is testable because the statement of relationship between the two variables is clearly stated, and it is specific in terms of population, time, and place. The concepts of knowledge of social service agencies and academic performance can also be operationally defined, and they are distinct. In addition, there is a sizable population that can be studied in urban areas, such as New York, where research observations pertaining to the concepts could be made.

Level 2: Measurement Accuracy and Representative Sampling

Measurement accuracy refers to the accuracy of processing data and to the validity and reliability of the measures used for producing quantitative descriptions. A measurement is reliable when it is relatively free from error and produces consistent results on repeated applications. Two common indicators of reliability are test-retest reliability and interrater reliability (I. Epstein & Tripodi, 1977). Test-retest reliability indicates the degree of consistency between responses obtained on the same measure over two periods of time. Interrater reliability indicates the extent to which two or more raters (observers) independently agree in their observations for the values of a variable or variables at a single point in time (Bostwick & Kyte, 1981).

Validity of measurement can be assessed in at least two ways: content validity, and predictive validity. Content validity refers to the extent to which the content of a measurement device is directly relevant to the concept being measured. If a measurement device predicts other phenomena that are expected to be associated with the concept being measured, there is evidence of predictive validity. In essence, then, validity refers to the extent to which instruments are measuring what they are intended to measure (Hudson, 1981).

For example, if an attitude questionnaire were used to measure the concept of community involvement of residents, the content validity of the questions (items) would refer to whether the questions measure what we generally mean by the term *community involvement*. An item such as "I feel very much a part of the community in which I live" would have high content validity. An item such as "I like to work near to where I live" would not. To measure predictive validity, we would see how these measures of attitudinal involvement in the community are associated with actual attendance at city council meetings, community activities, and the like.

Representative sampling is a criterion that is used when one is interested in generalizing quantitative descriptions. It involves the use of sampling procedures to provide samples from the study population that have characteristics similar to those of the population to which the results of a sample would be generalized. Probability sampling procedures that include simple random sampling are generally sufficient for obtaining random samples. If a sample is not representative, quantitative descriptions produced from the sample cannot be generalized to the larger population from which it was drawn.

For example, a population of clients from several social agencies in a community may be comprised of 50 percent black Americans and 50 percent white Americans. We could not generalize to that population on the basis of a sample of only white Americans. To be representative, the sample must also be comprised of approximately 50 percent black Americans and 50 percent white Americans.

Level 3: Empirical Relationships and Replications

There is evidence of an empirical relationship between two variables when one or more of the following conditions is met:

1. There is a statistically significant difference between the mean differences of the distributions of one variable with respect to another.
2. There is a correlation coefficient that is statistically significant.
3. There is a high correlation coefficient of sufficient magnitude to result in a relatively high degree of predictability.

For example, it is possible to provide evidence of an empirical association between the two variables of client's age and number of casework interviews completed by testing for and showing that the average number of interviews completed for older clients is significantly greater than the average number of interviews completed for younger clients. An alternative is to test for the statistical significance of the association between the two variables.

Associational knowledge can be generalized by providing evidence of representative sampling, as is done for quantitative-descriptive knowledge. Generalization can also be enhanced by replications, or repeated research studies with consistent results. The results of research studies that are repeated with different samples are replicated when certain conditions exist. These conditions are:

1. The associations between the independent and dependent variables are of approximately the same magnitude.
2. The associations between the independent and dependent variables are in the same direction (i.e., either positive or negative relationships).
3. The associations between the independent and dependent variabes provide similar levels of statistical significance.

Level 4: Time Order, Internal and External Validity

To show cause-effect knowledge between two variables requires more knowledge than that provided on the associational level. First, it should be demonstrated that changes in the independent variable occur earlier in time than changes in the dependent variable. If we are attempting to show that the activities of a community organizer result in the formation of a community organization, we should document the time-order relationship of activities which occur *prior* to the formation of a community organization.

Second, information should be provided about procedures, assumptions, and empirical evidence which show that potentially influential internal and external validity factors are controlled in the particular research investigation. Internal validity indicates the extent to which the observed changes in a dependent variable are not traceable to variables other than the independent variable. The degree of internal validity is directly proportional to the number of internal validity factors that are controlled, or shown to be noninfluential with respect to changes in the dependent variable. There are eight general sets of variables which are potential threats to internal validity (Campbell & Stanley, 1963). They are:

1. *History.* Events in addition to the independent variable which affect or occur between measurements, reflecting change of the dependent variable.
2. *Maturation.* Variables which indicate physical states occurring within research participants over time, such as fatigue, ennui, developmental growth, hunger, or aging.
3. *Initial measurement effects.* Responses of a second administration of an instrument (such as a test or questionnaire) that may be affected by responses to the first administration.
4. *Instrumentation.* Lack of standardized procedures in the process of obtaining measurements.

5. *Statistical regression.* The tendency of research groups selected on the basis of extreme measurement scores to regress to more average scores on subsequent measurements, irrespective of the influence of the independent variable.
6. *Selection biases.* The differential selection of research participants for two or more comparison groups.
7. *Experimental mortality.* The differential loss of research participants resulting in differences among comparison groups.
8. *Interaction effects.* The combined effects of any of the above factors, such as selection-maturation interaction.

Procedures for controlling internal validity factors include such notions as control groups, random assignment, and manipulation of the independent variable. The use of these procedures is discussed in the section on research designs below.

Generalizability can be achieved by the use of representative sampling procedures and experimental replications, as well as by selected experimental procedures for controlling external validity factors that might reduce the extent to which generalizations can be made. There are four of these external validity factors.

First, the interaction between initial measurement and the independent variable may not be generalizable to other populations. This factor is controlled for by using experiments that do not have initial measurements prior to the administration of the independent variable.

Second, there may be an interaction between selection biases and the independent variable. This is controlled for by replications of the independent variable with consistent results on different subpopulations.

Third, there may be reactive effects of experimental arrangements, such as the belief of participants that exposure to the independent variable will result in changes. This "placebo effect" can be minimized by providing a comparison group that receives the attention given by persons administering the independent variable but not its contents. For example, in assessing the effectiveness of a drug, an experimental group would receive the drug, while a comparison group would receive a relatively inert substance such as a sugar pill (or placebo).

Fourth, there may be multiple-treatment interference. This refers to the possibility that research participants may be receiving more than one independent variable from sources other than the researcher. For example, in assessing the effectiveness of a casework intervention as an independent variable, we would want to be sure that research participants have not received other casework interventions that would interact with the intervention being studied. This external validity threat can be minimized by studying participants who indicate they have not had prior treatment, by showing that experimental and control groups have an identical small amount of other treatment, and by replications with consistent results.

The Knowledge Objective Criteria Continuum

The continuum of criteria which must be met to produce evidence that each knowledge objective is being obtained results in cumulative requirements (see Table 13.1). Conceptual translatability and hypothesis researchability are necessary for the achievement of hypothetical-developmental knowledge (i.e., Level 1). Each of the three succeeding levels (2, 3, and 4) must also have Level 1 knowledge. Quantitative-descriptive knowledge, Level 2, requires evidence of measurement accuracy and representative sampling for empirical generality; that is also

TABLE 13.1

Continuum of Criteria Necessary for Obtaining Knowledge Objectives

Level	Knowledge Objective	Criteria for Meeting Objectives
1.	Hypothetical-developmental	1a. Conceptual translatability 1b. Hypothesis researchability
2.	Quantitative-descriptive	1a. Conceptual translatability 1b. Hypothesis researchability 2a. Measurement accuracy 2b. Representative sampling
3.	Associational	1a. Conceptual translatability 1b. Hypothesis researchability 2a. Measurement accuracy 2b. Representative sampling 3a. Empirical relationships 3b. Replications
4.	Cause-effect	1a. Conceptual translatability 1b. Hypothesis researchability 2a. Measurement accuracy 2b. Representative sampling 3a. Empirical relationships 3b. Replications 4a. Time order 4b. Internal and external validity

Source: Tripodi (1981).

required for Levels 3 and 4. Another criterion for associational knowledge, Level 3, is evidence of an empirical relationship. Cause-effect knowledge demands that all the criteria for Levels 1, 2, and 3 be satisfied, in addition to the provision of procedures for establishing the time order of independent and dependent variables and the control of internal and external validity factors.

RESEARCH DESIGNS

Research designs are logical strategies for planning research procedures and providing evidence for the development of knowledge. The logic of research design can be represented by the following three steps:

1. Research objectives are identified in terms of levels of desired knowledge.
2. Criteria that are necessary for establishing knowledge are specified.
3. Research designs are chosen that include procedures for meeting the criteria for establishing the particular level of knowledge.

Just as there is a continuum of knowledge objectives and a set of related criteria, there can also be said to be a continuum of research designs. Different research designs can be classified and identified in terms of their major purposes in providing evidence for the production of different levels of knowledge. There are designs for producing hypothetical-developmental, quantitative-descriptive, associational, and cause-effect knowledge, and research designs for higher levels of knowledge require more procedures and are devised to obtain more empirical data than research designs for lower knowledge levels.

A given research study may have more than one objective and may combine one or more research designs to meet those objectives. Correspondingly, a design whose major purpose is for the production of one level of knowledge may also provide the context for developing a different level of knowledge. For example, a study with the major function of verifying a cause-effect hypothesis might also lead to the development of hypotheses for future research, or, a case study with the primary task of developing concepts might also be used to verify hypotheses.

The major types of research designs which can be used to produce evidence to demonstrate that knowledge objectives are being obtained are identified in Table 13.2. The structure of these research designs will be represented in this chapter by the following symbols:

X = Administration of the independent variable
O = Observation or measurement of the dependent variable
R = Random assignment to a group
— — — = No random assignment to a group

TABLE 13.2
Knowledge Objectives and Appropriate Research Designs

Level	Knowledge Objective	Research Designs
1.	Hypothetical-developmental	1a. Cross-sectional case study
		1b. Longitudinal case study
2.	Quantitative-descriptive	2a. Cross-sectional survey
		2b. Replicated cross-sectional survey
3.	Associational	3a. One-group pretest-posttest
		3b. Static group comparison
4.	Cause-effect	4a. Classical experimental
		4b. Posttest-only control group
		4c. Nonequivalent comparison group
		4d. Interrupted time series

Source: Tripodi (1981).

Level 1: Hypothetical-Developmental Designs

Design 1a: Cross-Sectional Case Study

$$\boxed{X \; O}$$

The basic strategy of this design is to thoroughly describe a single unit during a *specific* period in time. A unit might include an individual, case, family, group, social agency, or community, for example. It is presumed that a thorough description of a unit would enable a social worker to develop insights, ideas, questions, and hypotheses for further study. Hence, the design entails a description of multiple experiences based on a variety of data.

Any type of research method can be used in the cross-sectional case study. However, data are typically obtained through observations (see Chapters 17 and 18) in interviews (see Chapter 16) with key informants (i.e., those judged to be knowledgeable about the unit being studied), and from available documents (see Chapter 19). The principal assumption is that one who is personally involved and is immersed in a variety of data will be able to induce hypotheses. The social worker must be skilled in deriving abstract, qualitative generalizations from direct observations.

The sampling process in this type of design is purposive rather than random. In this sense, the social worker selects cases that will provide contrasting experiences, which will aid in developing ideas. Thus, there may be more of an interest in "deviant" or "extreme" cases than in "normal" or "average" cases.

Adequate knowledge of the history of the unit is important in providing a sound perspective. The social worker seeks available documents pertaining to the phenomenon being studied and makes inquiries of key informants. In particular, the worker looks for changes that have taken place and attempts to locate any variables that may have been associated with such changes over time.

Example. In order to study the intake process in a social agency, a social worker may be interested in developing some ideas about which persons are accepted or rejected as clients. Such data might be obtained from documents regarding agency policies, eligibility requirements for services, annual reports, agency statistics, and the like. Careful study of these documents could lead the social worker to form questions such as:

Is there differential processing of black and white clients?

Are appropriate referrals made?

Are the policies implemented differently with different intake workers?

The worker decides to observe the intake process for two weeks. Permission is obtained from the agency and from the clients with whom direct contact will be made. The worker observes from three vantage points: the waiting room, during the treatment interview, and after the interview. Interviews are held with social workers who have accepted and rejected persons for agency services, clients who have been accepted, and clients who have been rejected. This method provides a range of contrasting experiences for the social worker to study. Clients are then asked for their opinions of the agency, whether there appeared to be any biases in their assignments, and so forth.

Data gathered from observations and from other data sources are summarized. The intake process at the agency is described in a detailed qualitative manner, with some quantitative data. In this case, the worker might report such quantitative data as the proportion of black applicants who received services or the number of persons refused services. With this information, it is possible to look for any tendencies that might be deduced from the descriptions and to develop general questions or formulate specific hypotheses for further study.

Design 1b: Longitudinal Case Study

$$X\ O_1\ O_2\ O_3\ \ldots$$

The longitudinal case study is also referred to as a panel, cohort, developmental, or dynamic case study (White, 1963). The strategy of this design involves the observation of repeated measurements on a dependent variable *over* time, coupled with the observation of a potentially independent variable that may be associated with changes in the dependent variable.

Example. In a social agency, a social worker might be interested in changes over time in the proportions of applicants accepted, referred to other agencies, and rejected for agency services. The dependent variable is determined by studying the proportions of applications the agency receives which fall in each classification. Measurements are obtained once a month. For a one-week period each month, the worker repeats a cross-sectional case study (Design 1a), and changes in the dependent variable over time are noted. That is, the social worker examines the rate of proportions of clients accepted, rejected, or referred and classifies it as greater or lesser. The worker also is sensitized to look for other independent variables which might be associated with the changes.

There are three basic features of this design. First, it provides a qualitative and quantitative description of a unit over an extended period of time. Hence it can be used to describe normative patterns of growth or maturation for the particular unit of interest. Second, it provides a context wherein a researcher may observe changes in one variable while thoroughly studying the unit. This provides contrasting measurements on one variable which could alert the worker to changes on other variables, thus facilitating the development of hypotheses. Third, it can be used for developing measurement instruments and for testing their reliability over time.

Designs 1a and 1b are not intended to be used for generalizing to units other than those that are studied. Moreover, internal and external validity factors are not controlled. It is especially evident that the biases of the worker are involved in the development of hypotheses, which would need verification by other research designs. Nevertheless, the strength of these two designs (1a and 1b) is in their flexibility, which enhances the social worker's creativity in developing major, meaningful general questions or specific hypotheses.

Level 2: Quantitative-Descriptive Designs

Design 2a: Cross-Sectional Survey

$$R \ X \ O$$

The cross-sectional survey design has the primary function of providing accurate quantitative-descriptive data which can be generalized to some designated population (Kerlinger, 1973). The R in the symbolic form of this design refers to a random sample from the designated population. When the entire population is studied, the symbol R is, of course, not necessary.

This design stresses representativeness of all elements for the unit under study. For example, a study might seek to obtain a representative sample of all clients in a social agency. The cross-sectional case study (Design 1a), in comparison, is not necessarily focused on representativeness, and it is consequently less comprehensive in its coverage of elements in the population. To accomplish the objective of representativeness in the quantitative-descriptive design, seven steps are involved.

First, general research questions or specific hypotheses are developed prior to the survey. The questions or hypotheses serve to focus the study in preconceived areas.

Second, independent and dependent variables are operationally defined in advance of the survey. Research instruments for gathering data, such as opinion questionnaires or structured interviews, are constructed.

Third, a population is defined. Often it is defined in terms of geographic and demographic characteristics, as well as with respect to a specific time period.

Fourth, depending on available resources and desired efficiency, the worker chooses the parameters of the study participants. The entire population may be used, as in a census or complete enumeration of all population elements, or a representative sample of the population may be obtained.

Fifth, the research instruments developed in Step 2 are pretested in a pilot study to establish evidence for their validity and reliability. The instrument is pretested with persons identified within the study's population, and appropriate revisions are made. If interviewers are employed, they are thoroughly trained to use the data collection instrument appropriately.

Sixth, permission is sought from persons and/or organizations to participate in the study. Obtaining cooperation and maintaining good interpersonal relationships with research participants are vital aspects of the research process. Lack of cooperation can lead to a nonrepresentative sample or, in extreme cases, no sample at all.

Seventh, individuals in the sample are contacted. Data are collected, coded (i.e., classified with respect to operational definitions used in the survey), tabulated, and analyzed.

Example.   Suppose that a community organizer is interested in the extent to which elderly residents in a particular neighborhood are aware of and potentially interested in using existing social service programs, as well as participating in the development of new programs. The community organizer decides to conduct a survey of elderly residents in order to gather data about developing new social programs and to determine the extent of people's knowledge about available social programs and services.

A structured interview is constructed which includes basic information relating to the study's questions. Because the community organizer is interested in the residents' knowledge of existing programs, the items are devised to ask them what they know about the services offered. These include old age assistance, Meals on Wheels, legal counsel for the aged, family services, and so on. Questions are asked about difficulties the residents would have in getting to programs (e.g., availability of transportation, program scheduling), whether they have any special needs (e.g., recreational, health, social, psychological, economic) that might be met by new programs, and whether they are interested in participating in such programs. Demographic data (such as age, gender, type of residence, and persons with whom they are living) also are obtained.

The population is designated as persons 65 years of age and older who reside within a specified area and who are not living in institutions for the aged. Since the potential population of the elderly in that area, as indicated by census data, is 2,150, the community organizer decides to obtain a 10 percent randomly drawn sample of 215 individuals ($2,150 \times .10 = 215$).

The interview schedule is pretested with 22 individuals to determine whether every question is adequately phrased, whether the interview is too fatiguing, and whether any biases can be removed from the interviewing process. After the instrument is refined to increase its content validity and reliability, the interview schedule is ready for the actual survey. Contact is made by door-to-door canvassing. Much care is taken to make sure that items are asked exactly in the same, standardized manner for each respondent and that the interviewer's biases are kept to a minimum.

The results of the survey summarize data pertaining to the proportion of respondents who knew of services, the proportion of respondents who said they already use existing services, and so forth. In addition, some associational data might be obtained. This type of information might indicate, for example, that older persons are less likely to use services than younger persons, or that older females desire more recreational activities than older males.

Design 2b: Replicated Cross-Sectional Survey

$$R \ X \ O_1 \ O_2 \ O_3 \ldots$$

Replicated cross-sectional surveys are surveys of a particular population that are repeated over selected time periods. For each survey, a new representative random sample is measured. Design 2b is analogous to the longitudinal case study (Design 1b) in that repeated measurements are taken over time. However, it is different in other ways.

First, the same individuals are not necessarily surveyed. Hence, net changes in the dependent variable can be observed, although the specific changes within individuals over time cannot. Second, the purpose of the design is quantitative-descriptive rather than exploratory. The independent and dependent variables are, therefore, operationally defined in advance of the survey. Third, the validity and reliability of the measurement instruments utilized must be high. Fourth, each sample is randomly drawn from the population. In addition, when it is possible to do so, relevant characteristics of the sample such as age, race, gender, and social class are compared to the population to provide evidence of similarity for inferring representativeness.

Basically, replicated cross-sectional surveys provide a description of net change over time. This design is commonly used to measure change in attitudes, opinions, perceptions, and facts.

Example. A public policy analyst may be interested in the extent to which the population believes first-time offenders for nonviolent crimes should be imprisoned. Representative random samples of the population are queried every 3 months, for 18 months, to determine whether public attitudes are changing. Evidence of attitude change favoring more incarceration may have implications regarding the development of new prison structures. These changes may be especially important if legislators are debating the topic.

Information regarding the characteristics of the population also is examined, as these characteristics also may be related to the survey results. Changes in these characteristics could also be observed, therefore, over time. Analysis of the data may reveal, for example, that increasing proportions of persons of voting age favor long-term prison sentences, regardless of the type of crime committed.

Survey designs (Designs 2a and 2b) can also be used to provide associational data at particular points in time. However, these two designs are not constructed fundamentally to provide such data. While they are excellent for providing accurate, comprehensive information about specific populations, they do not provide the intensive, in-depth description that results from Designs 1a and 1b. Internal validity factors of biased selection, experimental mortality, interactions, history, and maturation are not controlled. Changes reported from replicated cross-sectional surveys, therefore, cannot be easily explained or attributed to other independent variables.

Level 3: Associational Designs

Design 3a: One-Group Pretest-Posttest

$$O_1 \ X \ O_2$$

The strategy of associational designs is to determine if there is a significant difference between the dependent variable at pretest as compared to posttest. Statistically significant differences ($O_1 - O_2$ = difference) between measures of a dependent variable constitute evidence of an empirical association between the independent and dependent variables.

In the one-group pretest-posttest design, there is measurement of a dependent variable (0_1) when no independent variable (X) is present, and then an independent variable is introduced, followed by a repeated measurement of the dependent variable (0_2) at a subsequent time. Measures of the dependent variable, 0_1 and 0_2, are compared for two different states of the independent variable, within the same group (before and after). There must be reliable, valid, and accurate measurement, and all elements (or a random sample) in the unit studied must be measured. The time order is manipulated as well, which enables the practitioner/ researcher to note whether changes in the dependent variable are temporally associated with the independent variable.

As noted in the discussion of the knowledge objectives continuum, evidence of an association (Level 3) is a necessary, but insufficient, condition for inferring causality (Level 4). Absence of association implies absence of a causal relationship, but the presence of association does not imply causality. As history, maturation, initial measurement effects, instrumentation, statistical regression, and interactions among internal validity factors are not controlled for in this design, causality cannot be determined.

This is a popular design because it is easy to implement. It is properly useful for the generation of associational knowledge, as a first approximation to cause-effect knowledge. Likewise, it is a poor design when it is used to provide data that are to form the bases of causal assertions.

Example. Suppose the director of an alcoholic rehabilitation agency wishes to determine whether there is an association between the two variables of treatment administered by social workers in the agency and the reduction in alcohol consumption of its clientele. There are 50 clients who are operationally defined as alcoholic by relatives, physicians, and themselves. None of the clients has received previous treatment.

During the first contact, clients and relatives are queried about the amounts of alcohol consumed daily by the client. They are also questioned three months after the treatment is introduced. Prior to the implementation of the study, the variable of alcoholic consumption is operationally defined. In a pretest of the data collection instrument used to assess alcohol consumption, the clients' responses are judged to be reliable and are associated significantly with the observations of relatives, providing some evidence of predictive validity.

The treatment consists of intensive, two-hour daily group therapy sessions, coupled with positive reinforcements for each day of alcohol abstention. No statistically significant reduction ($0_1 - 0_2$ = difference) in alcohol consumption (i.e., no change) would indicate the treatment is not associated with the desired changes. Obviously, the treatment would not be causally related to reduced alcohol consumption.

Design 3b: Static Group Comparison

Experimental group: X O_1

– – –

Comparison group: O_1

In a static group comparison design, one group is the experimental group, which is exposed to the independent variable (X). The other group, the comparison group, is not exposed to X. The comparison group is compared to the experimental group for purposes of providing evidence of associational knowledge. Reliable, accurate, and valid measurement is necessary.

The broken line between the two groups serves to emphasize the fact that the groups were *not* obtained by random assignment. As a result, selection biases on other variables related to the dependent variable, O_1, may occur.

This design can control more internal validity factors than Design 3a. It controls for initial measurement effects, instrumentation, and statistical regression. It also makes it possible to control for history, if the social worker can demonstrate that both groups have had similar experiences. The design is still insufficient, however, for inferring causal relations, due to its lack of control of selection biases, experimental mortality, maturation, and interaction effects.

Example. Suppose that a community organizer is interested in the possibility of an association between the two variables of attendance at community meetings and voting in local elections. The worker specifies the nature of community meetings and operationally defines attendance. Two groups are then located: attenders, and nonattenders.

The worker seeks permission for participation of the group members. Those willing to participate in the study are queried about their voting patterns in local elections. If the proportion of voting for attenders is statistically higher than the proportion of voting for nonattenders, there is evidence of a relationship.

Design 3b can also involve three or more comparison groups. Three (or more) groups may be chosen to represent increasing amounts of an independent variable (X_1, X_2, X_3, . . .). A no-treatment comparison group need not be included in this design. For each group, measurements are obtained on the dependent variable (O_1, O_2, O_3, . . .). Statistically significant differences between the dependent variable (between O_1 and O_2, between O_2 and O_3, or between O_1 and O_3 etc.) would indicate that associational knowledge could be drawn.

Moreover, the direction of the association can be inferred. If there are positive increases in the dependent variable that correspond to increasing amounts of the independent variable, a direct association is apparent. Likewise, decreases in dependent variables as a function of increasing amounts of the independent variables provide evidence of a negative relationship.

This design can also be used to determine if there are any statistical differences between two or more groups of individuals on an independent variable, such as ethnicity. Or, one group could receive behavior modification, one reality therapy, and the other psychoanalytic therapy. An outcome measure (the dependent variable) could be utilized to determine if there were any statistically significant differences between the three groups.

Example. The static group comparison design with three or more groups might be used by a social worker wanting to learn the relationship between the number of completed social work interviews with parents of truant children and the frequency of children's school attendance. Truant children are operationally defined as those who have been officially designated truant by the school system; they have three or more unexcused absences within a two-week period. Children of junior high school age, 13 and 14, are selected for the study. Using reliable records of the number and type of absences, the worker selects four groups. Records of parent-social worker interviews also had been compiled for one school year, so the investigator examines the number of interviews in each case.

Analysis indicates that one group received no interviews; the second, 1-2; the third, 3-4; and the fourth, more than four interviews. The data might show that the average weekly absence rate is inversely proportional to the number of interviews; the highest absence rate occurs for the no-interview group, and the lowest for the group that received four or more interviews.

Cause-effect knowledge could not be established because the social workers in the school system may have been biased in selecting families for interviewing on the basis of the children's better attendance. To infer causality, the investigator would have to demonstrate that the individuals of each group were similar on all relevant characteristics (family composition, grades, achievement test scores, etc.) and that differential dropout rates (experimental mortality) were not responsible for the changes. Further, the social worker might interview the families, children, and the social workers to discern whether there is a perceived causal connection between family interviews with the school social worker and increased school attendance. Even under the best of circumstances, the internal validity factors of biased selection, maturation, and interactions are not completely controlled.

Level 4: Experimental and Quasi-experimental Designs

Design 4a: Classical Experimental

Experimental group: $R\ O_1\ X\ O_2$

Control group: $R\ O_1\quad O_2$

The classical experimental design, also known as the pre-test-posttest control group design, controls for all internal validity factors. It involves the manipulation of the independent variable by introducing it only to an experimental group. The control group receives no independent variable. Before (pretest) and after (posttest) measurements of the dependent variable are taken for both groups. Manipulation of the independent variable occurs prior to potential changes apparent in the second measurement of the dependent variable.

Random assignment to the experimental and control groups is mandatory. It controls for selection biases, especially when there are relatively large numbers of individuals in both groups. A careful social worker checks the extent to which random assignment is effective by comparing the distributions of meaningful variables between the two groups, which should be similar at the pretest. Evidence of similar distributions increases confidence in the effectiveness of random assignment for a particular study.

The control group, which does not receive the independent variable, is assumed to undergo similar maturational and historical influences as the experimental group. Moreover, it is used to check for the potential influence of initial measurement effects, statistical regression, and instrumentation. If there are no changes between O_1 and O_2, these internal validity factors are not operative.

Moreover, the worker attempts to show that the differences in the independent variable for the experimental group are greater than the differences for the control group. This difference is the net change due to the independent variable. This is based on the assumption that the joint effects of internal validity factors are additive and can consequently be reflected in differences between experimental and control groups. This net change provides evidence of an association between the independent and dependent variables.

Of course, the factor of experimental mortality cannot be controlled in advance, but it can be monitored. If dropout rates, for example, for experimental and control groups are low (say 5 percent or less), experimental mortality can be regarded as controlled. When the dropout rate is high and it results in differential loss of individuals in the experimental and control groups, the experimental design no longer is effective in controlling other internal validity factors. The random assignment process would no longer be probabilistic, and there would be a possibility of resulting selection biases among those participants who complete the experiment.

Example. Suppose that an administrator is interested in determining whether an incentive system would reduce the length of time it takes social workers to write summary recordings of their interviews. The independent variable is the provision of one vacation day for every three months that summary recordings are completed within one week of each client contact. The dependent variable is the length of time it takes for recordings to be completed.

The agency is a statewide child protective services organization where the social workers travel at least 40 percent of the time. Throughout the state there are 100 social workers. They are randomly assigned to either an experimental group or a control group. The random assignment is checked by determining if the experimental and control groups are similar with respect to the variables of age, race, gender, amount of experience, and case-load size. If the random assignment is not effective, it can be repeated until it is, for in this stage of the study the assignment of individuals to groups is on paper only. After a successful random assignment effort, the administrator contacts those in the experimental group to request their participation and confidentiality (i.e., not informing other social workers of the experiment until its completion).

Data are collected from all social workers regarding their lag time in completing summary recordings, prior to the introduction of the incentive system and after. The study is to take place for six months. When it is completed, results are tabulated, compared, and analyzed. The administrator puts into operation the same incentive system for the control group members, regardless of whether the study shows that the incentive system is causally related to reduced completion time at the end of the study. In that way, all social workers receive the same privileges, and the conduct of the study can be regarded as ethical.

Design 4b: Posttest-Only Control Group

Experimental group: $R \; X \; O_1$

Control group: $R \quad \; O_1$

The posttest-only control group design is identical to Design 4a, but there are no measurements of the dependent variable prior to the introduction of the independent variable. There is random assignment to the experimental and control groups. The experimental group receives the independent variable, and the control group does not. After a specified period of time, both groups are measured on the dependent variable. Differences between groups in the relative amounts of the dependent variable can provide evidence of any association between the independent and dependent variables.

Example.   The same example used for Design 4a can also be used for the posttest-only control group design. Random assignment can be tested on relevant characteristics. The dependent variable, time lag in completing summary recordings, is only measured *after* the independent variable is administered. The data are compiled after six months by questionnaires and agency records. The average length of time for completing summary recordings is compared for both groups. If the experimental group shows a significantly faster completion time than the control group, a causal relationship can be inferred.

Whereas Design 4a does not control for any external validity factors, Design 4b does. Since there is no premeasurement, there cannot be any combined effects of the independent variable and premeasurement. As previously indicated, representative sampling procedures can be used to increase the generalizability of studies. Furthermore, replications with similar results minimize the external validity threat of the interaction between selection biases and the independent variable.

Design 4c: Nonequivalent Comparison Group

Experimental group: O_1 X O_2

— — —

Comparison group: O_1 O_2

When true experimental designs, such as Designs 4a and 4b, cannot be implemented, social workers attempt to approximate them with quasi-experimental designs. The strategy in quasi-experimental designs, which do not use random assignment procedures, is to control as many internal validity factors as is possible. Two examples of quasi-experimental designs are Designs 4c and 4d.

The nonequivalent comparison group design is similar to Design 4a except that it does not use random assignment to the two groups.

The two groups, assumed to be comparable, are selected, and they are administered premeasurements on the dependent variable. One group receives the independent variable, and the other group does not. After a specified period of time, postmeasurements of the dependent variable are taken for both groups.

In this design, experimental mortality can be monitored but not controlled. The effects of statistical regression are most likely when the comparison groups are selected by extreme scores. Otherwise, the influence of statistical regression is not clear. Historical and maturational factors can be assumed to be minimized by using a comparison group that does not receive the independent variable. The effects of premeasurement and instrumentation are controlled by the use of valid and reliable measures of the dependent variable, in addition to the comparison group comparison.

The major problem of control is that of selection biases and their potential interactions with other variables. To approximate control of selection biases three major strategies can be used: control by definition, control by individual matching, and frequency distribution control. Control by definition involves an increase in the homogeneity of the comparison group. For example, if gender is a relevant or meaningful variable, the group selected may be only male or only female. Hence the internal validity threat of biased selection by gender would be controlled. However, external validity would be reduced because generalizations could be made only to males or only to females.

The second strategy used to control for selection biases is individual matching. Individual matching involves the comparison of pairs of individuals on relevant or meaningful variables. For example, a pair of individuals is selected who have the same social class, race, gender, and age. One individual is assigned to the group receiving the independent variable (experimental), and the other is assigned to the group not receiving the independent variable (comparison). The process is repeated until the desired number of individuals for each group is attained.

The third strategy, frequency distribution control, is a process whereby the frequency distributions of the two groups are matched. If, for example, one group has 40 females and 60 males, and 30 blacks and 70 whites, similar distributions are sought for the other group. It is less cumbersome than matching by pairs, since it is concerned with aggregate rather than individual matching. In individual matching, black females would be matched with black females, white males with white males, and so on. In frequency distribution control, the focus on matching is only on the group averages.

Before using any of the three strategies, the social worker specifies which variables are relevant for control. Relevant variables must be either theoretically or empirically related to the dependent variable.

The worker attempts to show that the two groups are equivalent with respect to relevant variables, ignoring the irrelevant ones.

Example.   Suppose that a social worker wishes to study the effectiveness of a film on sex education for sixth-grade elementary school students in a particular city. There are two elementary schools, and each has one sixth-grade class. On the same day, all children in both sixth-grade classes are measured for their knowledge of sex (the dependent variable) by a questionnaire that has demonstrated high validity and reliability. Relevant variables related to knowledge of sex are gender, age, social class, and religion. The distributions of these variables between both classes are compared and found to be similar. One week later, the film is shown to only one of the sixth-grade classes. After another week elapses, the questionnaire on sex knowledge is again administered to both sixth-grade classes. Comparisons between classes are made on the basis of the postmeasurement data.

Design 4d: Interrupted Time Series

$$O_1 \ O_2 \ O_3 \ O_4 \ X \ O_5 \ O_6 \ O_7 \ O_8 \ \ldots$$

The interrupted time-series design involves a series of repeated measures on the dependent variable, both before and after the introduction of an independent variable (Tripodi & Harrington, 1979). Each time-series study may involve a few or a large number of measurements. The series of measurements prior to X enables the social worker to monitor for statistical regression, premeasurement effects, and instrumentation. When the data pattern is stable (i.e., there are no significant declining or increasing trends in the measurements, which also show little variability), these factors are controlled. Since there is no control or comparison group, biased selection and experimental mortality are not relevant. Moreover, if the measurements (O_1, O_2, O_3, O_4) are stable and cover a relatively long period of time, the influence of maturation is minimal. Historical factors and their possible interactions with other internal validity factors are not controlled. However, the investigator can seek to reduce such influences by asking research participants to specify any significant events that might have occurred in their environments, from O_1 to O_8.

Evidence for an association is provided if the observations for O_5, O_6, O_7 and O_8 are significantly different from the observations for O_1, O_2, O_3, and O_4. The time-order relationship between the independent and dependent variables is clearly established with the introduction of X.

With stable patterns in the time series, significant changes in the data patterns following the introduction of the independent variable, and no historical influences apparent to the research participants, this design allows the worker to approximate cause-effect knowledge. In contrast, if there is a consistent trend in the time series prior to X, which continues after X, the design does not control for history, maturation, statistical regression, instrumentation, premeasurement effects, or interactions. In this instance, the interrupted time-series design would have the same control of internal validity as Design 3a, an associational design.

Example. Suppose that a social worker is interested in determining the effectiveness of a program designed to increase referrals to a family service agency. The number of referrals is measured weekly for six weeks. The average number of referrals from 19 referring agencies is 10, and the data are stable in that the number of referrals range from 9 to 11 for each week over the four-week period. A program involving information about the agency and discussion of its services is then administered to the 19 target agencies two days a week for two weeks. This is followed by measurements of the number of referrals for six more weeks, with a resulting average of 15 referrals, ranging from 13 to 17. No other historical factors are apparent. Hence, the worker concludes that the information and discussion program was effective.

SUMMARY

This chapter has provided information on four levels of knowledge and the specific criteria that must be met to produce evidence that the desired knowledge objective is attained. It also has demonstrated the basic research designs social workers can use in social work research to obtain a specific knowledge level.

PART THREE

Methods of Data Gathering

Contents of PART THREE

Chapter

Irwin Epstein

14. QUANTITATIVE AND QUALITATIVE METHODS

As presented in Chapter 5, a fundamental distinction in social work research is that between the use of quantitative and qualitative research methods. Quantitative research methods are utilized to count and correlate social and psychological phenomena (Lazarsfeld & Barton, 1971). Qualitative research methods determine to seek the essential character of social and psychological phenomena. Both methods attempt to describe and explain social reality (Dabbs, 1982; Morick, 1972).

The two methodological approaches have been available to social work practitioners and researchers throughout the history of our profession. There is little agreement among social workers on the exact differences and commonalities between quantitative and qualitative research methods (Dabbs, 1982). Many and probably most professionals perceive quantitative methods as more respectable and closer to the common understanding of science (Van Maanen, Dabbs, & Faulkner, 1982).

However, in the recent response to the high status in the use of the quantitative approach to practice in our profession, some social workers are beginning to advocate more use of qualitative approaches and are focusing on the conflicting aspects of the two methods (Geismar & Wood, 1982). In doing so, they create an erroneous impression that the choice between the two is political and that social workers must decide and declare which side they are on (DeMaria, 1981). In arguing their case, they have characterized quantitative research methods as archaic, politically conservative, and ill-suited to the social action and social change traditions of our profession (DeMaria, 1981; Geismar & Wood, 1982; Heineman, 1981; Hudson, 1982c; Ruckdeschel & Faris, 1981; Taylor, 1977; Weissman, 1981).

EPISTEMOLOGICAL ORIGINS

Quantitative methods have epistemological roots in logical positivism (Van Maanen, 1983). Logical positivism refers to a theory of meaning in which a proposition is acceptable *only* if it can be empirically verified and *only* if there is a quantitative research method for deciding whether the proposition is true or false. The theory requires that all meaningful propositions have to be tested by observation and experiment. Common to these philosophical orientations is the application of the logic and principles of measurement from the physical sciences to the social world with the goal of prediction and validation of these predictions (see Chapter 9). The ultimate purpose of such research is to generate universal "laws" of social behavior analogous to the laws of the physical sciences (Bernstein, 1976; Heineman, 1981).

Qualitative research methods assumes that the subjective dimensions of human experience are continuously changing and cannot be studied using the objective principles of quantitative research methodologies (Filstead, 1970; Watts, 1976). Instead, emphasis is placed on fully describing and comprehending the subjective meanings of events to individuals and groups caught up in them (Bogdan & Taylor, 1975; Walizer & Wienir, 1978).

The two research methods have existed side by side since the beginnings of contemporary social science. So, for example, in discussing the epistemological roots of psychoanalysis, Bettleheim (1982) remarks:

> In the German culture within which Freud lived, and which permeated his work, there existed and still exists a definite and important division between two approaches to knowledge. Both disciplines are called *Wissenschaften* (sciences), and they are accepted as equally legitimate.... These two are the *Naturwissenschaften* (natural sciences) and, ... the *Geisteswissenschaften* (which defies translation into English; its literal meaning is "sciences of spirit") and the concept is deeply rooted in German idealist philosophy. These disciplines represent entirely different approaches to understanding the world.

Attempting to explain some of the distortions that occurred when Freudian theory was translated into English, Bettleheim notes a division of knowledge between a "hermeneutic-spiritual knowing and a positivistic pragmatic knowing.... In much of the German world, and particularly in Vienna before and during Freud's life, psychology clearly fell into the realm of the first (*Geisteswissenschaften*); in much of the English-speaking world, on the other hand, psychology clearly belonged to the *Naturwissenschaften*."

Despite these philosophical differences and the theoretical distortions that may have occurred, psychology and psychoanalysis have flourished with significant contributions based on each of the epistemological approaches (Wechsler, Reinherz, & Dobbin, 1981).

Similarly, in describing the origins of organizational theory, Gouldner (1969) contrasts the perspectives of the early French social philosophers Saint-Simon and Comte. For the former, the first to recognize the significance of organizations for the modern state, organizational expertise and the "authority of the administrators would rest upon their possession of scientific skills and 'positive' knowledge." For Comte, on the other hand, organizations, and indeed, all social institutions were best maintained by subjective and spontaneous forms of knowledge and interventions which were indigenous to particular organizations and institutions. Saint-Simon's approach gradually evolved into the "rational model" of organizational analysis; Comte's into the "natural-systems" model. The former approach relies heavily on quantitative measurement and empirical testing of existing theory. The latter, relying heavily on qualitative case studies of single organizations, emphasizes conceptual and theory development. Without either approach and their cross-fertilization, our current understanding of organizations would be greatly diminished (Charlesworth, 1982).

PATTERNS OF UTILIZATION

Given the divergent philosophical underpinnings of quantitative and qualitative research methods, how have these different approaches been utilized by the social sciences in the study of social reality? Figure 14.1 presents some of the major differences in the ways quantitative

FIGURE 14.1

Major Differences in the Uses of Quantitative and Qualitative Methods

	Method	
Difference	*Quantitative*	*Qualitative*
Purpose	Prediction and testing	Description
Logic	Deductive	Inductive
Point of view	Objective	Subjective
Language	Numerical	Natural
Research techniques	Survey, structured interviews, census data, etc.	Participant observation, purposeful conversation, ethnomethodology, etc.
Research designs	Experimental and quasi-experimental	Nonexperimental
Type of theory	Sociological or psychological	Social-psychological

and qualitative research methods have tended to be used. Emphasis is placed on the differences and it is not meant to suggest that the two approaches are incompatible or that no exceptions exist (Filstead, 1970; Taylor, 1977).

As presented in Chapter 13, the ultimate purpose of quantitative research methodology has been in the testing and validation of predictive, cause-effect hypotheses about social reality. By employing qualitative methods, on the other hand, a social worker can assemble detailed descriptions of social reality, often useful in generating hypotheses (see Tables 13.1 and 13.2 in Chapter 13).

Each research method emphasizes a different form of logic. Thus, quantitative methods have tended to rely on deductive logic (i.e., applying social science theory to social reality). Qualitative methods have generally been used inductively (i.e., deriving concepts and theory from the social reality being studied). The use of qualitative research methods in theory development has been called *grounded theory* and is more suited to the study of relatively uncharted social terrain. The quantitative approach is best suited to studying phenomena which has previously had a high level of theory development and hypotheses testing (Glaser & Strauss, 1967).

Quantitatively oriented social work researchers attempt to describe social reality from an "objective" standpoint. The adjective (objective) is in quotes because one can never totally eliminate subjectivity from the social judgments that are inevitably involved in all forms of social science (see Chapter 5). Still, quantitative approaches place emphasis on the insight that an outside observer may bring to the study of a social system (see Chapters 15, 20, and 21). Qualitative methods, on the other hand, are employed to describe reality from the points of view of participants in the systems studied. It is based on the assumption that actors in a system can tell the social worker most about what they are doing and why (see Chapters 16 through 19).

Another indication of the difference in the two research methods is the language in which ideas are ultimately expressed. Thus, quantitatively oriented social workers translate constructs and concepts into operational definitions and hence—numerical indices (see Chapter 20). Their predictions are validated through the application and manipulation of numbers. Qualitative researchers, on the other hand, employ only natural language in their studies. Their ideas are expressed in the argot of system members. They are validated by logical induction and through detailed observation of and discussion with system numbers (Parsons, 1949, 1964).

DATA GENERATION

Quantitative researchers tend to utilize social surveys (see Chapter 15), structured interviews (see Chapter 16), self-administered questionnaires (see Chapters 15 and 16), census data (see Chapter 19), and the like. These methods, while efficient and systematic have the disadvantage of being imposed on the systems studied. As presented in Chapter 7, the data collection methods themselves may influence and distort the reality which they wish to describe through measurement effects and other threats to validity. The result may be gross inconsistencies between what system members tell the investigators and what they actually do (McCall & Simmons, 1969). Qualitative researchers have relied heavily on participant observation (see Chapters 17 and 18) and methods and purposeful conversation. Although qualitative methods create their own problems of inference, they come closer to being "unobtrusive" (Deutscher, 1966). In other words, they have minimal effects on the people and events being studied (Webb, Campbell, Schwartz, & Sechrest, 1966).

As indicated earlier, social workers utilizing quantitative research methods implement experimental and quasi-experimental designs. Such designs are best suited to testing causality. Their major disadvantage has been described as *design intrusiveness* (Thomas, 1978c). So, for example, the implementation of a single-case experimental design in a direct service agency may necessitate incomplete, delayed, or denied service; may impose extraneous requirements on the treatment situation; and may result in adverse client reactions. Qualitative researchers, on the other hand, emphasize nonexperimental designs. Although qualitative designs make definite cause-effect knowledge difficult to derive, they are indeed less intrusive.

Finally, one might contrast the type of theory used and/or generated by these divergent research methods. Although there is no inherent relationship between the theoretical discipline and method employed, quantitative studies have been more likely to remain within the disciplinary boundaries of psychology and sociology (Clark, 1983; Merton, 1957). Qualitative studies on the other hand, have generally been social-psychological.

In this discussion we have described and emphasized major differences in the application of quantitative and qualitative research methods, ignoring many exceptions to the generalizations. Thus, for example, quantitative studies are sometimes used for purely descriptive purposes (Tripodi, Fellin, & Meyer, 1983). Alternatively, qualitative studies are sometimes searching for causal explanation. Similar exceptions could be stated for most of the differentiating dimensions listed. Nevertheless, the discussion captures trends or emphasis in the actual application of these two methods (Dabbs, 1982).

Despite their differences, however, both research methods are planful, systematic, and empirical. By empirical (often incorrectly used as a synonym for quantitative), we refer to a reliance on practical experience and observation as a source of knowledge verification. In short, both methods are equally valid approaches to social work knowledge generation.

CRITIQUES OF QUANTITATIVE METHODS

Despite the scientific legitimacy of the two research methods, quantitative techniques have dominated social science research. This reference is in part a response to the requisites of professionalization of social science. Neo-Marxist critics of the social sciences have alleged that quantitative research methods are conservative instruments of the social science establishment (Mills, 1959).

Within social work research, quantitative approaches tend to enjoy greater respectability. And, in response to this intramural quantitative emphasis, a few social work researchers have recently begun their own rebellion. Thus, for example, in the most recent edition of *The Encyclopedia of Social Work,* Maas (1977) calls for a broader application of qualitative methods claiming that the total commitment to measurement and quantitative analysis seems now to have been premature in a field of inquiry still lacking a clear description of how things happen (Ruckdeschel & Farris, 1981).

Taking a similar position, Taylor (1977) suggests that the naturalistic qualitative approach, as compared with the "positivistic," quantitative one, often is more in keeping with the internal logic of our profession and often is more relevant to the problems of social work practice. Taylor cites the significant contributions that Becker (1958), Goffman (1959), Lewis (1966), Liebow (1967), and Whyte (1966) (all qualitative researchers) have made to social work thought. There is a paradigm conflict between the proof-oriented, nomothetic, quantitative research methods that are commonly taught and the discovery-oriented, idiographic work that social workers do (Beckerman, 1978).

Similarly, DeMaria (1981) argues that quantitative research methodology in particular and empiricism in general represent an "impoverished" research paradigm for social work because they fail to question social structure and dominant values. In other words, they maintain the institutional status quo. Moreover, DeMaria contends that empirically oriented research studies are incompatible with the reform tradition of social work. Finally, Heineman (1981) goes so far as to declare this form of research obsolete, outmoded, and overly restrictive (F. C. Johnson, 1981).

This critical orientation toward quantitative methods has expressed itself recently in challenges to particular practice-research methodologies (Bloom & Fischer, 1982). For example, it has been suggested that single-subject methodology in casework is scientifically simplistic and overly restricts the mode of treatment interventions (Jayaratne & Levy, 1979). It has also been suggested that a great deal of positivist research is not useful and the types of problems social workers deal with, whether they are working with groups or individuals, often require knowledge that, to date, can only be developed through qualitative means (Imre, 1984; Weissman, 1981).

METHODS

The anti-quantitative ideology that runs through the above critiques has been responsible for the creation of four major misconceptions about quantitative and qualitative research methods. These are as follows: (1) the myth that quantitative methods are inherently politically conservative and therefore unsuited to the reform tradition of our profession; (2) the myth that qualitative methods are inherently politically progressive and therefore ideally suited to social work; (3) the myth that qualitative methods are more likely to be utilized by practitioners than are quantitative ones; and (4) the myth that quantitative and qualitative methods are inherently incompatible.

Conservatism

The first myth is that quantitative methods are inherently conservative. This myth is easily dispelled by considering quantitative social work research that has a critical consciousness and that is change oriented. Consider, for example, Piven and Cloward's book, *Regulating the Poor: The Functions of Public Welfare* (1971). This book is a study of relief policies in the United States and employs extensive quantitative data to link relief policies to social control and the muting of potential civil disorder. The authors of this book, perhaps the most significant radical theoreticians in social work today and two of the architects of the welfare rights movement, apparently see no incompatibility between the requisites of social action and quantitative research methodology (Brager & Purcell, 1967).

Politics

The second myth is that qualitative methods are inherently politically progressive. Much could be written concerning the trivial preoccupations of the qualitative research studies that have been conducted and on the scant attention given to social and political influences in much of this literature. Instead, however, let us consider the qualitative research by a single author well known to social workers. It has been contended that Oscar Lewis's (1966) anthropological-oriented qualitative research studies have been largely responsible for promoting the concept of a "culture of poverty" that separates the poor from other social classes and contributes to their own lack of social mobility. Based on participant observation and lengthy in-depth, open-ended interviews, Lewis's work has been utilized to indict the poor rather than the social structure that creates and maintains poverty.

In a scathing criticism of Lewis's methods, data/analysis, and interpretation, Valentine (1971) comments:

> The scientific status of the "culture of poverty" remains essentially a series of undemonstrated hypotheses. With respect to many or most of these hypotheses, alternative propositions are theoretically more convincing and are supported by more available evidence. The complex of conceptions, attitudes, and activities that has grown up around the "culture of poverty" has had a predominantly pernicious effect on American society. This complex has been a keystone in the crumbling arch of official policy toward the poor.

Valentine goes on to show how Lewis's central idea has been used to blame poverty on the poor themselves and to justify programs designed to inculcate middle-class values and virtues among the poor and especially their children, rather than changing the conditions of their existence. Hence, Lewis's qualitative methodology did not ensure against the conservative practice of "blaming the victim."

Utilization

The third myth is that qualitative methods are more likely to be utilized by social workers. Although this has not been true historically, it is difficult to say what the future will bring. In a paper concerning the incorporation of research methodology into social work practice, Tripodi and I. Epstein (1978) hypothesize that the utilization of research methods by social workers will depend on the following five conditions: (1) the availability of research methods; (2) the correspondence of those methods to the informational requirements of social workers; (3) the compatibility of those methods with social work practice; (4) the extent to which those methods can be implemented; and (5) their costs.

Availability. Quantitative methods are currently much more readily available to social workers than qualitative ones. It could be argued that the social-psychological perspective which is characteristic of much of qualitative research today is more compatible with the "person-in-environment" perspective of direct practice (Germain, 1981). Nevertheless, with the advent and development of single-subject designs, practice research methodology requires knowledge of quantitative principles and methods as well (W. Gingerich, 1983; Grinnell, 1981a; Hudson, 1977; F. Johnson, 1981).

Compatibility. Compatibility is the extent to which the knowledge and values necessary to employ the research methods are congruent with the knowledge and value structures of social workers. On this dimension, qualitative approaches probably are more superior to quantitative ones. Thus, the descriptive, inductive, subjective, and unobtrusive approach to information gathering associated with qualitative methods is much closer to traditional social work practice. In addition, social workers are more likely to accept a method based on natural language than one based on numbers and statistical manipulation. Nevertheless, the implicit logic, specificity, and rigor of quantitative research can still make a significant contribution to social work data gathering and knowledge, even if quantitative methods, per se, are rejected (L. Epstein, 1981; Tripodi & I. Epstein, 1978).

Implementation. Implementation is the degree to which research methods can be used directly or indirectly (see Chapter 7). A research method is directly useful when it can be employed without any modification in format or procedures. In contrast, a research method that is indirectly useful is one that requires change so that it can be adapted to social work practice. The emphasis within qualitative methods on the use of nonexperimental, nonintrusive research designs suggests that these approaches would offer fewer problems of direct implementation than would classic experimental designs. Nonetheless, the quasi-experimental, "formative" quantitative evaluation designs that have been recently developed both at the program level and at the single-case level offer greater flexibility for those interested in the direct implementation of quantitative methods in social work practice (Tripodi & I. Epstein, 1978).

As for indirect uses, it could be argued that effective social work practice is based on the extent to which workers think systematically, test their intuitions with observation and analyze information through a disciplined use of logic (see Chapters 1 and 2). These elements are part of *both* quantitative and qualitative research methods.

Costs. Cost considerations are difficult to assess. Qualitative research studies are frequently time consuming and therefore often expensive. These difficulties render it inaccessible especially to social workers whose employing agencies expect them to be engaged in service delivery and in research only as it relates immediately to service delivery. However, while quantitative data gathering is often far more efficient, the costs of creating and maintaining the other requisites of quantitative research designs may be greater (Karger, 1983).

Thus, neither research method is clearly more suitable for social work utilization. Instead, a social worker needs to consider the context in which the research study is taking place and the question it is attempting to answer (Kazdin, 1982).

Compatibility

The fourth myth is that the two research methods are inherently incompatible because they rest on different epistemological assumptions (Leinhardt, 1984). Although it is true that there are epistemological differences between these two research methods, some of the most practical and innovative research to be published in recent years makes use of both quantitative and qualitative data. Thus, Maluccio's book, *Learning from Clients* (1979), makes use of quantitative and qualitative data collected from clients and social workers to generate ideas about the treatment process and the impact of environmental factors on service delivery in a family agency (Maluccio, 1979, 1983).

In a study of classroom structure and teaching style on student compliance, Bossert (1979) skillfully employed quantitative data concerning teacher and student behavior with narrative descriptions, verbatim accounts of conversations between pupils and teachers, interviews, and so on. A final example is Fabricant's (1982) work on juveniles in the family court. Here again, we find an effective interplay of quantitative and qualitative research methodology in a critique of the institutional processing of young offenders. Thus, to imply that social workers must make an existential choice between one or the other research method is nonsense. Each method can make a contribution to our understanding of the social world, and together they obviously augment it (Lowenberg & Dolgoff, 1983).

UTILIZATION GUIDELINES

Thus far, we have argued that quantitative and qualitative methods each have their uses, advantages, and disadvantages. As a result, it makes more sense to ask under what conditions should one employ either than to ask which is "better" than the other.

Figure 14.2 presents a few of the conditions under which quantitative or qualitative methods are generally preferred. Quantitative methods are probably most useful when the social worker has considerable knowledge of the culture and structure of the context in which the study is going to take place. Such studies often require ease of access and a

FIGURE 14.2

Conditions under Which Quantitative and Qualitative Methods
Are Preferred

	Preferred Method	
Condition	*Quantitative*	*Qualitative*
Extent of knowledge of culture of the research context	High	Low
Extent of difficulty of access to the research context	Low	High
Extent of control over elements in the research context	High	Low
Amount of previous research and theory development	High	Low
Type of knowledge sought	Cause-effect or quantitative descriptive	Process or qualitative descriptive

high level of legitimation. The worker must also be in control of the various elements of the research situation. If these conditions are not present, the research design, strategies of data collection, and other essential components are likely to be subverted. In addition, in areas of inquiry in which there has been considerable previous research findings and theory development, quantitative methods are usually preferable. Finally, quantitative methods are best suited to trying to establish cause-effect relationships between variables or to describe relatively straightforward objective characteristics such as demographic area.

Qualitative methods, on the other hand, are more suitable when the worker is entering a relatively unfamiliar research context in which the legitimacy of the study is not assured and where the worker has relatively little control over structural elements in the research situation. Under such circumstances, the greater flexibility of the qualitative approach recommends itself. Qualitative methods are also most suitable when there has been a relatively low level of previous conceptualization, theory building, and research findings in a given area of inquiry. They lend themselves to description of complex social processes and the subjective perceptions of these processes by people involved in them. Thus, qualitative methods are ideal for conceptual development and hypothesis formulation.

This is not to say that occasional departures from these generalizations would not have a positive effect on knowledge development. So, for example, the literature on social work professionalization is dominated by quantitative research findings (P. Wilson, Voth, & Hudson, 1980). However, it would be extremely interesting to explore the subjective meanings of the concept of professionalization to social workers (I. Epstein & Conrad, 1978). Alternatively, labeling theory which is firmly rooted in qualitative methodology has been uncritically welcomed by social workers despite the paucity of quantitative evidence to support its validity (Case & Lingerfelt, 1974; W. Gingerich, Kleczewski, & Kirk, 1982; C. Levy, 1981).

Overall, neither quantitative nor qualitative methodology is in any ultimate sense superior to the other. The two methods exist along a continuum on which neither pole is more "scientific" nor more suited to social work knowledge development. As Geismar and Wood (1982) state:

> Each research model is needed. But needed also is a more sophisticated awareness of what the questions are that are being posed, and the suitability of each type of research for particular practice problems. To attempt to decide the direction for social work research on any other ground such as those based on emotional faith in any model, subverts the principles of scientific inquiry on which research is based, and on which practice should be based.

SUMMARY

Quantitative research methods are utilized to count and correlate social and psychological phenomena. Qualitative research methods determine to seek the essential character of social and psychological phenomena. Both methods attempt to describe and explain social reality. The two research methods have existed side by side since the beginnings of contemporary social science. Each research method emphasizes a different form of logic. Thus, quantitative methods have tended to rely on deductive logic (i.e., applying social science theory to social reality). Qualitative methods have generally been used inductively (i.e., deriving concepts and theory from the social reality being studied). Despite their differences, however, both research methods are planful, systematic, and empirical. By empirical (often incorrectly used as a synonym for quantitative), we refer to a reliance on practical experience and observation as a source of knowledge verification. In short, both methods are equally valid approaches to social work knowledge generation. Thus, neither research method is clearly more suitable for social work utilization. Instead, a social worker needs to consider the context in which the research study is taking place and the question it is attempting to answer.

Michael J. Austin and Jill Crowell

15. SURVEY RESEARCH

Survey research provides a means the social worker can use in seeking data to answer research questions in collaboration with other people—colleagues, agency clients, staff members, or citizens of the community. It is important that any research study be coneucted *with* people rather than *on* people. The value base underlying social work research (as noted in Chapter 6) calls on the worker to recognize the integrkty of individual participants rather than seeing them as just subjects. It calls for commitments to provide respondents with feedback on the study's results, to preserve the confidentiality of responses, and to respect the rights of individuals to refuse, without penalty, to participate in a study.

In the public image, social and behavioral science investigators are often perceived as having cavalier attitudes toward people. Controlled psychological experiments with insufficient safeguares for the rights of people, and sociological studies which simply take ideas from community residents and fail to feed them back for purposes of local improvement, have contributed to this impression.

The social worker's efforts, in contrast, are devoted to increasing the base of knowledge about problems thct affect the needs of a wide variety of clients or the conduct of programs. The applied research approach, despite criticisms about lack of rigor and!regardless of the complexities of understanding and documenting the human condition, incorporates practice and research in a problem-solving process designed to provide evaluative data on specific social work problem areas.

This chapter builds on the information provided in Chapter 12 on the design and construction of questionnaires as measuring instruments and considers their application and use in!survey research. While the emphasis is on the group-administered questionnaire (particularly in the case study example), many of the same principles are related to mailed questionnaires, and their development and implementation are also described. Group-admimistered questionnaires, which cost less than mailed surveys, are emphasized because they particularly meet the needs of social workers who often receive minimal funding to conduct studies on problems whkch are imporuant to social work practice. As a result of their limited access to the public or private research funds devoted to basic or "pure" research, they have found that necessity again must be the mother of invention, and the group-administered questionnaire is one result.

ADVANTAGES AND DISADVANTAGES OF SURVEY QUESTIONNAIRES

The two methods most often used by social workers, the survey questionnaire and the interview, are compared in Figure 15.1.

The interview technique has been one of the major tools of social work practice since the profession began (Kadushin, 1983). It is a valuable method when used in the context of social work research, particularly in helping to identify the depth and breadth of problem areas and opinions in order to formulate meaningful researchable questions and hypotheses. Its strength as a research method has been its ability to *produce* hypotheses (Knowledge Level 1, as discussed in Chapter 13).

The survey questionnaire has also had a long history in social work community organizing and social planning as a method for collecting data about a population and for testing hypotheses. Its strength as a research method has been its ability to *test* hypotheses (Clark, 1983).

A more specific perspective on the survey questionnaire method can be gained by considering the advantages and disadvantages of this method, as stipulated by Bailey (1978). The advantages of survey questionnaires as a research method include:

1. Considerable savings in comparison to the higher costs of conducting interviews.
2. Considerable time saving, in comparison to the many hours involved in face-to-face interviewing and travel time.
3. Questionnaire completion at respondents' convenience.
4. Greater assurance of anonymity.
5. Standardized wording.
6. No interviewer bias.
7. Possibility of gathering relevant data from personal records or colleagues before answering items.
8. Respondents more accessible by mail than with face-to-face interviews.

The disadvantages of the survey questionnaire method include:

FIGURE 15.1
Comparison of Survey Questionnaires and Interviews

Survey Questionnaire	Interview
Individuals may be less embarrassed and more open in their responses.	Responses can be obtained in areas where specific questions are difficult to construct.
Probing questions cannot be used, and questions must always be direct.	Probing techniques can be used.
A wide variety of subjects is potentially available over a large geographic area.	Identity of respondents is known.
Individuals who would not be approachable by an interviewer can be used. If there is nonresponse, it may be difficult to determine who answered and who did not.	Some individuals may take the time to answer if confronted by an interviewer but would not respond by mail.
Cost per questionnaire is low.	Most expensive method.
No field staff necessary.	Field staff must be trained and supervised.
Individuals have more time to think and may respond when they want to.	Time requirements are very flexible if a semi- or unstructured schedule is used.
Nonresponse may be great.	Nonresponse is usually very low.
Difficult to deal with missing data, although easier to use.	Responses from unstructured schedules must be handled.
Interpretations often more clear-cut.	Results are often a matter of interpretation.
It may be difficult to generalize findings if there is a high nonresponse rate, and it may not be possible to generalize to certain types.	Since more control is possible, generalization of findings may be more certain.

Source: Adapted from pages 289–290 from *Research Methods and Analysis: Searching for Relationships* by Michael H. Walizer and Paul L. Wiener. Copyright©1978 by Michael H. Walizer and Paul L. Wienir. Reprinted by permission of Harper & Row, Publishers, Inc.

1. Lack of flexibility in question format, which prevents varying the items or probing (as is possible in interviewing).

2. High potential for low response rate.

3. Use of written responses only; nonverbal behavior and other personal characteristics cannot be documented.

4. No control over the environment of the respondent (e.g., distractions, censorship, or use of another person's answers).
5. No control over the manner in which respondents choose to answer items.
6. Possibility that many items will be left unanswered.
7. Difficult to record spontaneous first responses to items; respondents may record only what they perceive to be requested.
8. Difficult to determine whether questionnaires are not returned because of wrong addresses or because recipients are uninterested in the questionnaire.
9. No control over the date on which respondents answer the items.
10. Complex questionnaire format cannot be used.
11. Possibility of a biased sample, since motivated and curious people might respond and others might not.

The debate over the pros and cons of using questionnaires in applied research continues in the literature, including many standard behavioral science and research methodology texts which can be consulted for details.

Many of the disadvantages in the use of survey questionnaires are related to the mailing of the questionnaires, the usual technique in this method. A fairly recent innovation, group administration of the questionnaires, can avoid many of these difficulties. This method is illustrated in the case study below and discussed in the section that follows it.

The development and implementation of a questionnaire survey by a novice social work researcher described in the case study in the next section demonstrates how learned research skills can be refined by conducting actual studies in social agencies.

CASE STUDY

While there is a rough chronological order to the following case study, the flow of events is modified in order to describe the logical development and use of a questionnaire survey method in social work research. The journal includes a modified research process (as in Figure 2.1 in Chapter 2) which consists of clarifying the research problem, the compilation of the literature review, the development of the research design, the design and modification of existing questionnaires, and the administration of the questionnaire in the field. In developing these components, it captures some of the unplanned realities of the research process as well as frequent serendipitous events.

From the Journal of a Beginning Practitioner/Researcher

When I began my studies in social welfare with a background in psychology, my accumulated research experience included participation in a few laboratory studies where the parameters of the studies were narrowly defined and readily amenable to control. It was "pure" research as opposed to "applied" research, which reflects the orientation of social work. As a newcomer to the social work profession, I soon became an advocate of applied research and the practitioner/researcher model. However, I was quick to discover the lack of research texts specifically oriented to the problems and needs of social workers. This is not surprising in view of the profession's historically practice focus and the only very recent attempts to integrate practice and research. Accordingly, the novice investigator is largely left to wade through literature from other academic disciplines such as anthropology, business, psychology, sociology, and so on—to extrapolate, synthesize, and apply the knowledge in some fashion that makes sense at the moment.

My research interests and the events related to the conception, development, and implementation of my study were in a large part a reflection of who I am. In other words, my study was not attached to, or a part of, an ongoing research project. It grew out of my own passions and intrigue with human behavior in work settings, my experiences in mental health organizations, and my convictions that the quality of work life in social welfare organizations can always be improved. My study and the lessons I learned along the way were also influenced by my tendency to conceptualize broadly, to acknowledge and insist upon multiple perspectives and interpretations, and a willful determination to have my own way. These attributes both facilitated my study and at the same time thwarted a smooth transition from problem identification, definition, and specification to evaluation and dissemination of findings. Had it not been for externally imposed time frames that were critical to the study, in all likelihood I would still be floundering in a mass of variables unwilling to compromise for less than a total picture of the event to be studied. All this is to say that novice social work researchers are up against meager relevant literature, and, like other investigators, up against themselves.

It is well known that standard research texts characterize the research process as a logical process, from beginning to end. Recalling the true sequence of research events related to my own study brings to mind the observation that research literature concerns itself with "ways in which the scientist *ought* to think, feel, and act. It does not necessarily describe in needed detail the way scientists *actually* do think, feel, and act." Another investigator, anticipating the introspective task of describing the events of research activities, called to mind as models "not the great researchers, but the confessors." I found comfort in knowing that experienced practitioner/researchers also deviated from the precision of research models portrayed in standard textbooks. Particularly in field research, the best laid plans are subject to events beyond the control of the researcher.

Phase 1:   Problem Identification, Definition, and Specification

My concerns regarding quality of work life and management practices in social welfare organizations led me to explore a broad range of
literature prior to identifying a specific research problem. I was particularly interested in organizational change and had experience-based hunches
(later to become hypotheses) about the relationship of certain factors in
the change situation. I wondered, for example, if certain organizational
characteristics or variables (e.g., organizational communication, staff morale, the agency's political environment) predisposed agencies to more or
less successful implementation of change. Was management style related
to the speed with which an innovation was adopted in agencies? Did the
nature of a particular change (e.g., its compatibility with staff norms and
values, the magnitude of change, its cost) affect the success of a change
effort? Or does the manner in which change is brought about (e.g., collaborative decision making, directives from above) affect the change process?
These questions later became important variables in my study that examined the implementation of a statewide management information
system in mental health centers.

The management, policy implementation, program evaluation, and
organizational analysis literature helped me to validate some of my own
thinking and provided sources of new ideas for understanding the complexities of human behavior in organizations. Rather than narrowing my
already broad focus, the literature exploration increased my awareness
of variables at play in organizations and increased my belief that to
understand a small piece of a large picture, one had to understand the
whole system. It was difficult for me to imagine, for example, that one
could talk about or understand managerial decision making without considering managerial style, organizational climate, organizational communication, the goals of the organization, the physical environment of the
organization, the organization's political climate, and so on. I therefore
studied systems theory.

While I appreciate this propensity of mine to consider the interactive effects of multiple factors in order to understand human and organizational phenomena, it was this tendency that most plagued me throughout
the study. My first written review of the literature, for example, which
included only the organizational change variables, was 85 pages long and,
from my perspective, was sketchy at best. I attempted only to highlight
some of the major variables at play in organization change situations.
From this review, I began to formulate hypotheses and to sketch out a
tentative research design.

At the time, the design, which identified over 20 major variables,
seemed neither overwhelming nor impractical. It was simply a systems
perspective of organizational change identifying those variables which
needed to be accounted for in a study of change implementation. The
next step, I assumed, was to select, from the available questionnaires, an
instrument or items to measure the variables.

Two related processes were set in motion at this time: responding
to my advisor's prodding to operationally define the concepts in the form
of specific measurable variables; and identifying and assessing potentially
relevant measuring instruments. Logically these two processes go hand
in hand. It is impossible to adequately assess the appropriateness of a
measuring instrument to measure a variable if the variable has not been

operationally defined. But this was the procedure I elected to follow—resisting operationally defining the variables.

Phase 2: Generation of Alternatives and Selection of Strategies for Problem Solution

It's difficult to talk about this phase of the research process without at the same time discussing my reluctance to operationally define the variables, since both processes were highly related. However, for the purposes of the discussion, I'll attempt to deal with them separately.

To illustrate some of the difficulties in selecting, assessing, and modifying questionnaires, I shall work with the concept of organizational readiness. This is a relatively new concept in the organizational literature and one that is of considerable interest to me. In its broadest sense, organizational readiness refers to the characteristics of an organization which predispose the organization to more or less successful implementation of change. In broad hypothetical terms, one could argue that the greater the organization's readiness to implement a specific change, the greater the likelihood of successful implementation.

Looking back, I realize that much of the struggle with the variable of organizational readiness and subsequent selection of questionnaire items was related to my own lack of conceptual clarity. On the one hand, I conceptualized organizational readiness broadly to include an array of organizational variables, such as organizational communication, morale, decision-making processes, and political climate, as well as specific change variables, such as staff attitudes about the proposed change, the agency's need for the proposed change, and the availability of resources for implementing the change. The underlying assumption of this conceptualization is that the nature of organizational politics and environmental factors at a given point in time contribute in some way to the organization's readiness for change. For example, an organization's political climate may reflect a legislature's current preoccupation with accountability issues and therefore help ripen conditions for implementing a computerized management information system. Viewed from this perspective, organizational readiness is a highly inclusive concept to be understood in terms of the cumulative and interactive effects of a rather large number of change-related variables. Alternatively, organizational readiness can be seen more narrowly in terms related only to the proposed change (i.e., staff attitudes about the proposed change, availability or resources to implement the change, etc.). My early attempts to arrive at a research design reflected this more narrow perspective of organizational readiness.

Only retrospectively have I seen how my ambivalence regarding the choice between perspectives blocked the articulation of clear guidelines for assessing relevant questionnaires and items. For example, at one point I had located a questionnaire for gathering data about an organization's readiness for program evaluation that could be easily modified for my own study. The questionnaire reflected the comprehensive view of organizational readiness rather than the narrow focus that I had identified in my study. The questionnaire had great appeal to me for four reasons: it reflected much of the organizational change literature; it was an appropriate length for the study; it had been developed and used by researchers interested in the same target population with which I was concerned; and a decision to use this questionnaire in its entirety would bring a quick and much needed closure to the task of instrument selection. Additionally, the literature stresses the critical need for replication of research studies, and I became enamoured with the notion of using questionnaires that had been developed and used by reputable people in the field. As a result of this flirtation with the organizational readiness questionnaire, the!questionnaire itself became the guiding force for my study. I lost sight of my own research priorities, discarding variables that were not addressed in the questionnaire, adopting the more inclusive definition of orgcnizational readiness, and opting for a nonsystems model of organizational change.

Prodded by my advisor to generate my own operational definitions of the variables and to prioritize my research interests, I undertook a more critical examination of the existing questionnaire. I began to verbalize my reservations about some of the questionnaire's items, variable definitions, format, and so on that heretofore had been vague and largely unarticulated. As I came to trust my own hunches, I realized I had been operating on the assumption that published and often quoted work had intrinsic merit and was above criticism from the novice practitioner/ researcher. The process of demystifying the existing questionnaire led to a reclaiming of my earlier research design and a keener sense of knowing why I selected, rejected, or modified certain items.

Constructing a questionnaire by bringing together in new combinations items from already existing questionnaires draws upon both the logical-rational and creative-intuitive processes of the investigator. I like to think of the item selection as a product of a systematic and/or theoretically based analysis of the issues. For example (see Figure A), there is a branch of the *organizational behavior and analysis* literature that is concerned with *planned organizational change*. Within the organizational change literature is a concept called *organizational readiness* for change. Some professionals speculate that the *organizational climate* (i.e., the internal state and characteristic ways of working of an agency which result in a particular atmosphere) partially determines an organization's success with change and is therefore a component of organizational readiness for change. One indicator of climate is the nature of the organization's *communication,* or the manner in which information and meaning is transmitted. Communication can be characterized along an open-closed dimension and some studies indicate that *open communication* is a major component of a healthy climate for change.

I hypothesized, therefore, that greater openness of organizational communication will lead to greater success in implementing a management information system. But what is open communication? I defined one component of this variable as *the existence of norms for the expression of differences among staff.* The definition then served as a basis for selecting items. Three items used in the questionnaire to measure this specific variable are noted in the bottom of Figure A; individuals could indicate their degree of agreement with these statements.

This deductive process of moving from the abstract to the concrete is only a partial reflection of the processes that led to the selection of my items. In fact, the logical process can be seen more accurately as an overlay to the creative-intuitive processes. Hunches, based on work experiences and observations of organizational behavior, were in fact what led to the interest in communication. I looked at numerous items related

FIGURE A

From Concepts to Questionnaire Items

Organizational Behavior and Analysis

Planned Organizational Change

Organizational Readiness

Organizational Climate

Communication

Open/Close

Open

Open communication: The existence of norms for the expression of differences among staff.

Item 1. Most mental health staff in our agency feel free to express disagreement with their supervisors.

Item 2. It is difficult to have a complaint dealt with fairly in this agency.

Item 3. Our staff meetings are characterized by free *and* open communication, particularly in relation to controversial issues.

to organizational communication before operationalizing the variable for the purpose of my study. Without the guideline of a definition, my assessments were more intuitive, such as "I like the sound of this item," "I like the idea of this item but the item itself is awkward," or "The format here might be useful but the response categories are vague." Encouraged by my advisor to explore the logic behind the intuitive judgments led to a more systematic appraisal of items and frequently to refinements of the conceptual framework of the study.

Over time my own experience-based criteria for assessing questionnaires emerged. Frequently these criteria were identical to guidelines outlined in the literature regarding item construction, but the "hands-on" experience gave depth to my intellectual understanding of the issues. I recall my early attraction to vague items such as "Our activities with each client are recorded at least fairly systematically." I learned to ask myself, "What will a response to this item tell me?" This critical perspective led to the development of more specific items, such as:

Do you record activities with each client on a daily basis?

Do you have a good system for tracking client progress within the program?

Are client records kept up to date?

Does each client record portray the range of agency services that your clients are receiving at a given point in time?

A number of factors accounted for my reluctance to define the variables in operational terms. First, I waffled for some time regarding which specific variables I would include in the study and from what perspective they would be defined. Second, I did not fully grasp the level of specificity required and the necessarily tight connection between the definitions and the specific items. For example, I conceptualized job satisfaction in broad terms and expected that a single score from a job satisfaction scale would serve as my indicator of a person's job satisfaction. Later I broke this concept into several subvariables, such as: satisfaction with peer relations, satisfaction with supervisory relations, satisfaction with intrinsic rewards, satisfaction with extrinsic rewards, and so on. Factoring out the pieces of each variable provided a basis on which to define the variables in operational terms and to prioritize and select variables for the study.

The process of factoring out the components of the variables also forced me to realize what an enormous task lay ahead of me. To reduce the size of the study I had already given up many variables that were important to me, and this process made clear that I was still dealing with too many variables to be included in one study. Conceivably, each of the major variables to be included in the measuring instrument could be broken into over ten factors. Each factor then had to be defined operationally, its importance related to the literature, items selected or identified for each factor, and hypotheses generated for the relationships among the factors. Since the size of the task now seemed overwhelming, I simply resorted to resisting defining the variables, feeling more comfortable in the realm of abstraction.

At the same time that I was coming to appreciate the necessity for greater specificity in definitions, the variable definitions in the literature seemed vague and very broad. For example, one existing questionnaire purported to measure "values" and defined this variable as "the degree of accord (of the specific change about the be implemented) with the organization's philosophy and operating style." And "resistance" was defined as "the organizational or individual disinclination to change, for whatever reason." I felt caught between what was now seeming to be a more precise and proper manner for defining variables and what was available in the literature to serve as models. Again, as with my assessments of existing questionnaires, it took time before I trusted my own critical evaluations of variable definitions.

Phase 3: Implementation

A consequence of my reluctance to define the variables was that the fine tuning of the design—narrowing the focus of the study—came only shortly before data collection began. Again, it was the time frame of the field situation that ultimately forced the choices that I was resisting. In order to keep the questionnaire length within practical limits, many variables or subvariables had to be sacrificed at the last minute. The letting-go process at times seemed almost unethical, and my insistence to look at multiple and interactional explanations of phenomena haunted me till the end. While the letting-go process was difficult, the final product was cleaner, more focused, and considerably more manageable than what I had earlier proposed.

I was to learn at first hand (and the hard way) the difference between a pretest and a pilot study. My questionnaire was designed to be self-administered. In other words, an individual could complete and return the questionnaire without my assistance. The mail survey is the typical method for distributing self-administered questionnaires and the method that receives most attention in the literature. However, there is increasing evidence that the appearance of an investigator or assistant delivering and explaining the questionnaire, and picking it up, produces a higher return rate than is normally expected for mailed questionnaires. For this reason, I elected to group administer the questionnaire at each agency, meet with the staff during a regularly scheduled staff meeting to describe the study and related procedures, request staff participation, distribute the questionnaires, and respond to staff questions and comments. A test site for the pilot study was identified and a time arranged to group administer the questionnaire. This would be the first time that persons similar to the proposed study sample would respond to the questionnaire. Having labored over the strategy for presenting the study and motivating people to participate, I was anxious to test its impact. Upon arrival at the test site I was informed by my contact person that only two of the agency's administrative staff would meet with me. As circumstances would have it, summer vacation had left the agency understaffed, and the regular meeting I was to attend had been canceled. Therefore, the two persons with whom I would meet would take responsibility for distributing and collecting the questionnaires.

I was initially disappointed not to have the opportunity to "dress rehearse" my prepared remarks and concerned that the two administrative personnel would not be able to convince the social workers to complete and return the questionnaires. My concerns were quickly alleviated by a warm and animated conversation. There was a good return rate on the questionnaires, and not until I began the formal study did I learn what I had lost by not personally group-administering the questionnaires at the test site. It was at this point that I learned the difference between a pretest and a pilot study. In essence what I had conducted was a pretest—a pretest of the questionnaire—and not a pilot test of the study. While the feedback on the questionnaire was informative and resulted in important modifications, the situation had prevented an *in vivo* rehearsal, or dry run, of the study procedures. For example, at the first agency in the formal study I realized that I needed additional written instructions for returning the questionnaires and consent forms. I forgot to leave the questionnaire for the director and had to return to the meeting to drop it off, and my own anxiety, created by both my investment in the study and my awareness of the needed impact of this presentation, resulted in a less than polished presentation. Had a comprehensive pilot study been conducted, implementation problems would likely have been identified and problem-solved prior to the formal study. A good pilot study would also have permitted firsthand experience in responding to staff comments and questions. As it was, my skills in this area developed and improved from one agency to the next in the formal study.

Another painful lesson grew out of my initial attempts to contact agency directors. Directors were to be contacted initially by telephone, followed by a letter detailing the study purposes and procedures and a formal request to participate in the study. A preaddressed return letter and stamped envelope accompanied the invitation which the agency director would sign to indicate the agency's agreement to participate in the study. I confess that I expected this process to take about two weeks. Since I had about six weeks before it became critical to begin data collection, and since I was in an energy slump (i.e., depressed), I put off making this initial telephone contact until the last minute. Unfortunately, just getting through to the agency directors was a feat in itself. They were "out of town," "out to lunch," "stepped out momentarily," "in conference," and so on. And, in my case, it was the month of August and many directors were on vacation or going to be on vacation. As a consequence, I lost three agencies that would have been willing to participate in the study had I not put off the initial contacts.

I might add here that I found this initial task of contacting agency directors very unpleasant, cringing when I thought about saying, "Hello Mr. L. This is Joan Avery speaking. I'm a student in the School of Social Welfare at the University of Washington, and I'm doing a research project ...," and visualizing another cringing person on the other end of the line. Student status seldom contributes to one's sense of being a competent professional. Also, I heard from one director after another about their being deluged with requests for participation in research projects. Those situations where I either knew the director or agency program evaluator were considerably easier to tackle. In two situations a friend who knew the agency director made the initial contact for me. This was a successful strategy.

In most cases, the response to the letter of invitation was unusually prompt. In cases where considerable time lapsed, I was reluctant to call the director—not wanting to make a pest of myself. However, without exception, the agency director expressed gratitude for the reminder and responded immediately. I came away from this part of the research process learning the importance of leaving adequate time for establishing contacts with agencies, that follow-up calls are appreciated, and that unpleasant tasks ultimately have to be done anyway and are seldom as unpleasant in reality as anticipated.

I had intended to send identical letters to each agency director. However, in response to telephone contacts with directors, I personalized each letter either in the introduction or conclusion, leaving the body of the letter identical for each agency. I initially questioned the lack of standardized procedures from one agency to another; however, the risk seemed minimal in terms of the potential payoff. Sometimes the personalized comments took as much as one or two paragraphs. While I struggled anyway with business letters, particularly those which are needed to make a definite and positive impression, I suspect that the extra effort paid off in terms of the director's response to me as an investigator and the energy that would be necessary in coordinating the data collection.

Two factors that helped facilitate the working relationship with agency directors prior to any face-to-face interactions were a clear, concise, and thorough description of the study, its procedures, and the expectations of the agencies, and the use of a form letter and a return addressed envelope for agency directors to indicate their willingness to participate. Persons from three different agencies gave me unsolicited positive feedback regarding the letter. In most cases, the letters of agreement to participate were received by return mail, in part, I suspect, because the task was uncomplicated and required little time.

With the exception of one agency, the questionnaire return rate ranged from 85 to 100 percent. I attribute this exceptionally high return rate largely to the fact that the questionnaires were group administered. The questionnaires had been developed in such a manner that they could have been mailed. However, the literature indicates that a 50 percent return rate on mailed questionnaires is generally considered good, 70 percent to 80 percent possible but unusual. Since it was advantageous to have a high return rate, the questionnaires were group administered. Group administering the questionnaire permitted the introduction of the human factor into the research situation. This involved attending staff meetings at the various agencies to present the proposed study and distribute the questionnaires in person.

The face-to-face contact with potential respondents was critical for me. I was aware that historically the relationship between practitioners and researchers in the human services had not been compatible, often resulting in a lack of cooperation by social workers in research studies. Since the study sample would be largely social workers, the strategy for motivating them addressed this population. To avoid using too much of the agency staff meeting time, I planned a 20-minute time period for introducing myself, introducing the proposed study, describing the study procedures, distributing the questionnaires, and responding to questions and comments. In retrospect, I was able to accomplish many objectives in a very short period of time. In addition to presenting information about the study and related procedures, the major goal was to elicit staff support and cooperation. Towards this end, several objectives needed to be met. For example, respondents would need to see me as being competent, trustworthy, holding similar values and concerns as their own, able to relate on a collegial level, and committed to and capable of assuring that the study's findings would be utilized for the purposes indicated. And, too, I think they needed to like me on first impression. These factors seemed particularly critical in view of the sometimes sensitive and controversial nature of the study content.

With this audience in mind, I worked on a presentation that would facilitate meeting these objectives by identifying myself as a former social worker and grounding the research question in my own work experiences in a mental health center. Since I had personally experienced the organizational change that these agencies were about to undergo, it was a relatively easy matter to anticipate the kinds of concerns and issues that would be important to the workers. While the study had both theoretical and applied interests for me, and with the agency staff, I focused entirely on the applied aspects relating the study to service delivery and quality of work life in human service organizations. For example, I was interested in the relationship between staff attitudes about a proposed change and the degree of agency success in implementing the change. During the staff meetings, however, I directed the discussion to topics such as the amount of paperwork that a management information system implied for social workers, the limitations of information systems for evaluating service delivery programs, and the importance of clinical input for resolving accountability-related problems.

There are obviously many ways to present a research study to an audience, and I was conscious of the very different manner in which I talked with these audiences, in contrast to my academic language. I think my willingness to relate on a professional line level (free of research jargon) was an important factor in eliciting staff cooperation. I was perceived as "one of them" rather than a "researcher" operating out of an ivory tower.

Phase 4: Evaluation and Dissemination of Findings

The conduct of research frequently requires making promises to individuals—promises regarding confidentiality of responses and promises regarding what will be done with the study's findings. As a practitioner/researcher interested in data analysis, it was difficult for me to imagine how or for what purpose I would reveal individual responses. Yet questions about confidentiality were raised in almost all agencies. For example, some staff were concerned that the study's findings would be identified by agency name. I responded to this concern by discussing the importance of aggregated versus individual data for research purposes and the steps I had taken and would take to protect confidentiality of responses. Respondents ultimately had to decide for themselves about my trustworthiness regarding these issues, but had the questionnaires been mailed, the opportunity to raise questions and hear from me directly would not have been available.

Questions were also raised about what would be done with the study's findings. They were concerned not that the findings would be shared with a state agency that was interested in the findings but that the findings would never be used. In other words, given that they took the time to express their views, would the feedback to the state agency have any impact—would it be heard? The discussions increased my awareness of the importance of establishing channels through which the data would be utilized prior to conducting the study. Because these channels were well established prior to data collection and because I had ongoing contact with state personnel who were invested in the study findings, I was able to share my optimism and belief about data utilization in a very personal way.

All of these issues—the purpose of the study, the study procedures, confidentiality of responses, utilization of research findings, and so on—can be described to some extent in the cover letter of a group-administered questionnaire (see Figure B). But it is difficult to anticipate all possible staff reactions and to deal with them thoroughly or convincingly in a cover letter. I was frequently surprised, for example, by hostile staff reactions to what I viewed as a fairly innocuous individual consent form and appreciated the opportunity to clarify and reassure. The face-to-face

FIGURE B
Cover Page and Consent Form:
Staff Perceptions of Change in Agency Life

As part of my research program in Social Welfare at the University of Washington, I am seeking information about the attitudes and perceptions of mental health agency staff regarding program evaluation, accountability, information systems, computerized information systems, organizational change, job satisfaction, and characteristics of mental health agencies. Better understanding of employee attitudes and perceptions can hopefully lead to improved practices in mental health agencies.

As an employee of one of the mental health agencies in this state, you are being asked to complete two questionnaires regarding the subjects mentioned above. The first questionnaire is attached. The second questionnaire will follow in approximately four months. Each questionnaire will take about 20-30 minutes to complete. Should you complete the first questionnaire, I ask that this be an expression of your intent to complete the second questionnaire although participation in both cases is entirely voluntary. You are free to withdraw your consent to participate or discontinue participation at any time. You may find some of the questions to be intrusive or disconcerting. For example, you will be asked to indicate how much you agree or disagree with the following statements: (1) Decisions made by administrators are typically regarded with suspicion; and (2) Some of our staff have good reason to fear program evaluation. However, you may refuse to answer any specific question that you wish.

Since I am interested in not just individual responses but the responses of an aggregate of employees, reporting of results will take place on a group level. Neither your agency's name nor your name will be identified with any of your responses and will not appear on the questionnaires. I would eventually like to treat both questionnaires as if they were one questionnaire so it is important that I be able to match your first questionnaire with your second questionnaire. Since I want to avoid using a coding system that would require my having access to the names of respondents, I am asking you to identify each of your questionnaires with your birth date, your sex, and the *third* letter of *your first* name. This information will be requested on each questionnaire. All questionnaires will be kept in a locked file and I am the only person who will have access to this file. All questionnaires will be destroyed 6 months following completion of the study.

I hope you will be willing to help in this project but wish to assure you that your participation is entirely voluntary. You are welcome to ask questions regarding the study and your participation in it. I will be visiting your agency when I distribute the questionnaires or you may contact me at the University. I wish to remind you that your comments will remain strictly confidential. Thank you for your assistance and cooperation.

_____ Investigator   _____ Date
          Joan Avery

I voluntarily agree to complete this questionnaire and have the opportunity to ask questions.

_____ Respondent   _____ Date

Copies: Respondent (1)
          File (1)

Source: M. Austin & Crowell (1981).

interaction between potential respondents and myself afforded the opportunity to inform, to clarify, to share values, and to provide assurances, and it introduced a very human element into the entire data collection process.

I have focused primarily on the content of the interaction between agency staff and myself. Implied throughout, however, is the importance of interpersonal style and the manner in which information is communicated, staff concerns are heard and dealt with, and trust is established. Reflecting on one's own interpersonal skills in a particular situation and describing them to others can be a rather awkward task. And yet I am convinced that the personal relationships established with agency staff in a period of 20 minutes contributed in a large way to the high return rate of the questionnaires. If I were to characterize my presentation of self in those agencies where the interpersonal factor worked most successfully, I would use words like *enthusiastic, warm, empathic, friendly, spontaneous, concerned,* and so on—not unfamiliar terminology to social workers.

I am reminded of a paper I wrote several years ago on the practitioner/researcher relationship. The paper grew out of my frustrations as a social worker with investigators who were both "clinically unaware" and "lacked interpersonal finesse." The literature confirmed some of my own impressions that "practitioners" and "researchers," particularly in social work, often inhabit two very different worlds. Differences in value systems, priorities, modes of thinking, and so on contribute to serious communication problems that inhibit collaborative or cooperative efforts. I advocated then (and do so now) that the training of capable social work practitioner/researchers should include attention to the interpersonal and social aspects of the research enterprise.

Group-administered questionnaires allow for the introduction of the human element into the data collection process. The investigator can benefit from some of the advantages inherent in the interview approach to data collection and yet minimize the costs that are associated with individually administered interview schedules. While the cost, time, and effort requirements of group-administered questionnaires exceed those for mailed survey questionnaires, the payoffs in terms of return rate plus the rich data obtained through informal contacts with agency staff far outweigh these additional costs.

GROUP-ADMINISTERED QUESTIONNAIRES

The group-administered questionnaire, as noted above, represents a method of data collection based on survey questionnaires which is very appropriate for social work research. It involves the researcher in direct contact with the population in introducing the study verbally and in writing, as well as administering the data collection process. The respondents may be agency staff members, as in the case study above, a group of community residents (as in a Community Action Program), or a number of clients considered collectively. For example, the social worker might administer a questionnaire to a group of clients in an agency waiting room, might involve staff in administering a questionnaire to clients completing a treatment or activity session, or might organize a special session of clients in a residential setting to complete a questionnaire. Social workers must be particularly sensitive to the issue of confidentiality when bringing a group of people (clients or otherwise) together.

There are several reasons why use of a group-administered questionnaire should be considered by a social worker. First, this method of data collection provides an opportunity to come in contact with the study's population. While this contact is also possible with the interview method (see Chapter 16), the group-administered questionnaire facilitates acquiring the largest number of participants in the shortest amount of time. Since individual interviews are quite time-consuming and mailed survey questionnaires are often completed in uncontrolled settings, with varying degrees of compliance, the group-administered questionnaire is more efficient and potentially more effective in capturing respondent data.

Sampling

The problems of efficiency and effectiveness are also related to the issue of sampling a range of individuals. All research methods use some form of sampling in order to locate a representative group of individuals so findings can be generalized to as wide a population as possible. Random sampling procedures were noted in Chapter 8, but the technique most frequently associated with group-administered questionnaires is called accidental sampling. This procedure involves selecting individuals by stratifying a population of potential respondents by some specific criteria. Examples of accidental samples would be staff from three urban agencies in cities of over 300,000 population and three rural agencies in communities of under 50,000 population, or clients selected from different program areas in an agency on the basis of the time of the month in which they appeared at the agency.

Once the tentative sampling plan has been developed, the investigation must enter the field by talking to the staff of an agency where a pilot study might be conducted or to clients about their possible involvement in the study. This helps assess the adequacy and feasibility of the sampling plan. The best laid plans usually require revisions due to unexpected changes in the lives of agency staff, clients, or community residents. The sampling plan may have to be modified, for example, to include agencies in one county rather than a hoped-for statewide representation (provided significant differences between the agencies can be identified), or to include clients from one agency program rather than hoped-for representation from all the programs in the agency (provided the sampling goal is to include all clients served by a particular program).

The goal of sampling is to provide a secure foundation for generalizing the study's findings. The question of how secure can be answered, in part, by the ethics of research. If the study honestly reflects the sampling goal and sets forth the qualifications that must be made about the findings if the goal is not reached, the results are most likely to be credible. The research process involves slow, steady accumulation of the results of studies of all sizes, and even the smallest one (e.g., small sample, brief questionnaire, short study period) can make a contribution to the growth of knowledge of human, organizational, or community behavior.

Entering the Field

There are some important principles for entering the field to collect data and conduct the actual study. The researcher should:

1. Communicate with a person from every important subgroup related to the study population (e.g., agency director, supervisor of service workers, service workers, clients, clerical staff), since every level either lacks knowledge of the activities of others or is biased by its own position.
2. Utilize agency and/or community informants who have a wide variety of contacts.
3. Consult with informal leaders inside and outside the staff group or client group, as well as formal leaders (e.g., agency administrators, presidents of organizations).
4. Use discrepancies in the accounts of various informants as the basis for further exploration.
5. Assess information from informants in terms of the respondents' social role or position (e.g., client's views toward participating in a study will be different from staffs' views) and their personal views about the value of the study. Beware, also, of positional lag in information; for example, a recently promoted supervisor may no longer have a complete picture of worker or client views.
6. Plan to spend considerable time as a participant-observer with the population which will ultimately be asked to participate in the study, since there are often discrepancies between what people *say* privately on a questionnaire and the ways they *behave* in a group.
7. Seek out personal and private beliefs of informants as well as the socially accepted climate of opinion (e.g., "I hate participating in research studies, but research is good for our agency").

8. Keep a detailed note file on the names and views of the entire range of contacts made in setting up the study population in advance of the group-administered questionnaire. Initial impressions and global judgments should not be discarded.
9. Study all available records and secondary sources carefully, as well as relevant procedures (e.g., client records in relationship to a study involving clients, agency procedures and manuals related to a study of staff, census data in relationship to studying the community).

These principles are drawn from the experience of professionals who have learned them as a result of many experiences using questionnaires or interview schedules to conduct studies. Their applicability will be recognized by social workers who are educated to engage in effective interpersonal communications and who learn to gather and analyze data from a variety of sources (verbal and written, formal and informal) before a plan is developed, to seek further data where gaps or contradictory evidence emerge, and to analyze data in terms of both human behavior and the contextual social environment from which it emanates. Such people are aware of the need to observe actual human behavior in efforts to understand discrepancies between what people *say* and what people *do,* as well as the difference between *public* and *private* beliefs.

Administration

Once entry has been achieved and the questionnaire has been field-tested to eliminate as many confusing elements as possible, the carefully laid-out questionnaire can be taken into the field for administration. Some of the principles to be applied in introducing and administering the questionnaire to a group of clients, staff members, or community citizens are indicated in the checklist for group-administered questionnaires in Figure 15.2.

FIGURE 15.2

Checklist for Implementation of Group-Administered Questionnaires

---

	YES	NO
A. QUESTIONNAIRE INTRODUCTION		
1. Does the face sheet of the questionnaire include general information about the purpose of the study?	___	___
2. Is there an indication of how much time it should take to complete the questionnaire?	___	___
3. Is a separate consent form attached to the questionnaire for the respondent to sign?	___	___
4. Does the face sheet include all necessary instructions for completing all items? (e.g., "Don't skip around," "Answer all items to the best of your ability.")	___	___
B. QUESTIONNAIRE ADMINISTRATION		
5. Are there enough questionnaires?	___	___
6. Have plans been developed for persons unable to attend the questionnaire completion session to complete and return the instrument at another time?	___	___
7. Have all staff been notified in writing and verbally at a staff meeting about the date and time of the group administration?	___	___
8. Has the physical environment been checked in advance to make sure there will be sufficient space and adequate lighting for writing?	___	___
9. Have efforts been made to anticipate and eliminate possible sources of noise or distraction during the questionnaire completion session?	___	___
10. Are there plans to read aloud the instructions on the face sheet at the questionnaire completion session?	___	___
11. Will specific instructions be given on how to mark the questionnaire or answer sheet?	___	___
12. Is sufficient time allowed for questions from respondents before beginning to complete the questionnaire?	___	___
13. Will clarification announcements based on respondents' questions about an item on the questionnaire be made slowly, in a clear voice which is loud enough for all to hear?	___	___

FIGURE 15.2 (continued)

	YES	NO
14. Are all questionnaires to be collected immediately after completion and checked for completed identification information and consent form signature?	____	____
15. Have all respondents been informed of a sign-up roster to receive copies of the results of the study?	____	____
16. Will each respondent be personally thanked when the questionnaire is returned?	____	____
17. Are follow-up letters to be sent to agency administrators and key staff members who facilitate the implementation of the group-administered questionnaire?	____	____

Source: Clemens (1971).

These commonsense principles involve clarity of communication, effective use of feedback, specification of expectations, proper agency protocol, attention to the way in which the agency or community environment affects the behavior of the respondents, and respect for each individual participating in the study. While many of these principles are obvious, they can be easily forgotten under the intensity of questionnaire administration or pressure to complete the study. Checking the 17 items in the checklist in Figure 15.2 can help the worker make plans for implementation prior to group administration of the questionnaire, or it can serve as an evaluative instrument following the administration.

One of the attributes of good social work researchers is the capacity to understand and effectively relate to where a potential respondent is "coming from," in order to capture a perspective which may be different from their own views or experience. This sensitivity should be reflected both in the language used in the construction of the instrument and in the implementation of a group-administered questionnaire (Mindel, 1981).

MAILED SURVEY QUESTIONNAIRES

The success of a survey using mailed questionnaires will primarily be determined by the response rate achieved. Some of the many factors which affect the number of recipients of a questionnaire who will complete and return it are:

1. *Sponsorship.* Potential respondents must be convinced of the study's legitimacy and value (scientific, government, university, or well-known organization auspices).
2. *Questionnaire format.* Printed or photocopied questionnaires appear to be equally effective. Using both front and back of paper may be acceptable because it results in less bulk.
3. *Questionnaire length.* Adequate and feasible length is best determined in the pretest of the questionnaire. The least cluttered format is preferable.
4. *Cover letter.* Clarity of purpose and benefit of study are critical elements.
5. *Ease of completing and returning questionnaire.* Explicit mailing instructions and a self-addressed, stamped return envelope should be provided.
6. *Inducements to reply.* Potential respondents must be convinced that the study is worthwhile and that their cooperation is important.
7. *Nature of respondents.* Members of special groups are usually good respondents, and socioeconomic class differences contribute to variable response rates.
8. *Type of mailing.* First-class mailing and prestamped return envelopes stimulate the highest return rate.
9. *Timing of mailing.* Holidays, vacation periods, or school opening should be avoided.
10. *Follow-up letters and telephone calls.* Written or verbal follow-up should be given after allowing two or three weeks for response to initial mailing.

There is considerable "practice wisdom" about ways to increase questionnaire response rates. The key factors seem to be the clarity of the cover letter, the format and length of the questionnaire, the type and timing of the mailing, and the use of follow-up mechanisms. The details of developing a cover letter, mailing the questionnaire, and follow-up are covered in the checklist in Figure 15.3.

The 24 items on this checklist should be viewed as suggestive rather than prescriptive; alternate methods may be preferable in some circumstances. They simply reflect some of the practice wisdom gained from implementing mailed surveys. Like the implementation checklist for group-administered questionnaires (Figure 15.2), the checklist in Figure 15.3 can be used in planning or evaluating mailed questionnaires.

FIGURE 15.3
Checklist for Implementation of Mailed Questionnaires

	YES	NO
A. DEVELOPING COVER LETTER		
1. Does the letter communicate the appeal to respondents?	____	____
2. Does it include a reasonable explanation of the study by anticipating and countering respondents' questions?	____	____
3. Does it set forth the benefits of the study?	____	____
4. Does it describe the importance of the respondent to the study and indicate that no one else can be substituted?	____	____
5. Does it exceed the maximum of one page?	____	____
6. Does it appear under an appropriate letterhead?	____	____
7. Does the individualized name and address and the date appear on the letter?	____	____
8. Is the investigator's individually applied signature included?	____	____
9. Does the letter include a confidentiality statement and explanation of the coding procedure?	____	____
10. Does the attachment to the cover letter include a stamped, self-addressed questionnaire reply envelope?	____	____
11. Does the letter indicate how results will be shared with respondents?	____	____
12. Are there instructions for indicating that a copy of the results is wanted (e.g., placing name and address on back of return envelope)?	____	____
13. Is the letter reproduced on an electric typewriter or printed by multilith or high-speed computer printer for greater efficiency and better appearance?	____	____
B. MAILING PROCEDURES		
14. Is the envelope an unusual size, shape, or color to attract attention, along with embellishments such as "Immediate reply requested"?	____	____
15. Has the size of the questionnaire and envelope been determined in relationship to using first-class postage and minimizing the appearance of bulky contents?	____	____

FIGURE 15.3 (continued)

	YES	NO
16. Has a mailing list been developed which includes the number of the questionnaire beside the name of the respondent?	_____	_____
17. Are the envelope contents folded together when inserted so that respondents will find all relevant materials on opening the envelope?	_____	_____
18. Is the mailing planned for early in the week in anticipation of time needed to forward mail to new addresses?	_____	_____
19. Will the mailing avoid a holiday period when respondents are likely to be away from home, and will it avoid December and the crush of holiday mail?	_____	_____

C. FOLLOW-UP

20. Is there a preprinted follow-up postcard for mailing one week after mailing of cover letter?	_____	_____
21. Does the postcard include the respondent's name and address and the investigator's signature?	_____	_____
22. Does it thank the respondent if the questionnaire has already been returned?	_____	_____
23. Is a second follow-up letter ready for sending three weeks after mailing of the cover letter, with a replacement questionnaire and return envelope?	_____	_____
24. Is a third follow-up letter ready for certified mailing to remaining nonrespondents seven weeks after original mailing, with a replacement questionnaire and return envelope?	_____	_____

Source: Don A. Dillman, Mail and Telephone Surveys: The Total Design Method. Copyright©1978 by John Wiley & Sons, Inc. Reprinted by permission of John Wiley & Sons, Inc.

QUESTIONNAIRE SELECTION AND MODIFICATION

The development and use of indexes and scales for measuring variables relevant to social work practice were discussed in Chapter 11 which pointed out that the worker is frequently confronted with the option of choosing from among existing instruments or constructing new measures. Using existing instruments can save time, money, and energy. From the perspective of increasing our understanding of social phenomena, it is also important to use standardized measures of social variables.

Standardization refers to the extent to which different researchers use the same measures when studying the same concepts. If different measures are used, differences in study findings can always be attributed to differences in measurement. When the same measures are used, comparisons of findings are easier because differences in measurement are eliminated. For example, if we wish to determine differential effects on client self-esteem of three therapeutic modes, equivalent or identical measures of self-esteem are needed for each mode. Or, if a state mental health agency wants to determine the distribution of income for mental health center clients throughout the state, standardized means for determining and recording client income are required.

Standardization in measurement is our rationale for recommending the use of already existing measures. Standardized instruments usually have documented levels of validity and reliability (see Chapters 10 and 11). While it should not be assumed that all published measurement instruments provide data about their validity and reliability, there is a greater probability, particularly in the case of beginning social workers, that these issues will be ignored if new measures are constructed.

Since much social work research is conducted within limited time frames, the construction of highly valid and reliable measures can be very difficult to accomplish. Understanding the importance and significance of validity and reliability requires a good deal of hands-on experience. Lack of such awareness can lead investigators to selectively avoid these issues, in much the same way as lack of understanding of statistics can lead them to skip over data analysis sections in research reports. Therefore it is important to take the time to assess potentially relevant instruments carefully and critically in order to look for and report validity and reliability indicators.

One additional reason for using existing measuring instruments is that, despite their sometimes simplistic appearance, questionnaires can be deceivingly difficult to construct. For beginning social work researchers, it is preferable to use existing questionnaires as a way of grasping measurement concepts and item construction. Experience with existing instruments provides a meaningful learning base for constructing them.

If a good measure of a particular concept exists, there is little to be gained by constructing a new measure. The question remains, however, whether adequate or good measurement instruments do in fact exist. It is not uncommon for social workers to lament the lack of sound measuring instruments for social work concepts. While there is considerable basis for this concern, particularly in view of the complex nature of human phenomena, the temptation may be to assume too readily that appropriate measures are unavailable, when in fact they do exist as presented in Table 11.3 in Chapter 11. There are thousands of exciting instruments, and it may be difficult to find one's way through the mass.

Assessing Existing Questionnaires

While standardization in measurement is a recommendation for using existing instruments, it should not be assumed that any instrument developed or used by reputable persons in the field is beyond scrutiny or is superior to a personally constructed questionnaire (see Table 11.3 in Chapter 11). It is important to remember that published instruments may be developed by novices or others who are working under time pressures, have a narrow perspective of the questionnaire content, or are so deeply involved in the subject area that they cannot communicate clearly to those who are less knowledgeable. Assuming the fallibility of other professionals may help to develop trust in one's own critical assessments (intuitive or otherwise) of existing instruments.

Questionnaires should not be assessed solely in terms of their availability, frequency of use, or validity or reliability in other situations. Rather, the assessment should reflect the nature of the concepts under investigation and the circumstances in which the study is to be conducted. The 12 items in the checklist in Figure 15.4 provide a guide to assessing the compatibility of existing questionnaires with the needs of a particular study.

Modifying Existing Questionnaires

The decision to modify an existing questionnaire is often based on the attractiveness or appropriateness of some of the items. Modifying a questionnaire makes it possible to build on the work of others and at the same time to avoid the compromises inherent in rigid adherence to an existing questionnaire.

There are a number of dimensions along which measuring instruments can be characterized and, therefore, assessed and changed. Decisions about the use of questionnaire items for a particular study are often based on the anticipated level of statistical analyses, the time frame for data collection, the nature of the variables, or the respondents' level of sophistication.

The serendipitous nature of the research enterprise and the importance of the investigator's intuitive and subjective hunches and impressions of an existing questionnaire item should also be taken into account. For example, the search for relevant measuring instruments

FIGURE 15.4
Checklist for Assessing Existing Questionnaires

	YES	NO
1. Will the responses to the questionnaire provide the data needed to answer the research question?	——	——
2. Does the questionnaire address the same types of variables that are to be studied (i.e., value, attitude, personality trait, behavior, knowledge, skill, perception, judgment)?	——	——
3. Is the level of measurement appropriate for the intended statistical analyses?	——	——
4. Is the format of the items appropriate to the level of inquiry?	——	——
5. Does the questionnaire have known reliability? Are the circumstances in which reliability was established known?	——	——
6. Does the questionnaire have known validity?	——	——
7. Have there been other applications of the instrument? Or has the instrument been reviewed by other professionals in journals, books, or other publications?	——	——
8. Is the language of the questionnaire appropriate for the intended sample or population?	——	——
9. Are the instructions clear and easy to follow?	——	——
10. Do the items meet standards for item construction (i.e., clear, precise, not double-barreled, or biased)?	——	——
11. Is the flow of the questionnaire logical and easy to follow?	——	——
12. Is the questionnaire the appropriate length for the time available for data collection, the attention span of intended respondents, or other circumstances related to the design?	——	——

Source: M. Austin, & Crowell (1981).

can begin at different points in the research process, even before the variables have been operationally defined and the ultimate format of the questionnaire is clear. The social worker may have an intuitive sense about the appeal of particular instruments, as in the case study in this chapter. Subjective impressions, even without a clear basis, can facilitate the development of criteria for assessing, constructing, and modifying questionnaires.

Some of the ways in which questionnaires can be modified, including changes in length, level of specificity, levels of measurement, and language, and the pooling of items from different questionnaires, have been discussed in preceding chapters, and they may appear obvious. However, they are often overlooked in the search for the "perfect instrument" and thus merit attention here.

Length. Questionnaires can be shortened, lengthened, or used only in part. It is possible to expand a particular section or subsection of an instrument in order to gather more data, or limited access to a particular client population may require a shortened version. Perhaps only one section of a questionnaire is relevant. It is important to bear in mind that as changes are made in the instrument, the validity and reliability of the questionnaire items change as well. Steps must be taken to establish the validity and reliability of the modified instrument through pilot studies with a representative sample of respondents and a panel of judges, such as other social workers who are familiar with the research topic.

Level of Specificity. Instrument items vary in their level of specificity. Some items, for example, may address an issue broadly, such as open-ended Item A:

A. Do you feel you have enough freedom in making decisions about your work?

The same issue can be addressed more specifically, such as open-ended Item B:

B. Do you feel you have enough freedom in making decisions regarding:
   1. Client treatment plans?
   2. Size of client load?
   3. Nature of client load?
   4. Your work hours?
   5. Where you see your clients?

Conceivably, an existing questionnaire could address the investigator's interests in a study, but the level of specificity may need to be modified.

Levels of Measurement. The four levels of measurement discussed in Chapter 9—nominal, ordinal, interval, and ratio—represent another area in which measuring instruments can be modified. Consider a question like Item C:

C. What is your major responsibility in your place of employment? (Circle one number below.)
   1. DIRECT SERVICES
   2. INDIRECT SERVICES
   3. SUPERVISION
   4. PROGRAM MANAGEMENT

    5. ADMINISTRATION
    6. RESEARCH
    7. OTHER (SPECIFY)

In this example the response categories distinguish among potential responses related to the nominal variable, major responsibility. The seven categories are perceived to be mutually exclusive in order to suggest that there is no relationship between the items. The use of nominal measurement limits the range of alternatives for statistical analyses.

    If interval data were desired, the item could be changed to read as in Item D:

D. What percentage of your time is spent in each of the following activities? (Place percent of time to the right of each activity.)

DIRECT SERVICES	____%
INDIRECT SERVICES	____%
SUPERVISION	____%
PROGRAM MANAGEMENT	____%
ADMINISTRATION	____%
RESEARCH	____%
OTHER (SPECIFY)_____	____%

                                           Total. 100%

Language. Existing questionnaires should be assessed for their suitability for the respondent population (e.g., age, experience, level of sophistication, ethnicity). An instrument developed originally for college-age students might be modified for a younger age-group by simplifying the language, for example, or language designed for professionally trained staff could be adapted for clients who may not be familiar with the technical language of the social worker.

Pooling Items from Different Questionnaires. If the social worker likes some items from various questionnaires which deal with the same concept or variable, it is possible to combine items to create a new index or scale. It is also possible to include entire sections of several different instruments by bringing them together in new combinations to reflect particular research interests. The sources used in this approach to instrument modification and construction should always be cited.

    Modifying existing questionnaires is an artistic endeavor. Like a sculptor, the social worker molds and shapes the instrument until it adequately reflects the research question of the study. Social workers should have the confidence to experiment with various combinations of questionnaire items and to trust their own judgment in assessing the utility of existing questionnaires (Marsh, 1982).

PILOT STUDIES AND FIELD-TESTING

A basic tenet of social work research utilizing questionnaires is the commitment to field-test the instrument as part of a pilot study prior to using the final instrument in the actual study. It is not always clear what constitutes a pilot study, as the social worker found in the case study in this chapter.

The first step in questionnaire implementation is a pilot study, which consists of at least three parts: (1) entry assessment, (2) instrument administration field test, and (3) preliminary data reduction. Thus, the pilot study consists of more than simply field-testing the instrument.

In the first part of the pilot study, actual steps are taken to gain access to a small sample which is similar to the population chosen for the larger study. While there are no clear specifications for the size of a pilot study sample, it is advisable to test the instrument on 15 to 20 people. The issue of access is concerned with the problems of gaining the people's interest; time commitments and schedules; and agency, administrative, or board approval (or human subjects review clearance) for a sample of the most sensitive questionnaire items. In this part of the study the worker can also gain experience in answering the potential respondents' question, "What is in it for me?"

Next the worker tests the instrument under actual conditions. Potential respondents may need clarification of the language on certain items or may demonstrate a tendency to skip items which do not appear to apply to them. A review of completed questionnaires, along with a group discussion with respondents about their difficulties in answering them, is one of the most valuable ingredients of the pilot study.

The final step of the pilot study is to aggregate the data from the 15-20 questionnaires by hand tabulation to see if the responses reflect sufficient variation to test the study's hypothesis or to reflect findings which appear to have some validity (Beless, 1981). This step should also provide some insights about how the codebook should be developed for managing the completed questionnaires resulting from the larger study.

SUMMARY

This chapter serves as a bridge between Chapter 12, on instrument design and construction, and Chapter 16, on research interviewing. The bridge was built on one side of the ravine with pillars comparing questionnaires and interviews and describing the pros and cons of questionnaires, and on the other side with pillars describing the development and implementation of group-administered and mailed questionnaires. The bridge itself was constructed out of personal and professional experiences, including a journal of a beginning social work practitioner/researcher. Those who see such a bridge as contributing to their expertise as social workers should remember that it can only be strengthened through the personal experience of conducting social work research.

16. RESEARCH INTERVIEWING

Interviewing is at the core of social work practice and is the most consistently and frequently employed social work technique (Kadushin, 1983). Social work education emphasizes the skills and purposes of the interview; therefore it is not surprising that social workers are most comfortable with interviewing as a method of collecting data for research studies. Indeed, the goal of much of the interviewing social workers do is to gather data about clients and their situations or data on which program evaluation can be based. Familiarity with the purposes and techniques of interviewing, therefore, is a necessity in conducting research studies which depend on data elicited from interviews (Wasser, 1957, 1962).

The two major sources of self-reported data in research studies are material presented by individuals in written form through questionnaires, and information elicited from respondents through interviews. Characteristics and problems of survey questionnaire research were discussed in the preceding chapter. This chapter describes the uses of research interviews in the social worker's problem-solving process, suggests some procedures for conducting effective research interviews, and considers the advantages and disadvantages of interviews for collecting research data.

ADVANTAGES OF RESEARCH INTERVIEWING

The advantages of interviewing as a data collection method are primarily related to naturalness and spontaneity, flexibility, and control of the environment. Combined with a high response rate, they provide a good argument for the use of this method when compared to mailed survey questionnaires (see Chapter 15).

Naturalness and Spontaneity

Interviews usually create a natural situation for individuals to present information in. For most people, it is easier and more natural to respond to questions orally than in writing, and a casual, relaxed setting leads to more spontaneous answers. What people say "off the top of their heads" may be free of the self-censorship often encountered in written responses. Also, it is more difficult in an interview than in a mailed survey questionnaire to "erase" an answer and replace it with a more "appropriate" and perhaps less valid answer.

High Response Rate

Respondents may leave out answers in mailed survey questionnaires because they lack reading or language skills, do not understand the questions, are unmotivated to answer the instrument, or simply overlook some items. In a research interview, the interviewer is there to see that each item is answered, and the interviewer can interpret or reword the item if necessary without distorting it. Many people not only are more comfortable expressing their ideas in speech than in writing, they may even enjoy talking to an interviewer, whereas they would consider filling out a survey questionnaire a nuisance and toss it in a wastebasket. Interviewers also are much harder to avoid than survey questionnaires, particularly survey questionnaires that arrive in the mail. The presence of a trained interviewer allows for a far more detailed and complex set of questions than is possible in a mailed questionnaire. The interviewer can slowly and carefully go over intricate items and make sure every question is covered.

Flexibility

Interviews permit far more flexibility than survey questionnaires. In talking with an interviewee, areas which might be difficult to frame in specific questions can be explored, and probing questions can be used to give responses greater depth. The interviewer can also adapt the sequence and timing of questions, the way items are phrased, and even which questions can be eliminated, according to the characteristics of a particular respondent (such as age, ethnic group, intelligence, or experience).

In studies of sexual behavior, for example, Pomeroy (1972) soon learned that the areas with which people are most uncomfortable tend to vary with their socioeconomic levels. Thus, the interviewers were instructed to ask people from lower socioeconomic levels about premarital intercourse (a behavior they tended to be comfortable about) early in the interview, while items about masturbation (a behavior they tended to be more uncomfortable about) were to be asked later. The reverse order was used with respondents of higher socioeconomic levels because of their different relative ease with these two behaviors.

Access to Serendipitous Information

Since interviewers are present, they can make use of any unanticipated data interviewees offer. Content thus "stumbled on" can provide useful data for the study and, perhaps, subsequent investigations. The concept of unexpected events is expanded on in Chapter 17, on participant observation.

For example, in the pretest of a study conducted on postplacement adoption services by Gochros (1970), an adoptive parent mentioned quite casually the extent to which she and her husband had lied to their social worker during their adoptive study. Her degree of comfort in sharing this information impressed the interviewer, and in subsequent interviews a question about parents misinforming and withholding information from the social workers was added.

Nonverbal Responses

Skilled social workers are sensitive to their clients' nonverbal responses, which also can supply significant data in research interviews. The tone of the interviewee's voice, an interruption of eye contact, an unexplained smile or frown, can all reflect on the verbal response it accompanies and lead the interviewer to probe for explanations.

Observation of and Control over the Environment

In mailed survey questionnaires, social workers have little or no control over when, where, or how the measuring instruments are answered, or even who answers them. The interviewer can both observe, and to some extent, control these factors. For example, with group-administered survey questionnaires (see Chapter 15), respondents may have little control over who is looking over their shoulders. Indeed, they may choose to have others in their environment help them with their answers. The interviewer can see to it that respondents answer the questions in private and without the prompting or influence of others. Thus, the answers are clearly the respondents' own.

DISADVANTAGES OF RESEARCH INTERVIEWING

There are problems and limitations in any research method which depends on respondents' self-reports, whether the data come from a survey questionnaire or an interview. According to Bailey (1978), there are four major sources of respondent errors and biases in self-reported data. Respondents may: (1) deliberately lie because they do not know an answer, (2) make mistakes without realizing it (often because they are not able to admit socially undesirable feelings, attitudes, or traits, even to themselves), (3) give inaccurate answers by accident simply because they misunderstand or misinterpret the question, or (4) be unable to remember, despite their best efforts. Respondents may even blend truth with fiction to cover up their memory gaps.

In addition to these problems, which are endemic to self-report studies, there are other problems which particularly affect research based on the interview method in comparison to survey research. These are principally related to time and cost constraints, the reactions of respondents, and possible interviewer influence or distortion.

Time and Expense

Perhaps the most obvious limitation of interview research is its high cost and the considerable amount of time involved. The postage involved in mailing questionnaires in surveys is far less expensive than hiring, training, and supervising interviewing staff, let alone paying for the long hours of the interviews, as well as the time and expense involved in getting to and from them. Further, translating data from interview notes and completed instruments adds an extra, often expensive, step in the research process which may not be necessary with the relatively simpler survey questionnaire forms.

Unless an extravagantly large interviewing team is accessible—and affordable—interview research is a slow process. Especially in situations in which it is necessary to go to the respondents (which is often the case), the number of interviews any one interviewer can cover in a day is quite limited. In contrast, large numbers of mailed survey questionnaires can be accumulated and coded in a relatively short time. There are also problems in coding responses which are associated with interviewers wording the items differently. The time problems are aggravated when respondents are hard to reach, fail to keep appointments, or do not complete interviews because of outside distractions. These are old stories to social workers who are experienced with home visits with clients, but the motivation for being a research respondent is usually weaker than that for receiving social work services. The number of interviews which may be needed to accumulate a large enough sample for many research studies adds to the difficulty of conducting these interview-based research projects.

Interview Intensity

While many people enjoy the attention and stimulation of being interviewed, others may consider it a nuisance, particularly if the interview comes at a time when they are tired, preoccupied, or uncomfortable. With mailed surveys, respondents can determine when and where they will answer the questionnaire; they may even choose to answer it in dribs and drabs. When interviewers are seated opposite respondents, urging them on, they have little choice but to stay with the interview until the end, and the resulting fatigue, discomfort, and even anger may well influence their responses. Respondents may provide poor answers in an interview situation merely because the interviewer arrives when the baby is crying, the dog is barking, dinner is burning, or they need to go to the bathroom.

Inaccessibility to Respondents

An obvious limitation of research interviews is that the social workers may have a hard time getting to the respondents. Sampling procedures may suggest a group of respondents who are geographically widely distributed or located in areas which are hard to reach, such as the hollows of West Virginia or distant military bases.

Loss of Anonymity

Mailed survey questionnaires, especially those asking for little identifying data, can provide anonymity for respondents, who can feel relatively sure their participation will have no negative effects. Responding to a research interview can pose greater anticipated and perhaps real threats to respondents, despite reassurances of confidentiality. The interviewer not only sees respondents in person but, if the interview is in the home, may come to know their address and observe their homes as well as their families, neighbors, and friends. Some people could consider such observations embarrassing or even incriminating. For example, in the postplacement adoption study referred to earlier, respondents may well have feared the interviewer's impressions of their handling of their adopted children. Furthermore, interviewers may be seen by neighbors and others entering or leaving respondents' homes, with possibly uncomfortable implications.

Interviewer Distortion

The research interviewer adds a link in the chain from respondents' responses to the data which does not exist in mailed survey questionnaire research. In mailed questionnaires, respondents read the questions and place their answers directly on the instrument. In interview research, the interviewer asks items in what may or may not be a standardized format, listens to the answers, and then summarizes or attempts to put the full response into notes which may be later rewritten or reformulated and then put into the data bank.

While the presence of the interviewer can facilitate the gathering of more meaningful data, for reasons stated above, there are risks of interviewer distortion or error at several points in the process. Interviewers may misread or badly phrase a question, or interpret or hear a respondent's answer incorrectly. It is also possible for the interviewer to check an answer on the wrong line or in other ways fail to record responses accurately. Further distortion may occur later if the interviewer misreads or cannot understand the notes taken during interviews (Crittenden & Hill, 1971).

There are four common interviewer distortions based on various types of errors, as follows:

1. *Asking errors.* Interviewers may change the wording of questions or even fail to ask a particular item.
2. *Probing errors.* Interviewers may negatively affect respondents' answers by asking follow-up questions or probes which are unnecessarily challenging, hostile, biased, or irrelevant.
3. *Recording errors.* Unless interviewers use tape recorders or have excellent memories, they must record respondents' answers by either the cumbersome and time-consuming process of writing exactly what their respondents say or by summarizing the responses. Such processes have a high potential for error.
4. *Cheating.* Interviewers are subject to the same temptations as any other employed mortal. Whatever the motivation, an interviewer may deliberately fill in gaps in interviews or even record a response for an item which was never asked.

Interviewer Influence

Interviewers can influence respondents not only by the phrasing of questions and tone of voice but by their own apparent comfort or discomfort with a particular question. This can be demonstrated, for example, by a change in eye contact or the rapidity with which a question is asked.

Even the words that are emphasized in an item can influence the response. Consider the different implications of these two questions:

Did you *ever* feel like hurting your children?
Did you ever feel like *hurting* your children?

Other characteristics of the interviewer, in addition to specific behaviors in the interview, may have an effect, for better or worse, on the reliability of the data gathered from a research interview. Such variables as the interviewer's age, sex, physical appearance, racial or ethnic group, or language and accent, can affect the quality of respondents' responses. Moreover, these same variables and other characteristics of the interviewees (such as "apparent intelligence") may well elicit diverse patterns of behavior from interviewers, and this can affect the way they carry out the interview and the resulting data.

CONSIDERATIONS IN RESEARCH INTERVIEWS

Once an area of study has been selected which lends itself to self-reports elicited through research interviews, and the necessary resources for conducting such interviews have been assembled, the social worker is concerned with how to prepare for, conduct, and record the data from such a study. The remainder of this chapter will consider some of the points to consider in going through these stages in research interviewing. The procedures include: determining the degree of structure in content, developing the interviewing schedule, determining the format of interview items, selecting interviewers, gaining access to interviewees, deciding where to conduct the interviews, checking the interviewers' appearance, developing the interviewer-respondent relationship, formulating and asking questions, and recording the data.

Determining the Degree of Structure in Content

The preparation of the interview instrument or schedule (a written instrument that sets out the overall plan for the interviews and determines the structure, sequence, and content of the specific items to be asked) is crucial to the outcome of the study. Many of the considerations in the development of the instrument as well as the overall plan for research conducted through interviews are somewhat similar if not identical to those associated with mailed survey questionnaire construction (Chapter 12) and group-administered survey research (Chapter 15).

An important variable in planning research interviews, however, is the degree to which the interview is to be structured. Structure refers to the extent to which the interview schedule or instrument includes predetermined, specific items. There are three options for structure in research interviews: structured, semi-structured (or focused), and unstructured. Each has particular purposes, advantages, and disadvantages.

Structured Interviews. In a structured interview, the instrument prescribes exactly what items will be asked, their sequence, and even their specific wording. Both open- and closed-ended items may be used. This is the easiest type of interview to code, since all interviewees are asked exactly the same items in the same order.

Predetermining the exact wording of the items reduces the risk that interviewers may introduce their biases by the way they word questions. Structured interviews also provide consistency in the nature of the data collected from interview to interview. The social worker can use interviewers with relatively little training, since individual decisions are kept at a minimum and they need only follow specific instructions.

Structured interviews have a number of limitations, however. Interviewers have little freedom to draw fully on respondents' knowledge of the research question or to explore or expand on answers with probing questions. They may not even seek clarification of ambiguous or vague answers. Thus, structured interviews provide few of the advantages of interviews over mailed survey questionnaires, yet they are more expensive and time-consuming.

Semistructured or Focused Interviews. The semistructured interview schedule may include some specific items, but considerable latitude is given to interviewers to explore in their own way matters pertaining to the research question being studied. A form of the semistructured interview called the focused interview centers on selected topics and hypotheses, but the specific items used are not entirely predetermined. Usually this form of interview is used for respondents who have shared a common experience, such as having received a particular type of social work service, been the victim of a particular crime, or suffered a certain illness.

The semistructured interview requires a more skilled and better trained interviewer than does the structured form. Interviewers must learn as much as possible about the particular attribute or experience the respondents have shared. On the basis of this knowledge, they decide before the interviews what aspects of the respondents' experience are to be explored, and they may develop hypotheses about these experiences to be tested in the interviews (Bailey, 1978). Thus, the general areas to be explored are determined before the interviews, although few, if any, of the questions may be formulated in advance. The process has been described by Merton, Fiske, and Kendall (1956) as follows:

First of all, the persons interviewed are known to have been involved in a particular situation: they have seen a film, heard a radio program, read a pamphlet, article or book, taken part in a psychological experiment or in an uncontrolled, but observed, social situation (for example, a political rally, a ritual, or a riot). Secondly, the hypothetically significant elements, patterns, processes and total structure of this situation have been provisionally analyzed by the social scientist. Through this content or situational analysis, he has arrived at a set of hypotheses concerning the consequences of determinate aspects of the situation for those involved in it. On the basis of this analysis, he takes the third step of developing an interview guide, setting forth the major areas of inquiry and the hypotheses which provide criteria of relevance for the data to be obtained in the interview. Fourth and finally, the interview is focused on the subjective experiences of persons exposed to the pre-analyzed situation in an effort to ascertain their definitions of the situation. The array of reported unanticipated responses gives rise to fresh hypotheses for more systematic and rigorous investigation.

Since the hypotheses may be formulated before a semistructured interview, the interviewer must avoid biasing the items to confirm the hypotheses. Moreover, although respondents have a right to be informed about the general purposes of a study in which they are participating, it may not be advisable to inform them of the specific hypothesis being tested, because knowing this might bias their responses.

Semistructured interviews allow for the introduction of unanticipated answers from interviewees. For example, Gochros (1970) had not anticipated before the pretest for the study of postplacement adoption services mentioned above that adoptive parents would volunteer how they had misled their adoption study worker and were concerned that their postplacement workers would discover their deceptions. As a result, probes in this area were later introduced.

Such exploration in semistructured interviews often is accomplished with "funneling" techniques, in which a general item is followed up with more specific probing questions. An example of this procedure was used in an interview study of 300 mothers whose children had been placed in foster care. The interviewers were all trained social workers who visited the mothers in their homes. After explaining the purposes of the study and obtaining the mothers' agreement to explore their experiences with foster care, they recorded the responses as accurately as possible following a very detailed semistructured instrument, the opening segment of which is shown in Figure 16.1. The full interview instrument covered 34 pages and required an interview approximately two hours long. It included open- and closed-ended questions, checklists, and scales. This obviously long and complicated instrument was necessitated by the quantity and complexity of the data the researchers hoped to gather.

FIGURE 16.1

Opening Segment of a Semistructured Interview Instrument

A. MAIN QUESTION: Respondent's Statement of Problem

    1. First of all, would you tell me in your own words what brought about the placement of _____ away from home in foster care?

        (Probe if not spontaneously answered)

        1A. Who first had the idea to place _____?
            (1) Did anyone oppose it or disagree with it?
            If yes:
            a. Who?
            b. Why?
        1B. Were any attempts made to make other arrangements for _____ other than placement?
            If yes:
            a. What?
            b. Who did this?
            c. Why didn't it work out?
        1C. Was there anyone whom you usually depend on who couldn't or didn't help out?
            If yes:
            a. Who? (relationship)
            b. Why not?
        1D. Did all your children who were in your home go into placement at that time?
            If no:
            a. Which children were not placed at that time (name, age, sex, father)?
            b. Why weren't they placed?
        1E. Who was caring for _____ just before he/she was placed?
            If other than natural mother:
            a. For how long had she been caring for _____?
            b. Why was she caring for the child (rather than the child's mother)?

Source: S. Jenkins & E. Norman, *Filial Deprivation and Foster Care* (New York: Columbia University Press), ©1972. Reprinted by permission of the publisher.

    Semistructured and focused interviews allow for considerable latitude in the length and detail of the instrument. If only one or two researchers who are intimately familiar with the phenomenon being studied and the goals of the study will be conducting the interviews, the instrument can be comparatively shorter and less detailed. In Gochros's study of postplacement adoption services, he was the sole interviewer. While there may be considerable hazard of interviewer bias when the social worker is both the hypothesis formulator and interviewer, such economy of personnel does allow for a much simpler measuring instrument. The instrument used for the interviews with each of the 114 adoptive parent respondents (and a similar one used with their 18 postplacement social workers) was less than two pages in length. This schedule is shown in Figure 16.2.

The brevity of the instrument in Figure 16.2 leads to less disconcerting paper shuffling during the interview and fuller attention to respondents. Extensive use of abbreviations (e.g., AP = adoptive parent, CW = caseworker, SP = supervisory or postplacement period) allows the instrument to be further condensed. The instrument does not need to conform to the strict design and construction methods as presented in Chapter 12 because only the interviewer sees it.

The guide to the determination of the degree of detail in the instrument for the semistructured or focused interview is threefold:

1. What is it that is to be learned, and how much is already known about it?
2. To what extent are the interviewers trained, prepared, and able to elicit data on their own from respondents?
3. To what extent is the simplicity of coding responses (with its implications for validity) to be a determining factor?

Unstructured Interviews. In unstructured interviews, only the general problem area to be studied is determined in advance of the interviews. The interviewers choose the timing, structure, and content of items to be asked, not unlike the procedures used in worker-client fact-gathering interviews.

The major advantage of unstructured interviews is that the interviewer has almost unlimited freedom to ask interviewees wide-ranging items, to seek in-depth clarification of their answers, and to explore any possibly profitable avenues which may emerge in the interview. The respondent is clearly at the center of this form of interview. Responses are often elicited from neutral probes provided by the interviewer. This form of research interview is derived from the field of psychotherapy (Rogers, 1945). It often seeks to probe the respondents' deepest feelings and experiences and may well uncover emotions, attitudes, and beliefs they were not even aware of prior to the interview.

This type of research interviewing depends heavily on the competence and self-awareness of the interviewer. It requires well-trained interviewers who are skilled in techniques for developing working relationships and eliciting data from respondents. They must be able to make quick decisions about what to ask and when and how to ask productive questions. They must also be knowledgeable about the gen-

FIGURE 16.2
Interview Schedule with Adoptive Parents

1. What were you told about the purposes and content of the SP?
   By whom:
2. What did you expect the visits to be like?
3. How were they different from what you expected?
4. Why do you think there is a SP?
5. How many SP visits were there?
6. Average length?
7. How many AP initiated? Why?
8. How many unexpected? Opinion
9. How many were you present:
10. Ever feel left out?
11. What did you talk about?
12. What do you think CW wanted you to bring up or discuss in SP visits?
13. Subsequent contacts.
14. What sort of problems did you run into during the SP?
    Freedom
    Rel: Husband-Wife
    Rel: Parent-Child
    Depressed
    Neglected
15. Books recommended? Why? Read? Useful?
16. Did you think of CW more as a friend or caseworker?
17. What did you like most about CW?
18. What did you like least about CW?
19. Did CW create the kind of atmosphere where you felt free to talk over your real feelings about things?
20. Did you ever withhold any information or feelings from CW?
21. How much do you think CW knew about child care and development?
22. What did you think about when you knew a visit was scheduled?
23. What did you think about just after the visit was over?
24. Did your feelings change about the visits during the SP?
25. What did you find the most helpful result of the visits?
26. What did you find to be the least helpful or most unpleasant aspect of the visits?
27. Any way agency could have been more helpful during the SP?
28. How helpful was the SP to you, overall?
29. Can you think of any way that the visits may be helpful to you in the future?
30. How did you feel when the decree was finally granted?
31. Do you think there should be a waiting period?
32. If yes, how long?
33. Should there be CW visits? Why?
34. Compulsory? Why?   (continued)

FIGURE 16.2 (continued)

---

35. If they had been voluntary, would you have requested any?
36. If adopt again and if voluntary, would you have requested any?
37. Groups for parents of 5-year-olds, interested?
38. Groups for parents of adolescents, interested?
39. If ran into a problem with a child, contact worker?
40. Second child: planning, applied, placed, not planning
41. If worker was different from study, was transition difficult?
42. Comments:

Source: Gochros (1970, 1981).

eral subject they are exploring. Further, they must be fully aware of the dangers of leading or biasing interviewees, which are greater because of the nature of the unstructured give-and-take.

One of the most significant limitations of this type of interview is the problems it creates in coding. However, if little is known about the research question being studied or if the question is a sensitive one, unstructured interviews may lead to the acquisition of useful data for more structured future inquiries. Indeed, unstructured interviews are generally not as useful for testing out hypotheses or for deriving accurate measurements of specific phenomena as they are for developing preliminary data in relatively uncharted areas which may lead to the formulation of later hypotheses (Knowledge Level 1, as presented in Chapter 13). Such research may require very small samples.

For example, a social worker contacted six former male clients who were homosexually oriented and heterosexually married, and asked to interview them regarding their hopes and expectations from treatment and their reactions to it, as well as their subsequent experiences. While the general purposes of these interviews were clear to both the interviewer and interviewees (i.e., what they wanted and what they got from their social work contact), the interviews were entirely unstructured. The report of the study included hypotheses about counseling gay husbands derived from the interviews, illustrated with extensive direct quotations from the former clients. Such a study can provide a stepping stone to larger, more detailed, and more structured investigations (Knowledge Levels 2, 3, and 4 as discussed in Chapter 13).

Developing the Interview Schedule

There are probably far more similarities than differences in the formulation of both effective interview schedules and respondent-recorded questionnaires. Guidelines presented in the preceding chapter for questionnaire formulation, therefore, can be adapted to interview schedule formulation.

As noted in Chapter 12 there is no "right" way to construct an instrument, despite advances in research methods and techniques—many of which are reported in this text. Decisions on how to structure and design an instrument must generally be based on informed hunches which are pretested before being used with the sample or population. One of the few generalities which can be drawn from the experience (especially the early experience) of interview research designers is that usually far more data are elicited from the interviews than will subsequently be used in the research analysis and report. The social worker, having the typical limitations of time and money, may be well advised to be parsimonious in deciding what will be covered in a measuring instrument.

In deciding what is to be covered and how the items can best elicit this information, a number of questions must first be answered:

1. What do we want to know that we don't know already?
2. Who can tell us what we don't know and what we want to know?
3. How can we formulate and ask questions that will increase the probability that they will tell us what we want to know?
4. What would keep them from telling us what we want to know or would lead them to deceive us or present us with incomplete data?
5. How can we override these sources of withholding and distortion?

The answers to the first three questions have been presented in Part One of this text. To answer the remaining two questions it is necessary to consider some successful strategies which have been developed to elicit desired information through research interviews.

Sequencing of Questions. Generally, the funneling techniques referred to earlier have been found to be useful in gaining honest and complete answers from respondents (Gochros, 1978a). This involves starting the interview with broad, general questions and then moving on to narrower, more specific—and perhaps more difficult and sensitive—questions as the interview progresses. The advantage of this approach is that rapport can be established early in the interview with questions which do not make the respondent particularly uncomfortable. As interviewees establish more trust and confidence in the interviewers, more challenging questions can be asked.

Bailey (1978) has suggested six guidelines for establishing an order for questions in an interview. These suggestions are the basis for the discussion in this section.

First, open-ended questions, and those which are likely to be sensitive or difficult to answer, should be placed late in the interview. If difficult items come early, the respondent may become resentful or immobilized and could refuse to continue. What is sensitive to one respondent, however, may not be sensitive to another. For example, Pomeroy's finding that respondents of low socioeconomic standing tended to be uncomfortable with questions about masturbation but were relatively comfortable with items about premarital sex was noted above. The degree of sensitivity was generally reversed among respondents of higher socioeconomic levels.

Thus, interviewers may need some flexibility in the order in which they ask such items. Even if open-ended questions are not sensitive, they should generally be placed last, because answers to this type of question take more time and energy. For example, in studying reactions to group therapy, it may be easier for respondents to answer such items as "How often did you meet?" and "Was the group therapist always there?" than a question like "How did you feel when other group members were confronting you?"

Second, easy-to-answer items should be asked first in the interview. Such questions usually ask for facts rather than feelings, beliefs, or opinions. Thus, interviews usually start with such demographic variables as age, gender, home address, marital status, occupation, and place of employment. (In survey research, demographic variables are asked last; see Chapter 15). Although even such seemingly innocuous items can cause discomfort, they are usually at least clear and nonthreatening (demographic variables about race, income, and religion are more likely to be discomforting). Whenever possible, opening questions should also be interesting and perhaps mildly provocative so as to gain the respondents' interest and clarify the subject matter of the interview.

Third, answers should be obtained early in the interview to items that may be necessary to guide the remainder. For example, getting the names, sex, and ages of siblings and determining whether they are still living would be a logical, early step in studies of family relationships.

Fourth, items should be asked in a logical order. This provides a flow to the interview which facilitates moving easily from item to item. The most obvious and frequently used organizing theme is time sequence. In describing children, for example, it would seem most logical to ask about them in order of birth. Indeed, that is the sequence in which most people usually present this information. The frame of reference of the interview should also be clear and orderly. Each segment should be covered completely before moving on to the next. It is both awkward and confusing to the respondent to move back and forth between topics.

For example, in Gochros's study of adoptive parents' experiences with postplacement services, the unstructured interview (see Figure 16.2) was constructed in the following sequence:

1. How parents were prepared by the agency for postplacement services (Item 1).
2. What they expected postplacement services to be like (Items 2 through 4).
3. What the postplacement services were like (specific facts, such as number of visits, followed by more difficult questions, including reactions) (Items 5 through 15).
4. Evaluation of the social workers and the usefulness of their services (Items 16 through 28).
5. Suggestions for how services could be improved (Item 29).
6. Reactions to the postplacement period itself (Items 30 through 35).
7. Anticipation of any future problems and whether agency services might be used in the future (Items 36 through 41).
8. Any other comments (Item 42).

Fifth, the creation of a "response set" should be avoided. The suggestion that there should be a logical sequence of questions and the interviewer should avoid skipping around from topic to topic should not be regarded as a rigid requirement. Indeed, if the researcher senses that asking items in a particular order will lead an interviewee to answer in a particular way, that order should probably be changed. This avoids what is called a response set, whereby the interviewer causes respondents to reply in a way that does not reflect the questions' content or the respondents' accurate answers. One of the most common response sets is a function of social desirability, or the tendency to reply to items in a way respondents perceive as conforming to social norms. The order of items may well encourage such a response set. An exaggerated example would be asking an item such as "Do you think most people love their mothers?" followed by another item such as "Do you love your mother?" When respondents are asked to give their salaries in a succession of jobs, they may well have a response set to report increased salaries from job to job, whether or not such a pattern really existed.

The probability of response sets can be reduced by changing the order of questions or the answer format. This has the disadvantage of possibly confusing the respondent, but if it is done with moderation such a procedure may also lessen the boredom of a long series of items. In the postplacement adoption study, items about parents' perceptions of the social worker's activities were interspersed with an activity in which respondents were presented with a deck of index cards on which various worker activities were written and asked to rearrange them in order of what they believed their social workers were trying to do—from "most trying to do" to "least trying to do."

Sixth, reliability—question pairs should be asked at various points in the interview. In this procedure two questions, one phrased negatively and the other phrased positively, are asked to check the reliability of respondents' answers. For example, at one point in an interview, the interviewer may ask, "Did you think your social worker generally understood what you were up against?" and at another, "Did you get the feeling that your social worker didn't understand the problems you were facing?" Such a procedure can be used to double-check the reliability of particularly strategic items for either a particular respondent or for an entire sample. Where disparity in responses is encountered, the interviewer can ask probing items in order to amplify or clarify respondents' ideas. This procedure should be used cautiously for a variety of reasons, most conspicuously because the respondents may perceive the device—accurately—as a trick.

Determining the Format of Interview Items

It is often desirable to vary the format of items in an interview schedule. For example, the respondent may be asked to read a statement, then be asked some questions about it. The length and type of answers expected can also be varied; at various times, facts, beliefs, opinions, or experiences can be requested. In addition to adding variety to an interview and thus avoiding response sets and maintaining interest in the interview, different types of items can achieve different purposes. The relative merits of the two primary forms of items, open- and closed-ended questions, were discussed in Chapter 12, and we need only summarize some of their advantages and disadvantages in research interviews.

Utilizing Open- and Closed-Ended Questions. In closed-ended questions, the respondent has a limited, predetermined range of answers, such as, "yes or no", and "male or female." With open-ended questions, respondents can give any answer they choose, rather than selecting from a range of options. For example, "Do you get along with your children?" is a closed-ended question which invites a yes or no response, while "How do you get along with your children?" is an open-ended question allowing for a wide range of answers. Open-ended questions are relatively easy to formulate and to ask, but the answers are difficult to code and categorize. For example, the item, "If you had three wishes, what would they be?" can produce data that may be a practitioner's dream but a researcher's nightmare (Jenkins, 1975). However for the price of agonizing over more complex response categories, the worker may gain a greater range of responses, many of which may not have been anticipated.

It may seem logical that open-ended questions would elicit answers reflecting greater depth and feelings from respondents, but this is not necessarily the case. There is no evidence that open-ended questions produce answers of greater depth or validity than closed-ended questions do (Dohrenwend, 1965). Indeed, with situations in which respondents are considered resistant, the closed-ended, "objective" questions often provide more valid results. Additionally, closed-ended questions are most useful when specific categories are available against which the respondents' replies can be measured and when a clear conceptual framework exists in which respondents' replies will logically fit (Dohrenwend, Colombatos, & Dohrenwend, 1968).

Using Probes.   Perhaps the most useful type of item in semistructured interviews is the probe, or follow-up question. The intent of such items is to seek greater depth or clarity about answers the interviewee has already given. Often vague or general replies will be given to open-ended items because respondents have not completely thought through their replies or are not sure how to answer. They may also be holding back from giving a complete answer for fear of appearing sick, bad, stupid, or worthless. This is when a probe is called for. The intent of such questions is to help interviewees provide more complete and accurate data.

Probes may also be used to increase the probability that all areas of interest to the interviewer have been explored. For this purpose, the need for probes may be anticipated and included in the interview schedule, based on the investigator's experience with responses to particular areas of questioning in the pretest. These predetermined probes can then be used as "contingency questions" the interviewer can draw up if the interviewee answers—or fails to answer—questions in certain anticipated ways.

There is a variety of interviewing techniques which can be used as probes to encourage respondents to amplify, expand, or clarify responses. These probes need not be included in the interview schedule but should become part of the interviewer's standard repertoire to be called upon when respondents' answers suggest their use. Bailey (1978) has described the procedures researchers can use in probing for responses. They are:

1. *Repeating the question.*   This is done whenever the respondent hesitates or appears not to understand the question.
2. *Repeating the answer.*   This type of neutral probe can be used by an interviewer who is not certain about understanding the respondent's answer correctly. Repetition of the answer can

correct errors and assure both respondent and interviewer that the answer is recorded carefully. Repetition also gives the respondent an opportunity to think about elaborating it further.

3. *Indicating understanding and interest.*   The interviewer indicates that the answer has been heard and approved of, thus stimulating the respondent to continue.

4. *Pausing.*   The interviewer pauses and says nothing if the response is obviously incomplete. This indicates that the interviewer knows the respondent has begun to answer and is waiting for the rest of the reply.

5. *Using a neutral question or comment.*   "How do you mean that?" or "Tell me more" indicates to the respondent that an answer is on the right track but more data are desired.

Selecting Interviewers

It would appear logical for social workers to do their own research interviewing, since their training and experience should have made them knowledgeable about human behavior and social problems and skilled in interviewing. This background would seem to equip them for interviewing in sensitive areas (Hamovitch, 1963). However, there are a number of significant differences between social work practice interviewing and research interviewing. As a result, years of service-oriented practice may, paradoxically, be both a limitation and an asset for the social worker as research interviewer. Moreover, trained social work researchers are expensive to employ and may be hard to recruit for research interviewing positions.

The choice of the particular level of training required for a research interviewing assignment should be determined by a review of the population to be interviewed, the content of the interview, and the availability of supervisory staff and other resources for the study. Interviewers who lack social work training, such as indigenous community residents, graduate students, paraprofessionals, and social work moonlighters, have been used effectively in a wide range of social work research efforts. Indeed, such classifications of researchers are used more often than full-time trained social workers. Since there is some evidence that the personality of interviewers is more predictive of effectiveness than is education or social status, there is good reason to at least consider alternatives to social work staff (Summers & Beck, 1973). Nevertheless, as Jenkins (1975) suggests: "Where feasible and appropriate . . . filling the role of research interviewer is one way for the practitioner to contribute to social work research." Indeed, doing so may provide social workers with new and useful perspectives on their practice, and it is one way to introduce them to the practitioner/ researcher concept. Matching other characteristics of the respondent and interviewer may be more significant for the quality of the data derived from research interviews than the formal, professional training of the interviewer.

Matching Interviewer and Interviewee Characteristics. Social workers usually have limited financial resources and thus have little control over which interviewers will interview which respondents, regardless of similar or different characteristics. However, the differences or similarities of interviewers and respondents can have considerable influence on the usefulness of the data acquired. Thus, if the luxury of choice is available, deliberately matching interviewers to respondents may be desirable. But what should be matched to what? Generally, respondents and interviewers seem to do best when they can identify with each other. However, the means to achieve such empathy is not always simple or clear. This section will review the effects of a number of physical and social characteristics of interviewers on the answers of respondents and also on interviewers' reactions to the respondents. These variables are sex, age, language, socioeconomic disparity, and race or ethnicity.

Sex. Since rapport is usually (but not always) better when interviewer and respondent have somewhat similar characteristics, it would seem likely that interviewers who are of the same sex as their respondents would get better results. Such would certainly seem to be the case in such situations as research on rape (Jenkins, 1975). Sex-linked patterns of relating may also affect perceptions of interviewers. Investigators asked male and female interviewers who had surveyed political attitudes to rate each of their respondents in terms of their honesty. The male interviewers rated 68 percent of their male respondents and 56 percent of their female respondents as "completely frank and honest," while the female interviewers rated 79 percent of *both* their male and female respondents this way (Benney, Riesman, & Star, 1956). Another study found that both men and women rated whether they would like to see a particular movie in a way that they thought would please their interviewers on the basis of the interviewer's sex, especially if the interviewer was of the other sex (Hyman, 1954).

Age. Considerable disparity in age between interviewers and interviewees may also contribute to the biases of either. One study examined the effect of age differences with the hypothesis that the closer in age respondents and interviewers were, the more rapport there would be. Although the results of the study were inconclusive, interviewers who were considerably older or younger than respondents often rated them as equally or more frank and honest than did interviewers who were in the same age group as respondents. However, when both age and sex were considered together, it was found that young female interviewers rated young male respondents significantly higher for honesty than they did older males. Older interviewers did not display such a disparity (Benney, Riesman, & Star, 1956).

Language. Matching the interviewer and respondent in language and accent has been found to be of considerable importance (Welch, Comer, & Steinman, 1973). If respondents are more comfortable in a language other than English, it would, of course, be desirable to use bilingual interviewers. Obviously, also, translations of items originally composed in English must not distort the meaning of the original item. This might best be accomplished by having a professional with competence in both languages develop the items to be used.

Word use also is important in interviewing respondents who use a particular argot or slang words peculiar to their particular situation. Such populations as drug users, prostitutes, homosexually oriented individuals, and ethnic minorities often develop a unique vocabulary to describe concepts important to them. Terms such as *honkey, closet queen,* or *angel dust* which are part of some group's everyday vocabulary may be incomprehensible to the uninitiated.

Interviewers with life situations similar to their respondents may be more comfortable and conversant with this language than those who have merely been tutored in the argot. Professionals studying former drug users have successfully involved them in developing the interview schedule and doing the actual interviewing, thus permitting the meaningful, unstilted, and appropriate use of the vernacular of addicts (Jenkins, 1975). Indeed, with most categories of respondents, interviewers who ask questions in simple language compatible with the everyday speech of respondents tend to get better results. One study examined low-income families and found that abstract and complex items elicited far fewer responses than items which were simply phrased.

Socioeconomic Disparity. It is sometimes difficult to separate socioeconomic differences from racial disparity in matching interviewers to potential interviewees. They are often interrelated; one study, for example, found an inverse relationship between biased data and the social distance between respondents and interviewers. In the case of white interviewers, there was a stronger bias against lower-socioeconomic-class black respondents than against those who were in a higher socioeconomic class. Another study which asked white interviewers what variables (sex, age, race, and economic level) they preferred in the respondents they interviewed found that those interviewers who preferred not to interview older people also rejected poor people and blacks in general.

In a discussion of social work interviewing, Kadushin (1983) introduced the concept of *homophily,* the idea that social workers and clients from similar cultural backgrounds will be more comfortable with each other and thus will work together more effectively. However, it may be dangerous to translate this observation from social work practice to research interviewing. Overidentification, lack of control of bias, and confusion of roles are possible consequences of overemphasis on matching. As an example, in a study of welfare mothers in which both interviewers and respondents were black, the social distance between the interviewers and respondents was examined in relation to their rapport and the validity of the study. Surprisingly, the results indicated that it was similarity in background rather than difference which was associated with interviewer bias. Furthermore, the interviewers who had the greatest rapport with their respondents were the most biased (Weiss, 1969).

There is evidence that interviewers who are socially "too close" to their respondents may become too involved with them, rather than relating to the task of the study (Hyman, 1954). It may be that either too little or too much social distance between interviewer and interviewee can create biases which reduce the value of a study.

In the past, most research interviewers in studies of interest to social workers were from middle socioeconomic classes, white, and well educated, while most of the respondents were less educated, from a lower socioeconomic class, and often nonwhite. In a classic study on interview bias in polls conducted in 1942, Katz (1942) demonstrated a lack of rapport between interviewers and lower socioeconomic-class respondents which led to a clear bias in respondents' answers on matters of concern to them. Socioeconomic disparity between respondents and interviewers continues to be a problem in social work research.

Race or Ethnicity.   The effects of racial differences and similarities between interviewer and respondent are long-standing social research topics. A study conducted during World War II found that blacks interviewed by black interviewers gave significantly more responses indicating racial protest and discrimination in the Army than those interviewed by whites (Hyman, 1954). For another 1942 study in Memphis, Tennessee (a southern city during a period of considerable racial tension), 1,000 black respondents were randomly assigned to black and white interviewers, and there were significant differences in the responses to the interviews of the two groups. Black social aspirations and problems were presented in a more passive way to white interviewers than to black interviewers. Further, the white interviewers obtained significantly higher proportions of what might be called "proper" or "acceptable" answers (Hyman, 1954).

Much has changed, of course, in black-white relations of today, but differences in blacks' responses to black and white interviewers still are apparent. One recent study reported that this difference showed up most clearly when questions were directed at race relation issues and were less significant in questions related to family patterns and other aspects of daily living (Schuman & Converse, 1970). In terms of social work services, both black and white research interviewers asked blacks' preferences for black or white workers. The study found that blacks preferred receiving their social services from blacks, assuming equal competence for black and white workers, and this preference was expressed more strongly to black interviewers than to whites (Brieland, 1969).

Racial and ethnic bias is not limited to black-white differences. In a study of the effects of Gentile respondents interviewed by Gentile and Jewish interviewers in New York City, respondents were asked whether they believed Jewish people had too much, not enough, or about what they should have of influence in the business world. When the interviewer was also a Gentile, one half of the respondents reported that they believed Jewish people had too much influence. However, only 22 percent stated that they thought Jewish people had too much influence when they were asked the question by a Jewish interviewer (Hyman, 1954).

Many of these studies concerning the impact of ethnic and racial differences between interviewers and respondents were conducted when racial, religious, and ethnic biases were socially more acceptable than they are today (D. Robinson & Rhodes, 1946). There is little doubt, however, that such biases still exist and may be a factor in both respondent and interviewer behavior. Indeed, growing minority assertiveness among such racial and social groups as women, gays, Latinos, and blacks may maintain biases which can well affect interview behaviors on both sides of the notepad.

In any case, matching interviewers and respondents can enhance the value of social work research. The biases of both interviewers and respondents on the basis of sex, age, race, and social distance must be considered. However, it is important to recognize that women interviewers *can* be sexists, old people *can* be ageists, gays *can* be homophobic, and blacks *can* be racists. These biases can be minimized by careful selection of interviewers, open exploration of biases, and consideration of how to minimize the impact of any residual biases on the interview process.

Gaining Access to Interviewees

It is often necessary to get permission to approach potential respondents. When an organization is involved, this may entail going through a chain of command. For example, in order to interview prisoners, the investigator may have to ask not only the prisoners but also the warden, who might in turn have to seek permission from the commissioner of corrections, who might then have to check with the governor. For most populations or samples social workers study, such official permission will be necessary, and it is not always easy to obtain. Some communities, such as Beverly Hills, California, require a city permit before some forms of interview research can be undertaken (Bailey, 1978).

Governmental and organizational regulations pertaining to access to samples should be examined to determine to what extent the population has already been studied. Many social work studies call for interviews of lower income groups, ethnic minorities, or other populations which already consider themselves "overstudied." Their resentment and feelings of being used as guinea pigs for more affluent, mainstream researchers may impair the formal or informal group acceptance of the study. Many blacks, for example, have suggested that what needs to be studied is white racism, not black family dynamics. Similarly, some gays feel that research studies should explore the homophobia of non-homosexuals, and some women feel that male investigators should study their own sexism.

Obtaining Organizational Consent. Measures have been adopted in recent years to protect people who are asked to participate in research studies. Studies supported by federal or other institutional funds or conducted under university auspices generally must be subjected to review by research committees, which must be satisfied that no harm will be done to respondents. The National Institute of Health requires that statements to that effect be filed for studies it funds. Such reviews usually cover the measurement instruments to be used and the methods to be undertaken to safeguard the confidentiality of respondents. The risks to respondents as well as the benefits anticipated from the study must be specified.

It is appropriate that social workers protect the rights of respondents as carefully as social work ethics and agency policies protect the rights of clients. The ethics involved in social work research are presented in Chapter 6.

Obtaining Respondent Cooperation. Once organizational consent has been obtained, the worker must secure evidence of the proposed respondents' willingness to be interviewed. If the sample refuses, the result is nothing but a list of nonrespondents. The two most important elements in achieving respondent cooperation are convincing them that their participation is important and that the study is legitimate, and appealing to their self-interests by showing how the results of their participation will be worthwhile to them.

Demonstrating the Importance and Legitimacy of the Study. Prospective interviewees will be more likely to participate if they are made aware that the proposed study is sponsored, approved by, or conducted under the auspices of a prestigious organization, agency, or philanthropic association. This is especially valuable if they are familiar with the organization and have positive experiences and feelings for it.

The endorsement of the organization can be demonstrated in a cover letter under the organization's letterhead endorsing the project and encouraging the respondent's cooperation (see Figure 16.3 and

FIGURE 16.3
Cover Letter Requesting a Research Interview

[Agency Letterhead]

Dear Mr. and Mrs. _____

Our agency recognizes research as a basic method for evaluating old ways and developing new ways of providing more effective services for couples adopting children. The State Division of Child Welfare, in cooperation with this and other twin city adoption agencies, is currently conducting a study of the supervisory period in adoption.

Because you have recently adopted a child through this agency, your experiences and opinions would be of much value. We are therefore asking your cooperation in this study. Your participation will involve an interview between each of you and a researcher from the State Division of Child Welfare.

We wish to emphatically assure you that the information requested in your interview will be treated confidentially by the researcher. Your observations and comments will in no way be identified with your name to this agency. Your information will be known only to the researcher who is conducting this study and will be incorporated anonymously, with that of many other adoptive parents, into the final research report.

Within the next few weeks you will be called by Mr. Harvey Gochros to arrange an appointment with you. We hope you will be able to participate in this most important study. Thank you for your anticipated cooperation.

Sincerely yours,

Executive Director

Source: Gochros (1981).

Figure B in Chapter 15). Such a letter should spell out the purposes of the study and reassure the potential respondents of the legitimacy of the project and the "safety" of their participation. The letter can also prepare the respondents for a direct contact from the interviewer.

In the study of adoption postplacement services, letters to adoptive parents were sent to the sample selected for the study from the agencies that had placed babies with the parents. The request letter attempted to communicate the following five points to the sample:

1. The agency considered research important for improving services, and their participation in the present study would be helpful in accomplishing this.
2. The project had been legitimized by the involvement of both the adoption agency and the state division of child welfare.
3. There were reasons why the particular parents had been chosen to participate.
4. The parents were guaranteed confidentiality, and there were ways to safeguard this confidentiality.
5. The interviewer, identified by name, would contact them soon.

Appeal to Respondents' Self-Interests. The cover letter in Figure 16.3 also appealed to the adoptive parents' self-interest. Many wished to show their appreciation to the agency for having had a baby placed with them, and participating in the study afforded this opportunity. Many also wanted to help in any way they could to improve the quality of the agencies' services, in view of their hopes to adopt more children. Others wanted a chance to express dissatisfaction with the services they had received.

There are also more general ways in which participating in interviews may appeal to respondents' self-interest. Being "selected" for a study in itself may be valued by those who enjoy the prospect of the attention they will receive. Participating in social work studies may appeal to the altruism of respondents and provide a chance to contribute to the common good, while demanding relatively little. The purposes of a study can often be phrased in a way to convey the idea that the findings will help improve life, create a better society, aid individuals, or in some other fashion be beneficial to people or organizations.

Other techniques can enhance the belief of potential respondents that they will get some benefit from being interviewed. When they are contacted to get their agreement to participate and to arrange for an appointment, they should be told the limits of time and data to be required. The idea that the interview should be interesting—perhaps even fun—can be conveyed, and the respondents can be offered a summary of the research findings if they request it. For example, when unmarried couples were approached to be interviewed for a student research project studying the patterns and problems encountered in such relationships, a number expressed considerable interest in receiving the results of the study. They wanted to be able to compare their relationships to those of other couples who were studied. As perhaps a final resort, respondents may be paid a fee for participating in study. Such a procedure has been used in a study of delinquents and their rehabilitation, for example.

Of course, any promises, offers, and incentives given by the interviewer must be honored. Generally, prospective respondents will make themselves available if they feel a study is legitimate, will not demand excessive time, will respect their limits on what they choose to disclose, will protect their confidentiality, and will in some way be advantageous to them.

Another approach to encourage respondent cooperation is to involve representatives, especially acknowledged leaders, of the population to be studied in the development of the research procedures and measurement instruments. This gives such populations greater commitment to the study, since it is not only *about* them but *for* them, and, at least partially, *by* them as well. The involvement of representatives of the sample also provides useful inputs on such matters as areas to explore, access to the sample or population, and the language and phrasing of items.

Deciding Where to Conduct the Interviews

Several locations may be available for conducting the interview: the social worker's office (social agency or university), the respondent's home, the setting which is the focus of the study (such as the respondent's place of employment), or a "neutral" setting (such as a coffee shop or park bench). The determination of which option to select may boil down to what is available, or where the respondent is willing to be interviewed. However, if the interviewer has a choice, the advantages and disadvantages of the more common settings should be considered.

Offices.   Conducting interviews in the offices of the sponsoring organization (assuming that space is available) is certainly the most economical arrangement in terms of money and time. Furthermore, it provides the worker with the most control over environmental conditions such as privacy, temperature, lighting, and seating arrangements. However, if respondents have to come to the site of the interviews, they are more vulnerable to the vagaries of motivation—they simply may not show up. The formality of the office setting may be intimidating to some respondents, who may make their discomfort evident by withholding or distorting responses.

This distortion is most likely if the office represents an organization whose services the respondents are evaluating. They may be understandably cautious about giving honest feedback regarding services from an agency in whose offices they are sitting. Such an arrangement would well call into question any promises of confidentiality.

Respondents' Homes. Conducting the interview in the respondent's home poses a number of problems. It takes time and money to get to and from respondents' homes, and they may not even be there when the interviewer arrives, regardless of previous arrangements. Privacy may be limited if children and other family members and neighbors wander in and out. The physical surroundings (furniture arrangement, for example) also may not be conducive to interviewing.

The home interview also offers a number of advantages, however. In the postplacement adoption services study, all parent respondents were interviewed in their homes, and the social workers were interviewed in their offices. It was anticipated that the adoptive parents would be more relaxed and would behave and respond more naturally on their own turf. They would be less inhibited at home evaluating the services they had received than in an agency office. Furthermore, the interviewer would have the opportunity to observe interactions between parents and their children in their natural settings.

A special problem with this setting was that both parents were to be interviewed separately, using the same instrument, and it was preferable that neither parent be biased by hearing the responses of the other. This would have been comparatively easy to arrange in an office by having one parent wait outside while the other was being interviewed. It was possible, however, to arrange for nearly the same privacy in the parents' home by starting the interview with both parents present and then instructing one parent to fill out some written checklist in another room while the other was being interviewed. Since there was nothing particularly confidential in the interviews, the fact that one parent would occasionally overhear the other was not considered a drawback to using the home as the site for the interviews.

Neutral Places. Some research interviews are best conducted on neutral territory: neither the interviewer's office nor the respondent's home. With such respondents as teenagers or people with deviant lifestyles (e.g., prostitutes), a public setting may be the most acceptable setting for an interview. Although such settings may not be very private in terms of the proximity of strangers, they may be preferable to some respondents because of the absence of family and acquaintances.

Checking the Interviewers' Appearance

Most research interviewers spend considerably less time with their respondents than social workers do with their clients. Because rapport must be established relatively quickly, the physical appearance of the interviewer is important.

Few studies have reported the effects of grooming and clothing on interviewers' effectiveness, but, as with other social work roles, an unobtrusive, neat, and conservative appearance which is compatible with the respondents' standards of proper dress for someone in their role seems advisable. Interviewers should dress in a fashion fairly similar to that of the people they will be interviewing. A too well-dressed interviewer will probably not get good cooperation and responses from disadvantaged respondents, and a poorly dressed interviewer will have similar difficulties with other respondents.

Too much jewelry, sexually provocative clothes, unorthodox hairstyles, or excessive makeup can all be distracting to respondents. In brief contacts such as occur in research interviews, first appearances, including clothing and grooming, are cues which can profoundly affect the way people subsequently relate to each other (Jenkins, 1975).

The interviewer must create a climate in which respondents will be able and willing to provide clear, complete answers. Therefore they should appear the way they anticipate the interviewees will expect them to.

The University of Michigan Survey Research Center (1960) employs interviewers throughout the United States to carry out studies on a wide variety of topics. The center's *Interviewer's Manual* instructs its interviewers to:

> Aim for simplicity and comfort: a simple suit or dress is best. Avoid identification with groups or orders (pins or rings, for instance, of clubs or fraternal orders). The respondents should be led to concentrate on you as a person and the interview you want to take, and not the way you are dressed.

The manual goes on to recommend that the interviewer always carry the "official blue folder" (University of Michigan Survey Research Center, 1960). Interviewers may or may not have an official folder to carry with them, but a neat binder carried in a clean, untattered briefcase can enhance the image of a purposeful, well-organized interviewer, while a pile of dogeared papers balanced precariously could shatter it.

Developing the Interviewer-Respondent Relationship

There are both similarities and differences between worker-client and interviewer-respondent relationships. Ideally, both are purposeful, goal-directed relationships. Both are, or should be, guided by basic social work values and ethics regarding clients and respondents, such as respect for personal dignity, protection of confidentiality, and acceptance of the right to self-determination, including the right to refuse to answer any question. In both situations the social worker tries to create a climate in which the client or respondent will be able to provide honest and complete information (Geismar & LaSorte, 1963).

But there are differences between the worker-client relationship and the interviewer-respondent relationship which some interviewers may have difficulty adjusting to. The social worker who either conducts or supervises research interviews must understand these differences and accommodate them. The social work practice interview is generally focused on establishing a helping relationship and eliciting data in order to provide services to clients. In the research interview, acquiring data is an end in itself, although the long-range effect of the study may be beneficial to the respondents. Again, since the time for research interviews is limited and the parameters for the data to be obtained are predetermined (as opposed to the generally more open-ended goals of social work treatment interviews), research interviews tend to be much more focused. Social work relationships are often ongoing; research relationships are almost always relatively brief. The goal of social work *practice* interviews is to help a particular client system. The goal of *research* interviews is to obtain data about and from a particular population. The social worker represents help to be offered to the client; the research interviewer cannot make promises or commitments.

These differences in purpose account for the differences between worker-client and interviewer-respondent relationships. In the research interview, the interviewer takes the major (if not entire) responsibility for the direction of the interview, including the topics covered and the sequence of questions asked. In a social work interview, it is often preferable to follow the client's lead. The social work *practice* interview is for the *client;* the social work *research* interview is for the *interviewer* .

There is considerable evidence in research of clinical relationships that the therapists' communication of warmth, empathy, and genuineness to clients is positively associated with effective treatment. Whether similar communication by the research interviewer would enhance research interviews has not been determined; no studies are yet available comparing the effectiveness of research interviewers who have high ratings on any or all of these dimensions with those who do not. We could hypothesize that since these attributes in an interviewer seem to be effective because they allow interviewees to be truly themselves, to trust the interviewer, and to explore their feelings and experience more easily, then they would be equally useful in enabling the research respondent to provide more valid and reliable data. However, a number of the factors which differentiate research from treatment interviewing raise questions about just how much, and what kind of, warmth, empathy, and genuineness should be communicated in research interviews.

While research interviewers who communicate empathy may indeed be brought closer to respondents, at the same time this could make them "anticipate" or even prejudice respondents' answers. The interviewers might project themselves into their respondents' feeling and beliefs, rather than objectively eliciting and recording their answers.

The warmth emanating from the interviewer also could delay or inhibit respondents from sharing personal data. It is sometimes easier to convey sensitive information to a neutral stranger than to a friend; witness the ease with which people reveal personal details to fellow passengers on an airplane. Objectivity and even professional detachment on the part of the interviewer may be more effective in obtaining valid and reliable answers.

It is neither fair to respondents nor effective use of research time to involve them in a pseudotherapeutic relationship, which the active communication of warmth and empathy may do. If respondents reveal problems amenable to professional treatment intervention during the course of research interviews, and they indicate a desire to seek help, it would certainly be appropriate for interviews to refer them to appropriate resources. But offering professional social work services is not the intent of research interviews.

Since there have been few studies to guide investigation of the interviewer-respondent relationship, and since worker-client relationship research may be of limited applicability, we can only suggest some attributes of interviewers which may guide research interview relationships. Interviewers should:

1. Clearly communicate to respondents the purposes and limits of their contact.
2. Be trustworthy, friendly, courteous, and kind to respondents, yet focus clearly on the goals of their contact.
3. Communicate to respondents that their only interest in their answers is for the purposes of the study, and they have no personal interest in the responses. In conducting the sexual behavior interviews in Pomeroy's study (1972) cited at the beginning of this chapter, for example, the interviewers communicated to their respondents that, personally, they didn't care what sexual behaviors their respondents reported, other than for the contribution it could make to the study.

Certainly research interviewers, as social workers and human beings, care about any pain or suffering they may be told about, and they may well communicate this caring to respondents. However, research nonjudgmentality calls for neutral reactions to any information provided.

Formulating and Asking Questions

Most of the guidelines for formulating and asking questions in interviews are similar to those that have already been suggested for survey measuring instruments (see Chapters 12 and 15). Some of the basic guidelines which are *especially* applicable to asking questions in interviews are described in this section.

Keeping the Language Simple. The wording of questions should generally be simple, clear, and unobtrusive. Words from the average person's vocabulary, rather than the jargon of graduate social workers, should be used. "Meaningful others" is meaningless to most respondents. Generally, "angry" is better than "hostile," "sad" is better than "depressed," and certainly "brothers and sisters" is better than "siblings." It has been suggested that the interviewer should use the type of vocabulary usually found in most newspapers and popular magazines (*not* professional journals). Further, the use of slang expressions such as "getting stoned," "giving head," or "being ripped-off" may be unclear to respondents and may also "turn them off" to the interviewer.

Avoiding Double-Barreled Questions. The respondent should only be asked for one reply at a time. There are three ways in which double-barreled questions can confuse respondents, thereby leaving the interviewer unsure about the intent of their answers. The first is by essentially asking two questions at once. For example, medical students on psychiatric rotation were given an interviewing schedule prepared by the staff psychiatrists to be used in obtaining a brief sexual history. One of the items was clearly double-barreled: "Have you ever masturbated *or* participated in a homosexual activity?" Of course most patients hurriedly answered "no" (much to the relief of the medical students). What they were saying no to remained obscure.

A second type of double-barreled question starts with a statement of alleged fact which is the premise on which the question is based. For example, parents could be asked: "Of course, you wanted your daughter to finish high school. How did you go about keeping her going?" Such a question has a built-in bias which may or may not be true.

The third type of double-barreled question is built on a hidden premise, such as the classic, "When did you stop beating your child?" Some assumptions may be useful in facilitating questioning, but these must be used cautiously. It's best to assume very little. Assumptions often lead the respondent to offer socially desirable but inaccurate answers.

Avoiding Double-Negative Questions. Double negatives imply a positive, and such questions can be confusing. "Do you feel that most married women would really prefer not to work if they were not under financial stress?" might better be phrased, "Do you feel most married women prefer to work only if they are under financial stress?"

Discouraging Biased Responses. Questions should be asked in such a way that respondents will not feel constrained to give only those answers they perceive would fit generally accepted social norms. Respondents often choose to give answers that sound good—whether they're true or not. For example, pupils in a third-grade class were asked to tell the teacher their greatest wish. Most of the children replied with such answers as "to go to Disneyland" or "to get a bicycle," but one boy said "to have peace on earth." The teacher was impressed and sent home a laudatory note to his parents. The student confided a few years later that he knew that answer would get him "strokes" from the teacher, and that what he really wanted to answer was "to be able to fly"!

It will help respondents be more open about sensitive areas if such items are phrased in a way to convey the idea that the interviewer knows there is a wide range of human behaviors, most people have problems, and there is nothing (well, almost nothing) that will shock the interviewer.

One of the most effective ways to encourage respondents to answer questions truthfully, even if the answers might be embarrassing or violate social norms, is the "many people" technique. This approach enabled Pomeroy's researchers to uncover data about sexual behavior that might otherwise have been impossible to obtain. For example, rather than asking a married adult "Do you masturbate?" which might prompt an immediate and defensive "no," the interviewer might say "Many married men and women find that stimulating themselves to orgasm is a satisfying supplement to other sexual experiences," and then ask, "Have you found this to be true for you?" It is unlikely that such a question would lead respondents to answer "yes" if they did not masturbate at least occasionally, but it does provide support for a yes answer if that is the case. It also could pave the way to subsequent, more detailed items. Note that in the rephased question the emotionally laden "masturbation" was replaced with the more cumbersome but less emotionally charged euphemism "stimulating yourself to orgasm." As long as a concept is clear in meaning, it is best to use the least emotionally charged word or phrase—even a euphemism—which describes it. For example, it might be better to ask, "How often is your behavior altered by drinking alcoholic beverages?" than "How often do you get drunk?" Similarly, "How often has an employer let you go?" may be a less threatening question than "How often have you been fired?"

Investigators also found that presenting a wide range of options for answers in random order enables respondents to avoid biasing their answers according to what might be expected of them. Thus, after asking the questions, "How often do you and your husband have sexual intercourse?" the interviewers would add, "Once a month? Twice a day? Less than once a year? Four times a week? Every six months?" This provides respondents with considerable latitude to answer what might otherwise be an embarrassing item (Williams, 1964).

It is often difficult for respondents to give negative evaluations of services, agencies, and experiences. A technique which can help them overcome this resistance is to ask paired questions which make it possible to offer both praise and criticism, ideally in that order. For example, "What did you like most about your social worker?" can be followed with "What did you like least about your social worker?" The overall effect of such pairs of questions is to elicit a balanced evaluation which can justify the expression of negative opinions or observations.

Avoiding Interviewer Bias. Respondents may feel or be made to feel that the research interview is essentially an examination or trial, and they must somehow please or satisfy the interviewer. Often, therefore, they will try to get the interviewer's opinions or experiences on particular questions before they respond.

Interviewers may bias answers by the way they phrase questions or by the expressions on their faces. They can also bias subsequent answers by their verbal and nonverbal reactions to responses. Asking the questions as consistently as possible, and reviewing tape recordings of interviewer-respondent interchanges, can reduce this bias.

Reinforcing Respondent's Answers. Respondents, like everyone else, respond to reinforcement. If interviewers demonstrate that they appreciate and value respondents' answers, the quality of subsequent answers will generally be enhanced. A study on the effects of experimental interviewing techniques used in health interview studies reported by the U.S. Public Health Service showed that verbal reinforcement by the interviewer increased both the amount and quality of respondents' recall in interviews. Without overdoing it, the interviewer can follow respondents' answers with reactions ranging from a simple head nod and "uh-huh" to "Thanks for giving me such a detailed answer." Comments which do not evaluate the content of the response but do reinforce its completeness need not bias the respondent.

Recording the Data

The final consideration in research interviewing is recording the respondents' answers. The conversion of these answers to a pool of valid, useful data challenges the interviewer's skill to avoid distortion or omission of data.

Generally, the recording procedure chosen should meet the following criteria:

1. It should accurately record the manifest intent if not the exact wording of the respondents' answers.
2. It should be as unobtrusive as possible so that it does not inhibit the flow of the interview or distract the respondent from giving complete, candid answers.
3. It should facilitate transmittal of the data from the recording instrument to the data bank.

Interviews which rely on closed-ended questions are the easiest to record and run the least risk of recording distortion and bias. All the interviewer has to do is check, underline, or circle the appropriate answer on the interview schedule. At most, it is necessary to record a few words per answer.

Semistructured and unstructured interviews pose greater problems in recording (Crittenden & Hill, 1971). Two alternatives are available to interviewers: handwritten and mechanical recording.

Using Handwritten Recording. In the unlikely event that interviewers are skilled at taking shorthand, they would still have difficulty taking down respondents' answers verbatim. And, even if that were possible, excessive note taking can be distracting to some respondents as well as some interviewers. Furthermore, verbatim responses are rarely necessary for recording useful data. The interviewer may choose to wait until the interview is over and then try to recall and record answers as completely and accurately as possible. However, this procedure is risky. The interviewer may forget significant answers and nuances. Furthermore, if the interviewer has seen a number of respondents in a relatively short time, one respondent's answers may blur with another's thus seriously distorting the data.

A safer procedure is for the interviewer to record summaries of responses from time to time throughout the interview, supplemented with direct quotations for illustrative purposes. If necessary, the interviewer may interrupt or slow down the respondent with such comments as "Wait a second, that was an interesting point, I want to get it down in my notes." Again, the social work research interview is different from a social work practice interview. The purpose of research interviews is clearly defined as data gathering, not service delivery.

Therefore, while note taking may be distracting and even inappropriate in a treatment interview, it can be an acceptable and integral part of the research interview.

However, the recording procedures used by research interviewers should be as brief and uncomplicated as possible. This can be achieved by developing a coding procedure and other shortcuts to recording data—as long as the interviewer can remember what the notes and codes mean. Pomeroy's sexual behavior investigators, for example, developed a code by which they could record extensive, detailed sexual life histories on a single index card.

Using Mechanical Recording. The development of compact, reliable cassette recorders makes it possible to record exactly what is said by respondents. Furthermore, once the recorder is turned on, it provides none of the distractions to either interviewers or respondents that handwritten recording can. Clients generally have no objection to being recorded (Kogan, 1950). Respondents should, of course, be informed that an interview is being recorded. However, no extensive discussion of its use or a respondent's reaction is necessary unless the respondent initiates such a discussion.

Although there are obvious advantages to the absolute accuracy that mechanical recording can provide, tape-recorded data has its limitations. Machines can break down, tapes can break, and microphones can pick up background noises which obscure the comments of the respondent. Occasionally respondents will object to having their comments recorded. The greatest limitation, however, is the considerable time and expense of either transcribing the recording or listening to the entire recording for research analysis. In some ways, this is a duplication of energy, since the respondents' answers have already been heard by the interviewer while the interview was being taped. It is possible, however, that after the taped interviews have been analyzed, the social worker will choose additional variables to study and return to the original tapes for reanalysis. Thus, taped interviews provide more comprehensive and flexible data.

SUMMARY

This overview of interviewing in social work research began with a consideration of the advantages of research interviewing over questionnaires in self-report surveys and some of the limitations of interviews in research. The tasks in planning and organizing interview-based research were then discussed: determining the content of interviews and developing the interview schedule, phrasing the questions, selecting the interviewers, gaining access to respondents, deciding where to conduct the interviews, how interviewers should be groomed and dressed, and the nature of effective interviewer-respondent relationships. Finally, the manner in which questions should be asked in the interview and procedures for recording answers were explored.

Throughout this discussion, differences and similarities between treatment and research interviews have been described. While there are numerous differences, the significance of social work skills, knowledge, and values for research interviewing must be stressed.

17. PARTICIPANT OBSERVATION

Participant observation is a research method the social worker can utilize to learn about the lives of those being studied, from their own points of view. It is a qualitative method which has two implications about the data being collected on the people being studied: The data are descriptive, and they are usually expressed in a qualitative form. Thus, participant observation is useful in generating Knowledge Level 1, hypothetical-developmental, and Level 2, quantitative-descriptive, as presented in Chapter 13.

CASE STUDY: FIELD PLACEMENT

A university instructor supervises social work students in their field placement within the Department of Social Services (DSS). The instructor spends several hours a week with these students in their field placements in order to provide adequate supervision and discuss their progress. By participating in the practice experiences of these students as well as in the activities of the DSS, the instructor is able to collect data on both aspects of the field placements.

During the field work, one of the students, Mary, conducts an intake interview with a prospective client, Opal. Following their interview, the instructor discusses their reactions to the experience, one at a time. Mary's and Opal's interpretations of the interview are tape recorded, as follows:

> *Opal* (welfare client): I sat in the waiting area for an hour or so. The baby was with me, and he was fussing. I was tired. Besides his fussing, he had kept me up half the night. So, to keep my mind occupied, I watched and talked to people as I waited to be called. You know how you do when you're kept waiting. So, I watched and talked and listened to the people being called. I kept my ear out to catch who interviewed the people around me. I was nervous, and I wanted to get an idea of who was going to talk to me.

I got a woman named Mary Appleton. I went to her office. She said hello and all, and she tried to be friendly. She wasn't mean or rude, but her smile had a forced look about it. I first thought she didn't feel well. Then, you know, from her questions and tone of voice, I got the idea she didn't like my answers. When I realized this I began to get more nervous and to feel shabby. You know, I began to notice how she was dressed and how I was dressed.

Then to make matters worse, the baby threw up. She didn't offer to help or anything. She just asked why I didn't leave him with a sitter. This kinda talk made me angry. Didn't she know? If I could've left him at home, I would've. Anyway, she didn't help me. She only asked me to come again for more interviews. So, we made another appointment.

Mary (intake worker): It's difficult to relate to all people. The problem is part the client's fault and part the office, the agency. Let's take Opal. She was hard to communicate with. She hesitated when answering my questions. And, I became suspicious about her need. Then her kid up-chucked on the floor. You can still smell the sour milk. This and the woman's general appearance turned me off. This is also a part of the problem.

The other part is the agency. I'm supposed to process these people and at the same time make sure they're not cheaters. So you look for things that reveal who they really are. This is hard to do. Some of us, at least I do, when in doubt about their honesty, have them come back again. I do this so I can compare what they tell me on the first visit with the second visit. This would be okay, except I don't process as many people as I'm expected. So I keep wondering how my supervisor is viewing this. You know, that I don't process as many people as the other workers. People like this woman, then, are a problem. You look them over and you listen to them, but it's not easy to find out who they really are.

A Working Definition of Participant Observation

From this example, we can arrive at a working definition of participant observation. It is a research method in which the worker (the instructor, in this example) is also a participant in the social setting being studied. And it is a method by which people's actions and verbalizations are observed and recorded in a description of small-group life and the micro aspects of social order.

In the welfare setting, the instructor was a participant *and* an observer. But the investigator was not the only participant-observer on the scene; in a sense, both Mary and Opal were also participant-observers, because they were acknowledging what was going on and trying to make sense out of it. Opal "... watched and talked and listened to the people being called," so that she would know what to do when her turn came. Mary looked for "... things that reveal who they really are." Although they did not record data for a specific research purpose, they had at least adopted the attitude of participant-observers.

Of course, just having the attitude of a participant-observer will not necessarily result in useful data. What is needed is a plan of action. After the basic format of participant observation has been mastered, it can be enlarged upon until it becomes an innovative, creative research method capable of expanding present notions of human behavior. The process of participant observation has basically eight phases, as described in the next section.

THE PROCESS OF PARTICIPANT OBSERVATION

The phases in the participant observation process are:

1. Selecting the research question.
2. Gaining entry into the group.
3. Gaining rapport with group members.
4. Getting involved with group members.
5. Depth interviewing.
6. Recording the data.
7. Ending the study.
8. Writing the report.

Phase 1: Selecting the Research Question

As presented in Chapter 3, the first phase of any study, choosing a research problem, is very important and requires careful thought. Who should be studied? On what aspects of persons' lives should the study focus? Why should these people be studied, and of what benefit will the resulting data be? The social worker or participant-observer must answer these questions before beginning the study.

Phase 2: Gaining Entry into the Group

How a setting is entered is influenced by the setting itself. The worker should choose a research problem because of an interest in it, and this normally means also having some knowledge of the problem area and of the people who comprise the members of the group to be studied. Thus, persons known to social workers can introduce as well as integrate them into target groups.

If the worker must start cold (not knowing the area to be studied or any people who can help), then other approaches must be considered. A letter of introduction to the director of the agency or group to be studied, for example, can serve as an entry point. Such a letter must ask permission to do the study (Denzin, 1970a). If the focus of the study concerns certain aspects of a community, participant-observers can actually move into it and begin to meet the neighbors and other people who will interact with them (Filstead, 1970).

Phase 3: Gaining Rapport with Group Members

It is not enough to live among the people under study or to move in their circles. The social worker cannot learn about the frame of reference used by the people under study until some measure of rapport is gained. Probably the researcher's basic temperament or personality has as much to do with gaining rapport as anything. A person who is friendly, tactful, willing to listen to others, and not pushy or judgmental is more likely to succeed in this than an aggressive person who expects others to disclose personal aspects of their lives immediately. Time and patience are required, as well as the sensitivity to know whether or not rapport has been gained.

Phase 4: Getting Involved with Group Members

Unfortunately, a person who has the sensitivity to gain rapport may also be most likely to become emotionally involved with the people under study. The participant-observer must constantly deal with the problem of "going native," or staying close enough to the group, while at the same time maintaining enough distance emotionally to be able to see other points of view.

A related problem occurs when participant-observers become attached too quickly to a few of the people under study. In this instance, they may find that these people are manipulating them for their own purposes. Or a worker may find that the close alliance with one or several persons has cut off access to other people in the social setting.

Phase 5: Depth Interviewing

Depth interviewing is a logical partner with participant observation. A depth interview is an unstructured interview in which the worker asks general questions pertaining to the research question. Although the investigator may decide in advance on the first questions to be asked, subsequent questioning will emerge in response to the subject's answers and the ongoing discussion. Depth interviewing is most fruitful after the investigator has gained significant rapport. Much of the participant-observer's data will come from depth interviews which have been recorded.

Phase 6: Recording the Data

There are basically three ways for the participant-observer to record data: by writing down what is observed or heard (field notes), by tape recording, or by videotaping. The choice of method will depend on such factors as the physical location of the study, the availability of equipment, and the agreement of the people under study to be recorded. Closely associated with the choice of method is the decision to record overtly or covertly. Not only the ethical aspects of recording data covertly but the advantages and disadvantages of informing people they are being studied must be weighed. This decision is one the social worker alone must make.

How to record data is only part of the problem. The participant-observer may find it equally difficult to decide just what events (data) to record. A general rule of thumb is to record anything which relates in any way to the central focus of the study (the research problem). This includes not only recording what is said but also taking notes on physical aspects of the scene, nonverbal behavior, smells, and so on. In many cases, more data will be recorded than are necessary, but this is better than having too little data.

Phase 7: Ending the Study

The participant-observer must decide when to stop the study. This can present a problem at times, since there are no clear-cut indications. The study should be brought to an end when the social worker feels that a reasonable account of the people or scene has been acquired.

Phase 8: Writing the Report

Because the data collected in participant observation are descriptive, the report is usually written in the form of a case study or ethnography (see Chapter 18 on ethnomethodology). In writing a case study, the social worker includes a detailed description of an individual or a group of individuals, along with an analysis of the importance of the description. For example, Liebow (1967) spent a year doing participant observation of black men who habitually hung around a particular street corner. Then he used his observations as the basis for a case study detailing the lives of the people and analyzing the life and problems of low-income blacks.

EXTENDING PARTICIPANT OBSERVATION
THROUGH UNEXPECTED EVENTS

Like all social work skills, the ability to do participant observation increases with experience (Lofland, 1971). After completing several research studies, researchers begin to develop their own individual styles for doing participant observation. And as they read case studies done by others, they incorporate new techniques or methods in their research efforts.

It is possible to extend participant observation by attending to unexpected events as they reveal the behind-the-scenes features of everyday life. The remainder of this chapter will be built around the notion of using unexpected events as an aspect of participant observation, as illustrated with another case study.

Since unexpected events are unanticipated, the participant-observer cannot have the assistance of a plan for study. In a methodological sense, and as suggested in the ethnomethodological literature (Chapter 18), unexpected events aid the social worker because in experiencing them people reveal the commonsense knowledge they use to manage their practical, everyday affairs (Heller, 1971). Furthermore, unexpected events can also be used as research strategies to discover the boundaries of the research setting. The use of unexpected events as a research tool is most easily understood in the context of an actual case study (Van Maanen, Dabbs, & Faulkner, 1982).

CASE STUDY: THE GARZA FAMILY

The ethnographic study from which the data were taken for this case study was conducted in a small, northern Colorado town. The participant-observer, Mr. Ramos, was employed as a family contact person for an elementary school. He was responsible for making home visits to students' families in an attempt to resolve problems between the students, their families, and other community members. Since the job provided a natural entree into the common culture of the school, the students and their families, and community agencies, it evolved as an ethnographic post. Depth interviewing and participant observation were therefore possible as difficulties between these social networks were observed.

While working for the elementary school, the Garzas were introduced to Mr. Ramos. They are a family of seven; Mr. Garza earns less than $4,000 a year; he and his wife are resident aliens from Mexico; and both of them have had approximately three years of formal education in Mexico. Their children are one to two years behind their grade levels in school.

The First Unexpected Event

On one occasion, Mr. Ramos visits the Garzas's home to learn why the youngest child, a first-grader, is frequently absent from school. Mrs. Garza also had not attended a parent-teacher conference in some time, and the teachers of the Garza children want to encourage her to come to discuss their progress.

While Mr. Ramos is talking with Mrs. Garza, a stranger, Mr. Jones from the state university, comes to the front door. When Mrs. Garza answers the door, she opens it only about a foot and does not bother to unlock the screen door, so she and Mr. Jones talk with it between them.

> *Jones:* Hello. I'm Mr. Jones from the state university, and I'm doing a survey. Could I take a little bit of your time to ask some questions?
>
> *Garza* (in broken English): No, my husband does all the talking.
>
> *Jones:* Is he at home?
>
> *Garza:* No.
>
> *Jones:* Is he at work? And, could I come back this evening?
>
> (Garza tilts her head to one side and shrugs her shoulders to convey to Mr. Jones that she does not know if he could come in the evening.)
>
> *Jones:* Does he work at the foundry?
>
> (Garza nods "yes.")
>
> *Jones:* Thank you very much.

This was an ordinary conversation. As Mr. Ramos listened and recorded the above conversation, he was puzzled by Mrs. Garza's behavior. She presented herself in a naive and helpless way, although she was known as a very gregarious and talkative woman. While she did not speak English well, she used her Spanish and what little English she knew to manage her affairs quite effectively. It was her out-of-character behaviors which prompted Mr. Ramos to ask about the way in which she dealt with Mr. Jones.

In this situation, Mr. Jones's arrival was an unexpected event, although it was used as a research method to learn more about Mrs. Garza. These events, neither planned nor expected, proved fruitful in helping Mr. Ramos understand something about the ways in which one specific Mexican American woman managed her everyday life and about the importance of using unexpected events as field guides in doing participant observation.

Discovering the Garzas' Family Life

Mr. Ramos decides to pursue the issue of how Mrs. Garza handled Mr. Jones, rather than continuing the discussion of the parent-teacher conference. The discussion goes as follows:

Ramos: Can I ask you why you didn't let him in? You always invite people in, especially when there are others in the house.

Garza: Because I didn't know him, and I didn't want to bother with whatever nonsense he wanted to ask me.

Ramos: I'm surprised by what you tell me. When I first came here, I was a stranger and you let me in. Why?

Garza: Correction, you were *not* a stranger. True, we had never met, but I knew who you were. Mrs. Gomez—you visited her two days before coming here the first time—told me about you. She said you were a nice person who worked for the school and that you were trying to help the kids. I also know that your wife is a teacher. You also live on K Street. No?

Don't think I'm snoopy. I just keep my eyes and ears open like everybody else around here (i.e., in the neighborhood). We may not know how to speak English, but we know what's going on around here. For example, someone has been going into people's houses and most of us think it's a stranger and not someone from around here. That's another reason I didn't let that Mr. Jones in. How do I know, he may simply want to come in here to see what we have that's worth stealing. People do that. A man did that some time ago. Now what is your other surprise? (laughing). Any more surprises?

Ramos: Why did you tell him your husband did all the talking? I've heard you do a lot of talking, not only in Spanish but also in English.

Garza: I told you I didn't want to bother with him. When people, nosy people, come around here and I don't want to bother with them, I tell them to see Pedro—who is always at work. So, people don't talk with me and they certainly don't bother him. No?

Ramos: Does Pedro really do all the talking for the family?

Garza: Only when I let him (laughing). Don't get me wrong. I don't boss him. We have our understandings. He doesn't step all over me or the kids as they say men in Mexico do. Even when he appears to boss us, he knows how far to go. The same goes for me; I know how far to go with him. I may not say anything to him when he is mad, sometimes I do, but he knows that I know how to get even. I'm not going to tell you what way that is. We have our understandings.

When you live together for a long time you know the character or particulars of the other. This also goes for the kids. We all seem to know each other's moods and we try to keep out of each other's way when we're in a bad mood. For example, when the old man comes home after work and I'm putting down pots and pans a little extra hard as I cook supper, he knows that things aren't right, so he takes it easy with me. He can see that I'm mad and sometimes he knows why I'm mad. That's when he's in hot water with me. When one of us is going around the house with a long face and grumpy, we seem to know why. Half the time we (parents and other family members) are the ones who made him mad.

A family knows each other. We know how to manage each other, and we can guess who is in one of his *moviditas* (schemes or strategies). Sometimes we gang up on each other. So, when one person takes advantage of the others, it's because the others let him. When they do that (let someone take advantage of them), it's because everyone knows what is going on. It's like that. I don't know how to explain it to you, but people just know what is going on around here. Maybe we don't know 100 percent, but at least 90 percent of the time we have a sense of why we punish or let someone punish us. It's an awareness (*conocimiento*) of what we do to each other.

Do you know Carmela, the skinny woman from down the street? Her husband beats her up, goes out drinking, and treats her like dirt. All of us around here (women in the community) tell her not to take all that nonsense. She always answers with, "What can I do?" and continues getting kicked and God knows what else. Most of us think she's a little innocent. We keep telling her that her husband saw her coming with a "P" on her forehead and that's why he takes advantage of her. (The letter *P* stands for *pendeja* in Spanish, which means fools. Mrs. Garza used the expression to mean he saw her as a fool.)

I tell my girls to look at Carmela, especially when they get out of hand and they want to go out with people (boys) we don't know. "She found a sharpy and look at the beautiful life he gives her," I tell them. "Find yourself one like him. Keep fooling around with boys that don't go to school and that's what you'll find."

Depth Interviewing

In dealing with Mr. Jones's visit, Mr. Ramos also conducted depth interviewing with Mrs. Garza. His observations helped to select the topics of conversation and formulate the questions he asked her. In depth interviewing, topics of conversation between the investigator and the subject of study, and the questions that emerge from the data gathered by observation, tend to be meaningful to the subject. The conversation emerges from the subject's life experiences. Thus, people can feel that they are *participants* in the conversation, as opposed to *subjects* who are being "interviewed" with questions that do not have any face validity. For these reasons, depth interviewing must be incorporated into any study involving participant observation (Mehan, 1974).

A good question the novice participant-observer might ask concerns Mrs. Garza's credibility. How does one know if she was telling the truth? After listening to Mrs. Garza's account of her family, Mr. Ramos could either believe her or assume that she was putting him on, as she managed Mr. Jones. As Mr. Ramos had already been to the Garza home many times before and was familiar with the family, the event and Mrs. Garza's account were accepted as truth. Mrs. Garza's behavior in managing Mr. Jones was out of character. By contrast, the remarks about herself and her family were more in keeping with those aspects of her family known to Mr. Ramos, both from observation and previous conversations. The main difference between what was known about the family before and after the unexpected event was in terms of quantity and quality. Mr. Ramos learned more specific things about how the family members managed their family affairs. For example, before the unexpected event, Mr. Ramos had generally categorized the family structure as being democratic, but he did not have many specifics to back up the assumption. After the unexpected event, Mr. Ramos knew more specifically what "democratic family structure" meant for the Garza family.

Therefore, by not ignoring the opportunity created by Mr. Jones's interruption, Mr. Ramos obtained a great deal of data about Mrs. Garza and her family. Mrs. Garza explained in very concrete terms how her family life was structured and managed in terms of her common-sense understandings of the world in which she operates.

The Second Unexpected Event

A few hours later at a local community action center, both Mr. Jones and Mr. Ramos attended a meeting on the recruitment of minority parents for the basic adult education class. At that time the two were formally introduced, and Mr. Ramos learned the following: Mr. Jones is a graduate student from a nearby university; he is collecting data for his doctoral dissertation; he is interested in learning how Mexican American parents motivate their children to succeed in getting an education; and he was given Mrs. Garza's name, as well as the names of other Mexican American families, by the community worker who has introduced them to each other.

During the conversation, Mr. Ramos also learned what Mr. Jones thinks about Mrs. Garza and the other Mexican American women who had turned him down when he tried to interview them. In part, Mr. Jones said to Mr. Ramos that evening:

> *Jones:* . . . She's typical (referring to Mrs. Garza). The way she and the other women around here have responded to me, by and large, is typical of the group, don't you think?
>
> (Ramos does not answer affirmatively or negatively. He simply smiles.)
>
> *Jones* (taking the smile to be an affirmative answer): It's part of the culture. The husband rules the roost, and there are no two ways about that. I don't know how you people (community action center workers) are going to get the women involved. If the old man says "no" you've had it. You will not be able to get the women into the adult education classes without their husbands' permission.

Meeting Mr. Jones a second time was an opportunity for Mr. Ramos to get Mr. Jones's version of his interaction with Mrs. Garza, as well as with other Mexican American women in the community. In addition to this, Mr. Ramos was able to get a sense of the boundaries of the social setting. Before the occurrence of these unexpected events, the social setting had been defined as consisting of the school and the home of the families. After the second unexpected encounter with Mr. Jones, the community action center was included as part of the research setting.

The advantages of expanding the research boundaries were several. First, some of the families under study were members of the community action center. As a result, Mr. Ramos could observe the families in a setting other than the public school and their respective homes. Second, the employees of the center worked with some of the people being studied. It would be advantageous to interview these employees periodically to learn about other aspects of the families' lives which were not accessible at the school or in their homes. Third, by going regularly to the center, Mr. Ramos increased the chances of meeting other persons, such as Mr. Jones, who might have an interest in and a different idea about the people being studied. In conclusion, the unexpected event of meeting Mr. Jones at the center had the effect of enlarging the obvious, but unnoticed, boundaries of the research setting.

ADVANTAGES OF PARTICIPANT OBSERVATION

Participant observation is a time-consuming research method. When pairing participant observation with depth interviewing, and when allowing plenty of time for dealing with unexpected events, the investigator must be committed to long-term study which focuses on detail. Why would a social worker want to do this? There are many advantages to participant observation, but two of them are particularly pertinent to the field of social work: rethinking stereotypes, and improving social work skills (H. Schwartz & Jacobs, 1979).

Rethinking Stereotypes

Social workers deal with people from all segments of society. Many published studies describe segments of a population in terms of general characteristics which have been synthesized from the results of survey data. One example of this is in the study of minority groups. The beginning social worker can find in any introductory social work text a list of so-called cultural traits for blacks, Mexican Americans, and other ethnic minority groups. It was obvious that Mr. Jones had read of such cultural traits in the literature when he said, "It's part of the culture."

The first advantage of participant observation and the use of unexpected events is that these research methods cause us to rethink traditional notions about American ethnic minorities. For example, we can question how the data from the case study with the Garzas, a Mexican American family, differ from traditional accounts.

Mr. Jones's arrival at the Garza's home was an unexpected event, and the way in which Mrs. Garza managed it provided an opportunity to learn more about her and her family. In explaining her out-of-character behavior, she revealed certain things, such as male-female roles in the family. From what she said it can be concluded that the relationship she has with her husband is a democratic one. Neither one bosses the other, and, as she puts it, "understandings" exist between family members.

What she had to say was important because it is different from what we find in the literature on the Mexican American family. In most studies, the Mexican American family structure is said to be based on the norm of male and age superiority (Garfinkel, 1967). Family authority rests with the males, who are ranked according to age. The husband is inherently entitled to obedience from his wife and children, who think of his needs before their own and accept abuse without complaint (Madsen, 1964). This typification of sex roles in Mexican American families does not fit the Garza family. It might even be suggested that it describes a pathological relationship, like the one Carmela (Mrs. Garza's neighbor) has with her husband. That relationship was seen by Mrs. Garza and her other neighbors as the exception and not the rule.

In talking about herself and her family, Mrs. Garza discussed another aspect of her family's life, family coalitions. She pointed to how family members are constantly interpreting situations and gauging the appropriateness of certain role performances in terms of what they know about the world in which they live. As Mrs. Garza said, "A family knows each other. We know how to manage each other. . . ."

Again, this information which is made available as a result of the unexpected events is important. Coalitions within Mexican families have been neglected in Mexican American studies, largely because Mexican American family life has traditionally been viewed from a culturally deterministic perspective (Grebler, Moore, & Guzman, 1970). From such a perspective, Mexican Americans are not presented as people capable of creating strategies, but as people who dutifully behave according to the norms of Mexican American culture. But it is certainly obvious that Mexican American family members can and do organize themselves into family coalitions in order to deal with the practicalities of family life. Family coalitions do take shape because Mexican American family members, like family members in other culture groups, do not manage their everyday lives solely in terms of the ideal norms attributed to them by "social scientists" in traditional explanations of human behavior (Ramos, 1973). Instead, they rely upon their commonsense knowledge of the world in which they live to interpret the norms (whether Mexican American or otherwise) in order to create effective ways for managing.

Because of the unexpected event, Mrs. Garza revealed other things about her family which are different from the cultural typifications attributed to Mexican Americans in the literature. For example, we can learn something about how Mexican American women like Mrs. Garza and people like Mr. Jones participate in maintaining the stereotypical notions of the passive Mexican American female. We also can learn that Mexican Americans know more about their communities than they have been given credit for in the literature. Mrs. Garza knows and interacts with the other members of her community (Romano, 1968). She and her neighbors do not peep out from behind their curtains like frightened children, as has been suggested in a description of the Chicano community as an atomistic-type society (Rubel, 1966). Finally, we can learn something about female socialization. Persons like Mrs. Garza belittle the passive female role, in direct contrast with the literature, which states that Mexican American females espouse it (Vaca, 1970).

In short, the use of unexpected events as a research tool in participant observation can enlarge current notions of human behavior by causing us to rethink the stereotypes that exist in the literature, whether they concern ethnic groups, sex roles, or the roles played by organizations within a community (Schwitzgebel, 1964).

Improving Social Work Skills

A second advantage of participant observation as a research method is that it helps social workers become more skillful in helping people. Some individuals who ask social workers for help either intentionally or unintentionally fail to document their situations adequately, which makes it difficult to learn about them. The helping process can also be impeded by bureaucratic procedures in departments of social services and by the actions of other community members who may inadvertently make trouble for the social worker. How can the social worker become more skillful in dealing with these eventualities?

Much of the social worker's job involves learning how to cope with the variables that hinder the helping process. Some strategies are needed, and participant observation can play an important role. When an unexpected event occurs, clients may reveal how and why they manage the events in their everyday lives. In so doing, they may reveal more than was apparent in an initial interview or would be apparent to a casual observer.

Social workers can become skillful participant-observers who know how to utilize unexpected events as a research tool, even though they

may not be participating in an "official research project." By assuming
the attitude of the participant-observer, they can arrive at new knowledge. As a result, they will be better able to do the job of helping
effectively and in a way that is meaningful to the client.

SUMMARY

This chapter can serve as a step-by-step guide for conducting
participant observation. It has examined the use of this research method
by social workers through unexpected events that occur daily and consistently cause trouble for the social worker. Such events actually provide opportunities for participant-observers to use them to learn more
about the ways in which those being observed manage their everyday
lives.

Thomas D. Watts

18. ETHNOMETHODOLOGY

Ethnomethodology is less a discipline and more a subject matter: the methodology employed by ordinary people in their everyday life when they reason about their society and its activities (H. Schwartz & Jacobs, 1979). One of the main values of the ethnomethodological approach for the social worker is that it attempts to go inside social scenes, to look at the client's perspective from the inside out. Social workers need this inside-out perspective because of its value in improving their understanding of the clients they serve. Ethnomethodology can also be used to study social programs, community action programs, and so on.

The objective of this chapter is to discuss the basic presuppositions, principles, and methodological approaches of ethnomethodology. Ethnomethodology and participant observation (Chapter 17) share a common base: They are both qualitative research methods. Ethnomethodologists use participant observation as one method for collecting data. They are interested in discovering the knowledge that the persons under study are using to interpret the norms of their culture and environment and to cope with their practical circumstances. Other professionals who are not ethnomethodologists use participant observation to collect observations of people's actions and behaviors (Turner, 1972).

The ethnomethodologists' use of participant observation is different because they are looking for the reasoning behind people's actions (that is, the meaning people give to their own actions). Other methods may look for actions and behaviors and then attribute reasons to these behaviors according to some predetermined scheme. In many respects, ethnomethodology is a more intensive and risky qualitative method, the reality of which will be demonstrated in detail throughout this chapter.

Ethnomethodologists have not always been clear on how their use of participant observation is different from others', and they are working to clarify this distinction. An example of this effort is the notion of unexpected events to extend the use of participant observation as a research method which was presented in the preceding chapter.

Ethnomethodology provides a somewhat different perspective in studying social phenomena, while supplementing and augmenting traditional research methods. It is a theoretical and methodological method aimed at describing how people in everyday interactions construct definitions for their situations and shape their realities (B. Phillips, 1976). An abiding concern of ethnomethodology has been to identify ways in which members of society come to recognize, interpret, and make sense of the world (Hilbert, 1977). This distinguishes ethnomethodology from other research methods in that it stresses the contingent, self-created nature of the world in which we live (Gellner, 1975). Ethnomethodology is intended to parallel ethnoscience, as used in anthropology, which refers to the knowledge constructs of primitives (Watts, 1974). In a similar way, ethnomethodology refers to the methods people employ in carrying out the activities that make up their everyday life (Churchill, 1971).

Like all research methods, ethnomethodology has deep roots in philosophy (Zimmerman, 1979). It has been said that developments in the social sciences are several years or decades behind their antecedent movements in philosophy. To a large extent, ethnomethodology springs and draws its sustenance from phenomenology, an important philosophical movement emphasizing the subjective, which has a number of similarities to existentialism. Phenomenology is critical of the positivist notions that knowledge is inherently neutral and can be garnered by examining social scenes from the "outside in," usually by imposing empirical tools on the social phenomena to be studied. Phenomenology has had an increasing influence on the social sciences for several years (Watts, 1976).

Ethnomethodologists view the social world as held together by a complex, intricate, collective structure of so-called tacit understandings (what people know and know others know) concerning uhe most ordinary and seemingly trivial of daily affairs (Cicourel, 1973).

This chapter is divided into two main sections. The first section examines the ethnomethodological quest for understanding social phenomena and the documentary interpretation method which is often used to accomplish this task. It also suggests a framework of common elements in ethnomethodological studies and considers some of the advantages and disadvantages of the method. The second section considers some ethnomethodological research in areas that have particular import for the social workers.

ETHNOMETHODOLOGY: A TERRITORIAL MAP

Ethnomethodology can be explained and demonstrated with the example of Mrs. Larsen, an 82-year-old resident of Magnolias Manor Nursing Home for the past six years. She has one daughter who lives 40 miles away and who visits whenever she can. Mrs. Larsen came to the nursing home when her daughter could no longer care for her as her health declined.

Mrs. Larsen's best friend among the 60 residents of the home is Mrs. O'Leary, who is 84 years old. They enjoy crocheting and talking with other residents in the recreation room. A favorite conversational item is the general conditions of the home and what Mrs. Larsen and several others feel is the rude and unpleasant behavior of some of the nursing aides and other personnel. They ventilate their frustrations in these sessions and complain that nothing is ever done by the administrators about these workers.

Looking Inside Out: Structuring Activities

Ethnomethodology is interested in probing and unearthing the meanings that Mrs. Larsen and the other residents (the clients) in this complex social scene attach to what they say and do. These meanings are difficult to uncover. Indeed, some ethnomethodologists have maintained that most traditional research methodologies, in a search for regularities in social structures, have ignored the structuring activities that have created those structures (Mehan & Wood, 1975a).

The structuring activities that the residents at Magnolias Manor are engaged in on a day-to-day basis are complex, intricate, and can only be uncovered by examining the meanings the residents attach to their activities. A study of the residents in the home using survey research methodology would not necessarily explicate the meanings within the social scenario there. To accomplish this, ethnomethodologists are interested in probing and investigating the linguistic aspects of human interchange, the use of norms, and reflexivity. All three are interrelated and interconnected, but they nevertheless represent different emphases or orientations.

Linguistic Aspects of Human Interchange. Ethnomethodologists are intrigued with indexical expressions, which can be looked at as situation-specific words and phrases whose meaning might change from one situation to another, depending on who is speaking, how they might be saying it, and where. In this sense, indexical expressions are accounts whose meaning cannot be separated from the occasions of their use, and the accounts are thus linked to the meaning conveyed in such occasions (Mitchell, 1978). They are utterances that require contextual data to be thoroughly understood (Bar-Hillel, 1964).

According to ethnomethodologists, conventional social workers are more concerned with converting indexical expressions into objective nonindexical expressions, or in substituting objective expressions for indexical ones, than they are in studying the rules by which sense is made of indexicals by persons in ongoing, everyday conversation (Bailey, 1978). Hence, if the indexicals employed by Mrs. Larsen and other residents were left untouched in a traditional survey research study conducted at Magnolias Manor, then the true picture would be incomplete. We cannot fully understand the unfolding scenario until we have a firm grasp on the indexicalities employed. For example, Mrs. Larsen may employ different kinds of expressions, tones of voice, and so on, in speaking with different kinds of people in the nursing home.

Another aspect of the ethnomethodologist's concern with linguistics and everyday language is the *et cetera* clause, a kind of filling-in process with human interchange (Garfinkel, 1964). The speaker and the hearer "fill in" when the rest of the speaker's message is obvious. It could be argued that the et cetera clause is probably employed frequently between Mrs. Larsen and Mrs. O'Leary, or between any two (or more) people who know each other well. It is likely that any list of social rules, conventions, or agreements contains an et cetera clause, which is treated as binding by participants and as "being there all along." For example, Mrs. Larsen may not bother to complete a sentence she expresses to Mrs. O'Leary, who is well acquainted with the notion or thought expressed.

Use of Norms.   Ethnomethodologists are also interested in the norms applied in social scenes. Norms specify which behavior, utterance, or activity is appropriate and relevant for a person with a given status and in a given context at a particular moment. Most norms in use are not consciously thought about by the individual. Ethnomethodologists are frequently interested in penetrating social situations to uncover norms in use (Emerson & Pollner, 1978).

Reflexivity.   The concept of reflexivity implies that persons actively cooperate with others to create and maintain social structures. They actively organize their daily lives and make their activities accountable in some way to themselves, significant others, and outsiders (Gidlow, 1972). There is a continuous (reflexive) feedback with the environment. Talk is itself reflexive, in that to say "hello" both creates and sustains a world in which, according to Mehan and Wood (1975a), people acknowledge that:

1. They sometimes can see one another.
2. A world exists in which it is possible for them to signal to one another.
3. They expect to be signaled back to.

4. They expect to be signaled back by some people but not all.

With talk and in the absence of talk, reflexivity is operating in social situations to provide a continuous feedback to participants about the routine sense of what is transpiring (Cicourel, 1968). The body language of Mrs. Larsen, Mrs. O'Leary, and the other residents of Magnolias Manor may be illustrative of this principle, without any verbal language being employed.

Documentary Interpretation

Ethnomethodology often uses documentary interpretation, a method which consists of treating an actual appearance as an indicator of a presupposed underlying pattern. The underlying pattern is derived from its individual documentary evidences. The individual documentary evidences, in their turn, are interpreted on the basis of what is known about the underlying pattern. Each is used to elaborate the other. For example, what is known about the mannerisms and behaviors of the residents is indicative of underlying social patterns. The behaviors and the perceived underlying social patterns are juxtaposed and examined in order to achieve a better understanding of each and of the whole.

With the documentary method of interpretation there is a concerted, exhaustive attempt to reconstruct the social realities of the actors (those being studied). Those employing this method take as problematic all of their own and the actors' behaviors and pay careful attention to how concepts are linked to observations (Dreitzel, 1970). They make public and observable all documentary activities carried out and treat background features of situations (the dress of respondents and the like) as important data contributing to the final research product (Denzin, 1970a).

A model is constructed by the worker, one that might reflect the ideal standards for the investigation. A person is selected as a methodological anchor point and employed as the standard of scientific comparison (Mrs. Larsen in the example). Since social workers can never fully enter the complex, everyday lives of people, the "here and now" world, the model of the person is employed as a way of at least approaching such a world. Such a model could be employed at Magnolias Manor to help explicate the hidden background expectancies, indexicalities, norms in use, and the like that play out every day. For example, the model employed in the example is of an elderly individual with normal abilities, intelligence, and interactional skills, coping with everyday life as it presents itself in the home (Denzin, 1970b).

A Framework for Ethnomethodological Studies

As in all research methods, there is no single organized way to do an ethnomethodological study (Goffman, 1959). Ethnomethodologists are careful about the dangers of refining or absolutizing almost anything, including their work. However, ethnomethodological studies might be said to reflect a basic framework with the common elements described below for studying the nursing home.

First, the worker attempts to "bracket" all preconceived ideas, biases, and attitudes about the phenomenon being studied. The social worker may not have a particular liking for Mrs. Larsen as a person or may have some definitely negative feelings about nursing homes, but these attitudes and feelings must be disregarded as much as possible. A conscious and deliberate decision must be made to bracket these attitudes and preconceived ideas and put them aside, such as any ideas or notions about what friends (or society) say Magnolias Manor is. Then the investigator can go about the business of attempting to understand the complex social phenomena taking place there on its own reckoning—as much as it is humanly possible to do (Heap, 1977).

Second, the social worker attempts to enter into the interpretative procedures of each client being studied, to understand the social phenomena from the client's point of view. Here the social worker does some conscious role playing, attempting to get into the shoes of Mrs. Larsen and the other residents as they go about their daily routines in the nursing home. It is necessary to imagine what it is like to think their thoughts, to be in their particular phase of life. What is it like for Mrs. Larsen to be notified that it is time for supper at 4:30 P.M., for example, when she is accustomed to eating much later in the day? What might be going on in her mind about this?

Third, the social worker obtains the trust and confidence of the residents of the home. This involves discussing the social worker's interest in bringing the views of the residents to the forefront and a willingness to wait as long as necessary to gain their trust. Trust is often not easily given by people, and a deliberate effort must be made to merit and obtain it. The social worker must inform Mrs. Larsen and her friends of the purposes of the study and how it is being conducted and discuss the necessity for openness, honesty, and trust on all sides. Furthermore, the worker must be willing to devote the time and effort necessary to achieve rapport with the residents. Several visits before launching the study, to carry on conversations with Mrs. Larsen and others, could provide an opportunity to indicate the time and energy that will be devoted to obtaining a more intensive knowledge about the people and the social phenomena at the nursing home.

Fourth, the social worker employs whatever tools are helpful in bringing out the clients' points of view, such as videotape, tape recordings, extensive note taking, or extended conversations at a nearby restaurant. Various kinds of tools that might be helpful in penetrating and understanding the interaction and the social scenario at the nursing home are considered. Since Mrs. Larsen and the other residents might find certain tools threatening (videotape, for example), note taking might be considered the only tool that could be usefully employed in studying this situation (Mehan & Wood, 1975b).

Fifth, the social worker pays particular attention to the linguistic styles and indexical expressions employed by the residents, in attempts to understand reality as they perceive it. Mrs. Larsen has the particular linguistic style, appropriate to her generation, sex, ethnic and cultural background, and socioeconomic status. Her use of language depends on the social situation in which she finds herself, on the mood she might be in at the moment, and on many other variables. The worker must attempt to understand all these variables and how they influence the perception of reality held by the residents of the home. For example, the worker might notice that when Mrs. Larsen is tired, her speech becomes more staccato-like and noticeably irritating to some of the other residents.

Sixth, the social worker views as problematic all client and social worker behaviors, taking into account at every step in the research process how concepts are linked to observations and how behaviors are interpreted by clients and the social worker. Behind every behavior or action exhibited by Mrs. Larsen or the other residents are attitudes, thoughts, intentions, and meanings. This is true of the social worker as well. How the social worker interprets what is going on in the nursing home, and why the actions and behaviors are interpreted in that way, must be carefully detailed. For example, the social worker's interpretation of why some residents were noticeably irritated with Mrs. Larsen in the late afternoon (staccato-like speech, interpreted by the worker as due to fatigue) must be stated, as well as the fact that the worker may or may not have felt something like that same irritation.

Seventh, the social worker treats the background features of situations (e.g., the dress of clients) as important pieces of data to be recorded and interpreted, alongside the interpretations given the same phenomena by the client. Mrs. Larsen's bodily mannerisms and expressions may be interpreted in one way by the social worker and in other ways by other residents. Each interpretation has its own merit and worth and is to be considered in its own right, and each is important for understanding the whole. For example, Mrs. Larsen may interpret the attire of another woman resident as slovenly and act accordingly toward her, while some of the other women may not feel the same way about that resident.

Eighth, the social worker treats actual appearances as the documents of underlying patterns. Ultimately, care must be taken to explicate the interpretation alongside other possible interpretations that could be made (and are being made) of the same phenomena by residents of the home, by readers of the study, and by others. For example, a particularly unhappy resident of the nursing home might interpret slovenly attire as a kind of protest against the conditions in the home, while other residents (and perhaps the social worker) may interpret the same behavior in a very different way. All interpretations must be explicated in juxtaposition to the individual resident wearing the allegedly slovenly attire and her interpretations, all placed alongside the perceived underlying social patterns in the home (Myrdal, 1969).

Ninth, the social worker makes public all research activities, from the very beginning to the end of the effort. Readers of the study must be completely aware of all the activities carried out by the worker, in order to understand the social scenario at the nursing home in a holistic context. The worker's activities are not "value free" but "value full," since the goal of objectivity cannot be totally reached. The social worker must attempt to become part of the social scenario at the nursing home by experiencing it as much as feasible. The explication of the social worker's activities can be of much assistance to readers and to the worker as well.

Some of the elements of this framework sound at least something like participant observation techniques (see Chapter 17). There are close ties between ethnomethodology and participant observation, but there are differences as well. One of the limitations of participant observation is that the unstated assumptions, concepts, and theories of the participant-observer may be substituted for an analysis of the point of view of the clients being studied (Silverman, 1972). The client's point of view and perspective, and the indexicalities and norms in use in a given social scene, may not appear in a definitive way (or at all) in a traditional participant observation study. Still, ethnomethodologists are quite sympathetic to the process of firsthand observation of social phenomena that has been so much a hallmark of participant observation studies (Bruyn, 1966; McCall & Simmons, 1969; Whyte, 1966).

ADVANTAGES AND DISADVANTAGES OF ETHNOMETHODOLOGY

Advantages

One advantage of ethnomethodology as a research method is its attempts to bring the client's point of view to the surface. The social worker in the example attempts to explicate Mrs. Larsen's perspective by viewing the social scenario at the nursing home from the inside out. It is basic for the social worker to understand social reality from the point of view of the person experiencing that reality. Ethnomethodology provides a possible avenue for increasing that understanding.

Ethnomethodology also attempts to bring to the forefront the background expectancies and exigencies that are a fundamental element in any social scenario. The worker examines the background expectancies of nursing home life, the expectations that the home has in respect to resident actions and behaviors, and the expectations that the residents have in this same regard. These are elements that frequently do not rise to the surface in most traditional qualitative research methods.

Ethnomethodology can serve as a valuable cross-check for traditional research methodology. An example might be an answer to the following question: Would an ethnomethodological study and a traditional research study on the Magnolias Manor nursing home coincide in their findings? They might or might not. If they did coincide, then both could contribute to a more holistic research understanding of the home and the people who live there. If they did not, then it may be a clue for the worker of either method to return to the drawing board. Perhaps more valid or reliable research instruments need to be constructed and employed in both approaches.

Disadvantages

Among the disadvantages of ethnomethodology are that it may be difficult to conduct. The larger the study, the more difficult and time-consuming it will be. To understand something from the inside out is, on the face of it, a considerable undertaking. In the example, the initial steps of gaining the trust and understanding of the residents itself can take considerable time. Time and expense are important considerations in launching an ethnomethodological study. A considerable array of variables are incorporated, and the larger the study, the more variables are involved. The Magnolias Manor Nursing Home situation could involve so many variables that the investigator might be engulfed by their number and complexity.

Another disadvantage of ethnomethodology is that the concepts and methods employed are not well defined and often are not easily understandable. Since the ethnomethodological approach was originated only within the past few years, the concepts are still poorly formulated and have not met the test of time or experience to any considerable degree. In addition, ethnomethodologists are quick to point out that the phenomena they attempt to study are as elusive and at times as indecipherable as the concepts themselves. Ethnomethodologists are often not fond of excessive pigeonholing, preciseness, and absolute clarity in their formulations, arguing that such absolutism may do an injustice to the very intricate and at times bewilderingly complex phenomena they hope to understand and explicate. Terms such as *indexicalities, documentary interpretation,* and the like simply do not have the preciseness that is characteristic of concepts in traditional quantitative research (B. Phillips, 1979).

While in the example ethnomethodology is a notable attempt to bring the residents' point of view to the forefront, there may be as many interpretations of the phenomena as there are residents. The "Rashomon effect" describes the wide number of interpretations that individuals may have about a single event. Carried to a logical extreme, there may be as many underlying patterns in the event or social scene as there are individual perceivers and interpreters of the patterns. The very complexity that ethnomethodology stresses as characteristic of social phenomena ultimately may limit its effectiveness as a research method. For example, an ethnomethodological study may encounter so many interpretations of only one behavior (such as slovenly attire) that the ongoing study will be in danger of becoming bogged down by the number of possible interpretations and the complexity of the social scenario.

EXAMPLES OF ETHNOMETHODOLOGICAL RESEARCH

Ethnomethodology has not had a lengthy history, although a number of ethnomethodological and ethnomethodologically based research studies have appeared in recent years. A study of the activities and processing of juveniles through the juvenile justice system in two San Francisco area counties was one of the first and most influential of such research studies. This study will be examined in some detail, as well as studies in education, public assistance, and other areas.

Correctional Settings

Cicourel's study of two San Francisco Bay area probation departments took four years to complete (Cicourel, 1968). He was interested in looking at juvenile probation departments from the inside out, from the point of view of the main client in the drama: the juvenile. Cicourel, who was indebted to labeling theory, considered the police officer to be often the prime definer of "the problem situation." "Criminal" statistics were viewed as creatures of the day-to-day activities of corrections personnel.

With these assumptions, Cicourel made use of verbatim materials whenever possible to obtain some of the best data on how the police really viewed the juvenile delinquent. Three years were spent building relationships with individual police and probation officers in lengthy conversations in informal settings, such as favorite police bars. These exchanges brought seminal data, as the officers opened up in a way they probably would not have in a formal work setting.

Cicourel relates in considerable detail the various contingencies associated with court, police, and probation work. The indexicalities of the social scene were brought out, and the categorization of juveniles into "punks," "good kids," and so on was explicated. With open eyes and ears, and a strong desire to obtain the juvenile's point of view in respect to hidden norms in use and indexicalities, the author observed the complex juvenile justice processing system in the two counties and described it with considerable detail. The study demonstrates that simply examining quantitative data cannot lead to a full understanding of the negotiated character of phenomena labeled delinquency, unless the process by which these "official data" became "official statistics" is examined at the same time.

Other studies also have been helpful in "getting into" the corrections scenario (Emerson, 1969; Emerson & Pollner, 1976; Pollner, 1974; Sacks, 1972b; Sudnow, 1965). Studies of correctional settings bring home the concepts of definition of the situation, indexicalities, norms in use, and the like. Ethnomethodologists are particularly intrigued with the study of broad-scale deviance settings.

Educational Settings

Various aspects of educational settings have been studied with ethnomethodological procedures. A series of studies of school settings applied ethnomethodology to describe the practices school officials and students employ to produce reified educational statistics (Mehan & Wood, 1976). Other investigators have examined how placement counselors work to process students through educational structures to produce outcomes (Erickson, 1975).

Public Assistance Settings

Zimmerman's (1979) study of a public assistance agency attempted to answer these questions:

1. What is it that confers upon a particular piece of paper in a public assistance agency its authority for the determination of matters of fact?

2. How do such records reach the level of authority which purports to represent an objective and impersonal account of a life?

3. What features give these records currency—that is, what permits their utilization in various contexts and situations, sometimes distinct from the purposes for which they were originated?

The study found that there was a continual interplay between the routine and problematic use of documents by employees. The taken-for-granted use of documents, as analyzed by accounts given in this setting, was found to be dependent on an ordered, rational world. Public assistance recipients were processed through the ordered world of the public assistance organization, and the processing was accompanied by a highly intricate recording operation. Records became reified over time, coupled with the interpretations of client behaviors by employees and other elements. Zimmerman's study attempted to go inside that complex process in order to observe and interpret it (Zimmerman, 1969).

Mental Health and Health Settings

In the mental health area, some ethnomethodologists have studied the factors affecting how psychiatric emergency teams evaluated, legitimated, or discounted the calls of those in need of assistance (Emerson & Pollner, 1978). One study explored the origins and consequences of duties considered "dirty work" in a mental health setting, while another examined therapy talk (Emerson & Pollner, 1976). Other medical settings also have been studied by ethnomethodologists (Sudnow, 1969).

Other Settings

Ramos's studies of Mexican Americans, such as those described in Chapter 17, often use ethnomethodological methods. One study which looked at a poor Mexican American widow and her family suggested that social workers should take into account the background knowledge Mexican Americans take for granted in managing their everyday lives (Ramos, 1973). Others of Ramos's studies have examined the concept of *movidas* among Mexican Americans (Ramos, 1973, 1978, 1979a, 1979b, 1979c, 1981).

Some ethnomethodologists have studied conversational practices such as openings, topic selection, turn-taking, and closings. Language and conversational practices, as mentioned earlier, are of particular interest to ethnomethodologists (Sacks, 1972a, 1972b, 1972c, 1975, Schenkein, 1972; Turner, 1970).

SUMMARY

This chapter has defined the basic terminology of ethnomethodology and constructed a territorial map which focuses on investigating the meanings that people attach to their words and actions. It has examined documentary interpretation, common elements involved in an ethnomethodology study, advantages and disadvantages of the method, and examples of ethnomethodological research.

Perhaps the main value of ethnomethodology for the social worker is that it attempts to go inside social scenes, to look at the actors' perspective from the "inside out." This is in contrast to the "outside in" view that is characteristic of traditional research methodologies. Social workers need the inside-out perspective because it can be of inestimable value in improving their understanding of the clients they serve or the settings they wish to investigate.

An invariant claim of ethnomethodologists is that all action is irremediably indexical; that is, the sense or meaning of any action depends on its context (Heap, 1975). This underlining of the indexicality of all social action, of all social phenomena, can be of considerable aid to social workers. Those who can garner an understanding of indexicalities can be most effective in working inside the structures and frameworks of social scenes and situations. The helper must be able to understand social reality from the point of view of the client who experiences that reality.

Ethnomethodology is a topic of considerable discussion (Attewell, 1974). Some critics argue that it amounts to an orgy of subjectivism, a self-indulgent enterprise in which the discovery of the ineffable qualities of the mind of the analyst and its private construction of reality serve to obscure the tangible elements of the world (Coser, 1975). Others say ethnomethodology leads toward a kind of solipsism, meaning that the self is the only thing that can be known and verified.

In any case, ethnomethodology supplements traditional research techniques. It may be looked at as a healthy enrichment for the collection of research methods available to help the social worker understand and explicate social phenomena. Ethnomethodology is the heir to a noted qualitative tradition, a tradition that has much to offer anyone who seeks a better understanding of the incredibly complex workings of social phenomena.

George Hoshino and Mary Martin Lynch

19. SECONDARY ANALYSES

All social work research does not require the social worker to collect original data. Quite frequently, data that have been collected by others can be analyzed to investigate a problem area. Census data, for example, can be used to describe a community for a study, although the data were not collected personally by the worker. The use of existing data sources, or data that have been collected without the prior direct control or involvement of the worker, is referred to as secondary analysis (Hoshino & McDonald, 1975).

Secondary analyses are common in social work. Indeed, the techniques of analyzing existing data are well developed by those who regularly pursue research questions. Data are available from such agencies as the Census Bureau, the Social Security Administration, and thousands of social agencies throughout the country. Three developments have converged to make possible the rapid and sophisticated analysis of available data: the emergence of personal social services as a distinct system of social welfare, advances in computer technology, and the development of management information systems (MISs) in social service agencies. Together, they have opened up new possibilities for research and evaluation in social services (Hoshino & Lynch, 1981).

Secondary analysis of existing data may involve the analysis or reanalysis of data originally gathered by others for research purposes (Berger & Piliavin, 1976). This chapter, however, is concerned primarily with the analysis of data that have been collected by social agencies for administrative or client service purposes and that are stored in existing agency data banks (Brieland, 1980). A study of the personal social service program of a large urban public social service agency will be used as a case example to illustrate the feasibility, techniques, and problems of conducting large-scale research and evaluation efforts through this research method.

The existence in an MIS of a large amount of data that is easily accessible to workers and administrators helps make the role of a social worker a reality. This chapter provides information that increases the capacity of social workers to engage in and use secondary analyses of existing data.

Although the focus of the chapter is on secondary analysis of data stored in computerized information systems, analysis of existing data need not be restricted to large agencies or computerized files. "Canned" or standard statistical computer programs make it possible to process data in an agency information system that has not been computerized (Lindsey, 1981).

For example, only an elementary knowledge of research methods, statistical analysis, and computers was necessary to evaluate the services of a small, private residential treatment center for emotionally disturbed children with the methods presented in this chapter. This study attempted to determine how certain preadmission characteristics of emotionally disturbed children were related to the final outcomes of treatment, as well as to explore possible uses of these variables in treatment. Data on various characteristics of the children, their service experience with social agencies, and workers' ratings of them as expressed in client records were collected from the agency's records. This project illustrates the feasibility and efficiency with which noncomputerized data in existing agency records can be tapped and computer processed.

The trend in agency records, however, is toward social service data systems in which data are stored in computer-readable media (Reid, 1978b). This trend has been accompanied by greater standardization of social services data and an increase in the amount of data collected on clients, services provided, and their outcomes. In addition, individual agency information systems have been linked to larger central management information systems such as those of the United Way and departments of social services (Reid, 1975a).

DEVELOPMENTS ENCOURAGING USE OF SECONDARY ANALYSIS

The enactment in 1974 of Title XX of the Social Security Act authorized federal grants to the states for social services. The new title symbolized the emergence of personal social services, in which the social work profession plays a pivotal role, as a distinct and increasingly important component of social welfare. Significant features of Title XX are the requirement that services be directed to specified goals, and the inclusion of specific references to needs assessment, planning, accountability, and evaluation. This act has therefore encouraged agencies to collect data on a regular basis to help account for and evaluate their services.

In response to the reporting requirements in Title XX and the increasing demands for detailed social service data, many agencies have developed management information systems to collect, store, and process data. The computerized MIS is rapidly becoming a reality in public and private social service agencies, and the development has deeply involved social workers in research and evaluation. The data collection task, hitherto the costly and time-consuming responsibility of the "research specialist," is now increasingly a major task of the individual social worker. Detailed records must be kept regarding client characteristics, service activities, and client-worker interactional outcomes (Reid, 1975b).

Social service agency record-keeping activities have developed in response to state and federal reporting requirements and the new emphasis on evaluation. Title XX reporting, which is required by the Department of Health and Human Services, has moved many agencies to computerize because of the tremendous amount of data they must collect. These requirements, the advances in computer technology, and the thrust for accountability have fostered the widespread development of MISs throughout social service agencies. These MISs have created an enormous volume of detailed and readily accessible data that allows a range of research activity which until recently has been beyond the capacity, if not the interest, of social workers and administrators. The analysis of data stored in a MIS is the type of secondary analysis most frequently used by social workers when tapping data sources in the social services.

METHODOLOGICAL CONCERNS

Several methodological concerns are unique to secondary analysis, or the investigation of data which have been collected without the prior control or involvement of the researcher. These include the issues of validity and reliability, the emphasis on inductive rather than deductive methods, and the problem of missing data. The absence of the social work researcher from the data collection stage eliminates any interviewer influence or bias, and this helps ensure validity or reliability in these concepts of the research process. In secondary analysis, research questions tend to flow inductively from the data, in contrast to the more classical deductive situation in which the research questions determine the types of data collected. The issues of validity, reliability, induction versus deduction, and missing data require special consideration in the legitimization of secondary analysis as a research method.

Validity

Assuming reasonable reliability of the data, the first consideration is validity. Discussions of validity tend to focus on the measurement instrument, such as a questionnaire or an interview schedule (see Chapters 15 and 16). The question of validity (see Chapter 10) is more complex in respect to the data in an elaborate MIS.

The validity question is: Do MIS data measure what they intend to measure? The data in most systems tend to be straightforward. They typically describe demographic characteristics of clients, daily services, and financial transactions between workers and clients. There is no reason to believe that MIS data do not describe what actually occurs or exists (Bostwick & Kyte, 1981).

The areas that could present validity questions are goal status and client outcome measures. These are the variables that tend to be excluded from an agency MIS. Precise operational definitions of these variables are difficult, and the measurements may be the workers' perceptions of their own performance, the effectiveness of the agency's services, or the clients' characteristics. Validity can be a problem in respect to such variables. The straightforward demographic, financial, and descriptive data normally found in an MIS pose less of a problem. As MISs become more sophisticated and agencies begin to use them for evaluation purposes, and so require additional types of data, the question of validity will undoubtedly become more serious.

Reliability

Social work researchers typically take great pride in the degree of exactness in the data collection process. Attention to consistency, correctness, and precision of the data ensures reliability (see Chapter 9). But the very nature of secondary analysis, which by definition is removed from the data collection stage, frustrates the social worker who seeks to be personally confident of the data being analyzed. Therefore, steps must be undertaken to give the worker sufficient confidence to proceed to the analysis stage.

Data collectors for an agency MIS must understand that accuracy or precision is not an end in itself but is relative to the purpose it is to serve. Given other demands on a worker's time, the effort required for consistent reporting of data will be undertaken only if the purpose of the reporting is clear. Agency administrators can demonstrate their commitment to the MIS through an investment in training and updating workers' data collection skills. A systematic effort can be launched to determine what workers need to know to improve their practice. Efforts can be made to present clearly the problems that the MIS is meant to address—whether these be management, fiscal, or evaluative. When secondary analysis is undertaken in an agency, the question of reliability is relatively straightforward. If the climate of the agency is such that the reporting of data for the MIS is valued as an important effort that will benefit both clients and workers, accuracy will be more apt to prevail.

More sophisticated secondary analyses are conducted with data that have been collected by academic research centers and governmental bodies. The data that are stored in such computer banks should conform to standards such as those being developed by the Council of Social Science Data Archives. Such data as census tract data and social or poverty indicators should be thoroughly investigated for reliability before use. Because these data have been collected for research purposes, however, they are likely to be more reliable than those in an agency MIS.

Inductive Research

Social service systems characteristically lack adequate definitional and conceptual underpinnings. The confusion surrounding the rapid growth of social services has made even simple descriptive analysis difficult. Consequently, much study of social services is most appropriately inductive. Inductive methods result in an implicit understanding of what is observed, whereas deductive methods explicitly indicate what to observe (Merton, 1957).

A distinction is often made between the purposes of data collection. Some social workers may "explore" given phenomena (theory building), while others may "test" specific hypotheses (theory testing). Secondary analysis of existing data should not be viewed simply as exploratory research or purely descriptive, and the social worker should not be limited to the "counting and categorizing" of the stereotypical empiricist. Rather, the process of induction, from observation to empirical generalization to theories, with the appropriate intervening synthesis, should be emphasized (Wallace, 1973).

Generalizing from empirical observations is an important research activity. The process of applying research to theory begins when the uniformities of a set of interrelated propositions are tentatively established (Merton, 1957). Social workers are legitimately concerned with observing phenomena and considering their interrelationships as they build generalizations, concepts, and finally, theories (Reynolds, 1971). In this sense, the research process is "directed" toward theory building through an inductive process. It is through analysis of the MIS data base that social services can be so examined. The social worker can therefore take into account that a research design in an exploratory study can also examine theories.

It is possible to observe social service systems in great detail because of the development and expansion of the MIS concept. Elaborate MISs provide data that enable users to achieve quickly the practical equivalent of products yielded by conventional research undertakings. Theoretical interest tends to shift to those areas in which there is an abundance of pertinent available data. Despite the problems of validity and confidentiality, as well as the limited potential of generalization, the massive amounts of raw data still cry out for analysis. Undoubtedly, they will be analyzed as the capabilities of computers are expanded and the possibilities of secondary analysis become recognized (Shyne, 1975).

The difficulty of using such existing data for effectiveness studies has been attributed to lack of controls of the experimental design. It seems more appropriate at this point to use such data in exploratory efforts (Knowledge Level 1, as presented in Chapter 13) as the basis for subsequent manipulation of more clearly conceptualized variables in experimental research. As agencies become more sophisticated and selective in their MIS data collection and analysis, they will also move toward the incorporation of outcome variables which will allow more traditional deductive designs.

Missing Data

Secondary analysis may be difficult because some data may be missing, may not be uniform, may not be readily accessible, or may be in a form in which they cannot be efficiently converted to a form needed by the social worker. Missing data are observations that have not been recorded (P. Stuart, 1981). They cause special problems because almost all statistics assume complete data. In the case study described in the next section, missing data surfaced in the MIS and were not retrievable. Data that were not necessary for agency reporting or financial purposes were not regularly updated or even uniformly collected. Consequently, missing data were a serious shortcoming in the study, one that could not be readily remedied.

CASE STUDY: USING EXISTING DATA

A study by Lynch (1978) of the social service program of a large, public social service department demonstrates the feasibility of conducting large-scale research and evaluation through secondary analysis of existing agency data. The research questions, methods, and findings are presented briefly in order to demonstrate the context within which the secondary analysis was undertaken. Emphasis is placed on the steps involved in the process of analysis.

Purpose of the Study

The purpose of the study was to extend knowledge of the personal social services by examining the social services of a large metropolitan social services department. The three research questions were:

1. Can social services provided by the department be more parsimoniously classified?
2. How significant is the maintenance function in the social service agency?
3. How do combinations of clients, workers, and services affect client outcomes?

The Agency's Management Information System

The MIS at the agency was installed in 1975 and had been converted to facilitate Title XX reporting requirements. Three components of the system were used in the study: the Welfare Information System (WIS), the Social Service Information System (SSIS), and the Purchased Service Information System (PSIS). WIS contains demographic variables such as age, race, eligibility, and place of residence on all clients and is periodically updated. SSIS contains variables that are tabulated daily by each worker regarding service activities for each client served including such variables as type of service, type of social work intervention, and minutes spent in interviews. PSIS contains financial variables for all clients.

In the 10-month period of the study, 13,170 clients appeared on WIS, over 200,000 incidents appeared on SSIS, and 32,180 incidents appeared on PSIS. It was possible to match WIS, SSIS, and PSIS data on each client involved in the study to produce a composite profile of each client. MIS data are especially useful because of their broad scope. The social service system can be studied in a normal state of operation, rather than in an artificial or experimental light. Data on interrelated conditions can be examined simultaneously, thus permitting a systems-oriented study. And, of course, the greatest advantage is the volume of data available, owing to the rapidity of data collection and the number of observations recorded. This volume is dramatic when contrasted with the notion of a single social worker collecting the thousands of incidents within the MIS.

An MIS is useful when it is reliable, that is, if it can be ascertained that it provides consistent data. In this sense, WIS, which contained relatively straightforward demographic data about each client, could logically be considered fairly reliable. Workers and clerical staff constantly use WIS data for administrative purposes and find it useful and accurate, an indication of reliability.

The SSIS data were collected from activity sheets completed daily by each worker. The MIS staff had aggregated the amount of time spent by workers according to program area and had found a high degree of similarity from month to month—an indication of reliability.

The PSIS is primarily an accounting tool and corresponds to the financial aspects of client services in the agency. Workers used the data as a decision-making tool; thus subversion seemed unlikely to occur.

Admittedly, none of these considerations was sufficient to establish conclusively that a high level of reliability existed in the data of the information system. However, the MIS staff constantly attempted to simplify the reporting system for workers in an environment where cooperation between staff and workers was evident. The staff routinely checked for missing data and gross discrepancies, checking personally with workers in order to correct errors. Considerations such as these were felt to justify the use of the MIS data for the exploratory study.

Sample and Primary Data Sources

A 10 percent random sample was drawn from the population of the 13,170 clients served in the 10-month period. Demographic data were obtained on the clients sampled from the agency MIS. Outcome data, which were not available on the MIS, were obtained by a measuring instrument applied to client records of the 1,317 sampled clients. This instrument measures client behaviors indicated in six programs or goals on a goal progress chart (Hoshino & Lynch, 1981). The Title XX goal structure provided the framework for a behavioral scale which was individualized for the major program areas in the department. Worker data, also not computerized, were derived from a questionnaire administered to workers involved with the sampled clients. Thus, three sources of data were utilized in the study: MIS (WIS, SSIS, and PSIS), clients' records, and workers' questionnaires.

The existing data sources in the MIS and the two primary data sources (client records not in the MIS and worker data) provided a detailed description of the clients, the workers, and the social services of the agency. It was not possible to specify how varying combinations of variables affected service outcomes. However, the findings of the study did substantiate the existence and importance of the maintenance (social care) function in public social services.

Data Processing

Preprogrammed statistical packages have become a common tool for statistically analyzing data. Such standard or "canned" statistical programs, which are available universally at colleges and universities and increasingly in larger public agencies, enable social workers to apply a wide range of statistical methods with a minimum of training (Lindsey, 1981).

In this study, processing the data to make it usable for the statistical program was of greater complexity than initially anticipated. The task was time-consuming for both people and the computer, due partially to the large sample size but more especially to the fact that the data were collected and stored in a way that they were accessible only through the agency's data processing system. Converting the data in the agency's MIS into a form usable by the investigator required three tasks: creating the sample, creating three data tapes, and reading and merging the data onto one tape.

Task 1: Creating the Sample. Each client who receives social services from the agency is given a case number. Data collected at different points—whether for the WIS, the SSIS, or the PSIS—are identified by case number. Thus, it was possible to request all case numbers served in the 10-month period from the agency programmer, who made a data tape with a list of the case numbers of the 13,170 individuals served in the time frame. From this tape the university computer center programmers wrote a simple randomizing computer program to generate a 10 percent random sample. The creation of the sample enabled the worker to begin the collection of the primary data through client case reading and questionnaire distribution to the workers (see Chapter 8).

This was the first of many such interactions between the agency and the university programmers. The agency agreed to provide the data needed but was financially not able to provide the programming and computer time necessary to process the data. Therefore, many additional steps were required to adapt the agency data, which had been collected and stored for use in one computer language (Cobalt), to permit its use in the university computer, which utilized another language (Fortran). This transfer of data from one form to another would have been unnecessary if the agency staff had been able to provide the computer time, or if the agency and university systems had been compatible. However, given the financial constraints of the agency and the probability that most theory-based research will take place in universities, similar intermediate steps in data processing may well be necessary. At least this will be the case as long as different data processing units use different computer systems and languages.

Task 2: Creating the Data Tapes. The variables of interest had been recorded in the three parts of the MIS: the agency service variables in the SSIS; the demographic variables in the WIS; and the purchased service variables in the PSIS. Consequently, all data relating to the sampled clients were retrieved from each of the three data sources, put on three separate data tapes, and then transferred to the university computer center. This illustrates some of the complications when the analysis is not done in the agency which can be anticipated and which may present difficult but not insurmountable problems.

Task 3: Merging the Three Existing Data Sources on One Tape. Differences between the agency and university computer systems, compounded with basic computer language differences, caused difficulty in reading the data on the tapes. Moreover, codebooks with variable and coding information were not uniformly consistent or updated.

Discussions between the social worker and agency and university programmers, however, eventually resulted in a successful reading of the agency tapes.

Data from the three existing secondary sources were merged so that each client in the sample had a single computerized case record. These three secondary data sources were then merged with the primary data collected from the clients' records and workers' questionnaires. Finally, all the variables of concern were grouped together for each individual in the sample and statistically analyzed.

Conclusions

Although this case study of the personal social services of a large public social service agency was undertaken to expand knowledge about them in order to improve the conceptualization of this emerging and increasingly important component of social welfare, it also demonstrated the feasibility of secondary analysis of data that are routinely collected during the normal course of an agency's operations. Many problems were encountered, but each was largely overcome. Some problems were technical, for example, those arising from the different computer systems used by the agency and the university. Other problems, such as the lack of data on service outcomes that had to be collected as primary data, reflect the state of development of service effectiveness measures. Until consensus on outcome measurement is achieved and such measures are adopted, it will be difficult to incorporate such variables in an MIS.

SUMMARY

It is generally accepted that within the next few years virtually all social agencies will have computerized many if not all of their MISs. There are many reported uses of computers in direct practice—in caseload management, eligibility determinations, assessments, and even in child placement (Schoech & Arangio, 1979). The social work researcher's increased familiarity and facility with the computer, coupled with advances in computer technology, will make secondary analysis an increasingly efficient and effective research method in social work.

Richard A. Polster and Mary Ann Lynch

20. SINGLE-SUBJECT DESIGNS

Single-subject designs serve a primary function in social work practice and research. The characteristics of these designs make them adaptable to use by the social worker involved in direct services, planning and administration, or grant-funded research.

Single-subject designs are particularly suited to the practitioner/ researcher concept because they incorporate research procedures as an integral part of intervention procedures. Unlike classical experimental designs (see Chapter 13), which typically evaluate the strength of intervention effects *after* the interventions have ended, single-subject designs provide ongoing, *continuous* feedback on these effects, and this in turn shapes intervention strategies (Hersen & Barlow, 1976). Problems are delineated within a specific framework, with the problem, or some aspect of it, defined as the dependent variable and the intervention (proposed solution) defined as the independent variable. The effectiveness of the proposed solution is evaluated through analysis of repeated measurements of the dependent variable.

The fine-grained (precise) analysis produced by single-subject designs provides specific data about the process of implementing the solution. According to Bloom and Fischer (1982), the advantages of single-subject designs are as follows:

1. They can be built into every social worker's practice with each and every case/situation without disruption of practice.
2. They provide the tools for evaluating the effectiveness of our practice with each client, group, or system with which we work.
3. They focus on individual clients or systems. If there is any variation in effect from one client or system to another, single-subject designs will be able to pick it up.
4. They provide a continuous record of changes in the target

problem over the entire course of intervention, not just a pre- and posttest.

5. They are practice-based and practitioner-oriented. Single-subject designs provide continuous assessment and outcome data to practitioners so that they can monitor progress and make changes in the nature of the intervention program if so indicated. Unlike traditional group designs and the intervention programs they are used to evaluate, which ordinarily cannot be changed once the study has begun, single-subject designs are flexible; the worker can change the intervention and the design depending on the needs of the case.

6. They can be used to test hypotheses or ideas regarding the relationship between specific intervention procedures and client changes, ruling out some alternative explanations and allowing an inference regarding causality: Was the intervention program responsible for the change in the target problem?

7. They can be used to help the worker *assess* the case/situation, leading to selection of a more appropriate program of intervention by clarifying what seem to be the relevant factors involved in the problem.

8. They essentially are theory-free; that is, they can be applied to the practice of any practitioner regardless of the worker's theoretical orientation or approach to practice.

9. They are relatively easy to use and understand. They can be applied within the same time frame the social worker is currently using in seeing clients or others. In fact, use of single-subject designs can actually enhance the worker's efficiency by saving time and energy in trying to record and evaluate the social worker's practice.

10. They avoid the problem of outside researchers coming into an agency and imposing a study on the social workers. Single-subject designs are established and conducted by practitioners for their benefits and for the benefits of the client/systems.

11. They provide a model for demonstrating our accountability to ourselves, our clients and consumers, our funding sources, and our communities. Systematic, consistent use of single-subject designs will allow practitioners, and agencies, to collect a body of data about the effectiveness of practice that provides more or less objective information about the success of our practice.

On the basis of the ongoing measurement of the dependent variable, referred to as the target behavior, the measurements which indicate its status or variability are represented graphically as the frequency of the target behavior over time. Repeated measures of the target behavior prior to the introduction of the intervention serve as a representation of its "normal trends," against which the intervention data can be compared. This phase, referred to as the *baseline,* serves as a control for the experimental phase. A change in the frequency of the behavior which is not consistent with the trends established during the baseline, and which is temporally associated with the systematic introduction of the intervention, strengthens the conclusion that there is a causal relationship between the target behavior change and the intervention (Thomas, 1983).

CHARACTERISTICS OF SINGLE-SUBJECT DESIGNS

Single-subject designs have several distinguishing characteristics. First, they may be used to evaluate the effects of an intervention on a single individual (the subject). Properties of the designs give validity to their use with a single individual who is able to serve both experimental and control functions. Second, the designs can be used with both individuals and groups. Group data, however, are derived by combining the individual group members' data and using the mean or total frequency of behavior. The data are then analyzed as if they were representative of a single individual. Third, they utilize repeated measures to establish trends and analyze change. Multiple data points provide detailed data on how the intervention affects the target behavior over time. This level of information about individual or group behavior produces a fine-grained analysis. Fourth, they base analyses of behavior on comparisons of trends during interventions (experimental condition) with trends established prior to intervention (control or baseline condition). This method highlights changes in the individual's responses over time and emphasizes variations in responding between different individuals. Finally, single-subject designs rely on feedback from ongoing data recording to determine when changes in the intervention should take place. The data indicate whether the frequency of the behavior has changed or remained stable in response to the intervention.

As open-ended, responsive approaches to experimental evaluation of intervention effects, single-subject designs make it possible to conduct a study (practice or research) which is sensitive to the needs and constraints of applied social work settings. They allow for the generation of new knowledge and techniques while the study is in process, resulting in a rapid feedback—adjustment—feedback cycle which provides the flexibility and responsiveness needed in social service agencies.

CONCEPTUALIZATION AND OPERATIONALIZATION OF VARIABLES

Target Behaviors

The primary emphasis in single-subject designs is not on proof or disproof of hypotheses, as in group designs, but on the observations and analyses of the effects of interventions on specific target behaviors (Zimbalist, 1983). As with group designs, however, the selection and definition of target behaviors are critical steps in the research process.

Any measurable aspects of the problems social workers are investigating may be selected as target behaviors. Social workers in direct services may select as the dependent variable a problem behavior which has been identified as interfering with the client's functioning, such as parent-child fighting. An administrator of an agency may select a dependent variable which relates to a problem in service provision, such as hours of direct service provided, or a worker behavior such as attendance and completion of paperwork and charting. A social planner or community organizer may choose a target behavior relating to a problem such as utilization of community services. In each of these examples the goal is to alleviate the severity of the problem. The study conducted should evaluate the effectiveness of the intervention in producing the desired change in the target behaviors.

Target behaviors can also be selected to evaluate the relationship between particular behaviors and specific environmental variables. The target behavior need not have been identified as a problem, and the goal may merely be to document that a relationship exists between the behavior and environmental variables. Environmental changes could influence the performance of a particular behavior, so that, for example, the relationship between changes in laws or regulations and the number of persons seeking services or the types of services requested might be investigated. Or executive policy changes in response to funding availability could affect staff performance, so that, for example, a program director would want to investigate the relationship between the change in policy and staff absenteeism, turnover, and amount of direct service provided.

Since it may not always be possible to measure all aspects of the desired change, the target behaviors selected must be representative of the changes which must occur to indicate successful accomplishment of the intervention goals. The target behavior must also be one which the worker, other cooperative persons (collaterals) in the environment, or the individual (subject) have opportunities to measure. Behaviors which are covert and leave no reliable evidence of having occurred, or which occur in places or at times when no one is available to record them, are not suitable as target behaviors unless the behavior leaves an observable product which can be recorded.

Operationalization of the Dependent Variables

The reliability of data in single-subject designs is determined by the ability of two observers (raters) to obtain a high level of agreement on the occurrence or nonoccurrence of the target behavior. Demonstration of the reliability of data recording is basic to the analysis of single-subject designs and is necessary before conclusions can be drawn on the relationship between the intervention and the frequency of behavior. To produce reliable data the target behavior must be operationally defined in terms of its observable characteristics.

Unobservable or private events, such as thoughts or feelings, can be recorded by the individual, but these data cannot be considered reliable due to the inability of an independent observer to observe and record the target behavior. Measurement of observable manifestations of the thoughts and feelings or products of the behavior, however, can produce reliable data (Skinner, 1974). Examples are:

Private Event	*Observable Manifestation*
Fear	Avoidance of feared objects or places, such as refusing to enter an elevator or a house in which there is a dog.
Anxiety	Stammering, shaking, sweating, or failure to complete tasks.
Depression	Isolable behaviors, such as staying indoors, sleeping, low rate of verbalization.
Helplessness	Passive behavior, such as not responding to another's aggression, lack of assertiveness in most or all situations (e.g., not requesting correct change when salesclerk makes error).

The first step in developing an operational definition of a target behavior is to gather data about it, either by direct observations or by talking to those who have an opportunity to observe the behavior regularly. Characteristics of the target behavior which distinguish it from all other behaviors should be noted. For example, an administrator may want to study the effects of a policy change on employees' work behavior. Observation of the employees indicates two possibly interrelated problems:

1. Employees spend a high proportion of their time in nonwork-related activities, such as personal phone calls, snack breaks, and talking with other employees. They spend little time in their offices alone, working at their desks.
2. Employees are failing to complete paperwork and charting according to defined standards and within expected time limits.

Following the gathering of information, an operational definition of the discrete characteristics of the behavior is developed, along with the specific rules for how the behavior will be recorded. This description referred to as a *behavioral observation code,* must enable an independent observer to distinguish easily between the target behavior and other behaviors. What to include in the definition of the target behavior may involve arbitrary decisions so as much of the problem behavior as possible is recorded, while other behaviors are excluded. The worker should emphasize aspects of the dependent variable that appear to be most closely related to the solution of the problem. The administrator, for example, might develop the following code for work behavior:

1. Employees will be recorded as being "at work" when they are in their assigned offices, sitting on a desk chair, and facing their desk which has work-related materials on it. Work materials include: charts, reports, note pads, phone messages, journals, or books. Employees can also be facing exposed work materials located on their shelves and in their file cabinets. They will not be recorded as working if other employees are in their offices.
2. Paperwork and charting will be recorded as complete if it is turned in by the assigned date and if the entries are complete according to the instructions in the *Clinical Records Procedures Manual.*

Notice the conscious decision to record only solitary, at-desk, work behavior. Clearly, the definition of work behavior does not include occurrences which necessitate consultation with another employee or completion of work outside the office. Although these aspects of work may be important to overall job functioning, this definition is appropriate if the administrator is primarily concerned with increasing solitary, in-office work behavior and completed paperwork. This operational definition of work behavior avoids the difficulty of distinguishing between work-related and nonwork-related conversations among employees. Thus, the likelihood that independent observers would obtain a high level of agreement (reliability) on the occurrence of work and nonwork behavior is increased.

Some clients' problems are initially presented conceptually, so their behaviors are interpreted rather than defined. To measure the problem and evaluate the effects of an intervention, an operational definition specifying the behaviors to be observed must be developed (Reid & L. Epstein, 1977). For example, a client is referred with the problem of having a poor self-concept. Observation and data gathered from the client or collaterals can identify behaviors the client exhibits which result in that label, such as making negative statements about self, refusal to participate in new activities, and failure to initiate interactions with other persons. The specific behaviors to be recorded may be defined as follows:

1. *Negative statements.* Clients make statements indicating inability to accomplish an activity or goal, listing negative self-attributes, or judging performance as inadequate.
2. *Participation in new activities.* Client engages in new activity within five minutes, after only one verbal prompt by the person initiating the activity.
3. *Initiation of interactions with others.* Client makes first statement to another person within 30 seconds of coming into contact with the other person.

In this example, desired behaviors are defined as participation in new activities or initiation of interactions, as opposed to refusal to participate or failure to initiate. A decrease in the first behavior and an increase in the second and third behaviors will indicate an improvement in the client's self-concept. The behaviors that originally instigated the referral will be changed.

Operationalization of the Independent Variables

In addition to operationally defining the target behavior, it is crucial to operationalize the intervention, or the modification of the environment which is expected to produce a change in the target behavior. Failure to operationally define an intervention limits the support for strong conclusions about the study in two ways. First, it allows the worker to be casual about what constitutes the intervention, and this makes it difficult to assure uniform application of the intervention with all individuals during all phases of the study. Second, it makes it impossible to provide sufficient detailed data to enable others to replicate the intervention in other settings and with other people.

If the intervention procedures are not clearly defined and measurable, an independent observer could not reliably detect whether the intervention has been correctly applied. To produce the same intervention consistently, the intervention procedures *must* be written, and all persons who are responsible for implementing them *must* be trained and monitored. The operational definition *must* identify the discrete elements or steps of the intervention and describe the criteria for implementing each one. Conceptual descriptions such as family systems therapy or parent training are obviously not precise and need to be operationally defined.

A first step in operationally defining a community education program designed to influence the social behavior of nonhandicapped children toward handicapped individuals, for example, is to describe the elements of the program. A handicap is considered to be any physically disabling condition which manifests itself in uncommon physical characteristics, such as uneven gait, lack of sight or hearing, or contorted limbs. In most situations, artificial or mechanical assistance, such as wheelchairs or hearing aids, is required. Social behavior includes initiating contact through verbalization or physical means, such as shaking hands or saying "hello." The community education program includes a 90-minute multimedia presentation to be shown to children in Grades 1-5. The presentation consists of a 20-minute videotaped documentary on the lives of three handicapped individuals, a 10-minute presentation of a short play by handicapped children depicting common prejudices encountered by handicapped persons, and a 20-minute discussion by handicapped children about what it is like to be handicapped. There also are three exercises designed to allow nonhandicapped children to experience a handicapping condition:

1. *Blind.* Children are blindfolded and asked to find their way from the classroom to the bathroom.
2. *Deaf.* Children's ears are covered, and they are asked to get directions from another person.
3. *Physically handicapped.* Children are placed in a wheelchair and allowed to navigate through the classroom.

This provides a clearer idea about what is included in the intervention, but there is not yet sufficient information to replicate it. The content of the video presentation and the play must be clearly and specifically defined, and the procedures to be followed in presenting the discussion and the exercises must be specified.

Interventions such as changes in agency policy or procedure must define both the content of the changes and the methods of implementing them. For example, specifics of how the staff or the public will be informed about the changes must be outlined, and new performance expectations which will affect staff compliance must be defined.

Therapeutic interventions may seem difficult to operationalize since therapy typically involves an ongoing interaction between the client and the social worker. The intervention is defined generally, in terms such as psychosocial therapy, family therapy, or behavior therapy, but the discrete therapeutic techniques which comprise the intervention must be clearly defined. The definitions indicate differences or similarities of the therapeutic intervention with others.

In order to study the results of family therapy on a particular problem, for example, the family therapy techniques that will be employed and the conditions under which they will be implemented must be operationally defined. For example, a social worker may want to study the effects of family therapy on the occurrence of physical and verbal aggression between children and their parents. The intervention might be defined as one 60-minute session per week, for 10 weeks, at which all family members must be present. Communication exercises to be practiced are to consist of the following five components:

1. Presentation of a communication model.
2. Guided application of the model to a hypothetical disagreement.
3. Application of the model to a real disagreement.
4. Videotape replay of the family's performance during the disagreement.
5. Discussion of each family member's reactions on:
   a. Positive communication by other family members.
   b. Communication which seemed effective or not effective.
   c. Own ideas that occurred during the communication practice.

This operational definition of the intervention specifies in measurable and observable terms what the worker will be doing, to whom, when, how often, and where. This information constitutes a format which ensures uniform application of the intervention, provides adequate information to compare it to other treatment interventions, and allows the social worker to replicate the intervention or use it with other populations, behaviors, or settings (Mutschler, 1979).

RECORDING METHODS

Evaluation of the intervention in single-subject designs is accomplished through systematic recording and analysis of the data. Data refers to information that has been quantified and recorded, thereby facilitating comparison of behaviors before, during, and after interventions. There are six basic methods of recording data: (1) interval, (2) frequency, (3) duration, (4) magnitude, (5) spot-check, and (6) permanent product procedures. The selection of the most suitable method for recording data in a study is made by matching the type of data a recording method can capture with the characteristics of the target behavior and the requirements of the study. Two additional variables that may influence the choice of data recording methods are the type of data recorder (observer) needed, and the amount of training necessary to produce reliable data (Gambrill, 1977, 1983).

Interval Recording

Interval recording involves continuous direct observations of individuals in their natural environments during specified observation periods divided into intervals of equal time. The shorter the intervals, the more precisely when the behavior occurred can be determined. The reliability can, therefore, be more clearly demonstrated. Recording the behavior within short time intervals produces a temporal picture of the occurrence of the behavior over time and therefore provides a basis for a fine-grained analysis. Ten-second intervals are common in research requiring a fine-grained analysis.

Data can be recorded within the time intervals in several ways. Occurrence data are obtained by recording the first occurrence of the behavior during each time interval. Subsequent occurrences of the behavior during the same interval are not recorded. Nonoccurrence data can be obtained by recording those intervals in which the behavior does not occur. The resulting data will show the number of intervals during which the behavior occurred at least once and the number of intervals during which the behavior did not occur. Interval data do not indicate the number of times the behavior occurs. Instead, the data are presented in terms of the percentage of intervals in which the behavior did or did not occur.

When duration of the behavior is of interest, data are recorded when the behavior occurs for the entire interval. Behavior which occurs for only a portion of the interval is not recorded. For example, this procedure might be used to record the duration of on-task behavior for a child consistently working at a task. On-task behavior would be recorded for an interval if the child was on-task for the entire interval, and an interval during which the child exhibited both on-task and off-task behavior would be recorded as off-task. The resulting data would indicate the number of intervals during which the child sustained on-task activity, but it would not indicate the precise amount of time the child was on-task.

In recording interval data, a recording form is used which has spaces for each interval of the observation period for each behavior to be recorded. The observer typically uses a clipboard with the recording form held securely in place and a stopwatch fastened to the top so the passage of time can be accurately noted. A location which is unobtrusive and does not respond to environmental stimuli is best. The observer notes occurrence or nonoccurrence of the target behaviors by placing a check mark or a specified symbol in the space corresponding to each time interval.

Figure 20.1 is an example of how a specific behavior might be recorded in the second, third, fourth, and sixth 10-second time intervals of a one-minute observation period. The data indicate that the behavior occurred at least one time during each of the four intervals, or in 67 percent of the intervals shown. If the observer was recording

FIGURE 20.1

One Minute of Ten-Second Interval Recording

Time in Seconds

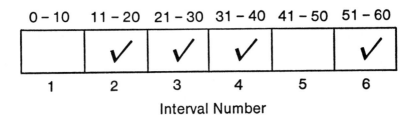

Interval Number

duration of the behavior instead of frequency, the figure would indicate that the behavior occurred continually for at least 30 seconds during one episode and at least 10 seconds during a second episode.

Figure 20.2 presents a variation of Figure 20.1 in that more than one behavior can be recorded on the same form.

Data obtained through interval recording will be highly detailed, providing a temporal picture of the behavior in addition to information about frequency or duration. Small changes in the rate or pattern of behavior can usually be observed in the data. Interval recording, however, is more suitable for recording behaviors that occur frequently or that have varying frequencies, as it involves intense use of observers over a relatively short time. The procedure is not economically feasible for recording behaviors that occur at low frequencies.

Interval recording will indicate patterns of occurrence of target behaviors, which may be useful information in planning interventional strategies. The temporal relationships between different behaviors of one individual or the behaviors of people interacting with one another also can be studied using this procedure. Relationships in dyads such as parent-child, teacher-student, or husband-wife and in small groups can be studied, such as the effects of an increase in a teacher's use of contingent reinforcement on a student's rate of task completion.

Reliability. Reliability of the data collected with interval recording is computed by having at least two independent observers record the same behaviors simultaneously. The common formula for computing overall reliability in interval recording is:

$$\frac{\text{Agreements}}{\text{(Disagreements + Agreements)}} \times 100 = \text{Percentage of Agreement}$$

Agreement is calculated by comparing the recording forms and counting the intervals for which both observers recorded occurrence of the behavior (occurrence agreement) and nonoccurrence of the behavior

FIGURE 20.2
Interval Recording Form for More than One Behavior
(from Figure 20.1)

Client's Name   Recorder's Name

Behaviors to be Observed:

A. _____

B. _____

C. _____

Time Period: _____

Duration of Each Interval: _____

Interval

Minute	Behavior	1	2	3	4	5	6	7	8	9	10
	A										
1	B										
	C										
	A										
2	B										
	C										
	A										
3	B										
	C										
	A										
4	B										
	C										
	A										
5	B										
	C										

Source: Martin Bloom, Joel Fischer, *Evaluating Practice: Guidelines for Accountable Professional,* © 1982. Reprinted by permission of Prentice-Hall, Inc., Englewood Cliffs, N.J.

(nonoccurrence agreement). Disagreement is said to occur when one observer records the occurrence of the behavior and the other records nonoccurrence for the same interval.

Uses. Interval recording is a complex and time-consuming procedure which requires the use of trained observers to record the data. Before beginning the study it is advisable to conduct practice recording sessions until the observers are able to produce reliable data using the observational code. Interval recording is not recommended for use by indigenous observers unless the behavior code is simple and discrete and the intervals are large. Since the behavior of recording data is performed to the exclusion of other behaviors, this procedure cannot be used by individuals to record data on their own behavior.

Compared to the other data recording methods to be discussed, interval recording is the most rigorous, precise, and expensive. Baring cost, the decision to use this method should depend on whether the behavior occurs at a high enough frequency to warrant its use and whether, for practical purposes, the practice or research problem necessitates such detailed data.

Frequency Recording

Frequency recording also involves direct observation of individuals in the natural environment, but the techniques of recording data are less complex than those used in interval recording. As a result, the behavior can be observed over a longer period of time, and frequency recording is appropriate for use with both high- and low-frequency behaviors.

During the specified observation period, each occurrence of the target behavior (as defined in the observational code) is noted on the data recording form as a symbol, check, or tally mark. The notations are totaled for each observation period and can be expressed as the number of occurrences of the target behavior per the length of the observation period. This is an expression of rate (frequency/time). An example of frequency recording during a three-hour observation period in which there were 18 recorded occurrences of the target behavior would be shown as:

Observation Period	*Frequency*
10:30 A.M.–1:30 P.M.	卌 卌 卌 III

The rate of behavior can be expressed as 18 (occurrences)/3(hours), or 6 occurrences per hour.

FIGURE 20.3
Frequency Recording Form for One Period of Time

Client's Name		Recorder's Name
Behavior to be Observed: _____		
Time Period (Hours/Day): _____		
Date	Frequency	Additional Comments

Source: Martin Bloom, Joel Fischer, *Evaluating Practice: Guidelines for Accountable Professional,* °1982. Reprinted by permission of Prentice-Hall, Inc., Englewood Cliffs, NJ.

Figure 20.3 displays a frequency recording form for one period of time while Figure 20.4 displays a frequency recording form for recording frequencies for different periods of time.

Reliability. While reliability can be determined by having two observers simultaneously and independently record data on the same behaviors, frequency data is a gross measure indicating the total number of times the behaviors have occurred during a specific time. Therefore comparison of the data recorded by the observers shows only

FIGURE 20.4
Frequency Recording Form for Varying Periods of Time

Client's Name				Recorder's Name	
Behavior to be Observed _____					
Date	Frequency	Total	Time	Rate	Additional Comments

Source: Martin Bloom, Joel Fischer, *Evaluating Practice: Guidelines for Accountable Professional,* ®1982. Reprinted by permission of Prentice-Hall, Inc., Englewood Cliffs, NJ.

whether they recorded the same number of behaviors. The common formula for computing reliability in frequency recording is:

$$\frac{\text{Lowest frequency observed}}{\text{Highest frequency observed}} \times 100 = \text{Percentage of Agreement}$$

This reliability computation will not indicate whether the observers recorded the same occurrences of the behavior. Each observer could have missed 25 percent of the occurrences and still have arrived at the same number of occurrences. This method is not highly accurate, but it can support the conclusion that the data are representative of the frequency of behavior. Confidence in the reliability of frequency recording can be increased when both observers record the actual time the behavior occurred, so it is possible to determine if the same behavior was recorded by both observers at the same time.

Uses. Frequency recording is suitable when the number of times the behavior occurs is the relevant measure. An administrator might use frequency recording to evaluate the effect of a policy change on the completion of work by measuring important work behaviors such as number of referrals processed, or number of clients served. Community organizers might use frequency recording to evaluate the effectiveness of a community action program by recording number of requests for services.

This type of recording can be used effectively by collaterals and by the individuals themselves, provided the behaviors are limited in number and are characterized by clear and mutually exclusive operational definitions. Behaviors such as hitting, arguments, completion of tasks, temper tantrums, compliance, and physical affection can all be measured with frequency recording.

Rates of behavior may vary for different activities, particularly in settings such as homes or schools in which the schedule of activities constantly changes. Therefore frequency data should be recorded under the most standard conditions possible. For example, the number of arguments a couple has between 6:00 and 10:00 P.M. might vary according to the activities in which they are involved. An evening at the movies or a party might result in few arguments; an evening at home might include many. Comparisons of data recorded prior to and during interventions must be made across similar environmental conditions: nights at home *prior* to the intervention compared to nights at home *during* the intervention.

The amount of observer training required to reliably record frequency data is related to the number and complexity of the behaviors to be recorded. If the behavior definitions require fine discriminations, or if many behaviors are to be recorded, observers may need extensive practice. However, in social work, especially when collaterals are recording data, the observational code can be simple and clearly defined, so frequency recording can be easily learned and implemented.

If the recording of data is done by the individual or collaterals, frequency data recording is relatively inexpensive. If trained observers are used or extensive training is necessary, it may be as costly as interval recording.

Duration Recording

Duration data are obtained by directly observing the target behavior in the natural environment and recording the length of time each episode lasts within the specified observation period. The procedure requires the observer to attend to the behavior each time it occurs and to record the length of time the behavior persists. The observer may measure the duration of each occurrence in seconds or minutes by watching a clock or triggering a stopwatch, or simply by noting the time the behavior begins and ends for each occurrence and calculating the duration later.

In the example of duration recording illustrated below, the observer recorded the length of time the behavior persisted for each of the three episodes of the target behavior that occurred during a one-hour observation period. The first episode lasted for 3 minutes, the second lasted 25 minutes, and the third continued for 5 minutes:

Observation Period	*Episode Duration in Minutes*
6:00 P.M.–7:00 A.M.	**3, 25, 5**

Figure 20.5 displays a duration recording form for one behavior.

Reliability.   When the reliability of duration data is assessed by two observers simultaneously and independently recording data, synchronized timepieces are used to note the time of onset and completion of each behavior. Comparison of the times indicates whether the observers were recording the same occurrence of the behavior.

Uses.   Duration data can be used in several ways. The duration of each occurrence of the behavior during the intervention can be compared with duration of occurrences prior to intervention. Durations of each occurrence during each observation period can be added to indicate the cumulative amount of time the person engaged in the behavior during the observation period. This figure divided by the total length of the observation period produces the percentage of time the person engaged in the behavior. The duration of each occurrence during the observational period may also be averaged, but this may obscure variations in the person's responding. For example, in the example above the episodes of behavior range in duration from 3 to 25 minutes, with one occurrence of 5 minutes. The average of these episodes is 11 minutes, but the average hides the fact that the longest episode was more than twice that length.

Duration can be recorded by trained observers, collaterals, or the individual. If the behavior is highly noticeable and occurs infrequently the observer can engage in other activities until the onset of the behavior. However, if the behavior is subtle at onset or is of high frequency or extremely long in duration, the observer's time may be dominated by the need to record data. Unless the behavior is difficult to discriminate, observer training should be minimal. Simple recording rules and explicit behavior definitions should be sufficient (Ballard & Glynn, 1975).

FIGURE 20.5
Duration Recording Form for One Behavior

Date	Length of Time Behavior Occurred (e.g., minutes)	Total Time (minutes)	Additional Comments

Client's Name   Recorder's Name

Behavior to be Observed: _____

_____

Time Period for Observation: _____

Source: Martin Bloom, Joel Fischer, *Evaluating Practice: Guidelines for Accountable Professional,* ©1982. Reprinted by permission of Prentice-Hall, Inc., Englewood Cliffs, NJ.

Duration recording should be used when the length of time a behavior persists is the relevant issue. Many behaviors can be measured both in terms of duration and frequency. The selection of techniques depends on the aspect of behavior to be studied or changed. Some examples of behaviors that can be measured by duration recording are length of episodes of crying, length of arguments, length of work breaks, duration of illness, and length of time engaged in a task without interruption.

Duration recording can also be used to measure the length of time between the presentation of a stimulus and the onset of behavior, such as the elapsed time between a call for emergency services (stimulus) and the delivery of the services (behavior), or the time between a parent's request and a child's compliance.

If trained observers are used, duration recording will be as expensive as interval recording, but training time will most likely be less. In many cases duration data can be recorded by collaterals or the client at minimal expense (Blackman, Howe, & Pinkston, 1976).

Magnitude Recording

Magnitude recording involves recording data on the amount, level, or degree of the target behavior during each occurrence. It can also be accomplished by rating the target behavior at prescribed intervals according to the frequency of severity of behavior. Ratings are made on a scale which delineates the most minor level of the behavior at one end of the scale and the most major at the other, as in the following example of a scale to measure the magnitude of a child's temper tantrums:

1. Child cries and whines—low volume.
2. Child screams or shouts—high volume.
3. Child uses body to hit or throw inanimate objects: stomping feet on floor, kicking furniture, throwing objects (but not in the direction of a person), hitting furniture with hands.
4. Child uses body to strike other persons or self, throws an object in the direction of, or hits another person.

Points on the scale should be operationally defined whenever possible, but a simple four-point subjective rating scale may be implemented for collaterals to rate their observations of the client's behavior. Clients can also use subjective recording of their own behavior to rate private events such as their amount of pain or anxiety.

Reliability. When simultaneous and independent ratings by two observers are used as a reliability check, the data should correspond not only for the number of occurrences but also for the magnitude rating. As in frequency recording, it is not possible to ensure that the observers have recorded and rated the same occurrence of the behavior unless the exact time of occurrence is noted. Figure 20.6 is an example of reliability computation for magnitude recording. Because the observers achieved 100 percent agreement on the time the behaviors occurred, they were able to compare their ratings on each episode. There was agreement on the ratings of two or three occurrences, for a 67 percent level of agreement.

Uses. Magnitude recording is an appropriate measure for behaviors which are characterized by a wide range or degree of responses and where the degree of responding is the relevant issue. Measures of magnitude can provide data on the appearance of behavior which would not be reflected in a duration or frequency measure. For example, a

FIGURE 20.6
Reliability Computation for Magnitude Recording

Observer 1		Observer 2	
Time	*Magnitude*	*Time*	*Magnitude*
10:02	3	10:02	3
10:57	2	10:57	3
11:17	3	11:17	3

Time agreement = 100%
Magnitude agreement = ⅔ or 67%

Source: Polster and Lynch (1981).

social planner who wants to know if a training program affects the degree to which school board members use community complaints as input for planning could rate the board's responses to each citizen complaint according to this scale:

1. Refuses to hear complaint.
2. Gives time for complaint but does not respond.
3. Discusses complaint but does not attempt to solve problem.
4. Devises solution to citizen problem.
5. Devises solution, discusses implications for future planning, and implements plan.

Magnitude recording requires more training than frequency or duration recording do because the observer needs to make judgments about the degree of behavior, in addition to merely noticing its occurrence. Minor distinctions between levels of behavior may necessitate the use of trained observers. However, for most behaviors with distinct levels of behavior and clear definitions, one practice session is likely to afford sufficient training.

This is a relatively inexpensive method of data recording unless outside observers are used. Recording of magnitude requires attention to all the discrete elements of the behavior, so it may be time-consuming if behaviors are of long duration (Browning & Stover, 1971).

Spot-Check Recording

Spot-check recording calls for observing the target behavior at specified intervals. Unlike the previously discussed procedures, spot checks involve intermittent rather than continuous observations. At the specified observation time the observer looks at the individual and records whether or not the individual is engaged in the target behavior at that moment. Spot-check recording produces occurrence-nonoccurrence data on the target behavior. Figure 20.7 presents an example of spot-check recording in which the target behavior was recorded as occurring in the second, third, and fifth spot checks.

The percentage of spot checks in which the behavior occurred can be determined by dividing the number of spot checks in which the behavior was recorded by the total number of spot checks conducted. If the behavior is spot-checked a number of times during the day, the percentages can be compared, and the daily data may be averaged to compare data from day to day. Behaviors of groups of individuals can be expressed as the percent of group members who were engaged in the behavior.

Reliability. Reliability of data in spot-check recording is determined on the basis of data collected by two independent observers recording simultaneously. The level of reliability is computed with the same formula used to determine reliability in frequency recording. Because observation periods last only a moment, the two observers must be precisely synchronized. The greater the degree to which exactly simultaneous recording is achieved, the stronger the conclusion of reliable data can be.

The amount of observer training needed is minimal unless the target behavior is difficult to distinguish from other behaviors. Instructions alone may be sufficient, but a practice session would be advisable (Witkin & Harrison, 1979).

Uses. Spot checks can be conducted by persons who are normally part of the environment or by outside observers. Individuals may

FIGURE 20.7
Reliability Computation for Spot-Check Recording

Spot Check	Behavior Was Occurring	Behavior Was Not Occurring
1.		✓
2.	✓	
3.	✓	
4.		✓
5.	✓	

Source: Polster and Lynch (1981).

react more to outside observers with this method, since the observer is present only intermittently and may continue to be a novel stimulus longer. Individuals can record spot-check data on their own behavior by using a timer to signal when to record whether or not they are engaged in the target behavior. They can also use naturally occurring time intervals, such as lunch breaks, coffee breaks, and end of work, as signals to record data.

Spot checks are typically the least expensive direct observation method available, since the behavior is only observed intermittently. This also enables collaterals and clients to record data with minimal interruption of normal activities.

This is a useful technique for assessing the behavior of individuals in a group. For instance, the social behavior or nursing home residents in the Magnolias Manor Nursing Home (Chapter 18) could be measured by counting the number of residents who are alone in their rooms. Continued spot checks at prescribed intervals would indicate the level of social activity among the residents, and activity programs designed to affect social behavior also could be evaluated using this measure. This technique can be used by observers who spend minimal time in the settings or indigenous observers who have little time to record data. Generally, spot checks are best suited for measuring behaviors that occur at a high frequency or are sustained over a long period of time, such as social interaction, play, and work. Low-frequency behaviors may not be accurately represented by this technique.

Permanent Product Recording

Permanent product recording does not necessitate direct observation of the performance of the target behavior. Instead, occurrence of the behavior is determined by observing the product of the behavior. Examples of permanent product recording include records of social service usage, teachers' records, and end products of work activity, such as "empty wastebaskets and vacuumed carpets for custodial work." Data are recorded at a convenient time after the occurrence of the behavior but before the product of the behavior is altered or obliterated by subsequent behaviors. Occurrence or nonoccurrence of the behavior is recorded according to a *product observation code* which is identical in form and purpose to the behavioral observation code.

Reliability. As in other data recording techniques, observers must learn to record the permanent product according to a product observation code. Since the product is fixed the observer may take more time during recording and may refer back to the code if necessary. Reliability is determined by having two independent observers code the product.

However, reliability measures do not have to be made simultaneously. In most instances, durable records can be stored indefinitely for future reference.

Uses. Permanent product recording is appropriate for measuring behaviors that alter the state of the environment or that are recorded in a lasting form. Behaviors that involve written reporting, such as school attendance, report completion, and reports of rape to the police, can be measured by inspecting the records maintained on these behaviors, rather than by observing performance of the behaviors. For example, a staff trainer may be interested to know if staff-developed treatment plans improve after the introduction of a new program which teaches special techniques for maintaining clinical records. Frequency of record completion or duration of work on treatment plans would not reflect an improvement in quality. A frequency count could be made of all treatment plans that meet minimal standards, but those data would only indicate how many plans do or do not meet these standards. However, the records could be compared over time according to a standard of "completeness" or quality which was taught in the training session. The permanent product of the case reports then could be used to demonstrate fine-grained changes in the quality of work over time.

Behaviors that produce an observable change in the environment can be measured by observing and recording the changes rather than observing the behavior as it occurs. For example, a parent can record data on a child's completion of assigned chores, such as taking the garbage out, by looking to see if the garbage has been removed after the deadline for completion of the chore. Or introduction of a new policy on recruiting and hiring members of racial minority groups can be evaluated by recording the number of minority staff hired. Permanent product recording also can be used to measure behavior which otherwise could not be observed. The cognitive process of learning how to perform a mathematical function such as multiplication would be indicated by consistently producing the correct answers to multiplication problems.

Measurement instruments such as questionnaires or tests can create permanent products which may be scored to indicate individual's feelings, attitudes, or understanding of a topic. To use this type of data in single-subject designs, repeated measures or applications of the instruments are necessary prior to and during intervention (Cautela, 1977).

Permanent product data can be recorded by trained observers, collaterals, or individuals. Since the measure relies on ongoing recording of environmental changes, this type of recording can usually be implemented in the absence of the individual, and therefore it is inherently the least intrusive method. However, permanent product recording provides data only on the end result of the behavior, not on the appearance of the behavior. Other data recording methods, such as interval recording, must be implemented to measure the process of the behavior.

Permanent product measures are effective and inexpensive to use in systems utilizing ongoing reporting. Because the data on any behavior can only be as accurate as the reporting, however, if a system is suspected of inaccurate or incomplete reporting, use of other data recording methods is advisable.

BASIC PROCEDURES

There are basic procedural similarities in these six data recording methods. The data are recorded according to a standardized format, which must be determined *prior* to the start of the study or treatment. It is generally preferable that the target behavior be recorded for a uniform period of time, at the same time of day or night, during the same activity, and in the same setting. The optimal length of observation period depends in part on the rate of occurrence of the behavior; behaviors that occur often can be more accurately represented in a short time frame. For example, children who are considered hyperactive may perform a great number of different behaviors in a short time, so that a 20-minute observation period supplies a large amount of data. Conversely, children who are considered fighters may have low rates of occurrence of the problem behavior; during a 20-minute observation period it is likely that very few fights will occur, and longer observation periods would be necessary to obtain a representative sample. The severity and frequency of a target behavior should be a primary consideration in deciding the duration of observation periods. The literature can indicate accepted standards for length of observation periods for particular behaviors.

Constructing a Behavioral Observation Code

Rules for recording data and the operational definitions of target behaviors are outlined in an instrument called a *behavioral observation code*. An example is Figure 20.8, an observational code used to record data on the classroom behaviors of a child (Sam) and his teacher. The code states the operational definitions of the target behavior, giving characteristic examples and listing any exceptions. Exceptions are behaviors which fit the operational definitions of the target behavior but which, for the purposes of the study, are not to be recorded as occurrences of the target behavior. Recording rules such as how often and when to record behaviors and an example of the recording form and the symbols to be used in recording are included.

FIGURE 20.8
Behavioral Observation Code for Sam and His Teacher

DEFINITIONS

1. In-seat behavior—Sam is resting with the full weight of his body on the seat of the chair. Sam may have one foot or leg under his body. Sam's bottom should be positioned fully over the seat of the chair. Sam may be tipping chair. Sam must be in his seat for the full recording interval to be recorded as "in-seat."

   Exceptions: Kneeling on chair or sitting with both his legs under him. Sitting with only one-half of bottom on the chair seat.

2. Teacher attention to Sam—attention may be verbal or nonverbal.
   a. Verbal attention—statement by the teacher directed to Sam by name. Examples—"Sam, sit down and do your work." "Sam is the only one doing his work." "Sam!"

      Exceptions: Teacher addressing entire class, but not mentioning Sam by name.
   b. Nonverbal attention—teacher is located within 3 feet of Sam with body and face oriented toward him. Teacher touching Sam. Examples—teacher watching Sam while standing within 3 feet of him. Teacher grabbing Sam and directing him to desk. Teacher putting hand on Sam's back or patting his head.

      Exceptions: Teacher standing within 3 feet of Sam but with attention or speech directed toward another child. Teacher standing within 3 feet of Sam while reading a story or talking to the entire class.

FIGURE 20.8 (continued)

RECORDING RULES

1. All behaviors may occur within the same 10-second interval. Each behavior that occurs within the 10-second recording interval is recorded the first time it occurs. It is, therefore, possible to record in-seat and teacher attention once in each interval. Each behavior is recorded by placing a check (✓) in the interval it occurs.

2. If Sam leaves the room after obtaining teacher permission, a line (/) is placed through the entire 10-second column. If Sam leaves the room without teacher permission, an X (X) is placed through the entire 10-second column.

RECORDING EXAMPLE

Each of the six columns represent a 10-second interval. The top (first) row is for recording in-seat behavior. The bottom (second) row is for recording teacher attention.

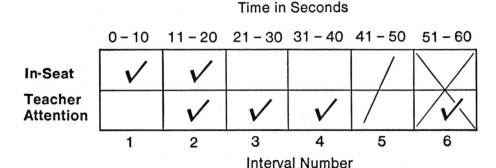

In this hypothetical one-minute sample Sam was in his seat during the first 20 seconds (Intervals 1 and 2), out of his seat at least once during each of the next three 10-second intervals, and out of the room with permission in the fifth 10-second interval. In the last 10-second interval the teacher called Sam back into the room, and Sam refused to return. Therefore, Sam is recorded as out of the room without permission, and the teacher is recorded as attending to Sam. The teacher attended to Sam in the second, third, fourth, and sixth intervals.

Source: Polster and Lynch (1981).

Selecting Observers

All of the data recording methods, with the exception of permanent product recording, require direct observation of the target behavior. The social worker can employ several means of recording data via direct observation: Observations can be made by outside observers who enter the setting solely for the purpose of recording data, by persons who are naturally part of the environment (indigenous persons) in which the target behavior is to be observed, and by individuals who can be taught to record data on their own behavior.

There are some important factors to consider when choosing outside observers, indigenous observers, or self-observers. Use of outside observers is expensive and may not be an available alternative. The social worker may serve as the data recorder if the setting in which the behavior is being measured is accessible. For example, a school social worker may record data on student classroom behavior, or an agency administrator may record data on employee behavior. A less expensive alternative is to train indigenous persons such as teachers, parents, spouses, and peers to record data. Care must be taken, however, to ensure that their data recording activities do not interfere with the other functions they are expected to perform concurrently. Although some indigenous observers may be capable of following sophisticated data recording procedures, they are more suited to procedures which are less time-consuming and require comparatively less training and skill. The amount of preliminary training observers need in order to produce accurate, reliable data depends on the data recording method chosen, the complexity of the behavior definitions, the number of behaviors to be recorded, and the level of prior experience or training of the observer.

If private behaviors such as thoughts and feelings, which can only be felt by those who experience them, are to be studied, individuals must be taught to record data on their own feelings. An individual may also be the observer of choice when the situation in which the behavior occurs precludes the possibility of other observers, the presence of an observer might significantly alter the environment, or the problem is one in which confidentiality must be assured (R. Levy & Olson, 1979).

Reliability of Data

Although an individual's self-reports on nonobservable behavior cannot be easily assessed for reliability, operationalization of variables and standardization of procedures are still essential. If these guidelines for observation are not followed, the data cannot be considered comparable from one observation period to another. Concurrently gathered additional measures of observable behaviors, such as collateral reports or periodic observations by outside or indigenous observers, can be used to support self-report data. For example, a client may report that the severity of depression is lessening. A collateral person asked for verification may indeed indicate the client's episodes of crying and long periods of sleeping have decreased. Thus, the collateral report supports the client's self-report data.

Regardless of the type of recording procedure used, the reliability of the data must be established. The reliability or accuracy of the data recording according to the observational code is evaluated by performing reliability checks. These involve the simultaneous recording of data by two independent observers and comparison of the data obtained, using simple formulas to calculate the percentage of agreement between the observers. Reliability should be checked as often as possible. The more data are shown to be accurately recorded, the stronger is the argument that the rest of the data are accurate. Minimally, reliability must be checked at least once during each experimental condition and whenever the data show a major change in the frequency of behavior. Such changes could be due to a change in the target behavior or a change in the accuracy of the recorded data.

Environmental Constraints Affecting Choice of Recording Methods

Environmental constraints may limit the amount or kind of data that can be recorded (Lin, 1976). When trained observers are not available, the complexity of the target behavior and the choice of the data recording method must be matched with the willingness and the ability of persons in the natural environment to record data. The benefits of the data in the development of effective interventions may have to be stressed in order to sell the idea of data recording. Clear, easily understood definitions and simple recording procedures should be developed, to diminish the difficulties of data recording and increase the likelihood that reliable data will be recorded.

A fundamental principle of single-subject designs is that change in the target behavior that is not apparent when data are represented graphically is not important. (The representation and analysis of data will be discussed later.) Therefore the social worker must choose, given the constraints of time, money, and reliability of observers, the method of data recording that is the most responsive or sensitive to the changes sought in the dependent variable.

Considerations in Recording Data

Choosing the Data Recording Method. Each of the six methods for data recording described earlier can be used in single-subject designs, but each method varies with regard to the type of data and amount of detail it can provide about the target behavior. The choice of one recording method over another must be based on the type of data needed, as well as when and where the behavior is to be observed and who is to record data. Data recorded by collaterals or the individual are generally considered to be less reliable than that recorded by trained observers.

Several different data recording methods may be conjointly implemented to expand the picture of the behavior and substantiate the data. Self-report data on nonobservable behaviors should be augmented by recording of observable behaviors. For example, self-reports on feelings of not being able to be assertive might be augmented by collaterals' recording of instances of assertive behavior. Interval recording could be used to provide a fine-grained analysis of the process of behavior, while permanent product recording could be used to measure the end products of behavior.

Reactivity to Data Recording. In single-subject designs repeated observations are essential. Since most data recording procedures require direct observation of individuals, the effects of the presence of observers and data recording procedures must be considered. Preferably, individuals should be unaware of data recording in order to produce "normal" samples of their behavior, but the introduction of a new person into the environment for data recording purposes may be necessary. This may alter some behaviors; for example, employees may reduce nonwork-related social interactions in the presence of an unexplained visitor, or the presence of an observer may increase attention-attracting behavior.

These effects can usually be minimized if the observers spend some time in the setting, until novelty of their presence diminishes. During observations the observer should interact as little as possible with the individual being observed or other persons in the environment. Most importantly, the observer should not respond contingently to the target behavior; that is, no recognition, positive or negative, should be given it. Failure to adhere to this rule increases the potential that the observer will affect the behavior. If an observer responds contingently to the performance of the target behavior, the presence of the observer must be considered as an intervention strategy in itself. If the observer remains neutral, within several observation periods the individual will be likely to behave the same way as when the observer is absent (Rosenthal, 1966).

In direct treatment with clients, data recording prior to intervention and without the client's knowledge is of the same nature as information gathered from a referral source or collaterals. The basic difference is that recorded data is a systematic procedure for gathering information which quantifies the behavior and provides an objective reference for behavior change. Once clients have agreed to treatment they should be told that records (data) will be kept which will be used in designing the treatment strategies, but data recording may be presented as simply a way to take notes on what is happening.

A change in behavior may occur when an individual is informed that data recording is being done. Typically the behavior change is temporary, but occasionally the target behavior will be permanently altered. Therefore baseline data recording should be continued until the target behavior becomes stable, and the intervention should not be implemented until stability has been established. The issue of stability of the target behavior is very important and is discussed later in this chapter.

Self-recording by an individual also may affect the target behavior, and recording data on one's own behavior can directly affect the frequency of the behavior. However, these effects of self-recording usually decrease over time (Kazdin, 1979, 1982). Initially, self-recording increases the client's attention to the target behavior, and this may produce an increase or decrease in the frequency of behavior (McFall, 1970). The worker can capitalize on this potential effect by defining the target behavior so that the focus of self-recording is the preferred alternative to the problem behavior. For example, a client wishing to decrease the number of episodes of eating might record periods during which no eating occurred. This puts the emphasis on *not* eating; the client is directly attending to the direction in which the behavior must be changed.

Recorded data by the client or collaterals may contradict their own impressions of the target behavior, which may differ considerably from the actual recorded frequency of occurrence (Mann, 1976). The knowledge that the behavior is closer to, or further from, the desired frequency than originally thought may cause them to redefine the target behavior. For example, parents who complain that their child is "always" nagging and whining may find that nagging only occurs once or twice a week. The information that their problem is not as serious as they believed can be used to build a case for the good things the child does, and the parents may interact with their child in more positive ways.

CONTROLLING EXTRANEOUS EFFECTS

In single-subject research extraneous effects are controlled through five procedures:

1. Stable environmental conditions must be maintained.
2. There must be repeated and reliable measurements throughout the study (the independent variable).
3. There must be a demonstration of a stable rate of behavior prior to intervention (baseline data must be stable).
4. There must be systematic and repeated introduction of the independent variables (the intervention).
5. There must be a demonstration of stable rates of behavior during each introduction of the independent variables.

Stability of Environmental Conditions

To diminish the possible effects of nonintervention-related variables on the target behavior, the environment of the individual (the subject) should ideally remain unchanged throughout the study, except for the introduction of the intervention. Those controlling the environment should be asked to postpone changes if possible, until after the conclusion of the study. In particular, changes in contingencies, rules, policies, or procedures which could affect the performance of the target behavior should be avoided. For example, if an intervention is directed at increasing the percentage of their time social workers devote to direct service, a change in procedures for reporting client progress could interfere with the study by affecting the amount of time they have for it, thereby altering the rate of the target behavior.

The worker, however, may not be able to control the stability of the environment. It is not uncommon for an intervention to spur other changes in the environment. The content of such a change and the dates of beginning and end should be noted, and these variables should be taken into account in analyzing the effects of the intervention. If the effects of the environmental change are overpowering, the study may have to be discontinued.

Failure to control for stability of the environment greatly reduces the strength of conclusions that can be drawn from the study. However, the data that are produced in such circumstances may be useful in planning new interventions or procedures.

Stability of Data

Baseline data are recorded on the frequency of the individual's behavior prior to the introduction of the intervention. In order to make a valid comparison between baseline frequencies of behavior and intervention frequencies of behavior, the trend of behavior within each condition must be stable (Sidman, 1960). Stability of the data is determined by graphically plotting the frequencies of behavior over time.

In single-subject designs, graphs are usually drawn so that the vertical axis represents frequency of behavior and the horizontal axis represents periods of data recording (see Figure 20.9). Plotting the frequency of the behavior according to these axes over time will visually represent the trend of the behavior.

A stable baseline has several characteristics. The frequency of behavior is steady, remaining at a constant level over three to five measurement sessions, or the frequency is changing in some identifiable, orderly fashion. These characteristics are necessary to permit the conclusion, with some assurance, that the changes in behavior associated with the intervention are a result of intervention, not of normal fluctuations in the frequency of behavior.

Trends become visible when baseline data are graphed and the consecutive data points are joined. Steady frequencies of behavior appear as a virtually horizontal line (Figure 20.10A). Variable frequencies that are stable appear in recurring patterns within identifiable upper and lower bounds which show no trend toward the upper and lower right of the graph (Figure 20.10B). Gradually increasing behaviors appear as a trend moving toward the upper right (Figure 20.10C), and

FIGURE 20.9
Basic Single-Subject Design Graph Layout

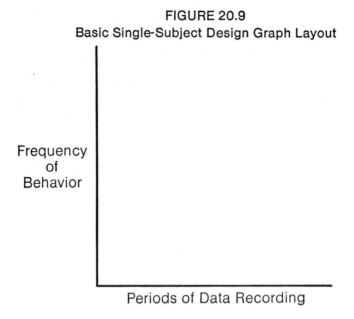

Periods of Data Recording

gradually decreasing behaviors as a trend toward the lower right (Figure 20.10D).

Although each of the four trends in Figure 20.10 can be considered stable, the appropriate baseline trends for an investigation depends on the expected effect of the intervention on the target behavior (Parsonson & Baer, 1978). If the intervention is directed at decreasing the frequency of behavior, the baseline trend should be steady or increasing in an orderly fashion. If it is directed at increasing the frequency of the behavior, the baseline trend must be steady or decreasing in an orderly fashion (Rabin, 1981).

The number of baseline observation sessions necessary to indicate a stable trend in behavior depends on the variability of the behavior from session to session. In general, the less variation in frequency over observation sessions, the sooner the trend will be apparent. Figure 20.11 illustrates this point. By the fifth day of data recording, the frequency of Behavior 1 (represented by the solid line) has remained at a fairly constant level across observation periods, so the baseline for this behavior can be considered stable. But Behavior 2 (represented by the dashed line and triangles) has not yet produced a recognizable pattern or trend, so the baseline is not considered stable and more data must be recorded. While both behaviors may change during the sixth observation period, the data indicate that Behavior 2 is more likely to change radically than Behavior 1. Five observation periods are sufficient

FIGURE 20.10
Stable Baseline Trends

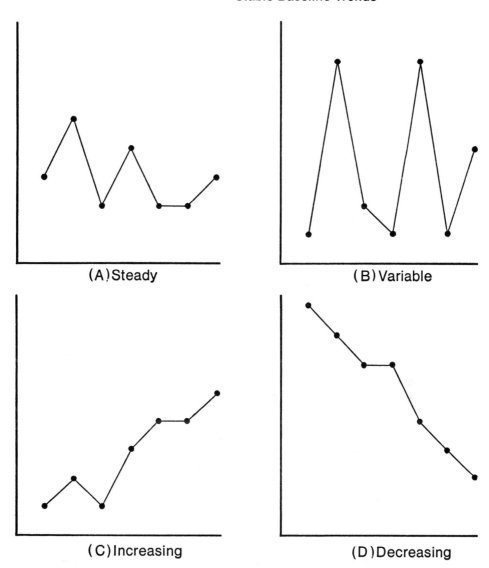

(A) Steady

(B) Variable

(C) Increasing

(D) Decreasing

to predict that the frequency of Behavior 1 during the sixth observation period will continue if the environmental conditions remain the same. Behavior 2 must be observed for more sessions before a trend, and hence predictability of future frequency, can be determined.

Figure 20.12 shows the same behaviors after 10 baseline observation sessions. Behavior 1 has remained stable, and the trend of Behav-

FIGURE 20.11

Hypothetical Model of Effects
of Stable and Variable Frequencies of Behavior

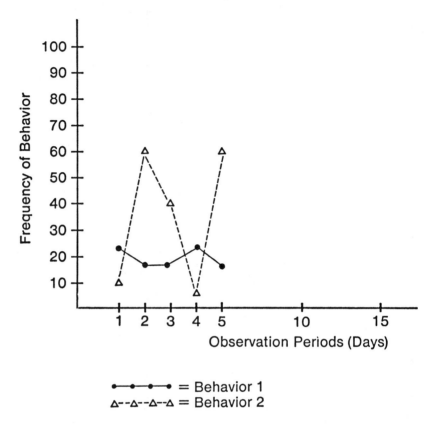

●——●——● = Behavior 1
△--△--△--△ = Behavior 2

ior 2 is now established; the behavior is still occurring at a variable
frequency, but it is variable around a specific trend. The trend established in both behaviors provides a reference for predicting the future
direction of each one.

Predictability is based on the assumption that the frequency of
behavior will remain stable if the conditions in the environment remain stable, but introduction of the intervention constitutes a change
in environmental conditions. If the environmental change alters contingencies that affect the occurrence of the dependent variable, a corresponding change in the frequency of behavior should be observed.
Once the intervention is introduced, a trend must be established in the
intervention phase. Effective comparison of baseline and intervention
data is possible only if baseline trends have been established. If data
during the intervention phase do not also establish a stable trend,
conclusions about the effects of the intervention cannot be drawn.

FIGURE 20.12

Hypothetical Model of Trend Established by Consistent Observation of a Variable Frequency of Behavior over Time

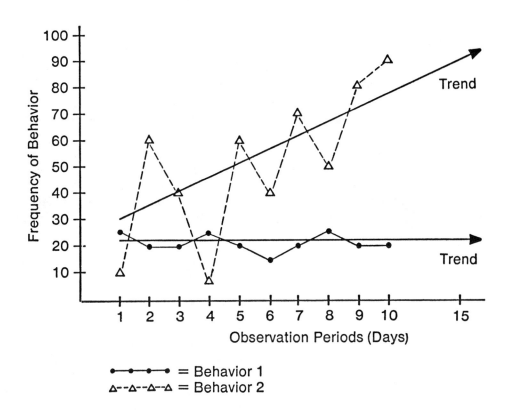

SINGLE-SUBJECT DESIGNS

The basic format for single-subject designs is based on the measurement of a stable baseline (A) followed by the introduction of the intervention (B). This is referred to as the AB design. Three variations of this format, the reversal, multiple-element, and multiple-baseline designs, are described in this section.

In all the single-subject designs, intervention is implemented only after a stable baseline trend has been established. A minimum of three data recording sessions is necessary to begin to show a trend, and more are needed for behaviors which are highly variable in frequency from one recording session to another. Once a stable trend has been established, the intervention is introduced prior to or at the beginning of the next recording session. Intervention data recording should be continued until the frequency of behavior stabilizes so that a clear comparison can be made between baseline and intervention trends. Typically two weeks of stable intervention data are sufficient to indicate a durable and stable trend.

Basic Design (AB)

The AB design involves a single introduction of the intervention (Figure 20.13). A change in the frequency of the target behavior associated with the introduction of the intervention suggests a causal relation between the independent and dependent variables, or between the solution and the problem. A single presentation of the intervention, however, cannot rule out the possibility that the change in behavior was produced by an extraneous variable. Repeated application of the intervention with the same individual, as required for the other single-subject designs, is necessary before any conclusions can be drawn.

Despite the weakness of the AB design, it is useful when more

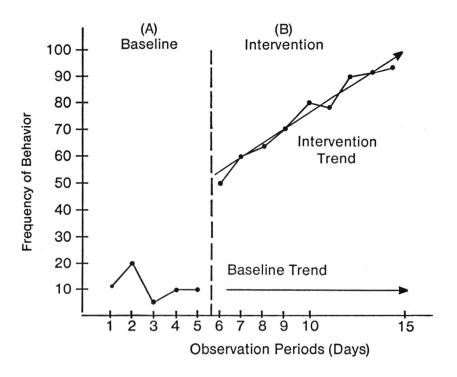

rigorous designs are not feasible. It provides ongoing feedback on the frequency of behavior during baseline and intervention periods and permits a limited appraisal of the effectiveness of the intervention. The AB design also clearly indicates the interventions that are effective in producing the desired change, so that these interventions can be used with other individuals for similar target behaviors. Each successful replication further supports the effectiveness of the intervention.

Reversal Design (ABAB)

The reversal (or withdrawal) design consists of four experimental conditions: baseline (A); intervention (B); return to baseline (A); and reintroduction of the intervention (B), or ABAB. As in the basic AB design, the reversal design involves the recording of baseline data (A) to establish stable trends and the time for introduction of the intervention, and the recording of intervention data (B) until another stable trend has been indicated. Control of the intervention over the behavior is demonstrated by withdrawing the intervention, allowing the environment to return to its preintervention condition (A). Behavior that is under the control of the intervention will revert to baseline levels. Reintroduction of the intervention (B) again demonstrates the control of the intervention if the behavior returns to levels established during the first application (see Figure 20.14).

The strength of the reversal design is in the withdrawal and repeated introduction of the intervention. Failure of the behavior to return to baseline levels indicates the behavior is not under control of the intervention. This may occur under two possible conditions. First, the behavior may not have been affected by the intervention; the associated change in the frequency of behavior during the initial introduction of the intervention may have been caused by extraneous variables. Second, the frequency of the behavior may have initially been changed by the introduction of the intervention, but then control of the behavior shifted to other variables. This can occur when the individual has "learned" or when the behavior is supported by the existing environment at its new rate more effectively than at the preintervention rate.

Reversal, or bringing the behavior back to its preintervention level, is not always possible. In some situations the social worker may have to consider whether it is desirable or ethical to attempt to reverse the behavior. In treatment, the ethics of intervening to improve a client's functioning and subsequently withdrawing the intervention to demonstrate causality must be questioned. In each instance, the potential experimental and clinical consequences of reversal must be balanced. These concerns are not necessarily antithetical, however. Reversal

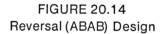

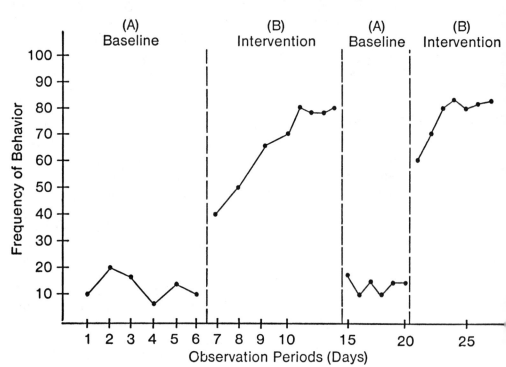

FIGURE 20.14
Reversal (ABAB) Design

may be an effective way to demonstrate the importance of continuing with an effective intervention. A recurring phenomenon in treatment is the gradual discontinuance of the intervention after behavior changes have become stable. A planned reversal may alert the individual to the relationship between the behavior and the intervention.

Reversal designs can also be used to check whether the intervention is still needed to maintain behavior. If the worker suspects that the behavior is under the control of other environmental conditions, withdrawal of the intervention can be employed to measure durability. Continuation of the behavior at intervention levels even when the intervention is withdrawn indicates that it may no longer be needed. Moreover, systematic, intermittent introduction and withdrawal of the intervention may help increase the likelihood of maintenance and generalization of behavioral change (Stokes & Baer, 1977).

Multiple-Element Design (ABCD)

The multiple-element design involves the recording of baseline data (A) and the successive introduction of different interventions (B,C,D). Rather than returning to baseline conditions between interventions, each intervention is introduced after the previous one has produced a stable change in the target behavior (or no change at all) (Ulman & Sulzer-Azaroff, 1975).

Figure 20.15 illustrates a multiple-element design evaluating three successive interventions. The A condition (baseline) indicates a steady frequency of responding. The B condition (Intervention 1) produces a decrease in the frequency of behavior after a slight increase. This intervention is continued until a stable level of behavior is shown, and then the C condition (Intervention 2) is introduced with a corresponding increase in response. The D condition (Intervention 3) produces a sharp decline in the frequency of responding which reaches a stable low level.

FIGURE 20.15
Multiple-Element (ABCD) Design

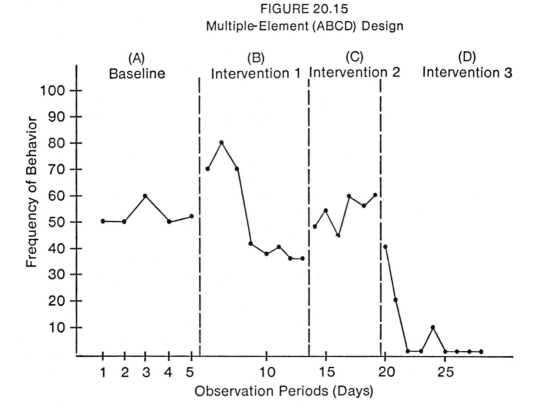

A visual analysis of Figure 20.15 would indicate that Intervention 1 is associated with a decline in the target behavior, Intervention 2 is associated with an increase to a level consistent with the baseline frequency of behavior, and Intervention 3 is associated with a decrease below any previous level. Two explanations can be offered of the effects during Intervention 2. One possibility is that Intervention 2 does not affect or control the behavior and condition C is, in effect, a return to baseline conditions. An alternative is that condition C does affect control over the behavior but produces a level of behavior similar to baseline. Without further implementation a strong argument cannot be made for accepting one explanation over the other.

Conclusions cannot be drawn about the separate effectiveness of each intervention. By inspecting the data, we might fallaciously conclude that Intervention 3 would have had the same effect on the behavior had it been presented singly. However, interventions are presented successively, and each succeeding intervention can only demonstrate its effect at that particular step in the process.

Multiple-element designs are practical, given the typical contingencies of social service delivery. A hypothetical example of how this design could be used to test the effects of communications media on utilization of social services is given in Figure 20.16. In this example, different forms of advertisements are the independent variables and utilization of agency services is the dependent variable. During baseline (A), service utilization averaged about 20 persons per day. In the B condition newspaper advertisements were run explaining available services, and utilization rose to approximately 35 clients per day. In the C condition radio advertisements were broadcast, but the data showed no additional increase in utilization. In the D condition television advertisements were shown and service utilization increased to approximately 65 clients per day, representing a major increase over other forms of advertising and baseline. When television and newspaper advertisements were implemented simultaneously (B + D), they appeared to produce slightly greater utilization than television alone. Television alone was again implemented, again followed by television and newspaper advertisements simultaneously.

The last four phases of the study actually constitute a reversal design (ABAB). Television alone in the D condition serves as a baseline (A) against which the addition of newspaper advertisements can be tested (B). Then newspaper advertisements are withdrawn (A) and reimplemented (B). This study within a study is an additional control to show that the combination of television and newspaper ads results in the greatest social service usage. It is not possible to determine whether the level of service utilization achieved in B + D could have been reached without the cumulative effects of newspaper ads alone

FIGURE 20.16

Example of Multiple-Element Design: Effects of Communications Media on Utilization of Social Services

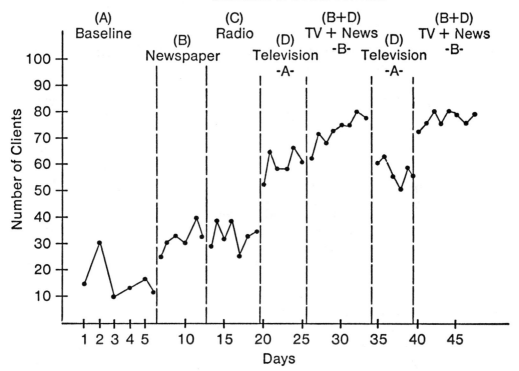

followed by radio advertisements, and both preceding television ads. A new study with a new sample would have to be conducted to test the necessity of newspaper and radio ads preceding television ads.

Successive implementation of interventions without reversion to baseline allow the investigator to respond promptly to changing problems or conditions by utilizing basic evaluation methods. Although the multiple-element design allows flexibility, however, it does not permit distinct empirical conclusions about each element. When reversal is acceptable, the investigator may want to combine multiple-element and reversal designs to create an ABACAD design, which produces additional data about each of the interventions. In the above example, however, there is no control for the cumulative effects of the B and C conditions that precede each other and the D condition. If the behavior returned to baseline levels during the D condition a conclusion for no cumulative effect could be drawn. Still, combining multiple-element with reversal design can contribute to stronger conclusions for causality than multiple-element design alone. Each return to baseline should reestablish a preintervention level of behavior against which comparisons of the following interventions can be made.

Multiple-Baseline Designs

These designs incorporate the basic AB design format, but instead of repeated introduction and withdrawal of the intervention to a single behavior, an AB design is replicated by applying the same intervention to two or more behaviors. Measurement may be across behaviors (Figure 20.17), across subjects (Figure 20.18), or across settings (Figure 20.19).

Baseline data are simultaneously recorded on each of the behaviors, and the interventions are not introduced until a stable baseline has been established for each one. The intervention is successively introduced to each of the behaviors. Baseline data recording is continued for remaining behaviors until the interventions are introduced, and data recording is continued on each of the behaviors during all the interventions. Experimental control is demonstrated through change in each behavior associated with the introduction of the intervention to that behavior.

Across Behaviors. This design measures the effects of one intervention as it is applied to two or more different behaviors of a single individual which occur in the same setting. Multiple-baseline design across behaviors should not be implemented with behaviors which are interrelated, since change in the frequency of one behavior may automatically produce a change in the frequency of the others.

Figure 20.17 illustrates the design across three behaviors of a seven-year-old girl in her home: hitting siblings, name-calling and swearing, and minutes late to bed. The intervention is introduced to the first behavior after stable baseline data are established for each behavior (baseline is represented by all data points left of the dashed line). The intervention includes parent training in child management techniques, which the parents then systematically apply to each behavior in succession. The data show a direct and repeated association between introduction of the intervention and a change to lower levels of each behavior. Introduction of the intervention to successive behaviors is delayed until the prior interventions have produced stable levels. Baseline and intervention frequencies should remain stable; change in frequency of behavior should be noted only when the intervention is applied to that behavior. It is important that the *same* intervention be introduced successively to each behavior.

Across Subjects. This design measures the effects of an intervention as it is applied to the same target behavior performed by two or

FIGURE 20.17
Multiple-Baseline Design across Behaviors

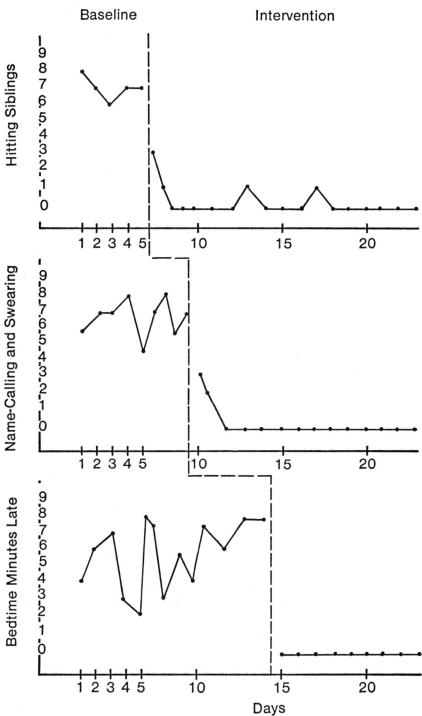

more individuals (subjects) within the same setting. It is best used with subjects whose rates of behavior are not related, as interrelation may cause all subjects' behavior to change when the behavior of one of the subjects changes (Polster & Pinkston, 1979).

Figure 20.18 is a multiple-baseline graph across three students in a special education classroom. The on-task behavior of each student is recorded, and the intervention is applied successively to each one's behavior. The intervention, represented by the data points on the right of the dashed line, consisted of a home-school communication system in which the teacher sent home individual daily reports on the students' in-class performance.

Across Settings. This design measures the outcome of the intervention as it is applied to a single behavior of a single individual performed in two or more settings. If the intervention is generalizable across settings, change in the frequency of behavior in each setting will be associated with the introduction of the intervention.

Figure 20.19 shows a multiple-baseline design across settings used to evaluate the effectiveness of an intervention with a 16-year-old boy's tardiness at school, home, and work (Long & Williams, 1973). The intervention consisted of the allowance of weekend privileges contingent on being on time.

In multiple-baseline designs, failure of the behavior to respond to the introduction of the intervention indicates a lack of control by the independent variable, and change in the behavior not associated with the introduction of the intervention might indicate an unplanned change in the environmental conditions. Investigation of these conditions can provide clues to controlling variables which might be incorporated into intervention efforts. For example, a school social worker may implement token programs in the school to reward the absence of temper tantrums at kindergarten, at a day-care center, and at home. A decrease in the frequency of tantrums in the home prior to introduction of the intervention in that setting might be traced to a new practice of the parents to spend a half-hour playing with the child before bedtime if there have been no tantrums at home that day. The use of parent time as a reward then might be incorporated into an intervention to be applied in all settings.

Changes in baseline rates of behavior associated with the introduction of the intervention when it is applied to another behavior indicate that unplanned generalization of treatment effects has occurred. In other words, the individual is applying what was learned in one situation to other experiences in another situation.

Multiple-baseline designs have several characteristics which make them appropriate for social workers. Because they do not require reversal or withdrawal of the intervention, they can be used with behaviors

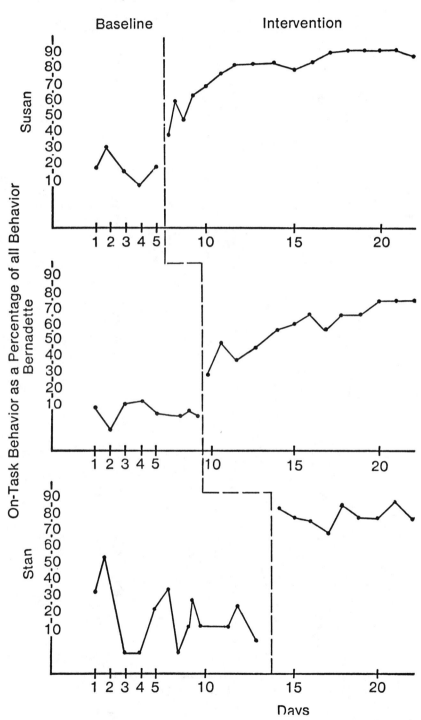

FIGURE 20.18
Multiple-Baseline Design across Subjects

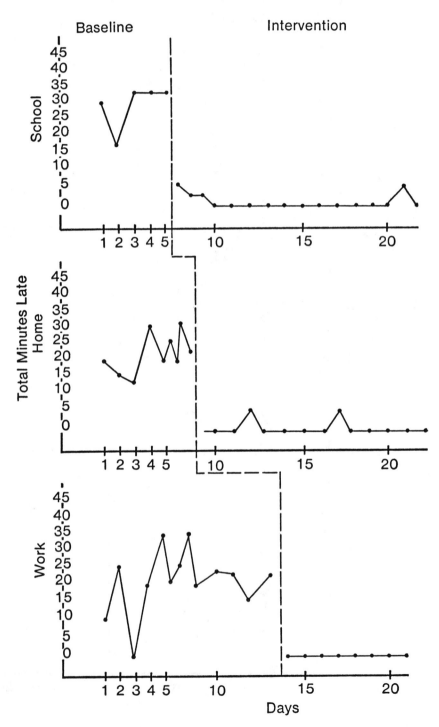

FIGURE 20.19
Multiple-Baseline Design across Settings

which are not likely to reverse or for which reversal would be unethical or undesirable. Multiple-baseline designs are also cost efficient because interventions can be simultaneously tested across behaviors, individuals, or settings, and this can yield data on a number of variables at once. By evaluating the effectiveness of an intervention across behaviors, individuals, or settings, multiple-baseline designs are able to demonstrate the generalizability of interventions to diverse populations and problems such as are encountered in the delivery of social services.

DATA ANALYSIS

Visual versus Statistical Analysis

Data analysis with single-subject designs is accomplished through the visual comparison of trends from one condition to the next. The effectiveness of the intervention is determined by the visual overall change in the behavior indicated by the data. There is a basic disagreement about whether a statistically significant change must be demonstrated via statistical tests or can be visually discernible through graphic representation of the data. Although there has been considerable discussion among professionals concerning the "most appropriate" procedures for determining the statistical significance of behavior change in single-subject designs, no consensus has been reached on the value of statistical analyses, nor has any particular statistical approach gained widespread acceptance (Gottman & Leiblum, 1974).

Criteria for making conclusions of significant changes are generally derived visually from graphic representation of the data and two additional factors. First, the consumers (e.g., individuals or collaterals who derived benefits from the intervention) should be consulted as to whether the change in behavior produced by the intervention was "sufficient." Second, the worker should have a preconceived notion of the degree of change which can be considered important in the functioning of the individual (W. Gingerich, 1978, 1983).

In single-subject designs, the most basic analysis of data involves a visual comparison of baseline and intervention periods, and meaningful change is characterized by a decrease or increase in the frequency of behavior. If the target behavior has increased or decreased, the majority of data points should correspondingly be above or below the mean of the baseline data (see Figure 20.13). Both the number of data points above or below the mean *and* the degree of change indicate the extent of "meaningfulness." Behaviors that have a steady trend but are highly variable may demonstrate a change in the degree of variability but not in the means of the trend. For example, a graph of the amount of time spent sleeping by a person exhibiting shifts in behavior characteristic of the manic-depressive might resemble Figure 20.20. Baseline levels indicate a regular curve-shaped trend, the extremes of which were dampened during intervention periods. Although the mean levels of behavior during baseline and intervention may be similar, the change has occurred in the decrease of variability of the behavior.

Establishing Baseline Trends

Failure to establish stable trends during baseline and intervention periods or to consider the appropriate direction of the baseline trend in relation to the desired change of the target behavior during intervention will diminish the value of the study. Figure 20.21 graphically represents some of the difficulties in analysis which arise when the procedures of single-subject designs are not followed. This is a hypothetical representation of data recorded on the completion of work assignments per day by sheltered workshop employees. The desired

FIGURE 20.20

Relation of Baseline and Intervention Means to Variability of Behavior

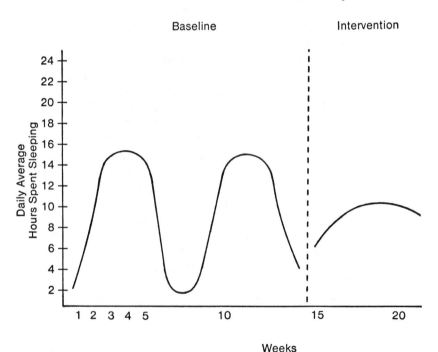

direction of behavior change as a result of the intervention is an increase in the rate of behavior. Guidelines for introduction of the intervention would have indicated that the trend of the baseline should have been steady or decreasing in a stable, orderly fashion. In this example the worker failed to continue the baseline until a stable trend was indicated, and therefore the future baseline trend of the behavior cannot be predicted. The same deficiency exists for data in the other phases of the study, due to the failure to record sufficient data to assess trends. Since comparison of intervention data with baseline data shows no clearly discernible differences, no conclusions can be drawn.

Consumer, Clinical, and Statistical Significance

Although there are no absolute rules for determining significance of behavior change, the social worker must be aware of and respond to three different but related issues: consumer satisfaction, clinical

FIGURE 20.21

Problems in Data Analysis Related to Failure to Establish Stable Baselines

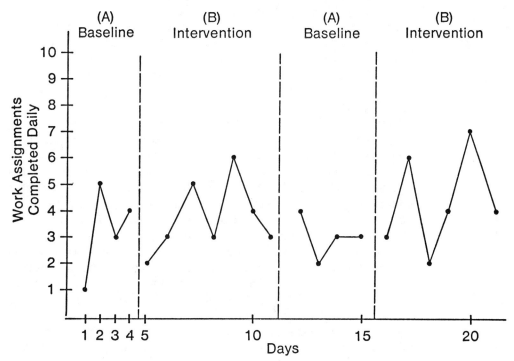

significance, and statistical significance (Carver, 1978; Labovitz, 1970; Morrison & Henkel, 1970; Winch & Campbell, 1969). Consumer satisfaction is determined by the client, collaterals, or other consumers of the effects of the intervention. In keeping with their role of solving social problems, social workers must determine whether the "solution" has sufficiently solved the problem for the consumer. Sensitivity to the consumers' standards gives an indication of how much solution or improvement is necessary to achieve their satisfaction with the intervention. While consumer satisfaction cannot stand alone as a determinant of significance of change, there may be occasions when the data do not show change in the target behavior but the consumers report satisfaction with the changes that have taken place. For example, while there may have been no actual changes in behavior for a client referred for the problem of low self-esteem, the referral collateral may claim that the client's self-esteem has improved markedly. Consumer satisfaction in this case is important but not sufficient to allow a claim of significant change. The investigator cannot accept responsibility for any client changes because there are no data to support a conclusion for a cause-effect association between the intervention and the collateral's claim for change in the client's self-esteem.

Clinical significance and statistical significance are sometimes the same issues, but they can be widely disparate. Consider the example of an 11-year-old boy who, because he starts fires, is referred to a social worker. The boy has a history of starting an average of seven fires a week, sometimes as many as three in one day. After one month of social work intervention, the boy reduces his behavior to setting only two fires per week. This change may be statistically significant, but from a clinical (and probably consumer satisfaction) perspective, two fires a week is still an unacceptable level of behavior. A total elimination of fire setting may be the only acceptable level of clinical significance. Clients, collaterals, and others who may be responsible for identifying the target behaviors are fundamental factors in determining criteria for clinical significance. Normative data may also be referred to in order to establish criteria for appropriate levels of behavior. In single-subject designs clinical significance is of utmost importance, but an apparent difference between baseline and intervention data is also essential in empirically establishing the effectiveness of an intervention.

Even though inferential statistics are not accepted as necessary in single-subject designs, studies which incorporate the recording of data on a control or comparison group can utilize tests of statistical significance to determine the effectiveness of the intervention (Polster & Lynch, 1981; Polster, Lynch, & Pinkston, 1981). The single-subject design portion of the experiment is conducted as usual, and the comparison of the experimental group to the control group is made using inferential statistics. The type of design will not only demonstrate the control of the intervention on the target behavior but also indicate the extent to which the behavior of the nonexperimental population changes during the same period.

Data analysis is an ongoing process in the application of single-subject designs and cannot be considered separate from their implementation. The data on the subject's behavior are analyzed to determine the stability of the behavior trends and the proper time for introduction or withdrawal of the intervention. Ongoing analysis of the data can also influence the content of the intervention in multiple-element designs in which design and implementation of each new intervention are based on the effectiveness of the prior interventions in producing the desired change.

SUMMARY

The special properties of single-subject designs make them practical for use by social workers in all areas of social service development and delivery. These designs permit simple evaluations utilizing readily available data, and more comprehensive research projects can be designed to answer specific questions. These projects would incorporate specific data recording procedures and highly controlled independent variables but would use similar strategies to evaluate effects.

Single-subject designs lend themselves to a variety of situations, and each one has characteristics which make it suitable for specific research endeavors. The design which answers the practice or research question most fully is the best one to use. Selection of design, therefore, should always be based on the type of data sought. The limits of the application of these designs are determined by environmental constraints and the worker's creativity and interest in assessing the effects of the intervention.

In times of budgetary restrictions and a demand for accountability, social workers must show evidence that what they do is effective and important (Biestek, 1977). Single-subject designs provide a technology for ongoing evaluations and adjustment of interventions to meet identified social service goals.

21. PROGRAM EVALUATION

The demand for accountability in the social work profession and the need to demonstrate the effectiveness of social work programs have led to the development and dissemination of a type of evaluation research called *program evaluation* (Gelman, 1983). This chapter explores the need, meaning, process, and some of the problems encountered in program evaluation and suggests program evaluation techniques which can be used by the social workers.

THE NEED FOR PROGRAM EVALUATION

It is likely that the emphasis on program evaluation in social agencies will continue in the coming years. The reasons for this emphasis are related to the environment that sanctions social agencies, the client groups these agencies serve, and the agencies themselves (Tripodi, 1983).

Several developments in the environment are resulting in closer public scrutiny of the effectiveness and efficiency of social programs. As these programs continue to expand, more money is needed for their operation. Additionally, inflationary pressures are increasingly requiring more tax dollars for all forms of public programs. Taxpayers, faced with higher taxes at a time when the value of the dollar is decreasing, are demanding to know if the social programs for which their tax dollars are being spent are worthwhile. The highly publicized failure of some social experiments has heightened the skepticism of citizens about publicly funded social programs in general.

Clients themselves are also pressing for accountable social programs. The 1970s has been described as the era of consumerism, a time when clients began to demand that the services they received were of acceptable quality. Now that we are halfway through the 1980s, clients' rights groups are becoming more vocal, and some success is being realized in making social programs more responsive to needs.

Within the social work profession the call for greater accountability is due in part to the influence of the environment and clients on developments in the field. More importantly, professional social workers are developing an increased awareness of the need for social programs that are responsive to client needs and that are of demonstrable quality. Historically social workers have always sought new or improved ways to serve clients. Today, however, the profession is shifting the focus to ends rather than means, or to the "what" instead of the "how." Whereas the historical development of social work has been characterized by an emphasis on discovery and utilization of the best methods of practice, now the profession is devoting more attention to describing the products of its practice in terms that are clear, objective, and measurable (Raymond, 1977). It is in this climate that the concept of the practitioner/researcher has emerged.

These external and internal developments have led social workers to seek ways to become more accountable and to demonstrate their worth (Raymond, 1981). Accountability is a broad concept which places numerous requirements on social agencies, such as determination through quantitative means that the services offered are optimally effective and efficient. The formal methods and analyses of program evaluation provide the tools agencies can use for this purpose (Tripodi, Fellin, & I. Epstein, 1971).

THE MEANING OF PROGRAM EVALUATION

Program evaluation is applied research which utilizes the various methods and types of analyses presented in the chapters of this text. It is distinguished from pure research, which has as its main objective the accumulation and analysis of data in order to formulate hypotheses and theories for the sake of the knowledge itself. When the purpose of social work research and evaluation is to determine how successful a social program is in fulfilling its mission, what effects the program is having, or whether it is performing as expected, the research process may be considered to be program evaluation.

Bigman (1961) has identified six primary purposes of program evaluation. They are:

1. To discover whether and how well objectives are being fulfilled.
2. To determine the reasons for specific successes and failures.
3. To uncover the principles underlying a successful program.
4. To direct the course of experiments with techniques for increasing effectiveness.

5. To lay the basis for further research or to determine the reasons for the relative success of alternative techniques.
6. To redefine the means to be used for attaining objectives, and even to redefine subgoals, in the light of research findings.

Program evaluation is concerned, therefore, with measurement of the degree to which a social program succeeds in reaching its predetermined objectives (Suchman, 1967a). The reasons why a particular social program fails or achieves success in meeting program objectives are also relevant, since they provide agency administrators and planners with information they can use to restructure programs and make them more effective (Weiss, 1972a, 1972b).

THE PROCESS OF PROGRAM EVALUATION

Program evaluation is a process which consists of five phases:

1. Determining program objectives.
2. Establishing outcome measures (dependent variables).
3. Identifying independent and intervening variables.
4. Utilizing research designs.
5. Assessing program efficiency.

Phase 1: Determining Program Objectives

One of the most difficult steps in program evaluation is the clarification of objectives. As presented in Chapter 3, often the objectives of social programs are stated in such vague and general terms that it is impossible to demonstrate with certainty whether or not they are being attained. Examples of nebulous and vague objectives are "to strengthen family life," "to enhance social functioning," or "to improve mental health." The problem of ill-defined objectives is reduced if those who will evaluate a social program participate in developing its objectives. If the evaluator is an outside observer and not an agency staff member, objectives should be developed with the administrative staff and others only after studying the agency's organizational structure and functioning.

The overall objectives of a social program should be defined in terms that are clear, specific, and measurable. They should be clear so evaluators know exactly what to look for, specific so they can be translated into operational definitions and made visible, and measurable so data collection and analysis methods can be applied. Examples of measurable objectives are "to reduce the use of specific illegal addicting drugs by 100 percent in 50 clients following one year of treatment," or "to reduce the rate of a specific reported juvenile crime in Cook County by 10 percent by December 1, 1985."

After the overall objectives for a social program have been defined, lower level supporting subobjectives, or program activities or steps necessary for the overall objectives to be attained, must be identified. Then the objectives at the next lower level that must be met for the subobjectives to be achieved are defined. This process may continue for several levels, resulting in a hierarchy of objectives. At each level, the objectives must meet the criteria of clarity, specificity, and measurability.

Often each objective in the hierarchy corresponds to an organizational division, department, or office that is responsible for meeting that objective. The division of labor in an organization such as a department of social services is such that the technique or methods to be used at any level are the objectives of the next lower level. In turn, the objectives at any level form the methods of the next higher level. A social program can be divided into a chain of events in which each event is the result of the one that comes before it and a necessary condition to the one that comes after it. Program evaluation, then, consists of validating the means-end relationships between each adjacent pair of objectives comprising the program—that is, demonstrating that the objectives at each level are being successfully achieved through the methods used.

Phase 2: Establishing Outcome Measures (Dependent Variables)

Outcome measures assess the degree to which a program's objectives are achieved. These measures are the dependent variables in the evaluation.

Many types of outcome measures may be used to determine the degree of success in meeting program objectives. The selection of these measures depends on the intent of a program as set forth in its objectives. Outcome measures may reflect attitudes, values, knowledge, behavior, productivity, services offered, and so on. Usually outcome measures focus on changes in the clients being served, although they also can be concerned with the agencies offering the services, those affected by changed patterns of the services, the neighborhood or community, or the public at large.

In any case, the outcome measures must reflect as closely as possible the real changes the agency is concerned with producing, or the stated written objectives. There are times when these changes cannot be measured directly. It is then necessary to establish objectives and related outcome measures which approximate these changes or are assumed to reflect them. For example, a mental health program concerned with treating neuroses of clients may not be able to measure directly the reduction of neurosis. Instead, judgments of "experts," behavior scales, or questionnaires could be utilized. Or a program endeavoring to improve the self-concept of juvenile offenders would not be able to assess the psychological construct of self-concept directly but could instead administer a self-concept scale to clients.

Indirect outcome measures such as these involve assumptions that may be of questionable validity, however, and workers should endeavor to use direct measures whenever possible. When the use of indirect measures is unavoidable, it is advisable to employ measures that have already been developed and have been shown to have a high degree of validity and reliability, rather than to create new ones. A number of outcome measures have been pretested (as noted in Chapter 10), and such measures should be utilized whenever possible (Posavac & Carey, 1980).

Often a social program's success cannot be adequately assessed by analyzing a single outcome measure. It is then useful to employ multiple measures. For example, a health care program concerned with improving the health of a group of elderly outpatients might use several outcome measures, such as rate of illness, level of functioning of specific organs, and self-reports from patients regarding how they feel. Each of these is a partial measure of a larger concept, but no single measure would be an adequate indicator of the program's success. Combining these criteria can provide a more complete and accurate picture of the program's outcome. When multiple measures are used, however, it is essential that the various measures be complementary rather than assessments of the same dimension. It is also necessary to weigh the relative importance of the different outcome measures utilized.

Phase 3: Identifying Independent and Intervening Variables

In addition to determining the success of a social program, the worker must assess why the outcome has occurred. Rather than viewing the social program as a "black box" whose contents are unknown or unimportant, one must also be concerned with what is producing the desired change and why the change is occurring. To accomplish this analysis it is necessary to define and quantify the independent and intervening variables. Independent variables might include the agency's or program's purpose, principles, methods, staffing, location, size, and length of service, as well as characteristics of clients such as race, sex, age, socioeconomic status, and attitudes. (The dependent variables, as noted above, are the outcome measures which assess the degree to which the problem is solvable.)

Intervening variables may be of two types. The first type, termed *program operation variables,* is concerned with the way in which the program functions. Examples of program operation variables are clients' frequency of attendance, degree of acceptance by professional peers, degree of stress, and participation in related social programs. These variables aid in the identification of the factors that influence client outcome. Delineation of these variables may help administrators or planners to control for the conditions of program operation that are essential for successful client outcome.

In the evaluation of any social program a multitude of intervening program operation variables can be measured. Few social programs, however, have the resources to assess all these variables, nor is it necessarily desirable that all of them be assessed. The variables used in program evaluation analyses must be selected on the basis of prior research, knowledge of the field of practice under study, familiarity with the social program being evaluated, or the application of theory.

The second type of intervening variables is known as *bridging variables.* These variables are concerned with the attainment of the program's subobjectives. As noted above, a social program is organized around a mean-ends chain of objectives and supporting subobjectives. Theoretically, for a given objective to be attained, the next lower level of supporting subobjectives must have been met. Thus, the subobjectives may be considered bridging variables, and measurement of these variables tests the validity of the theory around which the social program is organized.

In the example of a program with the overall objective of improving the health care for a group of elderly citizens, a subobjective, or bridging variable, may be to provide all clients with three meals each day. Measuring the extent to which all the clients receive three meals a day, and then relating this to the overall objective of improved health care, would provide data about the relationship of the subobjectives to the final objective. These data would make it possible to modify program assumptions and the related structure and functioning of the agency.

Phase 4: Utilizing Research Designs

To determine the degree to which a program's objectives are being achieved as a result of the program or intervention, quasi-experimental or experimental designs can be employed. Because lack of adequate control or comparison groups or inability to manipulate the independent variables may make true experimental designs unsuited to program evaluation, quasi-experimental designs are frequently utilized. The various types of designs and data collection techniques that can be used in the evaluation of social programs are described in this text.

The application of a particular research design depends on the purpose or intent of the evaluation and the nature of the program being evaluated. For example, a worker interested in the reasons for a program's success would use a design which permits examination of associational or cause-effect relationships. A social worker wanting to measure the extent to which a program's objectives have been achieved might utilize a quantitative-descriptive design. These types of designs are among those identified in Chapter 13 which describes research designs according to their major purposes in a knowledge-building continuum. Illustrations of these designs as they apply to program evaluation are given here, but Chapter 13 should be consulted for a complete list (Table 13.2) and a detailed discussion to their meaning and purposes.

Knowledge Level 1. Hypothetical-development designs seek to describe a single unit thoroughly during a *specific* period of time. Such a description of an agency or program would enable a social worker to develop ideas, questions, or hypotheses for subsequent study. These designs are, therefore, valuable for formative purposes or to provide a preliminary look at the effectiveness of a program. A cross-sectional case study (Design 1a), for example, could be utilized to determine the effects of a treatment program for drug abusers. The worker might first isolate and define the term *drug abuse* by reviewing clients' retrospective reports concerning drug use. This information might be used to develop a drug abuse scale or to isolate specific characteristics of persons described as drug abusers for purposes of future study.

Knowledge Level 2. Quantitative-descriptive designs make it possible to generalize results beyond the study's sample to a population because randomization procedures have been employed. Such designs seek to answer simple, descriptive questions, usually in terms of frequency or percentages for a variable as identified by another variable. For example, a worker might use a cross-sectional survey design (Design 2a) to examine satisfaction with a parent training program. A number of those who entered the training sessions are randomly sampled and administered a parent satisfaction test. The test results reflect the proportion of persons who were satisfied with the style and content of the sessions. As the sample was randomly selected, the results can be generalized to all persons attending the sessions.

Knowledge Level 3. Associational designs analyze the presence or direction of relationships between two or more variables. For example, a one-group pretest-posttest design (Design 3a) might be used to assess the outcome of a marital counseling program. Marital adjustment, as defined by predetermined criteria, is measured *before* and *after* the counseling process. Qualitative analysis of the counseling program can be used to supplement the quantitative analysis of changes occurring during the program. Although investigators may be able to conclude that positive change actually did occur, they cannot state unequivocally that these changes were brought about by the program rather than by history, maturation, or other influences on internal validity.

Knowledge Level 4. Cause-effect designs enable investigators to determine the independent variables that produce change in the dependent variables during the course of a study. When used in program evaluation, these designs enable social workers to state that changes occurring during the course of a program were, in fact, due to the results of the program. The interrupted time-series design (Design 4d), for example, involves a series of measurements of the outcome indicator *before* the program begins, *during* the program, and *after* the program has been completed. Thus, it is possible to pinpoint the times at which changes occur and to determine if these changes coincide with the introduction of the intervention.

For example, a group of 16-year-olds may be provided with an experimental course in school to help them raise their self-concepts, based on the assumption that self-concept affects adolescent behaviors such as drug use, dropping out of school, or running away. A self-concept scale could be administered to sophomores several times before the course begins, during the course, and several times afterward. If self-concept improves during the course and shows little changes at other times, one could surmise that the course produced these changes.

Phase 5: Assessing Program Efficiency

When research designs such as those described above are used for program evaluation purposes, the focus is on assessment of outcome measures and determination of how well these measures achieve the program's objectives. They make it possible to assess a program's effectiveness, or the degree to which a program's objectives were attained through the program's efforts.

Often in the process of program evaluation it is necessary to go beyond program effectiveness and assess program efficiency, or the costs involved in achieving the program's objectives. The most common technique used to assess program efficiency is *cost-benefit analysis*. These procedures enable social workers to assess the relative costs of various alternative means of achieving a program's objectives and, on the basis of this analysis, to identify the preferred approach. Cost-benefit analysis concentrates on the output of a program, weighs the contribution of each alternative against its effectiveness in serving the desired objectives, and compares the costs of each in terms of its effectiveness. Thus, it requires the same clear delineation of objectives and establishment of outcome indicators that program evaluation does. The new feature is consideration of cost-analysis data such as a cost accountant would be concerned with.

In the analysis of the cost-benefit relationships of various program alternatives, the "cheapest" or even the "best" social program is not necessarily favored. Rather, the optimal program in terms of the available resources (money, trained personnel, facilities) is sought. Thus, the decision criteria may include achieving a given objective at the least cost, attaining it with the resources available, or providing for a trade-off for effectiveness, especially in the light of other objectives (Thompson, 1980).

Often a program's subobjectives can be evaluated as alternative means of achieving the objective. Each subobjective can be evaluated in terms of its effectiveness (benefits) and its efficiency (costs). For example, an alcoholism treatment program may have the ultimate objective of enabling all clients to reach total abstinence. To achieve this objective, the program may offer individual counseling, family counseling, and group counseling components. Each component would have its own set of objectives, which are leading to the attainment of the larger program objective. The effectiveness analysis would determine the extent to which each component contributes to the achievement of the overall objective. Cost-benefit (or efficiency) analysis would determine the same thing, but it would also determine the relative costs of these components. The decision maker concerned with selecting which program component (or components) to use would have the cost-benefit analysis data to aid in examining the various alternatives.

PROBLEMS IN PROGRAM EVALUATION

Program evaluation is seldom a simple procedure, and a number of methodological problems may be encountered. These include:

1. Objectives are seldom clear and measurable.
2. Outcome measures usually do not exist and thus must be developed.
3. It is problematic to randomly select and then randomly assign clients to experimental and control groups.
4. It is sometimes not possible to manipulate the independent variable.
5. It is difficult to control for the intrinsic factors that may jeopardize the internal validity of the evaluation.

These problems can be minimized, however, through careful design and implementation of the evaluation effort.

In addition to these methodological problems, other difficulties can be encountered in the process of evaluating a social program. The first has to do with determining objectives. Not only may formal organizational objectives lack clarity and measurability, but agencies may also have informal objectives they seek to meet. Any organization has maintenance and survival objectives, and much of its energy may be directed toward meeting these informal standards. In evaluating the effectiveness and efficiency of a social program, the possible existence of informal objectives must be recognized.

Etzioni (1960) has suggested that a better approach to program evaluation than the objective-attainment model described in this chapter would be a systems model. Rather than emphasizing the degree of success in reaching specific, formal objectives, the systems model would be concerned with establishing the degree to which an agency realizes its objectives under a given set of conditions. Accordingly, attention would be given to optimum distribution of resources among all objectives, both formal and informal.

Another problem encountered in program evaluation, particularly by outside evaluators, is resistance from agency personnel (Gelman, 1983). Personnel at all levels may well resent having what they are doing evaluated. The attention social program evaluation inherently focuses on issues such as accountability, effectiveness, and efficiency can create anxiety about job security, personal reputation, the agency's status, and so on. Moreover, the personnel may have interests and professional norms which are different from those of the evaluators. Personnel who are concerned with client service may feel that program evaluation creates only disruption and delay. While the problem of personnel resistance may be diminished when the evaluation is done by organization employees, it cannot be totally eliminated.

A related difficulty often experienced in program evaluation is that personnel may view it as a one-time-only effort. Ideally, program evaluation is of a repetitive nature; the results of an evaluation effort are used to improve the social program, which is later reevaluated and further improved, and so on. The program evaluation process should be an intrinsic part of the agency's formal feedback system.

There are several reasons why it is difficult to design and implement an evaluation system that will operate on a continuous basis. First, the evaluation may be designed only to determine whether a program should be continued or discontinued, with little concern about how to improve the program. Second, the evaluation may be intended only to determine whether or not a program's approach is effective or efficient, or whether the theory behind it is valid. Third, the purpose of program evaluation may be to determine how to allocate resources among competing social programs, and nothing more. Fourth, the evaluation may be designed only to comply with the requirements of an initial Request for Proposal (RFP) from a government agency granting funding, and the agency may have little real interest in the evaluation effort. Finally, the results of the evaluation may reflect negatively on the agency and, rather than using them as a means of improving services and seeking subsequent evaluation, the agency may question the value or desirability of all evaluation efforts.

In spite of all of the problems encountered in conducting program evaluation, research of this type can be of significant benefit to human service organizations by providing a means to enhance accountability. Program evaluation can help social program planners reach more rational designs and improve their capacity to develop and implement social programs which will effectively and efficiently meet human needs.

SUMMARY

In examining the meaning of program evaluation and exploring the reasons for the growing use of this type of research in social agencies, attention has been given to the difficult tasks of determining program objectives and establishing outcome measures to assess the extent to which objectives have been achieved. Since it is also important to understand why objectives are or are not attained, the identification of independent and intervening variables was also examined. Various experimental and quasi-experimental designs that can be used to assess program effectiveness have been discussed, as well as cost-benefit analysis techniques for measuring program efficiency. Some of the problems commonly encountered when program evaluation is carried out in social agencies have also been considered.

PART FOUR

Proposals, Reports,
and Knowledge Utilization

Contents of PART FOUR

Chapter

Kathryn E. Moss

22. RESEARCH PROPOSALS

A research proposal is a written request for permission and/or financial assistance to undertake a research study which is generally prepared for a grant-awarding agency or an academic committee. Thus, a research proposal is defined as a document that identifies a specific topic (general question or specific hypothesis) that is the subject area for the study, explains the importance of conducting the project, provides detailed plans for carrying it out, and itemizes the financial and physical resources that will be needed for implementation of the project.

CHARACTERISTICS OF RESEARCH PROPOSALS

Authors of research proposals take into account the functions, forms, and styles of proposals before they start writing.

Function

The purpose of a research proposal is to provide information on a general question or a specific hypothesis to be investigated in regard to the importance of answering the question or hypothesis, the explicit methodology for examining it, the social worker's ability to execute the study, and the resources (if any), needed for successful completion of the project.

A well-thought-out research proposal is as necessary to any successful research study as an architect's plans are to the construction of a building (Leedy, 1980, 1981). It is quite obvious that a home builder would not start to build a house by rushing out and digging a hole for the foundation without knowing in detail (and in advance) what the house will look like when finished. Like any home builder, a social worker leaves as little as possible to chance. Through the process of clearly articulating the general question or the specific hypothesis and spelling out every detail of how the study will be conducted, problems which arise throughout the course of the study are, to the greatest extent possible, anticipated, and minimized.

Form

The organization of proposals varies with regard to the information they require. In some simple cases, it is only necessary to fill out an application form. At other times a "letter of intent" may be all that is required. Such a letter provides information in concise form about the major points usually addressed in a full-length proposal (to be discussed later). However, favorable reception by a funding source to a letter of intent does not mean that the potential study will be approved. Typically, the next step is a request by the funding organization for a full-length proposal.

The information and format required in a proposal varies according to whether the proposal is submitted to an academic committee or to a funding organization. A proposal for an academic committee typically is more detailed and scholarly than one submitted to a funding organization. Similarly, different types of funding organizations have varying requirements. In some cases, funding organizations provide quite detailed instructions about the format and length of proposals they wish to receive. In other instances, *Requests for Proposals,* commonly termed *RFPs* are sent to outside reviewers. RFPs usually supply instructions prepared by funding organizations; they specify research topics that will be funded along with the proposal's format requirements. Most commonly, however, funders usually allow a great deal of latitude, leaving the form of research proposals to the discretion of their authors.

Style

Notwithstanding their differences, research proposals have many similarities. One similarity is their style. There are basically three stylistic characteristics common to all research proposals that are adhered to by their authors; research proposals are: (1) clearly worded; (2) written in a nonliterary style; and (3) clearly organized.

Clearly Worded. Research proposals are clearly written, well organized, and effectively worded. Those which are disorganized or contain unrelated or unessential information usually give the impression that their authors will not be able to execute the research study logically and objectively. Research proposals never explain in detail why the authors became interested in the proposed problem that is under investigation. Proposal review committees are never interested in autobiographical excursions by proposal authors. Rather, a well-written proposal is a straightforward document that begins with a clear statement about the topic to be investigated. Information that is necessary for understanding the proposed topic and its importance, the general question or specific hypothesis to be studied, and the study's design are included. Anything else usually obscures the proposal and diverts the reviewers' attention. A research proposal contains only the information that is absolutely necessary—not one detail more (Leedy, 1980).

Nonliterary in Style.   Research proposals require clear and precise writing; they are not meant to be literary classics, nor are they the occasions for "fine writing." On the contrary, most proposal reviewers frown upon elegant composition and written extravagance (Tallent, 1983). The specific wording of a research proposal is simple, matter-of-fact, and unadorned. This is not to say that writing a research proposal is an unscholarly process. It is simply an opportunity to be clear and precise in presenting the general question or the specific hypothesis to be investigated (American Psychological Association, 1983).

Clearly Organized.   Proposal reviewers usually have a difficult and time-consuming task. They are often faced with numerous proposals to evaluate at a given time. A majority of proposals submitted to funding agencies must be turned down due to the scarcity of funds. However, despite the number of proposals to be reviewed and the differences in their quality, most proposal reviewers read each proposal very carefully. Thus, the more clearly organized a proposal is the easier it is to read. And the easier the proposal is to read, the better the chance that the proposal's reviewers will react to it favorably.

Several factors facilitate clear organization. As noted above, a clear, unadorned prose style is absolutely essential. Short and simple paragraphs are required. Such paragraphs help proposal reviewers quickly assess whether the authors know what they are talking about. In contrast, paragraphs which ramble can so obscure main points that they become difficult or even impossible to follow. Major and minor headings also enhance a proposal's organization. They highlight important points and allow proposal reviewers who may be more interested in one substantive (or methodological) issue than another to thumb back and forth through the proposal with ease.

COMPONENTS OF PROPOSALS

Most funding agencies and academic committees leave the structure of research proposals to the discretion of their authors. However, proposal reviewers need, and thus obviously look for, certain basic types of information in assessing proposals. This basic information is usually broken into 11 general components, or parts, which parallel the actual working steps of the proposed research study. Although there is no one specific format to follow in writing research proposals, the ordering of the components in the following discussion is typical. Other approaches, however, may be chosen if they are more suitable to particular research areas. To illustrate the sequential development (or parts) of most proposals, the discussion below discusses the 11 common parts and draws from an ongoing example: the adjustment of former residents of psychiatric institutions in community settings. The 11 parts of most research proposals are: (1) specifying the research topic; (2) creating a literature review; (3) providing a conceptual framework; (4) delineating the general research question to be answered or the specific hypothesis to be tested; (5) constructing operational definitions of the independent and dependent variables; (6) specifying the specific research design; (7) delineating the population and sample; (8) describing the method(s) of data collection; (9) describing the method(s) of data analysis; (10) detailing the study's limitations; and (11) describing the study's administrative procedures.

Part 1: Research Topic

As distinguished from the general research question or specific research hypothesis to be investigated, the term *research topic* refers to the overall area of investigation. The term *topic statement* refers to a succinct description of the research topic.

On occasion, research topics are so complex that introductory information is provided before the area of investigation can be identified. If possible, however, the topic statement sets forth the research topic at the outset of the proposal. For example, in proposing a study of why some former residents of psychiatric institutions adjust more successfully than others in community settings, the proposal might state at the beginning: "The concern of the proposed study is the successful adjustment in community settings by former residents of psychiatric institutions."

The next part of the proposal usually discusses the significance of the proposed study to our profession (as presented in Chapters 3, 4, and 5). Proposal reviewers may be familiar with the proposed area of investigation and its relative importance; facts nonetheless are marshaled for reviewers who are unfamiliar with the proposal's topic and its significance for our profession.

Social work research proposals usually require their authors to address three areas of the study's significance: social policy significance; theoretical significance; and practice significance (or implications for social work practice). Vaguely worded statements such as "An increased knowledge of factors contributing to the successful adjustment in communities by former psychiatric patients is important to social work," would be insufficient. Rather, in describing the policymaking significance of the study, the proposal must provide specific ways in which the findings would facilitate some aspect of the policymaking process (D. Austin, 1981). In discussing the theoretical significance of the study, the proposal must delineate how the study would either test existing theory or generate new theory of potential use by our profession (E. G. Brown, 1981). The implications for social work practice must include a discussion of how knowledge obtained from the proposed study may enhance the effectiveness of individual social workers in their everyday practices (Briar, 1981). Sometimes the theoretical significance and implications for practice are treated as separate components and placed either immediately following the discussion on the social policy significance or at the end of the proposal. This is acceptable practice and is commonly followed (Reid, 1981).

Although all three elements of a proposal's significance are usually fully explicated in those submitted to academic committees, funding organizations attach varying degrees of importance to these elements. It is, therefore, important to assess both formally and informally a funding organization's priorities and to emphasize these elements accordingly before submitting proposals.

Part 2: Literature Review

An effective literature review achieves five objectives (Krathwohl, 1965):

1. It demonstrates that the social worker has mastered the available and relevant literature.
2. It demonstrates the similarities between the proposed study and past research findings of similar studies.
3. It describes the differences between the proposed investigation and past research findings of similar studies.
4. It discusses how the proposed investigation will contribute to the knowledge-base of the social work profession.
5. It supports and interacts with the conceptual framework by introducing and, together with the conceptual framework, conceptually defines the key variables that are the subject of the study.

As presented in Chapter 3, the primary consideration in developing a literature review concerns how much literature to summarize (Heffernan & Turman, 1981). In general, literature reviews in research proposals submitted to academic committees are far more comprehensive than in those proposals submitted to funding organizations. In either case, the literature review must be brief enough not to become tedious but extensive enough to inform proposal reviewers about the study's topic. Failure to carefully think through how much information is too much or too little may result in a proposal which is either burdensome to read or which presents an inadequate basis by which to understand the conceptual framework and subsequent components of the study (Zinsser, 1976, 1980).

Another consideration is the discussion on what information to present. Although the literature review usually discusses how the proposed study will mesh with and differ from past studies, there are frequently too many related studies to allow discussion of all pertinent past findings. In general, when there is an extensive body of related studies, the literature review concentrates on the most recent findings. In addition, if there are "classic" studies related to the proposed investigation, it is advisable to present them as well (Reid, 1981).

Conversely, the body of directly relevant studies may sometimes be too limited to provide adequate information on the research topic. In this case, the literature review contains findings which are indirectly pertinent. If, for example, there were a scarcity of existing studies concerning the adjustment of former residents of psychiatric institutions in community settings, the literature review might present research findings related to the adjustment of mentally retarded persons in community settings. As presented in Chapter 14, qualitative studies are also useful in the absence of related quantitative ones. Qualitative literature demonstrates in a persuasive manner the importance and background of the proposed study and may present alternative ways of conceptualizing it.

All independent and dependent variables are discussed in the literature review; they must be also conceptually defined. That is, semantic clarifications drawn primarily from the relevant literature rather than operational definitions of them are provided. For example, for one person, the variable community adjustment may suggest comfortable living arrangements, a job, and recreation in a community setting. For another person, the variable community adjustment may also include a supportive family. The social worker avoids such ambiguity through clear conceptual definitions. For example, authors of proposals may make clear that their conceptualization of community adjustment includes not only comfortable living arrangements, a job, and recreation, but *also* meaningful interaction with family. Key independent and dependent variables that are not conceptually defined in the literature review are defined in the conceptual framework.

Part 3: Conceptual Framework

The next part of the proposal provides a conceptual framework for the study. A conceptual framework is a frame of reference that serves to guide the study. It is developed from theories, quantitative and qualitative studies, and the social worker's personal experiences and values. It helps formulate the study's research problem or hypothesis; it defines what are and are not relevant data; and it provides a basis for interpreting these data.

As presented in Chapters 3, 4, and 5, the process of constructing a conceptual framework involves the review of relevant research findings, theories, experiences, and value assumptions to identify the key independent and dependent variables in the study and the predicted relationships among them. This process overlaps with that of reviewing the literature. For example, the development of a conceptual framework for undertaking a study of the adjustment in community settings by former residents of psychiatric institutions will include, as in the literature review, a review of studies related to the adjustment of former residents of institutions. Unlike the literature review, however, it will also require the identification of one or more theories not necessarily directly related to community adjustment (e.g., psychosocial or behavioral theories) which are useful in selecting and understanding the independent and dependent variables and identifying their relationship to one another. Personal experiences and value assumptions of the investigators may also be used to identify independent and dependent variables and their predicted relationships.

The next step is to develop a written version of the conceptual framework. The author identifies independent, dependent, intervening, and control variables, defines those which have not already been defined in the literature review, specifies predicted relationships among them, and provides a detailed explanation about why each variable and relationship has been selected for examination in the proposed study. One or more theories are usually employed in discussing these variables and explaining why they are thought to be related. For example, psychosocial variables suspected to affect the adjustment of former residents of psychiatric institutions would be presented. Research findings specific to community adjustment may be used in this discussion, although many will already have been placed in the literature review. Experiences and value assumptions of the proposal's author which influenced the decision to select particular independent and dependent variables may be included either in the conceptual framework or in the literature review. Where to include them is based on logical and stylistic considerations. In some proposals, little attention is paid to the author's personal experiences and values, while in others these data will enhance understanding of why certain variables are emphasized and others omitted.

Part 4: Questions and Hypotheses

In contrast to research topics, both general questions and specific hypotheses clearly identify the specific aspects of the topic to be studied. The general question may not always indicate precisely the variables which are the subject of the study. However, hypotheses, by definition, always contain predetermined specific independent and dependent variables (E. G. Brown, 1981). A general question about the topic of community adjustment might be: "What social and interpersonal factors are most important in explaining the successful adjustment of former residents of psychiatric institutions in community settings?" In contrast, a specific hypothesis related to this topic might be: "The more contact former residents of psychiatric institutions have with relatives and friends (independent variable), the more successful their adjustment in community settings" (dependent variable). In this specific hypothesis, the terms *contact, former residents, psychiatric settings, relatives, friends, adjustment,* and *community settings* would all be operationally defined (to be discussed in Part 5).

The general research questions or specific hypotheses flows from prior components of the proposal. First, both are derived logically from the original topic. For example, it would make little sense to state at the outset of the proposal that the planned study concerns the adjustment of former residents of psychiatric institutions within community settings and then to set forth general research questions or specific research hypotheses which deal with factors influencing the adjustment of persons within psychiatric institutions. In addition, the general questions and specific hypotheses are clearly understandable in terms of the perspective and definitions provided by the literature review and conceptual framework. Thus, for instance, a precondition for including the independent variable—contact with relative and friends by former residents of psychiatric institutions—in the specific research hypothesis is to have conceptually defined it in the literature review or conceptual framework of the proposal.

The general question and specific hypothesis also mesh with the methodological components that follow. Specifically, if questions or hypotheses are introduced in this component, they are always considered in subsequent components. If they are not introduced in this component, they are usually not discussed in the following components. For instance, if the data collection and analysis components specify that data will be collected and analyzed to account for the influence of available psychiatric support services in communities on the adjustment of former residents of psychiatric institutions, this must be reflected in the question or hypothesis.

Some research proposals contain both general questions *and* specific hypotheses, others have only a question *or* a hypothesis. Frequently, hypothetical-developmental studies (Level 1 as presented in Chapter 13) provide no basis for generating research hypotheses prior to data collection. In contrast, when cause-effect studies (Level 4 as presented in Chapter 13) are used, it is common practice to omit a research question and to identify only the specific research hypothesis to be verified.

Part 5: Operational Definitions

This component sets forth operational definitions for each independent and dependent variable under investigation. Whereas conceptual definitions facilitate agreement about the meaning of variables, operational definitions provide an even more concrete understanding by specifying specific data to be collected for each variable. Thus, when scales or indexes are utilized to measure certain variables, the operational definitions identify the specific scales or indexes employed (e.g., Index of Marital Satisfaction scale in Table 2.1 in Chapter 2). When other data collection techniques are utilized, the operational definitions state precisely the nature of the data to be collected. For example, with the hypothesis "The more contact former residents of psychiatric institutions have with relatives and friends in community settings, the more successful their adjustment in community settings," the independent variable contact with relatives and friends leaves room for confusion, even after being conceptually defined. Exactly how much contact is meant? What constitutes contact? With which relatives and what types of friends is contact established? And, with the variable successful adjustment, what if the nature of one person's adjustment is substantially different from that of another person, but both have remained in community settings? Have both "successfully" adjusted or has one person's adjustment been more successful than the other's and, if so, in what way and to what extent?

In fact, it is not uncommon for research proposals to omit the operational definitions component and instead to answer such questions in the data collection component instead (Part 8). Yet, successful research proposals enable proposal reviewers to visualize the precise meaning of each independent and dependent variable in terms of what will be observed and/or measured and how observations and/or measurements will occur. A clear listing of operational definitions for each pertinent independent and dependent variable enhances the ability of proposal reviewers to do so.

Part 6: Research Design

The proposal describes the research design utilized in obtaining answers to the general question and/or verifying the specific hypothesis. As presented in Chapter 13, there are four major designs most frequently used in social work research: case study designs, descriptive survey designs, comparative designs, and experimental designs. After selecting the design of the study, this component furnishes summarized information about: *who* will be studied; *what* will be observed or measured; *when* the observations and/or measurements will occur; and *how* these data will be gathered. For example, after proposing a descriptive survey design to examine the adjustment of former residents of psychiatric institutions in community settings, the design component would next briefly describe the sample for the survey (e.g., a stratified random sample of all former residents of the Greenwood State Hospital discharged to the community in the last year), what data are to be collected from the sample (e.g., data concerning contact with relatives and friends, residential circumstances, and vocational and social adjustment), when data collection will occur (e.g., between January and March of the next fiscal year), and the data gathering procedures (e.g., mailed questionnaires or interviews).

The research design links the component just prior to it (operational definition) with the two components that follow (population and sample; and data collection). In particular, in addressing what will be observed and/or measured, this component summarizes the operational definitions. In discussing who will be studied, when the observations or measurements will occur, and how these data will be gathered, material to be presented in detail in the sample and data collection components is briefly identified in the design component.

Part 7: Population and Sample

As presented in Chapter 8, this part of a research proposal provides a description of: the population to whom the study's findings will be generalized; the study's sample and sampling strategy; and the potential generalizability of the study's findings. Usually, the description of the population is not long or detailed. Armed with information from earlier parts of the proposal, reviewers often have determined what the population will be prior to reaching this section of the proposal. Nevertheless, since research studies are usually undertaken in order to generalize to larger populations rather than to make statements about their samples, a succinct statement describing the population is needed. Such a statement is typically included in this part, regardless of the extent to which the population has been described earlier in the proposal. For example, in the community adjustment proposal a statement is needed that identifies the study's population as all former residents of a specific psychiatric institution discharged between January 1, 1985 through December 31, 1986 and presently living in community environments.

The population is also differentiated from the study's sample. In some instances, the population and sample are the same. When this is the case, the proposal makes this clear. Most of the time, however, researchers generate data derived from samples rather than populations, and this component describes in detail the nature of the sample and the strategy for selecting it.

Describing the study's sample and sampling strategy involves specifying the unit of analysis (the group of persons or things to be studied); the precise procedures to be used in selecting the sample; the reasons for choosing the procedures; and the actual, estimated, or minimum number of persons or objects to be included in the sample. The description of a sample is usually a detailed discussion; it is a primary means by which proposal reviewers can assess the potential generalizability (external validity) of the study's findings.

In addition to the information contained in the discussion of the sample and sampling strategy, proposal reviewers also need to know the study's potential for generalization to the larger population. Thus, this component includes the author's assessment about the generalizability of the study's findings, the reasoning behind this assessment, and a discussion of limitations in generalizing from the sample to the larger population from which it is drawn.

Part 8: Data Collection

A detailed description of the data gathering procedures for the planned investigation is needed. This description covers the specific techniques to be employed, the specific measuring instruments to be utilized, and the specific series of activities to be conducted in implementing the measuring instruments. When original measuring instruments are to be constructed, as discussed in Chapters 10, 11, and 12, the data gathering component will contain a detailed discussion of the procedures to be employed in constructing them and will also discuss their validity and reliability. When existing measuring instruments are to be utilized, their validity and reliability are also discussed. Finally, the study's general research question or specific research hypothesis, the questions asked, the sample selected, the ethical considerations (or any other factors may result in problems in obtaining access to data), and the steps to be taken to overcome these potential problems are then detailed.

If, for example, interviews are utilized to gather data from former residents of psychiatric institutions to assess their adjustment in community settings, the data collection component would then contain detailed information about the type of questions to be asked, the procedures for constructing, administering, and ensuring the validity and reliability of the interview instruments, the progression of activities to be undertaken in arranging and conducting the interviews, and the steps to be taken to ensure a high response rate (external validity) to the interviews, despite the probably sensitive nature of the questions. Alternatively, where participant observation is used to collect data on adjustment (as presented in Chapters 14, 17, and 18), the data collection component would then describe the setting, individuals, behaviors, and interactions to be observed, whether people would be aware that they were being observed, whether the observer would observe as a participant, quasi-participant, or nonparticipant, how the observer would gain access to data, and the planned duration of the observational period.

Part 9: Data Analysis

The procedures that are utilized to analyze the data must be described. When employing statistical analyses, this involves specifying each specific procedure to be employed for each general research question to be answered or specific research hypothesis to be verified. An example would be identifying the particular tests of significance and correlational procedures to be employed in verifying the relationship between the independent and dependent variable. The majority of social work studies utilize statistical procedures to analyze data. However, as presented in Chapters 14, 17, 18, and 20, there are many situations where the use of statistical analysis is not only impossible but also inappropriate (Gorsuch, 1981; Royer, 1981).

Part 10: Limitations

Potential limitations are often numerous in even the most carefully planned research study (Fischer, 1981a), and it is therefore important that these be listed in the proposal. Generally, identification of limitations involves considering:

1. The validity and reliability of all data collection instruments (see Chapters 10, 11, and 12).
2. The generalizability of the sample to the population from which it was drawn (see Chapter 8).
3. Access to data (see Chapter 3, 4, and 5).
4. Ethical problems (see Chapter 6).
5. The ability to control for extraneous factors in the environment and in respondents (see Chapter 13).

For example, a limitation in the community adjustment proposal may be the inability to obtain access to a truly representative random sample of former residents of psychiatric institutions which, in turn, would limit the social worker's ability to generalize to the larger population of such persons that the sample was drawn.

Although all problems are never completely eliminated from any social work research study, it is necessary that the various means to be used to try to reduce the problems are spelled out. For example, having specified that a truly representative random sample of former residents of psychiatric institutions cannot be obtained, the specific steps that will be taken to try to ensure that the sample is as representative as possible of the population from which it is to be drawn, must also be detailed.

Part 11: Administration

All proposals address the resources that are available and that are needed to carry out the study. As presented in Chapter 4, all studies must develop organizational, work, and financial plans. A majority of funding organizations specify that these plans be addressed as separate components in the proposal. Although it is useful to consider them separately in determining which resources are available and which are necessary to execute the study, all three areas involve considerations of basic resources and can be seen as one component (Mayer & Greenwood, 1980).

A number of questions are addressed in the development of the proposal's organizational plan. Which organization, department, or departmental subunit will assume administrative responsibility for the study? Where will the project be physically housed? What personnel are needed to carry out the study? What are their specific responsibilities? What should their qualifications be? What will the chain of authority be? What is the procedure for access to specialized facilities (e.g., computer time)? Answering these questions provides an organizational chart that illustrates the proposed study's organizational context, the personnel to be employed, and the flow of authority that connects them.

The development of a work plan includes the identification of the sequence of activities necessary to execute the study, the person(s) responsible for carrying out each activity, and the anticipated dates for beginning and completing each specific activity. Research projects usually have explicit time frames. Time periods for developing the research operation and for data analysis and report preparation are usually underestimated. Based on the principles of management planning, the work plan promotes efficient organization in the execution of the research project. In addition, the work plan aids proposal reviewers to judge the extent to which the study will be efficiently organized.

Finally, the administration component translates the work plan into dollars in providing a detailed budget description. The budget identifies resources that are needed to accomplish the activities described in the work plan and estimates the cost of each activity. Line-item budgets show exactly what amount of money will be needed for each activity. Typically, the items included in a line-item budget in social work research proposals are: personnel (including secretarial, research assistant, etc.); consultants; travel; supplies and equipment; telephone expenses; computer service; facilities; and special categories. Provision for institutional overhead costs may be a critical factor over which the study may have little control, but which nevertheless must be taken into account in the budget.

SUMMARY

The need to obtain approval to undertake research studies in the organizations for which they work, to seek funds from grant awarding agencies, or to fulfill the requirements of their academic committees requires many social workers to prepare research proposals. Such proposals involve detailing a variety of significant features relevant to most social work research effort. This chapter has discussed the importance of a clear, straightforward, and well organized style in proposal writing. It has also explored eleven common parts of the research proposal and has suggested a format for presenting them.

After a research proposal has been subsequently funded, the next step in the research process is writing a research report that is derived from the study's data (or findings). The next chapter describes the process on how to write and publish a research report derived from quantitative data techniques.

William J. Reid

23. WRITING RESEARCH REPORTS

Research reports serve an important function in social work research and evaluation because they contribute to the knowledge base of our profession in written form. Without published research reports, the assumption of a scientific knowledge base for social work would have little basis.

The knowledge obtained by social workers can be reported in a variety of forms. In length, a report may range from a brief note to a full-scale report of several hundred pages. It may stand by itself or be imbedded in a larger work. It may be so highly technical that only readers who have a high degree of research sophistication will understand it, or expressed in language that can be readily comprehended by any literature person. Reports can also be communicated in the form of films.

The audience reading the report accounts for an even more important source of variation. A report may be read (or heard) by a handful of persons, or it may reach thousands. The scope of the audience reached depends largely on the medium of distribution. Among other possibilities, a report may be circulated informally, read at a conference, distributed through mailing lists, or published as a journal article, monograph, or book.

This chapter will concentrate on one general type of report: a report suitable for publication in a professional social work journal. Most reports range in length from about 10 to 25 double-spaced, typewritten pages, including tables, figures, and references. The report is usually based on a single study and is written for a potentially wide readership. This type of report is probably both the most common and the most important means of sharing the results of studies with other social work professionals. Journal articles (published reports) generally provide the core of knowledge in any given field.

In social work, many reports are based on student projects, particularly doctoral dissertations. Master's students are also encouraged to try to publish their studies if they are of sufficient merit and interest. Some social work instructors make a particular effort to help students achieve this goal (Kane, 1978). The bulk of the unpublished social work literature is comprised of reports of article length and format. Such reports include conference papers, presentations of student projects, and shorter reports to sponsoring agencies.

THE PURPOSE OF A REPORT

The major purpose of a research report is to communicate to others the knowledge that has been derived from a particular study (Tallent, 1983). To achieve this purpose, the author customarily provides a rationale for conducting the study, reviews what is already known in the area under investigation, and states the research problem. The author then lays out the design and methods of the study and presents the findings and the conclusions that the author has drawn from the data.

All aspects of a study should be related to the fundamental purpose of communicating the knowledge that has been determined in the study. The distinction between what has been found out and the author's use of the findings must always be clear. If this distinction is not maintained, and if the findings and the means of obtaining them are distorted to advance the author's points of view, the purpose of the report will be badly subverted (American Psychological Association, 1983).

The Audience

Since a report is written to be understood and utilized by its readers, assumptions regarding the intended audience are critical. In social work, readers vary considerably in their ability to comprehend research and evaluation concepts, in their interest in technical detail, and in the criteria they use for assessing findings and conclusions. Social workers who specialize in research and evaluation may desire a range and depth of information about a study's methodology. But this may be of secondary concern to social workers who specialize in direct practice. They may be more interested in the author's speculations concerning applications they can make of the study's findings to their own practice. The concept of the practitioner/researcher presented in this text would minimize such differences in audience orientations (Weed & Greenwald, 1973).

Authors understandably would like to satisfy both interests. There are various ways of doing this, but none of them is completely satisfactory. A hard-line approach taken by some authors is to write for an audience of research specialists, without a great deal of concern about other readers. In another approach, sometimes referred to as spoonfeeding, the author glosses over technical aspects of the study and concentrates on delivering "useful" information to social workers. A more technical version of the same study may also be prepared for an audience of researchers.

A more satisfactory solution avoids either of these two extremes. The essential technical aspects of a study should be presented. It is impossible to divorce the meaning of a study's findings from the methods used to obtain them. That is, how these methods are applied within a study needs to be understood by readers if the findings are to be properly assessed. But authors can help readers with the task of comprehension by providing explanations of technical procedures. In addition, they can make an effort to enhance the practice relevance of a study's findings, implications, and conclusions.

In terms of the development of our profession and the services it provides, the best long-run solution is to raise the level of the research literacy among social workers. Professional education provides one means to this end. What students learn about research at schools soon fades, unless, as professionals, they are continually exposed to research concepts by reading reports of interest to them. If research writing is stripped of essential technical content, incompetence in the utilization of social work research will surely result.

WRITING A RESEARCH REPORT

This section is concerned with the "how to" of social work report writing. The best way to get a sense of how social work research is reported is to read articles that have been published in professional social work journals (Souther & White, 1977). Many additional resources also are useful in learning to write reports. These include books, articles, and manuals on writing skills and report preparation (Mendelsohn, 1982, 1983; Strunk & White, 1979; Tallent, 1983; Turabian, 1973; Zinsser, 1976, 1980).

Organization and Content

The general format of the article-length report usually follows a standard sequence (Ewing, 1974).Within this sequence, there may be a good deal of variation in how different parts of the report are labeled, in the attention given to each part, and in the nature and internal

TABLE 23.1
Organization of Parts in a Research Report

Part	Contents
1. Problem	Background, rationale, and significance of the study; review of relevant research and theory; presentation and explanation of the research problem and variables
2. Method	Delineation of the strategy (design) and methods of the investigation, including a description of the setting and the sampling plan; description of data collection procedures, instruments, and measurement approach
3. Findings	Presentation of findings, including data displays (tables, graphs, etc.); textual exposition of data; description of relevant analytic procedures
4. Discussion	Discussion of findings, including interpretation of data, implications for theory, practice, education, and research; limitations of study; relationship to other research; summary and conclusions

Source: Reid (1981).

organization of the content. A commonly used framework is presented in this section. The four parts of this sequence and the topics each is likely to contain are listed in Table 23.1.

In most reports headings follow this general progression, although they reflect a report's particular emphases. The example outlined in Table 23.2 illustrates how the headings used in an actual published report were related to these four parts. In this example, the author elicited from hospital patients critical incidents (important examples) of helpful and nonhelpful staff behavior (J. Rosenberg, 1977). These incidents were then classified and analyzed to present a picture of the patients' perception of their hospital care.

As the example in Table 23.2 shows, the basic structure of the report follows the four-part scheme. The headings are dictated by the particulars of the study. The example also illustrates a point worth noting in relation to headings. The first few paragraphs of a report, which presents some aspects of Part 1, often have no heading.

A useful way to outline a report prior to actually writing it is to generate major headings directly from the four-part structure presented

TABLE 23.2
Headings in a Published Research Report

Part	Heading in Report	Contents
1. Problem	Unheaded introduction	Review of previous research
2. Method	Plan of study	Study design; setting; sampling plan; critical incident technique
	Classifying the Incidents	Method of classifying incidents; reliability of the classifications
3. Findings	Major findings	Frequency distribution of helpful and nonhelpful incidents; relation of patients' perceptions to different factors
4. Discussion	Discussion	Reasons why findings may differ from those of previous research
	Implications for practice	Importance of patients' perceptions in shaping hospital services and staff behavior
	Implications for training	Use of patient questionnaire in staff monitoring and training

Source: Reid (1981).

in Table 23.1. The major headings can then be broken down into whatever subheadings are applicable to the specific study. This creates an outline which can be used to organize the divisions to be used in writing the report.

There is a significant deviation from this structure when a study is conducted in stages. For example, an evaluation of an intervention upon its termination may constitute the first stage of a study, and a follow-up of clients six months later may comprise the second stage. In such cases, the report may begin with a fairly standard Part 1 (statement of the problem). Then each stage might be presented as if it were a separate study, with description of the methods, presentation of findings, and discussion of findings for each stage. The report may conclude with an overall discussion and summary. This type of narration makes the most sense when the different stages of the study are sufficiently distinct in methods and findings to warrant presentation as separate units (Marks, 1975).

Part 1: Problem

Often the introduction to a report proves the most difficult section to write. Although the author wishes to put the study in some perspective, any study is potentially connected to a wide range of topics. It is difficult to know where to begin or end. If a study evaluates a method for helping marital partners with communication problems, should something be said about marital conflict as a social problem? What about theories of family communication? Or other methods of marital treatment?

A pragmatic way to approach the writing of Part 1 of a report is to begin with its most essential element—the statement of the research problem in the form of specific study aims, questions, and hypotheses. We can then ask: What do readers need to know in order to understand the problem, to place it in appropriate context, to appreciate its significance, and to determine how its solution will contribute to existing knowledge?

The amount of attention given to these facets depends on the nature of the research problem and the assumptions about the audience to which the report is primarily directed. If the research problem involves concepts or theoretical formulations that are likely to be unfamiliar to readers, then some explanation of these ideas is in order. The significance of some research problems will be self-evident and need not be belabored; the importance of other problem areas may need to be made clear. The relevance of the study's problem area to social work practice should be articulated if it is not obvious.

The expected contribution of the report to existing knowledge can be stated through a review of the literature that is directly related to the problem area of the study. The review should not consist of a string of paragraphs each presenting a capsule summary of a study. Rather, it should organize relevant findings pertinent to the research, with emphasis on identifying gaps in knowledge that the report intends to fill. These preliminaries can be overdone, however. The introduction to a report is not the place for a lengthy review of the literature that may have some degree of relevance to the problem at hand. It also should not be used as a vehicle for an incidental essay.

Part 2: Method

Part 2 sets forth the methodology of the study. It usually includes descriptions of the research design, the sampling plan, data collection procedures, and instruments. If an evaluation of a program or an experiment is being reported, the section should describe the setting, social workers (if any were used), and the nature of the program and the experimental variables.

Substantive findings (findings bearing directly on the study question or hypothesis) are not presented in this part. However, data on the validity and reliability of the instrument(s) and on characteristics of the setting may be included. Information concerning the sample may also be presented here rather than in Part 3, particularly if there is only a small amount of data to be reported. Aspects of methodology that may be better understood in conjunction with presentation of findings may be deferred until Part 3. Methods of data analysis or secondary measures obtained from manipulations of the data may be best discussed in the context of data presentation.

The most common shortcoming in Part 2 is insufficient or unclear presentation of the study's methods. The author's intimate familiarity with these methods may breed insensitivity to readers' ignorance of them. As a result, the study methodology may be presented in an elliptical, cryptic manner. Putting oneself in the readers' position is an excellent device to avoid this problem. It is particularly important to provide a clear picture of how the problem area of this study is connected to the data obtained. In order to accomplish this objective, some description of the study instruments, including a presentation of sample questions or items, is usually necessary. Ideally, the instrument or key portions of it should be included as an appendix, but this is usually not feasible if the report is to be published in a professional journal.

The steps in transforming the data into the measurements used should be delineated. It may then be well to restate the original problem in operational language. For example, the study hypothesis may be stated as a prediction that certain scores will be correlated or that statistically significant differences between sample groups will be found on critical variables.

Part 3: Findings

The essential purpose of Part 3 is to present findings that have been anticipated by the statement of the research problem. Not all findings of a study need to be reported in an article-length report, but all important results that bear on the problem area of the study should be shared.

Data Displays. A useful first step is to prepare the tables, graphs, figures, or other data displays that will form the core of the presentation. The narrative portion of the findings section can then be organized according to these displays. Statistical tables are the most widely used form of data displays. An example is Table 23.3.

The first principle in displaying data is to make the display sufficiently clear so that it can be readily understood, given the infor-

TABLE 23.3

Example of Table as Data Display: Client Satisfaction with Social Work
Services by Educational Level of Workers

| | Educational Level of Workers | | | | | |
| | MSW | | BSW | | Totals | |
Satisfaction	Number	Percent	Number	Percent	Number	Percent
Satisfied	23	57.5	28	50.0	51	53.1
Neutral	16	40.0	13	23.2	29	30.2
Dissatisfied ..	1	2.5	15	26.8	16	16.7
Totals	40		56		96	

$\chi^2 = 10.7$, $df = 2$, $p < .01$
Source: Reid (1981).

mation presented up to that point in the report. Table 23.3 meets this
criterion by providing descriptive titles and labels. In fact, the main
point of the findings can be quickly grasped without knowing anything
about the study.

The data in Table 23.3 also are reasonably complete. Percentages
are given to facilitate comparisons between the two groups of clients,
although the actual data on which the percentages are based are also
given.

Information concerning the statistical test of significance used is
given at the bottom of the table. As a matter of convention, routine
statistical procedures are not explained, either as a part of the table or
in the text. This creates obvious communication difficulties for readers
who lack knowledge of statistics.

The purpose of a data display is to communicate information to
the reader in a graphic manner. If a display has achieved this purpose
efficiently, there should be no need to repeat the information it contains
in the text of the report. Textual commentary on data displays should
be used to emphasize the main points of the data or to draw attention
to characteristics of the data that might be overlooked. Thus, in interpreting Table 23.3, the text should not be used to plod through the
obvious—"57.5 percent of the clients who had M.S.W. social workers
were satisfied; 40 percent were neutral," and so on. Rather, the author
might observe that clients who had M.S.W. social workers were relatively more satisfied with service than clients who had B.S.W. social
workers. In addition, the author might note that dissatisfied clients
accounted for the largest share of the difference.

If the purpose of data displays is adhered to, displays of inordinate complexity, such as a graph with a half dozen crisscrossing lines, will not be used. Nor will displays be used for basic information which can be more simply expressed in the text. In the example, if satisfaction data had been obtained only for clients served by M.S.W. social workers, Table 23.3 would not have been necessary.

Narrative Description. The text of the findings of the report should follow a logical sequence. Data describing biographical characteristics (demographic data) of clients are generally presented first, as a means of defining the group to which the findings of substantive interest relate. A convenient way to proceed from that point is in order of the hypotheses or questions set forth in the formulation of the research problem. Findings not anticipated in this formulation may then be introduced.

In order to present the findings in a coherent manner, it may be necessary to describe additional measurement procedures as well as analytic methods. The amount of detail and explanation necessary to elucidate techniques used in the analysis of data varies. Certainly routine data processing procedures that are of no consequence to the study findings need not be reported. For example, informing readers that the data were coded, keypunched, and analyzed with a computer adds nothing of value to the report.

Common statistical techniques, such as standard measures of association and tests of statistical significance, are neither explained nor referenced. It is good practice, however, to clarify their function so that the essential meaning of the statistical findings can be easily grasped. Thus, in describing a correlation between expenditures for social work services and the patient discharge rate, across a number of mental health facilities, an author might say, "The correlation coefficient between expenditures and the discharge rate was .76, which suggests a relatively high degree of association between these two variables." Specialized methods which are not yet in common use should be described (Kolevzon, 1981).

The usual practice in writing Part 3 is to present and clarify the study's findings but not to discuss them at length. There may be reasons to deviate from this format. For instance, if a study produces an assortment of findings, the author may wish to summarize some of them. In such a circumstance, the discussion section can be confined to those findings that the author wishes to emphasize. In other situations, however, the findings and their significance may be fairly clear. Whatever discussion is needed can be done in passing. The final section of the report might be devoted to recommendations based upon the findings.

With studies using primarily qualitative rather than quantitative methods, the presentation and discussion of the findings are often combined. The principle of organization may be the themes that emerge in the author's analysis of the qualitative data. Brief examples, often in the form of quotes from clients, may be used, for purposes of both illustration and documentation. Such examples may also be used to illustrate and enliven reports of quantitative studies.

Reports based on qualitative data are not likely to contain technical information that readers may have difficulty comprehending. But these studies can suffer from needless imprecision caused by the author's reluctance to use quantitative descriptions. In summarizing the results, an author may describe selected behaviors or attitudes as if they were characteristic of everyone in the sample. Although excessive discriminations (one person said this, a second said that, a third said something else) should be avoided, some quantification may be useful to avoid such overgeneralization. The number or proportion of deviant cases that might qualify a generalization could be noted, for example.

Part 4: Discussion

There are variations in form and content, but Part 4 is primarily concerned with the meaning and importance of the findings reported in Part 3. The place for presenting data has been passed. Now discussion of what the findings add up to and where they may lead is in order.

Two shortcomings are frequently found in this part. One is to turn the discussion into a repetition of findings previously presented, without much commentary on their practical or theoretical significance. While it may be useful to remind readers of certain results that will be the focus of discussion, there is no need for simple repetition. If findings were discussed in Part 3, Part 4 can focus on further implications, general conclusions, and so on.

The second shortcoming falls somewhat on the opposite extreme. This is to ignore the findings and concentrate on an exposition of the author's own point of view—perhaps because the findings did not meet expectations. The findings from any study, no matter how trivial or inconclusive, merit some discussion, even if it does little more than give reasons why the findings were not more revealing.

The content of the discussion section varies according to the nature of the findings and what has been previously said about them. In most studies, the findings are sufficiently complex (or ambiguous) to warrant explication of what was in fact learned about the sample studied. Causal connections between variables which are found to be associated should be discussed. For example, the length of social work treatment may be found to be positively correlated with outcome. Does this mean that greater amounts of treatment played a causative role in the outcome, or does it mean that clients who were getting better on their own tended to remain in treatment longer? Any evidence or argument that can be brought to bear on this point should be presented.

In examining such relationships, and in determining the meaning of descriptive findings, possible sources of bias or error in data collection and measurement should be mentioned. Were the interviewers' perceptions influenced by knowledge of the study hypotheses? Is it possible that clients were giving socially desirable responses? An attempt should be made to construct patterns from isolated results. Inconsistencies in the findings, such as discrepancies among measures of the same phenomenon, need to be identified and accounted for. The author's speculations about the reasons for unanticipated findings may also be offered. In trying to understand and explain the meaning of a study's findings, however, the author is limited to the events actually investigated.

A rather different question concerns the importance of meaningfulness of the study's findings to other situations. This is the payoff question. An understanding of events actually studied should have a broader application. Since most social work studies are not based on representative samples, however, it is usually not possible to generalize within known margins of error to larger populations. Nevertheless, some kinds of generalizations, often referred to as *implications,* are needed. Without such generalizations there would be little point in conducting the study.

In stating the implications, fatuous statements like "Since the sample studied was not representative, generalization of the findings is not possible" should be avoided. Claims that the findings necessarily reflect universal truth also are needless. In most studies, an appropriate position is to assume that the findings have some implications for the field of social work. Even findings based on small, nonrepresentative samples may provide some support for, or challenge to, existing hypotheses or social work practice. Such findings might also be used as a basis for suggesting new hypotheses or practices.

While the findings may not "prove" or "establish" a great deal, they may "provide evidence for," "suggest the possibility that," or "raise question about." Using appropriately qualified language, an author can usually present implications that readers will find useful but not misleading. Many authors often do not push either their imaginations or their data far enough. Ultraconservative interpretations of findings may have the dubious advantage of avoiding criticism from other professionals, but they may also fail to extract useful ideas and suggestions from the findings.

The limitations of a study, particularly major shortcomings that may affect how the findings are interpreted or applied, should be made explicit. This is sometimes done in a separate subsection in which specific limitations are cited. Alternatively, they may be made clear in the process of interpreting findings or in developing implications for social work. For example, a study of the needs of older people in a community may have used a sample that overrepresented the younger, healthier people among the aged. In discussing implications of the findings for community planning, the author can point out the limiting effects of the sample bias.

The conclusions of a study may be strengthened or qualified by references to related literature, which may have been reviewed in Part 1. In fact, the review of related literature can be deferred to Part 4 in order to connect the findings of the study more closely to the results of other investigations. Introducing other authors' findings in Part 4 may be particularly appropriate when the study's findings have been seren-dipitous, or perhaps not encompassed in the literature referred to in the introduction.

Some authors make recommendations for further study based on the findings. Such recommendations should be informative. If nothing more specific can be said than, "It is important to do more research in this area," it is better to say nothing. To be helpful, a recommendation for further study should specify particular research questions, variables, and designs that would not otherwise be obvious.

Recommendations for changes in policies, programs, practices, and so on are most likely to appear in reports addressed to particular decision makers, such as key agency staff, who might be able to initiate them. In making these recommendations the findings of the study should be synthesized with assumptions about desirable goals and some knowledge of the relevant policy or program.

The final section of Part 4 may be devoted to a brief summary of important findings and conclusions of the study. This format is perhaps most needed if the preceding discussion has dealt with a range of findings in a somewhat lengthy or discursive fashion. It is less necessary if the discussion is brief, well focused, and in itself summarizes the major findings. A summary also may not be needed if an abstract of the study is furnished.

Longer Reports

While this section has dealt with article-length reports, much of the material also applies to longer reports such as master's theses, doctoral dissertations, and reports to sponsoring agencies. These reports are usually richer in detail and provide a more complete picture of the findings of a study. An article-length report, in fact, may be based on only a portion of the findings from a study.

Because of their length and comprehensiveness, longer reports should have good summaries. In fact, a common way of using such reports is to read only the summary and portions that are of particular interest. Agency decision makers particularly require a nontechnical summary of a study, with emphasis on major findings. Often such an "executive summary" is presented at the beginning of the report.

Use of footnotes and appendixes helps unburden the text of longer reports. This suits readers who are not interested in plowing through a great deal of technical detail, but at the same time it provides valuable information for those who wish to pursue the topic further.

PUBLICATION

Authors are interested in communicating their work to audiences that will find it of interest or potential value. The generic term for exposure of a study to others is *dissemination*. Extensive dissemination is accomplished through publication (Weinberger & Tripodi, 1969). More limited forms include distribution of copies to the staff of an organization, mailing copies to a list of prospective readers, presentations at staff meetings and conferences, and interlibrary circulation of master's theses and doctoral dissertations.

Although a simple distinction between published and unpublished reports is commonly made, there is a considerable gray area between these categories. Many reports, particularly the more lengthy ones, may be "quasi-published" by schools, agencies, conferences, and so forth. For example, several hundred copies of a report may be duplicated (or even printed), advertised, and sold by an agency. Such reports lack the imprimatur of established publishing organizations, and they are sometimes referred to as "near print."

This section of the chapter will be devoted to one form of dissemination, journal publication. The importance of the other forms should not be overlooked, however. Through a little imagination and initiative, an unpublished report that may be of interest to others can often be put into broader circulation. For example, a state department of mental health may be able to distribute a study to its field offices. Copies of an unpublished report might also be sent to a small number of individuals for whom it may be of particular interest and who may cite it in their own publications.

Journal Publication

The most common means of large-scale dissemination of a report is in a professional journal (Markle & Rinn, 1977). These journals have certain characteristics which make them particularly important as vehicles for research products. They provide ready accessibility to studies, regardless of when the studies are published, because present and past issues can usually be found in libraries serving the field. Moreover, a variety of information-retrieval tools, such as abstracts publications, computerized abstract services, and citation indexes, have been designed as aids in searches of the journal (or periodical) literature. Thus, a study reported in a periodical becomes part of an information network, and it has a better chance of being located and utilized. Finally, most professional journals use some form of expert review for papers submitted. This provides some assurance that the articles that are published meet certain standards (Lindsey, 1978b).

The number of social work journals now being published is difficult to determine exactly because of problems in defining both *journal* and *social work.* According to one recent estimate, there are 34 social work journals, yielding a combined annual harvest of close to a thousand articles (Else, 1978, 1979; Grinnell, 1983). Most of these journals are geared to special-interest groups, defined by field of practice, region, auspices, social work method and so forth. With the one exception of *Social Work,* the journals have limited numbers of subscribers. A sizable proportion of subscribers is likely to be represented by libraries. At least two journals are run primarily by students, and several of them expressly encourage students to submit work for possible publication.

Unsolicited reports of research are not always received with great enthusiasm by social work journals. Editors may be concerned about their readers' ability to comprehend highly technical content. Problems may be posed by the length of a report, the cost of reproducing data displays, or difficulties in securing expertise needed to do reviews and technical editing. If a report is accepted, the editor may want the author to revise it and perhaps to tone down technical content, eliminate tables, or reduce the length (Mullins, 1977).

The lack of receptivity for quantitatively based reports was a motivating factor in the recent inauguration of two social work journals specializing in research articles: *Social Work Research and Abstracts* and *Journal of Social Service Research.* Although these two journals are providing a much-needed outlet for more technical and lengthier research reports, they have raised the not wholly unfounded concern that they may siphon reports away from journals that practitioners are more likely to read (Grinnell & Royer, 1983). As a result they may deprive the profession's practice arm of new research knowledge (Brieland, 1978, 1979; Khinduka, 1977; Reid, 1977).

In addition to social work journals, there are interdisciplinary journals and journals in allied fields which publish studies concerned with social work topics. In some cases, social workers publish in other types of journals for substantive reasons. In others, they choose journals which are receptive to quantitative reports. With the appearance of the two social work journals committed to publishing quantitative reports, and with the increasing emphasis on research methods in the profession, the difficulty of publishing a competent report of a worthwhile piece of research in a social work journal should be lessened.

Getting a Report Published

The surest way to get an article published is to write a good report based on a good study. The first step in writing a report for possible publication is to identify the journal to which it will be submitted initially. The report can be then written to relate to the interests of the readers and to meet special requirements concerning length, footnote style, and so forth. Information on journal policy is usually published in each issue as part of the journal's masthead. This includes a description of the types of reports the journal is interested in and details for submission procedures. It is important to consult various issues for actual models of reports the journal has published.

If the report is rejected by the journal originally selected, it may be submitted, with whatever reshaping may be advisable, to other journals. The submissions should be made successively, not several at once. Sending copies of a report to more than one journal at the same time is considered unethical. Moreover, it may prove embarrassing if a report is accepted simultaneously by two journals.

The submission of a report is simple. It is sent with the number of required photocopies (usually three or four) to the journal's editorial office, together with a brief cover letter stating that the report is being submitted for possible publication by the journal. At the journal's editorial office, a decision-making process begins which will determine whether the report will appear in the journal's pages (National Association of Social Workers, 1985). Key persons in this process are the editor and reviewers (referees). The reviewers are in most instances experts in the field covered by the journal, and they contribute their time on a voluntary basis.

The report is read independently by two or more reviewers who are usually not informed of the author's identity. They make recommendations regarding whether the report is suitable for publication and give reasons for their decisions. Disagreements among reviewers are common. Agreement to reject a report is more usual than agreement to publish a report.

When reviewers disagree, the editor may make the final decision. The position of arbitrator gives the editor a good deal of influence over which reports are published. Journal contents therefore tend to reflect the standards and biases of their editors. An editor rarely has free rein, however. Few editors would refuse to publish a report universally endorsed by the journal's reviewers, regardless of their own biases.

Journals tend to reject more reports than they accept. However, most reports are appropriate for several journals, including publications outside the field of social work. Since acceptance criteria vary from journal to journal, it pays to be persistent. Journal policies vary concerning the amount and kind of feedback supplied in the event a report is rejected. Some send out an essentially form letter of rejection, while others supply the reviewers' comments. While these may be painful to read, they can be enormously helpful to an author who wishes to revise a rejected report for submission elsewhere.

The decision about a report frequently falls somewhere between total rejection and unqualified acceptance. The report may be rejected, but the author may be encouraged to revise and resubmit it. This, however, does not commit the journal to accept the revised report for publication.

Once a report is accepted, it is copy edited. The copy editor is mainly concerned with matters of style and form but may raise questions about clarity, redundancy, omissions, and the like. The author normally reviews the edited copy and may make additional changes. The author is discouraged from making changes after the manuscript has been typeset.

The processes of review, editing, and production take time. For authors, the clock ticks most slowly between the submission of a report and a final decision by a journal. This period of uncertainty may vary from a few weeks to several months, depending on the time absorbed by the review process. Reading and evaluating reports seldom is a first-order priority for volunteer reviewers, but an author does not wish to spend several years collecting rejection letters from journals just to learn that the report is not going to be published.

There is also a gap between acceptance and actual publication which may range from a few weeks to two years or more. A six- to nine-month delay is fairly typical among social work journals. This results from such fixed factors as the number of issues a journal publishes a year and the time consumed by editing, printing, and so forth. In addition, a journal may have accumulated a backlog of accepted manuscripts, perhaps enough for three or four issues. Some time lag is unavoidable and does have a positive side. For example, a backlog of manuscripts permits greater deliberation in the selection and editing of reports (Lindsey, 1977b).

Submitting Student Work

A few words of advice are in order for social work students who wish to publish reports of studies they do in their academic work. A good first step is to consult with an instructor about publication possibilities (Kane, 1978, 1980).

If students are serious about publication, they should rewrite their course papers with that objective in mind after selecting a journal to which the finished product will be submitted. As a rule, course papers should not be submitted as is. There is usually a great deal of distance between a first-class student paper and a report of publishable quality. In rewriting the paper, the student should be particularly sensitive to aspects of the study that may have been glossed over because of assumptions about the instructor's knowledge of those areas. Some requirements of the assignment also may be dispensed with in a published article.

In some cases the instructor may be willing to collaborate with the student in the rewriting and become a coauthor of the report. If the original work is a joint effort, senior authorship (the first author listed) is usually given to the one who has borne the greatest responsibility for the conduct of the study and the write-up of the results. It is usually assumed that the senior author has made a greater contribution to the work, but, some coauthors determine the order randomly.

Students should not confine submissions to the better known social work journals, where their work is more likely to be rejected. They may find greater receptivity and fewer delays with some of the lesser known social work journals, particularly those that are relatively new. And students should not be discouraged if their initial submissions are rejected. Even well-established authors must learn to live with the unpleasant reality that their work is not always welcome. If reviewers' comments are supplied, they can have considerable learning value.

SUMMARY

This chapter has presented the steps that are necessary to prepare a report for publication. The chapter also has detailed the information needed to submit a report to a professional journal for possible publication.

The next chapter provides criteria for evaluating quantitative articles published in social work journals. These criteria can also guide authors in preparing reports for possible publication in a journal, since they are typical of the ones by which professional social work journals review possible contributions.

Joel Fischer

24. EVALUATING RESEARCH REPORTS

Quantitative research reports are defined in this chapter as published articles based on studies designed to contribute to the social work knowledge base through rigorous, replicable means. A methodology for evaluating the significance and validity of the knowledge derived from such reports is suggested in a framework whose value rests on answers to two basic questions:

1. Why is it important to analyze social work research?
2. Why is the framework presented in this chapter recommended?

The first question is addressed in the theme of this text: Research and evaluation should be applicable in social work practice situations, and the field of social work should *not* be dichotomized into practice and research orientations. These concepts are based on the belief that systematic, orderly procedures of quantitative social work research and evaluation provide the most productive means to organize, understand, test, and develop social work knowledge. The capacity to perform competently in our profession, therefore, is based on the ability to analyze and utilize the results of social work research and evaluation.

As presented in Chapter 1, the issue of competency in our profession was critically examined during the 70s. This decade has been called the age of accountability because it emphasized social workers' responsibility to demonstrate their effectiveness. To demonstrate accountability, social work practice must be guided, as much as possible, by empirically validated principles and techniques.

Few (if any) quantitative studies of social work research or evaluation are without flaws. Nevertheless, the social worker must be able to analyze social work research and evaluation findings from reports and to make judgments as to their applicability. Otherwise, even minimum effectiveness in practice is unlikely.

The second question—why the framework presented in this chapter is recommended—relates to the accessibility and feasibility for use of this framework. The framework defines the key criteria for assessing research reports. It should aid social workers to develop the basic skills for analyzing reports and alert them to how these skills can be applied effectively and efficiently in conducting and writing up their own studies. The key evaluative criteria suggested for analyzing a quantitative research study can be applied on a point-by-point basis in the analysis of a single study, or they can be used in comparing several studies. Each criterion in the framework is related to a specific aspect of the research process. Analyzing a study criterion by criterion should make it relatively easy to draw accurate conclusions about the study. As in all social work skills, however, the case of using this framework increases with practice.

Figure 24.1 summarizes the framework for evaluating the strengths and weaknesses of quantitative social work research studies. It is composed of 80 specific criteria which can be applied in the evaluation of any study. The criteria highlight specific analytic dimensions and indicate their importance in an evaluation. Each criterion is distinct, although there is a clear overlap among them.

The framework was developed by abstracting and synthesizing criteria for analysis from a number of different sources, both from within the field of social work and outside it (Tripodi, Fellin, & Meyer, 1983). The criteria are grouped into the four major categories of a research report discussed in the preceding chapter: problem, method, findings, and discussion (Fischer, 1981a).

SUMMARY

The 80 criteria in the framework for evaluating quantitative research reports are specified in Figure 24.1 at the beginning of this chapter. Obviously, some of these criteria are far more important than others. There is a considerable overlap among them, to the extent that some are actually subcategories. Examples are the various internal and external validity criteria listed in the method section.

Ideal research conditions are rarely possible, due to any number of economic, personal, or organizational constraints. Most authors are forced to compromise on some of these conditions. Therefore the overall impact of a study's deficiencies should be taken into account in judging the applicability of the knowledge derived from the study to social work practice.

FIGURE 24.1

Framework for Evaluating Empirical Research Reports

Criteria	Scale			
	Low			High
A. PROBLEM				
1. Adequacy of the literature review	1	2	3	4
2. Clarity of the problem area (research question) under investigation	1	2	3	4
3. Clarity of the statement of the hypothesis	1	2	3	4
4. Clarity of the specification of the independent variable	1	2	3	4
5. Clarity of the specification of the dependent variable	1	2	3	4
6. Clarity of the definitions for major concepts	1	2	3	4
7. Clarity of the operational definitions	1	2	3	4
8. Reasonableness of assumption of relationship between the independent and dependent variables	1	2	3	4
9. Specification of confounding variables	1	2	3	4
10. Number of independent variables tested	1	2	3	4
11. Adequacy in the control of confounding variables	1	2	3	4
12. Clarity of author orientation	1	2	3	4
13. Clarity of the study's purpose	1	2	3	4
14. Clarity of the study's auspices	1	2	3	4
15. Reasonableness of the author's assumptions	1	2	3	4
B. METHOD				
16. Clarity of the specification of the kinds of changes desired	1	2	3	4
17. Clarity as to signs of client change	1	2	3	4
18. Appropriateness of the criterion measure in relation to the purpose of the study	1	2	3	4
19. Degree of validity of the criterion measure	1	2	3	4
20. Degree of reliability of the criterion measure	1	2	3	4
21. Degree of use of a variety of criterion measures (e.g., subjective and objective)	1	2	3	4
22. Clarity about how data were collected	1	2	3	4
23. Clarity about who collects data	1	2	3	4
24. Degree of avoidance of contamination in process of data collection	1	2	3	4
25. Clarity of the statement of the research design	1	2	3	4

FIGURE 24.1 (continued)

Criteria	Scale			
	Low			High
26. Adequacy of the research design (re: purpose)	1	2	3	4
27. Clarity and adequacy of the time between pretests and posttests	1	2	3	4
28. Appropriateness in the use of control group(s)	1	2	3	4
29. Appropriateness in the use of random assignment procedures	1	2	3	4
30. Appropriateness in the use of matching procedures	1	2	3	4
31. Experimental and control group equivalency (at pretest)	1	2	3	4
32. Degree of control for effects of history	1	2	3	4
33. Degree of control for effects of maturation	1	2	3	4
34. Degree of control for effects of testing	1	2	3	4
35. Degree of control for effects of instrumentation	1	2	3	4
36. Degree of control for statistical regression	1	2	3	4
37. Degree of control for differential selection of clients	1	2	3	4
38. Degree of control for differential mortality	1	2	3	4
39. Degree of control for practitioner bias	1	2	3	4
40. Degree of control for temporal bias	1	2	3	4
41. Degree of control for selection-maturation interaction	1	2	3	4
42. Overall degree of success in maximizing internal validity (32–41)	1	2	3	4
43. Adequacy of sample size	1	2	3	4
44. Degree of adequacy in the representativeness of the client sample	1	2	3	4
45. Degree of adequacy in the representativeness of the practitioner sample	1	2	3	4
46. Degree of control for reactive effects or testing (interaction with independent variable)	1	2	3	4
47. Degree of control for special effects of experimental arrangements (e.g., Hawthorne effect, placebo effect)	1	2	3	4

FIGURE 24.1 (continued)

Criteria	Scale			
	Low			High
48. Degree of control for multiple-treatment interference	1	2	3	4
49. Degree of control for interaction between selection and experimental variable	1	2	3	4
50. Overall degree of success in maximizing external validity (43–49)	1	2	3	4

C. FINDINGS

51. Adequacy of the manipulation of the independent variable	1	2	3	4
52. Appropriateness in the use of follow-up measures	1	2	3	4
53. Adequacy of data to provide evidence for testing of hypotheses	1	2	3	4
54. Appropriateness in the use of statistical controls	1	2	3	4
55. Appropriateness of statistical procedures	1	2	3	4
56. Use of between-group statistical procedures	1	2	3	4
57. Degree to which data support the hypothesis	1	2	3	4
58. Extent to which author's conclusions are consistent with data	1	2	3	4
59. Degree of uniformity between tables and text	1	2	3	4
60. Degree of investigator (author) bias	1	2	3	4
61. Clarity as to cause of client changes	1	2	3	4
62. Degree to which alternative explanations were avoided in the design	1	2	3	4
63. Degree to which potential alternative explanations were dealt with	1	2	3	4
64. Degree of control of confounding effects of practitioners	1	2	3	4
65. Degree of control for confounding effects of clients	1	2	3	4
66. Degree of control for confounding effects of nonspecific treatment	1	2	3	4
67. Reasonableness of author's inferences	1	2	3	4
68. Clarity as to meaning of change(s)	1	2	3	4
69. Adequacy in relating findings to previous literature	1	2	3	4

FIGURE 24.1 (continued)

	Scale			
Criteria	Low			High
70. Adequacy of conclusions in not generalizing beyond data	1	2	3	4
71. Extent to which the research design accomplished the purpose of the study	1	2	3	4
72. Appropriateness in the handling of unexpected consequences	1	2	3	4
D. DISCUSSION				
73. Degree of relevance to social work practice	1	2	3	4
74. Overall soundness of study	1	2	3	4
75. Degree of generalizability of the study's findings	1	2	3	4
76. Degree to which the independent variables are accessible to control by social workers	1	2	3	4
77. Extent to which a meaningful difference would occur if the independent variable were utilized in actual social work practice situations	1	2	3	4
78. Degree of economic feasibility of the independent variable if utilized in actual social work practice situations	1	2	3	4
79. Degree of ethical suitability of the manipulation of the independent variable	1	2	3	4
80. Extent to which the primary question is addressed (what methods, based on what theory, with what social workers, working with what clients, with what kinds of client problems, in what situations, are most successful?)	1	2	3	4

Source: Fischer (1981a).

As Figure 24.1 shows, each of the 80 criteria can be rated on a scale from 1 to 4. These ratings call for careful observation and personal judgment. In some instances, a study either meets a criterion or it does not. For example, on Criterion 28, a study which uses some type of control group would be rated with a 3 or 4, and a study which does not use a control group would be rated with a 1 or 2. In other situations, it is necessary to decide whether or not the study "adequately" meets a given criterion. An example is deciding whether there is a sufficiently clear specification of the independent variable. In other circumstances, the relative rating will be less judgmental. For example, a study using three independent criterion measures would be rated higher on Criterion 21, "Degree of use of a variety of criterion measures," than a study using only one.

Because there are clear differences in the importance of the various criteria, the overall rating given a study may be less important than ensuring that certain criteria are met. For example, it is more important for an experimental study to use a control group appropriately than to specify the theoretical orientation of the author. The implications for social work of research which meets the various criteria must always be considered.

In using this framework, one standard to consider is that if a study's results cannot be readily incorporated into the knowledge base of our profession, it is, for all intents and purposes, practically useless. A study may be designed and executed perfectly. Yet it will have only limited value to the profession if it does not address a meaningful problem area and if the results cannot be put into practice by social workers.

Edwin J. Thomas

25. DEVELOPMENTAL RESEARCH

A recent development in social work research and evaluation is interest in a social version of the research and development (R&D) approach employed in technical fields like engineering or in business organizations. Although research oriented to the generation of social work interventions and social technology is new and relatively undeveloped, it is a promising innovation in research methods. This chapter presents developmental research as a model of research for the generation of new social work intervention technology.

Traditionally, research in social work has been directed primarily to what has come to be known as *knowledge development.* It draws its methods largely from the behavioral sciences and uses them to examine research questions relevant to social work and social welfare. This model of research in social work is referred to here as the *behavioral science model* because its objective is to make contributions to knowledge of human behavior, and the research methods are those of one or another of the behavioral sciences. Most social work practitioner/researchers have been trained in this model, and it guides their conception and practices of research.

Developmental research, in contrast, is very different and is not well known. A primary objective of this chapter is to explain how the purposes, outcomes, phases, operations, methods of injury, and sources of data of the developmental research model differ from other social work research methods which are oriented to the development of knowledge (Thomas, 1978a, 1978b).

SOCIAL TECHNOLOGY AND SOCIAL WORK OBJECTIVES

Social work has a technology, just like engineering, medicine, and all other fields dealing with applied and practical matters. Social work, of course, consists of much more than a social technology, and it is guided by important values and humane commitments. Nevertheless, human service work is done with a *social technology*. Developmental research is concerned precisely with the social technology of social work, and newly developed social technology is the product of such inquiry.

Technology is concerned with the study of practical arts. In social work, technology consists of all the technical means by which social work objectives are achieved. Without such technical wherewithal, social work could not achieve its goals. There are at least nine general types of social technology. The characteristics of these types and examples of each one are presented in Table 25.1.

This typology is one specification of the social technology that is relevant for developmental research; the types identified may not provide an exhaustive list. Some are more general than others and therefore include some subcategories (e.g., service systems include service programs), and any given instance of technology may illustrate more than one type (e.g., a computer is an electromechanical device that may also be part of an information system). The types embrace the technological components that are the person-made instruments for achieving social work objectives. As such, they are subject to modification and creative alteration.

Today's social technology generally has a brief period of use. One reason is that the technological components of most innovations, when examined in detail, would generally be judged as incomplete, not fully adequate, and deserving of change. There are also frequent changes in resources, priorities, and social objectives that provide impetus for alterations in the goals, tasks, and methods bearing on social work. Further, data and technological resources relevant to new social technology are constantly appearing, and at an increasingly rapid rate. Behavioral science research steadfastly continues to provide new findings, and a rapidly developing physical technology inevitably (but not always immediately) paces developments in social technology. Because of these factors, the social technology applicable to social work will doubtless be subject to continuing change in the foreseeable future.

THE NEED FOR NEW METHODOLOGY

At present, the methodology of behavioral science is the single best set of methodological tools the social worker has. These tools have been the dominant methodology applied in the social work research process. Since they originally evolved in behavioral science, the research is directed to knowledge development in the form of the genera-

TABLE 25.1
Principal Types of Social Technology

Types	Characteristics	Examples
Physical frameworks	Static physical structures that passively control space, light, sound and/or temperature variables, with some structural elements that may be moveable or changeable*	Room size and arrangements in agencies and residential facilities
Electromechanical devices	Electronic or mechanical devices	Timers, counters, audio and video recorders, chart recorders, transducers, computers
Information systems	Methods of collecting, processing, storing, retrieving, and/or displaying information by human or electromechanical means	Problem Oriented Medical Recording, automated intake, computer-assisted agency record keeping
Assessment methods	Principles and procedures for gathering and evaluating diagnostic information about clients, families, and other clientele	Interviewing guidelines, intake questionnaires, family observational procedures
Intervention methods	Principles and procedures for carrying out intervention and evaluating progress of clinical and service activity	Particular change methods of behavior modification, task-oriented casework, insight treatment, transactional analysis, group treatment methods
Service programs	Service components with distinctive objectives and clientele, usually part of larger systems of service	Day care, foster-home care, adoption, Aid to Families with Dependent Children
Organizational structures	Structures of social agencies which provide financial and social services	Arrangements of power, authority, responsibility, and distribution of work and labor in agencies
Service systems	Organizational structures designed to coordinate and deliver aspects of one or more human service programs	State and local departments of social welfare, community mental health agencies

(continued)

TABLE 25.1 (continued)

Types	Characteristics	Examples
Social and welfare policy	Prescriptions, directives, rules, or regulations oriented to guide action in regard to particular financial and social service objectives	Systematic positions on preferred approaches to income distribution, welfare benefits, governmentally provided health services, equal rights

Source: Edwin J. Thomas, "Generating Innovation in Social Work: The Paradigm of Developmental Research," *Journal of Social Service Research,* 2 (Fall 1978), pp. 95–117. ©1979, The Haworth Press (reproduced with permission of publisher).

tion of facts, empirical relationships, and the testing of hypotheses and theories. The methodology of behavioral science research will no doubt continue to be the mainstay of research in social work that is oriented to knowledge building, in contrast to research directed to the development of social technology. It is not the appropriate model for research directed to technological development, but some of the component methods do have a place in developmental research. For example, hypothetical-developmental (Knowledge Level 1 as presented in Chapter 13) studies may be useful in the earlier stages of developmental research, and cause-effect (Knowledge Level 4 as presented in Chapter 13) studies are especially valuable in carrying out the evaluation of interventions and other technological innovations. Indeed, the entire field of evaluative research has been enriched immensely by the methodological contributions of behavioral science methods. However, because they yield knowledge about human behavior rather than social technology itself, behavioral science methods at best contribute only indirectly to the actual process of generating innovation. New methods are needed to involve the worker actively in the process of social-technological innovation in social work and related fields of human service.

There have been important changes in conceptions of applied research and practice which have provided an intellectual climate favoring the introduction of a model of developmental research. Among these changes are inquiry into the phases of research utilization (such as the R&D phases of research, development, diffusion, and adoption in engineering and science), identification of selection criteria in research utilization (such as content relevance, knowledge power, and referent features), the development of literature retrieval models to generate interventional guidelines, the formulation of action models, social program evaluation, and the movement toward empirically-oriented practice (Mullen, 1978, 1981, 1983). Each of these areas has made some contribution to the emerging methodology of developmental research (Bloom, 1975; Havelock, 1973; Specht, 1968).

DEVELOPMENTAL RESEARCH AND THE DR&U MODEL

A model of developmental research ideally should be applicable to the main activities and conditions relating to all the various efforts in the development of social technology. In such a general model, a phase of analysis should precede a development phase, and each should be explicated in terms of its main constituent features. A phase for evaluation of the innovation should follow the developmental phase, and the subsequent phases of diffusion and adoption should be recognized. The first three phases—analysis, development, and evaluation—are distinguished here as *developmental research*. The other two phases—diffusion and adoption—are mainly concerned with utilization of the innovation and are called *utilization research*. Thus, developmental research is seen as the early essential phases that come before the phases involving utilization. The full sequence of phases, with their constituent steps and conditions, is called *developmental research and utilization* (DR&U). The framework for this model is presented in Figure 25.1 (Thomas, 1978a, 1978b).

The DR&U model is superficially similar to that of social R&D, which has assumed the phases of research, development, diffusion, and adoption in scientific and organizational R&D. There is increasing interest in the applicability of social R&D in social work and related areas. The DR&U model proposes important differences, however, that deserve brief comment at the outset. In social R&D, the phase of research precedes development. This is too narrow; in DR&U, a phase of *analysis* precedes the development phase. There are many other sources of basic data for interventional innovation besides research (a look ahead at Figure 25.2 should make this evident). These other sources are also critical for innovation; in some cases, they are more important than the findings of research. In addition, interventional innovation requires evaluation that is sufficiently complex and important to be distinguished as a separate phase following the development phase. Without careful repeated evaluation, first in trial use and later in field implementation, it would be difficult if not impossible to progress beyond the evolution of an early prototype to a mature, reliable, and usable technological achievement.

In DR&U, in addition to the phases, there are operational steps that deal with important components of each phase and embrace a set of specific activities to be carried out. These operational steps are the

FIGURE 25.1
Phases, Material Conditions, and Operational Steps of DR&U

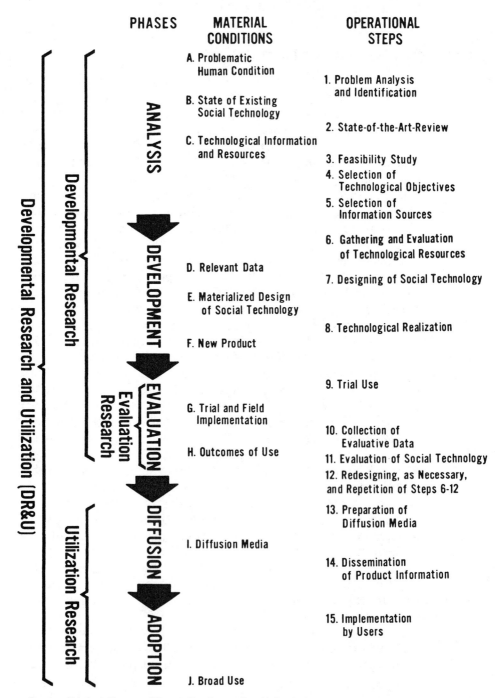

PHASES   **MATERIAL CONDITIONS**   **OPERATIONAL STEPS**

Developmental Research and Utilization (DR&U)

Developmental Research

Evaluation Research

Utilization Research

ANALYSIS

A. Problematic Human Condition

B. State of Existing Social Technology

C. Technological Information and Resources

1. Problem Analysis and Identification

2. State-of-the-Art-Review

3. Feasibility Study
4. Selection of Technological Objectives
5. Selection of Information Sources

DEVELOPMENT

D. Relevant Data

E. Materialized Design of Social Technology

F. New Product

6. Gathering and Evaluation of Technological Resources

7. Designing of Social Technology

8. Technological Realization

EVALUATION

G. Trial and Field Implementation

H. Outcomes of Use

9. Trial Use

10. Collection of Evaluative Data
11. Evaluation of Social Technology
12. Redesigning, as Necessary, and Repetition of Steps 6-12
13. Preparation of Diffusion Media

DIFFUSION

I. Diffusion Media

14. Dissemination of Product Information

ADOPTION

J. Broad Use

15. Implementation by Users

Source: Edwin J. Thomas, "Generating Innovation in Social Work: The Paradigm of Developmental Research," *Journal of Social Service Research*, 2 (Fall 1978), pp. 95–117. ©1979, The Haworth Press (reproduced with permission of the publisher).

how-to-do-it features of this framework, although there are many constituents of each step that cannot be detailed here. Of the 15 operational steps of the DR&U model, 12 relate directly to developmental research. These are the steps that are most relevant to this chapter. The framework also distinguishes a number of material conditions, or real, objective phenomena associated with the phases and the consequences of carrying out the operational steps. Most of these material conditions are the real-world outcomes of the DR&U activity (Rothman, 1980a, 1980b).

The Analysis Phase

Analysis, the first phase in this model, embraces the relevant activities that necessarily precede the developmental effort itself. In this phase there are three material conditions: problematic human conditions, state of existing social technology, and technological information and resources. Each condition is critical to whether or not subsequent development may be engaged in and, if so, the decision it should take. The activities involved in the analysis phase are presented as operational steps, each of which relates to one or more of the material conditions.

Problematic Human Condition. At the outset, before any developmental activity occurs, there is some problematic human condition. One possible direction for change is the development of social technology to be directed at prevention or remediation of the condition. For example, child abuse is now recognized as a problematic human condition for which new procedures, programs, and policies should be worked out for prevention and intervention.

Step 1: Problem Analysis and Identification. Although the existence of a problematic condition is necessary before developmental effort can be directed at it, such a condition does not necessarily or automatically receive professional or public recognition. To bring about such recognition, there must be evidence that there is a problematic condition, combined with the presence of values that make it possible to judge this condition as meriting attention and alteration. The problem presents an opportunity to carry out problem analysis and identification, Step 1 in the series of operational steps. Thus, although child abuse has been with us for a very long time, such abuse—particularly child battering—has emerged as a social issue of greater importance through the efforts of a small group of concerned physicians. Radiologists had reported multiple bone breaks in very young children in the 1940s and the 1950s, but it was not until 1961, when investigators at the Denver Medical Center coined the emotionally charged diagnostic term *battered child syndrome,* that professional and public interest in child abuse began to develop (Antler, 1978).

Activities relating to problem analysis and identification have been carried out by professionals, scholars, and investigators for some time. For example, social policy analysis is one way in which human conditions are evaluated and gaps in service are identified. The empirical methodologies of needs analysis also are often employed to obtain objective data concerning the nature and extent of particular human problems. Even so, much more attention needs to be devoted to explicating and systematizing the methodologies involved in problem analysis and identification.

State of Existing Social Technology. Another material condition bearing directly on whether or not developmental inquiry can or should be embarked upon is the state of existing social technology. To justify investments of time and money in developmental inquiry, the existing social technology must somehow be inadequate to address the problematic condition. In an analysis of prior interventional efforts in regard to child abuse, for example, Antler (1978) discerned many limitations. Child abuse was being addressed as a crisis rather than as a complex set of problems requiring sustained intervention, and as a medical problem calling for protection rather than as a social problem with implications for social, economic, and other services as well. Antler noted that until recently the focus was on abuse, at the expense of attending to problems of neglect, and that greater emphasis had been placed on rehabilitation than on prevention. An alternative approach was proposed in which intervention and social services would be directed toward rectifying these shortcomings.

Step 2: State-of-the-Art-Review. This step consists of activities involved in the review and appraisal of the state of existing social technology. It might include the assessment of published and unpublished literature, firsthand observation in on-site visits to determine new technologies, discussion with knowledgeable informants, or attendance at conferences, conventions, and workshops where new developments are presented. Such a review and appraisal is essential because it can identify the precise strengths and limitations of existing social technology. Without thorough, critical review of the state of the art, directions for the development of new technology cannot be intelligently charted.

Technological Information and Resources. Developmental research derives its data and resources for technological development from a large number of sources. Investigation of the eight principal sources of basic information for the DR&U model shown in Figure 25.2 is part of the analysis phase. The figure shows how the results of this information are transformed through a generation process (see Step 7) to provide data for the development phase.

FIGURE 25.2
Sources of Basic Information for Development of Social Work Technology

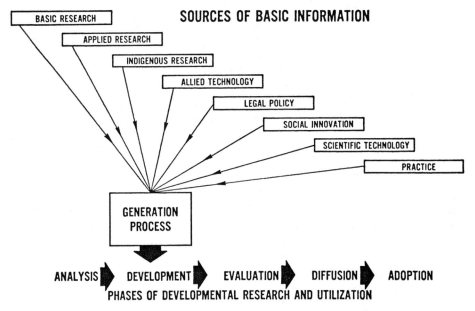

Source: Adapted from Edwin J. Thomas, "Generating Innovation in Social Work: The Paradigm of Developmental Research," *Journal of Social Service Research,* 2 (Fall 1978), pp. 95–117. ©1979, The Haworth Press. Reproduced with the permission of the publisher.

Basic research, such as the research findings and methods of the behavioral and social sciences, as well as selected findings from natural science, is one source of information. Another is applied research, such as applied behavior analysis and psychotherapy research. A third is indigenous research, such as that done on social work problems in the field of social work. Research of these three types, when transformed through research utilization (or generation) processes, provides important contributions to many aspects of social work technology. They are the main sources of information for development in social R&D and in utilization models of research application and development. As rich as the contributions are from these research sources, however, they are still too limited and slow in coming, and, in any case, they are not sufficiently comprehensive to support the continuing pressing demand for new and improved social technology in social work.

In addition to the research sources, data for generating social work technology may be derived from at least five other sources of information. These are:

1. *Allied technology.* Examples are use of selected principles of hospital administration in social welfare administration and use of behavior modification in interpersonal helping.
2. *Legal policy.* An example is development of guidelines for ethical practice from court decisions and judicial rulings.
3. *Social innovation.* Examples are applications of feminist therapy or self-help group practices in social work practice.
4. *Scientific technology.* Examples are design of a computer-assisted record system in an agency and use of closed-circuit television in social work practice.
5. *Practice.* An example is codification of new procedures developed in direct practice.

Step 3: Feasibility Study. The existing technological information and resources are applied in the feasibility study, a fact-finding inquiry to determine whether the development effort is technologically feasible. They should indicate that the effort is likely to result in improved social technology. In general, sufficient technological data and resources must be available to justify developmental effort, and the effort, in the judgment of professionals, must have a reasonable chance of producing the intended improvement.

Technological feasibility is based on the data supplied by one or more sources of basic information such as those depicted in Figure 25.2. One example is relevant research findings from behavioral science that have not yet been applied, such as new empirical generalizations in applied behavior analysis which are related to discrimination training but which have not yet been incorporated in interventional methods intended to bring about transfer and generalization of planned change. Another is relevant scientific technology not yet applied, such as compact, inexpensive, reliable microprocessors for use in computer-assisted practice or administration. Allied technology not yet transferred to social work, such as recent developments in management information systems in business and industry which are relevant to social service administration, is another source of such data. The other types of basic data—from applied research, legal policy, social innovation, indigenous research, and practice—are likewise potentially relevant sources that must be surveyed in the feasibility study.

Although the feasibility study at this point should be addressed largely to questions of technological feasibility, there are other aspects of feasibility that cannot be overlooked. One is the economics of the anticipated costs and benefits of the study. Clearly, anticipated costs must somehow be justified in terms of anticipated benefits. Although research costs are often difficult to anticipate, they can be projected, with ample allowance for unanticipated factors and error. Anticipated benefits, in contrast, very often entailed qualitative human factors which are presently difficult if not impossible to translate into quantitative or monetary terms (Masters, Garfinkel, & Bishop, 1978). However, often some component of the effort can be at least grossly quantified in monetary terms. Although it is difficult to quantify the benefits of interventions in terms of improved living conditions for alcohol abusers and their families, for example, the economic costs associated with alcohol abuse have been quantified (Krimmel, 1971).

Still another aspect of feasibility is organizational in nature. Among the questions to be considered are whether there would be organizational constraints on the use of innovations, whether they would have the intended consequences, and whether they could be employed without adverse effects. Organizational feasibility is important in the long run and has particular bearing on the diffusion and adoption of innovations once they have been developed. But lack of feasibility for an anticipated innovation because of present-day organizational limitations need not and generally should not be a deterrent to developmental research that has technological feasibility and promises, if successful, to yield large benefits. Organizational arrangements for agencies, programs, and services are themselves aspects of social technology. As such, they also can be studied in developmental research efforts to make them compatible with social-technological innovations such as intervention methods.

Step 4: Selection of Technological Objectives. The technological objective in developmental research is analogous to the research problem or hypothesis to be investigated. That is, it is the new social technology to be developed. The objective is a specific aspect of social technology, such as a new assessment or intervention method, service program, organizational structure, service system, or welfare policy (see Table 25.1), or some specific combination such as a particular intervention method with a distinctive service program and organizational structure. In the case of child abuse, for example, an objective could be to evolve a new child management approach to assist abusive parents to employ less aversive and more appropriate practices with their children.

Step 5: Selection of Information Sources. This step consists of selecting the most appropriate sources of basic data for the developmental task. More than one source of data is generally relevant to any developmental task. For example, if the effort is to develop a procedure to help clients who have great pain and for whom medical solutions have been exhausted, the experience of social workers working in pain clinics (practice) would be an important source of data. So would medicine (allied technology), research on operant factors in pain-expressive behavior (applied research), and scientific findings on the neurophysiology of pain (basic research). Although selection of information sources is presented here as the last step of analysis, it may be thought of as overlapping with the developmental phase to be described below.

The analysis phase is important because its successful completion makes subsequent development possible and assures that the investment of time and resources in a developmental effort is likely to be worthwhile.

The Development Phase

The development phase, the second one in the DR&U model, is central because it is here that the interventional innovation is created. Through a series of additional operational steps, relevant data bearing on the developmental objective are transformed and shaped into a new product. Critical as it is, this is probably the least-well-understood phase of developmental research.

Step 6: Gathering and Evaluation of Technological Resources. The developmental phase proper begins with this step. For example, to determine the findings of social science that apply to social planning and community organization, Rothman (1978) reviewed the applicable social science studies. Over 900 relevant studies were reviewed and processed. In Rothman's conceptualization of the research utilization process, the transition from raw, basic research to consensus generalizations is seen as dependent on such constituent operations as retrieval, codification, and generalization of research findings. Illustrative activities are location of pertinent studies; assessing data for validity, reliability, and applicability; codifying data into suitable categories; constructing consensus findings within the selected data; and drawing appropriate generalizations and propositions from the consensus findings.

Literature review and evaluation of research findings from applied and basic research have so far been the main forms of developmental research (Thomas, 1980). However, it is also important to consider the potential relevance of all the other information sources. Each of the eight sources of basic information in Figure 25.2 can contribute to the development of social technology. For instance, to learn more about the applicability of the Problem-Oriented Medical Record method of record keeping in social work, it would be appropriate to turn to medical practice (an allied technology), where this form of recording has been used, and to visit facilities where such recording was being carried out, examine the records, and consult with those who have had experience with this type of recording. The selection, evaluation, and assembly of relevant basic information for purposes of technological innovation are important aspects of developmental research.

Relevant Data. After the data gathered in Step 6 have been collated and evaluated, the result is a research-produced material condition which consists of relevant data and which serves as a basis for generation of the innovation. Because this is the point at which use is made of relevant data to bring about something that is technologically different, it is a critical juncture that calls for a creative transition.

Step 7: Designing of Social Technology. A central activity of developmental research is the design of the social technology. In moving from research findings to concrete action principles, Rothman speaks of processes of translation, conversion, and operationalization of the findings (Rothman, 1978). In the *utilization of knowledge,* a critical feature in this transition consists of converting descriptive generalizations to action prescriptions. However, different generation processes are suggested for other informational sources, as described elsewhere (Thomas, 1980). For example, if we were interested in making use in social work of contributions from scientific technology such as computers, a critical innovative activity might consist of a novel assembly of existing computer components combined in a relevant manner for purposes, say, of processing data in a social work agency. This generation process is called *technological transfer,* in contrast to the knowledge utilization process described above. Another method is *novel application,* also an aspect of transfer. Here, for instance, a new method of budgeting developed in an allied field such as business might be applied directly in social welfare budgeting. Still another generation process involves an *experimental synthesis,* an "invention," as it were, in which the technological innovation is not analogous or related to other innovations, nor is it an extrapolation and operationalization of research findings. Such a synthesis thus tends to generate that which is truly new. Consider, for example, the entirely different group procedure that social workers might invent on the basis of their own practice experience in trying to evolve new methods of change.

Materialized Design of Social Technology. The result of the operations related to the innovation of a product is the materialized design for the innovation. When the design is sufficiently precise, it may take its material, real-world form. For example, when the Signal System for the Assessment and Modification of Behavior (SAM) and the computerized version (CASAM) were conceived, the rendition of product design consisted of drawings of the mechanical components, their interrelationships, the electrical schematics and computer programs (for CASAM), along with a conception of how these light-signal apparatuses could be helpful in the assessment and modification of family verbal behavior (Thomas, Carter, Gambrill, & Butterfield, 1970; Thomas, Walter, & O'Flaherty, 1974).

Step 8: Technological Realization. This step consists of actually bringing the product into being. If the product is a device, the realization would be a prototype apparatus; if it is a practice procedure, its realization would consist of carrying it out in practice; if it is a service program, it might consist of mounting a pilot program. The consequence of such product realization, of course, is a new technological product.

The Evaluation Phase

New Product

Much of the evaluation phase is embraced in evaluation research. However, unlike some evaluative research in which the evaluation component turns out to be an end in itself, disembodied from earlier development and subsequent events, the evaluation activities in the DR&U model are an integral part of a research-innovation process which begins with the phases that generate social technology. The process employs evaluation to appraise and, if appropriate, revise the innovation, and continues on to utilization in the forms of diffusion and adoption.

Step 9: Trial Use. After a product has been created, its use must be tested. Trial use generally begins with pilot implementation. Later on, demonstration projects and, eventually, large-scale evaluation studies conducted in the field are also initiated.

Trial and Field Implementation

Step 10: Collection of Evaluative Data. The trial and field implementation in turn leads to the collection of evaluative data. It is at this point that evaluative research methodology and, indeed, the full range of behavioral science research methodology (e.g., experimental and quasi-experimental designs, data gathering procedures, and cost-benefit analyses) may be drawn on to gather data systematically for purposes of evaluating the innovation. For example, single-subject experimental designs may be particularly useful in the early stages of evaluation, when it is not known whether a prototype or social-technological innovation is effective. Control group experimental designs may be informative later on for purposes of systematic and comparative evaluation of better developed technology that needs to be tested in the field under conditions approximating normal operation (Campbell & Stanley, 1963; Herson & Barlow, 1976).

Outcomes of Use

Step 11: Evaluation of Social Technology. The outcome data that result from the collection of evaluation data provide the basis for embarking on evaluation of the social technology. Through evaluative research, the innovation is appraised in terms of such criteria as its effectiveness in the attainment of given objectives, its efficiency, and its costs and benefits. For example, Thomas and Walter (1978) evaluated and developed a new stepwise procedure for conducting behavioral assessment and modification with individuals in open community settings (the PAMBOS procedure). When the procedure was employed in practice with a sample of 32 cases embracing 66 problem areas, it was found to be associated with a high degree of effectiveness (93 percent of the 48 problem areas that progressed to the point of modification demonstrated success), it was relatively efficient, and it was adequate inasmuch as the procedural steps systematically guided the practice activities of the participating social workers.

It is accurate and realistic to view evaluation as a process and an ongoing activity preceding satisfactory development of new social technology. This is because it is generally necessary to revise the innovation, repeat trial use, collect new evaluation data, and reappraise the revised product—and often to do so repeatedly, depending on the results of evaluations. Revision of the innovation combined with its evaluation may occur many, many times before a satisfactory technical achievement is obtained.

Step 12: Redesigning, as Necessary, and Repetition of Steps 6-12. This step completes the evaluation phase of the DR&U model. The subsequent phases of diffusion and adoption, while relevant to the full sequence of DR&U, are summarized only briefly because there has been a great deal of prior work on these aspects of utilization.

The Diffusion Phase

Diffusion Media. After the innovation has been evaluated and found to be worthy of use, information concerning its nature and applicability should be prepared and disseminated. Such diffusion media require prior preparation.

Step 13: Preparation of Diffusion Media. This step consists of such activities as writing articles and books and preparing training materials. (See Chapter 23 for how to prepare research reports for publication.)

Step 14: Dissemination of Product Information. In this step, the diffusion media are made available for the consideration of potential consumers. Dissemination consists of such activities as publication, inservice training, professional education, and field demonstration.

The Adoption Phase

Step 15: Implementation by Users.   Implementation by users consists of the use in social work practice of such contributions as new practice methods, program changes in the case of new service programs, and legislative enactment and administrative follow-through in the case of welfare policy.

Broad Use.   Broad use is achieved if there is widespread diffusion and adoption of the technology. The goal is to have the innovation broadly used by large numbers of those who are potentially the primary consumers.

A WORKING DEFINITION OF DEVELOPMENTAL RESEARCH

The framework presented in Figure 25.1 provides the basis for a working definition of developmental research. As inquiry directed toward the development of social technology for social work, developmental research involves those methods by which social technology is analyzed,.designed, created, and evaluated. Data necessary to the design and innovation of social technology may be derived from such basic sources as research (basic, applied, or indigenous) technology (scientific or allied), legal policy, practice, or social innovation. The generation processes by which data from these basic sources are transformed into designs for innovation involve methods that are critical to the development of social technology and are distinctive to the evolving developmental research methodology.

The three phases of developmental research proper are analysis, development, and evaluation, each of which has distinctive operational steps. These phases of developmental research are the essential phases in the DR&U model that come before the phases of diffusion and adoption or utilization. The full sequence of phases (analysis, development, evaluation, diffusion, and adoption), with their constituent steps and conditions, is termed *developmental research and utilization* (DR&U).

EPILOGUE AND CONCLUSION

An engineering professor assigned all first-year engineering students the difficult project of making a contraption that would drop raw eggs from a 50-foot fire tower without breaking them. The devices had to be original and inexpensive. In the most ingenious device, which cost around 20 cents, the student inventor forced the egg inside a balloon, then blew up the balloon and surrounded it with four other balloons to make a pyramid-shaped object in which the egg survived the test.

Counterparts of such training in social work and in related fields, given present educational philosophy and methods, would be most unusual indeed. The mission of social workers, however, like that of engineers, consists of more than learning about, using, and presiding over in existing technology. They can be active participants in developing the technological innovations upon which the social work profession depends.

Developmental research may be the most appropriate model of research in social work because it consists of methods directed explicitly toward the analysis, development, and evaluation of the technical means by which social work objectives are achieved—namely, its interventional technology. Conventional research methodology oriented to knowledge development should continue to be studied, but developmental research should also be taught as a research methodology. Orienting social work instruction, training, and research toward the generation of interventional innovations would move developmental research more rapidly toward status as a mature methodology for social work research and development.

REFERENCES

Afidi, R. J. (1971). Informed consent: A study of patient reaction. *Journal of the American Medical Association, 216,* 1325-1329.

Agnew, N. M., & Pyke, S. W. (1969). *The science game: An introduction to research in the behavioral sciences.* Englewood Cliffs, NJ: Prentice-Hall.

American Association on Mental Deficiency. (1977). *Consent handbook* (No. 3). Washington, DC: Author.

American Psychological Association. (1973). *Ethical principles in the conduct of research with human participants.* Washington, DC: Author.

American Psychological Association. (1977). *Standards for providers of psychological services.* Washington, DC: Author.

American Psychological Association. (1983). *Publication manual* (3rd ed.). Washington, DC: Author.

Anastasi, A. (1976). *Psychological testing* (4th ed.). New York: Macmillan.

Antler, S. (1978). Child abuse: An emerging social priority. *Social Work, 23,* 58-62.

Arkava, M. L., & Lane, T. A. (1983). *Beginning social work research.* Boston: Allyn & Bacon.

Arkava, M. L., & Snow, M. (1978). *Psychological tests and social work practice.* Springfield, IL: Charles C Thomas.

Aronson, S. H., & Sherwood, C. (1967). Researcher versus practitioner: Problems in social action research. *Social Work, 12,* 89-96.

Atherton, C. R., & Klemmack, D. L. (1982). *Research methods in social work.* Lexington, MA: D. C. Heath & Co.

Attewell, P. (1974). Ethnomethodology since Garfinkel. *Theory and Society, 1,* 179-210.

Attkisson, C. C., Hargreaves, W. A., Horowitz, M. J., & Sorensen, J. E. (Eds.). (1978). *Evaluation of human service programs.* New York: Academic Press.

AuClaire, P.A. (1984). Public attitudes toward social welfare expenditures. *Social Work, 29,* 139-144.

Austin, D. M. (1978). Research and social work: Educational paradoxes and possibilities. *Journal of Social Service Research, 2,* 159-176.

Austin, D. M. (1981). Policy research. In R. M. Grinnell, Jr. (Ed.), *Social work research and evaluation* (pp. 291-315). Itasca, IL: F. E. Peacock Publishers.

Austin, M. J., Cox, G., Gottlieb, N., Hawkins, D. J., Kruzich, J. M., & Rauch, R. (1982). *Evaluating your agency's programs.* Beverly Hills, CA: Sage Publications.

Austin, M. J., & Crowell, J. (1981). Survey research. In R. M. Grinnell, Jr. (Ed.), *Social work research and evaluation* (pp. 226-254). Itasca, IL: F. E. Peacock Publishers.

Babbie, E. R. (1979). *The practice of social research* (2nd ed.). Belmont, CA: Wadsworth.

Babbie, E. R. (1982). *Social research for consumers.* Belmont, CA: Wadsworth.

Bailey, K. D. (1978). *Methods of social research.* New York: Free Press.

Bailey, K. D. (1982). *Methods of social research* (2nd ed.). New York: Free Press.

Baker, R. (1975). Toward generic social work research—A review and some innovations. *British Journal of Social Work, 5,* 193-215.

Ballard, K. D., & Glynn, T. (1975). Behavioral self-management in story writing with elementary school children. *Journal of Applied Behavior Analysis, 8,* 387-398.

Bar-Hillel, Y. (1964). Indexical expressions. *Mind, 63,* 359-379.

Barlow, D. H., Hayes, S. C. & Nelson, R. O. (1983). *The scientist practitioner: Research and accountability in clinical and educational settings.* Elmsford, NY: Pergamon Press.

Barth, R. P. (1981). Education for practice-research: Toward a reorientation. *Journal of Education for Social Work, 17,* 19-25.

Bartlett, H. M. (1958). Toward clarification and improvement of social work practice. *Social Work, 3,* 3-9.

Basom, R. E., Jr., Iacono-Harris, D. A., & Kraybill, D. B. (1982). Statistically speaking: Social work students are significant. *Journal of Education for Social Work, 18,* 20-26.

Baumrind, D. (1964). Some thoughts on ethics of research: After reading Milgram's "Behavioral study of obedience." *American Psychologist, 19,* 421-423.

Beals, R. (1969). *Politics of social research.* Hawthorne, NY: Aldine Publishing.

Beck, A. T. (1967). *Depression: Causes and treatment.* Philadelphia: University of Pennsylvania Press.

Becker, H. (1958). Problems of inference and proof in participant observation. *American Sociological Review, 23,* 652-660.

Beckerman, A. H. (1978). Differentiating between social research and social work research: Implications for teaching. *Journal of Education for Social Work, 14,* 9-15.

Beecher, H. K. (1966). Consent in clinical experimentation: Myth and reality. *Journal of American Medical Association, 195,* 124-125.

Beere, C. A. (1979). *Women and women's issues: A handbook of tests and measures.* San Francisco: Jossey-Bass.

Beless, D. W. (1981). Univariate analysis. In R. M. Grinnell, Jr. (Ed.), *Social work research and evaluation* (pp. 445-460). Itasca, IL: F. E. Peacock Publishers.

Bell, W. (1983). *Contemporary social welfare.* New York: Macmillan.

Benney, M., Riesman, D., & Star, S. (1956). Age and sex with the interview. *American Journal of Sociology, 62,* 143-152.

Berger, R., & Piliavin, I. (1976). The effect of casework: A research note. *Social Work, 21,* 205-208.

Berkman, B. (1981). Knowledge base needs for effective social work practice in health. *Journal of Education for Social Work, 17,* 85-90.

Berkum, M., Bialek, H. M., Kern, R. P., & Yagi, K. (1962). Experimental studies of psychological stress in man. *Psychological Monographs: General and Applied, 76,* 1-39.

Bernstein, R. (1976). *The restructuring of social and political history.* New York: Harcourt Brace Jovanovich.

Bettelheim, B. (March 1, 1982). Reflections: Freud and the soul. *New Yorker,* 52.

Biestek, F. P. (1977). The supreme value in social work: Its meaning and implementation. In D. C. Woods (Ed.), *Personal values and professional decisions* (pp. 1-12). Chicago: Loyola University Press.

Bigman, S. K. (1961). Evaluating the effectiveness of religious programs. *Review of Religious Research, 2,* 97-108.

Billups, J. O. (1984). Unifying social work: Importance of center-moving ideas. *Social Work, 29,* 173-180.

Black, J. A., & Champion, D. J. (1976). *Methods and issues in social research.* New York: John Wiley & Sons.

Blackman, D. K., Howe, M. W., & Pinkston, E. M. (1976). Increasing participation in social interaction of the institutionalized elderly. *The Gerontologist, 16,* 69-76.

Blalock, H. M., Jr. (1969). *Theory construction.* Englewood Cliffs, NJ: Prentice-Hall.

Blalock, H. M., Jr. (1972). *Social statistics* (2nd ed.). New York: McGraw-Hill.

Blalock, H. M., Jr. (1982). *Conceptualization and measurement in the social sciences.* Beverly Hills, CA: Sage Publications.

Blalock, H. M., Jr. (1984). *Basic dilemmas in the social sciences.* Beverly Hills, CA: Sage Publications.

Blalock, H. M., Jr., & Blalock, A. B. (Eds.). (1968). *Methodology in social research.* New York: McGraw-Hill.

Bloom, M. (1975). *The paradox of helping: Introduction to the philosophy of scientific practice.* New York: John Wiley & Sons.

Bloom, M., & Block, S. R. (1977). Evaluating one's own effectiveness and efficiency. *Social Work, 22,* 130-136.

Bloom, M., & Fischer, J. (1982). *Evaluating practice: Guidelines for the accountable professional.* Englewood Cliffs, NJ: Prentice-Hall.

Bloom, M., & Gordon, W. E. (1978). Measurement through practice. *Journal of Education for Social Work, 14,* 10-15.

Bogal, R. B., & Singer, M. J. (1981). Research coursework in the baccalaureate social work curriculum: A study. *Journal of Education for Social Work, 17,* 45-50.

Bogdan, R., & Taylor, S. (1975). *Introduction to qualitative research methods.* New York: John Wiley & Sons.

Borowski, A. (1980). The adequacy of social security retirement benefits: Simulation projections. *Social Work Research and Abstracts, 16,* 7-13.

Bossert, S. T. (1979). *Tasks and social relationships in classrooms.* New York: Cambridge University Press.

Bostwick, G. J., & Kyte, N. S. (1981). Measurement. In R. M. Grinnell, Jr. (Ed.), *Social work research and evaluation* (pp. 93-129). Itasca, IL: F. E. Peacock Publishers.

Brager, G. A., & Holloway, S. (1978). *Changing human service organizations: Politics and practice.* New York: Free Press.

Brager, G. A., & Purcell, F. P. (Eds.). (1967). *Community action against poverty.* New Haven, CT: College and University Press.

Brenner, M. N. (1976). The quest for viable research in social services: Development of the ministudy. *Social Service Review, 50,* 124-137.

Briar, S. (1968). The casework predicament. *Social Work, 13,* 5-12.

Briar, S. (1973). The age of accountability. *Social Work, 18,* 2, 14.

Briar, S. (1980). Toward thtegration of practice and research. In D. Fanshel (Ed.), *Future of social work research* (pp. 31-37). Washington, DC: National Association of Social Workers.

Briar, S. (1981). The project on research utilization in social work education. In S. Briar, H. Weissman, & A. Rubin (Eds.), *Research utilization in social work education* (pp. 1-5). New York: Council on Social Work Education.

Briar, S., & Miller, H. J. (1971). *Problems and issues in social casework.* New York: Columbia University Press.

Briar, S., Weissman, H., & Rubin, A. (Eds.). (1981). *Research utilization in social work education.* New York: Council on Social Work Education.

Brieland, D. (1969). Black identity and the helping person. *Children, 16,* 170-176.

Brieland, D. (1978). A report for the new year. *Social Work, 23,* 2, 84.

Brieland, D. (1979). Journals: Will more be better? *Social Work, 24,* 86, 165.

Brieland, D. (1980). Public and voluntary agencies. In D. Brieland, L. B. Costin, & C. R. Atherton (Eds.), *Contemporary social work* (pp. 54-55). New York: McGraw-Hill.

Bronowski, J. (1973). *The ascent of man.* London: British Broadcasting Corporation.

Brown, E. G. (1981). Selection and formulation of a research problem. In R. M. Grinnell, Jr. (Ed.), *Social work research and evaluation* (pp. 35-45). Itasca, IL: F. E. Peacock Publishers.

Brown, J. A. (1975). Research by practitioners. *Social Work, 20,* 501.

Brown, L. B., & Levitt, J. L. (1978). Some comments on training practitioner researchers in social work education. *Social Service Review, 52,* 644-647.

Browning, R. M., & Stover, D. O. (1971). *Behavior modification in child treatment.* Hawthorne, NY: Aldine Publishing.

Bruyn, S. T. (1966). *The human perspective in sociology: The methodology of participant observation.* Englewood Cliffs, NJ: Prentice-Hall.

Bucher, R., & Strauss, A. (1961). Professions in process. *American Journal of Sociology, 66,* 325-334.

Buros, O. K. (Ed.). (1968). *Reading tests and reviews.* Highland Park, NJ: Gryphon Press.

Buros, O. K. (Ed.). (1978). *The eighth mental measurements yearbook,* 2 Vols. Highland Park, NJ: Gryphon Press.

Butler, H., Davis, I., & Kukonnen, R. (1979). The logic of case comparison. *Social Work Research and Abstracts, 15,* 3-11.

Callahan, D., & Jennings, B. (Eds.). (1983). *Ethics, the social sciences, and policy analysis.* New York: Plenum Press.

Campbell, D. T., & Stanley, J. C. (1963). *Experimental and quasi-experimental designs for research.* Skokie, IL: Rand McNally.

Campbell, N. R. (1952). *What is science?* New York: Dover.

Carkhuff, R. R. (1973). *Art of problem solving.* Amherst, MA: Human Development Press.

Carr, L. W. (1980). Social work research at Howard University. In R. W. Weinbach, & A. Rubin (Eds.), *Teaching social work research: Alternative programs and strategies* (pp. 52-57). New York: Council on Social Work Education.

Carver, R. (1978). The case against statistical significance testing. *Harvard Educational Review, 48,* 378-399.

Case, L. P., & Lingerfelt, N. B. (1974). Name-calling: The labeling process in the social work interview. *Social Service Review, 48,* 75-86.

Casselman, B. L. (1972). On the practitioner's orientation toward research. *Smith College Studies in Social Work, 42,* 211-233.

Cautela, J. R. (1977). *Behavior analysis forms for clinical intervention.* Champaign, IL: Research Press.

Chambers, D. E. (1976). The trouble with secrets: A radical revision of the teaching of research in the social work curriculum. *Arete, 4,* 1-13.

Champion, D. J. (1970). *Basic statistics for social research.* New York: Harper & Row.

Charlesworth, M. (1982). *Science, neo-science and pseudo-science.* Geelong, Victoria, Australia: Deakin University Press.

Chatterjee, P. (1984). Cognitive theories and social work practice. *Social Service Review, 58,* 63-80.

Chun, Ki-Taek, Cobb, S., & French, J. R., Jr. (1975). *Measures for psychological assessment: A guide to 3,000 original sources and their applications.* Ann Arbor, MI: Institute for Social Research.

Churchill, L. (1971). Ethnomethodology and measurement. *Social Forces, 50,* 182-191.

Cicourel, A. V. (1968). *The social organization of juvenile justice.* New York: John Wiley & Sons.

Cicourel, A. V. (1973). *Cognitive sociology.* New York: Free Press.

Clark, A. (1983). *Social science: Introduction to theory and method.* Englewood Cliffs, NJ: Prentice-Hall.

Clemens, W. V. (1971). Test administration. In R. L. Thorndike (Ed.), *Educational measurement* (2nd ed., pp. 108-119). Washington, DC: American Council on Education.

Compton, B. R., & Galaway, B. (1984). *Social work processes* (3rd ed.). Homewood, IL: Dorsey Press.

Comrey A., Barker, T., & Glaser, E. (1975). *A sourcebook for mental health measures.* Los Angeles: Human Interaction Research Institute.

Coser, L. A. (1975). Presidential address: Two methods in search of a substance. *American Sociological Review, 40,* 691-700.

Council on Social Work Education (1982). Curriculum policy for the master's and baccalaureate degree programs in social work education. *Social Work Education Reporter, 30,* 5-12.

Crane, J. (1966). Utilizing the fundamentals of science in educating for social work practice. *Journal of Education for Social Work, 2,* 22-29.

Crittenden, K. S., & Hill, R. J. (1971). Coding reliability and validity of interview data. *American Sociological Review, 36,* 1037-1080.

Cronbach, L. J. (1951). Coefficient alpha and the internal structure of tests. *Psychometrika, 16,* 297-334.

Cronbach, L. J. (1970). *Essentials of psychological testing* (3rd ed.). New York: Harper & Row.

Dabbs, J. M., Jr. (1982). Making things visible. In J. Van Maanen, J. M. Dabbs, Jr., & R. R. Faulkner (Eds.), *Varieties of qualitative research* (pp. 97-123). Beverly Hills, CA: Sage Publications.

Dea, K. L. (1981). Project recommendations. In S. Briar, H. Weissman, & A. Rubin (Eds.), *Research utilization in social work education* (pp. 66-73). New York: Council on Social Work Education.

DeMaria, W. (1981). Empiricism: An impoverished philosophy for social work research. *Australian Social Work, 34,* 3-8.

Denzin, N. K. (Ed.). (1970a). *The research act: A theoretical introduction to sociological methods.* Hawthorne, NY: Aldine Publishing.

Denzin, N. K. (1970b). Symbolic interactionism and ethnomethodology. In J. D. Douglas (Ed.), *Understanding everyday life* (pp. 259-284). Hawthorne, NY: Aldine Publishing.

Department of Health, Education and Welfare. (1978). *Code of federal regulations, title 45: Public welfare.* Washington, DC: U.S. Government Printing Office.

Deutscher, I. (1966). Words and deeds. *Social Problems, 13,* 235-254.

Dewey, J. (1933). *How we think* (rev. ed.). Lexington, MA: D. C. Heath & Co.

Diener, E., & Crandall, R. (1978). *Ethics in social and behavioral research.* Chicago: University of Chicago Press.

Dillman, D. A. (1978). *Mail and telephone surveys: The total design method.* New York: John Wiley & Sons.

Dohrenwend, B. S. (1965). Some effects of open and close questions on respondents' answers. *Human Organization, 24,* 197-184.

Dohrenwend, B. S., Colombatos, J., & Dohrenwend, B. P. (1968). Social distance and interview effects. *Public Opinion Quarterly, 32,* 410-422.

Downs, W. R., & Robertson, J. F. (1983). Preserving the social work perspective in the research sequence: State of the art and program models for the 1980s. *Journal of Education for Social Work, 19,* 87-95.

Dreitzel, H. P. (Ed.). (1970). *Recent sociology number 2.* New York: Macmillan.

Duehn, W. D. (1981). The process of social work practice and research. In R. M. Grinnell, Jr. (Ed.), *Social work research and evaluation* (pp. 11-34). Itasca, IL: F. E. Peacock Publishers.

Duehn, W. D., & Mayadas, N. S. (1976). The effects of practice orientations on clinical assessment. *American Journal of Orthopsychiatry, 46,* 629-636.

Duehn, W. D., & Mayadas, N. S. (1977a). Entrance and exit requirements in professional social work education. *Journal of Education for Social Work, 13,* 22-29.

Duehn, W. D., & Mayadas, N. S. (1977b). The use of stimulus/modeling videotapes in assertive training for homosexuals. In J. Fischer, & H. L. Gochros (Eds.), *Handbook of behavior therapy with sexual problems* (Vol. 2, pp. 431-438). Elmsford, NY: Pergamon Press.

Duehn, W. D., & Mayadas, N. S. (1979). Starting where the client is: An empirical investigation. *Social Casework, 60,* 67-74.

Duehn, W. D., & Proctor, E. K. (1974). A study of cognitive complexity in the education for social work practice. *Journal of Education for Social Work, 10,* 20-26.

Durkheim, E. (1966). *The rules of sociological method.* New York: Free Press.

Eaton, J. W. (1962). Symbolic and substantive evaluative research. *Administrative Science Quarterly, 6,* 42-44.

Eaton, J. W. (1967). Training social work researchers: A curriculum innovation. *Social Work Education Reporter, 15,* 16-17, 32.

Edsall, G. (1969). A positive approach to the problem of human experimentation. *Daedalus, 98,* 463-479.

Eldridge, W. D. (1983). Conceptualizing self-evaluation of clinical practice. *Social Work, 28,* 57-61.

Else, J. F. (1978). Social work journals: Purpose and trends. *Social Work, 23,* 267-273.

Else, J. F. (1979). Else replys. *Social Work, 24,* 68-69.

Emerson, R. M. (1969). *Judging delinquents.* Hawthorne, NY: Aldine Publishing.

Emerson, R. M., & Pollner, M. (1976). Dirty work designations: Their features and consequences in a psychiatric setting. *Social Problems, 23,* 243-254.

Emerson, R. M., & Pollner, M. (1978). Policies and practices of psychiatric case selection. *Sociology of Work and Occupations, 5,* 75-96.

Epstein, I., & Conrad, K. (1978). The empirical limits of social work professionalization. In R. C. Sarri, & Y. Hasenfeld (Eds.), *The management of human services* (pp. 163-183). New York: Columbia University Press.

Epstein, I., & Tripodi, T. (1977). *Research techniques for program planning, monitoring and evaluation.* New York: Columbia University Press.

Epstein, L. (1981). Teaching research-based practice: Rationale and method. *Journal of Education for Social Work, 17,* 51-55.

Erickson, F. (1975). Gatekeeping and the melting pot: Interaction in counseling encounters. *Harvard Educational Review, 45,* 44-70.

Etzioni, A. (1960). Two approaches to organizational analysis: A critique and a suggestion. *Administrative Science Quarterly, 5,* 257-278.

Evans, P. (1976). The Burt affair . . . sleuthing in science. *American Psychological Association Monitor, 7,* 1, 4.

Ewalt, P. L., Cohen, M., & Harmatz, J. S. (1972). Prediction of treatment acceptance by child guidance clinic applicants: An easily applied instrument. *American Journal of Orthopsychiatry, 42,* 857-864.

Ewing, D. (1974). *Writing for results in business, government and the professions.* New York: John Wiley & Sons.

Fabricant, M. (1982). *Juveniles in the family courts.* Lexington, MA: Lexington Books.

Fairweather, G. (1967). *Methods for experimental social intervention.* New York: John Wiley & Sons.

Falck, H. S. (1984). The membership model of social work. *Social Work, 29,* 155-159.

Fanshel, D. (Ed.). (1980). *Future of social work research.* Washington, DC: National Association of Social Workers.

Fay, B. (1975). *Social theory and political practice.* Winchester, MA: Allen & Unwin.

Fellin, P. (1984). Book review. Review of *Research and evaluation in the human services. Social Service Review, 58,* 154-155.

Filstead, W. J. (Ed.). (1970). *Qualitative methodology: Firsthand involvement with the social world.* Chicago: Markham Publishing.

Finestone, S., & Kahn, A. J. (1975). The design of research. In N. A. Polansky (Ed.), *Social work research: Methods for the helping professions* (rev. ed., pp. 38-67). Chicago: University of Chicago Press.

Fischer, J. (Ed.). (1973a). *Interpersonal helping: Emerging approaches for social work practice.* Springfield, IL: Charles C Thomas.

Fischer, J. (1973b). Is casework effective: A review? *Social Work, 18,* 5-21.

Fischer, J. (1976a). Do social workers understand research? *Journal of Education for Social Work, 12,* 63-70.

Fischer, J. (1976b). *The effectiveness of social casework.* Springfield, IL: Charles C Thomas.

Fischer, J. (1978). *Effective casework practice: An eclectic approach.* New York: McGraw-Hill.

Fischer, J. (1981a). A framework for evaluating empirical research reports. In R. M. Grinnell, Jr. (Ed.), *Social work research and evaluation* (pp. 569-589). Itasca, IL: F. E. Peacock Publishers.

Fischer, J. (1981b). New and emerging methods of direct practice: The revolution in social work. In N. Gilbert, & H. Specht (Eds.), *Handbook of the social services* (pp. 525-547). Englewood Cliffs, NJ: Prentice-Hall.

Fischer, J. (1981c). The social work revolution. *Social Work, 26,* 199-207.

Fischer, J. (1983). Evaluations of social work effectiveness: Is positive evidence always good evidence? *Social Work, 28,* 74-77.

Fischer, J. (1984). Revolution, schmevolution: Is social work changing or not? *Social Work, 29,* 91-74.

Fischer, J., & Gochros, H. L. (1975). *Planned behavior change: Behavior modification in social work.* New York: Free Press.

Fischer, J., & Hudson, W. W. (1976). An effect of casework? Back to the drawing board. *Social Work, 21,* 347-349.

Fischer, J., & Hudson, W. W. (1980). Increasing the relevance of research education: The University of Hawaii program. In R. W. Weinbach, & A. Rubin (Eds.), *Teaching social work research: Alternative programs and strategies* (pp. 23-29). New York: Council on Social Work Education.

Fischer, J., & Hudson, W. W. (1983). Measurement of client problems for improved practice. In A. Rosenblatt, & D. Waldfogel (Eds.), *Handbook of clinical social work* (pp. 457-471). San Francisco: Jossey-Bass.

Fiske, D. W. (1971). *Measuring the concepts of personality.* Hawthorne, NY: Aldine Publishing.

French, J. L. (1979). Intelligence: Its measurement and its relevance for education. *Professional Psychology, 10,* 753-759.

Friedrich, W. M., Greenberg, M. T., & Crnic, K. A. (1983). A short form of the questionnaire on resources and stress. *American Journal of Mental Deficiency, 88,* 41-48.

Friedrichs, R. S. (1970). *A sociology of sociology.* New York: Free Press.

Gambrill, E. D. (1977). *Behavior modification: Handbook of assessment, intervention and evaluation.* San Francisco: Jossey-Bass.

Gambrill, E. D. (1983). *Casework: A competency based approach.* Englewood Cliffs, NJ: Prentice-Hall.

Gambrill, E. D., & Barth, R. P. (1978). Single-case experimentations: Conflicts and choices. *Social Work Research and Abstracts, 14,* 20-31.

Gambrill, E. D., & Richey, C. A. (1975). An assertion inventory for use in assessment and research. *Behavior Therapy, 6,* 550-561.

Garfield, S. L., & Bergin, A. E. (Eds.). (1978). *Handbook of psychotherapy and behavior change: An empirical analysis* (2nd ed.). New York: John Wiley & Sons.

Garfinkel, H. (1964). Studies of the routine grounds of everyday activities. *Social Problems, 11,* 225-250.

Garfinkel, H. (1967). *Studies in ethnomethodology.* Englewood Cliffs, NJ: Prentice-Hall.

Garvin, C. D. (1981). Research-related roles for social workers. In R. M. Grinnell, Jr. (Ed.), *Social work research and evaluation* (pp. 547-552). Itasca, IL: F. E. Peacock Publishers.

Garvin, C. D., & Seabury, B. A. (1984). *Interpersonal practice in social work: Processes and procedures.* Englewood Cliffs, NJ: Prentice-Hall.

Geismar, L. L. (1982). Comments on "The obsolete scientific imperative in social work research." *Social Service Review, 56,* 311-312.

Geismar, L. L., & LaSorte, M. A. (1963). Research interviewing with low-income families. *Social Work, 8,* 10-14.

Geismar, L. L., & Wood, K. M. (1982). Evaluating practice: Science as faith. *Social Casework, 63,* 266-272.

Gellner, E. (1975). Ethnomethodology: The re-enchantment industry or the Californian way of subjectivity. *Philosophy of the Social Sciences, 5,* 431-450.

Gelman, S. R. (1983). The board of directors and agency accountability. *Contemporary Social Work, 64,* 83-96.

Germain, C. B. (1981). The ecological approach to people-environment transactions. *Social Casework, 62,* 323-331.

Gibbons, D. C. (1975). Unidentified research sites and fictitious names. *American Sociologist, 10,* 32-36.

Gidlow, B. (1972). Ethnomethodology: A new name for old practices. *British Journal of Sociology, 23,* 395-405.

Gilbert, J. P., Mosteller, F., & Tukey, J. W. (1976). Steady social progress requires quantitative evaluation to be searching. In C. C. Apt (Ed.), *The evaluation of social programs* (pp. 67-81). Beverly Hills, CA: Sage Publications.

Gilbert, N., & Specht, H. (1976). Advocacy and professional ethics. *Social Work, 21,* 288-293.

Gingerich, O. (1982). The Galileo affair. *Scientific American, 247,* 119-127, 134.

Gingerich, W. J. (1978). Measuring the process. *Social Work, 24,* 251-252.

Gingerich, W. J. (1983). Significance testing in single-case research. In A. Rosenblatt, & D. Waldfogel (Eds.), *Handbook of clinical social work* (pp. 124-134). San Francisco: Jossey-Bass.

Gingerich, W. J., & Feyerherm, W. H. (1979). The celeration line technique for assessing client change. *Journal of Social Service Research, 3,* 99-113.

Gingerich, W. J., Kleczewski, M., & Kirk, S. A. (1982). Name-calling in social work. *Social Service Review, 56,* 336-374.

Giuli, C. A., & Hudson, W. W. (1977). Assessing parent-child relationship disorders in clinical practice: The child's point of view. *Journal of Social Service Research, 1,* 77-92.

Glaser, B. G., & Strauss, A. L. (1967). *The discovery of grounded theory: Strategies for qualitative research.* Hawthorne, NY: Aldine Publishing.

Glisson, C. (1982). Research teaching in social work education. *Social Service Review, 56,* 629-639.

Gochros, H. L. (1970). The caseworker-adoptive parent relationships in post-placement services. In A. Kadushin (Ed.), *Child welfare services* (pp. 86-97). New York: Macmillan.

Gochros, H. L. (1978a). Counseling gay husbands. *Journal of Sex Education and Therapy, 4,* 6-10.

Gochros, H. L. (1978b). Foreword. In J. Fischer. *Effective casework practice: An eclectic approach* (pp. ix-xi). New York: McGraw-Hill.

Gochros, H. L. (1981). Research interviewing. In R. M. Grinnell, Jr. (Ed.), *Social work research and evaluation* (pp. 255-290). Itasca, IL: F. E. Peacock Publishers.

Goffman, E. (1959). *The presentation of self in everyday life.* Garden City, NY: Doubleday-Anchor Books.

Goldman, B. A., & Saunders, J. L. (1974). *Directory of unpublished experimental mental measures* (Vol. 1). New York: Human Sciences Press.

Goldstein, H. K. (1969). *Research standards and methods for social workers.* Wheeling, IL: Whitehall Co.

Goldstein, H. K., & Horder, L. (1974). Suggested teaching plans for maximizing research learning of three types of social work students. *Journal of Education for Social Work, 10,* 30-35.

Goldstein, H. K., & Proctor, J. (1980). Program evaluation training. In R. W. Weinbach, & A. Rubin (Eds.), *Teaching social work research: Alternative programs and strategies* (pp. 58-67). New York: Council on Social Work Education.

Goldstein, H. K. (1973). *Social work practice: A unitary approach.* Columbia, SC: University of South Carolina Press.

Goode, W., & Hatt, P. K. (1952). *Methods in social research.* New York: McGraw-Hill.

Gorden, J. E. (1984). Creating research-based practice principles: A model. *Social Work Research and Abstracts, 20,* 3-6.

Gordon, W. E. (1983). Social work revolution or evolution? *Social Work, 28,* 181-185.

Gordon, W. E. (1984). Gordon replies: Making social work a science-based profession. *Social Work, 29,* 74-75.

Gorsuch, R. L. (1981). Bivariate analysis: Analysis of variance. In R. M. Grinnell, Jr. (Ed.), *Social work research and evaluation* (pp. 500-529). Itasca, IL: F. E. Peacock Publishers.

Gottlieb, N., & Richey, C. (1980). Education of human services practitioners for clinical evaluation. In R. W. Weinbach, & A. Rubin (Eds.), *Teaching social work research: Alternative programs and strategies* (pp. 3-12). New York: Council on Social Work Education.

Gottman, J., & Leiblum, S. S. (1974). *How to do psychotherapy and how to evaluate it: A manual for beginners.* New York: Holt, Rinehart, & Winston.

Gould, J., & Kolb, W. (Eds.). (1964). *A dictionary of the social sciences.* New York: Free Press.

Gouldner, A. W. (1969). Organizational analysis. In R. K. Merton, L. Broom, & L. S. Cottrell, Jr. (Eds.), *Sociology today* (pp. 400-410). New York: Basic Books.

Gouldner, A. W. (1970). *The coming crisis of western sociology.* New York: Basic Books.

Grebler, L., Moore, J. W., & Guzman, R. C. (1970). *The Mexican American people.* New York: Free Press.

Greer, S. (1969). *The logic of inquiry.* Hawthorne, NY: Aldine Publishing.

Grinnell, R. M., Jr. (1981a). Becoming a knowledge-based social worker. In R. M. Grinnell, Jr. (Ed.), *Social work research and evaluation* (pp. 1-8). Itasca, IL: F. E. Peacock Publishers.

Grinnell, R. M., Jr. (Ed.). (1981b). *Social work research and evaluation.* Itasca, IL: F. E. Peacock Publishers.

Grinnell, R. M., Jr. (1982a). Book review. Review of *Social welfare in society. Journal of Education for Social Work, 18,* 121-122.

Grinnell, R. M., Jr. (1982b). The educational needs of private practitioners: A research note. *Contemporary Social Work Education, 5,* 59-67.

Grinnell, R. M., Jr. (1983). Quantitative articles in social work journals: A research note. *Arete, 8,* 33-38.

Grinnell, R. M., Jr., & Hill, L. S. (1979a). Do agency administrative changes affect the effectiveness and efficiency of DHR employees? *Journal of Sociology and Social Welfare, 6,* 503-508.

Grinnell, R. M., Jr., & Hill, L. S. (1979b). The perceived effectiveness and efficiency of DHR employees. *Social Service Review, 53,* 116-122.

Grinnell, R. M., Jr., & Jung, S. (1981). Children placed with relatives. *Social Work Research and Abstracts, 17,* 31-32.

Grinnell, R. M., Jr., & Kyte, N. S. (1976). Measuring faculty competence: A model. *Journal of Education for Social Work, 12,* 44-50.

Grinnell, R. M., Jr., & Kyte, N. S. (1977). A model for bridging the gap between undergraduate research and practice. *Journal of Education for Social Work, 13,* 30-36.

Grinnell, R. M., Jr., & Kyte, N. S. (1979). Anxiety level as an indicator of academic performance during the first semester of graduate work. *Journal of Psychology, 101,* 199-201.

Grinnell, R. M., & Lieberman, A. A. (1981). Helping mentally retarded persons get jobs. In S. P. Schinke (Ed.), *Behavioral methods in social welfare* (pp. 209-222). Hawthorne, NY: Aldine Publishing.

Grinnell, R. M., Jr., & Royer, M. L. (1983). Authors of articles in social work journals. *Journal of Social Service Research, 6,* 147-154.

Gripton, J. M. (1978). Research education for clinical social workers: An intermediate approach. *Journal of Education for Social Work, 14,* 49-55.

Grossman, B. (1980). Teaching research in the field practicum. *Social Work, 25,* 36-39.

Guilford, J. P. (1965). *Fundamental statistics in psychology and education* (4th ed.). New York: McGraw-Hill.

Hakim, C. (1982). *Secondary analysis in social research: A guide to data sources and methods with examples.* London: Allen & Unwin.

Hammersley, M., & Atkinson, P. (1983). *Ethnography: Principals in practice.* London: Tavistock Publications.

Hamovitch, M. (1963). Research interviewing in terminal illness. *Social Work, 8,* 4-9.

Haselkorn, F. (1978). Accountability in clinical practice. *Social Casework, 59,* 330-336.

Havelock, R. G. (1973). *Planning for innovation through dissemination in utilization of knowledge.* Ann Arbor, MI: Institute for Social Research.

Haynes, C., & Wilson, C. (1979). *Behavioral assessment.* San Francisco: Jossey-Bass.

Hays, W. L., & Winkler, R. L. (1971). *Statistics: Probability, inference and decision.* New York: Holt, Rinehart, & Winston.

Haywood, H. C. (1977). The ethics of doing research . . . and not doing it. *American Journal of Mental Deficiency, 81,* 311-317.

Heap, J. L. (1975). Non-indexical action. *Philosophy of the Social Sciences, 5,* 393-409.

Heap, J. L. (1977). Verstehen, language and warrants. *Sociological Quarterly, 18,* 177-184.

Heffernan, J., & Turman, B. (1981). Searching the literature. In R. M. Grinnell, Jr. (Ed.), *Social work research and evaluation* (pp. 46-56). Itasca, IL: F. E. Peacock Publishers.

Heineman, M. B. (1981). The obsolete scientific imperative in social work research. *Social Service Review, 55,* 371-397.

Heller, C. (1971). *New converts to the American dream: Mobility aspirations of young Mexican Americans.* New Haven, CT: College & University Press.

Hersen, M., & Barlow, D. H. (1976). *Single case experimental designs: Strategies for studying behavior change.* Elmsford, NY: Pergamon Press.

Hershey, N., & Miller, R. D. (1976). *Human experimentation and the law.* Germantown, MD: Aspen Systems Corp.

Hess, E. H. (1965). Attitudes and pupil size. *Scientific American, 212,* 46-54.

Hilbert, R. A. (1977). Approaching reason's edge: "Nonsense" as the final solution to the problem of meaning. *Sociological Inquiry, 47,* 25-31.

Hobbs, N. (Ed.). (1975). *Issues in the classification of children: A sourcebook on categories, labels and their consequences* (2 vols.). San Francisco: Jossey-Bass.

Hollingshead, A. B., & Redlich, F. C. (1958). *Social class and mental illness.* New York: John Wiley & Sons.

Hollis, F., & Woods, M. E. (1981). *Casework: A psychosocial therapy* (3rd ed.). New York: Random House.

Hoshino, G., & Lynch, M. M. (1981). Secondary analysis of existing data. In R. M. Grinnell, Jr. (Ed.), *Social work research and evaluation* (pp. 333-347). Itasca, IL: F. E. Peacock Publishers.

Hoshino, G., & McDonald, T. P. (1975). Social agencies in the computer age. *Social Work, 20,* 10-14.

Howe, M. W. (1974). Casework self-evaluation: A single-subject approach. *Social Service Review, 48,* 1-23.

Howie, J. (1982). *Ethical principles for social policy.* Carbondale, IL: Southern Illinois University Press.

Hudson, W. W. (1977). Elementary techniques for assessing single-client/single-worker interventions. *Social Service Review, 51,* 311-326.

Hudson, W. W. (1978a). First axioms of treatment. *Social Work, 23,* 65-66.

Hudson, W. W. (1978b). Research training in professional social work education: Issues and problems. *Social Service Review, 52,* 116-121.

Hudson, W. W. (1981). Development and use of indexes and scales. In R. M. Grinnell, Jr. (Ed.), *Social work research and evaluation* (pp. 130-155). Itasca, IL: F. E. Peacock Publishers.

Hudson, W. W. (1982a). *The clinical measurement package: A field manual.* Homewood, IL: Dorsey Press.

Hudson, W. W. (1982b). *The index of spouse abuse.* Tallahassee, FL: Walmyr Publishing.

Hudson, W. W. (1982c). Scientific imperatives in social work research and practice. *Social Service Review, 56,* 246-258.

Hudson, W. W. (1982d). *SPPC manual: A statistical package for the pocket calculator.* Tallahassee, FL: Walmyr Publishing.

Hudson, W. W., & Glisson, D. H. (1976). Assessment of marital discord in social work practice. *Social Service Review, 50,* 293-311.

Hudson, W. W., & Proctor, E. K. (1977). Assessment of depressive affect in clinical practice. *Journal of Consulting and Clinical Psychology, 45,* 1206-1207.

Hudson, W. W., Wung, B., & Borges, M. (1980). Parent-child relationship disorders: The parent's point of view. *Journal of Social Service Research, 3,* 283-294.

Hull, D. B., & Hull, J. H. (1978). Rathus assertiveness schedule: Normative and factor-analytic data. *Behavior Therapy, 9,* 673.

Hunter, M., & Grinnell, R. M., Jr. (1978). A privacy issues scale for social workers. *Journal of Psychology, 100,* 67-69.

Hunter, M., & Grinnell, R. M., Jr. (1983). Social workers' perceptions of privacy: A research note. *Social Work, 28,* 68-69.

Hunter, M., Grinnell, R. M., Jr., & Blanchard, R. (1978). A test of a shorter privacy preference scale. *Journal of Psychology, 98,* 207-210.

Hyman, H. H. (1954). *Interviewing in social research.* Chicago: University of Chicago Press.

Imre, R. W. (1984). The nature of knowledge in social work. *Social Work, 29,* 41-45.

Isaac, S., & Michael, W. B. (1971). *Handbook in research and evaluation.* San Diego: Robert R. Knapp.

Jayaratne, S., & Levy, R. L. (1979). *Empirical clinical practice.* New York: Columbia University Press.

Jenkins, S. (1975). Collecting data by questionnaire and interview. In N. A. Polansky (Ed.), *Social work research: Methods for the helping professions* (rev. ed., pp. 131-153). Chicago: University of Chicago Press.

Jenkins, S., & Norman, E. (1972). *Filial deprivation and foster care.* New York: Columbia University Press.

Jensen, A. R. (1977). Did Sir Cyril Burt fake his research on heritability of intelligence? Part 2. *Phi Delta Kappan, 58,* 471-492.

Johnson, F. C. (1981). Practice versus research: Issues in the teaching of single-subject research skills. *Journal of Education for Social Work, 17,* 62-68.

Johnson, L. C. (1983). *Social work practice: A generalist approach.* Newton, MA: Allyn & Bacon.

Johnson, O. G., & Rommarito, J. (1971). *Tests and measurements in child development: A handbook.* San Francisco: Jossey-Bass.

Jones, L. V. (1971). The nature of measurement. In R. L. Thorndike (Ed.), *Educational measurement* (2nd ed., pp. 335-355). Washington, DC: American Council on Education.

Julian, J., & Kornblum, W. (1983). *Social problems* (4th ed.). Englewood Cliffs, NJ: Prentice-Hall.

Kadushin, A. (1983). *The social work interview* (2nd ed.). New York: Columbia University Press.

Kagle, J. D. (1984a). Restoring the clinical record. *Social Work, 29,* 47-50.

Kagle, J. D. (1984b). *Social work records.* Homewood, IL: Dorsey Press.

Kane, R. A. (1978). Encouraging MSW students to write for publication: A realistic goal of the research curriculum. *Journal of Education for Social Work, 14,* 78-85.

Kane, R. A. (1980). Testing incentives to encourage research activities in newly graduated practitioners: A follow-up study. In R. W. Weinbach, & A. Rubin (Eds.), *Teaching social work research: Alternative programs and strategies* (pp. 68-80). New York: Council on Social Work Education.

Kaplan, A. (1964). *The conduct of inquiry: Methodology for behavioral science.* New York: Harper & Row.

Karger, H. J. (1983). Science, research and social work: Who controls the profession? *Social Work, 28,* 200-205.

Katz, D. (1942). Do interviewers bias polls? *Public Opinion Quarterly, 6,* 248-268.

Katzenberg, A. C. (1975). *How to draw graphs.* Kalamazoo, MI: Behaviordelia.

Kazdin, A. E. (1979). Data evaluation for intrasubject-replication research. *Journal of Social Service Research, 3,* 79-97.

Kazdin, A. E. (1982). *Single case research designs: Methods for clinical and applied settings.* New York: Oxford University Press.

Kelman, H. C. (1968). *A time to speak: On human values and social research.* San Francisco: Jossey-Bass.

Kerlinger, F. N. (1973). *Foundations of behavioral research* (2nd ed.). New York: Holt, Rinehart, & Winston.

Kershaw, D., & Fair, J. (1976). *The New Jersey income-maintenance experiment* (Vol. 1). New York: Academic Press.

Khinduka, S. K. (1977). Editorial. *Journal of Social Service Research, 1,* 3-4.

Kim, P. K. (1977). Research way to the remedy for a professional dilemma in social work. *Arete, 5,* 139-152.

Kirk, S. A., & Fischer, J. (1976). Do social workers understand research? *Journal of Education for Social Work, 12,* 63-70.

Kirk, S. A., & Kolevzon, M. S. (1978). Teaching research methodology from Z to A. *Journal of Education for Social Work, 14,* 66-72.

Kirk, S. A., Osmalov, M. J., & Fischer, J. (1976). Social workers' involvement in research. *Social Work, 21,* 121-124.

Kirk, S. A., & Rosenblatt, A. (1981). Research knowledge and orientation among social work students. In S. Briar, H. Weissman, & A. Rubin (Eds.), *Research utilization in social work education* (pp. 29-39). New York: Council on Social Work Education.

Kish, L. (1965). *Survey sampling.* New York: John Wiley & Sons.

Kogan, L. S. (1950). The electrical recording of the social casework interview. *Social Casework, 30,* 371-378.

Kogan, L. S. (1975). Principles of measurement. In N. A. Polansky (Ed.), *Social work research: Methods for the helping professions* (rev. ed., pp. 68-92). Chicago: University of Chicago Press.

Kolevzon, M. S. (1975). Integrational teaching modalities in social work education: Promise or pretense? *Journal of Education for Social Work, 11,* 60-67.

Kolevzon, M. S. (1981). Bivariate analysis: Correlation. In R. M. Grinnell, Jr. (Ed.), *Social work research and evaluation* (pp. 481-499). Itasca, IL: F. E. Peacock Publishers.

Kolevzon, M. S., & Maykranz, J. (1982). Theoretical orientations and clinical practice. *Social Service Review, 56,* 121-129.

Kramer, R. M., & Specht, H. (1983). *Readings in community organization practice* (3rd ed.). Englewood Cliffs, NJ: Prentice-Hall.

Krathwohl, D. R. (1965). *How to prepare a research proposal.* Syracuse, NY: Syracuse University Press.

Krause, M. S. (1966a). A cognitive theory of motivation for treatment. *Journal of General Psychology, 75,* 9-19.

Krause, M. S. (1966b). Comparative effects on continuance of four experimental intake procedures. *Social Casework, 47,* 515-519.

Krause, M. S. (1966c). Ordinal scaling for convergent validity, object discrimination and resolving power. *Multivariate Behavioral Research, 1,* 379-385.

Krause, M. S. (1967). Behavioral indexes of motivation for treatment. *Journal of General Psychology, 76,* 426-435.

Kraybill, D. B., Iacono-Harris, D. A., & Bascom, R. E., Jr. (1982). Teaching social work research: A consumer's approach. *Journal of Education for Social Work, 18,* 55-61.

Krimmel, H. (1971). *Alcoholism: Challenge for social work education.* New York: Council on Social Work Education.

Krippendorff, K. (1981). *Content analysis: An introduction to its methodology.* Beverly Hills, CA: Sage Publications.

Kuhn, T. S. (1970). *The structure of scientific revolutions* (2nd ed.) Chicago: University of Chicago Press.

Kuhn, T. S. (1977). *The essential tension: Selected studies in scientific tradition and change.* Chicago: University of Chicago Press.

Kurtz, N. R. (1983). *Introduction to social statistics.* New York: McGraw-Hill.

Labovitz, S. (1970). The nonutility of significance tests: The significance tests of significance reconsidered. *Pacific Sociological Review, 13,* 142-147.

Labovitz, S., & Hagedorn, R. (1976). *Introduction to social research* (rev. ed.). New York: McGraw-Hill.

Laird, J. (1984). Sorceres, shamans, and social workers: The use of ritual in social work practice. *Social Work, 29,* 123-129.

Lake, D. G., Miles, M. B., & Earle, R., Jr. (Eds.). (1973). *Measuring human behavior.* New York: Teachers College Press.

LaPiere, R. T. (1934). Attitudes vs. behavior. *Social Forces, 14,* 230-237.

Lazarsfeld, P. F., & Barton, A. (1971). Qualitative measurement in the social sciences. In B. J. Franklin, & H. W. Osborne (Eds.), *Research methods: Issues and insights* (pp. 85-97). Belmont, CA: Wadsworth Publishing.

Lazarus, R. S. (1964). A laboratory approach to the dynamics of psychological stress. *American Psychologist, 19,* 401-411.

Lazerwitz, B. (1968). Sampling theory and procedures. In H. M. Blalock, Jr., & A. B. Blalock (Eds.), *Methodology in social research* (pp. 298-308). New York: McGraw-Hill.

Leedy, P. D. (1980). *Practical research planning and design* (2nd ed.). New York: Macmillan.

Leedy, P. D. (1981). *How to read research and understand it.* New York: Macmillan.

Leinhardt, S. (Ed.). (1984). *Sociological methodology.* Beverly Hills, CA: Sage Publications.

LeMasters, E. E. (1976). *Blue collar aristocrats.* Madison, WI: University of Wisconsin Press.

Levitt, J. L., & Reid, W. J. (1981). Rapid assessment instruments for social work practice. *Social Work Research and Abstracts, 17,* 13-19.

Levy, C. S. (1974). Advocacy and the injustice of justice. *Social Service Review, 48,* 39-50.

Levy, C. S. (1976). Personal versus professional values: The practitioner's dilemma. *Clinical Social Work Journal, 4,* 110-120.

Levy, C. S. (1981). Labeling: The social worker's responsibility. *Social Casework, 62,* 332-342.

Levy, R. L. (1983). Overview of single-case experiments. In A. Rosenblatt & D. Waldfogel (Eds.), *Handbook of clinical social work* (pp. 321-332). San Francisco: Jossey-Bass.

Levy, R. L., & Olson, D. G. (1979). The single-subject methodology in clinical practice: An overview. *Journal of Social Service Research, 3,* 25-49.

Lewis, H. (1982). *The intellectual base of social work practice: Tools for thought in a helping profession.* New York: Haworth Press.

Lewis, O. (1966). *La vida: A Puerto Rican family in the culture of poverty.* New York: Random House.

Liebow, E. (1967). *Tally's corner.* Boston: Little Brown.

Likert, R. (1967). The method of constructing an attitude scale. In M. Fishbein (Ed.), *Readings in attitude theory and measurement* (pp. 90-95). New York: John Wiley & Sons.

Lin, N. (1976). *Foundations of social research.* New York: McGraw-Hill.

Lindsey, D. (1976). Distinction, achievement and editorial board membership. *American Psychologist, 31,* 799-804.

Lindsey, D. (1977a). Participation and influence in publication review processings: A reply. *American Psychologist, 32,* 579-582.

Lindsey, D. (1977b). The processing of self-criticism by social work editorial boards. *American Psychologist, 32,* 1110-1115.

Lindsey, D. (1978a). The operation of professional journals in social work. *Journal of Sociology and Social Welfare, 5,* 273-282.

Lindsey, D. (1978b). *The scientific publication system in social science.* San Francisco: Jossey-Bass.

Lindsey, D. (1979). Social work editorial boards: A debate continued. *Social Work, 24,* 67-68.

Lindsey, D. (1981). Data analysis with the computer. In R. M. Grinnell, Jr. (Ed.), *Social work research and evaluation* (pp. 530-544). Itasca, IL: F. E. Peacock Publishers.

Lindzey, G. (1950). An experimental examination of the scapegoat theory of prejudice. *Journal of Abnormal and Social Psychology, 45,* 296-309.

Locke, H. J., & Wallace, K. M. (1959). Short marital-adjustment and prediction tests: Their reliability and validity. *Journal of Marriage and Family Living, 21*, 251-255.

Lofland, J. (1971). *Analyzing social settings.* Belmont, CA: Wadsworth Publishing.

Lofland, J., & Lofland, L. H. (1984). *Analyzing social settings: A guide to qualitative observation and analysis.* Belmont, CA: Wadsworth Publishing.

Long, J. D., & Williams, R. L. (1973). The comparative effectiveness of group and individually contingent free-time with inner-city junior high school students. *Journal of Applied Behavior Analysis, 6*, 465-474.

Lorr, M. (1983). *Cluster analysis for social scientists.* Beverly Hills, CA: Sage Publications.

Lowenberg, F., & Dolgoff, R. (1983). *Ethical decisions for social work.* Itasca, IL: F. E. Peacock Publishers.

Lukton, R. C. (1980). Barriers and pathways to integrating research and practice in social work: Suggestions for innovations in the MSW curriculum. *Journal of Education for Social Work, 16*, 20-25.

Lynch, M. M. (1978). *An exploratory study of public personal social services.* Unpublished doctoral dissertation, University of Minnesota, St. Paul, MN.

Maas, H. S. (1977). Research in social work. In J. B. Turner (Ed.), *Encyclopedia of social work* (pp. 1189-1190). Washington, DC: National Association of Social Workers.

MacKay, R. (1973). Conceptions of children and models of socialization. In H. P. Dreitzel (Ed.), *Childhood and socialization* (pp. 27-43). New York: Macmillan.

Madsen, W. (1964). *The Mexican Americans of south Texas.* New York: Holt, Rinehart, & Winston.

Mahoney, B., & Mahoney, W. M. (1975). Policy implications: A skeptical view. In J. Pechman, & P. M. Timpane (Eds.), *Work incentives and income guarantees: The New Jersey negative income tax experiment* (pp. 183-205). Washington, DC: Brookings Institution.

Maluccio, A. N. (1979). *Learning from clients.* New York: Free Press.

Maluccio, A. N. (1983). Planned use of life experiences. In A. Rosenblatt, & D. Waldfogel (Eds.), *Handbook of clinical social work* (pp. 58-69). San Francisco: Jossey-Bass.

Mandell, B. R. (1983). *Human services: An introduction.* New York: John Wiley & Sons.

Mann, R. A. (1976). Assessment of behavioral excesses in children. In M. Hersen, & A. S. Bellack (Eds.), *Behavioral assessment: A practical handbook* (pp. 459-491). Elmsford, NY: Pergamon Press.

Mannheim, K. (1936). *Ideology and utopia.* New York: Harcourt Brace Jovanovich.

Markle, A., & Rinn, R. C. (1977). *Author's guide to journals in psychology, psychiatry and social work.* New York: Haworth Press.

Marks, R. (1975). Research reporting. In N. A. Polansky (Ed.), *Social work research: Methods for the helping professions* (rev. ed., pp. 284-302). Chicago: University of Chicago Press.

Marsh, C. (1982). *The survey method: The contribution of surveys to sociological explanation.* London: Allen & Unwin.

Martin, G. & Pear, J. (1983). *Behavior modification: What it is and how to do it.* Englewood Cliffs, NJ: Prentice-Hall.

Martin, R. (1975). *Legal challenges to behavior modification: Trends in schools, corrections and mental health.* Champaign, IL: Research Press.

Masters, S., Garfinkel, I., & Bishop, J. (1978). Benefit-cost analysis in program evaluation. *Journal of Social Service Research, 2,* 79-95.

Mayadas, N. S., & Duehn, W. D. (1975). Toward an empirically-based practice stance. *Iowa Journal of Social Work, 6,* 81-99.

Mayadas, N. S., & Duehn, W. D. (1977). Stimulus-modeling (SM) videotape for marital counseling: Method and application. *Journal of Marriage and Family Counseling, 3,* 35-42.

Mayadas, N. S., & Duehn, W. D. (1982). Stimulus-modeling videotape formats in clinical practice and research. In J. L. Fryrear, & R. Fleshman (Eds.), *Videotherapy in mental health* (pp. 85-97). Springfield, IL: Charles C Thomas.

Mayer, R. R., & Greenwood, E. (1980). *The nature of social policy research.* Englewood Cliffs, NJ: Prentice-Hall.

McCall, G. J., & Simmons, J. L. (Eds.). (1969). *Issues in participant observation: A text and reader.* Reading, MA: Addison-Wesley Publishing.

McCord, J. (1978). A thirty-year follow-up of treatment effects. *American Psychologist, 33,* 284-289.

McFall, R. M. (1970). Effects of self-monitoring on normal smoking behavior. *Journal of Consulting and Clinical Psychology, 35,* 135-142.

McLoed, D. L., & Meyer, H. J. (1967). A study of values of social workers. In E. J. Thomas (Ed.), *Behavioral science for social workers* (pp. 401-416). New York: Free Press.

McReynolds, P. (Ed.). (1978). *Advances in psychological assessment* (4 vols.). Palo Alto, CA: Science and Behavior Books.

Mehan, H. (1974). Ethnomethodology and education. In D. O'Shea (Ed.), *Sociology of the school and schooling* (pp. 141-219). Washington, DC: National Institute of Education.

Mehan, H., & Wood, H. (1975a). An image of man for ethnomethodology. *Philosophy of the Social Sciences, 5,* 362-371.

Mehan, H., & Wood, H. (1975b). *The reality of ethnomethodology.* New York: John Wiley & Sons.

Mehan, H., & Wood, H. (1976). De-secting ethnomethodology. *American Sociologist, 11,* 13-21.

Mendelsohn, H. N. (1982). Social work journals: A review. *Serials Review, 8,* 9-13.

Mendelsohn, H. N. (1983). *An authors guide to social work journals.* Washington, DC: National Association of Social Workers.

Merton, R. K. (1957). *Social theory and social structure.* New York: Free Press.

Merton, R. K., Fiske, M., & Kendall, P. (1956). *The focused interview.* New York: Free Press.

Meyer, H. J., Borgatta, E. F., & Jones, W. C. (1965). *Girls at vocational high: An experiment in social work intervention.* New York: Russell Sage Foundation.

Middleman, R. R. (1984). How competent is social work's approach to the assessment of competence? *Social Work, 29,* 146-153.

Milgram, S. (1963). Behavioral study of obedience. *Journal of Abnormal and Social Psychology, 67,* 371-378.

Milgram, S. (1964). Issues in the study of obedience: A reply to Baumrind. *American Psychologist, 19,* 848-852.

Miller, D. C. (1977). *Handbook of research design and social measurement* (3rd ed.). New York: David McKay.

Miller, G. A. (1956). The magical number seven, plus or minus two. *Psychological Review, 63,* 81-97.

Miller, H. J., & Tripodi, T. (1967). Information accrual and clinical judgement. *Social Work, 12,* 63-69.

Miller, R. S. & Rehr, H. (1983). *Social work issues in health care.* Englewood Cliffs, NJ: Prentice-Hall.

Mills, C. W. (1959). *The sociological imagination.* New York: Oxford University Press.

Mindel, C. H. (1981). Instrument design and construction. In R. M. Grinnell, Jr. (Ed.), *Social work research and evaluation* (pp. 156-179). Itasca, IL: F. E. Peacock Publishers.

Mitchell, J. N. (1978). *Social exchange, dramaturgy and ethnomethodology.* New York: American Elsevier.

Moore, J. (1973). Social constraints on sociological knowledge: Academics and research concerning minorities. *Social Problems, 21,* 65-77.

Moos, R. H. (1974). *Evaluating treatment environments.* New York: John Wiley & Sons.

Morick, H. (1972). Introduction: The critique of contemporary empiricism. In H. Morick (Ed.), *Challenges to empiricism* (pp. 1-25). Belmont, CA: Wadsworth.

Morgan, G. (Ed.). (1983). *Beyond method: Strategies for social research.* Beverly Hills, CA: Sage Publications.

Morrison, D. E., & Henkel, R. E. (Eds.). (1970). *The significance test controversy.* Hawthorne, NY: Aldine Publishing.

Mullen, E. J. (1978). The construction of personal intervention models for effective practice: A method for utilizing research findings to guide social interventions. *Journal of Social Service Research, 2,* 45-65.

Mullen, E. J. (1981). Development of personal intervention models. In R. M. Grinnell, Jr. (Ed.), *Social work research and evaluation* (pp. 606-632). Itasca, IL: F. E. Peacock Publishers.

Mullen, E. J. (1983). Personal practice models. In A. Rosenblatt, & D. Waldfogel (Eds.), *Handbook of clinical social work* (pp. 235-247). San Francisco: Jossey-Bass.

Mullen, E. J., Bostwick, G. J., & Ryg, B. (1980). Toward an integration of research and practice in the social work curriculum: A description and evaluation of a one-quarter course. In R. W. Weinbach, & A. Rubin (Eds.), *Teaching social work research: Alternative programs and strategies* (pp. 30-41). New York: Council on Social Work Education.

Mullen, E. J., & Dumpson, J. R. (Eds.). (1972). *Evaluation of social intervention.* San Francisco: Jossey-Bass.

Mullins, C. J. (1977). *A guide to writing and publishing in the social sciences.* New York: John Wiley & Sons.

Mutschler, E. (1979). Using single-case evaluation procedures in a family and children's service agency: Integration of practice and research. *Journal of Social Service Research, 3,* 115-134.

Myrdal, G. (1969). *Objectivity in social research.* New York: Random House.

National Association of Social Workers. (1980). *National association of social workers code of ethics.* Washington, DC: Author.

National Association of Social Workers. (1985). *Information on NASW professional journals.* Washington DC: Author.

Nelsen, J. C. (1978). Use of communication theory in single-subject research. *Social Work Research and Abstracts, 14,* 12-19.

Nelsen, J. C. (1981). Issues in single-subject research for non-behaviorists. *Social Work Research and Abstracts, 17,* 31-37.

Nelson, K. (1983). Differences in graduate and undergraduate performance in a core research course. *Journal of Education for Social Work, 19,* 77-84.

Northwood, L. K. (1966). Enriched training for researchers in the master's degree program. *Social Work Education Reporter, 14,* 34-35, 44-45.

Nunnally, J. C. (1975). *Introduction to statistics for psychology and education.* New York: McGraw-Hill.

Nunnally, J. C. (1978). *Psychometric theory* (2nd ed.). New York: McGraw-Hill.

Parsons, T. (1949). *The structure of social action.* New York: Free Press.

Parsons, T. (Ed.). (1964). *The theory of social and economic organization.* New York: Free Press.

Parsonson, B. S., & Baer, D. M. (1978). The analysis and presentation of graphic data. In T. R. Kratchowill (Ed.), *Single subject research: Strategies for evaluating change* (pp. 102-162). New York: Academic Press.

Patchner, M. A. (1983). The experiences of the DSW's and Ph.D.'s. *Journal of Education for Social Work, 19,* 198-106.

Patti, R. J. (1983). *Social welfare administration: managing social programs in a developmental context.* Englewood Cliffs, NJ: Prentice-Hall.

Pehm, L. P. (1976). Assessment of depression. In M. Hersen, & A. S. Bellack (Eds.), *Behavioral assessment: A practical handbook* (pp. 233-259). Elmsford, NY: Pergamon Press.

Perlman, H. H. (1957). *Social casework: A problem-solving process.* Chicago: University of Chicago Press.

Perlman, H. H. (1970). The problem-solving model in social casework. In R. W. Roberts, & R. H. Nee (Eds.), *Theories of social casework* (pp. 129-180). Chicago: University of Chicago Press.

Perlman, H. H. (1972). Once more with feeling. In E. J. Mullen, & J. R. Dumpson (Eds.), *Evaluation of social intervention* (pp. 191-209). San Francisco: Jossey-Bass.

Perlman, H. H. (1976). Believing and doing: Values in social work education. *Social Casework, 57,* 381-390.

Philliber, S. G., Schwab, M. R., & Sloss, G. S. (1980). *Social research: Guides to a decision-making process.* Itasca, IL: F. E. Peacock Publishers.

Phillips, B. S. (1976). *Social research: Strategy and tactics* (3rd ed.). New York: Macmillan.

Phillips, B. S. (1979). *Sociology: From concepts to practice.* New York: McGraw-Hill.

Phillips, B. S. (1984). *Sociological research methods: An introduction.* Homewood, IL: Dorsey Press.

Phillips, J. L., Jr. (1973). *Statistical thinking: A structural approach.* San Francisco: W. H. Freeman & Co.

Pincus, A., & Minahan, A. (1973). *Social work practice: Model and method.* Itasca, IL: F. E. Peacock Publishers.

Pinkston, E. M., Levitt, J. L., Green, G. T., Linsk, N. L., & Rzepnicki, T. L. (1982). *Effective social work practice.* San Francisco: Jossey-Bass.

Piven, F. F., & Cloward, R. A. (1971). *Regulating the poor: The functions of public welfare.* New York: Vintage Books.

Polansky, N. A. (1975a). Introduction: Social and historical context. In N. A. Polansky (Ed.), *Social work research: Methods for the helping professions* (rev. ed., pp. 1-17). Chicago: University of Chicago Press.

Polansky, N. A. (Ed.). (1975b). *Social work research: Methods for the helping professions* (rev. ed.). Chicago: University of Chicago Press.

Polansky, N. A. (1975c). Theory construction and the scientific method. In N. A. Polansky (Ed.), *Social work research: Methods for the helping professions* (rev. ed., pp. 18-37). *Chicago: University of Chicago Press.*

Pollner, M. (1974). Mundane reasoning. *Philosophy of the Social Sciences, 4,* 35-54.

Polster, R. A., & Lynch, M. A. (1981). Single-subject designs. In R. M. Grinnell, Jr. (Ed.), *Social work research and evaluation* (pp. 373-418). Itasca, IL: F. E. Peacock Publishers.

Polster, R. A., Lynch, M. A., & Pinkston, E. M. (1981). Reaching underachievers. In S. P. Schinke (Ed.), *Behavioral methods in social welfare* (pp. 41-60). Hawthorne, NY: Aldine Publishing.

Polster, R. A., & Pinkston, E. M. (1979). A delivery system for the treatment of underachievement. *Social Service Review, 53,* 35-55.

Pomeroy, W. (1972). *Dr. Kinsey and the sex institute.* New York: Harper & Row.

Popper, K. R. (1945). *The open society and its enemies.* Boston: Routledge & Kegan Paul.

Popper, K. R. (1961). *The logic of scientific discovery.* New York: Science Editions.

Posavac, E. J., & Carey, R. G. (1980). *Program evaluation: Methods and case studies.* Englewood Cliffs, NJ: Prentice-Hall.

Powers, M. G. (Ed.). (1982). *Measures of socioeconomic status: Current issues.* Boulder, CO: Westview Press.

Rabin, C. (1981). The single-case design in family therapy evaluation research. *Family Process, 20,* 351-366.

Ramos, R. (1973). A case in point: An ethnomethodological study of a poor Mexican American family. *Social Science Quarterly, 53,* 905-919.

Ramos, R. (1978). The use of improvisation and modulation in natural talk: An alternative approach to conversational analysis. In N. K. Denzin (Ed.), *Studies in symbolic interaction* (Vol. 1, pp. 319-337). Greenwich, CT: JAI Press.

Ramos, R. (1979a). A preliminary look at an alternative approach to the study of immigrants. In R. Bryce-Laport (Ed.), *The new immigration: Implications for American society* (pp. 379-388). New Brunswick, NJ: Transaction Books.

Ramos, R. (1979b). The Mexican American: Am I who they say I am? In A. D. Trejo (Ed.), *The Mexican American as we see ourselves* (pp. 49-66). Tucson, AZ: University of Arizona Press.

Ramos, R. (1979c). Movidas: The methodological and theoretical relevance of interactional strategies. In N. K. Denzin (Ed.), *Studies in symbolic interaction* (Vol. 2, pp. 141-165). Greenwich, CT: JAI Press.

Ramos, R. (1981). Participant observation. In R. M. Grinnell, Jr. (Ed.), *Social work research and evaluation* (pp. 348-360). Itasca, IL: F. E. Peacock Publishers.

Rathus, S. A. (1973). A thirty-item schedule for assessing assertive behavior. *Behavior Therapy, 4,* 298-306.

Raymond, F. B. (1977). A changing focus for the profession: Product rather than process. *Journal of Social Welfare, 4,* 9-16.

Raymond, F. B. (1981). Program evaluation. In R. M. Grinnell, Jr. (Ed.), *Social work research and evaluation* (pp. 419-428). Itasca, IL: F. E. Peacock Publishers.

Reamer, F. G. (1979). Fundamental ethical issues in social work: An essay review. *Social Service Review, 53,* 229-243.

Reamer, F. G. (1982). *Ethical dilemmas in social service.* New York: Columbia University Press.

Reamer, F. G. (1983). Ethical dilemmas in social work practice. *Social Work, 28,* 31-35.

Reid, W. J. (1974). Developments in the use of organized data. *Social Work, 19,* 585-593.

Reid, W. J. (1975a). Applications of computer technology. In N. A. Polansky (Ed.), *Social work research: Methods for the helping professions* (rev. ed., pp. 229-253). Chicago: University of Chicago Press.

Reid, W. J. (1975b). A test of a task-centered approach. *Social Work, 20,* 3-9.

Reid, W. J. (1977). A journal for research: An editorial. *Social Work Research and Abstracts, 13,* 2-3.

Reid, W. J. (1978a). Some reflections on the practice doctorate. *Social Service Review, 52,* 449-455.

Reid, W. J. (1978b). The social agency as a research machine. *Journal of Social Service Research, 2,* 11-24.

Reid, W. J. (1978c). *The task-centered system.* New York: Columbia University Press.

Reid, W. J. (1981). Research reports and publication procedures. In R. M. Grinnell, Jr. (Ed.), *Social work research and evaluation* (pp. 553-568). Itasca, IL: F. E. Peacock Publishers.

Reid, W. J. (1983). Developing intervention methods through experimental designs. In A. Rosenblatt, & D. Waldfogel (Eds.), *Handbook of clinical social work* (pp. 246-255). San Francisco: Jossey-Bass.

Reid, W. J., & Epstein, L. (1972). *Task-centered casework.* New York: Columbia University Press.

Reid, W. J., & Epstein, L. (Eds.). (1977). *Task-centered practice.* (New York: Columbia University Press.

Reid, W. J., & Hanrahan, P. (1982). Recent evaluations of social work: Grounds for optimism. *Social Work, 27,* 328-340.

Reid, W. J., & Hanrahan, P. (1983). Reply. *Social Work, 28,* 79.

Reid, W. J., & Shyne, A. (1969). *Brief and extended casework.* New York: Columbia University Press.

Reid, W. J., & Smith, A. D. (1981). *Research in social work.* New York: Columbia University Press.

Rein, M., & Peattie, L. (1981). Knowledge for policy. *Social Service Review, 55,* 525-543.

Rein, M., & White, S. (1981). Knowledge for practice. *Social Service Review, 55,* 1-41.

Reinherz, H., Grob, M. C., & Berkman, B. (1983). Health agencies and a school of social work: Practice and research in partnership. *Health and Social Work, 8,* 40-47.

Reinherz, H., Regan, J. M., & Anastas, J. W. (1983). A research curriculum for future clinicians: A multimodel strategy. *Journal of Education for Social Work, 19,* 35-41.

Reiss, A. J. (1971). *The police and the public.* New Haven, CT: Yale University Press.

Reynolds, P. D. (1971). *A primer in theory construction.* Indianapolis, IN: Bobbs-Merrill.

Richmond, M. E. (1922). *What is social case work?* New York: Russell Sage Foundation.

Ring, K., Walston, K., & Corey, M. (1970). Mode of debriefing as a factor affecting subjective reaction to a Milgram-type obedience experiment. *Representative Research in Social Psychology, 1,* 67-88.

Robinson, D., & Rhodes, S. (1946). Two experiments with an anti-semitism poll. *Journal of Abnormal and Social Psychology, 41,* 136-144.

Robinson, J. P., Athanasion, R., & Head, K. (1973). *Measures of occupational attitudes and occupational characteristics* (rev. ed.). Ann Arbor, MI: Institute for Social Research.

Robinson, J. P., & Shaver, P. R. (1973). *Measures of social psychological attitudes* (rev. ed.). Ann Arbor, MI: Institute for Social Research.

Rogers, C. R. (1945). The nondirective method as a technique for social research. *American Journal of Sociology, 50,* 279-283.

Romano, O. (1968). The anthropology and sociology of the Mexican American. *El Grito, 2,* 9-26.

Rosen, A. (1981). Toward a function-related organization of doctoral education. *Journal of Education for Social Work, 17,* 69-75.

Rosen, A., & Mutschler, E. (1982). Social work students' and practitioners' orientation to research. *Journal of Education for Social Work, 18,* 62-68.

Rosen, A., & Proctor, E. K. (1978). Specifying the treatment process: The basis for effectiveness research. *Journal of Social Service Research, 2,* 25-26.

Rosen, S., & Polansky, N. A. (1975). Observation of social interaction. In N. A. Polansky (Ed.), *Social work research: Methods for the helping professions* (rev. ed., pp. 154-181). Chicago: University of Chicago Press.

Rosenberg, J. (1977). Veterans' perception of their hospital care. *Social Work Research and Abstracts, 13,* 30-34.

Rosenberg, M. (1968). *The logic of survey analysis.* New York: Basic Books.

Rosenblatt, A. (1968). The practitioner's use and evaluation of research. *Social Work, 13,* 53-59.

Rosenblatt, A. (1981). Research models for social work education. In S. Briar, H. Weissman, & A. Rubin (Eds.), *Research utilization in social work education* (pp. 17-28). New York: Council on Social Work Education.

Rosenblatt, A., & Kirk, S. A. (1981). Cumulative effect of research courses on knowledge and attitudes of social work students. *Journal of Education for Social Work, 17,* 26-34.

Rosenman, L., & Ruckdeschel, R. A. (1981). Catch 1234B: Integrating material on women into the social research curriculum. *Journal of Education for Social Work, 17,* 5-11.

Rosenthal, R. (1966). *Experimenter effects in behavioral research.* New York: Appleton-Century-Crofts.

Rossi, P. H. (1979). *Evaluation: A systematic approach.* Beverly Hills, CA: Sage Publications.

Rossi, P. H., & Freeman, H. E. (1982). *Evaluation: A systematic approach* (2nd ed.). Beverly Hills, CA: Sage Publications.

Rothman, J. (1978). Conversion and design in the research utilization process. *Journal of Social Service Research, 2,* 117-133.

Rothman, J. (1980a). *Social R & D: Research and development in the human services.* Englewood, Cliffs, NJ: Prentice-Hall.

Rothman, J. (1980b). *Using research in organizations: A guide to successful applications.* Beverly Hills, CA: Sage Publications.

Royer, M. L. (1981). Expressing concepts and results in numeric form. In R. M. Grinnell, Jr. (Ed.), *Social work research and evaluation* (pp. 431-444). Itasca, IL: F. E. Peacock Publishers.

Rubel, A. (1966). *Across the tracks: Mexican Americans in a Texas city.* Austin, TX: University of Texas Press.

Rubin, A., & Rosenblatt, A. (Eds.). (1979). *Sourcebook on research utilization.* New York: Council on Social Work Education.

Rubin, A., & Zimbalist, S. E. (1981). Issues in the MSW research curriculum, 1968-1979. In S. Briar, H. Weissman, & A. Rubin (Eds.), *Research utilization in social work education* (pp. 6-16). New York: Council on Social Work Education.

Ruckdeschel, R. A., & Faris, B. E. (1981). Assessing practice: A critical look at the single-case design. *Social Casework, 62,* 413-419.

Russell, P. A., Lankford, M. W., & Grinnell, R. M., Jr. (1983). Attitudes toward supervisors in a human service agency. *The Clinical Supervisor, 1,* 57-71.

Russell, P. A., Lankford, M. W., & Grinnell, R. M., Jr. (1984). Administrative styles of social work supervisors in a human service agency. *Administration in Social Work, 8,* 65-77.

Sacks, H. (1972a). An initial investigation of the useability of conversational data for doing sociology. In D. Sudnow (Ed.), *Studies in interaction* (pp. 280-293). New York: Free Press.

Sacks, H. (1972b). Notes on police assessment of moral character. In D. Sudnow (Ed.), *Studies in interaction* (pp. 45-59). New York: Free Press.

Sacks, H. (1972c). On the analyzability of stories by children. In J. J. Gumperz, & D. Hymes (Eds.), *Directions in sociolinguistics.* New York: Holt, Rinehart, & Winston.

Sacks, H. (1975). Everybody has to lie. In M. Sanchez, & B. Blount (Eds.), *Sociocultural dimensions of language use* (pp. 57-80). New York: Academic Press.

Sammons, C. C. (1978). Ethical issues in genetic intervention. *Social Work, 23,* 237-242.

Sarkar, H. (1984). *A theory of method.* Berkeley, CA: University of California Press.

Sartori, G. (Ed.). (1984). *Social science concepts: A systematic analysis.* Beverly Hills, CA: Sage Publications.

Schegloff, E. (1968). Sequencing in conversational openings. *American Anthropologist, 70,* 1075-1095.

Schoech, D., & Arangio, T. (1979). Computers in the human services. *Social Work, 24,* 96-102.

Schenkein, J. (1972). Toward an analysis of natural conversation and the sense of heheh. *Semiotica, 6,* 334-377.

Schilling, R. F., Gilchrist, L. D., & Schinke, S. P. (1984). Coping and social support in families of developmentally disabled children. *Family Relations, 33,* 47-54.

Schinke, S. P. (1979a). Bridging the accountability gap. *Practice Digest, 1,* 28-29.

Schinke, S. P. (1979b). Evaluating social work practice: A conceptual model and example. *Social Casework, 60,* 195-200.

Schinke, S. P. (Ed.). (1981a). *Behavioral methods in social welfare.* Hawthorne, NY: Aldine Publishing.

Schinke, S. P. (1981b). Ethics. In R. M. Grinnell, Jr. (Ed.), *Social work research and evaluation* (pp. 57-70). Itasca, IL: F. E. Peacock Publishers.

Schinke, S. P. (1983). Empirical methods of practice. In A. Rosenblatt, & D. Waldfogel (Eds.), *Handbook of clinical social work* (pp. 345-361). San Francisco: Jossey-Bass.

Schinke, S. P., & Gilchrist, L. D. (1984). *Life skills counseling with adolescents.* Baltimore, MD: University Park Press.

Schram, B., & Mandell, B. R. (1983). *Human services: Strategies of intervention.* New York: John Wiley & Sons.

Schrodt, P. A. (1984). *Microcomputer methods for social scientists.* Beverly Hills, CA: Sage Publications.

Schuerman, J. R. (1981). Bivariate analysis: Crosstabulation. In R. M. Grinnell, Jr. (Ed.), *Social work research and evaluation* (pp. 461-480). Itasca, IL: F. E. Peacock Publishers.

Schuerman, J. R. (1983). *Research and evaluation in the human services.* New York: Free Press.

Schuman, H., & Converse, J. M. (1970). The effects of black and white interviewers on black responses in 1968. *Public Opinion Quarterly, 35,* 44-68.

Schwartz, A. C. (1976). Believing and doing: Values in social work education commentary. *Social Casework, 57,* 393-396.

Schwartz, A. C. (1982). *The behavior therapies: Theories and applications.* New York: Free Press.

Schwartz, H., & Jacobs, J. (1979). *Qualitative sociology: A method to the madness.* New York: Free Press.

Schwitzgebel, R. (1964). *Street-corner research.* Cambridge, MA: Harvard University Press.

Seaberg, J. R. (1981). Sampling procedures and techniques. In R. M. Grinnell, Jr. (Ed.), *Social work research and evaluation* (pp. 71-92). Itasca, IL: F. E. Peacock Publishers.

Seidl, F. W. (1973). Teaching social work research: A study in teaching method. *Journal of Education for Social Work, 9,* 71-77.

Selltiz, C., Wrightsman, L. S., & Cook, S. W. (1976). *Research methods in social relations* (3rd ed.). New York: Holt, Rinehart, & Winston.

Shaw, M. E., & Wright, J. M. (1967). *Scales for the measurement of attitudes.* New York: McGraw-Hill.

Shyne, A. W. (1975). Exploiting available information. In N. A. Polansky (Ed.), *Social work research: Methods for the helping professions* (rev. ed., pp. 109-130). Chicago: University of Chicago Press.

Sidman, M. (1960). *Tactics of scientific research: Evaluating experimental data in psychology.* New York: Basic Books.

Siegel, D. H. (1983). Can research and practice be integrated in social work education? *Journal of Education for Social Work, 19,* 12-19.

Silverman, D. (1972). Methodology and meaning. In P. Filmer, M. Phillipson, D. Silverman, & D. Walsh (Eds.), *New directions in sociological theory* (pp. 183-200). Cambridge, MA: MIT Press.

Simon, J. (1969). *Basic research methods in social science.* New York: Random House.

Siporin, M. (1975). *Introduction to social work practice.* New York: Macmillan.

Skinner, B. F. (1974). *About behaviorism.* New York: Alfred A. Knopf.

Slonim, M. J. (1960). *Sampling.* New York: Simon & Schuster.

Smith, M. J. (1983). Use of the computer in a course on data analysis in social welfare research. *Journal of Education for Social Work, 19,* 74-78.

Souther, J. W., & White, M. L. (1977). *Technical report writing* (2nd ed.). New York: John Wiley & Sons.

Spanier, G. B. (1976). Measuring dyadic adjustment: New scales for assessing the quality of marriage and similar dyads. *Journal of Marriage and the Family, 38,* 15-28.

Specht, H. (1968). Casework practice and social policy formulation. *Social Work, 13,* 42-53.

Spielberger, C. D., Gorsuch, R. L., & Lushene, R. E. (1970). *State-trait anxiety inventory.* Palo Alto, CA: Consulting Psychologists Press.

Spivack, G., Platt, J. J., & Shure, M. (1976). *The problem-approach to adjustment: A guide to current and effective intervention.* San Francisco: Jossey-Bass.

Steiner, I. D. (1972). The evils of research: Or what my mother didn't tell me about the sins of academia. *American Psychologist, 27,* 766-768.

Stern, P. C. (1979). *Evaluating social science research.* New York: Oxford University Press.

Stevens, S. S. (1951). *Mathematics, measurement and psychophysics.* New York: John Wiley & Sons.

Stinchcombe, A. L. (1968). *Constructing social theories.* New York: Harcourt Brace Jovanovich.

Stokes, T. F., & Baer, D. M. (1977). An implicit technology of generalization. *Journal of Applied Behavior Analysis, 10,* 349-365.

Strauss, M. A. (1969). *Family measurement techniques.* Minneapolis: University of Minnesota Press.

Strunk, W., Jr., & White, E. B. (1979). *The elements of style* (3rd ed.). New York: Macmillan.

Stuart, F., Stuart, R. B., Maurice, W. L., & Szasz, G. (1975). *Sexual adjustment inventory.* Champaign, IL: Research Press.

Stuart, P. (1981). Historical research. In R. M. Grinnell, Jr. (Ed.), *Social work research and evaluation* (pp. 316-332). Itasca, IL: F. E. Peacock Publishers.

Stuart, R. B. (1973). *Marital precounseling inventory.* Champaign, IL: Research Press.

Stuart, R. B., & Stuart, F. (1975). *Family precounseling inventory.* Champaign, IL: Research Press.

Suchman, E. A. (1967a). *Evaluative research: Principles and practice in public service and social action programs.* New York: Russell Sage Foundation.

Suchman, E. A. (1967b). The principles of research design and administration. In J. T. Doby (Ed.), *An introduction to social research* (2nd ed., pp. 81-96). New York: Appleton-Century-Crofts.

Sudnow, D. (1965). Normal crimes. *Social Problems, 12,* 255-276.

Sudnow, D. (1969). *Passing on: The social organization of dying.* Englewood Cliffs, NJ: Prentice-Hall.

Summers, G. F., & Beck, E. M. (1973). Social status and personality factors in predicting interviewer performance. *Sociological Methods and Research, 2,* 111-122.

Tallent, N. (1983). *Psychological report writing* (2nd ed.). Englewood Cliffs, NJ: Prentice-Hall.

Taylor, J. B. (1977). Toward alternative forms of social work research: The case for naturalistic methods. *Journal of Social Welfare, 4,* 119-126.

Teigiser, K. S. (1983). Evaluation of education for generalist practice. *Journal of Education for Social Work, 19,* 79-85.

Thomas, E. J. (1975). Uses of research methods in interpersonal practice. In N. A. Polansky (Ed.), *Social work research: Methods for the helping professions* (rev. ed., pp. 254-283). Chicago: University of Chicago Press.

Thomas, E. J. (1978a). Generating innovation in social work: The paradigm of developmental research. *Journal of Social Service Research, 2,* 95-117.

Thomas, E. J. (1978b). Mousetraps, developmental research and social work education. *Social Service Review, 52,* 468-483.

Thomas, E. J. (1978c). Research and service in single-case experimentation: Conflicts and choices. *Social Work Research and Abstracts, 14,* 20-31.

Thomas, E. J. (1980). Beyond knowledge utilization in generating human service technology. In D. Fanshel (Ed.), *Future of social work research* (pp. 91-104). Washington, DC: National Association of Social Workers.

Thomas, E. J. (1981). Developmental research: A model for interventional innovation. In R. M. Grinnell, Jr. (Ed.), *Social work research and evaluation* (pp. 590-605). Itasca, IL: F. E. Peacock Publishers.

Thomas, E. J. (1983). Problems and issues in single-case experiments. In A. Rosenblatt, & D. Waldfogel (Eds.), *Handbook of clinical social work* (pp. 560-571). San Francisco: Jossey-Bass.

Thomas, E. J., Carter, R. B., Gambrill, E. D., & Butterfield, W. H. (1970). A signal system for the assessment and modification of behavior. *Behavior Therapy, 1,* 252-258.

Thomas, E. J., & Walter, C. L. (1978). Guidelines for behavioral practice in the open community agency: Procedure and evaluation. *Behavior Research and Therapy, 11,* 193-207.

Thomas, E. J., Walter, C. L., & O'Flaherty, K. (1974). Computer-assisted assessment and modification: Possibilities and illustrative data. *Social Service Review, 48,* 170-183.

Thomlison, R. J. (1984). Something works: Evidence from practice effectiveness studies. *Social Work, 29,* 51-56.

Thompson, M. S. (1980). *Benefit-cost analysis for program evaluation.* Beverly Hills, CA: Sage Publications.

Thorndike, R. L. (Ed.). (1971). *Educational measurement* (2nd ed.). Washington, DC: American Council on Education.

Thorndike, R. L., & Hagen, E. (1969). *Measurement and evaluation in psychology and education* (3rd ed.). New York: John Wiley & Sons.

Torgerson, W. (1958). *Theory and methods of scaling.* New York: John Wiley & Sons.

Toseland, R. W. (1981). Choosing an appropriate research method. In R. M. Grinnell, Jr. (Ed.), *Social work research and evaluation* (pp. 183-197). Itasca, IL: F. E. Peacock Publishers.

Tripodi, T. (1974). *Uses and abuses of social research in social work.* New York: Columbia University Press.

Tripodi, T. (1981). The logic of research design. In R. M. Grinnell, Jr. (Ed.), *Social work research and evaluation* (pp. 198-225). Itasca, IL: F. E. Peacock Publishers.

Tripodi, T. (1983). *Evaluative research for social workers.* Englewood Cliffs, NJ: Prentice-Hall.

Tripodi, T., & Epstein, I. (1978). Incorporating knowledge of research methodology into social work practice. *Journal of Social Service Research, 2,* 11-23.

Tripodi, T., & Epstein, I. (1980). *Research techniques for clinical social workers.* New York: Columbia University Press.

Tripodi, T., Fellin, P. A., & Epstein, I. (1971). *Social program evaluation: Guidelines for health, education and welfare administrators.* Itasca, IL: F. E. Peacock Publishers.

Tripodi, T., Fellin, P. A., & Meyer, H. J. (1983). *The assessment of social research: Guidelines for the use of research in social work and social service* (2nd ed.). Itasca, IL: F. E. Peacock Publishers.

Tripodi, T., & Harrington, J. (1979). Uses of time-series designs for formative program evaluation. *Journal of Social Service Research, 3,* 67-78.

Tripodi, T., & Miller, H. J. (1966). The clinical judgement process: A review of the literature. *Social Work, 11,* 63-69.

Trochim, W. M. (1984). *Research design for program evaluation.* Beverly Hills, CA: Sage Publications.

Truax, C. B., & Mitchell, K. M. (1971). Research on certain therapist interpersonal skills in relation to process and outcome. In A. E. Bergin, & S. L. Garfield (Eds.), *Handbook of psychotherapy and behavior change: An empirical analysis* (pp. 299-334). New York: John Wiley & Sons.

Turabian, K. L. (1973). *A manual for writers of term papers, theses and dissertations* (4th ed.). Chicago: University of Chicago Press.

Turner, R. (1970). Words, utterances and activities. In J. Douglas (Ed.), *Understanding everyday life* (pp. 169-187). Hawthorne, NY: Aldine Publishing.

Turner, R. (1972). Some formal properties of therapy talk. In D. Sudnow (Ed.), *Studies in interaction* (pp. 367-396). New York: Free Press.

Ulman, J. D., & Sulzer-Azaroff, B. (1975). Multi-element baseline design in educational research. In E. Ramp, & G. Semb (Eds.), *Behavior analysis: Areas of research and application* (pp. 377-391). Englewood Cliffs, NJ: Prentice-Hall.

University of Michigan Survey Research Center. (1960). *Interviewer's manual.* Ann Arbor, MI: Institute for Social Research.

Vaca, N. (1970). The Mexican American in the social sciences, 1912-1970. *El Grito, 4,* 17-51.

Valentine, C. A. (1971). The culture of poverty: Its scientific significance and its implications for action. In E. B. Leacock (Ed.), *The culture of poverty: A critique* (pp. 193-225). New York: Simon & Schuster.

Van Maanen, J. (Ed.). (1983). *Qualitative methodology.* Beverly Hills, CA: Sage Publications.

Van Maanen, J., Dabbs, J. M., Jr., & Faulkner, R. R. (Eds.). (1982). *Varieties of qualitative research.* Beverly Hills, CA: Sage Publications.

Vigilante, J. (1974). Between values and science. *Journal of Education for Social Work, 10,* 107-115.

Walizer, M. H., & Wienir, P. L. (1978). *Research methods and analysis: Searching for relationships.* New York: Harper & Row.

Wallace, W. L. (1973). *The logic of science in sociology.* Hawthorne, NY: Aldine Publishing.

Warwick, D. P. (1975). Social scientists ought to stop lying. *Psychology Today, 8,* 105-106.

Waskow, I. E., & Parloff, M. B. (Eds.). (1975). *Psychotherapy change measures.* Rockville, MD. National Institute of Mental Health.

Wasser, E. (1957). The caseworker as research interviewer in follow-up studies. *Social Casework, 38,* 423-430.

Wasser, E. (1962). Research interviewing in social work research: Some formulations. *Social Service Review, 36,* 286-294.

Watts, T. D. (1974). Ethnomethodology: A consideration of theory and research. *Cornell Journal of Social Relations, 9,* 91-115.

Watts, T. D. (1976). Phenomenological social science and holistic social policy. *Journal of Sociology and Social Welfare, 4,* 58-72.

Watts, T. D. (1981). Ethnomethodology. In R. M. Grinnell, Jr. (Ed.), *Social work research and evaluation* (pp. 361-372). Itasca, IL: F. E. Peacock Publishers.

Webb, E. J., Campbell, D. T., Schwartz, R. D., & Sechrest, L. (1966). *Unobtrusive measures: Nonreactive research in the social sciences.* Chicago: Rand McNally.

Weber, R. E., & Polansky, N. A. (1975). Evaluation. In N. A. Polansky (Ed.), *Social work research: Methods for the helping professions* (rev. ed., pp. 182-201). Chicago: University of Chicago Press.

Wechsler, H., Reinherz, H. Z., & Dobbin, D. D. (Eds.). (1981). *Social work research in the human services* (2nd ed.). New York: Human Sciences Press.

Weed, P., & Greenwald, S. R. (1973). The mystics of statistics. *Social Work, 18,* 113-115.

Weinbach, R. W. (1981). Variations in social work research education. In S. Briar, H. Weissman, & A. Rubin (Eds.), *Research utilization in social work education* (pp. 40-47). New York: Council on Social Work Education.

Weinbach, R. W., & Gandy, J. T. (1980). The traditional approach to social work research education: Avant-garde or backward? In R. W. Weinbach, & A. Rubin (Eds.), *Teaching social work research: Alternative programs and strategies* (pp. 45-51). New York: Council on Social Work Education.

Weinberger, R., & Tripodi, T. (1969). Trends in types of research reported in selected social work journals, 1956-1965. *Social Service Review, 43,* 439-447.

Weiss, C. H. (1969). Validity of welfare mothers' interview responses. *Public Opinion Quarterly, 32,* 622-633.

Weiss, C. H. (Ed.). (1972a). *Evaluating action programs: Readings in social action.* Boston, MA: Allyn & Bacon.

Weiss, C. H. (1972b). *Evaluation research: Methods of assessing program effectiveness.* Englewood Cliffs, NJ: Prentice-Hall.

Weissman, H. (1981). Teaching qualitative research methods. In S. Briar, H. Weissman, & A. Rubin (Eds.), *Research utilization in social work education* (pp. 59-65). New York: Council on Social Work Education.

Weissman, H., Epstein, I., & Savage, A. (1983). *Agency-based social work: Neglected aspects of clinical practice.* Philadelphia: Temple University Press.

Welch, G. J. (1983). Will graduates use single-subject designs to evaluate their casework practice? *Journal of Education for Social Work, 19,* 42-47.

Welch, G. J., & Granvold, D. (1979). In defense of small N research. *Educational Research Quarterly, 4,* 2-11.

Welch, S., Comer, J., & Steinman, M. (1973). Interviewing in a Mexican American community: An investigation of some potential sources of response bias. *Public Opinion Quarterly, 37,* 115-126.

Wells, R. A., Figurel, J. A., & McNamee P. (1977). Communication training vs. conjoint marital therapy. *Social Work Reserach and Abstracts, 13,* 31-39.

White, M. (1963). *Sociological research.* New York: Harcourt Brace Jovanovich.

Whyte, W. F. (1966). *Street corner society.* Chicago: University of Chicago Press.

Wiersma, W. (1980). *Research methods in education: An introduction* (3rd ed.). Itasca, IL: F. E. Peacock Publishers.

Williams, J. A., Jr. (1964). Interview-respondent interaction: A study of bias in the information interview. *Sociometry, 27,* 338-352.

Wilson, P. A., Voth, V., & Hudson, W. W. (1980). Professionals and the bureaucracy: Measuring the orientations of social workers. *Journal of Social Service Research, 4,* 15-30.

Wilson, S. J. (1978). *Confidentiality in social work.* New York: Free Press.

Wilson, S. J. (1980). *Recording: Guidelines for social workers.* New York: Free Press.

Winch, R. F., & Campbell, D. T. (1969). Proof? No. Evidence? Yes. The significance of tests of significance. *American Sociologist, 4,* 140-143.

Witkin, S. L., & Harrison, D. F. (1979). Single-case designs in marital research and therapy. *Journal of Social Service Research, 3,* 51-66.

Wolpe, J., & Lang, P. (1964). A fear survey instrument for use in behavior therapy. *Behavior Research and Therapy, 2,* 27-30.

Wong, P. (1982). Social work research on minorities: Toward a comparative approach. *Journal of Education for Social Work, 18,* 69-76.

Wood, K. M. (1978). Casework effectiveness: A new look at the research evidence. *Social Work, 23,* 437-468.

Wood, K. M. (1980). Experiences in teaching the practitioner-researcher model. In R. W. Weinbach, & A. Rubin (Eds.), *Teaching social work research: Alternative programs and strategies* (pp. 13-22). New York: Council on Social Work Education.

Yeakel, M., & Ganter, G. (1975). Some principles and methods of sampling. In N. A. Polansky (Ed.), *Social work research: Methods for the helping professions* (rev. ed., pp. 93-108). Chicago: University of Chicago Press.

Zimbalist, S. E. (1983). The single-case clinical research design in developmental perspective: Mainstream or tangent? *Journal of Education for Social Work, 19,* 61-66.

Zimbalist, S. E. (1974). The research component of the master's degree curriculum in social work: A survey summary. *Journal of Education for Social Work, 10,* 118-123.

Zimbalist, S. E. (1977). *Historic themes and landmarks in social welfare research.* New York: Harper & Row.

Zimbalist, S. E., & Rubin, A. (1981). Contrasting extremes in research requirements for the MSW curriculum. *Journal of Education for Social Work, 17,* 56-61.

Zimmerman, D. H. (1969). Tasks and troubles: The practical bases of work activities in a public assistance organization. In D. A. Hansen (Ed.), *Exploration in sociology and counseling* (pp. 237-266). Boston: Houghton Mifflin.

Zimmerman, D. H. (1979). Record-keeping and the intake process in a public welfare agency. In S. Wheeler (Ed.), *On record: Files and dossiers in American life* (pp. 319-354). New York: Russell Sage Foundation.

Zinsser, W. (1976). *On writing well: An informal guide to writing nonfiction.* New York: Harper & Row.

Zinsser, W. (1980). *On writing well: An informal guide to writing nonfiction* (2nd ed.). New York: Harper & Row.

INDEX

THE BOOK MANUFACTURE

Social Work Research and Evaluation, Second Edition, was typeset by Compositors, Cedar Rapids, IA. It was printed and bound at Kingsport Press, Kingsport, Tennessee. The design was by F.E. Peacock Publishers' art department. The typeface is Times Roman with Helvetica display.